American Casebook Series
Hornbook Series and Basic Legal Texts
Nutshell Series

of

WEST PUBLISHING COMPANY
P.O. Box 64526
St. Paul, Minnesota 55164–0526

ACCOUNTING

Faris' Accounting and Law in a Nutshell, 377 pages, 1984 (Text)

Fiflis, Kripke and Foster's Teaching Materials on Accounting for Business Lawyers, 3rd Ed., 838 pages, 1984 (Casebook)

Siegel and Siegel's Accounting and Financial Disclosure: A Guide to Basic Concepts, 259 pages, 1983 (Text)

ADMINISTRATIVE LAW

Davis' Cases, Text and Problems on Administrative Law, 6th Ed., 683 pages, 1977 (Casebook)

Davis' Basic Text on Administrative Law, 3rd Ed., 617 pages, 1972 (Text)

Gellhorn and Boyer's Administrative Law and Process in a Nutshell, 2nd Ed., 445 pages, 1981 (Text)

Mashaw and Merrill's Cases and Materials on Administrative Law–The American Public Law System, 2nd Ed., 976 pages, 1985 (Casebook)

Robinson, Gellhorn and Bruff's The Administrative Process, 3rd Ed., 978 pages, 1986 (Casebook)

ADMIRALTY

Healy and Sharpe's Cases and Materials on Admiralty, 2nd Ed., 876 pages, 1986 (Casebook)

Maraist's Admiralty in a Nutshell, 390 pages, 1983 (Text)

Sohn and Gustafson's Law of the Sea in a Nutshell, 264 pages, 1984 (Text)

AGENCY—PARTNERSHIP

Fessler's Alternatives to Incorporation for Persons in Quest of Profit, 2nd Ed., 326 pages, 1986 (Casebook)

AGENCY—PARTNERSHIP—Cont'd

Henn's Cases and Materials on Agency, Partnership and Other Unincorporated Business Enterprises, 2nd Ed., 733 pages, 1985 (Casebook)

Reuschlein and Gregory's Hornbook on the Law of Agency and Partnership, 625 pages, 1979, with 1981 pocket part (Text)

Seavey, Reuschlein and Hall's Cases on Agency and Partnership, 599 pages, 1962 (Casebook)

Selected Corporation and Partnership Statutes and Forms, 555 pages, 1985

Steffen and Kerr's Cases and Materials on Agency-Partnership, 4th Ed., 859 pages, 1980 (Casebook)

Steffen's Agency-Partnership in a Nutshell, 364 pages, 1977 (Text)

AGRICULTURAL LAW

Meyer, Pedersen, Thorson and Davidson's Agricultural Law: Cases and Materials, 931 pages, 1985 (Casebook)

ALTERNATIVE DISPUTE RESOLUTION

Kanowitz' Cases and Materials on Alternative Dispute Resolution, 1024 pages, 1986 (Casebook)

AMERICAN INDIAN LAW

Canby's American Indian Law in a Nutshell, 288 pages, 1981 (Text)

Getches and Wilkinson's Cases on Federal Indian Law, 2nd Ed., approximately 870 pages, 1986 (Casebook)

ANTITRUST LAW

Gellhorn's Antitrust Law and Economics in a Nutshell, 3rd Ed., about 425 pages, 1987 (Text)

List current as of July, 1986

LAW SCHOOL PUBLICATIONS—Continued

ANTITRUST LAW—Cont'd

Gifford and Raskind's Cases and Materials on Antitrust, 694 pages, 1983 with 1985 Supplement (Casebook)

Hovenkamp's Hornbook on Economics and Federal Antitrust Law, Student Ed., 414 pages, 1985 (Text)

Oppenheim, Weston and McCarthy's Cases and Comments on Federal Antitrust Laws, 4th Ed., 1168 pages, 1981 with 1985 Supplement (Casebook)

Posner and Easterbrook's Cases and Economic Notes on Antitrust, 2nd Ed., 1077 pages, 1981, with 1984–85 Supplement (Casebook)

Sullivan's Hornbook of the Law of Antitrust, 886 pages, 1977 (Text)

See also Regulated Industries, Trade Regulation

ART LAW

DuBoff's Art Law in a Nutshell, 335 pages, 1984 (Text)

BANKING LAW

Lovett's Banking and Financial Institutions in a Nutshell, 409 pages, 1984 (Text)

Symons and White's Teaching Materials on Banking Law, 2nd Ed., 993 pages, 1984 (Casebook)

BUSINESS PLANNING

Painter's Problems and Materials in Business Planning, 2nd Ed., 1008 pages, 1984 (Casebook)

Selected Securities and Business Planning Statutes, Rules and Forms, 470 pages, 1985

CIVIL PROCEDURE

Casad's Res Judicata in a Nutshell, 310 pages, 1976 (text)

Cound, Friedenthal, Miller and Sexton's Cases and Materials on Civil Procedure, 4th Ed., 1202 pages, 1985 with 1985 Supplement (Casebook)

Ehrenzweig, Louisell and Hazard's Jurisdiction in a Nutshell, 4th Ed., 232 pages, 1980 (Text)

Federal Rules of Civil-Appellate Procedure—West Law School Edition, about 550 pages, 1986

Friedenthal, Kane and Miller's Hornbook on Civil Procedure, 876 pages, 1985 (Text)

Kane's Civil Procedure in a Nutshell, 2nd Ed., 306 pages, 1986 (Text)

Koffler and Reppy's Hornbook on Common Law Pleading, 663 pages, 1969 (Text)

Marcus and Sherman's Complex Litigation—Cases and Materials on Advanced Civil Procedure, 846 pages, 1985 (Casebook)

Park's Computer-Aided Exercises on Civil Procedure, 2nd Ed., 167 pages, 1983 (Coursebook)

CIVIL PROCEDURE—Cont'd

Siegel's Hornbook on New York Practice, 1011 pages, 1978 with 1985 Pocket Part (Text)

See also Federal Jurisdiction and Procedure

CIVIL RIGHTS

Abernathy's Cases and Materials on Civil Rights, 660 pages, 1980 (Casebook)

Cohen's Cases on the Law of Deprivation of Liberty: A Study in Social Control, 755 pages, 1980 (Casebook)

Lockhart, Kamisar, Choper and Shiffrin's Cases on Constitutional Rights and Liberties, 6th Ed., about 1300 pages, 1986 with 1986 Supplement (Casebook)—reprint from Lockhart, et al. Cases on Constitutional Law, 6th Ed., 1986

Vieira's Civil Rights in a Nutshell, 279 pages, 1978 (Text)

COMMERCIAL LAW

Bailey's Secured Transactions in a Nutshell, 2nd Ed., 391 pages, 1981 (Text)

Epstein and Martin's Basic Uniform Commercial Code Teaching Materials, 2nd Ed., 667 pages, 1983 (Casebook)

Henson's Hornbook on Secured Transactions Under the U.C.C., 2nd Ed., 504 pages, 1979 with 1979 P.P. (Text)

Murray's Commercial Law, Problems and Materials, 366 pages, 1975 (Coursebook)

Nordstrom and Clovis' Problems and Materials on Commercial Paper, 458 pages, 1972 (Casebook)

Nordstrom, Murray and Clovis' Problems and Materials on Sales, 515 pages, 1982 (Casebook)

Nordstrom, Murray and Clovis' Problems and Materials on Secured Transactions, about 500 pages, 1987 (Casebook)

Selected Commercial Statutes, 1389 pages, 1985

Speidel, Summers and White's Teaching Materials on Commercial and Consumer Law, 3rd Ed., 1490 pages, 1981 (Casebook)

Stockton's Sales in a Nutshell, 2nd Ed., 370 pages, 1981 (Text)

Stone's Uniform Commercial Code in a Nutshell, 2nd Ed., 516 pages, 1984 (Text)

Uniform Commercial Code, Official Text with Comments, 994 pages, 1978

UCC Article 9, Reprint from 1962 Code, 128 pages, 1976

UCC Article 9, 1972 Amendments, 304 pages, 1978

Weber and Speidel's Commercial Paper in a Nutshell, 3rd Ed., 404 pages, 1982 (Text)

White and Summers' Hornbook on the Uniform Commercial Code, 2nd Ed., 1250 pages, 1980 (Text)

LAW SCHOOL PUBLICATIONS—Continued

COMMUNITY PROPERTY

Mennell's Community Property in a Nutshell, 447 pages, 1982 (Text)

Verrall and Bird's Cases and Materials on California Community Property, 4th Ed., 549 pages, 1983 (Casebook)

COMPARATIVE LAW

Barton, Gibbs, Li and Merryman's Law in Radically Different Cultures, 960 pages, 1983 (Casebook)

Glendon, Gordon and Osakive's Comparative Legal Traditions: Text, Materials and Cases on the Civil Law, Common Law, and Socialist Law Traditions, 1091 pages, 1985 (Casebook)

Glendon, Gordon, and Osakwe's Comparative Legal Traditions in a Nutshell, 402 pages, 1982 (Text)

Langbein's Comparative Criminal Procedure: Germany, 172 pages, 1977 (Casebook)

COMPUTERS AND LAW

Maggs and Sprowl's Computer Applications in the Law, about 300 pages, 1986 (Text)

Mason's An Introduction to the Use of Computers in Law, 223 pages, 1984 (Text)

CONFLICT OF LAWS

Cramton, Currie and Kay's Cases-Comments-Questions on Conflict of Laws, 3rd Ed., 1026 pages, 1981 (Casebook)

Scoles and Hay's Hornbook on Conflict of Laws, Student Ed., 1085 pages, 1982 with 1986 P.P. (Text)

Scoles and Weintraub's Cases and Materials on Conflict of Laws, 2nd Ed., 966 pages, 1972, with 1978 Supplement (Casebook)

Siegel's Conflicts in a Nutshell, 469 pages, 1982 (Text)

CONSTITUTIONAL LAW

Barron and Dienes' Constitutional Law in a Nutshell, about 400 pages, 1986 (Text)

Engdahl's Constitutional Power in a Nutshell: Federal and State, 411 pages, 1974 (Text)

Lockhart, Kamisar, Choper and Shiffrin's Cases-Comments-Questions on Constitutional Law, 6th Ed., 1601 pages, 1986 with 1986 Supplement (Casebook)

Lockhart, Kamisar, Choper and Shiffrin's Cases-Comments-Questions on the American Constitution, 6th Ed., about 1200 pages, 1986 with 1986 Supplement (Casebook)—abridgment of Lockhart, et al. Cases on Constitutional Law, 6th Ed., 1986

Manning's The Law of Church-State Relations in a Nutshell, 305 pages, 1981 (Text)

Miller's Presidential Power in a Nutshell, 328 pages, 1977 (Text)

CONSTITUTIONAL LAW—Cont'd

Nowak, Rotunda and Young's Hornbook on Constitutional Law, 3rd Ed., Student Ed., approximately 1100 pages, 1986 (Text)

Rotunda's Modern Constitutional Law: Cases and Notes, 2nd Ed., 1004 pages, 1985, with 1986 Supplement (Casebook)

Williams' Constitutional Analysis in a Nutshell, 388 pages, 1979 (Text)

See also Civil Rights

CONSUMER LAW

Epstein and Nickles' Consumer Law in a Nutshell, 2nd Ed., 418 pages, 1981 (Text)

McCall's Consumer Protection, Cases, Notes and Materials, 594 pages, 1977, with 1977 Statutory Supplement (Casebook)

Selected Commercial Statutes, 1389 pages, 1985

Spanogle and Rohner's Cases and Materials on Consumer Law, 693 pages, 1979, with 1982 Supplement (Casebook)

See also Commercial Law

CONTRACTS

Calamari & Perillo's Cases and Problems on Contracts, 1061 pages, 1978 (Casebook)

Calamari and Perillo's Hornbook on Contracts, 2nd Ed., 878 pages, 1977 (Text)

Corbin's Text on Contracts, One Volume Student Edition, 1224 pages, 1952 (Text)

Fessler and Loiseaux's Cases and Materials on Contracts, 837 pages, 1982 (Casebook)

Friedman's Contract Remedies in a Nutshell, 323 pages, 1981 (Text)

Fuller and Eisenberg's Cases on Basic Contract Law, 4th Ed., 1203 pages, 1981 (Casebook)

Hamilton, Rau and Weintraub's Cases and Materials on Contracts, 830 pages, 1984 (Casebook)

Jackson and Bollinger's Cases on Contract Law in Modern Society, 2nd Ed., 1329 pages, 1980 (Casebook)

Keyes' Government Contracts in a Nutshell, 423 pages, 1979 (Text)

Schaber and Rohwer's Contracts in a Nutshell, 2nd Ed., 425 pages, 1984 (Text)

COPYRIGHT

See Patent and Copyright Law

CORPORATIONS

Hamilton's Cases on Corporations—Including Partnerships and Limited Partnerships, 3rd Ed., 1213 pages, 1986 with 1986 Statutory Supplement (Casebook)

Hamilton's Law of Corporations in a Nutshell, 379 pages, 1980 (Text)

Henn's Teaching Materials on Corporations, 2nd Ed., about 1200 pages, 1986 (Casebook)

LAW SCHOOL PUBLICATIONS—Continued

CORPORATIONS—Cont'd

Henn and Alexander's Hornbook on Corporations, 3rd Ed., Student Ed., 1371 pages, 1983 with 1986 P.P. (Text)

Jennings and Buxbaum's Cases and Materials on Corporations, 5th Ed., 1180 pages, 1979 (Casebook)

Selected Corporation and Partnership Statutes, Regulations and Forms, 555 pages, 1985

Solomon, Stevenson and Schwartz' Materials and Problems on Corporations: Law and Policy, 1172 pages, 1982 with 1986 Supplement (Casebook)

CORPORATE FINANCE

Hamilton's Cases and Materials on Corporate Finance, 895 pages, 1984 with 1986 Supplement (Casebook)

CORRECTIONS

Krantz's Cases and Materials on the Law of Corrections and Prisoners' Rights, 3rd Ed., 855 pages, 1986 (Casebook)

Krantz's Law of Corrections and Prisoners' Rights in a Nutshell, 2nd Ed., 386 pages, 1983 (Text)

Popper's Post-Conviction Remedies in a Nutshell, 360 pages, 1978 (Text)

Robbins' Cases and Materials on Post Conviction Remedies, 506 pages, 1982 (Casebook)

CREDITOR'S RIGHTS

Bankruptcy Code, Rules and Forms, Law School and C.L.E. Ed., about 800 pages, 1986

Epstein's Debtor-Creditor Law in a Nutshell, 3rd Ed., 383 pages, 1986 (Text)

Epstein and Landers' Debtors and Creditors: Cases and Materials, 2nd Ed., 689 pages, 1982 (Casebook)

LoPucki's Player's Manual for the Debtor-Creditor Game, 123 pages, 1985 (Coursebook)

Riesenfeld's Cases and Materials on Creditors' Remedies and Debtors' Protection, 4th Ed., about 800 pages, 1987 (Casebook)

White's Bankruptcy and Creditor's Rights: Cases and Materials, 812 pages, 1985 (Casebook)

CRIMINAL LAW AND CRIMINAL PROCEDURE

Abrams', Federal Criminal Law and its Enforcement, 882 pages, 1986 (Casebook)

Carlson's Adjudication of Criminal Justice, Problems and References, about 124 pages, 1986 (Casebook)

Dix and Sharlot's Cases and Materials on Criminal Law, 2nd Ed., 771 pages, 1979 (Casebook)

CRIMINAL LAW AND CRIMINAL PROCEDURE—Cont'd

Federal Rules of Criminal Procedure—West Law School Edition, about 465 pages, 1986

Grano's Problems in Criminal Procedure, 2nd Ed., 176 pages, 1981 (Problem book)

Israel and LaFave's Criminal Procedure in a Nutshell, 3rd Ed., 438 pages, 1980 (Text)

Johnson's Cases, Materials and Text on Criminal Law, 3rd Ed., 783 pages, 1985 (Casebook)

Kamisar, LaFave and Israel's Cases, Comments and Questions on Modern Criminal Procedure, 6th Ed., about 1600 pages, 1986 with 1986 Supplement (Casebook)

Kamisar, LaFave and Israel's Cases, Comments and Questions on Basic Criminal Procedure, 6th Ed., about 800 pages, 1986 with 1986 Supplement (Casebook)—reprint from Kamisar, et al. Modern Criminal Procedure, 6th ed., 1986

LaFave's Modern Criminal Law: Cases, Comments and Questions, 789 pages, 1978 (Casebook)

LaFave and Israel's Hornbook on Criminal Procedure, Student Ed., 1142 pages, 1985 with 1985 P.P. (Text)

LaFave and Scott's Hornbook on Criminal Law, 2nd Ed., Student Ed., about 800 pages, 1986 (Text)

Langbein's Comparative Criminal Procedure: Germany, 172 pages, 1977 (Casebook)

Loewy's Criminal Law in a Nutshell, 302 pages, 1975 (Text)

Saltzburg's American Criminal Procedure, Cases and Commentary, 2nd Ed., 1193 pages, 1985 with 1986 Supplement (Casebook)

Uviller's The Processes of Criminal Justice: Investigation and Adjudication, 2nd Ed., 1384 pages, 1979 with 1979 Statutory Supplement and 1986 Update (Casebook)

Uviller's The Processes of Criminal Justice: Adjudication, 2nd Ed., 730 pages, 1979. Soft-cover reprint from Uviller's The Processes of Criminal Justice: Investigation and Adjudication, 2nd Ed. (Casebook)

Uviller's The Processes of Criminal Justice: Investigation, 2nd Ed., 655 pages, 1979. Soft-cover reprint from Uviller's The Processes of Criminal Justice: Investigation and Adjudication, 2nd Ed. (Casebook)

Vorenberg's Cases on Criminal Law and Procedure, 2nd Ed., 1088 pages, 1981 with 1985 Supplement (Casebook)

See also Corrections, Juvenile Justice

DECEDENTS ESTATES

See Trusts and Estates

LAW SCHOOL PUBLICATIONS—Continued

DOMESTIC RELATIONS

Clark's Cases and Problems on Domestic Relations, 3rd Ed., 1153 pages, 1980 (Casebook)

Clark's Hornbook on Domestic Relations, 754 pages, 1968 (Text)

Krause's Cases and Materials on Family Law, 2nd Ed., 1221 pages, 1983 with 1986 Supplement (Casebook)

Krause's Family Law in a Nutshell, 2nd Ed., 444 pages, 1986 (Text)

Krauskopf's Cases on Property Division at Marriage Dissolution, 250 pages, 1984 (Casebook)

ECONOMICS, LAW AND

Goetz' Cases and Materials on Law and Economics, 547 pages, 1984 (Casebook)

See also Antitrust, Regulated Industries

EDUCATION LAW

Alexander and Alexander's The Law of Schools, Students and Teachers in a Nutshell, 409 pages, 1984 (Text)

Morris' The Constitution and American Education, 2nd Ed., 992 pages, 1980 (Casebook)

EMPLOYMENT DISCRIMINATION

Jones, Murphy and Belton's Cases on Discrimination in Employment, about 930 pages, 1986 (Casebook)

Player's Cases and Materials on Employment Discrimination Law, 2nd Ed., 782 pages, 1984 (Casebook)

Player's Federal Law of Employment Discrimination in a Nutshell, 2nd Ed., 402 pages, 1981 (Text)

See also Women and the Law

ENERGY AND NATURAL RESOURCES LAW

Laitos' Cases and Materials on Natural Resources Law, 938 pages, 1985 (Casebook)

Rodgers' Cases and Materials on Energy and Natural Resources Law, 2nd Ed., 877 pages, 1983 (Casebook)

Selected Environmental Law Statutes, about 850 pages, 1986

Tomain's Energy Law in a Nutshell, 338 pages, 1981 (Text)

See also Environmental Law, Oil and Gas, Water Law

ENVIRONMENTAL LAW

Bonine and McGarity's Cases and Materials on the Law of Environment and Pollution, 1076 pages, 1984 (Casebook)

Findley and Farber's Cases and Materials on Environmental Law, 2nd Ed., 813 pages, 1985 (Casebook)

Findley and Farber's Environmental Law in a Nutshell, 343 pages, 1983 (Text)

ENVIRONMENTAL LAW—Cont'd

Rodgers' Hornbook on Environmental Law, 956 pages, 1977 with 1984 pocket part (Text)

Selected Environmental Law Statutes, about 950 pages, 1986

See also Energy Law, Natural Resources Law, Water Law

EQUITY

See Remedies

ESTATES

See Trusts and Estates

ESTATE PLANNING

Kurtz' Cases, Materials and Problems on Family Estate Planning, 853 pages, 1983 (Casebook)

Lynn's Introduction to Estate Planning, in a Nutshell, 3rd Ed., 370 pages, 1983 (Text)

See also Taxation

EVIDENCE

Broun and Meisenholder's Problems in Evidence, 2nd Ed., 304 pages, 1981 (Problem book)

Cleary and Strong's Cases, Materials and Problems on Evidence, 3rd Ed., 1143 pages, 1981 (Casebook)

Federal Rules of Evidence for United States Courts and Magistrates, 337 pages, 1984

Graham's Federal Rules of Evidence in a Nutshell, 429 pages, 1981 (Text)

Kimball's Programmed Materials on Problems in Evidence, 380 pages, 1978 (Problem book)

Lempert and Saltzburg's A Modern Approach to Evidence: Text, Problems, Transcripts and Cases, 2nd Ed., 1232 pages, 1983 (Casebook)

Lilly's Introduction to the Law of Evidence, 490 pages, 1978 (Text)

McCormick, Elliott and Sutton's Cases and Materials on Evidence, 5th Ed., 1212 pages, 1981 (Casebook)

McCormick's Hornbook on Evidence, 3rd Ed., Student Ed., 1156 pages, 1984 (Text)

Rothstein's Evidence, State and Federal Rules in a Nutshell, 2nd Ed., 514 pages, 1981 (Text)

Saltzburg's Evidence Supplement: Rules, Statutes, Commentary, 245 pages, 1980 (Casebook Supplement)

FEDERAL JURISDICTION AND PROCEDURE

Currie's Cases and Materials on Federal Courts, 3rd Ed., 1042 pages, 1982 with 1985 Supplement (Casebook)

Currie's Federal Jurisdiction in a Nutshell, 2nd Ed., 258 pages, 1981 (Text)

FEDERAL JURISDICTION AND PROCEDURE—Cont'd

Federal Rules of Civil-Appellate Procedure—West Law School Edition, about 550 pages, 1986

Forrester and Moye's Cases and Materials on Federal Jurisdiction and Procedure, 3rd Ed., 917 pages, 1977 with 1985 Supplement (Casebook)

Redish's Cases, Comments and Questions on Federal Courts, 878 pages, 1983 with 1986 Supplement (Casebook)

Vetri and Merrill's Federal Courts, Problems and Materials, 2nd Ed., 232 pages, 1984 (Problem Book)

Wright's Hornbook on Federal Courts, 4th Ed., Student Ed., 870 pages, 1983 (Text)

FUTURE INTERESTS

See Trusts and Estates

IMMIGRATION LAW

Aleinikoff and Martin's Immigration Process and Policy, 1042 pages, 1985 (Casebook)

Weissbrodt's Immigration Law and Procedure in a Nutshell, 345 pages, 1984 (Text)

INDIAN LAW

See American Indian Law

INSURANCE

Dobbyn's Insurance Law in a Nutshell, 281 pages, 1981 (Text)

Keeton's Cases on Basic Insurance Law, 2nd Ed., 1086 pages, 1977

Keeton's Basic Text on Insurance Law, 712 pages, 1971 (Text)

Keeton's Case Supplement to Keeton's Basic Text on Insurance Law, 334 pages, 1978 (Casebook)

York and Whelan's Cases, Materials and Problems on Insurance Law, 715 pages, 1982, with 1985 Supplement (Casebook)

INTERNATIONAL LAW

Buergenthal and Maier's Public International Law in a Nutshell, 262 pages, 1985 (Text)

Folsom, Gordon and Spanogle's International Business Transactions – a Problem-Oriented Coursebook, 1160 pages, 1986 (Casebook)

Henkin, Pugh, Schachter and Smit's Cases and Materials on International Law, 2nd Ed., about 1200 pages, 1987 with Documents Supplement (Casebook)

Jackson and Davey's Legal Problems of International Economic Relations, 2nd Ed., about 1250 pages, 1986, with Documents Supplement (Casebook)

Kirgis' International Organizations in Their Legal Setting, 1016 pages, 1977, with 1981 Supplement (Casebook)

INTERNATIONAL LAW—Cont'd

Weston, Falk and D'Amato's International Law and World Order—A Problem Oriented Coursebook, 1195 pages, 1980, with Documents Supplement (Casebook)

Wilson's International Business Transactions in a Nutshell, 2nd Ed., 476 pages, 1984 (Text)

INTERVIEWING AND COUNSELING

Binder and Price's Interviewing and Counseling, 232 pages, 1977 (Text)

Shaffer's Interviewing and Counseling in a Nutshell, 353 pages, 1976 (Text)

INTRODUCTION TO LAW STUDY

Dobbyn's So You Want to go to Law School, Revised First Edition, 206 pages, 1976 (Text)

Hegland's Introduction to the Study and Practice of Law in a Nutshell, 418 pages, 1983 (Text)

Kinyon's Introduction to Law Study and Law Examinations in a Nutshell, 389 pages, 1971 (Text)

See also Legal Method and Legal System

JUDICIAL ADMINISTRATION

Nelson's Cases and Materials on Judicial Administration and the Administration of Justice, 1032 pages, 1974 (Casebook)

JURISPRUDENCE

Christie's Text and Readings on Jurisprudence—The Philosophy of Law, 1056 pages, 1973 (Casebook)

JUVENILE JUSTICE

Fox's Cases and Materials on Modern Juvenile Justice, 2nd Ed., 960 pages, 1981 (Casebook)

Fox's Juvenile Courts in a Nutshell, 3rd Ed., 291 pages, 1984 (Text)

LABOR LAW

Gorman's Basic Text on Labor Law—Unionization and Collective Bargaining, 914 pages, 1976 (Text)

Leslie's Labor Law in a Nutshell, 2nd Ed., 397 pages, 1986 (Text)

Nolan's Labor Arbitration Law and Practice in a Nutshell, 358 pages, 1979 (Text)

Oberer, Hanslowe, Andersen and Heinsz' Cases and Materials on Labor Law—Collective Bargaining in a Free Society, 3rd Ed., about 1200 pages, 1986 with Statutory Supplement (Casebook)

See also Employment Discrimination, Social Legislation

LAND FINANCE

See Real Estate Transactions

LAND USE

Callies and Freilich's Cases and Materials on Land Use, 1233 pages, 1986 (Casebook)

Hagman's Cases on Public Planning and Control of Urban and Land Development, 2nd Ed., 1301 pages, 1980 (Casebook)

Hagman and Juergensmeyer's Hornbook on Urban Planning and Land Development Control Law, 2nd Ed., Student Edition, approximately 580 pages, 1986 (Text)

Wright and Gitelman's Cases and Materials on Land Use, 3rd Ed., 1300 pages, 1982 (Casebook)

Wright and Wright's Land Use in a Nutshell, 2nd Ed., 356 pages, 1985 (Text)

LEGAL HISTORY

Presser and Zainaldin's Cases on Law and American History, 855 pages, 1980 (Casebook)

See also Legal Method and Legal System

LEGAL METHOD AND LEGAL SYSTEM

Aldisert's Readings, Materials and Cases in the Judicial Process, 948 pages, 1976 (Casebook)

Berch and Berch's Introduction to Legal Method and Process, 550 pages, 1985 (Casebook)

Bodenheimer, Oakley and Love's Readings and Cases on an Introduction to the Anglo-American Legal System, 161 pages, 1980 (Casebook)

Davies and Lawry's Institutions and Methods of the Law—Introductory Teaching Materials, 547 pages, 1982 (Casebook)

Dvorkin, Himmelstein and Lesnick's Becoming a Lawyer: A Humanistic Perspective on Legal Education and Professionalism, 211 pages, 1981 (Text)

Greenberg's Judicial Process and Social Change, 666 pages, 1977 (Casebook)

Kelso and Kelso's Studying Law: An Introduction, 587 pages, 1984 (Coursebook)

Kempin's Historical Introduction to Anglo-American Law in a Nutshell, 2nd Ed., 280 pages, 1973 (Text)

Kimball's Historical Introduction to the Legal System, 610 pages, 1966 (Casebook)

Murphy's Cases and Materials on Introduction to Law—Legal Process and Procedure, 772 pages, 1977 (Casebook)

Reynolds' Judicial Process in a Nutshell, 292 pages, 1980 (Text)

See also Legal Research and Writing

LEGAL PROFESSION

Aronson, Devine and Fisch's Problems, Cases and Materials on Professional Responsibility, 745 pages, 1985 (Casebook)

Aronson and Weckstein's Professional Responsibility in a Nutshell, 399 pages, 1980 (Text)

LEGAL PROFESSION—Cont'd

Mellinkoff's The Conscience of a Lawyer, 304 pages, 1973 (Text)

Mellinkoff's Lawyers and the System of Justice, 983 pages, 1976 (Casebook)

Pirsig and Kirwin's Cases and Materials on Professional Responsibility, 4th Ed., 603 pages, 1984 (Casebook)

Schwartz and Wydick's Problems in Legal Ethics, 285 pages, 1983 (Casebook)

Selected Statutes, Rules and Standards on the Legal Profession, 276 pages, Revised 1984

Smith's Preventing Legal Malpractice, 142 pages, 1981 (Text)

Wolfram's Hornbook on Modern Legal Ethics, Student Edition, 1120 pages, 1986 (Text)

LEGAL RESEARCH AND WRITING

Cohen's Legal Research in a Nutshell, 4th Ed., 450 pages, 1985 (Text)

Cohen and Berring's How to Find the Law, 8th Ed., 790 pages, 1983. Problem book by Foster, Johnson and Kelly available (Casebook)

Cohen and Berring's Finding the Law, 8th Ed., Abridged Ed., 556 pages, 1984 (Casebook)

Dickerson's Materials on Legal Drafting, 425 pages, 1981 (Casebook)

Felsenfeld and Siegel's Writing Contracts in Plain English, 290 pages, 1981 (Text)

Gopen's Writing From a Legal Perspective, 225 pages, 1981 (Text)

Mellinkoff's Legal Writing—Sense and Nonsense, 242 pages, 1982 (Text)

Rombauer's Legal Problem Solving—Analysis, Research and Writing, 4th Ed., 424 pages, 1983 (Coursebook)

Squires and Rombauer's Legal Writing in a Nutshell, 294 pages, 1982 (Text)

Statsky's Legal Research, Writing and Analysis, 2nd Ed., 167 pages, 1982 (Coursebook)

Statsky and Wernet's Case Analysis and Fundamentals of Legal Writing, 2nd Ed., 441 pages, 1984 (Text)

Teply's Programmed Materials on Legal Research and Citation, 2nd Ed., 358 pages, 1986. Student Library Exercises available (Coursebook)

Weihofen's Legal Writing Style, 2nd Ed., 332 pages, 1980 (Text)

LEGISLATION

Davies' Legislative Law and Process in a Nutshell, 2nd Ed., 346 pages, 1986 (Text)

Nutting and Dickerson's Cases and Materials on Legislation, 5th Ed., 744 pages, 1978 (Casebook)

LAW SCHOOL PUBLICATIONS—Continued

LEGISLATION—Cont'd

Statsky's Legislative Analysis: How to Use Statutes and Regulations, 2nd Ed., 217 pages, 1984 (Text)

LOCAL GOVERNMENT

McCarthy's Local Government Law in a Nutshell, 2nd Ed., 404 pages, 1983 (Text)

Reynolds' Hornbook on Local Government Law, 860 pages, 1982 (Text)

Valente's Cases and Materials on Local Government Law, 2nd Ed., 980 pages, 1980 with 1982 Supplement (Casebook)

MASS COMMUNICATION LAW

Gillmor and Barron's Cases and Comment on Mass Communication Law, 4th Ed., 1076 pages, 1984 (Casebook)

Ginsburg's Regulation of Broadcasting: Law and Policy Towards Radio, Television and Cable Communications, 741 pages, 1979, with 1983 Supplement (Casebook)

Zuckman and Gayne's Mass Communications Law in a Nutshell, 2nd Ed., 473 pages, 1983 (Text)

MEDICINE, LAW AND

King's The Law of Medical Malpractice in a Nutshell, 2nd Ed., 342 pages, 1986 (Text)

Shapiro and Spece's Problems, Cases and Materials on Bioethics and Law, 892 pages, 1981 (Casebook)

Sharpe, Fiscina and Head's Cases on Law and Medicine, 882 pages, 1978 (Casebook)

MILITARY LAW

Shanor and Terrell's Military Law in a Nutshell, 378 pages, 1980 (Text)

MORTGAGES

See Real Estate Transactions

NATURAL RESOURCES LAW

See Energy and Natural Resources Law

NEGOTIATION

Edwards and White's Problems, Readings and Materials on the Lawyer as a Negotiator, 484 pages, 1977 (Casebook)

Williams' Legal Negotiation and Settlement, 207 pages, 1983 (Coursebook)

OFFICE PRACTICE

Hegland's Trial and Practice Skills in a Nutshell, 346 pages, 1978 (Text)

Strong and Clark's Law Office Management, 424 pages, 1974 (Casebook)

See also Computers and Law, Interviewing and Counseling, Negotiation

OIL AND GAS

Hemingway's Hornbook on Oil and Gas, 2nd Ed., Student Ed., 543 pages, 1983 with 1986 P.P. (Text)

OIL AND GAS—Cont'd

Kuntz, Lowe, Anderson and Smith's Cases and Materials on Oil and Gas Law, 857 pages, 1986 (Casebook)

Lowe's Oil and Gas Law in a Nutshell, 443 pages, 1983 (Text)

See also Energy and Natural Resources Law

PARTNERSHIP

See Agency—Partnership

PATENT AND COPYRIGHT LAW

Choate and Francis' Cases and Materials on Patent Law, 2nd Ed., 1110 pages, 1981 (Casebook)

Miller and Davis' Intellectual Property—Patents, Trademarks and Copyright in a Nutshell, 428 pages, 1983 (Text)

Nimmer's Cases on Copyright and Other Aspects of Entertainment Litigation, 3rd Ed., 1025 pages, 1985 (Casebook)

PRODUCTS LIABILITY

Noel and Phillips' Cases on Products Liability, 2nd Ed., 821 pages, 1982 (Casebook)

Noel and Phillips' Products Liability in a Nutshell, 2nd Ed., 341 pages, 1981 (Text)

PROPERTY

Bernhardt's Real Property in a Nutshell, 2nd Ed., 448 pages, 1981 (Text)

Boyer's Survey of the Law of Property, 766 pages, 1981 (Text)

Browder, Cunningham and Smith's Cases on Basic Property Law, 4th Ed., 1431 pages, 1984 (Casebook)

Bruce, Ely and Bostick's Cases and Materials on Modern Property Law, 1004 pages, 1984 (Casebook)

Burke's Personal Property in a Nutshell, 322 pages, 1983 (Text)

Cunningham, Stoebuck and Whitman's Hornbook on the Law of Property, Student Ed., 916 pages, 1984 (Text)

Donahue, Kauper and Martin's Cases on Property, 2nd Ed., 1362 pages, 1983 (Casebook)

Hill's Landlord and Tenant Law in a Nutshell, 2nd Ed., 311 pages, 1986 (Text)

Moynihan's Introduction to Real Property, 254 pages, 1962 (Text)

Uniform Land Transactions Act, Uniform Simplification of Land Transfers Act, Uniform Condominium Act, 1977 Official Text with Comments, 462 pages, 1978

See also Real Estate Transactions, Land Use

PSYCHIATRY, LAW AND

Reisner's Law and the Mental Health System, Civil and Criminal Aspects, 696 pages, 1985 (Casebooks)

LAW SCHOOL PUBLICATIONS—Continued

REAL ESTATE TRANSACTIONS

Bruce's Real Estate Finance in a Nutshell, 2nd Ed., 262 pages, 1985 (Text)

Maxwell, Riesenfeld, Hetland and Warren's Cases on California Security Transactions in Land, 3rd Ed., 728 pages, 1984 (Casebook)

Nelson and Whitman's Cases on Real Estate Transfer, Finance and Development, 2nd Ed., 1114 pages, 1981, with 1986 Supplement (Casebook)

Nelson and Whitman's Hornbook on Real Estate Finance Law, 2nd Ed., Student Ed., 941 pages, 1985 (Text)

Osborne's Cases and Materials on Secured Transactions, 559 pages, 1967 (Casebook)

REGULATED INDUSTRIES

Gellhorn and Pierce's Regulated Industries in a Nutshell, 394 pages, 1982 (Text)

Morgan, Harrison and Verkuil's Cases and Materials on Economic Regulation of Business, 2nd Ed., 666 pages, 1985 (Casebook)

See also Mass Communication Law, Banking Law

REMEDIES

Dobbs' Hornbook on Remedies, 1067 pages, 1973 (Text)

Dobbs' Problems in Remedies, 137 pages, 1974 (Problem book)

Dobbyn's Injunctions in a Nutshell, 264 pages, 1974 (Text)

Friedman's Contract Remedies in a Nutshell, 323 pages, 1981 (Text)

Leavell, Love and Nelson's Cases and Materials on Equitable Remedies and Restitution, 4th Ed., 1111 pages, 1986 (Casebook)

McCormick's Hornbook on Damages, 811 pages, 1935 (Text)

O'Connell's Remedies in a Nutshell, 2nd Ed., 320 pages, 1985 (Text)

York, Bauman and Rendleman's Cases and Materials on Remedies, 4th Ed., 1029 pages, 1985 (Casebook)

REVIEW MATERIALS

Ballantine's Problems

Black Letter Series

Smith's Review Series

West's Review Covering Multistate Subjects

SECURITIES REGULATION

Hazen's Hornbook on The Law of Securities Regulation, Student Ed., 739 pages, 1985 (Text)

Ratner's Securities Regulation: Materials for a Basic Course, 3rd Ed., 1000 pages, 1986 (Casebook)

Ratner's Securities Regulation in a Nutshell, 2nd Ed., 322 pages, 1982 (Text)

SECURITIES REGULATION—Cont'd

Selected Securities and Business Planning Statutes, Rules and Forms, 470 pages, 1985

SOCIAL LEGISLATION

Hood and Hardy's Workers' Compensation and Employee Protection Laws in a Nutshell, 274 pages, 1984 (Text)

LaFrance's Welfare Law: Structure and Entitlement in a Nutshell, 455 pages, 1979 (Text)

Malone, Plant and Little's Cases on Workers' Compensation and Employment Rights, 2nd Ed., 951 pages, 1980 (Casebook)

SPORTS LAW

Schubert, Smith and Trentadue's Sports Law, 395 pages, 1986 (Text)

TAXATION

Dodge's Cases and Materials on Federal Income Taxation, 820 pages, 1985 (Casebook)

Dodge's Federal Taxation of Estates, Trusts and Gifts: Principles and Planning, 771 pages, 1981 with 1982 Supplement (Casebook)

Garbis and Struntz' Cases and Materials on Tax Procedure and Tax Fraud, 829 pages, 1982 with 1984 Supplement (Casebook)

Gelfand and Salsich's State and Local Taxation and Finance in a Nutshell, 309 pages, 1986 (Text)

Gunn's Cases and Materials on Federal Income Taxation of Individuals, 785 pages, 1981 with 1985 Supplement (Casebook)

Hellerstein and Hellerstein's Cases on State and Local Taxation, 4th Ed., 1041 pages, 1978 with 1982 Supplement (Casebook)

Kahn and Gann's Corporate Taxation and Taxation of Partnerships and Partners, 2nd Ed., 1204 pages, 1985 (Casebook)

Kragen and McNulty's Cases and Materials on Federal Income Taxation: Individuals, Corporations, Partnerships, 4th Ed., 1287 pages, 1985 (Casebook)

McNulty's Federal Estate and Gift Taxation in a Nutshell, 3rd Ed., 509 pages, 1983 (Text)

McNulty's Federal Income Taxation of Individuals in a Nutshell, 3rd Ed., 487 pages, 1983 (Text)

Posin's Hornbook on Federal Income Taxation of Individuals, Student Ed., 491 pages, 1983 with 1985 pocket part (Text)

Selected Federal Taxation Statutes and Regulations, about 1400 pages, 1986

Solomon and Hesch's Cases on Federal Income Taxation of Individuals, about 800 pages, 1987 (Casebook)

LAW SCHOOL PUBLICATIONS—Continued

TAXATION—Cont'd

Sobeloff and Weidenbruch's Federal Income Taxation of Corporations and Stockholders in a Nutshell, 362 pages, 1981 (Text)

TORTS

Christie's Cases and Materials on the Law of Torts, 1264 pages, 1983 (Casebook)

Dobbs' Torts and Compensation—Personal Accountability and Social Responsibility for Injury, 955 pages, 1985 (Casebook)

Green, Pedrick, Rahl, Thode, Hawkins, Smith and Treece's Cases and Materials on Torts, 2nd Ed., 1360 pages, 1977 (Casebook)

Green, Pedrick, Rahl, Thode, Hawkins, Smith, and Treece's Advanced Torts: Injuries to Business, Political and Family Interests, 2nd Ed., 544 pages, 1977 (Casebook)—reprint from Green, et al. Cases and Materials on Torts, 2nd Ed., 1977

Keeton, Keeton, Sargentich and Steiner's Cases and Materials on Torts, and Accident Law, 1360 pages, 1983 (Casebook)

Kionka's Torts in a Nutshell: Injuries to Persons and Property, 434 pages, 1977 (Text)

Malone's Torts in a Nutshell: Injuries to Family, Social and Trade Relations, 358 pages, 1979 (Text)

Prosser and Keeton's Hornbook on Torts, 5th Ed., Student Ed., 1286 pages, 1984 (Text)

Shapo's Cases on Tort and Compensation Law, 1244 pages, 1976 (Casebook)

See also Products Liability

TRADE REGULATION

McManis' Unfair Trade Practices in a Nutshell, 444 pages, 1982 (Text)

Oppenheim, Weston, Maggs and Schechter's Cases and Materials on Unfair Trade Practices and Consumer Protection, 4th Ed., 1038 pages, 1983 with 1986 Supplement (Casebook)

See also Antitrust, Regulated Industries

TRIAL AND APPELLATE ADVOCACY

Appellate Advocacy, Handbook of, 2nd Ed., 182 pages, 1986 (Text)

Bergman's Trial Advocacy in a Nutshell, 402 pages, 1979 (Text)

Binder and Bergman's Fact Investigation: From Hypothesis to Proof, 354 pages, 1984 (Coursebook)

Goldberg's The First Trial (Where Do I Sit?, What Do I Say?) in a Nutshell, 396 pages, 1982 (Text)

Haydock, Herr and Stempel's, Fundamentals of Pre-Trial Litigation, 768 pages, 1985 (Casebook)

Hegland's Trial and Practice Skills in a Nutshell, 346 pages, 1978 (Text)

Hornstein's Appellate Advocacy in a Nutshell, 325 pages, 1984 (Text)

TRIAL AND APPELLATE ADVOCACY—Cont'd

Jeans' Handbook on Trial Advocacy, Student Ed., 473 pages, 1975 (Text)

Martineau's Cases and Materials on Appellate Practice and Procedure, about 550 pages, 1987 (Casebook)

McElhaney's Effective Litigation, 457 pages, 1974 (Casebook)

Nolan's Cases and Materials on Trial Practice, 518 pages, 1981 (Casebook)

Parnell and Shellhaas' Cases, Exercises and Problems for Trial Advocacy, 171 pages, 1982 (Coursebook)

Sonsteng, Haydock and Boyd's The Trialbook: A Total System for Preparation and Presentation of a Case, Student Ed., 404 pages, 1984 (Coursebook)

TRUSTS AND ESTATES

Atkinson's Hornbook on Wills, 2nd Ed., 975 pages, 1953 (Text)

Averill's Uniform Probate Code in a Nutshell, 425 pages, 1978 (Text)

Bogert's Hornbook on Trusts, 5th Ed., 726 pages, 1973 (Text)

Clark, Lusky and Murphy's Cases and Materials on Gratuitous Transfers, 3rd Ed., 970 pages, 1985 (Casebook)

Gulliver's Cases and Materials on Future Interests, 624 pages, 1959 (Casebook)

Gulliver's Introduction to the Law of Future Interests, 87 pages, 1959 (Casebook)—reprint from Gulliver's Cases and Materials on Future Interests, 1959

McGovern's Cases and Materials on Wills, Trusts and Future Interests: An Introduction to Estate Planning, 750 pages, 1983 (Casebook)

Mennell's Cases and Materials on California Decedent's Estates, 566 pages, 1973 (Casebook)

Mennell's Wills and Trusts in a Nutshell, 392 pages, 1979 (Text)

Powell's The Law of Future Interests in California, 91 pages, 1980 (Text)

Simes' Hornbook on Future Interests, 2nd Ed., 355 pages, 1966 (Text)

Turano and Radigan's Hornbook on New York Estate Administration, approximately 575 pages, 1986 (Text)

Uniform Probate Code, 5th Ed., Official Text With Comments, 384 pages, 1977

Waggoner's Future Interests in a Nutshell, 361 pages, 1981 (Text)

Waterbury's Materials on Trusts and Estates, 1039 pages, 1986 (Casebook)

WATER LAW

Getches' Water Law in a Nutshell, 439 pages, 1984 (Text)

LAW SCHOOL PUBLICATIONS—Continued

WATER LAW—Cont'd

Sax and Abram's Cases and Materials on Legal Control of Water Resources in the United States, 941 pages, 1986 (Casebook)

Trelease and Gould's Cases and Materials on Water Law, 4th Ed., 816 pages, 1986 (Casebook)

See also Energy and Natural Resources Law, Environmental Law

WILLS

See Trusts and Estates

WOMEN AND THE LAW

Kay's Text, Cases and Materials on Sex-Based Discrimination, 2nd Ed., 1045 pages, 1981, with 1986 Supplement (Casebook)

Thomas' Sex Discrimination in a Nutshell, 399 pages, 1982 (Text)

See also Employment Discrimination

WORKERS' COMPENSATION

See Social Legislation

URBAN PLANNING
AND
LAND DEVELOPMENT
CONTROL LAW

Second Edition

By
The Late Donald G. Hagman
and
Julian Conrad Juergensmeyer
Professor of Law, University of Florida

HORNBOOK SERIES
STUDENT EDITION

WEST PUBLISHING CO.
ST. PAUL, MINN., 1986

COPYRIGHT © 1971 By WEST PUBLISHING CO.
COPYRIGHT © 1986 By WEST PUBLISHING CO.
                         50 W. Kellogg Boulevard
                         P.O. Box 64526
                         St. Paul, Minnesota 55164–0526

Library of Congress Cataloging-in-Publication Data

Hagman, Donald G.
    Urban planning and land development.

    (Hornbook series student edition)
    Includes index.
    1. City planning and redevelopment law—United States.
2. Zoning law—United States. I. Juergensmeyer, Julian
Conrad. II. Title. III. Series.
KF5692.H3   1986   346.7304'5   86–9225
                        347.30645

ISBN 0–314–99321–5
Urban Planning, 2d Ed. (H. & J.) HB

Dedication
(First Edition)

To Ilene, my wife
and to
Fred Bosselman
and
Daniel Mandelker
Admirable peers

Dedication
(Second Edition)

To Jane, Conrad & Erik
And to the Memory of
Donald Hagman

*

Preface and Acknowledgements
to the First Edition

This textbook on urban planning and controls is offered as a basic, simplified, comprehensive discussion. It attempts to distill, summarize and state textually the wisdom on planning and development control law collected in current casebooks.

The materials in the casebooks which are fairly within the scope of the subject matter of planning and development control law are the minimum subject content of this textbook. However, since it is almost the essential nature of a casebook to leave gaps, since the subject matter is a rapidly developing one, and since it is losing its physical or land use base and becoming more economic and social oriented, there are numerous areas I have covered that are not in all or in any of the casebooks.

Because the raw materials which form the base of this textbook are predominantly written by property professors, the textbook is somewhat biased in that direction. However, that bias is corrected by my approach to the subject, which comes from the tradition of local government rather than from property. My hope is that this book will constitute a bridge between property materials and government materials, since the subject matter of planning and development controls is not yet dominated either by property law or local government law professors. For a time, the property professors dominated the subject matter as more and more of the basic property casebooks included planning and development control materials. However, in recent years it is refreshing to see a new breed of local government professors develop, who are being spurred by the "urban crisis" to write new and exciting materials that depart from the sterile municipal corporation and local government casebooks.

The uses of a textbook are not controlled by an author, but this book is designed to be supplementary reading in a basic property course in which planning and development controls materials are included. Generally, the property text book writers have not included these materials in basic property texts as have property casebook authors. Similarly, it is supplemental reading for those local government and urban problems courses that cover planning and development controls subject matter. Of course, the text can be used as a supplement to those courses which focus exclusively on that subject matter. It is specifically designed to supplement D. Hagman, Urban Planning and Controls: Problems and Materials (Tent.Ed.1969, Supp.1970, Supp.1971). That book is offered for use in an advanced course which seeks to give depth of coverage by use of the problem method and relies on breadth of coverage by supplementary reading in this textbook. Students coming to the advanced course sometimes have not been exposed to basic planning and development controls materials in their basic property course. Those who have had such basic materials can use the textbook to refresh their recollection and to give a broader context for the problems they will be considering.

I have been most fortunate to have the able and cheerful secretarial assistance of Polly Kosche, Pat Nicholas and others, for which I am most grateful.

One of the delights of writing books is that law student research assistants can be used. The use of such students is rewarding because the relationship between the student and the professor can be more intensive than the typical one afforded by the classroom situation. In addition, through their work, students develop a good deal of insight and understanding about the subject matter—no doubt more than they would learn in class. The students, now lawyers, who have hopefully learned while enriching these materials are: Jonathan Berge, David Buxbaum, Linn Coombs, Sally Disco, Peter Douglas, Henry Fenton, Jeffrey Freedman, Steven Pepe, George Schraer, Calvin Young, and Richard Besone.

While I am responsible for any errors in the book, several colleagues were asked to review and comment on various parts of the book before the chapters were submitted to the publisher. They are all experts on the subject matter they reviewed. Chapters 1 and 2 were reviewed by Professor Daniel Mandelker, Washington University. Chapters 4, 5, and 6 on substantive aspects of zoning were reviewed by Professor Norman Williams, Rutgers University. Chapters 7 and 8 on procedural aspects of zoning were reviewed by Mr. David Heeter, Editor of several American Society of Planning Officials publications such as the Zoning Digest and Land Use Controls Quarterly. Chapter 9 was reviewed by Professor Michael Heyman, University of California, Berkeley. Professor Graham Waite, Catholic University reviewed Chapter 10 on official maps, and Fred Bosselman, Attorney at Law, Chicago reviewed Chapter 11 on building and housing codes.

Professor Kenneth York, University of California, Los Angeles reviewed Chapter 12 on nuisances and Dean Richard Maxwell, also of that school, reviewed Chapter 13 on private controls. Professor Robert Meiners from California Western reviewed Chapter 14 on eminent domain.

Professor Orlando Delogu, University of Maine reviewed part of Chapter 15 on taxation. Other parts were reviewed by Professors Ralph Rice and Herbert Schwartz of the University of California, Los Angeles. Attorney Richard Bellman of the National Committee Against Discrimination in Housing, Inc. reviewed Chapter 18 dealing with race, poverty and land use controls and Attorney James Erikson, Santa Ana, California, reviewed Chapter 19 on the legal literature of planning and development control law. I am most grateful to all of those gentlemen.

Donald .G. Hagman

Los Angeles, California
August, 1971

*

Preface and Acknowledgements
to the Second Edition

The tragic and untimely death of Don Hagman in 1982 left a void in the world of land use planning and control. Land use control law is a relatively new and rapidly evolving field of law with ill-defined boundaries which cut across several other academic disciplines and areas. As is often the case with new and rapidly evolving areas of the law, individuals and their personalities are extremely important. This was particularly true in 1971 when the first edition of this Hornbook was published. Professor Hagman was already recognized as original, innovative, and eclectic but the first edition placed him, in the eyes of most, at the very top of the land use control world. His influence was so great that his work greatly accelerated change in the area. At the time of his death, he had recently completed a second edition of his important casebook, Public Planning and Control of Urban & Land Development, but had just barely started revision of this Hornbook which thanks in large part to the considerable influence of his work was in considerable need of revision.

I agreed to undertake the preparation of the second edition soon after Don's death. My original plan was to concentrate on updating footnotes and to make as few textual changes, deletions and additions as possible in order to preserve Don's original work to the greatest extent possible. I spent over a year trying to prepare the second edition on that basis. I finally abandoned that approach and eventually rewrote, deleted and added material so that only about one-third of the current text is taken from the original edition. The law has simply developed too extensively in the last 15 years to do otherwise. Nonetheless, I have tried very hard to preserve Don's thoughts and—when possible—even his style. For some essential material not contained in the first edition, I have used (at times copied or paraphrased with the permission of the copyright owner) Don's publications which appeared after the first edition. For example, Chapter 11 of this edition concerns Windfalls and Wipeouts. I consider this area to be one in which Don's ideas and approaches were particularly innovative and distinctive. Rather than try to write his ideas I have "cut and pasted" his own words from articles and books on the subject for most of that chapter.

The inevitable flaw in the approach that I have used is the potential inconsistency of ideas and predispositions. Although I consider myself a disciple of Don Hagman, my perspective differs on many important points. For example, he used to comment on my equal concern for rural and urban problems—an approach that he respected but did not totally share as the use of the term, "urban" in the title of this Hornbook indicates. Even though I have retained the title, I have added a chapter on farmland preservation and have de-emphasized some urban problems.

Don's main themes, predispositions, or "prejudices" if you will, are well known. Mine are no doubt less well known by many so I will state them so that the reader may be wary of them. I am what Dan Mandelker has called a "police power hawk." I have little patience with vested property rights theories when important social goals conflict with them. In short, I belong to the social function theory of property rights school. Leon Duguit is one of my heroes. I am concerned about the exclusionary zoning issues that cause a confrontation between growth management and planning and constitutional protection of minorities but I am determined that land use control law not be viewed as just a branch of constitutional law so that land use lawyers and planners become simply drones responding to whatever happens to be the latest attempt of the Supreme Court to interpret an outdated and obscure Constitution drafted in an era that had no need for or appreciation of land use control.

The most distinctive aspect of the first edition of this Hornbook was, in my opinion, Don's success in combining "black letter law" commentary and innovative and original discussions. It is this approach that I have tried the hardest to preserve.

There has been so much reorganization of the materials preserved from the first edition that the following chart—even though only roughly accurate—may be of help to those who are constant users of that edition.

2nd Ed. Chapter	1st Ed. Chapter
1	New
2	1, 2, 10
3	4
4	5
5	6
6	7
7	9
8	11
9	New
10	18
11	New
12	15
13	20
14	New
15	New
16	17
17	16
18	12
19	13
20	14

2nd Ed. Chapter	1st Ed. Chapter
21	3
22	New
23	8
24	New

I have received more help than I could have ever hoped for in the preparation of this manuscript from colleagues, fellow attorneys, friends and research assistants. Special thanks are due to: Alan Armour, Anne Bell, Fred Bosselman, Caryl Brinson, Andrzej Burzynski, Barry Currier, Joe DiMento, Don Dowling, Bill Futrell, Clare Gray, Roy Hunt, Bruce Kaleita, Bruce Kramer, Brenda London, Robert McLean, Mike Morell, Jim Nicholas, Bill Perry, Clay Phillips, Bob Rhodes, Tom Roberts, Glenda Sawyer, Andrew Stansell, Nancy Stroud, Bill Turbeville, Brenda Valla, Jim Wadley and Clif Weaver.

Although I have included Fred Bosselman and Clif Weaver in the above list because of their help with some of the materials in the student edition, I would like to extend special thanks to them for co-authoring the four chapters prepared especially for practicing attorneys and included only in the practitioner's edition.

JULIAN CONRAD JUERGENSMEYER

Gainesville, Florida
November 1, 1985

*

WESTLAW Introduction

Hagman and Juergensmeyer's *Urban Planning and Land Development Control Law* offers a detailed and comprehensive treatment of basic rules, principles, and issues in urban planning and land development control law. However, readers occasionally need to find additional authority. In an effort to assist with comprehensive research of the law of urban planning and land development control, preformulated WESTLAW references are included after most sections of the text in this edition. The WESTLAW references are designed for use with the WESTLAW computer-assisted legal research service. By joining this publication with the extensive WESTLAW databases in this way, the reader is able to move straight from the hornbook into WESTLAW with great speed and convenience.

Some readers may desire to use only the information supplied within the printed pages of this hornbook. Others, however, will encounter issues in urban planning and land development control law that require further information. Accordingly, those who opt for additional material can rapidly and easily gain access to WESTLAW, an electronic law library that possesses extraordinary currency and magnitude.

The preformulated WESTLAW references in this text provide illustrative searches for readers who wish to do additional research on WESTLAW. The WESTLAW references are approximately as general as the material in the text to which they correspond. Readers should be cautioned against placing undue emphasis upon these references as final solutions to all possible issues treated in the text. In most instances, it is necessary to make refinements to the search references, such as the addition of other search terms or the substitution of different proximity connectors, to adequately fit the particular needs of an individual reader's research problem. The freedom, and also the responsibility, remains with the reader to "fine tune" the WESTLAW references in accordance with his or her own research requirements. The primary usefulness of the preformulated references is in providing a basic framework upon which further query construction can be built. The Appendix gives concise, step-by-step instruction on how to coordinate WESTLAW research with this book.

THE PUBLISHER

Summary of Contents

*

Table of Contents

CHAPTER 3. HISTORY, SOURCES OF POWER AND PURPOSES OF ZONING

I. THE HISTORY AND FUTURE OF ZONING

II. THE SOURCES OF ZONING POWER

III. PURPOSES OF ZONING

CHAPTER 4. TYPES OF ZONES AND USES

I. INTRODUCTION

II. USE, BULK AND HEIGHT ZONES

III. SETBACKS

IV. SPECIAL SITUATION ZONES

V. ZONING FOR PUBLIC, QUASI–PUBLIC, RELIGIOUS AND NONPROFIT USES

VI. OTHER USES SUBJECT TO EXTRAORDINARY ZONING CONTROL

VII. NONCONFORMING USES

CHAPTER 5. LIMITATIONS ON ZONING POWER

I. INTRODUCTION

CHAPTER 6. TYPES OF ZONING RELIEF

I. INTRODUCTION

II. LEGISLATIVE AND ADMINISTRATIVE RELIEF: IN GENERAL

III. VARIANCES

IV. SPECIAL PERMITS

CHAPTER 7. SUBDIVISION CONTROL LAW

I. INTRODUCTION

II. SUBDIVISION REGULATIONS

III. MAPPING FOR FUTURE STREETS AND OTHER PUBLIC IMPROVEMENTS

IV. PLANNED UNIT DEVELOPMENTS

V. SUBDIVIDED LAND SALES

CHAPTER 8. BUILDING AND HOUSING CODES

CHAPTER 9. GROWTH MANAGEMENT AND PLANNING

CHAPTER 16. NEW COMMUNITIES

I. INTRODUCTION

II. GOVERNANCE, PLANNING AND CONTROL

CHAPTER 17. URBAN RENEWAL AND DOWNTOWN REVITALIZATION

CHAPTER 18. NUISANCES

CHAPTER 19. "PRIVATE" LAND USE CONTROLS

I. PRIVATE USE OF "PRIVATE" CONTROLS

II. PUBLIC USE OF "PRIVATE" CONTROLS

CHAPTER 20. THE POWER OF EMINENT DOMAIN

I. INTRODUCTION

II. PROPERTY, PUBLIC USE AND CONDEMNATION ISSUES

III. JUST COMPENSATION

URBAN PLANNING
AND
LAND DEVELOPMENT
CONTROL LAW

Second Edition

*

Chapter 1

AN INTRODUCTION TO LAND USE PLANNING AND CONTROL LAW

Analysis

Sec.
1.1   The Development of Land Use Planning and Control Law.
1.2   Scope of This Hornbook.
1.3   Issues for the Balance of the Twentieth Century.

---

§ 1.1   Land Use Planning and Control Law

The purpose of this Hornbook is to explicate the law of land use planning and control. Although instances of governmental and private regulation of the use of land can be found in virtually all legal systems and societies since the beginning of history, land use planning and control law must be considered a relatively new area of the law in our legal system. Certainly, as just suggested, land regulation laws, court decisions, and private agreements can be found at the very beginning of our common law system. For example, the tenure and estates concepts which formed the basis of our property law at the birth of our legal system in Norman England in 1066 were means of land use regulation as well as the conceptual foundations of property ownership. Even in the colonial period of the United States, governments and individuals used the legal system to regulate land use.

Land use planning and control law did not begin to emerge as a separate and distinct area of the law until the early zoning ordinances and judicial decisions concerning them in the 1920's. Even then, little evidence would support the recognition of land use control as a legal speciality or distinct area from a conceptual and subject matter viewpoint. Planners and municipal law specialists began to think of "zoning" as a "special" area in the 1930's, 40's and 50's, but few treatises, hornbooks, casebooks, manuals or law school courses were devoted to the subject before the 1960's.

In the last two decades and the present one, the growth has been astounding. Only a computer could manage a list of relevant publications. Thousands of American lawyers consider land use as their speciality and/or belong to land use law committees and organizations.

In the 1985 American Association of Law School's Directory of Law Teachers 337 professors are listed as teaching land use law. Many more than that no doubt teach the subject in planning schools and other academic institutions.

The interest of the American public in land use regulation has expanded at least as rapidly. Today it is almost unusual not to find a political campaign in which land use regulation and its cohort environmental protection are not crucial issues.

 WESTLAW REFERENCES
di land use planning
di tenure

§ 1.2 Scope of This Hornbook

It is inevitable or at least natural that there be uncertainty and disagreement over the scope of the subject matter of a new and rapidly changing and developing area of the law. Land use control law has matured enough for there to be general agreement that the core of this subject is planning and regulation of land use by governmental entities through the police power. Thus, zoning and subdivision control should make everyone's list of land use control law subtopics. The law on these is so vast—i.e. the court decisions; statutes, ordinances and regulations; and books, articles and manuals are so numerous that even if one confined land use control law to these two land regulatory approaches there would be more than enough law for courses and hornbooks.

No one, it seems, would confine land use control law to zoning and subdivision control. The uncertainty centers around how many related areas should be included.

As explained elsewhere, the first edition of this Hornbook was a seminal work by a giant in the field—Professor Donald Hagman—who had a broad and far reaching concept of what could and should be included in the land use control law parameters. In the spirit of the first edition, the author of the second edition has expanded the original even further.

The title of this Hornbook is "Urban Planning and Land Development Control Law." The retention of the title seems necessary to correctly reflect the close relationship of the second edition with the first. However, it is one of the theses of the current edition that land use control law is no longer exclusively or even primarily "urban" oriented. In fact, regulation of rural land, the urban fringe, suburban and other undeveloped areas are probably of greater importance. Furthermore, "Development Control" must be understood to include controls designed to prevent or limit development as well as those which determine the type and intensity of development. "Planning and Land

Use Control Law" perhaps more accurately reflects the current subject matter of the Hornbook.

The scope of this work is best analyzed on a chapter by chapter and topic by topic basis.

Planning Law [Chapter 2]

Planning and land use control law have always been recognized as closely interrelated. Unfortunately, that recognition until recently was more theoretical than actual. The recent advent of statutes requiring state, regional and local planning and the birth of the consistency requirement, has at last created planning law as distinguished from planning theory. At least in some states planning law has been legislatively and judicially determined to be an integral part of the core of land use control law. Since one of the principal tenets of planning law is that planning should precede any and all land use regulations this chapter is strategically located as the first substantive chapter. Discussion of planning principles are included in subsequent chapters in relation to particular land use control devices.

Zoning [Chapters 3, 4, 5 & 6]

The traditional "core" of land use control law is included within these chapters. It should be noted however that the concepts and goals of land use control law have changed so drastically in recent years—and since the first edition was written—that some of the zoning material now reflects such innovations as contract zoning, non-cumulative zoning, and the like.

Subdivision Control [Chapter 7]

Subdivision control law is almost as old as zoning law in this country and is a well recognized part of the land use control law "core." The increased importance of "exactions" and planned unit developments ["PUDs"] make it also a field of change and recent innovative developments.

Building and Housing Codes [Chapter 8]

Building codes are even older than zoning and subdivision control laws. Housing codes are more recent but both are closely related to zoning since their implementation and enforcement are closely—often integrally—tied to the enforcement of zoning ordinances. Their land use regulation consequences are generally more indirect than direct since they are directed to improvements authorized pursuant to zoning and subdivision regulations. To omit coverage of them would seem unwise both because of their historic tandem development and purposes and because of their potential for being direct land use control devices through building specifications that make some uses impossible on certain types of tracts—for example coastal areas, flood plains, and environmentally sensitive and unstable land.

Growth Management and Planning [Chapter 9]

The future direction of land use planning and control law would seem to be its reformulation to fit and serve growth management and planning. All land use planning concepts can be used as growth management tools. This chapter is designed to assimilate planning law, zoning law, and subdivision control law and focus it on growth management.

Constitutional Limitations [Chapter 10]

Up to this point, the Hornbook focuses primarily upon the power of governmental entities through the exercise of the police power and specific statutes and constitutional provisions to plan for and regulate the use of land. The greatly increased frequency and severity of land use restrictions in recent years has made the limits of governmental power more important. For many years litigation over land use control regulations was confined almost exclusively to the state courts. In the past few years, interest of the Supreme Court and other federal courts in land use control law—an interest which was peacefully dormant for decades—has awakened. Some of the interest is confined to several old issues—for example the taking issues or increasingly sensitive issues such as exclusionary zoning. New issues have emerged as well—for example liability under Section 1983 of the Civil Rights Act.

Many of the constitutional issues are also discussed in other chapters in relation to specific land regulatory devices and programs. The chapter is intended as an overview and the reader should seek greater depth of analysis in constitutional law hornbooks and treatises.

Windfalls and Wipeouts [Chapter 11]

The omnipresent and seemingly insolvable constitutional issue is the so called taking issue which proves to be the ultimate determination of the limits of the land use planning and control power. Professor Hagman was a strong advocate of regulating land so as to avoid the taking issue by compensating financially damaged land owners through recoupment of a portion of the windfall of economic benefit frequently showered on other landowners. This chapter is designed to provide his analysis, suggestions and insights which constitute some of his most original and provocative contributions to land use control law jurisprudence. Comparative land use materials are included in indication of his belief that American land use control law will increasingly reflect English land use planning concepts.

Taxation as a Land Use Planning and Control Device [Chapter 12]

The effect of taxation on land use cannot be ignored. Unlike other land use control devices, the effects of taxation on land use is usually indirect rather than direct and frequently even unintentional. In the future, taxation may become a more direct tool as it is put to use in connection with infrastructure funding in the growth management area. At present, it is perhaps best described as a peripheral area that bears "watching."

Protection and Preservation of the Natural and Built Environment: Environmental Protection, Aesthetic Regulation, Historic Preservation, Farmland Preservation [Chapters 13, 14 & 15]

Perhaps the fastest growing area of land use control law is that relevant to and at times overlapping with that of protection of the natural and built environments. Environmental law is even newer than land use law and in its early days it ran parallel to rather than intertwining with land use planning and control. The first edition of this Hornbook consistent with the views at that time had virtually no reference to environmental protection. Professor Hagman added a chapter on environmental protection in 1975. Even that recently, such coverage in a land use control book was deemed unnecessary by many land use control lawyers.

Today, however, environmental protection and land use regulation overlap to such a great degree on many points that it is impossible to separate the two. Chapter 13 attempts an explication of "basic" environmental law as it is most relevant to land use control law. Chapter 14 focuses on the "built environment" through consideration of aesthetic regulation and historic preservation. Chapter 15 treats farmland preservation problems and land use planning and control techniques for its accomplishment. Both Chapters 13 and 15 are also designed to further destroy any pre-conceptions that land use planning and control law is exclusively urban in its orientation.

New and Revitalized Communities [Chapter 16 & 17]

The development of new communities in previously rural areas and the revitalization of existing communities are important subject areas for land use control law. The current attitudes are hopefully made more comprehensible through discussions of traditional urban renewal programs and their vestiges.

Private Land Use Control [Chapters 18 & 19]

Private individuals have for centuries regulated the use of land even absent governmental activities or interest. Nuisance suits, private contracts, and privately created land use restrictions have and continue to function as significant and often effective means of controlling the use of land. Public land use regulation has in many regards made private methods more rather than less important and the ever frequent use of traditionally private devices (restrictive covenants for example) have revitalized the importance of "private" land use control techniques.

Power of Eminent Domain [Chapter 20]

At this point in the book, the power of eminent domain has received considerable attention. It can be conceived of as the ultimate land use control power possessed by governmental entities since as long as the entity is willing to pay compensation, the government has the power to regulate land in virtually any way it wishes and even take title to it.

A few traditional techniques intentionally employ the power of eminent domain [ZSAFED, for example] but usually governments for practical fiscal reasons seek to regulate land through the exercise of the police power. The close relationship and even overlap between the two powers necessitates an overview of eminent domain law and that is attempted in this chapter.

Land Use Litigation and Practice [Chapters 21, 22, 23 & 24]

It is the intent of the authors to make every topic covered in the first twenty chapters relevant to the practice as well as the study of land use planning and control law but several subjects are explored in depth by and particularly for practicing land use control attorneys. These chapters are not included in the student edition. The four chapters are Chapter 21—Reorganization and Reform of Local Government Incorporation and Boundary Changes; Chapter 22—Adoption Procedures for Local Land Use Controls; Chapter 23—Judicial Review; and Chapter 24—Monetary Liability for Improper Exercises of the Land Use Control Power.

 WESTLAW REFERENCES
di zoning
di building code
di exclusionary zoning
148k124

§ 1.3   Issues for the Balance of the Twentieth Century

The chapters which follow focus on hundreds of issues. Some are old and have been discussed and disputed since the beginnings of land use control law. Others are only a few months old. Most if not all are interrelated so that it is difficult if not impossible to solve one without raising another. It would seem desirable to highlight the author's view of leading issues so that readers may reflect on what land use planning and control law will be like as the twentieth century draws to a close. The list that follows is not designed to be clever, exhaustive, or innovative. It is simply designed to establish greater rapport between writer and reader so that the latter can read the balance of the Hornbook with some insight into what the author of the second edition was worried about when the chapters which follow were written or revised.[1]

I. What Will Become of Traditional Euclidian Zoning?

Traditional zoning was indicted many years ago by Reps in a seminal analysis.[2] More recently, the abolition of zoning has been called for.[3] Certainly Euclidian zoning in its cumulative, static and negative sense should not and probably will not survive into the next century. Even a more enlightened noncumulative and mixed use oriented zoning system is of questionable value. But, what will replace it? Will local governments—especially those with severe budget and staff limitations—be able to effectively, efficiently and equitably administer point systems, development order systems and performance standards?

II. Will Impact Analysis Become the Universal Antidote to Land Use Complaints?

Fred Bosselman raised the question [4] in the mid 80's and linkage, mitigation, transfer and related concepts have gained widespread attention very rapidly.

III. Will Land Use Regulatory Fees Save Governments From Their Infrastructure Funding Dilemmas?

Land regulatory fees until recently, have been designed to simply cover the cost of administration of the regulatory system—or a portion of it. The use of impact fees grounded in impact analysis offer land regulation as a potential source of funding for infrastructure requirements. In an era in which tax revenues are less and less sufficient to permit governments to pay for capital improvement needs, the revenue potential of land use regulation looms as a potential fiscal resource for local governments.

IV. Will Environmental Regulation and Land Use Regulation Merge?

In spite of considerable overlap in goals, principles and approaches, the land use and environmental regulatory systems often work at cross purposes to the great detriment of landowners and society. What

§ 1.3

1. For another list, see Netter, Land-Use Law: Issues for the Eighties (1981).

2. Reps, Pomeroy, Memorial Lecture: Requiem for Zoning Paper presented at the 1964 ASPO National Planning Conference. Planning 1964. American Society of Planning Officials.

3. Krasnowiecki, Abolish Zoning, 31 Syracuse L.Rev. 719 (1980).

4. Bosselman, "Linkage, Mitigation and Transfer: Will Impact Analysis Become the Universal Antidote to Land Use Complaints?" (1985).

should happen is that one permit-performance (or impact analysis) system should develop for the unified implementation of both systems.[5]

V. Will the Farmland Preservation Crisis Prove to Be a Tempest in a Teapot?

The most troubled part of America's society and economy at the present time is the agricultural sector. Will the impending financial disasters in farming result in the demise of farmland preservation programs so that the loss of prime farmland may haunt future generations?

VI. Will the Coordination of Planning and Land Use Regulation and the Requirement That Land Use Regulations Be Consistent With Comprehensive Plans Become the Norm in All Jurisdictions?

Nothing would seem more basic and essential than that land use regulations should be consistent with and implement of comprehensive plans. Yet, only a few states have this requirement. Why is it taking so long to be accepted? Can there be any validity and long range effects to land use regulations not based upon comprehensive planning? Surely not.

VII. Will the Quiet Revolution Continue?

In 1972, Fred Bosselman wrote of the revesting of land use control power in state government.[6] Will the trend continue or will there be a revitalization of local government home rule power?

VIII. Will Land Use Control Law Become a Step-Child of Constitutional Law? Will Governmental Liability and Taking Limitations Seriously Restrict the Future Exercise of the Land Use Control Power?

Fred Bosselman tells the story of asking a law student interviewee what he thought of the land use control law course he was enrolled in. The student's reply was, "Oh, it is just Constitution Law II."

The constitutional issues—equal protection, due process, taking, etc.,—cannot be ignored but if governments are not allowed to effectively plan and regulate the use of land and resources in the long run society will suffer greater loss than some perceived freedoms and liberties. The limitation of rights to use real property should not be equated with essential freedoms such as speech, press, and religion. Our common law system has always recognized that ownership of land carries with it both benefits and burdens. The so-called absolute right to use real property is inconsistent with our traditional legal concepts and is not supportive of our societal goals and values. Certainly individuals merit protection from inequitable, prejudicial and ineffi-

5. Professor Hagman urged the purging of land use law and policy from the influence of environmental imposters. D. Hagman, Public Planning and Control of Urban and Land Development Cases and Materials 6 (2d ed 1980).

6. F. Bosselman and D. Callies, The Quiet Revolution in Land Use Control (1972).

cient regulation of land but society merits protection from selfish, unreasonable use of private property.

IX. What Will Become of Mount Laurel I & II?

The 120 page decision by the New Jersey Supreme Court in Mt. Laurel (II)[7] has intensified the controversy over the "fair share" and exclusionary zoning issues raised in Mt. Laurel (I).[8] Will other courts follow the New Jersey lead? What role will the state legislatures assume in the controversy?

 WESTLAW REFERENCES

euclidian /s zon***

"mount laurel" /p zon*** housing land

---

7. Southern Burlington County N.A. A.C.P. v. Township of Mount Laurel (II), 92 N.J. 158, 456 A.2d 390 (1983), on remand ___ N.J.Super. ___, 504 A.2d 66 (1984).

8. Southern Burlington N.A.A.C.P. v. Township of Mount Laurel (I), 67 N.J. 151, 336 A.2d 713 (1975), appeal dismissed, certiorari denied 423 U.S. 808, 96 S.Ct. 18, 46 L.Ed.2d 28 (1975).

Chapter 2

THE COMPREHENSIVE PLAN AND THE PLANNING PROCESS

Analysis

I. PLANNERS AND PLANNING

Sec.

2.1 The Practice of Urban Planning.

II. ANTECEDENTS OF LOCAL GOVERNMENT PLANNING

2.2 The Colonial Planning Era.

2.3 The Sanitary Reform Movement.

2.4 The City Beautiful Movement.

2.5 The Advent of Planning Commissions.

2.6 Early Conceptions of the City Plan.

III. RELATIONSHIP OF PLANNING AND ZONING

2.7 The Promulgation of Zoning Ordinances.

2.8 Zoning Displaces Planning.

IV. THE PROCESS OF PLANNING COMPREHENSIVELY

2.9 The Function of the Plan.

2.10 The Rational Planning Process.

V. THE LEGAL STATUS OF THE COMPREHENSIVE PLAN

2.11 Plans as Optional Policy Documents.

2.12 Plans as Mandatory Policy Documents.

2.13 The Consistency Requirement.

I. PLANNERS AND PLANNING

§ 2.1 The Practice of Urban Planning

There is no universally-accepted definition of urban planning, nor is there a definition of the urban planner which would be endorsed by all those who now practice urban planning. Currently, only two states have legislation concerned with defining or licensing the urban planner as a professional: New Jersey [1] and Michigan.[2] Nevertheless, those involved with urban planning would generally agree that the planner who deals with land use regulation has several principal characteristics.

First, the planner has technical training at the undergraduate or graduate school level, often in one of the many university urban planning programs, or possibly in another discipline such as engineering, architecture or landscape architecture.

Second, the planner is future-oriented. The urban planner believes that by analyzing existing conditions, forecasting future trends, and establishing normative goals and policies, an optimum path for the development or redevelopment of a geographic area may be formulated. This process usually results in a "plan." In addition, many urban planners also perform independent projections, statistical analyses, studies of housing needs and conditions in blighted or underdeveloped areas, and draft municipal ordinances for zoning, aesthetic regulation and environmental protection. These studies are often done in conjunction with the process of preparing a plan.

Third, the urban planner acts as a catalyst in the political process by which plans and land use regulations are developed, adopted, and implemented by a local government such as a county or city. This catalytic role arises from the planner's function as an analyst of conditions and trends in development or decline, and as a proponent of alternative means to guide the development, or redevelopment, of urban and rural areas. As the proponent of new regulations and of the plan, the planner exerts an influence through the legislative and administrative processes by which local governments plan for, and regulate, development.

Planners are most often employees of governmental agencies. According to a 1981 study of planners' employment trends performed by the American Planning Association, 63 percent of all planners responding to a nationwide survey were employed by governmental agencies as permanent staff.[3] These agencies included city departments of plan-

§ 2.1

1. N.J. Statutes Annotated 45:14A et seq.

2. Mich. Compiled Laws Annotated § 339.23.

3. J. Getzels & G. Longhini, Planners' Salaries and Employment Trends, 1981 (American Planning Association Planning Advisory Service, Report No. 366).

ning, county planning departments, joint city-county planning agencies, metropolitan or regional planning agencies, state agencies, and federal government agencies. Those planners not employed by government work for consulting firms, business, colleges and universities, and nonprofit institutions, according to the study.

The planning profession has been seeking recognition as a profession for several decades. Engineers, architects, and landscape architects are often found in planning positions, but many colleges and universities now offer bachelor and masters degrees in urban planning. Curricula in these academic programs range from a technical, design-oriented approach, termed "physical planning" by planning theorists, to a more policy-oriented approach at the opposite extreme. Considerable intermixing of the two disciplines in planning occurs in practice.

In an effort to foster professionalism, the American Institute of Certified Planners (the professional component of the American Planning Association) administers an examination and certification program for urban planners. Passing the application and examination criteria entitles the planner to present himself as a "certified planner." Increasingly, municipal agencies seeking to fill positions request applicants with such certification. However, it has not yet become a thoroughly-established prerequisite for the practice of urban planning in either government or the private sector.

Thus, the planner may be educated in a field other than urban planning, and if so, is likely to be a licensed engineer, architect, or landscape architect. In truth, these professionals have not recently invaded the field of urban planning. Rather, the modern science of urban planning grew out of the efforts of individuals in these fields to design cities to accommodate the rapid growth that has consistently characterized the history of the United States. A debate continues to take place among these professions regarding their respective entitlements, and qualifications, to practice urban planning. Thus, when a state undertakes to regulate or register urban planners, litigation may ensue regarding the rights of other professionals to qualify as planners.[4]

 WESTLAW REFERENCES

"urban planning"

"urban Planner"

urban /2 plan**** /s regulate register licens*** practice

---

4. See, e.g., New Jersey Chapter, Am. Inst. of Planners v. New Jersey State Bd. of Professional Planners, 48 N.J. 581, 227 A.2d 313 (1967) (state statute licensing planners did not violate equal protection clause by exempting, from examination requirements, any licensed engineer, land surveyor or registered architect of New Jersey), cert. denied 389 U.S. 8, 88 S.Ct. 70, 19 L.Ed.2d 8 (1967).

II. ANTECEDENTS OF LOCAL GOVERNMENT PLANNING

§ 2.2 The Colonial Planning Era

Town planning in the United States, from early colonial days, resembled the modern science of subdivision design. At this stage in the early development of the American city, the planning of frontier settlements was dominated principally by civil engineers and land surveyors. The seminal town plan during the colonial era was the plan for the new City of Philadelphia, commissioned by William Penn and drawn up in 1681.[1] A site between two rivers was selected, and a gridiron system of streets was devised. Open spaces in the central area of the city were set aside, and uniform building spacings and setbacks were prescribed. Penn's engineer Thomas Holme prepared this plan, which became the model for most early city plans prepared for other colonial-era towns and cities. The Philadelphia Plan thus left its gridiron-street imprint on many cities planned later.

Such early town plans were invariably drawn by surveyors and engineers, and so the man-made aspects of cities took the rectilinear forms preferred by those professions. A notable departure from this approach was the first plan for Washington, D.C., commissioned in 1791 by the new federal government, and prepared by engineer Pierre L'Enfant that year. This plan superimposed an impressive diagonal-street and radial-thoroughfare system upon a traditional gridiron street system, thus incorporating elements of French civil design. Today, L'Enfant's plan can still be seen in the broad, sweeping vistas that characterize the nation's capital.

The Philadelphia and Washington plans are only two well-known examples of early town planning. Many other plans were prepared, some taking a different, smaller-scale approach.[2] Most of these city plans were no more than early forms of land subdivision control, since they were usually maps showing street right-of-way lines, parcel boundaries, open spaces and water bodies. The towns themselves were often no larger than modern tract subdivisions, but they accommodated that era's primitive technology and simple, agrarian economy.

After the American Revolution, power became more centralized in state governments, with a corresponding loss of autonomy by cities. With the adoption of state constitutions, cities henceforth derived powers of self-government usually by an act of the state legislature delegating that power. Thus, without a delegation of specific powers to control land uses, a municipality, the mere creature of the state, could

§ 2.2

1. W. Goodman & E. Freund, Principles and Practice of Urban Planning 9–10 (1968).

2. Id. at 10–14.

not exert effective control over the use, and intensity of use, of private property. Land speculation became a new industry, and the practice of maximization of economic returns upon land investments made it difficult to implement the open space and civic design elements of city plans such as those for Philadelphia and the District of Columbia.

 WESTLAW REFERENCES

city town urban /2 plan**** /s history

gridiron /4 street

"william penn" /s city town urban /s plan****

"principles and practice of urban planning"

§ 2.3 The Sanitary Reform Movement

Along with the advent of widespread land speculation came the era of city-building. Factories were built in existing towns, attracting workers from abroad and from agrarian areas. Slowly, American cities became aware that urbanization might be a contributing factor to disease and poor sanitation. Because their growth had been unplanned (and perhaps unanticipated), no American cities had ever comprehensively addressed the problems of drainage and disposal of wastes. The typical American city, by the 1840's, was characterized by filth, stench and stagnant water in the streets, backyard privies, dampness, and the absence of sunlight in residential space. As a result, deadly diseases such as yellow fever, cholera, typhoid, typhus, scarlet fever and diptheria were commonplace.[1] Backyards, gullies, and even public streets became repositories of all kinds of waste matter, and drainage ditches became choked with debris, including fecal matter and animal carcasses.[2]

There was a remedy to this serious danger to the public health. English sanitary reformer Edwin Chadwick, commencing in 1842, began to champion the construction of "water-carriage sewerage systems." By use of an egg-shaped pipe, flushed with water, Chadwick learned, sewage and even the carcasses of animals could be carried away from homes and cities, and channeled into water bodies in which, presumably, they would disappear. The system required the construction of public potable water supply systems, and sewer lines to carry away wastes. Chadwick's ideas took root in the United States, during a brief period before the Civil War now referred to as the era of the Sanitary Reform Movement.

New York City opened its first public water piping system in 1842, recognizing early on the need to provide an adequate water supply system. Boston opened its first system in 1848. The delivery of water obviously led to the need to pipe it away again, laden with wastes. By

§ 2.3

1. J. A. Peterson, The Impact of Sanitary Reform upon American Urban Planning, 1840–1890, in Introduction to Planning History in the United States 13–17 (D. Krueckeberg ed. 1983).

2. Id. at 17.

1865, New York City had constructed about 125 miles of sewerage pipelines; Boston completed about 100 miles of sewers by 1873.[3] These early systems were mostly unplanned, and constructed in response to pressures from landowners and political interest groups. Thus, a sort of incrementalist, project-by-project approach typified these early efforts at sanitation reforms.

Installation of sanitary sewers grew more widespread after the Civil War, and by 1875 sanitary engineering was firmly established as a profession in the United States. During this time period, there was also a virtual renaissance in the development of the design professions: in 1866, the American Institute of Architects was formed and in 1871 the engineering professions were first organized.[4] However, none of these professions engaged in comprehensive planning for the future, in the modern sense. The first major, comprehensive American effort to plan for future public health was spurred by the spread of a massive yellow-fever epidemic in the lower Mississippi River Valley in 1878. The epidemic killed over 5,000 people in Memphis, Tennessee, then a city of only 45,000.

In 1879, in response to the plague, Congress created a National Board of Health to advise state governments and to regulate quarantines. The Board, at the request of Tennessee authorities, by 1880 completed an exhaustive, unprecedented study of physical and structural conditions in the City of Memphis, a study that filled 96 volumes and made over 12,000 recommendations for improvements of a remedial nature on property in Memphis—principally nuisance abatements.[5]

The recommendations also included major proposals for a new sanitary public water supply, a sewerage system, destruction of substandard buildings, enactment of a sanitary code for the entire city requiring elevation of buildings whose floors were less than two feet above the ground, repaving of many streets, ventilation of all city houses, and the appointment of a city sanitation officer to oversee all future sanitary work.[6]

This scheme is regarded by modern observers as the first major example of the modern "comprehensive" approach to urban problems, although limited to the goals of prevention of disease and sanitation problems caused by unregulated growth of an urban area. The Memphis scheme did not address many concerns now regarded as properly within the purview of urban planning, such as planning vehicular circulation, districting of incompatible land uses, and recreation space planning. But it was a sign of things to come.

A prophetic expression of the broad approach the planner of urban areas must take was expressed during this era by at least one writer. Horace Bushnell, in his essay "City Plans," observed in 1864 that

3. Id. at 19.

4. D. Krueckeberg, The Culture of Planning, in id. at 1.

5. Peterson, supra note 1, at 25.

6. Id.

Considering the immense importance of a right location, and a right planning for cities, no step should ever be taken by the parties concerned, without employing some person who is qualified by a special culture, to assist and direct. Our engineers are trained by a very different kind of service, and are partly disqualified for this by the habit of a study more strictly linear . . . . The qualifications of surveyors are commonly more meagre still . . . . We have cities for the new age that has come, adapted to its better conditions of use and ornament. So great an advantage ought not to be thrown away. We want, therefore, a city planning profession . . . .[7]

 WESTLAW REFERENCES

di,sy(city town urban /2 plan**** /s health safety welfare)

city town urban /2 plan**** /s sewer*** sanitation

§ 2.4   The City Beautiful Movement

The consciousness of a new age, with new opportunities for civic improvement, was not limited to those who advocated sanitary reforms. With the increasing congestion of urbanizing areas came a growing awareness that aesthetics also plays a role in the evolution of urban form and function.

American cities grew rapidly during the nineteenth century. In 1840, the census showed only twelve American cities with populations of over 25,000 and of these only three had populations of over 100,000. But as industry grew, so grew American cities. By 1880, seventy-seven cities had populations of over 25,000 and twenty cities had more than 100,000 residents. This rapid centralization of population in cities, where job opportunities were, led to an increased awareness of the need for civic beauty and amenities in America's unplanned urban areas.

The proponents of civic beauty would hardly have claimed the title, but their agitations for greater attention to aesthetics in city planning later became known as the City Beautiful Movement, the precursor to modern urban planning. The movement was really a groundswell, grass-roots concern with the physical appearance of towns and cities. Because they were largely the product of unrestrained private enterprise, towns across the United States were, before the advent of the twentieth century, largely unattractive, muddy, cluttered clusters of buildings. Individual residences sported trash-strewn alleys and yards, and there was little monumental civic architecture. But if sanitary reform could be planned, many believed, so could aesthetics.

The origin of the City Beautiful Movement is commonly traced to the Chicago World's Fair of 1893, a massive celebration of technology, art and architecture in which Americans were first introduced *en masse*

7. H. Bushnell, Work and Play 196 (1864), reprinted in id. at 1.

to classical design via the Columbian Exposition. The exposition was an array of neo-classical structures and sculpture forming part of the Chicago World's Fair. But the World's Fair exposition was only a symbol of a growing consciousness of the importance of the physical appearance of towns.

In villages and towns across the country, "village improvement associations," usually ad-hoc committees of townspeople, were being created during the 1890s. The village improvement associations championed street lighting, paving of dirt streets and sidewalks, the cleaning up of private yards and alleys, planting of public and private gardens, and setting aside of public, urban parks. By 1901, over 1000 such improvement associations had sprung up across the United States, advocating both urban aesthetics and sanitation.[1]

The City Beautiful Movement, like the Sanitary Reform Movement, was oriented to physical improvements to rectify a perceived evil: the lack of order and cleanliness in American towns. Well-kept streets, beautiful parks, attractive private residences, fresh air and sanitary improvements became its hallmarks. Many of the village associations were persuaded to join the National League of Improvement Associations, which crusaded for these causes. Renamed the American League for Civic Improvement in 1901, the national association created advisory panels of experts in municipal art, sanitation, recreation and related concerns. To a great extent the City Beautiful Movement reflected the ideals of the Progressive Era of reform in which it flourished. But it also planted the seeds for a more comprehensive view of the science of planning urban spaces.

City Beautiful proponents caused a great deal of municipal expenditure for civic architecture and municipal improvements. But the proponents of beautification did not necessarily espouse comprehensive regulation of land uses and development. In fact, there was a fear of governmental regulation, rooted in a fundamental aversion to the limitation of private enterprise by local government. As one early commentator observed:

> In America it is the fear of restricting or injuring free and open competition that has made it so difficult for cities to exercise proper and efficient control over their development. The tendency therefore has been to promote those forms of civic improvement which can be carried out without interfering with vested interests
> . . . .[2]

§ 2.4

1. Introduction to Planning History in the United States 46–49 (D. Krueckeberg ed. 1983).

2. J. Nolen, New Ideals in the Planning of Cities, Towns and Villages 133–34 (1919).

WESTLAW REFERENCES
"city beautiful movement"
di,sy(city urban town /s planning zoning /s aesthetic garden
    sidewalk beautification)
414k36

§ 2.5 The Advent of Planning Commissions

Proponents of the City Beautiful advocated the creation of citizens' advisory planning commissions, which were the precursors to modern local government planning commissions. The early advisory planning commissions were composed, usually, of locally-prominent merchants and professionals who had an interest in civic beautification, the construction of parks, and the financing of municipal outdoor art. Frequently, these early planning commissions engaged prominent architects and landscape architects to prepare advisory "plans" for civic improvement. These early plans by consultants were non-legal documents, principally maps and lists of suggestions for civic improvements. Several of the early advisory plans, however, attempted to achieve a comprehensiveness of scope that was similar to the modern local government comprehensive plan.[1]

The citizens' advisory planning commissions, in some instances, achieved the status of organs of municipal government. Hartford, Connecticut in 1907 created the first city planning commission. Milwaukee, Wisconsin initiated its city planning commission in 1908. In 1909, Chicago, Illinois appointed a 328-member city planning commission. These commissions, without powers conferred by statute or ordinance, could only recommend the plans they produced as guidelines for decisionmaking by the local municipal legislative body.

In 1909, Chicago became the first city in the United States to voluntarily adopt, only as a non-legal, advisory document, a "comprehensive plan" for its future development. The plan was prepared by famed architect Daniel H. Burnham, who had been director of works for the Columbian Exposition at the 1893 Chicago World's Fair. Backed by wealthy commercial interests in Chicago, and with a budget of $85,000, Burnham prepared a long-range plan for the Chicago region more comprehensive in scope than any plan previously prepared for an American city.

The plan did not focus solely upon the civic beautification and sanitation concerns that had, until then, been the hallmark of the Sanitary Reform and City Beautiful Movements. Instead, Burnham made recommendations in the plan's maps and text, for a host of planning considerations that have now become commonplace in local government comprehensive plans.

§ 2.5

1. J. Nolen, New Ideals in the Planning of Cities, Towns and Villages 133–34 (1919).

The Chicago plan addressed transportation and recommended a system of regional highways extending far outside the city. It made suggestions for improvement of traffic circulation within the city limits, including the development of new collector streets and consolidation of regional railroad terminals. It recommended new city shipping docks, new parks and beaches on Lake Michigan, and construction of a new city civic center. While the plan was to remain principally advisory in nature, it was nonetheless adopted as the official General Plan of Chicago, by the city's advisory planning commission, in 1911. Ultimately, implementation of its recommendations depended upon the degree of political influence over city government exercised by the businessmen who were members of the Chicago Planning Commission.

WESTLAW REFERENCES

comprehensive master city /2 plan /s traffic transportation

§ 2.6   Early Conceptions of the City Plan

In 1909, the First National Conference on City Planning and the Problems of Congestion was convened in Washington, D.C., and attended by many of the design professionals who were working, at that time, as consultants to advisory planning commissions across the United States. At this conference, Frederick Law Olmsted, a prominent landscape architect and planning consultant, described the city plan as a compendium of all regulations on building, physical development, "districting" of land, health ordinances, and "police rules" for the use and development of land. Olmsted drew many of his ideas on plans from earlier experiments in town planning in Germany and Switzerland.[1]

In 1911, Olmsted, again addressing the National Conference on City Planning, said the plan was a forecast of the best path for development to take, which should be followed by the local legislative body in making land use and development-related decisions:

> We must cultivate in our minds and in the minds of the people the conception of the city plan as a device or piece of . . . machinery for preparing, and keeping constantly up to date, a unified forecast and definition of all the important changes, additions, and extensions of the physical equipment and arrangement of the city which a sound judgment holds likely to become desirable and practicable in the course of time, so as to avoid as far as possible both ignorantly wasteful action and . . . inaction in the control of the city's physical growth. It is a means by which those who become at any time responsible for decisions affecting the city's plan may be prevented from acting in ignorance of what their predecessors and

§ 2.6

1. M. Scott, American City Planning Since 1890, at 97 (1969).

their colleagues in other departments of city life have believed to be the reasonable contingencies.[2]

Olmsted's conception of the city plan was prophetic of today's plans, in focusing on the role of the plan as a rational, policy document by which development-related decisions by successive, elected city officials should be guided. Later, Alfred Bettman, a land use attorney from Cincinnati, reinforced the concept of the city plan as a master development guide for the city or town. Addressing the National Conference on City Planning in 1928, Bettman said:

> A city plan is a master design for the physical development of the territory of the city. It constitutes a plan of the division of land between public and private uses, specifying the general location and extent of new public improvements, grounds and structures . . . and, in the case of private developments, the general distribution [of land areas] amongst various classes of uses, such as residential, business and industrial uses.[3]

 WESTLAW REFERENCES
"city plan" /s purpose history

III. RELATIONSHIP OF PLANNING AND ZONING

§ 2.7 The Promulgation of Zoning Ordinances

The comprehensive plan's emphasis on setting the distribution of classes of land uses caused some confusion by many local governments over the difference between comprehensive *plans* and comprehensive *zoning ordinances*. Unlike the plans adopted during this era, which were advisory documents of a policy nature, zoning ordinances were local statutes establishing land-use districts for residential, commercial, industrial and agricultural activities, and usually prescribing standards within each district for building height and bulk, setbacks from lot lines, and density or intensity of the use of individual lots within each district. When faced with the choice of either preparing a comprehensive plan, followed by adoption of a zoning ordinance to implement the policies in the plan, or just preparing and adopting a "comprehensive zoning ordinance," most local governments opted for the latter alternative.

The first modern, comprehensive zoning ordinance was enacted by New York City in 1916. The ordinance classified land uses and created zones for these uses, depicted on zoning maps. The purposes of zoning were to segregate residential uses from more intensive uses of land,

2. Proceedings of the Third National Conference on City Planning, Philadelphia, Pennsylvania, 1911, as reprinted in W. Goodman & E. Freund, Principles and Practice of Urban Planning 352 (1968).

3. Planning Problems of Town, City and Region: Papers and Discussions of the Twentieth National Conference on City Planning, reprinted in W. Goodman & E. Freund, supra note 2, at 352–53.

such as industrial, and thereby to provide safer, more quiet areas for family life. By 1921, zoning had become fashionable: its advocates had persuaded almost half of the state legislatures to adopt zoning enabling acts, conferring upon municipalities the power to adopt and enforce zoning ordinances.

The popularity of zoning was given a boost by the preparation of a model zoning enabling act by the United States Department of Commerce. The Act, published in 1924, was entitled the Standard State Zoning Enabling Act. It provided a ready-made model for legislatures to follow in delegating police power to municipalities to prepare, adopt, and administer zoning codes. The act authorized the appointment of zoning commissions by local governments, which would set district boundaries and regulations, hold a public hearing on the proposed zoning ordinance, and submit it to the city council for final hearings and enactment into law. Without such an enabling act, a municipal zoning ordinance was in danger of being invalidated as *ultra vires* if challenged in court.

By 1926, 564 cities and towns had adopted zoning ordinances, and several state courts had upheld zoning as a valid exercise of police powers delegated by states to their municipalities. In that year, the United States Supreme Court upheld the use of the police power to zone. In Village of Euclid v. Ambler Realty Co.,[1] the court heard a challenge by an Ohio landowner of a "comprehensive zoning plan" adopted by the city council of Euclid, Ohio. The ordinance established districts for land use, and district regulations for building heights and minimum lot sizes. The ordinance, the Supreme Court held, did not violate due process, and bore a rational relationship to valid governmental interests in preventing congestion and in segregating incompatible land uses.

But the attractiveness of zoning to the general public was due principally to the fact that a new zoning ordinance tended to validate existing land use patterns by including them on the zoning map, and also provided the opportunity to over-zone for profitable industrial and business uses. The comprehensive zoning ordinance of the City of New York, the first such ordinance in the nation, set aside enough land in business and industrial zones to accommodate an eventual city population of some 340 million persons.[2] Hence, zoning appeared to be a welcome device for facilitating land speculation and validating the existing pattern of land uses.

 WESTLAW REFERENCES
di,sy("comprehensive zoning ordinance")

di,sy(zoning /4 purpose)

"model zoning enabling act"

§ 2.7

1. 272 U.S. 365, 47 S.Ct. 114, 71 L.Ed. 303 (1926).

2. R. Walker, The Planning Function in Urban Government 11 (1941).

"standard state zoning enabling act"

zoning   /s   "ultra vires"

di,sy(zoning   /s   "police power")

414k6

§ 2.8   Zoning Displaces Planning

While "comprehensive zoning" proliferated, planning remained principally the province of advisory planning commissions. Few cities had created full-time planning staffs. By 1929, only forty-six cities had an annual city planning budget of more than $5,000.[1] Most city plans were prepared by consultants, and typically addressed a half-dozen principal elements of city design:

1.   A land use plan or zoning plan.

2.   A plan for streets.

3.   A plan for public transit.

4.   An element addressing rail and water transportation.

5.   A plan addressing parks and public recreation.

6.   An element addressing civic art or civic appearance.[2]

These plans exerted an influence upon the drafters of the first model act for planning, the Standard City Planning Enabling Act of 1927. The earlier Standard State Zoning Enabling Act had made little mention of planning. However, the Standard City Planning Enabling Act, also prepared by the U.S. Department of Commerce, addressed only city planning. The Act enabled local governments to prepare plans for five principal urban concerns (streets, public grounds, public buildings, utilities, and zoning) via a municipally-appointed planning commission:

> § 6.   General Powers and Duties—It shall be the function and duty of the commission to make and adopt a master plan for the physical development of the municipality . . . [showing] the commission's recommendations for the development of said territory, including, among other things, the general location, character, and extent of streets, viaducts, subways, bridges, waterways, water fronts, boulevards, parkways, playgrounds, squares, parks, aviation fields, and other public ways . . . [and] the removal, relocation, widening, narrowing, vacating, abandonment, change of use or extension of any of the foregoing . . . as well as a zoning plan for the control of the height, area, bulk, location and use of buildings and premises. . . . The commission may from time to time amend, extend, or add to the plan.

§ 2.8

1. Principles and Practice of Urban Planning 23 (W. Goodman & E. Freund, eds. 1968) [hereinafter cited as Principles].

2. M. Scott, American City Planning Since 1890, at 228 (1969).

§ 7. Purposes in View—In the preparation of such plan the commission shall make careful and comprehensive surveys and studies of present conditions and future growth of the municipality . . . . The plan shall be made with the general purpose of guiding and accomplishing a coordinated, adjusted, and harmonious development of the municipality . . . as well as efficiency and economy in the process of development. . . .

Thus, the Standard City Planning Enabling Act envisioned a more comprehensive approach to regulating land uses and providing municipal services for future growth than zoning could attempt. Zones for land uses were to be only one concern in preparation of the plan, and efficient provision of utilities, transportation and other public services figured as prominently as land use districting.

The Act, however, contributed to the confusion over the differences between city plans and zoning ordinances, by stating that the plan should include a zoning element. As a result of this confusion and because of the growing interest in zoning, many communities prepared and adopted zoning ordinances without ever making the general, comprehensive plan upon which zoning was supposed to be based. This practice tended to divert attention from the future-oriented, general policies of city planning in favor of squabbles over the details which dominated individual zoning decisions and controversies.[3]

In addition, under the Act planning was not mandatory, but optional. While the Act implied that zoning was distinct from planning, it did not expressly state that zoning should be enacted in accordance with an existing comprehensive plan document. The Standard State Zoning Enabling Act did expressly state that zoning should be enacted "in accordance with a comprehensive plan,"[4] but in view of the fact that planning was optional under the Standard Planning Enabling Act, most courts addressing this question have held that the plan with which zoning must be in accord could be found in the entirety of the zoning ordinance. A separate plan was generally not required.[5] However, a growing number of states are requiring their municipalities to prepare comprehensive plans with specific "elements" therein, and in a growing minority of these jurisdictions zoning ordinances and other land use regulations are required to be "in accordance with," or consistent with, policies and provisions of the comprehensive plan.[6]

The federal government has also supplied strong incentives to municipalities to prepare comprehensive plans. Under the Housing

3. Principles, supra note 1, at 353.

4. A Standard State Zoning Enabling Act, § 3 (1926): *"Purposes in view.* Such regulations shall be made in accordance with a comprehensive plan . . . ."

5. A minority of states require that plans be enacted and that zoning be in accordance with comprehensive plans. For a detailed discussion of this trend, see Mandelker, The Role of the Comprehensive Plan in Land Use Regulation, 74 Mich.L. Rev. 899 (1976).

6. See generally id. See also § 2.13, infra.

Act of 1949,[7] municipalities applying for federal financial assistance in slum clearance were required to prepare a comprehensive plan before funds would be provided. Later, Congress provided federal funds to municipalities to finance preparation of such plans, under the Housing Act of 1954.[8] As a result of both federal and state initiatives, many local governments across the nation now maintain planning departments and routinely prepare and revise comprehensive plans.

 WESTLAW REFERENCES
"standard city planning enabling act"
di,sy(city comprehensive /2 plan /s zoning)
"comprehensive plan" /s slum

IV. THE PROCESS OF PLANNING COMPREHENSIVELY

§ 2.9 The Function of the Plan

Traditionally, land use regulations such as zoning and subdivision ordinances adopted by local governments were written and promulgated without reference to any prior comprehensive municipal plan. However, in a growing number of states, the adoption of such regulatory ordinances in the absence of a general comprehensive plan may cast doubts upon the validity of the ordinances. The comprehensive plan, once viewed as primarily an advisory document to the local legislative body, is in many states becoming more of a legal, binding document as well as a prescription for future development patterns.

The plan serves as an overall set of goals, objectives, and policies to guide land-use decisionmaking by the local legislative body. When particular regulatory decisions are made by the county commission or the city council, the comprehensive plan's policies, goals, and objectives may be invoked as the "rational basis" upon which local government exercises of the police power to zone must be based. Planners have encouraged the use of the comprehensive plan as a rational basis for land-use decisions, and, in an effort to promote planning as a new profession, have developed a theory of urban planning as a rational process of choice between different policy alternatives.

 WESTLAW REFERENCES
"comprehensive plan" /s ordinance
"comprehensive plan" /s "rational basis"

§ 2.10 The Rational Planning Process

An overall definition of "comprehensive plan" has become necessary. The comprehensive plan is generally defined as an official public document, preferably (but often not) adopted as law by the local

7. 42 U.S.C.A. § 1441 et seq. 8. Id. §§ 1450–1469(c).

government, as a policy guide to decisions about the physical development of the community. Usually it sets forth, in a general way, using text and maps, how the leaders of local government want the community to develop in the future. The length of the future time period to be addressed by a comprehensive plan varies widely from locale to locale, and is often set by state legislation enabling or requiring local governments to plan.[1]

The growing importance of the comprehensive plan in local land-use decisions prompted urban planning practitioners and theorists to develop a theory of planning as a "rational process."[2] The rational, comprehensive planning process has four principal characteristics. First, it is *future-oriented*, establishing goals and objectives for future land use and development, which will be attained incrementally over time through regulations, individual decisions about zoning and rezoning, development approval or disapproval, and municipal expenditures for capital improvements such as road construction and the installation of municipal utilities.

Second, planning is *continuous*, in that the plan is intended not as a blueprint for future development which must be as carefully executed as the architect's design for a building or the engineer's plan for a sewer line, but rather as a set of policies which must be periodically reevaluated and amended to adjust to changing conditions. A plan that is written purely as a static blueprint for future development will rapidly become obsolete when circumstances change.

Third, the plan must be based upon a *determination of present and projected conditions* within the area covered by the plan. This requirement ensures that the plan is not simply a list of hoped-for civic improvements, as were many of the plans prepared during the era of the City Beautiful Movement. Substantial efforts have been made by public planning staffs, university planning departments, and planning consulting firms, to develop useful techniques for gathering data, analyzing existing conditions, and projecting future trends and conditions

§ 2.10

1. Principles and Practice of Urban Planning 349 (W. Goodman & E. Freund, eds. 1968) [hereinafter cited as Principles].

2. "Planning is a comprehensive, coordinated and continuing process, the purpose of which is to help public and private decision makers arrive at decisions which promote the common good of society. This process includes: (1) Identification of problems or issues; (2) Research and analysis to provide definitive understanding of such problems or issues; (3) Formulation of goals and objectives to be attained in alleviating problems or resolving issues; (4) Development and evaluation of alternative methods (plans and programs) to attain agreed upon goals and objectives; (5) Recommendation of appropriate courses of action from among the alternatives; (6) Assistance in implementation of approved plans and programs; (7) Evaluation of actions taken to implement approved plans and programs in terms of progress towards agreed upon goals and objectives; and (8) A continuing process of adjusting plans and programs in light of the results of such evaluation or to take into account changed circumstances." American Planning Association, Planning Policies, APA Action Agenda, APA News (in Planning) 24B (July 1979). See also Moore, Why Allow Planners to Do what They Do? A Justification from Economic Theory, 44 J.Am. Inst. of Planners 387 (1978).

within the geographic area covered by a comprehensive plan. This body of methods, procedure and models is generally termed *planning methodology.*

Fourth, planning is *comprehensive.* In the past, architects, and engineers who became involved in solving urban problems, such as those attacked in the Sanitary Reform Movement, tended to identify one problem perceived to be solvable by one solution. Having targeted in on that problem, these early planners preferred to develop and advocate one solution, usually expressed as a static blueprint which, if fully implemented, would solve that problem. This problem—solution approach was the product of the project orientation that was typical of traditional civil engineering and architecture.

Planning theorists over the past several decades have observed that this approach has led to a phenomenon termed "disjointed incremental-ism," in which successive municipal problems such as drainage, traffic circulation, or sewage treatment might be incrementally "solved" without reference to related concerns of municipal government. For example, sewer systems in the era of the Sanitary Reform Movement were usually designed without reference to any overall plan for the optimum future locations, and densities, of different land uses to be served by them. Highways were often laid out without reference to any long-range plans for the types of land uses they were to serve in the future.

The recognition, starting after World War II, that the entire range of municipal land use, transportation, and growth problems were all interrelated, led to advocacy of comprehensive plans as a means of identifying the key problems in land use regulation, and recommending alternative solutions to these problems which were the product of a rational planning process. The courts have recognized this role of planning, in defining planning as concerned with ". . . the physical development of the community and its environs in relation to its social and economic well-being for the fulfillment of the rightful common destiny, according to a 'master plan' based on 'careful and comprehensive surveys and studies of present conditions and the prospects of future growth of the municipality,' and embodying scientific teachings and creative experience." [3]

The rational planning process essentially subsumes four discrete steps: *data gathering, setting of policies, plan implementation,* and *plan re-evaluation.* Rather than resulting in a final plan effective for all time, the process is instead reiterative over a period of years: re-evaluation of the plan starts the process over again, resulting in a new set of policies which are attempted to be implemented, and the success of the new plan is again evaluated at a future date. Thus the rational planning process is both reiterative and continuous.

3. Angermeier v. Borough of Sea Girt,
27 N.J. 298, 142 A.2d 624, 629 (1958).

During the first step of the process, the planner preparing the comprehensive plan performs research and analysis of a wide range of present, and projected, physical, economic, and sociological conditions of the municipality. The data-gathering stage is aided by a wide variety of planning methodologies. Statistical surveying, population forecasting, mapping of existing conditions in land use, transportation, and environmentally-sensitive areas, mathematical modeling of economic trends, analysis of traffic flows on major highways, and techniques borrowed from other professions such as economics, geography and engineering have formed a part of the methods employed by planners in data gathering and analysis.[4]

The data-gathering and analysis phase of the process usually results in the identification of present and potential future concerns in land use, transportation, environment, utilities, housing, and other areas to be addressed in the plan. Thus, following the first stage of the process, the planner may identify and prioritize a range of municipal problems and opportunities which should be addressed in the policy-formation stage of the planning process.

Analysis of the data then leads naturally to the second phase, setting of policies for the plan. In this phase, the planner ceases being a data gatherer, and assumes a policy formation role.[5] Working closely with the planning commission and sometimes the local legislative body, the planner examines and proposes alternative means of solving or averting the problems identified in the first phase of the process. Through communication with the local legislative body and the planning commission (if one exists), the planner develops a set of policies, goals, and objectives which constitute the principal, future-oriented sections of the comprehensive plan. Thus, for example, the policies may include a provision that sewage-treatment services must be expanded to accommodate new development; that the legislative body should initiate a program to stimulate new economic development in the declining downtown; and that steps should be taken to prevent further flood-prone development in low-lying areas adjoining rivers and streams.

As a supplement to these general policies, or goals, of planning, the planner may suggest means of achieving these goals. In setting the goals and recommending alternative objectives, the planner may refer to standards and principles widely-accepted in the planning profession: that excessive use of septic tanks rather than public sewers tends to pollute groundwater; that decay of the central business district leads to devaluation of the tax base; that development in flood-prone areas is

4. For a detailed discussion of quantitative planning analysis methods, see generally D. Krueckeberg & A. Silvers, Urban Planning Analysis: Methods and Models (1974). See also Principles, supra note 1, at 49–242.

5. Planners, as a group, seem to share a number of biases that affect their approach to setting norms in the planning process. An interesting discussion of some of these biases is presented in H. Gans, People and Plans 57–75 (1968).

detrimental to public safety by exposing buildings and their occupants to flood hazards.

The mere statement of policies and objectives will not, in itself, ensure that action is taken. Thus, the third stage of the planning process, implementation of the plan, becomes the most important stage. Implementation involves three discrete steps: developing public support of the plan by means of various forms of citizen participation and a series of public hearings and media coverage; securing adoption of the plan, either as an advisory document (as in most states) or as a legally-binding ordinance (as in a growing number of states); and action by the legislative body to implement the policies and objectives.

Upon adoption of the plan, the adopting agency espouses the policies and objectives of the plan as guidelines for daily decision-making. Thus, to return to our three examples of policies, the local legislative body will undertake revisions of the municipal zoning map to bring it into accordance with the land-use recommendations of the plan. Similarly, the governing body may prepare plans for expansion of sewers and construction of new roads to serve new development. The legislative body may appoint a downtown revitalization authority to oversee efforts to attract new businesses back into the central business district. The governing body may authorize the city attorney to draft a new flood-plain protection ordinance prohibiting careless construction of new buildings in low-lying areas adjoining streams and rivers.[6]

 WESTLAW REFERENCES

"comprehensive plan" /3 define* definition

comprehensive /2 plan**** /s rational

find 142 a.2d 624

di,sy(city urban comprehensive /2 plan /s policy goal objective)

V. THE LEGAL STATUS OF THE COMPREHENSIVE PLAN

§ 2.11 Plans as Optional Policy Documents

The majority of the states whose legislation enables the preparation of comprehensive plans do not require local governments to prepare plans, and comprehensive plans in these states are principally land use policy documents without the force of law. The justification frequently given for the lack of legal status is that urban planning has not yet proven itself capable of solving urban problems, and there is no consensus among the states over what elements of urban development plans should always address. Furthermore, some commentators believe that the comprehensive plan serves an important "visionary

6. This synopsis of the process represents a synthesis of current theories on the planning process. For a more detailed discussion, see F. Chapin & E. Kaiser, Urban Land Use Planning 68–104 (3d ed. 1979); Principles, supra note 1, at 327–48.

function," unlike the regulatory function of ordinances and statutes, and that to require the plan to be a painstakingly—drafted, regulatory document would prevent plans from being suggestive and boldly-innovative.[1]

The fact that plans are usually neither mandated by state laws nor given the force of law is traceable to the standard planning and zoning legislation promulgated by the United States Department of Commerce in the 1920's. The Standard Zoning Enabling Act, published in 1926, required that zoning regulations and zoning decisions be made "in accordance with the comprehensive plan," but failed to address the obvious question of what a comprehensive plan was. Later, the Standard City Planning Enabling Act of 1928, while boldly setting forth suggested "elements" of comprehensive plans, and the manner in which a city might prepare and adopt them, failed to strictly define the legal relationship between plans and zoning ordinances. In addition, plans were optional under the Standard City Planning Enabling Act.

Many states adopted these acts verbatim or only in slightly-altered form. The task of defining the relationship between local zoning statutes and local comprehensive plans (if one existed at all) naturally fell to the courts. In the majority of states, since a separate plan was not required, courts considering challenges to zoning ordinances as not "in accordance with a comprehensive plan" looked to the overall land-use policies of the zoning ordinance, if an optional comprehensive plan did not exist.

The best-known case taking this position is Kozesnik v. Montgomery Township.[2] The case arose before New Jersey enacted legislation requiring municipalities to prepare plans. The existing zoning enabling legislation required zoning decisions to be "in accordance" with a plan, but the defendant township in the case had not prepared any plan. The state supreme court noted that New Jersey's zoning enabling legislation (like that of most states) pre-dated the adoption of its planning enabling legislation. Inferring from this that the legislature could not have possibly required zoning to be in accordance with non-existent "plans," the court concluded that the plan with which zoning had to accord could "readily be revealed in . . . the zoning ordinance . . . and no more is required by the statute." Thus, although it appears to be somewhat of a circular reasoning process, the court was willing to measure individual zoning decisions—even those that altered the community's zoning maps—for their "accordance" with the master zoning code for the municipality, which included the maps. This amounted to no more than a process of "discovering" a comprehensive plan and policies for land use within the dictates of a zoning code.

§ 2.11

1. See DiMento, The Consistency Doctrine: Continuing Controversy, F. Strom, ed., 1982 Zoning and Planning Law Handbook 77.

2. 24 N.J. 154, 131 A.2d 1 (1957).

This process, which has been followed by the majority of states,[3] does not always result in a validation of rezoning decisions when challenged. Indeed, it may be no more than a reflection of the general requirement, under substantive due process, that exercises of municipal police powers be reasonable. However, the majority position appears to be largely the result of the historical accident of zoning becoming a widespread practice before the advent of comprehensive planning. The result of this doctrine, however, has been to perpetuate the "optional" nature of comprehensive plans in most states, because zoning codes so often became the "comprehensive plan" against which individual rezoning decisions had to be measured for conformity.

In a variation on this position, the New York Superior Court in Udell v. Haas required that "accordance" between rezoning and the overall zoning plan be "rational" as well. Reviewing a challenge to a zoning decision regarding an individual lot of land, the court observed that

> the comprehensive plan is the essence of zoning. Without it, there can be no rational allocation of land use. It is the insurance that the public welfare is being served and that zoning does not become nothing more than just a Gallup poll.[4]

 WESTLAW REFERENCES
"comprehensive plan" /s optional
"zoning ordinance" /s accord! /s "comprehensive plan"
414k30
kozesnik +s montgomery
udell +s haas

§ 2.12 Plans as Mandatory Policy Documents

The traditional position, that individual zoning decisions could be compared to the general zoning code to determine whether they are "in accordance with a comprehensive plan," had a circularity of reasoning which did not make sense to planning advocates. Many urged reform of the planning enabling statutes so as to clarify the role and status of the comprehensive, or master, plan. Thus, Harvard Law School Professor Charles Haar wrote in 1955:

> . . . While the statutory references [to planning by municipalities] are cast in large and hopeful terms, they assign no clear legal position to the plan. The legal impact of planning is significant only as it imports governmental control of physical development . . . [and] no consistent pattern of interpretation of the effect of the plan on the real world has yet emerged in the legislation or judicial opinions . . . . The requirement in the Zoning Enabling Act that the zoning ordinance shall be made "in accordance with a

---

3. See 3 R. Anderson, American Law of Zoning § 21.01 et seq. (1977).

4. 21 N.Y.2d 463, 469, 288 N.Y.S.2d 888, 893, 235 N.E.2d 897, 900 (1968).

comprehensive plan" has apparently carried the courts no further than requiring that the ordinance be reasonable and impartial so as to satisfy the *constitutional* conditions for the exercise of a state's police power . . . . Some acts do not even require the adoption of the master plan in order to exercise subdivision controls.[1]

Clearly, Haar said, the plan ought to have some legal significance, and it ought to be a separate document from zoning ordinances.[2] This argument has since proven persuasive to a growing number of states, which now require preparation of comprehensive plans prior to the adoption of land use regulatory ordinances; by statute in some states and by court decisions in others.[3] These states, by requiring a separate comprehensive plan, have escaped from the confusion, caused by the standard planning and zoning acts, over the role of the comprehensive plan. In these jurisdictions, a zoning challenge does not draw the court into a process of "discovering" a comprehensive plan inside a general zoning ordinance. As a result, these states have also become laboratories for case law experimentation with the concept of "consistency" between comprehensive plan policies and individual zoning and development approval decisions.

 WESTLAW REFERENCES
master comprehensive /2 plan /s mandatory
master comprehensive /2 plan /s consisten**

§ 2.13   The Consistency Requirement

In a broad sense, consistency refers to the relationship between planning and zoning. The concept can be traced back to the Standard State Zoning Enabling Act's (SZEA) requirement that zoning be "in accordance with a comprehensive plan."[1] Controversy regarding the term's precise meaning has existed for many years.[2] Much of this confusion stems from a difference in terminology used in the SZEA, referring to a comprehensive plan, and in the Standard City Planning Enabling Act (SPEA),[3] calling for a "master plan".[4] The SPEA provid-

§ 2.12

1. Haar, The Master Plan: An Impermanent Constitution, 20 Law & Contemp. Prob. 353, 366 (1955).

2. Id. at 367.

3. Those states include California, Florida, Kentucky, Nebraska, New Jersey, Oregon, and Vermont. See J. DiMento, The Consistency Doctrine and the Limits of Planning 18–21 (1980).

§ 2.13

1. U.S. Dep't of Commerce, A Standard State Zoning Enabling Act § 3 (rev. ed. 1926). See also § 2.11, supra.

2. See generally Haar, In Accordance With A Comprehensive Plan, 68 Harvard L.Rev. 1154, 1158 (1955).

3. U.S. Dep't of Commerce, Standard City Planning Enabling Act (rev. ed.1928).

4. An explanatory note to the SZEA indicated the comprehensive plan's purpose: "This will prevent haphazard or piecemeal zoning. No zoning should be done without such a comprehensive study." Id. § 3, note 22. Compare this with the SPEA's explication of master plan: "By this expression is meant a comprehensive scheme of development of the general fundamentals of a municipal plan. An express definition has not been thought desir-

ed for establishment of a local planning commission whose duty was to produce a master plan, to be used as a guide for orderly future development. The master plan was meant to serve as a substantive document, stating the goals of a locality to direct subsequent implementing legislation.[5] Because the SPEA's master plan was not considered binding, and because it has not traditionally been equated with the SZEA's comprehensive plan, implementation of the consistency mandate has been slow and controversial.

An unfortunate effect of this confusion has been a judicial tendency to interpret the "in accordance with" directive as meaning nothing more than that zoning ordinances be comprehensive or uniform in scope and coverage.[6] Thus many courts have looked to the zoning ordinance itself to fulfill the requirement and have regarded as sufficient elements of internal consistency and rationality within the ordinance.[7] This is a fairly common judicial response to the consistency requirement in those jurisdictions which do not statutorily mandate consistency.[8]

The scope of the consistency doctrine today is wide, and a number of different forms of the requirement have evolved. As noted above, consistency refers to the relationship between a comprehensive plan and its implementing measures. Not only does this mean that the plan and regulations promulgated under it must be consistent, it also means, in a growing number of jurisdictions, that any development orders and permits issued must be consistent with the local plan.[9] From a practi-

able or necessary. What is implied in it is best expressed by the provisions of this section which illustrate the subject matter that a master plan should consider." Id. § 6, note 32. See generally Haar, The Master Plan: An Impermanent Constitution, 20 Law & Contemp.Probs. 353 (1955).

5. See J. DiMento, The Consistency Doctrine and the Limits of Planning, 9 n. 1 (1980). (Portions of this work are reproduced herein with the author's permission.)

6. See Haar, supra note 2 at 1157.

7. See Kozesnik v. Township of Montgomery, 24 N.J. 154, 131 A.2d 1 (1957) (finding that the zoning statutes' comprehensive plan is not identical with the planning act's master plan and that there is no requirement that the comprehensive plan exist in some physical form apart from the ordinance). This view of the consistency requirement is still prevalent in a number of jurisdictions. See e.g., American University Park Citizen's Association v. Burka, 400 A.2d 737 (D.C.App.1979) (pending adoption of comprehensive plan, home rule act requires only that commission zone on a uniform and comprehensive basis); Town of Nottingham v. Harvey, 120 N.H. 889,

424 A.2d 1125 (1980) (subdivision regulations enacted without a comprehensive plan were valid where zoning ordinance constituted a comprehensive system for their application); Drake v. Craven, 105 Idaho 734, 672 P.2d 1064 (App.1983) (plan apparent in zoning regulations); McBride v. Town of Forestburgh, 54 A.D.2d 396, 388 N.Y.S.2d 940 (1976) (requirements of planning statute are met if implicit in zoning ordinance there is an element of planning which is both rational and consistent with community's basic land use policies).

8. See generally, J. DiMento, supra note 5.

9. See e.g. West's Ann.Cal.Gov't Code § 65567 mandating that development requiring a building permit, subdivision approval, or open space zoning be consistent with the local open space plan. See generally the Florida Environmental Land and Water Management Act of 1972, West's Fla.Stats.Ann. ch. 380, in particular, §§ 380.04(1) (defining development) and 380.06 (mandating local and regional review of developments of regional impact and requiring that such projects be consistent with the comprehensive plans before development orders are issued). See also

cal standpoint, the plan—implementation form is probably the most important type of consistency. It is from this relation that the bulk of inconsistency challenges are mounted.[10]

Jurisdictions that statutorily mandate planning frequently also require that the individual elements of the plan be consistent with one another. As one commentator has noted,

> [i]nternal consistency refers to compatability within the general plan—that is, dimensions of planning are to be addressed with cognizance of other dimensions. Where several separate plan elements are mandated, for example, integration of elements is required.[11]

Thus, internal consistency requires coordination between the various elements of a plan so that they can operate in an effective and comprehensive manner.

Still another form of consistency, appearing with greater frequency, is the type mandated between local, regional, state, and even federal [12] comprehensive plans. A number of state planning acts now require this form of consistency.[13] This has caused a certain amount of controversy as some regard it as an affront on local land use autonomy.[14] Although the purpose of this form of consistency is to assure that individual local and regional plans operate in a rational and coordinated manner, the effect has been to place even greater control over local land use policy in the hands of state government.[15]

The consistency doctrine did not exist at common law and is purely a creature of statute and some fairly recent case law.[16] Attempts to define the concept precisely have proven largely unsuccessful. As Professor DiMento notes:

West's Fla.Stat.Ann. § 163.3194(3) (requiring consistency between land development regulations and the adopted comprehensive plan).

10. See generally J. DiMento, supra note 5. See also note 22, infra.

11. Id. at 16.

12. See e.g., The National Coastal Zone Management Act of 1972, 16 U.S.C.A. § 1456(c)(1), requiring that federal activity affecting coastal zones be consistent with state management programs. Section 1456(d) makes the act cut in both directions by requiring state and local coastal activities to be consistent with the federal plan as a prerequisite to receiving federal assistance.

13. See e.g. West's Ann.Cal.Gov't Code § 65030.1 (stating that local growth decisions should proceed within the framework of officially adopted statewide goals and policies); Or.Rev.Stat. 197.251 (creating an acknowledgement process wherein local

plans are tested by a state agency for compliance with statewide planning goals); West's Fla.Stats.Ann. ch. 186 (the state and regional planning act, mandating state and regional plans with which local plans must be consistent). See also the 1985 amendments to Florida's Local Government Comprehensive Planning Act § 163.3177(9) (requiring the state land planning agency to establish guidelines for evaluation of local plans to ensure consistency with state and regional plans). For other examples of regionalism and federalization of comprehensive planning, see also Mandelker, The Role of the Local Comprehensive Plan in Land Use Regulation, 74 Mich.L.Rev. 900, 915 (1976).

14. See e.g., F. Bosselman & D. Callies, The Quiet Revolution in Land Use Controls (1971).

15. Id.

16. See e.g., Fasano, note 22 infra.

[e]ven in those states where legislation has been passed to effect consistency, there is no generally accepted understanding of the term in affected local governments. This is certainly a common state of affairs in statutory interpretation; however, differences in terminology need to be addressed if other issues surrounding the legal effect of the comprehensive plan are to be resolved.

In California, for example, several attempts have been made to clarify the cryptic language in the consistency statutes. The major consistency mandate notes:

A zoning ordinance shall be consistent with a city or county general plan only if:

(i) The city or county has officially adopted such a plan, and

(ii) The various land uses authorized by the ordinance are compatible with the objectives, policies, general land uses and programs specified in such a plan. Cal.Gov't Code § 65860(a) (1977).[17]

This definition is neither very helpful nor clear, as zoning deals with more than just uses.[18] If consistency is limited to uses—as the definition suggests—then an ordinance permitting greater density than the plan might not be within the scope of the requirement, and as such might not be regarded as inconsistent with the plan.[19]

The difficulty in defining consistency has undoubtedly been influenced by the use of similar terms; the "in accordance with" requirement of the SZEA, for example. Other synonymous terms include "substantially consistent with," "in conformity with," "in furtherance of," "closely attuned to," and "in basic harmony with" a comprehensive plan. None of these, however, has provided much in the way of progress toward an understanding of the term's meaning.

Another uncertain aspect of the doctrine concerns the phasing of consistency. Some jurisdictions might be willing to allow as consistent a less intensive use than the one contemplated by the plan on the theory that this type of development will lead toward achievement of the planned goal; for example, single family homes in an area with a plan designation approximating multi-family residential would be considered consistent. This holding zone approach reflects the planner's awareness of timing constraints, and recognizes the validity of interim development measures not inconsistent with the plan's long-term objectives.[20] Other jurisdictions might reject this as inconsistent, favoring

17. See J. DiMento, supra note 5 at 18.

18. See Hagman & DiMento, The Consistency Requirement in California, 30:6 Land Use L. & Zoning Dig. 5, 6 (1978).

19. But see Twain Harte Homeowners Ass'n, Inc. v. County of Tuolumne, 13 Cal. App.3d 664, 188 Cal.Rptr. 233, 254 (1982), where the state planning act was held to

require that population density be expressed numerically, and not merely in terms of uses (e.g., dwelling units per acre).

20. See J. DiMento, supra note 5 at 22. But see Phillippi v. Sublimity, 294 Or. 730, 662 P.2d 325 (1983) (plan favored agricultural designation until such time as needed for urban development, subdivision permit

instead a more literal one-to-one relationship between planning and zoning. A number of different approaches to the phasing problem have been suggested: i) requiring revision of the zoning ordinance to occur when the plan is adopted, ii) resolving the question through litigation on a case-by-case basis, iii) allowing a reasonable transition period, and iv) applying the comprehensive plan in a prospective manner only.[21]

Almost every zoning challenge contains an allegation that the contested action is inconsistent with some aspect of the comprehensive plan. Until recently, however, such challenges were seldom based solely on the grounds of inconsistency. In 1973, the Oregon Supreme Court in Fasano v. Board of County Commissioners[22] held that the state's planning act required that zoning ordinances and decisions be consistent with the adopted comprehensive plan. The court invalidated a rezoning which was determined to be inconsistent with the comprehensive plan. Fasano is seen by many as one of the earliest and strongest judicial endorsements of both consistency and comprehensive planning.[23]

As a practical matter, the meaning of consistency is in large part determined by what action courts will take for failure to meet the mandate. Remedies available include a reprimand,[24] injunctive relief, development moratoria,[25] and invalidation of the zoning ordinances.[26] It is clear that the impact of consistency will be greatly blunted unless an effective set of judicially enforceable remedies exists.[27] Thus the statutory remedies available for failure to meet the mandate will play an important role in defining consistency in a given jurisdiction.

Finally, an additional insight into the meaning of consistency can be gained by a consideration of some of the arguments for and against the doctrine. Proponents of consistency argue that the effectiveness of planning as a rational mechanism for allocating public resources will be weakened considerably by failure to mandate consistency. They additionally argue that planners can identify community objectives through a variety of means and present alternatives for rational and informed decisionmaking.[28] It has further been suggested that consistency helps prevent the taking challenge by putting landowners on notice well in advance as to what types of uses can be made of their property.[29] Thus proponents contend that only if consistency—the

denial affirmed even though zoning permitted single family residential).

21. See J. DiMento, supra note 5 at 22.

22. 264 Or. 574, 507 P.2d 23 (1973).

23. The case is perhaps better known for the surprising approach it took in regard to judicial review of local land use decisions. See § 6.4, infra.

24. See J. DiMento, supra note 5 at 24.

25. Allen v. Flathead County, 184 Mont. 58, 601 P.2d 399 (1979).

26. Manley v. Maysville, 528 S.W.2d 726 (Ky.1975).

27. See J. DiMento, supra note 5 at 23.

28. See generally Long, Making Urban Policy Useful and Corrigeable, 10 Urb.Aff. Q. 379 (1975). See also J. DiMento, supra note 5 at 45.

29. See Housing for All Under Law: New Directions in Housing, Land Use and Planning Law, Report of the A.B.A. Advisory Comm'n on Housing and Urban Growth, 379 (Fishman ed. 1978).

"missing link" between planning and zoning—is mandated can rational planning find any hope of successful implementation.

On the other hand, opponents of consistency argue forcefully that the doctrine creates more problems than it solves.[30] An interesting counter to one of the proponent's views is the argument that not only does mandatory consistency not prevent the taking challenge, it actually moves forward the point in time at which the taking occurs. Opponents suggest that if consistency really means that the plan controls, then planning is in reality regulatory, and such regulation results in "planning blight," potentially giving rise to claims of inverse condemnation.[31] They also contend that consistency does not prevent the spot zoning problem, but instead causes "spot planning".[32] Thus, rather than isolating planning from outside forces, consistency in reality subjects planning to the pressures of political and economic influence.[33]

The consistency debate continues even today. Although only a relatively small number of states are currently experimenting with the requirement,[34] it is significant that several of these—California, Florida and Oregon—are regarded as innovaters in land use and environmental law. Uncertainty about its true meaning will undoubtedly continue to plague the concept, but a growing number of statutory and judicial interpretations should help make a practical understanding of the concept possible.

 WESTLAW REFERENCES

zoning /s consisten** /s plan

mcbride +5 forestburgh

plan /s "internal consistency"

16 +5 1456(e)(1)

find 662 p.2d 325

414k14

fasano +5 "board of county commissioners"

---

30. See generally Tarlock, Consistency With Adopted Land Use Plans As A Standard of Judicial Review: The Case Against, 9 Urb.L.Ann. 69 (1975).

31. See generally DiMento, "But It's Only Planning": Planning and the Taking Issue in Land Development and Environmental Control Law, 1984 Zoning and Planning Law Handbook, ch. 5 (Clark Boardman 1984).

32. Spot planning occurs when instead of adhering to the existing plan designation, a locality allows both a comprehensive plan amendment and a zoning change to occur simultaneously without valid justification. Another definition was recently suggested in an article on Florida's new growth management legislation; spot planning, the practice of post-hoc consistency by amending plans or planning maps to coincide with or follow individual rezoning approvals. Davidson, Florida Restructures State and Local Growth Management Laws, 9:5 APA Planning & Law Div. Newsletter 7, 10 (Sept. 1985). See e.g. Dalton v. City and County of Honolulu, 51 Hawaii 400, 492, 462 P.2d 199 (1969) (purpose of plan was to prevent compromise of planning goals; simultaneous plan and zoning amendments declared void).

33. See generally J. DiMento, supra note 5, ch. 3.

34. See e.g., West's Ann.Cal.Gov't Code § 65860; D.C.Code 1981, § 5–414; West's Fla.Stat.Ann. § 163.3194; Ky.Rev.Stat. 100.213; 30 Me.Rev.Stat.Ann. § 4962; Neb.Rev.Stat. § 23–114–03; N.J.Stat.Ann. 40:55D–62; Or.Rev.Stat. 197.010(3).

zoning /s plan /s consisten** inconsisten** /s reprimand
"injunctive relief" "development moratoria" invalidation

find 462 p.2d 199

Chapter 3

HISTORY, SOURCES OF POWER AND PURPOSES OF ZONING

Analysis

I. THE HISTORY AND FUTURE OF ZONING

Sec.
3.1   Early History.
3.2   Zoning in the U.S. Supreme Court.
3.3   The 1920's.
3.4   Present.
3.5   Future.

II. THE SOURCES OF ZONING POWER

3.6   In General.
3.7   Development Control by State and Regional Agencies.
3.8   Home Rule.
3.9   Charter.
3.10   Inherent and Implied Powers.
3.11   Enabling Acts.
3.12   Initiative and Referendum.
3.13   Special Enabling Acts.

III. PURPOSES OF ZONING

3.14   In General.
3.15   Maintain Property Values.
3.16   Stabilize Neighborhoods.
3.17   Homogenized Areas.
3.18   Move Traffic Rapidly and Safely.
3.19   Regulate Competition.
3.20   Limit Densities: "Snob" Zoning.
3.21   Increase Tax Base.
3.22   Promote Morals.

I. THE HISTORY AND FUTURE OF ZONING

§ 3.1 Early History

PreComprehensive and Comprehensive Zoning

Regulations that have some of the features of zoning have existed as long as land and buildings in cities have been regulated, which means that zoning started with the growth of cities. Some early regulations were onerous and perhaps could not be sustained today. For example, an ordinance passed January 7, 1632, in the Town of Cambridge, Mass. provided for erection of buildings only with consent of the mayor. Since no standards were provided, such legislation might be invalid today.[1] No buildings could be built in outlying areas until vacant spaces within the town were filled in. Today where market forces indicate land should be developed, it is generally invalid to preclude it entirely. It is also generally not possible to deny subdivision permission on the ground that existing subdivided land is available.[2] Roofs had to be covered with slate or board rather than with thatch. As a safety measure against fires such a provision might be valid, but it would be of doubtful validity if for aesthetic purposes.[3] Heights of all buildings had to be the same. Maximum height limitations are valid today, but absolute uniformity is of questionable validity.[4] Lots were forfeited if not built on in six months. Obviously, land in Cambridge was a community resource that was to be used in the public interest.[5]

Other early ordinances excluded certain kinds of buildings and uses, such as wooden buildings or horse stables, from particular areas of the city and had bulk requirements providing for setbacks and yards.

What is generally regarded as the first modern zoning ordinance was enacted in 1916 by New York City and was upheld in Lincoln Trust Co. v. Williams Bldg. Corp.[6] It was comprehensive in the sense that it covered all but "unrestricted" or "undetermined" zones of the city and it classified uses and created zones for all uses, which zones were then mapped. The ordinance also included height and bulk controls which are distinctive features of zoning today.[7]

§ 3.1

1. See infra ch. 5.

2. See infra ch. 7.

3. See infra ch. 14.

4. See infra § 4.6.

5. The ordinance is reprinted in Gallagher, Report of Committee on Zoning and Planning, 18 NIMLO Mun.L.Rev. 373 (1955).

6. 229 N.Y. 313, 128 N.E. 209 (1920).

7. On early zoning, particularly in New York, see E. Bassett, Zoning (1940); S. Makielski, The Politics of Zoning: The New York Experience (1966); J. McGoldrick, S. Graubard & R. Horowitz, Building Regulations in New York City (1944); S. Toll, Zoned American (1969); F. Williams, The Law of City Planning and Zoning (1922).

Zoning by Eminent Domain

Until the 1920's, the courts frequently held zoning ordinances invalid when nonnuisance uses were prohibited. Doubts about validity of zoning under the police power led to the use of zoning by eminent domain in a few jurisdictions. Under eminent domain, where the right to develop was taken, compensation was paid and benefits were assessed on areas benefitted by the taking. Minnesota exemplified the use of this technique.[8] Some parts of Minneapolis and St. Paul are still zoned under the statute authorizing eminent domain, which is probably why the statute remains on the books.[9] Some parts of Kansas City are also still zoned by eminent domain, and such zoning has been held valid.[10]

The notion that government should pay for the taking of development rights, should charge for the sale of those rights, and should compensate neighboring property owners who are damaged by the granting of developmental permission has an essential attraction of fairness that presently leads to proposals for taking-compensation rather than exclusive reliance on the police power.[11]

WESTLAW REFERENCES

zoning & da(before 1925)

"lincoln trust" /5 "williams building" /15 (229 +5 313) (128 +5 209)

land property building /3 regulat! & "police power" & da(before 1925)

land property building /5 regulation control zoning & "police power" & "eminent domain"

land property building /s regulation control zoning & "police power" & "eminent domain"

land property building /4 taking "eminent domain" zoning & compensation payment

§ 3.2 Zoning in the U.S. Supreme Court

The U.S. Supreme Court set guidelines for zoning in the 1920's and for forty years declined to address zoning issues. More recently the court has acted on unlawful delegation of power to zone, restrictions on billboards, free speech based zoning, taking issues, historic preservation, zoning and due process, standing, and civil rights.

PreComprehensive Zoning

There were a number of precomprehensive zoning cases which were decided on the way to sustaining comprehensive zoning. Barbier

---

8. Anderson, Zoning in Minnesota; Eminent Domain vs. Police Power, 16 Nat'l Mun.Rev. 624 (1927).

9. Minn.Stat.Ann. §§ 462.12–462.17. See infra § 11.5.

10. City of Kansas City v. Kindle, 446 S.W.2d 807 (Mo.1969).

11. Bosselman, The Third Alternative in Zoning Litigation, 17 Zoning Dig. 73 (1965); Clawson, Why Not Sell Zoning and Rezoning? (Legally, That Is), Cry California, Winter 1966–67, at 9. See infra ch. 11.

v. Connolly [1] and Soon Hing v. Crowley [2] upheld "antiChinese" San Francisco ordinances restricting the hours of operation of Chinese laundries in certain locations.　Yick Wo v. Hopkins [3] held invalid another "anti-Chinese" San Francisco ordinance prohibiting laundries in wooden buildings unless permission was obtained from the Board of Supervisors.　L'Hote v. New Orleans [4] upheld an ordinance designating certain areas of the city for prostitution.　Welch v. Swasey [5] upheld a Massachusetts statute setting height limitations in the City of Boston. Laurel Hill Cemetery v. San Francisco [6] upheld an ordinance precluding further burials in existing cemeteries.　Eubank v. Richmond [7] held invalid an ordinance allowing neighbors to establish setback lines. Reinman v. Little Rock [8] upheld an ordinance excluding stables from a commercial district.　Hadacheck v. Sebastian [9] upheld a Los Angeles regulation that precluded the operation of an existing brickyard within an area zoned to exclude them.　Cusack Co. v. Chicago [10] upheld an ordinance prohibiting signs in residential neighborhoods unless neighbors consented.　Buchanan v. Warley [11] held a Louisville zoning ordinance invalid that zoned for white only and nonwhite only areas. Pierce Oil Corp. v. Hope [12] upheld a Hempstead County, Arkansas ordinance precluding the storage of oil and gasoline within 300 feet of a dwelling house.

In summary, by 1919, the Supreme Court had upheld governmental power to set height limits and to eliminate near nuisance uses from particular zones or areas.　It had also indicated that the imposition of restrictions could not be delegated to neighbors and had held that zoning could not be used, at least openly, to discriminate on the basis of race.　Some state courts had by this time upheld one or more aspects of zoning and some had even upheld comprehensive zoning.

Comprehensive Zoning

From 1926 through 1928 the Supreme Court decided a number of zoning cases.　The major breakthrough was the leading zoning case Village of Euclid v. Ambler Realty Co.,[13] in which the Court upheld the validity of comprehensive zoning regulations in general.　Zahn v. Board of Pub. Works [14] added little to Euclid, and held that businesses could

§ 3.2

1. 113 U.S. 27, 5 S.Ct. 357, 28 L.Ed. 923 (1885).

2. 113 U.S. 703, 5 S.Ct. 730, 28 L.Ed. 1145 (1885).

3. 118 U.S. 356, 6 S.Ct. 1064, 30 L.Ed. 220 (1888).

4. 177 U.S. 587, 20 S.Ct. 788, 44 L.Ed. 899 (1900).

5. 214 U.S. 91, 29 S.Ct. 567, 53 L.Ed. 923 (1909).

6. 216 U.S. 358, 30 S.Ct. 301, 54 L.Ed. 515 (1910).

7. 226 U.S. 137, 33 S.Ct. 76, 57 L.Ed. 156 (1912).

8. 237 U.S. 171, 35 S.Ct. 511, 59 L.Ed. 900 (1915).

9. 239 U.S. 394, 36 S.Ct. 143, 60 L.Ed. 348 (1915).

10. 242 U.S. 526, 37 S.Ct. 190, 61 L.Ed. 472 (1917).

11. 245 U.S. 60, 38 S.Ct. 16, 62 L.Ed. 149 (1917).

12. 248 U.S. 498, 39 S.Ct. 172, 63 L.Ed. 381 (1919).

13. 272 U.S. 365, 47 S.Ct. 114, 71 L.Ed. 303 (1926).

14. 274 U.S. 325, 47 S.Ct. 594, 71 L.Ed. 1074 (1927).

be excluded from residential areas in Los Angeles. Gorieb v. Fox [15] upheld a Roanoke ordinance imposing a setback provision that provided a house could be no closer to the street than the average of 60 percent of the houses on a block. The case is an interesting one in comparison with Eubank, since neighbors were in a sense imposing a restriction. Furthermore, some courts had held these setbacks invalid as motivated primarily by aesthetic considerations.

Nectow v. Cambridge,[16] decided in 1928, is the second most important case in zoning law. The case held a zoning ordinance invalid as applied to a particular parcel because the property owner's land was so divided that a 100 foot residential strip was of little value and the public good was not promoted. The Court's concern with zoning temporarily ended with Washington ex rel. Seattle Title Trust Co. v. Roberge [17] in which, similar to Cusack, a use was prohibited unless neighbors consented. Cusack was distinguished, however, because the use prohibited unless neighbors consented in Roberge was an old folks home. The Court indicated that signs had near-nuisance qualities, so the consent of neighbors could be required, but the Court would not uphold a limited delegation of power to neighbors to consent or object to an old folks home.

Recent Zoning Related Cases

For forty years after deciding Roberge, the Supreme Court did not render a zoning decision but since 1969 zoning cases have appeared on the Court's docket with regularity.[18] The leading cases decided since then include the following. The Court in Hunter v. Erickson [19] held that requiring a referendum for approval of fair housing ordinances was racially discriminatory because it treated the ordinances different than others. In James v. Valtierra,[20] an attack on the California constitutional provision requiring a referendum on all subsidized housing as racially discriminatory was rebuffed by the Court. It held the provision was neutral on its face and impacted on subsidized housing in both racial areas and non racial areas. More recently, the Court upheld the validity of approval of zoning changes by a commission with a referendum vote of at least 55 percent. The Court said that the people may reserve part of the power to themselves. It rejected the plaintiffs due process argument but noted that state courts and consti-

15. 274 U.S. 603, 47 S.Ct. 675, 71 L.Ed. 1228 (1927).

16. 277 U.S. 183, 48 S.Ct. 447, 72 L.Ed. 842 (1928).

17. 278 U.S. 116, 49 S.Ct. 50, 73 L.Ed. 210 (1928).

18. Many of these cases are further considered herein. See Table of Cases. See generally Johnson, Constitutional Law

and Community Planning, 20 Law & Contemp.Probs. 199 (1955); Williams, Planning Law and the Supreme Court, 13 Zoning Dig. 57 (1961).

19. 393 U.S. 385, 89 S.Ct. 557, 21 L.Ed. 2d 616 (1969).

20. 402 U.S. 137, 91 S.Ct. 1331, 28 L.Ed. 2d 678 (1971).

tutions may prohibit such referendum votes. City of Eastlake v. Forest City Enterprises.[21]

The Court addressed substantive due process challenges to zoning restrictions on the number of unrelated persons permitted in a single family residence in Village of Belle Terre v. Boraas.[22] The Court upheld the restrictions because they were designed to secure the quality of the environment of single family residential zoned areas. In Moore v. East Cleveland,[23] the Court struck down a local housing code restriction that limited occupants of residences to related individuals. The plurality found the definition of relatedness was flawed on substantive due process grounds and as an invasion of the family. The ordinance was not related to community objectives such as controlling overcrowding.

The parameters for standing to challenge exclusionary zoning were defined by the Court in Warth v. Seldin.[24] Single family restrictive zoning was challenged on racial discrimination grounds by nonresidents. The Court held that the challengers lacked specific concrete facts proving harm to them individually and could not show that intervention by the Court would benefit them. In Village of Arlington Heights v. Metropolitan Housing Dev. Corp.,[25] a development corporation was given standing to challenge a zoning change denial, which kept it from pursuing the development of low income housing, despite some uncertainty of its ability to succeed. Though allowed standing, the challengers' property was not rezoned because they had failed to show the denial was racially motivated. According to the Court, a discriminatory result was not sufficient to demonstrate discriminatory motivation.

A zoning ordinance restricting parking on residential streets to residents only by a permit system was challenged on equal protection grounds by nonresidents of nearby industrial areas in County Bd. of Arlington County v. Richards.[26] In a per curiam decision, the Court upheld the permit and zoning exclusion of nonresident parkers.

The Court has dealt with several free speech challenges. In Young v. American Mini Theatres, Inc.,[27] a plurality upheld sex business zoning that required regulated businesses to be dispersed throughout the city. The plurality held that the regulation was to maintain

---

21. 426 U.S. 668, 96 S.Ct. 2358, 49 L.Ed. 2d 132 (1976), on remand 48 Ohio St.2d 47, 356 N.E.2d 499 (1976).

22. 416 U.S. 1, 94 S.Ct. 1536, 39 L.Ed.2d 797 (1974).

23. 431 U.S. 494, 97 S.Ct. 1932, 52 L.Ed. 2d 531 (1977).

24. 422 U.S. 490, 95 S.Ct. 2197, 45 L.Ed. 2d 343 (1974).

25. 429 U.S. 252, 97 S.Ct. 555, 50 L.Ed. 2d 450 (1977), on remand 558 F.2d 1283

(7th Cir.1977), cert. denied 434 U.S. 1025, 98 S.Ct. 752, 54 L.Ed.2d 772 (1978), on remand 469 F.Supp. 836 (D.Ill.1979), judgment affirmed 616 F.2d 1006 (7th Cir. 1980).

26. 434 U.S. 5, 98 S.Ct. 24, 54 L.Ed.2d 4 (1977), rehearing denied 434 U.S. 976, 98 S.Ct. 535, 54 L.Ed.2d 468 (1977).

27. 427 U.S. 50, 96 S.Ct. 2440, 49 L.Ed. 2d 310 (1976), rehearing denied 429 U.S. 873, 97 S.Ct. 191, 50 L.Ed.2d 155 (1976).

quality of life and not an invasion of free speech. A concurring opinion viewed it as an incidental interference with free speech.

Owners of an establishment that had live nude dancing challenged an ordinance prohibiting live entertainment in Schad v. Borough of Mount Ephraim.[28] The owners based their attack upon free speech grounds. The Court upheld the owners attack because discrimination against live dancing commercial establishments was not based on reasonable grounds and there was no evidence of harm caused by live entertainment businesses. Free speech restrictions were again raised in Metromedia, Inc. v. San Diego.[29] Limitations on content and use of billboards were challenged on both commercial and non commercial free speech grounds. The ordinance banned off site billboards within the city, but exceptions were allowed for religious, government, temporary political advertisements and others. The plurality found that substantial governmental interests permitted the ban on commercial speech and that on site signs addressed business owners' higher interests. However, regulation of non commercial free speech totally flawed the ordinance because, according to the plurality, the exemptions were too narrow. Restrictions on public discourse subject matter were not appropriate subjects for city sign regulation.

The historic preservation ordinance of New York City was upheld by the Court in Penn Central Transportation Co. v. New York City.[30] Owners of the Penn Central train station wanted to build a much higher structure above the station. The city denied them a permit. They challenged the historic preservation ordinance on taking, due process, and equal protection grounds. The Court upheld the ordinance in a fragmented opinion. The owners were found to have developable property elsewhere, the station was profitable under current conditions, and there were other options available to the owners such as transferable development air rights. All these weighed against a taking.

The Court took up the taking issue again in a facial challenge of a California land use restriction ordinance, in Agins v. Tiburon.[31] The owners' challenge was rejected by the court because the restriction had never been applied to the property and thus other alternatives had not been exhausted. The owners had never demonstrated restriction sufficient to be a taking. A second case from California based on the Agins decision brought the taking issue before the court in San Diego Gas & Elec. Co. v. San Diego.[32] The city had adopted an open space zoning ordinance and had intended to purchase the companies' proposed electrical plant site with municipal bonds. The bond issue was not ap-

---

28. 452 U.S. 61, 101 S.Ct. 2176, 68 L.Ed. 2d 671 (1981).

29. 453 U.S. 490, (1981), on remand 32 Cal.3d 180, 185 Cal.Rptr. 260 (1982).

30. 438 U.S. 104, 98 S.Ct. 2646, 57 L.Ed. 2d 631 (1978), rehearing denied 439 U.S. 883, 99 S.Ct. 226, 58 L.Ed.2d 198 (1978).

31. 447 U.S. 255, 100 S.Ct. 2138, 65 L.Ed.2d 106 (1980).

32. 450 U.S. 621, 101 S.Ct. 1287, 67 L.Ed.2d 551 (1981).

proved. The company brought inverse condemnation proceedings in state court where the court dismissed based on Agins. On appeal, the Supreme Court held that the case wasn't ripe for considering a taking issue because the state courts had not yet determined if a taking had occurred.

The most recent Supreme Court decision concerned unlawful vesting of zoning powers. Larkin v. Grendel's Den, Inc.[33] A local government had permitted either churches or schools to reject a permit for a liquor license. The Court found that the ordinance unlawfully vested legislative zoning powers in the schools and churches.

WESTLAW REFERENCES
Precomprehensive Zoning

```
113  +4  27   &  barbier
113  +4  703  &  "soon hing"
118  +4  356  &  "yick wo"
117  +4  587  &  l'hote
214  +4  91   /5  welch
216  +4  358  &  "laurel hill"
226  +4  137  &  eubank
237  +4  171  &  reinman
239  +4  394  &  hadacheck
242  +4  526  &  cusack
245  +4  60   &  buchanan
248  +4  498  &  pierce
414k30  &  comprehensive
comprehensive  /s  zoning
zoning  &  business commercial store office  /s  exclud! prohibit!
    reject!  /s  residential house housing non-commercial
di,sy(zoning  &  business commercial store office  /s  exclud!
    prohibit! reject!  /s  residential hous***  non-commercial)
di,sy(zoning  &  set-back  /s  residential)
414k43
to(414)  &  hous***  &  referendum vot! petition!  &  discriminat!
    unfair unlawful! segregat! separat!  &  da(after 1968)
hunter  +4  erickson  &  zoning
james  +4  valtierra  &  zoning
eastlake  +4  forest  &  zoning
zoning  &  "due process"  &  family "single family"  &  restriction
    ordinance
di,sy(zoning  &  "due process"  &  family "single family" relative
    "related individual"  &  restriction ordinance)
zoning  &  exclusionary restrictive  &  racial! discriminat!  &
    standing
zoning  &  exclusion! restriction  &  ordinance law statute  &  park!
    /3  permit license  &  "equal protection"
zoning  &  free  /2  speech expression  &  ordinance law statute  &
    sex entertainment billboard sign
```

33.　459 U.S. 116, 103 S.Ct. 505, 74 L.Ed. 2d 297 (1982).

to(414) & free! /2 speech expression & ordinance law statute
& sex entertainment billboard sign

"penn central" +4 "new york"

zoning & ordinance restriction statute law "open space" /p taking

larkin /4 grendel

459 +4 116

§ 3.3 The 1920's

After Euclid, so-called Euclidian zoning swept the country. The zoning was Euclidian in two senses—the kind of zoning adopted was similar to that used in the Village of Euclid—and the landscape was divided into a geometric pattern of use districts. Under this kind of zoning, there are at least three kinds of zones—industrial or unrestricted, commercial and residential. The validity of a designation of all land within the city within one of those kinds of zones is essentially the principle sustained by Euclid. Euclidian zoning was also cumulative, that is, only the "highest" zone was exclusive and that was the residential zone. Residential uses were permitted in commercial zones and all uses were permitted in industrial zones. While "lower" uses could be kept out of "higher" zones, Euclidian zoning did not attempt to keep residential uses out of "lower" zones. The number of zones was small, perhaps more than three, but frequently not, and the ordinance listed a large number of permitted and prohibited uses within each zone. A few uses such as funeral parlors or airports were so unique that they were not permitted in any zone but were allowed under an *ad hoc* determination as a special exception. The ordinance also called for an administrative variance, which could be used in those few instances where the ordinance created unique hardship.

Euclidian zoning swept the country for at least two reasons in addition to the Euclid decision. It was a movement the country was ready for and there was a good model provided by the Standard State Zoning Enabling Act.[1] After the release of the Standard Act, many states passed enabling acts based on the Standard Act. Few model or uniform laws have enjoyed such widespread adoption or influence. All 50 states eventually adopted enabling acts, substantially patterned on the Standard Act.[2]

 WESTLAW REFERENCES

to(414) & district zone & industrial unrestricted commercial
residential & cumulative

to(414) & high higher low lower /2 use & zone district area

§ 3.3

1. U.S. Dep't of Commerce 1926, reprinted in 3 A. Rathkopf, The Law of Zoning and Planning 100 (3d ed. 1967). See infra § 3.11.

2. See R. Anderson & B. Roswig, Planning Zoning & Subdivision: A Summary of Statutory Law in the 50 States (1966).

to(414) & "ad hoc" administrative /2 variance (special /s
    exception)

to(414) & "ad hoc" (administrative /2 variance) (special /2
    exception)

"standard state zoning enabling act"

§ 3.4 Present

While the Euclidian origins of most present-day zoning ordinances
can be recognized, there have been many changes, most of which
provide "flexibility," an euphemistic term, though purists tend to refer
to the development as *"ad hocery."* Even small cities have many more
types of zones—20 to 25 rather than 3 or 4. Cumulative zoning is "out"
and exclusive industrial and agriculture zoning is "in." Directly
counter to the trend to exclusive zoning is an increasing trend to
planned unit development zoning, which permits a mixture of various
types of residential uses, at least, and sometimes residential, and
commercial and industrial uses as well. The number of uses permitted
by right in any zone are fewer relative to the number of special
exceptions allowed. Variances are frequently issued by boards which
ignore standards and in many situations the actions should not be
upheld by courts, yet are.[1]

The zoning lexicon now contains such descriptive phrases as compensating benefits, open end zoning, overlay zones, potential zones,
transitional zoning, performance standards, holding zones, contract
zoning, conditional zoning, tentative zoning, X zones, Q zones, phased
zoning, floating zones, sinking zones, spot zones, and incentive zones—
all of which are attempts to apply zoning flexibly.

 WESTLAW REFERENCES

to(414) & exclusive /2 zoning "planned unit development zoning"

zoning & "compensating benefits" "open end zoning" "overlay
    zones" "potential zones" "transitional zoning" "performance
    standards" "holding zones" "contract zoning" "conditional
    zoning" "tentative zoning"

zoning & "x zones" "q zones" "phased zoning" "floating zones"
    "sinking zones" "spot zones" "incentive zones"

§ 3.5 Future

The Model Land Development Code

In 1963 the Ford Foundation financed an American Law Institute
effort to write A Model Land Development Code. It was compiled in
1976.[1] The Code deals with the physical development of land, but in

§ 3.4

1. See infra ch. 6.

§ 3.5

1. American Law Institute, A Model
Land Development Code (1976).

such a way as to maximize social and economic objectives. This feature of the Code is not particularly new. In fact, it falls short of expressing the view of modern planning which attempts to emphasize the unity of physical, social and economic planning. The new planning seeks to attack social and economic problems directly rather than rely on good physical arrangements as a way of curing social and economic ills.

The Code is also based on the same assumptions underlying the Standard State Zoning Enabling Act, (SZEA) and its companion, the Standard City Planning Enabling Act (SPEA)[2] which provided powers for planning, control of subdivisions, official maps and regional planning. These two assumptions are, first, that the Acts authorize control of privately initiated development rather than a system under which government is made the primary development agency as in some countries, and, second, local government as distinguished from some other level of government is to exercise most of the control power.

Nevertheless, the Code attempts to incorporate at least some of the new techniques for inducing as distinguished from controlling development. These techniques include public housing laws, urban development and renewal legislation, laws authorizing use of airspace,[3] laws authorizing public construction of off-street parking, and laws giving tax exemption or reduction and grants-in-aid. However, every code must have some parameters, and the Model Code does not deal in any substantial way with building and housing codes, fire codes, public health codes or real property taxation.

The Code also attempts to resolve the difficult problem of the need to plan before the application of development controls and inducements. The Code rejects the extreme that all controls or inducements can be used without a formally adopted plan and the other extreme that such a plan is necessary to the exercise of any control or inducement. The SZEA and the SPEA were unclear or inconsistent in several respects on this problem. The new Code does generally not require a plan as a precondition to adoption of controls (e.g., zoning), but will require a formally adopted plan as a precondition to the adoption of some of the more powerful, inducement-oriented provisions.

The Code also deals with the problem of allocation of decisionmaking power. For example, a local government perhaps should not have power to engage in "snob" zoning, should not be able to zone out motels and gasoline stations at a major highway interchange, should not be able to acquire and develop land within the jurisdiction of another governmental body without control, and should not be able to dictate locations of railroads or public utility transmission lines or schools or churches that serve people beyond the boundaries of the municipality. A state planning agency is authorized by the Code to handle those

---

2. U.S. Dep't of Commerce (1928).

3. See also Sackman, Air Rights—A Developing Prospect, 1968 Inst. on Eminent Domain I; Comment, Air Rights—Prospects for the Future, 6 Wake Forest Intra. L.Rev. 65 (1969).

kinds of "spillover" problems. The state agency may also be given power to set aside overly restrictive regulations, to review applications for federal assistance and to engage in some regulatory power of its own where public facilities are involved. Provisions on administration will seek to establish standardized procedures and to eliminate the multiplicity of local agencies now involved in giving permission for land development. Some power will also be decentralized. Local governments should perhaps be compelled to allow affected neighborhoods a larger voice in what transpires in the neighborhood.

The SZEA and the SPEA were based on the "cookie cutter" theory of development, since they assumed a lot by lot development. The use of floating zones, planned unit residential districts and new towns suggests that lot by lot development should not be the pattern of all development. Under the new Code, controls are sufficiently flexible to permit the new type development, which some courts hold invalid under existing law.

Any system can be made better or be made ineffective by its administration. There is much confusion as to what acts are legislative, what adjudicatory. Legislative and administrative standards are often nonexistent, too general or not made public. It is not clear in many cases whether or not judicial review is possible before exhaustion of administrative remedies. The ability to discover and clearly understand the effects of development controls on title makes acquisition and development a precarious business for purchasers, lenders and title examiners. The Model Code deals with these problems.

The Model Code is an enabling act and does not itself regulate. A local government need not implement all of the provisions. It can pick and choose. The appropriate kind of local government that should be enabled is not specified—other than that it be a general purpose government. As with present acts, the power to control future development is much more extensive than the power to require conformance of existing development to a change. The most important definition in the Code is the word "development" which essentially is any material change in the appearance of a parcel of land or in its shape. The master plan called the land development plan will have no legal effect on private or public landowners. The relationship among the plan, controls and public acquisition will be set forth. Zoning-like controls will be merged with subdivision-like controls. As distinguished from the SPEA and the SZEA, the Code deals with the power to acquire land by eminent domain and to dispose of it to private developers. These provisions replace urban redevelopment and urban renewal statutes. The Code also has provisions indicating when regulations become so onerous that compensation should be paid—a kind of legislative "inverse condemnation" provision. Other provisions of the Code set forth the ways in which the development controls can be enforced.

The Code also contains guidelines for judging validity that are more precise than constitutional constraints and create a stronger presumption of validity where the community has adopted a land development plan. Uniform procedures for applying for and complying with state and Federal grants-in-aid will be established and local governments will be enabled under some circumstances to make grants to stimulate certain desired private development. Finally, the Code creates a system for the recording of publicly imposed regulations and restrictions so that these can be more easily identified and known.

Other Future Developments [4]

If the Model Code is adopted widely, and it hasn't been to date, the enabling acts among the states will be substantially similar, as they are now. Otherwise, there is not likely to be any systematic, rational change. Several states have substantially revised planning and land use control statutes.[5] Predicting the future is difficult. Some likely futures include the following:

Regional planning will become more important and some zoning may be done by the regional or state government;[6] master and general plans will become less important but the planning process and the use of computerized information gathering will become more important; master plans will attempt to incorporate more of the economic and social aspects of development; the number of basic use districts will not increase but flexibility devices of many kinds will continue to be used and more development decisions will be *ad hoc;* zoning will become less important as new controls and inducements are developed; rigorous and widespread elimination of "favored" non-conforming uses will not transpire; zoning will be merged with other controls that affect development; courts will become more tolerant of flexibility devices, will give more weight to plans as a basis for regulation and will begin to invalidate schemes that segregate the poor, particularly the minority poor; the federal government will continue to support better coordination of controls and the extension of controls to governmental development; and public agencies will become more generous and begin to pay compensation for some restrictions that constitutionally may be within the scope of the police power.[7] Any list of futures should be discounted by the fact that they may well be biased by what the predicter thinks desirable as a self-fulfilling prophecy.

4. See generally Heeter, Toward a More Effective Land-Use Guidance System, 4 Land-Use Controls Q. 8 (1970).

5. West's Fla.Stat.Ann. § 163.3161 et seq.; West's Rev.Code Wash.Ann. 35A.63.061 (for cities).

6. See Evans, Regional Land Use Control: The Stepping Stone Concept, 22 Baylor L.Rev. 1 (1970).

7. See generally Levin, New Directions in Land Acquisition and Land Use, 1969 Wis.L.Rev. 848; Mandelker, Governmental Intervention in Community Development, 1 Ind.Legal F. 310 (1968); Reps, Requiem for Zoning, Planning 56 (1965); Comment, Government Control of Land: Protecting the I-Know-It-When-I-See-It Interest, 62 Nw.U.L.Rev. 428 (1967); Reps, The Future of American Planning: Requiem or Renascence?, Planning 47 (1967).

WESTLAW REFERENCES

"model land development code"

"standard city planning enabling act" zoning & "model land
    development code" & control regulation authority /p private
    non-government! /p develop! build! construction expansion

zoning & "model land development code" & local county city
    municipal /2 government!

zoning & "model land development code" & (public government
    /2 housing) (urban renewal /2 development) (air /1 space)
    (public municipal city /s construction building /s parking /s
    garage ramp facility) (tax /3 reduc! exempt!) (grant /2 aid)

zoning & plan design /s application apply /s development /s
    control inducement

zoning & "model land development code" & limit! curb /p
    power control authority spillover decentral!

"model land development code" & float! /4 zone (planned /s
    unit /s residential /s area)

zoning & "model land development code" & judicial /2 review
    /s exhaust! /s "administrative remedy"

zoning & "model land development code" & local /3
    government & power domain! control & future /3 develop!

zoning & "model land development code" & compensation /p
    owner holder & rule regulation provision

II. THE SOURCES OF ZONING POWER

§ 3.6 In General

Zoning is an exercise of the police power which resides in the
several states. The state can delegate its power to zone and by and
large has done so. Very few state legislatures exercise the power of
zoning themselves. The delegation is sometimes to statewide agencies,
but almost all delegation is to local governments. Among the local
governments, the power is distributed to municipal corporations—cities,
villages and towns—and frequently to counties and towns.[1] Limited
purpose governments such as special districts and school districts are
seldom given the power to zone. The term local government is used in
this Hornbook to refer to any and all political subdivisions which have
land use control power in a given jurisdiction.

The state delegates in a variety of ways and the power to zone may
come from more than one source. Frequently, the state constitution
provides for home rule as a way of distributing state power to local
governments. Home rule is also sometimes granted by the state
legislature, so the land use control power can be based on legislative
delegation. Land use control power can also be implied from a law

§ 3.6

1. Towns are mentioned twice because
a town sometimes is a municipal corporation, to be distinguished from a town which
is a subdivision of a county. A county is
also not a municipal corporation but a subdivision of the state.

generally authorizing the exercise of the police power by local government. The source of power for most zoning is the enabling acts of the various states. Rarely, land use control power may also be based on a doctrine of inherent powers, meaning that the mere creation of a political subdivision confers power to do the kinds of things local governments need to do, such as to zone.

Most of the power delegated to local government to zone goes to the legislative bodies of local governments, particularly where the source of power is not an enabling act. When the source is the enabling act, the power is sometimes divided among legislative and administrative bodies such as planning commissions and boards of appeals.[2] In many states the people retain the power of initiative and referendum and, where they do, these powers may sometimes be used to zone.

Finally, many states have special legislation or enabling acts authorizing zoning in special kinds of situations, such as airport zoning or flood plain zoning. These provisions may not be part of the general zoning enabling act.

The following sections cover these matters in more detail.

 WESTLAW REFERENCES

zoning & state & delegation & local city county town

municipal & "home rule" constitution! legislat! /3 delegat! (impl! /4 police /4 power)

zoning & state & enabling /3 act statute law

§ 3.7 Development Control by State and Regional Agencies

States have provided for state or regional development control only in specialized situations. For example, in Kentucky, a city can have its own planning program only if it first determines whether the county will enter into joint planning. If the county wishes to have joint planning, then no city in the county may thereafter form an independent planning unit.[1] Louisiana retains power to zone to protect housing and redevelopment projects.[2] The Environmental Improvement Commission in Maine must approve all large commercial, industrial and natural resource extraction uses.[3] In Massachusetts, if a locality zones out state or federal supported low income housing, the applicant for the use is entitled to review by the housing appeals committee of the state department of community affairs.[4]

2. Boards of Appeal are frequently called Boards of Adjustment.

§ 3.7

1. Ky.Rev.Stat. 100.117.

2. La.—LSA–Rev.Stat. 40:533(4).

3. Me.Rev.Stat.Ann. tit. 38, § 481 et seq. See also 1970 Vt. Acts 250.

4. Mass.Gen.Laws Ann. c. 40B, §§ 20–23. See Beal, Massachusetts Takes Steps to Remove Local Barriers to Low-Income Housing, 1969 Land-Use Controls Q. 33 (Fall).

When major areas are to be developed, some states have created special state agencies which preempt local control over development. New Jersey has created a special commission to control development of the Hackensack Meadowlands.[5] The corporation created under the New York State Urban Development Corporation Act[6] is given broad combined powers of renewal, industrial development, new community planning, financing and building and is not subject to local development controls. In several states, zoning decisions with regional impacts must be referred to a regional or state body. The recommendations of these bodies is usually only advisory, though in some instances an adverse report requires a greater than ordinary majority before an ordinance can be enacted and a statement of reasons why the report is not followed.[7] Florida has provided for regional planning councils to review projects of major impact within a council's jurisdiction.[8] In Wisconsin, shorelands and flood plains are controlled by ordinances of the State Department of Resource Development if appropriate local ordinances have not been adopted.[9] It is provided in the American Law Institute, A Model Land Development Code that the state will review zoning decisions of regional impact, though the recommendations may not call for a state veto, let alone provide for the state to exercise controls itself.[10]

 WESTLAW REFERENCES

zoning & state regional /s control authority power review approv! /p specified special unusual defined extraordinary /s situation case area zone

100.117 100.121

---

§ 3.8 Home Rule

Courts of the various states are not in agreement as to whether home rule power authorized by a constitution or a legislative enactment can be a source of a power to zone. In California and Ohio, for example, power to make and enforce local regulations is interpreted as authorizing zoning,[1] whereas in New York, the constitutional power of municipalities to enact local laws does not authorize zoning.[2] Even where zoning power is authorized by the constitution or by legislative home rule, it only applies to local matters and to matters not in conflict

5. N.J.Stat.Ann. 13:17–5 et seq.

6. N.Y.—McKinney's Unconsol.Laws § 6251 et seq.

7. N.Y.—McKinney's Gen.Mun.Law § 239–m.

8. Florida Regional Planning Council Act, West's Fla.Stat.Ann. § 186.501.

9. Wis.Stat.Ann. 59.971(6), 87.30. See Wood, Wisconsin's Statewide Requirements for Shoreland and Flood Plain Zoning, 10 Nat. Resources J. 327 (1970). See also West's Fla.Stat.Ann. § 380.06.

10. See Sussna, Local Zoning is Obsolete, 11 Current Mun.Probs. 335 (1970); Comment, Regional Planning and Local Autonomy in Washington Zoning Law, 45 Wash.L.Rev. 593 (1970).

§ 3.8

1. Brougher v. Board of Pub. Works, 205 Cal. 426, 271 P. 487 (1928); Pritz v. Messer, 112 Ohio St. 628, 149 N.E. 30 (1925).

2. R. Anderson, Zoning Law and Practice in New York State § 3.02 (1963).

with state law. In states with zoning enabling legislation, a conflict is possible, particularly on procedural as distinguished from substantive matters because there may be a greater state interest in uniformity in procedural matters. Courts in some states might well uphold legislation indicating that the enabling act was the exclusive source of authority. Zoning is not so clearly a local matter as not to be affected by a substantial state interest.

 WESTLAW REFERENCES

    zoning & "home rule" /3 power & constitution! (legislat! /3 enactment delegat!) & source & power ability authority & zone

    271 +4 487 & brougher

    149 +4 30 & pritz

    zoning & local city municipal county town /p power /p authorized allowed permissible acceptable legal lawful & conflict /p state /3 law

§ 3.9 Charter

A charter is the basic document of a local government, somewhat akin to a constitution. The state legislature can confer power on a city in a charter, including zoning power.[1] Sometimes home rule powers can be obtained only by adopting a charter, that is, the zoning enabling act governs unless there is a charter.

 WESTLAW REFERENCES

    137 +4 239

§ 3.10 Inherent and Implied Powers

The power to zone is seldom held to inhere by the mere creation of a municipal corporation.[1] Because zoning is a relatively new exercise of power, and it was possible historically to have a city without having it zoned (in fact Houston, Texas still has no zoning), a court is not likely to support zoning on the largely discredited theory that cities have inherent powers. Furthermore, the power to zone usually is not implied from typical legislation conferring general police power on a municipality.[2]

§ 3.9

1. Bartle v. Zoning Bd. of Adjustment, 391 Pa. 207, 137 A.2d 239 (1958).

§ 3.10

1. Detroit Osteopathic Hosp. v. Southfield, 377 Mich. 128, 139 N.W.2d 728 (1966).

2. City of Searcy v. Roberson, 224 Ark. 344, 273 S.W.2d 26 (1954); Stevens v. Salisbury, 240 Md. 556, 214 A.2d 775 (1965). See also Kline v. Harrisburg, 362 Pa. 438, 68 A.2d 182 (1949), which holds that a third-class city had no power to interim zone under the enabling act or under general police power or any other power, express, inherent or implied.

WESTLAW REFERENCES
de,sy(zoning) & power authority ability /p legislat! /p giv!
confer! /p police /3 power & implied inere**

§ 3.11　Enabling Acts

Provisions

While in some states there may be alternate sources of power, the place to look first for justification of the exercise of the power to zone is in the state enabling act. Most of these acts are substantially based on the Standard State Zoning Enabling Act.[1] The first three sections of the Standard Act state the purposes of zoning and define its scope.

Section 1. Grant of Power.—For the purpose of promoting health, safety, morals, or the general welfare of the community, the legislative body of cities and incorporated villages is hereby empowered to regulate and restrict the height, number of stories, and size of buildings and other structures, the percentage of lot that may be occupied, the size of yards, courts, and other open spaces, the density of population, and the location and use of buildings, structures, and land for trade, industry, residence, or other purposes.

Sec. 2. Districts.—For any or all of said purposes the local legislative body may divide the municipality into districts of such number, shape, and area as may be deemed best suited to carry out the purposes of this act; and within such districts it may regulate and restrict the erection, construction, reconstruction, alteration, repair, or use of buildings, structures, or land. All such regulations shall be uniform for each class or kind of buildings throughout each district, but the regulations in one district may differ from those in other districts.

Sec. 3. Purposes in View.—Such regulations shall be made in accordance with a comprehensive plan and designed to lessen congestion in the streets; to secure safety from fire, panic, and other dangers; to promote health and the general welfare; to provide adequate light and air; to prevent the overcrowding of land; to avoid undue concentration of population; to facilitate the adequate provision of transportation, water, sewerage, schools, parks, and other public requirements. Such regulations shall be made with reasonable consideration among other things, to the character of the district and its peculiar suitability for particular uses, and with a view to conserving the value of buildings and encouraging the most appropriate use of land throughout such municipality.

§ 3.11

1. Dep't of Commerce (1926 rev.). The Act is reprinted in full in C. Berger, Land Ownership and Use 762 (3d ed. 1983); 5 A. Rathkopf, The Law of Zoning and Planning 765 (4th ed. 1985).

Subsequent sections of the Standard Act provide a procedure for adopting the zoning and making amendments, including provisions for protest by neighbors. The Act calls for the establishment of a zoning commission, which may be a planning commission, which makes recommendations on zoning. The Act also permits the establishment of a Board of Adjustment to hear appeals from enforcement of the ordinance, to hear and decide special exceptions (i.e., special permits) and to give variances. Finally, the Act contains provisions for enforcement of the regulations.

Substantive Zoning Outside Act

Local zoning outside the scope of the enabling act can result in a holding of invalidity. For example, in Shuford v. Waynesville,[2] a one-block business section was established and filling stations were excluded. The court held the zoning invalid on several grounds. One-block zoning was not a comprehensive plan for zoning and it did not apply uniformly to each class or kind of building. In Albrecht Realty Co. v. Town of New Castle,[3] the town passed a zoning amendment limiting the construction of new residences to 112 per year. The probable reason for so doing was that school facilities would then not be overwhelmed with children living in the new developments. The court held that the town had no power to adopt such a provision. It was not one of the purposes of zoning. In DeSena v. Gulde[4] the city zoned property industrial and then rezoned it residential because Negroes living in the area threatened to picket and riot if it was not rezoned. The court held that avoidance of picketing and rioting was not a purpose of zoning and invalidated the rezoning to residential. Similarly, while a city may have power to regulate competition, that power does not come directly from the zoning ordinance, so unduly restricting the area zoned for business may be invalid.[5] When power over an aspect of zoning is delegated to a town zoning commission, the town council has no power to exercise the authority.[6]

Procedures Outside Act

Zoning can also be held invalid if the procedures established by the enabling act are not followed. For example, in Ellison v. Fort Lauderdale[7] a zoning ordinance was amended to exclude the keeping of horses in a residential zone. When the defendant was charged with violation of the ordinance he defended and won on the ground that no notice and hearing was provided as required by the statute. In City of Searcy v. Roberson[8] business zoning was held invalid where it was not preceded

---

2. 214 N.C. 135, 198 S.E. 585 (1938).

3. 8 Misc.2d 255, 167 N.Y.S.2d 843 (1957).

4. 24 A.D.2d 165, 265 N.Y.S.2d 239 (1965).

5. Pacific Palisades Ass'n v. Huntington Beach, 196 Cal. 211, 237 P. 538 (1925).

6. Poulos v. Caparrelli, 25 Conn.Supp. 370, 205 A.2d 382 (Super.1964).

7. 183 So.2d 193 (Fla.1966).

8. 224 Ark. 344, 273 S.W.2d 26 (1954).

by comprehensive study by the planning commission, as the statute required. In Holdredge v. Cleveland,[9] an amendment had not been submitted to the planning commission as required by the statute, so the rezoning was held invalid.

 WESTLAW REFERENCES

(state /3 enabling /1 act) "standard state zoning enabling act" & zoning planning /3 commission

zoning & "standard state zoning enabling act" & "grant of power" district "purposes in view"

zoning & enabling /3 act & outside beyond /s scope authority law

zoning & invalid unlawful & procedure act method enabling /3 act & disregard! not /3 observ! follow!

§ 3.12   Initiative and Referendum

In some states, the people can enact legislation through use of the initiative, and in many states, can pass on legislative acts by exercising the power of referendum. Use of the initiative for zoning is authorized by statute in some states.[1] Where the power to zone does not come from the enabling act, it is more likely that general authority authorizing an initiative will be upheld as a basis for zoning.[2] Where the source of power to zone is the enabling act, however, it may be difficult to comply with procedural requisites for zoning such as notice, hearing and referral to the planning commission, so the initiative process may not be possible.[3] Furthermore, some states have disallowed zoning by initiative reasoning that the comprehensiveness of zoning legislation would be destroyed.[4]

Zoning referenda likewise have been disallowed so as to avoid piecemeal attacks on comprehensive plans.[5] Compliance with the procedural requisites for zoning, however, is generally not difficult with referenda. A referendum comes after the enactment of legislation, so there are no procedural steps for zoning with which the referendum procedures may conflict.[6] Thus, a referendum on zoning legislation is possible in many states. Some states expressly authorize it,[7] in others

9. 218 Tenn. 239, 402 S.W.2d 709 (1966).

§ 3.12

1. Ariz.Rev.Stat. § 11–826; Mich.Comp. Laws Ann. § 125.271; Ohio Rev.Code § 303.25.

2. Fletcher v. Porter, 203 Cal.App.2d 313, 21 Cal.Rptr. 452 (1962).

3. City of Scottsdale v. Superior Court, 103 Ariz. 204, 439 P.2d 290 (1968). Contra Associated Home Builders v. Livermore, 18 Cal.3d 582, 135 Cal.Rptr. 41, 557 P.2d 473 (1976).

4. Gumprecht v. Coeur d'Alene, 104 Idaho 615, 661 P.2d 1214 (1983).

5. Township of Sparta v. Spillane, 125 N.J.Super. 519, 312 A.2d 154 (1973), certification denied 64 N.J. 493, 317 A.2d 706 (1974).

6. But see San Pedro North, Ltd. v. San Antonio, 562 S.W.2d 260 (Tex.App.1978), cert. denied 439 U.S. 1004, 99 S.Ct. 616, 58 L.Ed.2d 680 (1978), rehearing denied 439 U.S. 1135, 99 S.Ct. 1060, 59 L.Ed.2d 98 (1979). To allow a referendum would be to add a procedural step to zoning which is not required by the enabling act.

7. Mich.Comp.Laws Ann. § 125.282.

the general authority to have referenda is sufficient.[8] Where a referendum is permitted, the state law generally provides that legislation does not take effect until the expiration of a specified period of time so as to provide the opportunity to file a referendum petition. If a timely petition is filed and qualified, the legislation does not take effect unless the measure receives a favorable vote in the election.

Typically, the initiative and referendum can only be used with respect to legislative acts. Therefore a referendum is not possible on such administrative acts as variances and special permits.[9] Furthermore, since delay in adoption of a measure may adversely affect the public interest, a referendum can be avoided by a legislative declaration that the action constitutes an emergency ordinance and should take effect immediately. Courts may not uphold legislative determinations of emergency. Similarly, if the nature of the act is legislative, the municipality cannot call it something else in order to avoid the referendum. For example, Parr v. Fulton[10] held that a rezoning of a 44-acre tract for public housing by resolution was really an ordinance and that a referendum on the action was possible.

 WESTLAW REFERENCES
di,sy(zoning & referend** initiative)

§ 3.13 Special Enabling Acts

Airport and Flood Plains

Authority for some kinds of zoning may be provided by a separate enabling act rather than the general zoning enabling act. Airport zoning and flood plain zoning are two examples, both of which were stimulated by federal legislation. Airport zoning is encouraged by 49 U.S.C.A. § 1110(4) which provides grants of 50 percent for airport construction provided that uses adjacent to the airport are so regulated as to preclude interference with airport operation. Some states have passed special legislation to assure the protection.[1]

Much flood plain zoning enabling legislation in the states was passed after 1956 because of the passage of the Federal Flood Insurance Act of 1956.[2] These special enabling acts authorize the exclusion of or other limitations on the erection of buildings on flood plains.[3] The

8. Florida Land Co. v. Winter Springs, 427 So.2d 170 (Fla.1983).

9. Allen v. Humboldt County Bd. of Supervisors, 241 Cal.App.2d 158, 50 Cal.Rptr. 444 (1966); Schroeder v. Zehrung, 108 Neb. 573, 188 N.W. 237 (1922).

10. 9 Mich.App. 719, 158 N.W.2d 35 (1968).

§ 3.13

1. E.g., Airport Approaches Zoning Law, West's Ann.Cal.Gov't Code §§ 50485–50485.14. See also infra § 4.19 for discussion on Zoning for Airports.

2. 70 Stat. 1078, repealed by Pub.L. No. 90–448, 82 Stat. 573 (1968).

3. E.g., Tenn.Code Ann. § 13–701; Wis. Stat.Ann. 59.971(6). See flood plain zoning, infra § 4.9.

1956 Federal Act was never funded but flood plain zoning is stimulated by the National Flood Insurance Act of 1968.[4]

Enabling acts have also been amended to permit the creation of historic districts and to preserve historic and architecturally significant areas.[5]

Interim, Extraterritorial and Prezoning—In General

The Standard State Zoning Enabling Act (SZEA) did not provide for temporary or interim zoning but rather contemplated the adoption of permanent zoning after study and the following of several procedural steps. Similarly, it did not provide any special mechanism for zoning annexed territory. Nor did the text provide for extraterritorial zoning, though a note suggested that power could be added.[6] The omissions have led to problems that have been cured in many states by amendments to the basic legislation.

Interim Zoning

When an area has not been zoned or has been zoned but is under comprehensive study for rezoning, there may be a long time delay between the beginning of the zoning process and the ultimate adoption of the zoning ordinance. Meanwhile, developers can emasculate the proposed controls by developing in a manner which would be inconsistent with the proposed ordinance. In order to prevent development, legislative bodies have adopted what is called temporary or interim or stopgap or freeze zoning, to prevent development. The procedural safeguards of notice, hearing, referral to planning commissions and the like are usually not possible or required. Where interim zoning is valid, the landowner may be delayed in his development plans for years. Where valid, the temptation is great to use interim zoning, since it is easy to use, and its misuse permits the governmental body to adopt regulation at a leisurely rate. It has also been misused to prevent development where the governmental body contemplates acquisition of the property and wants to keep "just compensation" to as low a figure as possible.[7]

Particularly in earlier years, interim zoning was not authorized by statute and many courts held it invalid.[8] On the other hand, some courts, recognizing that zoning cannot take place in a day have upheld

---

4. 42 U.S.C.A. § 4001 et seq.

5. See, e.g., Mass.Gen.Laws Ann. c. 40c, § 2; Vernon's Ann.Mo.Ann.Stat. § 89.040. See cultural, historic, natural and governmental area, infra ch. 14.

6. SZEA, § 1, note 15a.

7. See Annot. 30 A.L.R.3d 1196 (1970); Note, Stop-gap Measures to Preserve the Status Quo Pending Comprehensive Zoning or Urban Development Legislation, 14 Case W.Res.L.Rev. 135 (1962); Comment:

Stop-Gap and Interim Legislation, A Device to Maintain the Status Quo of an Area Pending the Adoption of a Comprehensive Zoning Ordinance or Amendment Thereto, 18 Syracuse L.Rev. 837 (1967). See also infra § 4.12.

8. Alexander v. Minneapolis, 267 Minn. 155, 125 N.W.2d 583 (1963); State ex rel. Kramer v. Schwartz, 336 Mo. 932, 82 S.W.2d 63 (1935).

interim ordinances where the time delay was reasonable.[9] However, interim zoning is for the purpose of freezing or holding development, not for permitting it.[10]

Several states have now authorized interim zoning by special legislation.[11] The acts generally limit the period of time during which the interim ordinances are effective.

Extraterritorial Zoning

The Standard State Zoning Enabling Act only provided that municipalities could zone, but the power has also been extended to counties in most states. Without county power to zone, the fringes of city areas could be developed without zoning control, for the courts will seldomly imply authority in a municipality to exercise any significant amount of police power extraterritorially.[12] Limited extraterritorial power might be implied. For example, Raleigh v. Morand[13] upheld extraterritorial zoning that excluded trailer camps.

Some states have given their municipalities the power to zone extraterritorially, though extraterritorial power to plan and control subdivisions is more frequently conferred.[14] Extraterritorial zoning power is frequently conferred only on larger cities, is limited in terms of miles from the city, is permitted if the county does not zone, is permissible where the county approves, or is permitted where there is a city planning commission.[15] In metropolitan areas, there is a possibility of overlapping extraterritorial jurisdiction, which is usually solved by limiting power to points equidistant between the municipalities exercising the power. Regionalization of zoning in metropolitan areas remains a major problem, and the prospective loss of zoning power is one of the major reasons why municipalities in metropolitan areas resist metropolitan government.

Prezoning

If there is no extraterritorial zoning power, a problem can arise upon annexation. Absent any authority, previous zoning regulations usually terminate upon annexation.[16] The states have handled the

9. Miller v. Board of Pub. Works, 195 Cal. 477, 234 P. 381 (1925) is the leading case. See also Metro Realty v. County of El Dorado, 222 Cal.App.2d 508, 35 Cal. Rptr. 480 (1963). Interim ordinance upheld that precluded subdivision because county was studying whether site should be acquired for reservoir.

10. Silvera v. South Lake Tahoe, 3 Cal. App.3d 554, 83 Cal.Rptr. 698 (1970). Interim zoning held invalid when passed to permit construction of high-rise building.

11. See, e.g., Colo.Rev.Stat. 30–28–121; Utah Code Ann. § 10–9–18.

12. Smeltzer v. Messer, 311 Ky. 692, 225 S.W.2d 96 (1949).

13. 247 N.C. 363, 100 S.E.2d 870 (1957), appeal dismissed 357 U.S. 343, 78 S.Ct. 1369, 2 L.Ed.2d 1367 (1958).

14. See infra ch. 7.

15. See generally F. Sengstock, Extra-Territorial Powers in the Metropolitan Area (1962); Becker, Municipal Boundaries and Zoning: Controlling Regional Land Development, 1966 Wash.U.L.Q. 1; Cunningham, Land-Use Control—The State and Local Programs, 50 Iowa L.Rev. 367 (1965).

16. Louisville & Jefferson County Plan. & Zoning Comm'n v. Fortner, 243 S.W.2d 492 (Ky.1951).

problem in a variety of ways. In California, cities are permitted to prezone annexed territory so that the zoning ordinance takes effect immediately upon annexation.[17] A zoning ordinance may be part of the annexation ordinance.[18] Interim zoning has been used.[19] In other states, the statutes provide that on annexation the area will remain as previously zoned for a period of time.[20] Ordinances sometimes provide that upon annexation the territory is automatically zoned to the most restrictive zone available under the zoning ordinance, pending reclassification.

 WESTLAW REFERENCES

enabling & airport "flood plain" /3 zoning

"national flood insurance act of 1968" & zoning

temporary interim stopgap freeze /5 zoning

125 +4 583 & alexander

234 +4 381 & miller & zoning

silvera /s "lake tahoe"

zoning & imply give confer grant /s power ability right /s extraterritorial!

zoning & overlapping /s extraterritorial /5 jurisdiction

zoning & regulation rule statute /p terminat! /p annex! prezoning

zoning & prezon! /5 annex! /5 territory land area

III. PURPOSES OF ZONING

§ 3.14   In General

The Standard Zoning Enabling Act provisions[1] list certain purposes for zoning. Most zoning ordinances also contain a statement of purposes and may merely repeat the statutory purposes or be closely similar thereto.

Zoning for a particular purpose may be invalid because the exercise of power constitutes an act that is beyond the scope of the police power. For example, if zoning is exercised to lower the market value of property so that a governmental body can acquire it more cheaply under eminent domain, exercise of the power for that purpose would be unconstitutional.

If the purposes as set forth in the ordinance are reasonably close to those authorized by statute, zoning effectuating such purposes is likely to be valid. For example, while the enabling act does not specifically authorize it, an ordinance providing that a purpose of zoning is the

17. West's Ann.Cal.Gov't Code § 65859.

18. Beshore v. Town of Bel Air, 237 Md. 398, 206 A.2d 678 (1965).

19. Williams v. Village of Deer Park, 78 Ohio App. 231, 69 N.E.2d 536 (1946).

20. Ohio Rev.Code §§ 303.18, 519.08 & 713.14.

§ 3.14

1. Reprinted § 3.11 supra.

promotion of beneficial development [2] is not likely to be found invalid as *ultra vires* the enabling act. However, an ordinance may be invalid if the type of zoning utilized is too novel. Certain traditional patterns of what may be accomplished under zoning have developed and departing from tradition can be risky.

In the sections which follow, some of the purposes of zoning are considered in further detail. A particular zoning action often effectuates several purposes and the purposes often overlap.

WESTLAW REFERENCES
zoning (standard +2 "enabling act") particular certain narrow /s
    purpose objective /s invalid*** unlawful "ultra vires"

§ 3.15 Maintain Property Values

The Standard Act indicates that conserving the value of buildings is a purpose of zoning. It may be wondered whether values should also be enhanced and whether land as well as building value should be conserved.[1] In any event, to the extent zoning is effective, the sum total of real property values in a city should be increased by orderly rather than haphazard development.

However, if zoning depresses values of particular buildings or parcels of land it is still valid. While a most unusual result, zoning has been held valid where it totally destroyed land value.[2] Similarly, the zoning of a parcel can be valid though the value of neighboring property is adversely affected by the zoning.[3]

The maintenance of property values purpose is sometimes used to support zoning that preserves the property tax base and to justify controls designed to preserve or promote aesthetics, or historic or natural areas. These matters are discussed separately.[4]

WESTLAW REFERENCES
zoning & valid legal invalid illegal /s destroy! reduc! diminish!
    detract! /s land property building /s value worth
zoning & destroy! ruin! /s land property building /s valid
    acceptable legal

§ 3.16 Stabilize Neighborhoods

While not a purpose stated by the Standard Act, some enabling acts and ordinances indicate that zoning is to stabilize neighborhoods or to

2. Nevada County, Cal., Zoning Enabling Ord. § 2 (Supp.1964).

§ 3.15

1. Statutes, ordinances and courts reflect a bias in favor of buildings rather than land in at least one other context. See infra § 4.36.

2. Consolidated Rock Prods. Co. v. Los Angeles, 57 Cal.2d 515, 20 Cal.Rptr. 638, 370 P.2d 342 (1962), appeal dismissed 371 U.S. 36, 83 S.Ct. 145, 9 L.Ed.2d 112 (1962).

3. Braden v. Much, 403 Ill. 507, 87 N.E.2d 620 (1949).

4. Infra ch. 14.

preserve their character.[1] Persons unhappy with a proposed zoning change often argue their right to have the zoning affecting them remain unchanged. While zoning should provide some stability, it is not a guarantee against change.[2]

A few states permit a change only where the present zoning was a mistake from the beginning or where the circumstances affecting a parcel of land have occurred that justify a change in the zoning. Maryland judicial decisions are often mentioned as exemplifying such a doctrine.[3] The doctrine may mean little more than that the court will superintend and hold invalid those rezonings where there is little or no evidence of change.

 WESTLAW REFERENCES
di,sy(zoning & stabilize preserve maintain /p neighborhood area district)

358 +4 136 & lamb

---

§ 3.17   Homogenized Areas

The Standard Act provides that regulations should be uniform for each class or kind of buildings throughout each district.[1] Uniformity in part means equal protection of the laws within districts, that is, regulating like situations in the same manner. Uniformity within districts and the authority to classify uses into various districts has also produced homogeneity, especially in the exclusive single-family zones, but also in cumulative zones. If zoning for all uses was exclusive rather than cumulative, more complete homogeneity in all zones would prevail.[2]

The uniformity or homogeneity purpose is sometimes used by courts to hold spot and contract zoning invalid.[3] Of course, only a reasonable amount of homogeneity is desired. Homogeneity can sometimes become stifling as in "ticky-tack" housing developments. Such developments sometimes lead to the enactment of anti-look-alike ordinances.

§ 3.16

1. The Standard Act indicates that the zoning should take into consideration the character of the district, probably implying that it should not dramatically change the character.

2. Lamb v. Monroe, 358 Mich. 136, 99 N.W.2d 566 (1959).

3. See, e.g., Montgomery v. Board of County Comm'rs, 256 Md. 597, 261 A.2d 447 (1970), appeal after remand 263 Md. 1, 280 A.2d 901 (1971); Westview Park Improvement & Civil Ass'n v. Hayes, 256 Md. 575, 261 A.2d 164 (1970); Woodlawn Area Citizens Ass'n v. Board of County Comm'rs, 241 Md. 187, 216 A.2d 149 (1966).

§ 3.17

1. The requirement is part of the section entitled "districts" rather than under the section entitled "purposes."

2. See infra § 4.3 on exclusive and cumulative zoning.

3. DeBlasiis v. Bartell, 143 Pa.Super. 485, 18 A.2d 478 (1941). Ordinarily, however, spot and contract zoning is invalidated on the basis of failure to accord with a comprehensive plan. See infra § 5.4 (spot zoning); infra § 5.5 (contract zoning).

zoning & regulat*** /s uniform! homogen! /s district

zoning & uniform! homogen! /p spot contract /3 zoning /p
   invalid!

§ 3.18 Move Traffic Rapidly and Safely

The Standard Act provides that regulations should be made to
lessen congestion in the streets and to facilitate adequate provision of
transportation. The location and dimension of streets is typically not
controlled by zoning. However, there are several aspects of zoning
related to traffic. The purpose is used to argue against non-residential
development in residential areas because of the danger to children in
street crossing. The purpose is also effectuated by front yard and
setback requirements of zoning ordinances, so that vision will not be
impaired at street corners.

Offstreet parking requirements are also justified to promote public
safety and to maintain the traffic capacity of streets.[1] While generally
held valid, offstreet parking requirements have been vigorously opposed
because they add considerable expense to construction and limit use of
a lot for its primary purpose. Further, there is a spurious American
tradition that there is a "right" to park on a public street. Perhaps
such a thought is the underlying reason leading to holding in one case
that off-street parking requirements constituted a taking of property
without just compensation.[2] In another leading case, Ronda Realty
Corp. v. Lawton[3] the court held offstreet parking requirements invalid
on improper classification grounds when offstreet parking requirements
were imposed on apartment houses but not on hotels and rooming
houses.

All of the density controls, such as height limits, yard requirements, minimum lot sizes, and control of number of units per parcel,
can be used to lessen the amount of traffic generating activity.[4]

In recent years it has become constitutionally possible to require
dedication of streets as a condition for the granting of a variance or a
change in zoning.[5] Such dedications relate to the purpose of lessening
congestion in the streets.

While perhaps not related to the purpose discussed in this section,
automobile traffic relates to zoning in at least two other ways. First, a

§ 3.18

1. Chambers v. Zoning Bd. of Adjustment, 250 N.C. 194, 108 S.E.2d 211 (1959).
See also supra § 4.24.

2. Denver v. Denver Buick, Inc., 141
Colo. 121, 347 P.2d 919 (1959).

3. 414 Ill. 313, 111 N.E.2d 310 (1953).

4. Flora Realty & Inv. Co. v. Ladue, 362
Mo. 1025, 246 S.W.2d 771 (1952), appeal

dismissed 344 U.S. 802, 73 S.Ct. 41, 97
L.Ed. 626 (1952) (large lot zoning upheld
partially on traffic considerations).

5. Bringle v. Board of Supervisors, 54
Cal.2d 86, 4 Cal.Rptr. 493, 351 P.2d 765
(1960). See infra § 6.7. California courts
have generally upheld more onerous conditions than allowed in other states.

substantial increase in traffic along a street may be a change of condition making a rezoning of a residential area proper.[6] Second, automobile traffic and parking is a use of land which, when not on public streets or areas, is a use of land subject to zoning regulation.[7]

 WESTLAW REFERENCES

zoning & offstreet /s parking /s require!

111 +4 310 & ronda

zoning & density /2 control height yard size /p traffic vehicle congestion

zoning & "density control" height yard size /p lessen control dictate /p traffic vehicle /3 congestion flow activity

zoning & require! demand /p dedicat! /p street road /p variance /3 zoning classification

§ 3.19   Regulate Competition

Zoning is sometimes used to regulate competition or has that effect.[1] Regulation of competition is not a purpose of zoning. Because zoning should not be used to create a monopoly, a few courts will sometimes hold zoning invalid where there is no place in a community for a competitive business to be established.[2] On the other hand, the mere fact of districting has some effect on competition. Every business does not have a right to be as near to its market as its competitor. It is not necessary to rezone areas commercial near a cemetery to permit flower shops simply because a nearby flower shop has a natural monopoly due to its protected non-conforming use status. Furthermore, a zoning ordinance enacted pursuant to a comprehensive plan will help shield it from a regulation of competition attack.[3]

Improper regulation of competition is often argued with respect to spacing requirements between such uses as filling stations and bars. For example, in Mazo v. Detroit,[4] an ordinance prohibited the establishment of a bar within 1,000 feet of another. The regulation was upheld as applied to "skid-row" area which the legislative body thought would become worse if a large number of bars were permitted. Similarly, spacing requirements may be upheld for gasoline stations on the

6. Offutt v. Board of Zoning Appeals, 204 Md. 551, 105 A.2d 219 (1954). See also infra § 3.16.

7. City & County of San Francisco v. Safeway Stores, Inc., 150 Cal.App.2d 327, 310 P.2d 68 (1957) (traffic to and from store on private easement over land zoned residential held to be commercial use and therefore precluded by the zone).

§ 3.19

1. Mandelker, Control of Competition as a Proper Purpose in Zoning, 14 Zoning Dig. 33 (1962).

2. In re White, 195 Cal. 516, 234 P. 396 (1925).

3. Ensign Bickford Realty Corp. v. City Council, 68 Cal.App.3d 467, 137 Cal.Rptr. 304 (1977).

4. 9 Mich.App. 354, 156 N.W.2d 155 (1968).

grounds of an undesirable increase of traffic or fire hazards,[5] or even on the ground that there are too many stations.[6]

 WESTLAW REFERENCES

zoning & regulat! effect /3 competition (districting /s competition)

zoning & spacing /s require!

zoning & spacing /4 requirement & filling gas service /4 station

§ 3.20   Limit Densities: "Snob" Zoning

Since zoning authorizes a municipality to restrict the percentage of lots that may be occupied, the size of yards, the density of population and the location of buildings, and since zoning is to promote health and general welfare, provide adequate light and air, prevent the overcrowding of land and avoid undue concentration of population, there are several bases on which zoning can rely to lower densities. The opportunity to zone out "undesirables," such as poor minorities, by zoning that increases the cost of land and housing may be a basic reason why zoning has been adopted on so widespread a basis in this country.[1]

Minimum Lot Size

The requirement of large minimum lot sizes is a popular device used by suburban communities.[2] Minimum lot size is sometimes stated in terms of width, square footage or both. Minimums of 5,000 square feet,[3] 20,000 square feet,[4] 40,000 square feet,[5] one acre [6] and five acres [7] have been upheld in leading cases. Courts sustaining these minimums do so on the ground that ordinances are presumed valid. They are particularly inclined to uphold them in rural areas where there is no

---

5. Mosher, Proximity Regulation of the Modern Service Station, 17 Syracuse L.Rev. 1 (1965); Williams, The Numbers Game: Gasoline Service Stations and Land Use Controls, 2 Urb.L.Ann. 23 (1969).

6. Turner v. Cook, 9 Misc.2d 850, 168 N.Y.S.2d 556 (1957). Contra, West Whiteland Township v. Sun Oil Co., 12 Pa. Cmwlth. 159, 316 A.2d 92 (1974).

§ 3.20

1. City of Boca Raton v. Boca Villas Corp., 371 So.2d 154 (Fla.App. 4th Dist. 1979), cert. denied 381 So.2d 765 (Fla.1980).

2. Becker, The Police Power and Minimum Lot Size Zoning (pt. 1), 1969 Wash. U.L.Q. 263; Comment, One Acre Minimum Lot Size Requirement in Zoning Ordinance Held to be Invalid, 106 U.Pa.L.Rev. 292 (1957).

3. Clemons v. Los Angeles, 36 Cal.2d 95, 222 P.2d 439 (1950).

4. Padover v. Township of Farmington, 374 Mich. 622, 132 N.W.2d 687 (1965).

5. Josephs v. Town Board of Clarkstown, 24 Misc.2d 366, 198 N.Y.S.2d 695 (1960).

6. Simon v. Town of Needham, 311 Mass. 560, 42 N.E.2d 516 (1942); Bilbar Constr. Co. v. Easttown Township Bd. of Adjustment, 393 Pa. 62, 141 A.2d 851 (1958).

7. Honeck v. County of Cook, 12 Ill.2d 257, 146 N.E.2d 35 (1957); Fischer v. Township of Bedminister, 11 N.J. 194, 93 A.2d 378 (1952). A minimum of 160 acres was upheld in a rural context in Wilson & Voss v. County of McHenry, 92 Ill.App.3d 997, 48 Ill.Dec. 395, 416 N.E.2d 426 (1981). See § 15.7 infra.

pressure for development. The courts indicate that a community can always change the minimums, but in the interim, sizes can be kept large to prevent an influx of population before community facilities are readied, such as schools, transportation facilities and water and sewer systems.

On the other hand, a large number of leading cases have held minimum lot size ordinances invalid. The California Court held a 5,000 square foot minimum invalid as applied to a lot where other houses in the area were on smaller lots.[8] One-half acre,[9] 2-acre,[10] 100,000 square feet,[11] and 2½ acre [12] minimums have been invalid. Courts so holding indicate that a town might use its zoning power to lower densities where there is a danger to the public health, for example, from a lack of sewers, but if a sewer system exists or if the minimum lot size for septic tank use is larger than necessary, the lots need not be any bigger. Courts recognize devices intended to prevent people in the low income bracket from moving into developing areas. They also recognize that large minimums tend to promote sprawl and that while septic tanks, wells and roads may not be adequate, local government is obliged to provide sewer, water and road systems. Some courts are basing their decisions on grounds that the minimums are invalid as denying rights of persons excluded. Other courts base their decision on the conventional ground that large minimum lot sizes constitute an unreasonable burden on private property, bearing no reasonable relationship to the public health, safety and welfare.

The debate over minimum lot sizes is not likely to be resolved for some time. In clearly rural areas, it is likely to be upheld, but in areas subject to development and where there is no regional master plan for handling new population pressures, the courts are likely to react adversely to exclusionary zoning.

Minimum Floor Space

Snob zoning is also effectuated through minimum floor space requirements. These ordinances are not as common as the minimum lot size ordinances. Lionshead Lake, Inc. v. Township of Wayne [13] is the most famous case sustaining the validity of minimum floor space requirements, partially because of the debate it stimulated in the legal literature.[14] Wayne Township was located in the New York Metropoli-

---

8. Morris v. Los Angeles, 116 Cal.App. 2d 856, 254 P.2d 935 (1953), *distinguishing* Clemons v. Los Angeles, 36 Cal.2d 95, 222 P.2d 439 (1950).

9. Christine Bldg. Co. v. Troy, 367 Mich. 508, 116 N.W.2d 816 (1962).

10. Board of County Supervisors v. Carper, 200 Va. 653, 107 S.E.2d 390 (1959).

11. Aronson v. Town of Sharon, 346 Mass. 598, 195 N.E.2d 341 (1964); *distinguishing* Simon v. Town of Needham, 311 Mass. 560, 42 N.E.2d 516 (1942).

12. County of Du Page v. Halkier, 1 Ill. 2d 491, 115 N.E.2d 635 (1953).

13. 10 N.J. 165, 89 A.2d 693 (1952), appeal dismissed 344 U.S. 919, 73 S.Ct. 386 (1953).

14. An article, criticism, reply ends with Haar, Wayne Township: Zoning for Whom?—In Brief Reply, 67 Harv.L.Rev. 986 (1954). Previous parts of the debate are Haar, Zoning for Minimum Standards: The Wayne Township Case, 66 Harv.L.Rev. 1051 (1953); Nolan & Horack, How Small a

tan Area. The township sought to justify its ordinance requiring minimum floor area houses on the basis of a study showing that minimum house sizes were related to health. The court held the determination that small houses created health problems not to be unreasonable and that the ordinance preserved property values by precluding the construction of shanties and made the community attractive.

The New Jersey Supreme Court implicitly overruled Lionshead Lake, however, in Home Builders League of South Jersey v. Town of Berlin.[15] Berlin held that the ordinance prescribing minimum floor areas for residences was invalid because it appeared to be directed towards economic segregation, rather than the public health or safety or the preservation of the character of neighborhoods. Other courts also have disagreed with Lionshead Lake. The court in Appeal of Medinger[16] found an ordinance invalid which divided the area into zones requiring minimums of 1,000 square feet in some areas to 1,800 square feet in others. While the court was willing to admit that square footage had some relation to health, the court found the reason for the sliding scale to be aesthetic or to maintain property values, neither of which justified the ordinance. The court surely had a point, because if 1,000 square foot dwellings do not impair health, it is hard to justify a 1,800 foot requirement on the basis of health. Similarly, in Frischkorn Constr. Co. v. Redford Township Bldg. Inspector,[17] the court held an ordinance invalid where the house proposed met the square footage requirement but was not high enough to meet the cubic foot requirements. While admitting that size had some relation to health, the court concluded a low house could be just as healthy as a high house and that aesthetics or preservation of property values alone could not justify the ordinance.[18]

Density is also controlled by setback, yard and height provisions which are considered later.[19]

 WESTLAW REFERENCES

371 +4 154 & "boca raton"

zoning & minimum /2 lot /2 size /p valid invalid

89 +4 693 & lionshead

zoning & minimum /2 floor /2 space

House?—Zoning for Minimum Space Requirements, 67 Harv.L.Rev. 967 (1954). See also Williams & Wacks, Segregation of Residential Areas Along Economic Lines: Lionshead Lake Revisited, 1969 Wis.L.Rev. 827; Annot., 149 A.L.R. 1440 (1944).

15. 81 N.J. 127, 405 A.2d 381 (1979).

16. 377 Pa. 217, 104 A.2d 118 (1954).

17. 315 Mich. 556, 24 N.W.2d 209 (1946).

18. Some courts uphold an ordinance enacted to preserve property values. See supra § 3.15.

19. Infra §§ 4.6–4.8.

§ 3.21 Increase Tax Base

In some states the enabling act provides that protecting or enhancing the tax base is a purpose of zoning.[1] If the enabling act does not authorize zoning undertaken for the purpose of preserving or increasing tax revenues, the purpose must be inferred or some other purpose must be found for the zoning.[2] In states whose acts are based on the Standard Act, the tax purpose can be inferred from the preservation of property value purpose.[3] Minimum lot sizes[4] may also be justified on the basis that the tax base is not adequate to provide the public improvements that must be constructed to accommodate development. If in keeping with a comprehensive plan, courts have also held it proper to zone land exclusively industrial for the purpose of alleviating a heavy tax burden and harmful school congestion.[5]

However, regulation of the rate of growth by limiting the number of building permits has been held invalid on the ground that relieving the school district of the necessity of providing additional school facilities was not a purpose of zoning.[6] But if the zoning is otherwise valid, the fact that it incidentally results in the production of additional taxes does invalidate the zoning.[7]

WESTLAW REFERENCES

zoning & preserv! maintain! increas! /3 "property value" tax /3 base

zoning & "reservation of property value"

zoning & exclusive! /2 industrial & tax /3 burden (school /s congestion)

167 +4 843 & albrecht

§ 3.22 Promote Morals

The Standard Act provides that zoning can promote morals, but few cases rely on that purpose particularly. Early cases authorizing the banning of billboards did so on the rationale that immoral activities could be conducted behind them.[1] Some zoning ordinances provide that on sale and off sale liquor outlets must be a certain distance from schools and churches. Other ordinances regulate the location of sex businesses. They are arguably based on a morals purpose.

§ 3.21

1. Utah Code Ann. § 17–27–13.

2. Putney v. Abington Township, 176 Pa.Super. 463, 108 A.2d 134 (1954).

3. See supra § 3.15.

4. See supra § 3.20.

5. Gruber v. Raritan Township, 39 N.J. 1, 186 A.2d 489 (1962).

6. Albrecht Realty Co. v. Town of New Castle, 8 Misc.2d 255, 167 N.Y.S.2d 843 (1957). More recent cases have recognized the validity of building-permit limitation programs. See infra ch. 9.

7. Ward v. Township of Montgomery, 28 N.J. 529, 147 A.2d 248 (1959).

§ 3.22

1. St. Louis Gunning Advertising Co. v. St. Louis, 235 Mo. 99, 137 S.W. 929 (1911), dismissed 231 U.S. 701, 34 S.Ct. 325, 58 L.Ed. 470 (1913). See also McCarthy v. Manhattan Beach, 41 Cal.2d 879, 264 P.2d 932 (1953), cert. denied 348 U.S. 817, 75 S.Ct. 29, 99 L.Ed. 644 (1954).

WESTLAW REFERENCES
zoning & promot! /2 moral
235 +4 99 & st. louis
264 +4 932 & mccarthy

Chapter 4

TYPES OF ZONES AND USES

Analysis

I. INTRODUCTION

Sec.

4.1 Types of Zones: In General.

II. USE, BULK AND HEIGHT ZONES

4.2 Use Zones.

4.3 Cumulative, Exclusive, Highest and Intensive Use Zones.

4.4 Agricultural Zones.

4.5 Industrial and Commercial Zones.

4.6 Height Zones.

4.7 Bulk Zones.

III. SETBACKS

4.8 Setback Lines.

4.9 Flood Plain Zoning.

IV. SPECIAL SITUATION ZONES

4.10 Floating Zones.

4.11 Performance Zones.

4.12 Holding Zones.

4.13 Transition or Buffer Zones.

4.14 Potential Classification, Tentative, Qualified and Overlay Zones.

I. INTRODUCTION

§ 4.1 Types of Zones: In General

The Standard State Zoning Enabling Act [1] provides that a legislative body is empowered to

> regulate and restrict the height, number of stories, and size of buildings and other structures, the percentage of a lot that may be occupied, the size of yards, courts, and other open spaces, the density of population, and the location and use of buildings, structures and land for trade, industry, residence, or other purposes.[2]

In order to do so

---

§ 4.1

1. U.S. Dept. Commerce (rev. ed. 1926).

2. Id. § 1.

[T]he local legislative body may divide the municipality into districts of such number, shape and area as may be . . . best . . . and within such districts it may regulate and restrict the erection, construction, alteration, repair, or use of buildings, structures, or land.[3]

The authority provided is the basis for four basic kinds of districts: use, height, bulk and density. The ordinances implementing these statutes apply the regulations to the geographical space controlled by the government having jurisdiction to zone in an area. The use zones, for trade, industry, residence or other purposes, as the statute authorizes, are designated by an ordinance which either precisely describes the areas zoned in each category or incorporates a precise map showing the areas. There typically are several kinds of residential zones, e.g., single family, two family, four family, apartment and hotel; several kinds of commercial, more than a few industrial and, frequently other kinds of use zones.[4]

Similarly, an ordinance may establish a variety of height zones. Height regulations are usually stated in terms of maximum permitted heights or number of stories or both, and these zones are applied to the various areas of the community. Generally, though not necessarily, height zones have the same boundaries as the use zones.

Bulk zones are also frequently tied to the use zones, so that the zone boundaries are the same. While a height regulation is a control of building bulk, and while the term bulk control sometimes includes height control, bulk control primarily deals with horizontal rather than vertical measurements. For example, minimum lot size, percentage of lot that may be occupied and yard requirements are bulk regulations.

Since population densities can be controlled by use, height and bulk provisions which relate to buildings, density zones which relate to persons are not widely used. However, some ordinances will provide, for example, that density can only be so many persons or families per acre or per lot, which permitted densities may be different in various zoned areas.

The next part of this chapter describes various kinds of zones and some of the variations on the basic patterns. Where appropriate, the validity of the zones will be considered.

---

3. Id. § 2.

4. For a discussion of various specialized kinds of zones, see Fonoroff, Special Districts: A Departure from the Concept of Uniform Controls, in The New Zoning 82 (N. Marcus & M. Groves eds. 1970).

II. USE, BULK AND HEIGHT ZONES

§ 4.2 Use Zones

In General

When laymen think of zoning, they primarily think of use zoning. Such an emphasis is proper because the zoning "movement" that swept the country between 1910 and 1930 was use zoning. Euclid v. Ambler Realty Co.[1] is the most famous zoning case because it upheld the comprehensive division of a city into different use zones. Prior to 1910–1930, zoned height and bulk regulations were widely used, though they were frequently not part of an ordinance known as a zoning ordinance. In the typical zoning ordinance each use zone has three varieties of uses: permitted, accessory and conditional.

Permitted Uses

A permitted use is primary and is permitted as a matter of right anywhere within the zone. For example, the text of an ordinance describing permitted commercial uses in a commercial zone may have between a few to perhaps several hundred kinds of commercial uses, often listed alphabetically. For example, the Los Angeles County Zoning Ordinance Zone C–1 Regulations, Restricted Business begins and ends with

> (1) Antiques. The retail sale of genuine antiques. (2) Automobiles. [sale of new] . . . (3) Automobile parts. The retail sale of new automobile parts. (4) Automobile trailers, sale of new. (5) Bakeries, retail. (6) Banks . . . (60) Theatre. (61) Tile. The retail sale of glazed and ornamental tile. (62) Turkish baths.[2]

There are nine other commercial zones in the ordinance, all having similar long lists of uses. The theory behind these groupings is that the uses are compatible and can share reciprocal benefits or at least do not cast major external costs on other uses permitted in the zone.

In some ordinances, the list will close with language such as "and any other similar uses," since it takes a long ordinance to list every conceivable use.[3] Even if the phrase is not in the ordinance, the building inspector or some other lower level administrator or administrative body may be given authority expressly or by practice to permit similar uses. Sometimes the lists of permitted and prohibited uses in the various zones are such that a particular use is unintentionally not permitted anywhere.

§ 4.2

1. 272 U.S. 365, 47 S.Ct. 114, 71 L.Ed. 303 (1926).

2. Los Angeles County, Cal., Zoning Ordinance § 254 (1966).

3. S. Calif. Ass'n of Governments, Classification of Land Use (1968) lists about 6,100 different land uses.

Where the use is not expressly listed as permitted, there is some risk. There are many cases every year on whether a particular use is or is not within the meaning of a use listed in the ordinance. For example, a permit was issued to build a veterinary hospital in a zone where the ordinance permitted hospitals. A Board of Appeals held that veterinary hospitals were clearly not included within the term hospital, and but for a court decision applying equitable estoppel, the veterinarian might have been forced to abandon his use.[4] The safer course is to apply for a textual amendment, adding the use as expressly permitted, rather than rely on any "similar uses" provision.

There are at least a few cases per year on the meaning of the word "family," a basic term used to describe uses in residential zones. The courts have held that religious communities are families, particularly where family is defined as one or more persons occupying premises and living as a single housekeeping unit.[5] These cases may be thought to be precedent for operations such as Synanon, which provides community living for drug addicts, and others, but a Synanon house with a variable and changing family of 11 to 34 persons was not considered to be a family for purposes of zoning.[6] In Belle Terre v. Borass,[7] the Supreme Court held that a municipal zoning ordinance limiting the occupancy of one-family dwellings to traditional families or to groups of not more than two unrelated persons was not a deprivation of a "fundamental" right, such as association, privacy, or travel. Some state courts,[8] however, have recognized these constitutional rights and have invalidated zoning ordinances restricting the size of unrelated families.

Alcoholic rehabilitation centers are not popular neighborhood uses, but where a B residence zone permitted such uses as hospitals, sanitariums, philanthropic institutions, fraternities and boarding and rooming houses, the court held that a nonprofit rooming and boarding rehabilitation center for alcoholics was a permitted use. The name of the use, i.e., rehabilitation center, or the purpose motivating the use, i.e., rehabilitation of alcoholics, was held not determinative.[9]

4. Crow v. Board of Adjustment, 227 Iowa 324, 288 N.W. 145 (1939).

5. Carroll v. Miami Beach, 198 So.2d 643 (Fla.3d D.C.A.1967); Missionaries of Our Lady of La Salette v. Village of Whitefish Bay, 267 Wis. 609, 66 N.W.2d 627 (1954).

6. Planning & Zoning Comm'n of Westport v. Synanon Found., Inc., 153 Conn. 305, 216 A.2d 442 (1966).

7. 416 U.S. 1, 94 S.Ct. 1536, 39 L.Ed.2d 797 (1974). But compare Moore v. East Cleveland, 431 U.S. 494, 97 S.Ct. 1932, 52 L.Ed.2d 531 (1977).

8. See City of Santa Barbara v. Adamson, 27 Cal.3d 123, 164 Cal.Rptr. 539, 610 P.2d 436 (1980); State v. Baker, 81 N.J. 99, 405 A.2d 368 (1979).

9. Beckman v. Grand Island, 182 Neb. 840, 157 N.W.2d 769 (1968). As to meaning and application of zoning regulations to automatic vending machines, garages and hotels, see respectively Annots., 11 A.L.R.3d 1004 (1967), 11 A.L.R.3d 1187 (1967) and 28 A.L.R.3d 1240 (1969).

Accessory Uses

An accessory use is a permitted use that is incidental to one of the primary uses allowed in the zone. Generally, it must be on the same lot as the permitted use and must be used by the same person making the permitted use. A private garage is an example of an accessory use in a single family zone.

A professional office or a home occupation is a type of accessory use in residential areas. It is often involved in litigation.[10] Questions arise as to what is a profession, and over the proper interpretation of specific terms of the ordinance.[11] Typically, the use must not only be incidental but customarily incidental. For example, it may be customary for an independent traveling salesman to have an office and to conduct business from his home but not customary for a stockbroker to run a business from his home.

Conditional Uses

A conditional use is a permitted use, but it is permitted only if certain conditions set forth in the ordinance are met. Some administrative body passes on applications to determine that the conditions have been met. When they are met, the administrative body issues a conditional use permit—sometimes called a special permit, a special use permit or a special exception.

The language of the Standard Act authorizing the issuance of permits is as follows:

> the . . . board may, in appropriate cases and subject to appropriate conditions and safeguards, make special exceptions to the terms of the ordinance in harmony with its general purpose and intent and in accordance with general or specific rules therein contained.[12]

> The board . . . shall have the following powers: . . . 2. To hear and decide special exceptions to the terms of the ordinance upon which such board is required to pass under such ordinance.[13]

In many ordinances, conditional uses and their conditions are listed for each zone following the list of permitted and accessory uses. In other ordinances, conditional uses are all listed in one part of the ordinance, with an indication for each use of the zone or zones in which they may be permitted and the conditions for permission in the various zones.

While the terms conditional and special use are sometimes used as synonyms, the terms are sometimes distinguished. Particularly when

---

10. Annot., 24 A.L.R.3d 1128 (1969).

11. See, e.g., State ex rel. Hynek & Sons Co. v. Board of Appeals of Racine, 267 Wis. 309, 66 N.W.2d 623 (1954), upholding as reasonable a decision by the board that a photographic studio was neither a professional office nor a home occupation.

12. U.S. Dept. of Commerce, Standard State Zoning Enabling Act § 7 (rev. ed. 1926).

13. Id.

conditional uses are not listed under each zone, they are sometimes called special uses. Historically, almost everything was a permitted use in some zone. But a few uses involved so much discretion and so little opportunity to set uniform standards and were considered so unique, i.e. special, that they had to be considered on an *ad hoc* basis. An airport or a rendering plant are good examples. In modern zoning ordinances, there are typically so many conditional uses listed that they are hardly special, and uniform conditions could be established. The conditions are either met or they are not. If met, issuance may not involve a significant degree of discretion and issuance may be mandated.

 WESTLAW REFERENCES

In General

di(use bulk height +1 zone)

272 +3 365 & euclid

Permitted Uses

zoning & residential /3 zone & family

zoning & family /p religious /s group community

Accessory Uses

di,sy(zoning & accessory /3 use)

Conditional Uses

di,sy(zoning & conditional special /3 use exception)

§ 4.3   Cumulative, Exclusive, Highest and Intensive Use Zones

The zoning lexicon contains phrases such as highest use and lowest use and higher zones and lower zones. Unintensive and intensive use zones are also descriptive of zoning. These terms in turn relate to cumulative and exclusive zoning.

Higher and Lower Zones

The highest zone is the single-family use zone. It usually is the first zone described in the zoning ordinance. It may be highest in the sense that a "man's home is his castle," or that the great American dream is the cottage in suburbia that is protected from "lower" apartment, commercial and industrial uses. In any event, it is called the highest zone in a continuum of zones that extends to heavy industrial or unrestricted zones, which are the lowest zones.

The phrase "highest zone" is not to be confused with another phrase, "the highest and best use of land." The highest and best use of land is the use which will result in the most profitable use or the use conferring the highest market value on the land. It is the phrase most often used in connection with a rezoning. The witnesses for the landowner argue that property should be rezoned, for example, from residential to commercial, on the ground that the commercial use is the highest and best use of land. It is also the phrase used when determining just compensation in condemnation actions, because compensation is fixed at a price assuming the highest and best use of the land. Of course, planning and zoning is employed for the purpose of "encouraging the most appropriate use of land"[1] which is concerned about other factors than maximizing market values for each parcel. Therefore the highest and best use of land as zoned or regulated becomes the market price, including the price on which just compensation is based.

Intensive to Unintensive Zone

While there is no precise meaning of the term "intensive zone," the term is descriptive of those zones that permit a large variety of activities or uses, high and large buildings, great densities, and require little open space. The large lot, single-family zone and agricultural zones[2] are generally the least intensive use zones and the continuum of zones continues through the most intensive use zones, heavy industry or unrestricted.

Exclusive and Cumulative Zones

Historically, the highest, least intensive use zone, namely the single-family zone, was also an exclusive zone. Uses permitted in other zones were not permitted in the single-family zone, so the single-family zone was the highest, the least intensive and the only exclusive zone. All other zones were cumulative, that is, they permitted all uses permitted in any higher use, less intensive use zone. The other zones only excluded uses permitted in any lower, more intensive use zone.[3] For example, in a city with seven zones, the light commercial zone would permit those uses permitted in single-family, multiple-family, and apartment zones and exclude uses permitted in heavy commercial, light industrial and heavy industrial zones.

The theory of exclusive residential zones is that it is legitimate to protect homes from non-residential intrusions; that the police power could preclude such near-nuisance activities as commercial and industrial uses in residential neighborhoods. At least in earlier times, zoning was somewhat nuisance based, so that the "pig could be kept out of the parlor." Moreover, exclusive residential zoning was very much like the customary restrictive covenants that limited uses to residential.

It is somewhat anomalous that the "parlor" was allowed to join the "pigs," however, for cumulative zoning was not designed to preclude residences in commercial and industrial areas—it was not extended to protect people from their own foibles. Perhaps the difference is ex-

§ 4.3

1. U.S. Dept. of Commerce, Standard State Zoning Enabling Act § 3 (rev. ed. 1926).

2. Agricultural zones were not typical in early zoning.

3. See, e.g., City of Miami Beach v. Ocean & Inland Co., 147 Fla. 480, 3 So.2d 364 (1941) upholding the exclusion of general businesses from hotel district.

plainable on constitutional grounds. Early zoning was reviewed by courts willing to declare it invalid on due process grounds, and such restrictions would be sustained only where strong and universally held values such as the sanctity of the home were involved.[4] Early zoners might also have assumed that the land in low, intensive, cumulative zones would have high value so that residential uses could not and would not compete for land so zoned. Further, if zoning was motivated by snobbery, as sometimes alleged, a scheme which kept commerce from upper and middle class residential enclaves, while permitting the poor and minorities to live where they worked, was consistent with the allegation.[5] Other kinds of exclusive zoning are discussed in the next two sections.

 WESTLAW REFERENCES

Higher and Lower Zones

rezoning   &   "highest and best use"

"highest and best use"   /p   just fair adequate   /3   compensat!   /p
   condem!

Intensive to Unintensive Zone

intensive   /2   zone

Exclusive and Cumulative Zones

exclud!   /p   use!   /p   permit! allow!   /p   lower (less   /2   intensive)
   /p   zone

exclusive   /2   residential   /2   zone

128   +3   50   &   goldman

§ 4.4   Agricultural Zones

Early zoning was urban oriented. Only cities and incorporated villages were given the power to zone by the Standard Act [1] and the use zones contemplated by the act were for "trade, industry, residence, or other purposes." [2] The country still had much open space and prime agricultural land was not regarded as a limited resource. The phenomena of "urban sprawl" was not widely known and automobile and transit facilities were not so extensive as to permit the "leap-frogging" of urban development far out into the countryside. Particularly in small towns, but even in larger cities, the poor added to their income by keeping a garden or a few chickens. Agricultural uses were not considered to be industrial or commercial uses.

Over the years, this picture has changed in almost every respect. Agricultural zoning is common.[3] Agricultural zoning is usually unintensive use zoning, though it will typically permit industrialized

---

4. For a typical case holding zoning invalid see Goldman v. Crowther, 147 Md. 282, 128 A. 50 (1925).

5. See infra ch. 10.

§ 4.4

1. U.S. Dept. Commerce, Standard State Zoning Enabling Act § 1 (rev. ed. 1926).

2. Id.

3. See infra § 15.5.

agriculture, such as intensive stock feeding, canneries and other uses compatible with an agricultural economy. Typically, it will also permit such residential uses as single-family homes on large lots. But it will prohibit conventional subdivisions and other urban uses which encroach upon the preservation of the prime agricultural resource. It is used as a holding zone [4] to contain urban areas and force denser development rather than allowing sprawl and destruction of agricultural areas.

In some senses, agricultural zoning is now the highest, least intensive, most exclusive zone. This is not to say that all agricultural uses are permitted in single-family zones, for over the years various agricultural uses have been banned from residential zones. The keeping of chickens, cows, goats and horses is now precluded in most residential zones. The growing of crops, however, is usually permitted in all zones, including residential zones.

As society began to value its rural areas more highly, and as the cases sustaining zoning became legion, the courts upheld exclusive agricultural zoning. Industrial uses may be excluded.[5] Commercial uses, particularly if not related to agricultural may be excluded.[6] Intensive residential uses may be excluded [7] or are made a conditional use.[8]

WESTLAW REFERENCES

agricultural /2 zone

agricultur! /2 zone & urban /2 sprawl

agricultur! /2 zone /p highest (most /2 exclusive)

agricultur! /2 use /s permit! allow! /s residential "single family"
/s zone

animal horse cow chicken /s barred prohibit! /s residential single
/2 family

156 +4 519 & glasstex

§ 4.5 Industrial and Commercial Zones

Most industrial and commercial zones are cumulative. However, some communities have enacted ordinances creating exclusive industrial zones. Just as industry can be a near-nuisance in residential zones, prime industrial land may be forever spoiled by the intrusion of residential uses. The development of industrial parks may be incompatible with residential intrusion. Industries may be subject to nuisance actions if residential uses are permitted.

4. See infra § 4.12.

5. County of Cook v. Glasstex Co., 16 Ill. 2d 72, 156 N.E.2d 519 (1959).

6. Winter v. Guenther, 24 Misc.2d 537, 192 N.Y.S.2d 892 (1959).

7. Mang v. County of Santa Barbara, 182 Cal.App.2d 93, 5 Cal.Rptr. 724 (1960), excluding trailer park and gas station.

8. See infra § 6.13, ch. 15.

The Standard Act did not require cumulative zoning, so exclusive industrial zoning does not conflict with a typical enabling act.[1] Litigation has been based on arguments that it is beyond the police power to protect lower uses from higher uses and on the basis that exclusive industrial zoning is unreasonable as applied to particular property. Several courts have now upheld exclusive industrial zoning where residential uses are excluded. Courts doing so indicate that just as industrial uses can be excluded from residential areas to promote the public health, safety and welfare, people can be protected from themselves by precluding them from moving into industrial areas. Furthermore, exclusive industrial zoning may be upheld to promote and protect industrial uses.[2] In those states where zoning can be used to increase the tax base,[3] the zoning may also be justified as a measure to attract industrial uses on the basis that such uses will provide a tax base.[4]

Exclusive industrial zoning may be invalid as applied. Communities are frequently "overzoned" for commercial and industrial uses, that is, there is no demand for as much land as is zoned for commercial and industrial uses. Where the zoning is cumulative, the property owner is not unreasonably burdened by the zoning, for his land can be devoted to some use for which there is a market. But when exclusive industrial zoning is used, and there is no demand for using the property in that manner, it is in effect zoned for non-use, which is unreasonable and does not serve the public health, safety and welfare.[5]

Some communities have attempted to exclude commercial as well as residential uses from industrial areas. A leading case on the matter [6] held such zoning invalid by a 4 to 3 opinion. The court held that there was not a sufficient distinction between commercial and industrial uses to justify such a classification, and the classification was thus unreasonable. Note also that it is difficult to justify the exclusion of commercial uses on the ground that they should be protected from themselves, as in the case of the exclusion of residential uses from exclusive industrial zones.[7]

§ 4.5

1. Kozesnik v. Montgomery Township, 24 N.J. 154, 131 A.2d 1 (1957).

2. People ex rel. Skokie Town House Builders v. Village of Morton Grove, 16 Ill. 2d 183, 157 N.E.2d 33 (1959); State ex rel. Berndt v. Iten, 259 Minn. 77, 106 N.W.2d 366 (1960); Kozesnik v. Montgomery Township, 24 N.J. 154, 131 A.2d 1 (1957).

3. See supra § 3.21.

4. Mott & Wehrly, The Prohibition of Residential Developments in Industrial Districts, Urban Land Institute, Tech.Bull. No. 10 (Nov. 1948).

5. Corthouts v. Newington, 140 Conn. 284, 99 A.2d 112 (1953). See also Gruber v. Raritan Township, 39 N.J. 1, 186 A.2d 489 (1962) (exclusive industrial zoning held invalid after residential development had been partially completed).

6. Katobimar Realty Co. v. Webster, 20 N.J. 114, 118 A.2d 824 (1955).

7. See generally Annot. 38 A.L.R.2d 1141 (1954); Note, Industrial Zoning to Exclude Higher Uses, 32 N.Y.U.L.Rev. 1261 (1957).

WESTLAW REFERENCES

157　+4　33　&　"skokie town house builders"

industrial　/s　zon!　/p　increase　/s　tax　/s　base

§ 4.6　Height Zones

Height regulations state maximum heights either in terms of feet or number of stories or both. Their general validity was accepted by Welch v. Swasey,[1] and most litigation questions their validity as applied. The regulations are imposed to effectuate some of the purposes, as stated in the Standard Act, namely "to secure safety from fire," "to provide adequate light and air" and "to prevent the overcrowding of land." They also are adopted for aesthetic reasons.

While maximum height limits receive a generally favorable reception in the courts, that is, few cases find such regulations unreasonable, minimum height limit requirements have not generally been found valid. For example, where an ordinance required all facades of buildings to be at least 15 feet in height in a commercial area, the court held the regulation had no relation to the public health, safety and welfare.[2] Minimum floor size regulations have sometimes been approved[3] on the basis that minimums have some reasonable relation to health. No one has yet been able to establish that a 15 foot minimum height is required for good health.

Height variances, as are area variances, are usually less consequential than use variances and are relatively easy to obtain.[4] Most height regulations except roof top protrusions, such as elevator towers and heating and air conditioning vents. Where height is measured by stories, the ordinance must be checked to determine whether a basement is or is not counted as a story. Almost every year there are a few cases[5] construing ordinance provisions as to the level from which heights are measured.[6]

WESTLAW REFERENCES

214　+4　91　&　welch

minimum　/s　height　/s　regulation zone requirement　/s　invalid

height　/s　restriction　/s　variance

height　/3　restriction　&　level　/s　height　/s　measure!

---

§ 4.6

1. 214 U.S. 91, 29 S.Ct. 567, 53 L.Ed. 923 (1909).

2. City of North Miami v. Newsome, 203 So.2d 634 (Fla.3d D.C.A. 1967).

3. See supra § 3.20.

4. Wilcox v. Zoning Bd. of Appeals of Yonkers, 17 N.Y.2d 249, 270 N.Y.S.2d 569, 217 N.E.2d 633 (1966).

5. Katcher v. Home Sav. & Loan Ass'n, 245 Cal.App.2d 425, 53 Cal.Rptr. 923 (1966) (height measured from finished grade level rather than original ground level); Opendack v. Madding, 69 Wn.2d 171, 417 P.2d 849 (1966) (height measured from average grade).

6. See infra § 4.07 (discussion of floor area ratios); supra § 3.13 (discussion of flight plane zoning); infra § 4.19 (same).

§ 4.7   Bulk Zones

Bulk zone regulations are those which provide a zoning envelope for buildings by horizontal measurement. They include such regulations as minimum lot size, minimum frontage of lots, the area of a lot that may be covered, yard requirements and setbacks. FAR, meaning floor-area ratio, is a device that combines height and bulk provisions.

FAR

Under FAR, the ordinance designates a floor-area ratio for a particular zone. If the ratio is 1:1, for example, a one story building can cover the entire buildable area of the lot, a two story building can cover one half of the buildable area, a four story building can cover one-fourth of the buildable area and so on. In commercial office building areas in large cities the ratios may be 10:1, which would permit a twenty story building on half of the buildable area of the lot.

FAR may be used in conjunction with maximum height limits and other bulk controls, so that in a 10:1 area, it may not be possible to build a 200 story building on 1/20th of the buildable area of a lot or to eliminate yards entirely and build a 10 story building up to all lot lines. Nevertheless, FAR does give the builder some flexibility. In effect it provides an inducement to the builder to leave more of his lot open by permitting him to build higher.

Indeed, some cities induce builders to leave more open space by offering increases in FAR in return for on-site public facilities, such as plazas. FAR has been assumed to be valid, though there are no significant cases where the technique has been exhaustively considered.[1]

Lots and Yards

Minimum lot size requirements[2] and minimum frontage of lot requirements or both are a means of controlling densities. As with minimum lot sizes, minimum lot frontages are sometimes regulated by the subdivision ordinance instead of or in addition to the regulations in a zoning ordinance.[3] Reasonable frontage requirements are valid as are minimum lot size requirements. Where the lot frontage is not

§ 4.7

1. See Broadway, Laguna, Vallejo Ass'n v. Board of Permit Appeals, 66 Cal.2d 767, 59 Cal.Rptr. 146, 427 P.2d 810 (1967); People ex rel. Interchemical Corp. v. Chicago, 29 Ill.2d 446, 194 N.E.2d 199 (1963); Pondfield Rd. Co. v. Bronxville, 141 N.Y.S.2d 723 (Westchester County 1955), affirmed mem. 1 A.D.2d 897, 150 N.Y.S.2d 910 (1956), affirmed mem. 1 N.Y.2d 841, 153 N.Y.S.2d 221, 135 N.E.2d 725 (1956); LaSalle Nat'l Bank v. Evanston, 57 Ill.2d 415, 312 N.E.2d 625 (1974); Park Avenue Tower Associates v. New York, 746 F.2d 135 (2d Cir.1984), cert. denied __ U.S. __,

105 S.Ct. 1854, 85 L.Ed.2d 151 (1985). See also The New Zoning 139–90 (N. Marcus & M. Groves, eds. 1970); Fisher, San Francisco Height, FAR and Variance Requirements Upheld in Strong New Decisions by California Supreme Court, Land-Use Controls No. 4, 1967, at 1; Note, Zoning—Police Power—Minimum Floor Area Requirements Unrelated to Legitimate Purposes of Zoning Are Invalid, 10 Seton Hall L.Rev. 765 (1980).

2. See supra § 3.20.

3. See infra ch. 7.

straight, for example on a cul-de-sac, the proper construction of ordinances requiring minimum footages sometimes leads to litigation.[4]

The Standard Act provides that a community may regulate the percentage of lot that may be occupied. A typical ordinance, for example, may provide that in a multi-family zone, not more than 60 percent of the lot shall be covered by buildings. As with other bulk requirements, reasonable regulation is held valid.[5]

Almost all zoning ordinances also require minimum front, side and rear yards, particularly in residential districts. The Standard Act provides that a community may regulate the size of yards. Yard requirements are imposed to provide space, light and air and safety from fire as well as for aesthetic purposes. Reasonable yard requirements are valid. Yard requirements have long been imposed by private restrictive covenants.

Construction of the ordinances may be difficult. For example, while a tree would not be considered to be a structure to be kept off a yard, what about a tennis court? What is the front yard on a corner lot? Does a balcony that overhangs a yard violate the yard requirements? Some of these matters may be covered by a detailed ordinance.[6]

Ordinances may also provide that land comprising a yard cannot be sold off to become the yard for some other lot.[7] Special yard requirements may be imposed in transition zones.[8] Front yards in partially built-up areas that existed prior to zoning may be set at a line constituting the average yards already established in the block.[9] Under some ordinances, if larger than required yards are provided on one or more sides, smaller yards are required on other sides.

Conventional yard requirements are measured from the building to the lot line and are a prime manifestation of the zoning "cookie cutter" style of development. Modern development may not conform to this kind of lot by lot building. For example, in Akers v. Mayor and City Council of Baltimore[10] a builder planned a series of four family buildings built in an offset pattern so as to touch only at the corners. The roof and foundation for the series of buildings was to be continuous. The ordinance required that each building have two side yards of ten feet or one side yard of 15 feet. If the series was construed to be one building, it complied with the ordinance. However, if each four family building was considered to be a separate building, the side yard requirement could not be met for any but two of the buildings.[11] The court

---

4. See Annot. 96 A.L.R.2d 1367 (1964).

5. Annot. 96 A.L.R.2d 1396 (1964).

6. See Annot. 94 A.L.R.2d 398 (1964) (on side and rear yards); Annot. 93 A.L.R.2d 1223 (1964) (on front yards).

7. See Hartman v. Rizzuto, 123 Cal. App.2d 186, 266 P.2d 539 (1954).

8. See infra § 4.13.

9. See infra ch. 5 (on delegation of power to property owners); infra § 4.8 (on setbacks).

10. 179 Md. 448, 20 A.2d 181 (1941).

11. Each four-family building was closer than 10 feet to another. While two could be closer than 10 feet, they would have to be 15 feet from the third unit.

construed the matter sensibly and held that the series of buildings was one building.

Norwood Heights Improvement Ass'n v. Mayor and City Council of Baltimore [12] involved a development similar to the one in Akers. The application for the development showed no lot lines, but the applicant was nevertheless issued a building permit. The ordinance defined a lot and required and defined a rear, side and front yard. The court reversed the issuance of the permit on the ground that because no lot lines were shown, and the basic units of zoning are buildings and lots, compliance with the ordinance could not be shown. By dictum the court indicated that the project might be revised by providing lot lines for each building and it might then comply with the ordinance.

In order to avoid these kinds of problems, some ordinances provide for planned unit developments.[13] Special provisions have also been included in ordinances to make condominium development consistent with lot by lot zoning.

WESTLAW REFERENCES
FAR
floor /2 area /2 ratio

Lots and Yards
minimum /2 lot /2 size /p control! /2 density
minimum /2 lot /2 size & control! /2 density
di,sy(zoning & percent! portion /s lot land /s cover! taken use!
    /s building house structure)
minimum /2 yard /2 size space
20 +4 181 & akers

III.   SETBACKS

§ 4.8   Setback Lines

While some state zoning enabling acts authorize the regulation of setbacks, acts based on the Standard Act do not so provide. The setback may be called a building line and may be authorized by a separate statute. In theory, the setback is somewhat different than a front yard requirement in zoning. Setback lines are imposed to facilitate the subsequent widening of streets, since the land can be acquired for less expense when buildings have not been erected on the site. However, as with front yard requirements, they relate to traffic safety in improving vision at street corners, improve appearances with a uniform building line and result in greater light, space and air. Front yards are frequently measured from the setback rather than from the lot line.

Because the setback line is used to reserve future street sites, it is very similar to official map provisions, a distinction being that official maps reserve new street sites as well as sites for widening existing

---

12. 191 Md. 155, 60 A.2d 192 (1948).   **13.** See infra §§ 7.15–.19.

streets. As with official maps, the constitutionality of reserving street sites under the police power is not as secure as is the imposition of front yard requirements in zoning. Under zoning, private conduct is being regulated and the public is not acquiring anything, whereas the imposition of a setback line looking forward to future acquisition may be considered to be a taking.[1] However, the courts are often not precise or are confused over the distinction between setbacks and front yard requirements, and the generally accepted validity of the latter has led to approval of the former under the police power, particularly if the setbacks are part of the zoning ordinance and are imposed for the same reasons as front yard requirements.[2] Only if the setbacks unreasonably restrict the use of land are they likely to be considered invalid under the police power.[3]

There have been some United States Supreme Court cases involving the validity of establishing setbacks on the basis of a request by existing property owners or at the average of setbacks for existing buildings. These cases turn on the propriety of a delegation of power.[4]

In addition to flood plain zoning, which is a kind of setback provision,[5] and provisions for setback of outdoor advertising signs, setbacks may be imposed in other situations. For example, there have been proposals in California to map earthquake fault lines and to establish setbacks measured from these lines. In order to prevent hillside and house slippage, building, subdivision or zoning ordinances may require that buildings be built a certain distance from the top of the slope of a hillside or the top of a hill.[6]

 WESTLAW REFERENCES

set-back /2 line

set-back /2 line & future prospective /3 street road /p
    widen! construct!

set-back /2 line & future prospective /p acquisition acquire!
    condem! /p street road highway

set-back /p front /2 yard /p require! & valid legal

set-back /p invalid illegal & unreason! /p restrict /p use
    enjoy!

---

§ 4.9 Flood Plain Zoning [1]

The Standard Act did not provide for zoning to preclude development in flood plain areas, though some states have added protection

§ 4.8

1. See infra ch. 20 (eminent domain).

2. Gorieb v. Fox, 274 U.S. 603, 47 S.Ct. 675, 71 L.Ed. 1228 (1927). See also Kerr's Appeal, 294 Pa. 246, 144 A. 81 (1928).

3. See Board of Supervisors v. Rowe, 216 Va. 128, 216 S.E.2d 199 (1975). See also infra ch. 5.

4. See infra § 5.13.

5. See infra § 4.9.

6. See, e.g., Los Angeles, Cal., Mun. Code § 91.3009, as amended (May 14, 1969).

§ 4.9

1. See infra ch. 13.

from floods to their zoning enabling acts as a purpose of zoning.[2] Many states enacted special acts in response to the stimulus of the Federal Flood Insurance Act of 1956.[3]

Flood plain regulations frequently have two parts, one dealing with channel encroachment, and the other with the flood plain, which may be but usually is not part of the channel, even in times of high flows. There are several purposes of the legislation. It might be imposed so that flood control facilities can be more inexpensively built, to prevent restriction of the channel's carrying capacity, to prevent buildings from being erected that will float downstream to damage other property including public property, to reduce community costs for rescue and repair operations and to protect life and property of landowners from their own foolish acts. While some of these purposes may suggest a taking for which compensation must be paid, others suggest that the zoning is attempting to prevent a nuisance or to effectuate some other purpose legitimately within the police power.

The ordinances usually allow unintensive use of the land such as agricultural, park and recreation, riding academy, golf course and like uses. Usually the ordinances contain provisions for an administratively granted variance or use permit if the regulation causes a hardship or if a building can be located or built with minimal risk. Nevertheless, a leading case holds flood plain zoning invalid. In Dooley v. Town Plan & Zoning Comm'n of Town of Fairfield[4] the value of a 404 acre tract was depreciated 75 percent when land previously available for residential use was limited to park, boathouse, clubhouse, wildlife sanctuary or agricultural purposes. The landowner had not exhausted his administrative remedy, but the court said the tests provided for the variance would not have been met, and that the zoning constituted an unreasonable and confiscatory regulation amounting to a taking of private property for public use without just compensation. The court construed the regulation as one where most of the value of a person's property was sacrificed so that community welfare may be served, which constituted a taking. The case came to a surprising result, particularly in light of a previous Connecticut case which had upheld similar legislation. In Vartelas v. Water Resources Comm's.,[5] a state agency had established a setback line from a river which limited a property owner to 60 square feet of usable property. The property owner applied for a permit to build a retail store in the flood plain. The Commission refused to issue the permit. The property owner attacked the regulation as constituting an unreasonable limitation on the use of his property which constituted a taking for which compensation should be paid. The court held that the unconstitutionality of the

---

2. See, e.g., Conn.Gen.Stat.Ann. § 8–2.

3. 70 Stat. 1078, repealed by Pub.L. No. 90–448, 83 Stat. 573 (1968). See, e.g., West's Ann.Cal.Water Code §§ 8400–8415. See also supra § 3.13.

4. 151 Conn. 304, 197 A.2d 770 (1964).

5. 146 Conn. 650, 153 A.2d 822 (1959).

statute as applied could be established only by showing that no reasonable use of the property was permitted and the denial of the applied for use did not meet this burden. For example, the court suggested, the store might be permitted if built on pilings. No private property was taken for a public use, rather, the regulation was imposed to prevent the imposition of a public harm. Since the legislation was enacted to facilitate stream clearance, channel improvement and other flood control measures, the conclusion that the property was being regulated to prevent harm rather than to provide a public benefit is somewhat doubtful. Perhaps the court was influenced by the fact that four years prior to the decision, five stores and six apartment buildings had been destroyed by a flood on the same land.

Ultimately, the validity of flood plain zoning will be sustained under the police power where there is some risk of flooding and the regulations permit a reasonable degree of use or provide for administrative relief.[6]

WESTLAW REFERENCES

(flood /2 plain) (channel /2 encroachment) & zoning regulat!

flood /2 plain /2 zoning & taking "just compensation"

153 +4 822 & vartelas

IV. SPECIAL SITUATION ZONES

§ 4.10 Floating Zones

A floating zone takes its name from the analogy that it "floats" over the city until it is affixed to a particular parcel of land. In effect, the ordinance first creates a zone of certain characteristics, for example, a planned unit development zone, and then provides that land will be or may be designated by a second ordinance as being in such a zone when a property owner applies for it. Generally, the ordinance will provide that the zone can only be applied to certain kinds of property— for example, only to property of a certain minimum acreage, that is presently in one or more kinds of zones specified in the ordinance, where uses already established adjacent to the property are of a certain type, and where certain height, yard and other requirements are met. Upon receipt of an application meeting the criteria, the zone can float down to the surface by enactment of the second ordinance. Once affixed, it is similar to any other zone, except that the invitation remains open to apply it wherever else the conditions are met.

6. See Turner v. County of Del Norte, 24 Cal.App.3d 311, 101 Cal.Rptr. 93 (1st DCA Cal.1972); Turnpike Realty Co. v. Town of Dedham, 284 N.E.2d 891 (Mass. 1972). Cf. Usdin v. State, 414 A.2d 280 (N.J.L.1980), aff'd 430 A.2d 949 (N.J.App. Div.1981) (ecological purpose decides validity).

As is apparent from a description of spot zoning, a floating zone may be held invalid where spot zoning is held invalid.[1] There may be contract-like features of the floating zone that makes it invalid where contract zoning is held invalid.[2] Or, if the ordinance lacks sufficient criteria to guide decisionmaking, it may be held unconstitutional as an invalid delegation of legislative authority.[3]

Spot zoning is sometimes held invalid because it does not "accord with a comprehensive plan." Floating zones do not accord where the comprehensive plan is exclusively construed to mean the zoning plan as evidenced by the zoning map. A floating zone creates an "island" just as spot zoning. However, where zoning need accord only in the sense that it is not arbitrary, or need accord only to a master plan (and the master plan has embodied floating zones) or need accord only to a policy,[4] floating zones should be held valid.[5] The mere creation of the floating zone is some evidence that the legislative body has thought the matter through. The ordinance attaching the zone to a particular parcel is an embodiment of the policy. Thus, floating zones have been or should be held valid where the court does not construe zoning to mean only traditional zoning where every zone must be affixed to some parcel of property as it is created. Even courts wed to traditional zoning uphold amendments, and the two step feature—creation of the zone, then applying it—certainly is a rational way of amending. Some courts may declare floating zoning invalid as applied on traditional grounds that the zoning of a particular parcel cannot be amended without a change in circumstances, and there has been no change of circumstances.[6]

The floating zone technique was upheld in Rodgers v. Village of Tarrytown,[7] where an ordinance provided that parcels of 10 acres or more in size could be rezoned to a BB district permitting multiple family dwellings if certain standards of size, height and so forth were met. There was no parcel on the zoning map which was designated BB. Under the ordinance, an area zoned residential A was rezoned BB. The court held that there was a need for extra housing in the area, the ordinance set standards for the zone, and it exemplified a considered, comprehensive scheme. The zoning was for the general welfare rather than for the benefit of an individual owner.[8]

---

§ 4.10

1. See infra § 5.4. See also Annot., 80 A.L.R.3d 95 (1975).

2. See infra § 5.5.

3. See infra § 5.2. See also City of Miami v. Save Brickell Ave., Inc., 426 So. 2d 1100 (Fla.3d D.C.A.1983). See generally Prahl, Rezoning Dilemma: What May a Court Do with an Invalid Zoning Classification? 25 S.D.L.Rev. 116 (1980).

4. See infra ch. 2 for discussion of relation of zoning to planning.

5. See Floyd v. County Council of Prince George's County, 55 Md.App. 246, 461 A.2d 76 (1983).

6. See MacDonald v. Board of Comm'rs for Prince George's County, 238 Md. 549, 210 A.2d 325 (1965); supra § 3.16; infra ch. 6 (legislative relief).

7. 302 N.Y. 115, 96 N.E.2d 731 (1951).

8. For a case coming to the same result under a similar ordinance applied to a 2½ acre parcel, see Miss Porter's School, Inc. v. Town Plan & Zoning Comm'n of Farmington, 151 Conn. 425, 198 A.2d 707 (1964).

Eves v. Zoning Bd. of Adjustment[9] is the leading case holding floating zones invalid. The floating zone established by the ordinance was applied to a 103 acre tract in a residential neighborhood. As distinguished from Tarrytown, Lower Gwynedd was attempting to float in an industrial, rather than a residential zone, but that did not seem to bother the court.[10] Rather, the court held the scheme invalid because there was no plan; development itself would become the plan as development was solicited by individuals. The court held such zoning was not authorized by the statute and carried evils akin to spot zoning. Moreover, as distinguished from situations involving a zoning plan that is likely to continue, property owners had no way of foreseeing changes resulting from floating zones.

 WESTLAW REFERENCES

float! /2 zone

float! /2 zone & spot /2 zon! /p invalid

float! /2 zon*** /p valid

96 +4 731 & tarrytown

96 +4 731 & tarrytown & float /2 zone & valid legal
     lawful

float! /3 zone /s invalid

164 +4 7 & eaves

§ 4.11 Performance Zones

Particularly in industrial zones, an ordinance may provide performance standards rather than list permitted uses. In effect the ordinance provides that any manufacturing use is permitted which is compatible with other uses as measured by the external effects produced by the use. The ordinance establishes certain standards for smoke, noise, dust, toxic emissions, glare, vibration, radioactivity, electrical disturbance, heat, odors and so forth. If the standards are met, any manufacturing use is permitted within the zone.

Theoretically, performance standards could be applied to all zones. In effect, any list of permitted uses in a zone is based on expectations that the external effects of the various uses will not be materially damaging to other permitted uses. Theoretically it is possible to design performance standards so that industrial, commercial and residential uses could be mixed without any substantial adverse effects on one another. Planned unit development[1] embodies such a concept, though

See also Floyd v. County Council, 55 Md.App. 246, 461 A.2d 76 (1983). See generally Rose, Planning and Dealing: Piecemeal Land Controls As a Problem of Local Legitimacy, 71 Cal.L.Rev. 837 (1983); Comment, Zoning—The Floating Zone: A Potential Instrument of Versatile Zoning, 16 Cath.U.L.Rev. 85 (1966); Comment, Zoning Change: Flexibility vs. Stability, 26 Md.L. Rev. 48 (1966).

9. 401 Pa. 211, 164 A.2d 7 (1960).

10. Huff v. Board of Zoning Appeals, 214 Md. 48, 133 A.2d 83 (1957) upheld the floating in of a light industrial zone into a residential area.

§ 4.11

1. See infra §§ 7.15–.19.

the performance of the various uses is based on simple judgments rather than on scientific measurement schemes, as is the case where performance standards are applied to industrial development. Whether performance standards really work and whether their use should be expanded is the subject of considerable controversy.[2]

WESTLAW REFERENCES
zoning & performance /2 standard
industrial /2 zone & performance /2 standard

§ 4.12 Holding Zones

If a community is ready to decide on the zoning that it expects to maintain for an area until circumstances change, the area is placed in a permanent zone. If the plan for the area is in the process of development, interim zoning may be used to protect the area pending the adoption of a permanent zone.[1] However, there may be areas within the community where the proper use of the area has not yet been established by zoning and development pressures are not yet substantial. Alternatively, there may be areas which should not be developed because closer in or other areas should be developed first. In these kinds of situations, the community may zone for unintensive uses, such as agriculture or large lot single family residential uses, and require application for a special permit for every other kind of use. This kind of zoning is called hold zoning or open zoning.

A community is ordinarily hard pressed to provide a rationale for hold zoning other than a vague desire to control future development. That may not be a sufficient reason to preclude uses, so if a special permit is denied, the landowner may well obtain permission to develop through the courts.[2] On the other hand, hold zoning is not per se invalid, and may be upheld, particularly against uses that are not highly regarded, such as outdoor advertising signs.[3]

WESTLAW REFERENCES
''open zoning''
190 +4 294 & cook
27 +4 136 & national

---

2. See Gillespie, Industrial Zoning and Beyond: Compatibility Through Performance Standards, 46 J.Urban L. 723 (1969); Goodfriend, Noise Protection in Residence Zones, 15 Zoning Digest 233 (1963); Hirsch, Measuring the Good Neighbor: A New Look at Performance Standards in Zoning, 2 Land Use Controls 5 (1968); Kendig, Performance Zoning (1980).

§ 4.12

1. See supra § 3.13.

2. First Nat'l Bank v. County of Cook, 27 Ill.2d 586, 190 N.E.2d 294 (1963); Glen Rock Realty Co. v. Board of Adjustment of Glen Rock, 80 N.J.Super. 79, 192 A.2d 865 (App.Div.1963).

3. National Advertising Co. v. County of Monterey, 211 Cal.App.2d 375, 27 Cal. Rptr. 136 (1962). See also McQuail v. Shell Oil Co., 40 Del.Ch. 396, 183 A.2d 572 (1962).

§ 4.13 Transition or Buffer Zones

The adverse effects from a different adjacent use zone are minimized if the adjacent zone is the next lower or more intensive zone. Thus, a single-family zone is typically adjacent to a two family zone which is adjacent to a four family zone and so on. Such zoning is not always possible, so transition zoning is sometimes provided at the boundaries of zones. For example, multiple residential zoning was upheld as reasonable even though its primary purpose appeared to be to shield a single family zone from an industrial zone.[1] The multiple residential property owner lost his case because he could devote his property to a profitable use if used for multiple residential development. Transition zoning also takes the form of height and bulk zoning. For example, where commercial areas abut single family residential areas, the commercial uses may be limited in height, greater than ordinary setbacks may be required, and fencing and landscaping may be imposed.

 WESTLAW REFERENCES
di(transition buffer /2 zon***)
16 +4 131 & evanston & zon!

§ 4.14 Potential Classification, Tentative, Qualified and Overlay Zones

Communities have adopted variations of the basic use zones to provide more flexibility. Both contract and conditional zoning have come into increasing use. Yet both have limitations imposed upon them by courts. Courts typically disapprove of bilateral contracts and bilateral conditions.

Under conditional zoning an ordinance might provide that on the happening of certain events, property will be reclassified for a different use. For example, the ordinance might provide that property zoned agricultural will be zoned residential upon the opening of a major street. Such a zone might be called a potential classification zone and has the advantage of giving property owners and others some indication of the plans of the city.

In order to avoid the problem of property owners applying for a rezoning and then selling the land rather than developing it as promised, some cities have adopted tentative zoning. Under this scheme, the property is zoned for the applied for use, for example, for a commercial use, but if the property is not developed to that use within a period of time, it reverts back to its permanent classification. This scheme may help avoid the problem of overzoning for commercial uses.

§ 4.13

1. Evanston Best & Co. v. Goodman,
369 Ill. 207, 16 N.E.2d 131 (1938).

Contract zoning is an attempt to tailor-make zoning and also to avoid the problem of a developer building something different than his application for rezoning indicates he intends to build. For example, a developer might indicate that he wishes to build a flower shop on a parcel and seeks rezoning for commercial use. The legislative body of the city finds such a use unobjectionable and rezones the property. The property owner then builds a filling station, which the city would not have permitted. Theoretically under such circumstances, the city should not have rezoned unless it was willing to permit any commercial use on the parcel, but without qualified zoning, it is limited to a rezoning for any commercial purpose or to no rezoning at all. With the contract zoning, property is designated commercial, but the kinds of commercial uses permitted are contractually limited. For example, the zone might be designated commercial, except filling stations, assuming the legislative body is willing to permit any commercial use except filling stations. In effect, the legislative body can create an almost unlimited number of different kinds of commercial zones.

An overlay zone is used to place property simultaneously in two zones. For example, it might be zoned light commercial and multiple residential. An overlay zone might appropriately be used where the municipality is not certain which zoning is proper and wishes to permit flexibility.

Overlay zones may be combined with a sinking zone, that is, when the property is developed for a particular use, it becomes zoned for that use, the other zone "sinking" out of existence. In the example, upon residential development, the property could no longer be used for commercial development.

The overlay zone can also be used for certain special uses. For example, a city may be zoned single family residential and the keeping of horses may be prohibited. However, particularly in areas of large lot zoning, the residents may wish to keep horses, and it would not be contrary to the public health, safety and welfare for them to do so. Rather than permit the keeping of horses in such large lot single family zones, the ordinance might separately provide for an equestrian zone, with mapped boundaries showing the areas within the city where horses can be kept and ridden. Some property would then be in two zones, a single family zone and an equestrian zone. Floodplain zoning [1] may be accomplished by an overlay zone.

 WESTLAW REFERENCES

conditional /2 zoning /p reclassif!

contract /2 zoning

contract /2 zoning /p limit! /p use! develop!

overlay /2 zon!

§ 4.14

1. See infra § 13.20 (Floodplains); supra § 4.9 (same).

V. ZONING FOR PUBLIC, QUASI–PUBLIC, RELIGIOUS AND NONPROFIT USES

§ 4.15 In General

Among the vast number of uses of land that are controlled under zoning in the interest of the public health, safety and welfare there are many uses which, while perhaps as objectionable to neighbors as other kinds of uses, nevertheless generate or are thought to generate special benefits to the public. Therefore, they are or may be treated somewhat differently under zoning. These uses include those of the government itself—federal, state and local, public utilities, churches and nonprofit uses. This part considers these uses.

 WESTLAW REFERENCES
414k288

§ 4.16 Publicly Owned Facilities [1]

In General

Unless permitted to do so by the federal government, the police power of a state does not extend to the regulation of federally owned facilities by zoning.[2] Where the federal government has recognized the desirability of some local control, it has retained final decisionmaking power. For example under the Lanham Act, which provided for defense housing, the Administrator was directed as follows:

> Consultation shall be had with local public officials and local housing authorities to the end that projects constructed under the provision [for defense housing] shall, so far as may be practical, conform in location and design to local planning and tradition.[3]

The Federal Urban Land-Use Act of 1968[4] was the first law establishing a more general recognition of willingness to cooperate with local planning and zoning authorities. Under the Act, notice is given to the local government before disposing of land in urban areas, so that the land can be zoned in accordance with local comprehensive planning. Similarly, before acquiring or changing the use of land, the federal Administrator is to consider objections of local government to the extent practical, so that the proposed use will comply with local planning and zoning. Advance notice of acquisition is to be given, except where such notice would have an adverse impact on the pro-

§ 4.16

1. Comment, The Inapplicability of Municipal Zoning Ordinances to Governmental Land Uses, 19 Syracuse L.Rev. 698 (1968).

2. United States v. Chester, 144 F.2d 415 (3d Cir.1944).

3. 42 U.S.C.A. § 1545.

4. 40 U.S.C.A. §§ 531–535.

posed purchase.[5] Executive Order No. 11,512 [6] also requires that federal facilities, to the greatest extent practicable, be consistent with state, regional and local plans and programs.

When the federal government is the lessee of property, it is not governed by local regulation.[7] However, the lessee of federally owned property is governed by local regulation.[8]

State

Unless authority is delegated, a state is generally not bound by the zoning of its local governments because a locality's police power is derived from the state.[9] The state's immunity extends to departments and agencies of the state,[10] including local governments when they are carrying on state functions.[11] In recent years, however, some courts have indicated dissatisfaction with state exemption from local zoning and have instituted a balance of interests test.[12] This approach allows the court to consider the particular interests of both governments in resolving a zoning dispute.

Local Governments

Some local ordinances expressly deal with the matter of whether the local government is subject to its own ordinances. The matter is sometimes resolved by exempting governmental uses and sometimes by subjecting them to normal or almost normal controls.[13] Absent an express provision, a local government is usually held bound by its own regulations as to proprietary activities but not as to governmental activities.[14] Of course, since the local government is regulating itself, it can always change the zoning ordinance. Local governments frequently themselves engage in activities that would not be tolerated if con-

---

5. The adverse impact clause is an interesting one, perhaps related to condemnation. In eminent domain, property is valued at market, including recognition of those values generated by the probability of a rezoning in the near future. See infra ch. 6. In making purchases, the federal government should offer fair market value. If it is buying land zoned residential for a high rise office building, is the effect on value similar to a proposed rezoning for commercial use? If so, would the likely increased price constitute an adverse impact, therefore suggesting that advance notice need not be given?

6. 42 Fed.Reg. 3979 (1970).

7. Tim v. Long Branch, 135 N.J.L. 549, 53 A.2d 164 (Err. & App.1947).

8. Baltimore v. Linthicum, 170 Md. 245, 183 A. 531 (1936). See also Annot., 61 A.L.R.2d 970 (1958). See also infra § 4.18 (effect of local regulation on federal licensees).

9. Annot., 61 A.L.R.2d 970 (1958).

10. Town of Bloomfield v. New Jersey Highway Auth., 18 N.J. 237, 113 A.2d 658 (1955).

11. Green County v. Monroe, 3 Wis.2d 196, 87 N.W.2d 827 (1958).

12. See City of Temple Terrace v. Hillsborough Association for Retarded Citizens, 322 So.2d 571 (Fla.2d D.C.A.1975), affirmed 332 So.2d 610 (1976). But see Macon Association for Retarded Citizens v. Macon-Bibb County Planning and Zoning Commission, 252 Ga. 484, 314 S.E.2d 218 (1984), appeal dismissed ___ U.S. ___, 105 S.Ct. 57, 83 L.Ed.2d 8 (1984).

13. See, e.g., Sellors v. Town of Concord, 329 Mass. 259, 107 N.E.2d 784 (1952) (ordinance requiring municipality to apply for special permit).

14. Annot. 61 A.L.R.2d 970 (1958).

ducted by private individuals. For example, local governmental sewage disposal systems are one of the worst sources of water pollution.[15]

While a decision to proceed with a governmental use not complying with local zoning may result in greater public good than harm to the residents of a city, the public benefited is a different body than the public adversely affected where one governmental body utilizes property contrary to zoning within the geographical jurisdiction of another government. For example, in City of Scottsdale v. Municipal Court of City of Tempe,[16] a leading case, Scottsdale purchased land zoned single family residential in Tempe to build a sewage disposal plant. Scottsdale applied for a permit, which Tempe refused. The court held that Scottsdale could proceed in any event, since sewage disposal was a governmental function, and Scottsdale had been given the power by state statute to construct utilities and acquire lands within or without corporate limits.

The governmental-proprietary distinction is frequently not helpful because it varies from time to time and from context to context; for example, a governmental activity for purposes of determining municipal tort liability may not be a governmental activity for purposes of determining immunity from zoning regulation. Moreover, there is no unanimity as to what is a proprietary and a governmental function. For example, as distinguished from Scottsdale, Jefferson County v. Birmingham,[17] held a sewage plant to be a proprietary function, so that the county was bound by residential zoning within a city and was precluded from building a sewage plant. St. Louis County v. Manchester [18] evidences a balancing of interests approach. The county had zoned areas for sewage plants. The city, pointing to its statutory authority to acquire sewage plants and to locate them outside of the city boundaries, argued that the county could not regulate locations. The court concluded that the statute authorizing county zoning and the statute authorizing extraterritorial sewage plants could be reconciled by requiring the city to submit to reasonable county zoning ordinances. Authority to locate plants outside of boundaries did not mean they could be located anywhere.[19]

 WESTLAW REFERENCES

state /p police /2 power /p federal! /s owned own control! operat! /s facilit! property & zoning

144 +4 415 & chester

42 +4 1545 & lanham

federal /2 urban /2 land /2 use /2 act

15. See Town of Waterford v. Water Pollution Control Bd., 5 N.Y.2d 171, 182 N.Y.S.2d 785, 156 N.E.2d 427 (1959) (town litigated preliminary proceedings that might have led to order precluding town from discharging raw sewage in a river).

16. 90 Ariz. 393, 368 P.2d 637 (1962).

17. 256 Ala. 436, 55 So.2d 196 (1951).

18. 360 S.W.2d 638 (Mo.1962).

19. See also Wilkinsburg-Penn Joint Water Auth. v. Churchill Borough, 417 Pa. 93, 207 A.2d 905 (1965).

```
federal /2 government /s lessee & exempt! not /2 control!
    govern! & zoning

53 +4 164 & tim /s "long branch"

183 +4 531 & baltimore
```

State

```
state /p exempt! local /3 zoning
```

Local Governments

```
107 +4 784 & sellors

zoning & governmental proprietary /3 activit! function
```

§ 4.17   Schools, Public and Private

The main issues in zoning for schools are whether they can be excluded or at least regulated, whether public, parochial and private schools can be separately classified and the determination of what a school is.[1]

Public Schools

Most persons like to live within a block or two of a public school. Few public enterprises add as much to the marketability of residential properties as the presence of a good school. However, because of the noise, confusion and traffic attendant to the use, residential locations immediately adjacent to a school are not highly preferred. Nevertheless, most ordinances permit schools, particularly public schools, to locate anywhere, even in the most restrictive residential districts. They are sometimes controlled by special permit. Just as other governmental uses,[2] local regulation may be preempted because of the general view that education is not only a local governmental function but is also a state function.[3] The matter may be resolved by state legislation.[4]

Total exclusion of public schools from an entire municipality is not likely, though a few ordinances attempt to exclude them from particular zones. Depending on state statutes or case-made law and on the reasonableness of exclusion from particular districts, the exclusion may be held valid[5] or invalid.[6] States not permitting exclusion of schools

§ 4.17

1. See Note, The Immunity of Schools from Zoning, 14 Syracuse L.Rev. 644 (1963); Annot. 11 A.L.R.4th 1084 (1979); Annot., 64 A.L.R.3d 1087 (1973); Annot., 36 A.L.R.2d 653 (1954).

2. See supra § 4.15.

3. Town of Atherton v. Superior Court, 159 Cal.App.2d 417, 324 P.2d 328 (1958).

4. As a result of Atherton, West's Ann. Cal.Gov't Code §§ 53090–95 now provides

for a limited amount of regulation by localities over schools if the locality has provided for school location in a master plan.

5. Roman Catholic Diocese of Newark v. Borough of Ho-Ho-Kus, 42 N.J. 556, 202 A.2d 161 (1964), appeal after remand 47 N.J. 211, 220 A.2d 97 (1966); City of Toronto v. Roman Catholic Separate School Bd., (1926) A.C. 81.

6. State ex rel. St. Louis Union Trust Co. v. Ferriss, 304 S.W.2d 896 (Mo.1957).

usually permit their regulation,[7] though the contrary has also been held.[8]

Private and Parochial Schools

Where public schools are permitted, some courts conclude that private and parochial schools must also be permitted. They refuse to recognize any criteria for classifying public and private schools differently.[9] The Wisconsin court has discerned a difference and has upheld exclusion of private schools on the ground that they do not serve all comers from the community.[10]

While parochial schools do not have the benefit of law protecting governmental and state activities, they do benefit from first amendment considerations, so it may be held they cannot be excluded or regulated on that ground.[11] Even if the first amendment ground is not used, the courts are not disposed to indulge in the same presumption of validity of a regulation excluding parochial schools. For example, Archbishop O'Hara's Appeal [12] reversed a denial of a special permit that had been denied because of increased traffic, adverse effects on the neighborhood and the cost of required community facilities. The court indicated that on such grounds, a permit could never be obtained—but it is to be doubted that a denial would be reversed if those were the grounds for denial of a commercial use.

Private, nonparochial schools have no special first amendment protection, but may nevertheless be treated as parochial schools on the ground that there is no reasonable distinction between parochial and private nonparochial schools.[13]

What are Schools?

Some private schools are very much like typical public or parochial schools, but others may be called schools only to obtain favorable zoning treatment. Some are easily recognized as schools. For example, an ordinance was held invalid that permitted all schools in an apartment district except nursery schools. The court found that a nursery school was so like other schools that the exclusion was discriminatory and void.[14] The problem may be easier where a school is defined in the ordinance. If not within the definition, it is not likely that a

---

7. School Dist. of Philadelphia v. Zoning Bd. of Adjustment, 417 Pa. 277, 207 A.2d 804 (1965).

8. Hall v. Taft, 47 Cal.2d 177, 302 P.2d 574 (1956).

9. Catholic Bishop of Chicago v. Kingery, 371 Ill. 257, 20 N.E.2d 583 (1939).

10. Annot. 74 A.L.R.3d 14 (1974). State ex rel. Wisconsin Lutheran High School Conference v. Sinar, 267 Wis. 91, 65 N.W.2d 43 (1954), appeal dismissed 349 U.S. 913, 75 S.Ct. 604, 99 L.Ed. 1248 (1955) is a leading case. See generally J. Curry,

Public Regulation of the Religious Use of Land 164 (1964).

11. Diocese of Rochester v. Planning Bd. of Brighton, 1 N.Y.2d 508, 154 N.Y.S.2d 849, 136 N.E.2d 827 (1956).

12. 389 Pa. 35, 131 A.2d 587 (1957).

13. State v. Northwestern Preparatory School, Inc., 228 Minn. 363, 37 N.W.2d 370 (1949). See generally 8 Stan.L.Rev. 712 (1956).

14. City of Chicago v. Sachs, 1 Ill.2d 342, 115 N.E.2d 762 (1953).

court would find a ceramics factory and store to have the favorable status of a school merely because classes in ceramics were conducted there.[15]

While some private schools should be treated as having little more claim to favored status than any other commercial use, some private schools of great social utility have been given disfavored treatment by the same types of communities disposed to other kinds of snob zoning.[16] For example, after being barred from use of their property in two other communities, a private institution for the education and residence of handicapped and delinquent boys from New York City was excluded from a residential district of yet another community on the ground that it was not a school. The court held that it was a school and, moreover, it shared the immunity as if it were a state institution carrying out a similar function.[17] Obviously, few communities would seek to attract facilities such as the Wiltwyck School, but such facilities serve a high public purpose and are entitled to an adequate location somewhere. It is the kind of institution whose location should perhaps be controlled by a regional, rather than a local, body, because few courts would go so far as to clothe a private facility with state immunity. However, courts are generally willing to interpret ordinances so as to preclude local interdiction of these schools of high social utility.[18]

 WESTLAW REFERENCES

Public Schools

zoning & public /2 school /p local /3 regulat! (preempt! /4 state)

exclusion exclude /s public /2 school /p town city municipality

Private and Parochial Schools

exclusion exclude /s parochial catholic private /3 school

What are Schools?

zoning & school /s defin! & exclude exclusion /s invalid

zoning & school /s handicapped delinquent reform deaf blind

di,sy(zoning & school /p exclud! deny denied (not /3 permit! allow!))

---

15. Annot. 64 A.L.R.3d 1087 (1973). See also City of Chicopee v. Jakubowski, 348 Mass. 230, 202 N.E.2d 913 (1964).

16. See infra § 3.20.

17. Wiltwyck School for Boys, Inc. v. Hill, 11 N.Y.2d 182, 227 N.Y.S.2d 655, 182 N.E.2d 268 (1962), reargument denied 11 N.Y.2d 1017, 229 N.Y.S.2d 1028, 183 N.E.2d 772 (1962). The court's discussion on the sharing of state immunity is somewhat vague.

18. Note, 71 Yale L.J. 720 (1962). But see Devereux Foundation Inc., Zoning Case, 351 Pa. 478, 41 A.2d 744 (1945), appeal dismissed 326 U.S. 686, 66 S.Ct. 89, 90 L.Ed. 403 (1945) (court indicated that locality improperly permitted dormitory to be built adjacent to school for mentally deficient persons which was located in a residential zone).

§ 4.18 Public Utilities and Federal, State Licensees

Utilities [1]

Whether privately or publicly owned, public utilities are specially treated under zoning law. Sometimes, they are immune from local regulation because of express provisions of the state constitution or law which vests authority in a state commission and precludes local regulation.[2] Alternatively, since they are generally national, state or regional in scope, and are frequently given a state franchise and the power of eminent domain, it may be inferred that they are not fit subjects of local regulation.[3] Of course, many public utilities are governmentally owned, so they are immune from local zoning or not as other governmental uses.[4]

If given some power to regulate, localities can impose reasonable control on public utilities. They can be required to seek approval of the local legislative body.[5] The power to regulate may involve a limited power to control locations, but a court is quick to find regulations unreasonable and beyond the police power if the regulation excludes entirely, prohibits necessary expansion or requires termination of the utility as a nonconforming use.[6]

The point of greatest current controversy between utilities and municipalities concerns aesthetics and whether utilities can be required to underground their services.[7] Generally, municipalities have won, so that service in residential and commercial areas at least is now frequently undergrounded. Not only have municipalities imposed the requirements, but state commissions and the FHA, which finances new subdivisions, have been convinced that undergrounding is appropriate to eliminate aerial blight. Underground regulations have been held valid by the courts.[8] The dispute was resolved partly by technology, because undergrounding has become less and less expensive. However, the undergrounding of high tension lines is still very expensive, so local requirements for undergrounding such lines may not be valid unless clearly authorized.[9]

§ 4.18

1. See generally Note, Zoning and the Expanding Public Utility, 13 Syracuse L.Rev. 581 (1962).

2. See, e.g., Ohio Rev.Code § 519.21.

3. Cf. Pacific Tel. & Tel. Co. v. Los Angeles, 44 Cal.2d 272, 280, 282 P.2d 36, 41 (1955). "The business of supplying the people with telephone service . . . is a matter of state-wide concern"; Algonquin Gas Transmission Co. v. Zoning Board of Appeals, 162 Conn. 50, 291 A.2d 204 (1971). Annot. 87 A.L.R.3d 1265 (1973).

4. See supra § 4.16.

5. State ex rel. Kearns v. Ohio Power Co., 163 Ohio St. 451, 127 N.E.2d 394 (1955) (held a private power company had to ob-

tain approval from local legislative body where statute provided that legislative body had to approve "systems of transportation" whose public improvements departed from development plans).

6. Long Island Lighting Co. v. Griffin, 272 App.Div. 551, 74 N.Y.S.2d 348 (1947), affirmed mem. 297 N.Y. 897, 79 N.E.2d 738 (1948).

7. Miller, Public Utilities Underground, 1 Cal.W.L.Rev. 97 (1965).

8. Kahl v. Consolidated Gas, Elec. Light & Power Co., 191 Md. 249, 60 A.2d 754 (1948).

9. In Maun v. United States, 347 F.2d 970 (9th Cir.1965), the Atomic Energy Act was construed as allowing Woodsides, Cali-

Major public utility facilities are frequently permitted uses only in commercial and industrial areas, rather than in residential areas. They are also frequently permitted in residential zones and other zones only as special rather than permitted uses.[10] The special permit technique is useful because it allows a rather unique use to be conditioned, so as to better accommodate it with minimum disruption to the neighborhood and to the essential public service.

Relationship of State and Federal Licenses to Zoning

Unless the statute so provides, state and federally owned property is not usually subject to local zoning.[11] Whether local zoning is preempted when a person has a state or federal license to make a particular use of land in a particular place is a related question. Such licenses may be issued for uses such as airports, alcoholic beverage outlets, atomic energy facilities, cemeteries, hospitals, mobile home parks, outdoor advertising, racetracks, radio stations, rubbish dumps and the like. The problem of conflict is sometimes eliminated by the requirement that the applicant for the state or federal license indicate in his application that the zoning permits the licensed use.[12]

Absent statutory guidance, a court must resolve the conflict. In Town of Onondaga v. Hubbell[13] the court held that a state license to sell liquor did not permit the licensee to expand his nonconforming restaurant to sales of liquor as well as food. However, in Desert Turf Club v. Board of Supervisors[14] the court held a local ordinance precluding a state licensed race track invalid. The ordinance had been based on the ground that such activity was immoral. The Court held the morals question had been resolved by the state determination on the matter and was not a matter of local option. However, the court indicated the county might exclude the race track on some other proper ground.

Where a federal license is involved, the federal law may preempt local regulation if the zoning constitutes a substantial burden on interstate commerce. For example, where a federal licensee wished to construct a natural gas measuring and regulating station, the court held that the station was reasonably necessary, alternative sites were not readily available, the degree of harm was slight and efficiency and safety suggested the appropriateness of the site. Therefore, the zoning

---

fornia, to require the undergrounding of power lines to a linear accelerator, which lines passed through the community. After the favorable court decision, the Atomic Energy Act was amended to restore the AEC to supremacy. 42 U.S.C.A. § 2018, amending U.S.C.A. § 2018.

10. See infra §§ 6.11–6.13 (special permits).

11. See supra §§ 4.15–.16.

12. See, e.g., West's Ann.Cal.Bus. & Prof.Code § 23790 (to alcoholic beverage

outlets). Generally, state licensure in California does not preempt local regulation, and most statutes for state licensure either require the applicant to indicate the zoning is proper or permit the locality to exclude the licensed activity from a particular place.

13. 8 N.Y.2d 1039, 206 N.Y.S.2d 820, 170 N.E.2d 231 (1960).

14. 141 Cal.App.2d 446, 296 P.2d 882 (1956).

was held invalid.[15]   However, in Kroeger v. Stahl,[16] the court held that local zoning could preclude use of the property by a radio licensee. Local zoning was not held to constitute a substantial burden on interstate commerce.

 WESTLAW REFERENCES
Utilities
sy,di(public +3 utilit*** /s zoned zoning /s local)
414k238

Relationship of State and Federal Licenses
sy,di(preempt*** +s state federal /p zoned zoning)
414k14 & licens! /p zoned zoning

§ 4.19   Airports

Airports may be publicly owned, in which case the effect of zoning raises problems similar to those for other governmental uses;[1] they may be privately owned, in which case they have qualities similar to a privately owned public utility.[2] A private airport is a commercial use that can be excluded from a residential neighborhood. Airports are frequently handled by special permit rather than made a permitted use.[3]

Regulation of uses in and immediately around airports under conventional zoning presents no unique problems, except that an airport is a difficult land use to accommodate to other uses. A major airport needs a large space. Land adjacent to the airport, particularly that not under the flight path, is very valuable, and because of noise and safety problems, owners of residential properties are continuously attempting to push back the limitations of trespass, nuisance and inverse condemnation actions in order to secure damages. Presently, low, repetitious overflights by governmentally owned planes[4] or by planes landing or departing from publicly owned airports[5] constitutes the taking of an easement for which compensation is due. If there are not overflights, but mere proximity to the airport, there is no taking.[6]

While conventional zoning around airports, including conventional height limitations, are ordinarily held valid,[7] the cases holding that

15. New York State Nat. Gas Corp. v. Town of Elma, 182 F.Supp. 1 (W.D.N.Y. 1960).

16. 248 F.2d 121 (3d Cir.1957).

§ 4.19

1. See supra § 4.16.

2. See supra § 4.18.

3. See infra ch. 6.

4. Annot., 18 A.L.R.4th 542 (1980); Annot. 77 A.L.R.2d 1362 (1974); United States v. Causby, 328 U.S. 256, 66 S.Ct. 1062, 90 L.Ed. 1206 (1946).

5. Griggs v. Allegheny County, 369 U.S. 84, 82 S.Ct. 531, 7 L.Ed.2d 585 (1962), rehearing denied 369 U.S. 857, 82 S.Ct. 931, 8 L.Ed.2d 16 (1962).

6. Batten v. United States, 306 F.2d 580 (10th Cir.1962), cert. denied 371 U.S. 955, 83 S.Ct. 506, 9 L.Ed.2d 502 (1963), rehearing denied 372 U.S. 925, 83 S.Ct. 718, 9 L.Ed.2d 731 (1963). See infra § 10.7 for further discussion.

7. Morse v. County of San Luis Obispo, 247 Cal.App.2d 600, 55 Cal.Rptr. 710 (1967).

overflights in landings and departures constitute the taking of an easement have been influential in cases involving airport or flight plane zoning. Flight plane zoning, which may be imposed as a requirement of obtaining federal funds for airport construction [8] is height zoning which precludes any building in the flight plane, the flight plane being an inclined line to and from the airport.[9] Many courts have held that such zoning constitutes a taking.[10] While ordinary zoning merely regulates between property owners, courts read airport zoning as an attempt to confer a benefit on the public, or to acquire a resource for the public or to invade a property right, like a highway in the sky, and therefore hold the regulation invalid as a taking without just compensation.[11]

 WESTLAW REFERENCES

sy,di(airport /s zoned zoning /p taking)

airport /s zoned zoning /s height /p preempt***

§ 4.20   Churches

The problem of zoning for churches is similar to the problem of zoning for schools.[1] Churches generate noise, traffic, and confusion and depreciate property values in neighboring areas, but this does not mean they are treated as commercial uses having similar effects. Federal and state constitutions guarantee freedom of religion, which guarantees are frequently used as partial justification for limiting the effect of zoning on churches.

Preferential Treatment

Few zoning regulations treat churches as a commercial use and they are ordinarily permitted in residential districts, at least by special permit. If not favorably treated under zoning ordinances, the courts often give them favored treatment. For example, while some uses might be totally excluded from a community,[2] there is only one case

---

8. 49 U.S.C.A. § 2210(a)(5); U.S. Aviation Agency, Model Airport Zoning Ord. (A.C. 150/5190–3, 1967).

9. See also supra § 4.13.

10. Jankovich v. Indiana Toll Rd. Comm'n, 379 U.S. 487, 85 S.Ct. 493, 13 L.Ed.2d 439 (1965); Sneed v. County of Riverside County, 218 Cal.App.2d 205, 32 Cal.Rptr. 318 (1963); Roark v. Caldwell, 87 Idaho 557, 394 P.2d 641 (1964); Ackerman v. Port of Seattle, 55 Wn.2d 400, 348 P.2d 664 (1960).

11. Among the large number of secondary authorities, see R. Wright, The Law of Air Space (1969); Fleming, Aircraft Noise: A Taking of Private Property Without Just Compensation, 18 S.C.L.Rev. 593 (1966); Haar, Airport Noise and the Urban Dweller: A Proposed Solution, 36 Appraisal J. 551 (1968); Seago, The Airport Noise Problem and Airport Zoning, 28 Md.L.Rev. 120 (1968); Stoudemire, Airport Zoning: A Growing Need in South Carolina, 18 S.C.L. Rev. 609 (1966); Comment, The Validity of Airport Zoning Ordinances, 1965 Duke L.J. 792; 12 U.C.L.A.L.Rev. 1451 (1965); Annot. 18 A.L.R.4th 542 (1980); Annot. 77 A.L.R.2d 1355, 1362 (1961); Annot. 77 A.L.R.2d 1362 (1961).

§ 4.20

1. See supra § 4.16.

2. See infra ch. 8.

suggesting that churches might be totally excluded.[3] Where the issue has been directly faced, total exclusion has been held invalid.[4] As with other favored uses, an ordinance prohibiting churches unless neighbors consent is invalid.[5]

In a few states, courts allow churches to be treated as any other commercial use so that they can be excluded from residential zones.[6] In most states, however, exclusion from residential districts is not permitted.[7] Typically the court will so hold on the ground that the police power does not extend to the banning of such highly regarded uses, that zoning for churches is not authorized by the enabling act or that there is an undue interference with the free exercise of religion.[8]

Church officials sometimes purchase improperly zoned land under the assumption churches are exempt from zoning regulations, or that the zoning authorities will give the necessary zoning permission. The purchase is also sometimes motivated by the need to acquire property zoned for unintensive use because of its lower price. Ordinarily churches cannot economically compete with business uses. Church officials then express surprise or outrage that they are controlled by zoning, and under some circumstances, it is hard to sympathize with their plight. If they do check informally beforehand as to the probability of a rezoning or other permission, and purchase the property in reliance, courts will frequently invalidate regulation which defeats the expectation.[9] Such reliance would not be given much weight with respect to most users of land.[10]

When a special permit is required before a church is permitted, the courts are watchful that conditions imposed are not onerous or otherwise improper. For example, a special permit could not be denied a church in a residential area on the basis of a policy to deny permits where property zoned for business was available to the church.[11] The church may have to comply with some conditions, such as a setback

---

3. Corporation of Presiding Bishop v. Porterville, 90 Cal.App.2d 656, 203 P.2d 823 (1949), appeal dismissed 338 U.S. 805, 70 S.Ct. 78, 94 L.Ed. 487 (1949), rehearing denied 338 U.S. 939, 70 S.Ct. 342, 94 L.Ed. 579 (1950).

4. North Shore Unitarian Soc'y v. Village of Plandome, 200 Misc. 524, 109 N.Y.S.2d 803 (1951).

5. Pentecostal Holiness Church v. Dunn, 248 Ala. 314, 27 So.2d 561 (1946). See also infra § 5.3.

6. Mumaw v. Glendale, 270 Cal.App.2d 454, 76 Cal.Rptr. 245 (1969); Corporation of Presiding Bishop v. Porterville, 90 Cal. App.2d 656, 203 P.2d 823 (1949), appeal dismissed 338 U.S. 805, 70 S.Ct. 78, 94 L.Ed. 487 (1949), rehearing denied 338 U.S. 939, 70 S.Ct. 342, 94 L.Ed. 579 (1950); Miami Beach United Lutheran Church v. Miami Beach, 82 So.2d 880 (Fla.1955).

7. Ellsworth v. Gercke, 62 Ariz. 198, 156 P.2d 242 (1945); Congregation Temple Israel v. Creve Coeur, 320 S.W.2d 451 (Mo. 1959).

8. See generally Comment, Zoning Ordinances, Private Religious Conduct and the Free Exercise of Religion, 76 Nw.U.L. Rev. 786 (1981).

9. State ex rel. Synod of Ohio of United Lutheran Church in America v. Joseph, 139 Ohio St. 229, 39 N.E.2d 515 (1942); State ex rel. Lake Drive Baptist Church v. Village of Bayside, 12 Wis.2d 585, 108 N.W.2d 288 (1961).

10. See infra § 6.13.

11. State ex rel. Synod of Ohio of United Lutheran Church in America v. Joseph, 139 Ohio St. 229, 39 N.E.2d 515 (1942).

requirement, but not others, such as an offstreet parking requirement, where the number of vehicles is small and the provision of offstreet parking would substantially raise the costs for the church.[12]

Discriminatory Treatment

If a study were made of the number of churches and their number was compared to the number of reported zoning cases dealing with churches, it is likely that litigation would be found relatively more prevalent with respect to minor Protestant sects, Jewish synagogues and Catholic churches—perhaps in that order—as compared with major Protestant faiths. Some of the result can be explained on the ground that the minor faiths are shoestring operations, not able to buy large, well-sited, nicely landscaped properties. Some of the result is explainable only on the ground that local zoning bodies engage in subtle religious discrimination.

Of course, some groups hold themselves out as religious in order to secure favorable zoning or tax treatment or other favoritism, though the religious nature of the use is highly dubious. Courts are then caught between their precedents favoring religious uses and their great disinclination to define the limits of what is or is not religion. However, there are limits, so a healing center has been held not to be a church.[13] A religious use includes not only a church, but either as a religious use itself, or as a use accessory to a religious use, might include such things as a school, a cemetery, a gym, a social center, offices and a residence for ministers. It might even include a television programming, printing and publishing operation utilized to further church purposes.[14]

 WESTLAW REFERENCES
Preferential Treatment
sy,di(church religious /p zoned zoning /2 exempt!)
topic(414) /p church religious /s residential

Discriminatory Treatment
fi 117 ne2d 115
define* /7 church religious /p zon***

---

12. Board of Zoning Appeals v. Decatur, Indiana Co. of Jehovah's Witnesses, 233 Ind. 83, 117 N.E.2d 115 (1954).

13. Coe v. Dallas, 266 S.W.2d 181 (Tex. Civ.App.1953).

14. Walker, What Constitutes a Religious Use for Zoning Purposes, 27 Cath. U.L.Rev. 129 (1982). See also In re Faith for Today, Inc., 11 A.D.2d 718, 204 N.Y.S.2d 751 (1960), order affirmed 9 N.Y. 2d 761, 215 N.Y.S.2d 70, 174 N.E.2d 743 (1961). See generally J. Curry, Public Regulation of the Religious Use of Land (1964); Note, Church-State-Religious Institutions and Values: A Legal Survey—1964–66, 41 Notre Dame Law. 681 (1966); Annot., 11 A.L.R.4th 1084 (1979); Annot., 74 A.L.R.2d 377 (1960).

§ 4.21   Hospitals and Medical Facilities

Like other uses described in this chapter, many hospitals and other medical facilities are either publicly owned or are owned by nonprofit groups, and in any case provide a very useful social service. Therefore, despite the activity they generate, they are frequently permitted in residential zones, though not as often in single family zones.[1] Courts will uphold exclusion of hospitals from residential zones,[2] but are likely to hold total or near total exclusion from an entire community to be improper.[3]

As is the case with schools for delinquents [4] and cemeteries,[5] hospitals are reminders of death, disease and other social ills. Hospitals dealing with tuberculosis, particularly in an earlier day, and with mental disorders, handicapped persons and unwed mothers are frequently separately classified by ordinance, usually to exclude them or to confine them to less restricted zones. Courts have sometimes intervened to prevent municipalities from unreasonably limiting the opportunity for such institutions to exist somewhere, sometimes on the ground of the state interest in their location.[6]

Hospital buildings are frequently specially designed, involve large investments and are not easily used for other purposes. Therefore, regulations terminating nonconforming uses or restricting their expansion that might be upheld with respect to other kinds of uses will more likely be held invalid with respect to hospitals.[7]

The availability of good medical care to all persons is a high national priority and large sums of money are spent by federal and state government to subsidize medical facilities. Federal grants and loans for medical facilities require that their location accord with state plans.[8] Private planning groups also exist in many areas, so that the combined federal, state and private sanctions discouraging the establishment of hospitals in disfavored locations, and encouraging their location where needed, are strong inducements to local governments. A hospital needing a change in zoning to locate in an area disfavored by those groups can expect opposition. Conversely, if these groups favor the location, the municipality zoning the area will find that the petitioner seeking a change in zoning to permit the hospital has powerful advocates on his side.[9]

§ 4.21

1. See generally Annot. 27 A.L.R.3rd 1022 (1969).

2. Jones v. Los Angeles, 211 Cal. 304, 295 P. 14 (1930).

3. Sisters of Bon Secours Hosp. v. Grosse Pointe, 8 Mich.App. 342, 154 N.W.2d 644 (1967).

4. See supra § 4.17.

5. See infra § 4.22.

6. Jewish Consumptives' Relief Soc'y v. Town of Woodbury, 230 App.Div. 228, 243 N.Y.S. 686 (1930), affirmed mem. 256 N.Y. 619, 177 N.E. 165 (1931); Urban Farms Inc. v. Franklin Lakes, 179 N.J.Super. 203, 431 A.2d 163 (1981), certification denied 87 N.J. 428, 434 A.2d 1099 (1981).

7. Jones v. Los Angeles, 211 Cal. 304, 295 P. 14 (1930).

8. 42 U.S.C.A. §§ 291–291o, 2661–2697.

9. See generally Planning 1964, at 190.

VI. OTHER USES SUBJECT TO EXTRAORDINARY ZONING CONTROL

§ 4.22   The Death Industry: Cemeteries and Funeral Parlors [1]

But for the reminder of death, the park-like aspect of cemeteries would make them desirable neighbors. Obviously, they are a needed use of land and may well be permitted in residential, commercial or agricultural districts. An old U.S. Supreme Court case held that burials could be totally precluded in a city,[2] though modern public health concepts and lack of reliance on wells for water supplies may undercut the thrust of the decision. Cemeteries are often regulated by the state,[3] but are not usually subject to ordinary subdivision ordinances, even though cemetery lands are subdivided and sold. Sometimes special state statutes apply to cemetery subdivisions.[4]

The body of nuisance and zoning law on funeral homes is substantial.[5] Some courts conclude that funeral parlors are nuisances per se or can be nuisances in residential areas,[6] so it is not surprising that funeral parlors are not often a permitted use in residential areas. While they are a commercial use, some ordinances attempt to exclude them even there, and they may constitute a nuisance in a commercial area.[7] Despite the fact that they are often nicely landscaped and for some socio-economic groups may be an important social center, funeral parlors do generate traffic and may generate feelings of disquietude leading to depression of neighborhood property values. As a result, they are often handled on a special permit basis. Under such handling, the movement of bodies and traffic can appropriately be controlled through the use of screening and offstreet parking.

§ 4.22

1. For a case history of a rezoning for a cemetery, see D. Hagman, Wisconsin Zoning Practice 17 (1962). See also Annot. 96 A.L.R.3d 921 (1979).

2. Laurel Hill Cemetery v. City & County of San Francisco, 216 U.S. 358, 30 S.Ct. 358, 54 L.Ed. 515 (1910).

3. See, e.g., West's Ann.Cal.Bus. & Prof. Code §§ 9600–770.

4. See, e.g., Vernon's Ann.Mo.Stat. § 214.040.

5. Annot., 92 A.L.R.3d 328 (1976).

6. See infra ch. 18.

7. Sweet v. Campbell, 282 N.Y. 146, 25 N.E.2d 963 (1940).

§ 4.23 Natural Resource Extraction

Ordinances often permit resource extraction in agricultural and heavy industrial zones, though the use is frequently handled on a special permit basis even in such zones.[1] There may be special zones, for example, for the production of oil and gas. Ordinances may regulate in terms of distance from other uses, for example, the ordinance may prohibit wells within 400 feet of a residence. Wells may be subject to other spacing limitations such as one well per block. Wells and quarry operations may, of course, be regulated by other ordinances besides zoning, including state statutes which may deal with some aspects of location.[2]

Favored Status

The view of earlier cases was that natural resource extraction not only uses land, it consumes it. If the consumption is to occur, it must occur where the resource is located. The land has special value for resource extraction, and zoning which precludes the use is likely to substantially destroy values and more likely constitute a taking. Moreover, it is those deposits close to urbanization which are likely to be most valuable since the transport of rock, sand, gravel, topsoil and the like is a high-cost operation. While not as easily seen in the case of some natural resources, zoning permission given to one property owner in oil and gas production confers a monopoly position to a pool, with enormous benefits resulting, while those precluded from drilling by zoning cannot exploit their underlying property.

Therefore, courts have intervened on various pretexts to allow the extraction. They have held prohibitory ordinances invalid where extraction was permitted in more densely populated areas,[3] where the surrounding area was occupied by other intensive uses,[4] where the area involved was not densely populated [5] and where denial of rights to drill to one would confer a monopoly on others.[6] Prohibitory ordinances have also been held invalid where, for example, a quarry preexisted neighboring development,[7] where the value of the property is substantially reduced [8] or on the ground that the operation was temporary and that neighbors could be temporarily inconvenienced in order to permit

§ 4.23

1. See Callies & Quay, Zoning for Gravel Pits: Simultaneous Rehabilitation According to Plan, 4 Land-Use Controls Q. 43 (1970).

2. See, e.g., West's Ann.Cal.Pub.Res. Code §§ 3600–3608. Annot., 10 A.L.R.3d 1226 (1966).

3. Pacific Palisades Ass'n v. Huntington Beach, 196 Cal. 211, 237 P. 538 (1925).

4. City of North Muskegon v. Miller, 249 Mich. 52, 227 N.W. 743 (1929).

5. Clouser v. Norman, 393 P.2d 827 (Okl.1964).

6. Braly v. Board of Fire Comm'rs, 157 Cal.App.2d 608, 321 P.2d 504 (1958).

7. Herman v. Village of Hillside, 15 Ill. 2d 396, 155 N.E.2d 47 (1958).

8. East Fairfield Coal Co. v. Booth, 166 Ohio St. 379, 2 O.O.2d 289, 143 N.E.2d 309 (1957) (where prohibition of strip coal mining would reduce value from $1,000,000 to $17,000).

exploitation of the mineral value of the land.[9] Zoning of a site having natural resources for quarry operations is also not as likely to be held invalid as spot zoning.[10]

Disfavored Status

While there are cases such as the above creating the impression that courts are disposed to favor the right to extract natural resources and do not give prohibitory ordinances the same measure of validity as in other situations, many of the harshest applications of the zoning power resulting in destroying values have been sustained in cases involving natural resources extraction. The use of lands for oil and gas production, mining, quarrying, topsoil removal and sand and gravel operations is as difficult to reconcile with other uses of lands as any.[11] The exploitation of natural resources involves odors, dust, use of heavy equipment, large amounts of truck traffic, noise—and, in the case of oil and gas production—danger of fire and explosion. Moreover, few uses are as unaesthetic as an operating or abandoned site for natural resource extraction. Therefore, there are a number of grounds on which such activities can be precluded or regulated under the police power.

Convenient ground for doing so is that natural resource extraction has nuisance or near-nuisance qualities. Some of the more recent cases also conclude there should be no special right to have zoning that permits extraction. While resources must be extracted where they are located, if extracted anywhere, place has value in other situations too. For example, it is because a downtown area zoned for commercial high rise is there rather than elsewhere, that it has high value. Zoning the site for single family residential use may take as much value as prohibiting the drilling of oil from the site. A good corner for a filling station may result in unique values that are as substantially impaired by residential zoning as they would be if an ordinance prohibited the removal of sand and gravel which happened to the makeup of the soil on the corner.

The nuisance-like aspects of the use were sufficient in an early case, Hadacheck v. Sebastian,[12] to lead the court to uphold an ordinance requiring the immediate termination of an operating brickyard. The brickyard preexisted other development in the area and the economic effect of the closure was to reduce the value of the bed of clay surrounding the yard from $800,000 to $60,000. Consolidated Rock Products Co. v. Los Angeles [13] is frequently mentioned as exemplifying

9. Village of Terrace Park v. Errett, 12 F.2d 240 (6th Cir.1926).

10. Kozesnik v. Township of Montgomery, 24 N.J. 154, 131 A.2d 1 (1957).

11. See generally Bosselman, The Control of Surface Mining: An Exercise in Creative Federalism, 9 Nat.Resources J. 137 (1969).

12. 239 U.S. 394, 36 S.Ct. 143, 60 L.Ed. 348 (1915).

13. 57 Cal.2d 515, 20 Cal.Rptr. 638, 370 P.2d 342 (1962), appeal dismissed 371 U.S. 36, 83 S.Ct. 145, 9 L.Ed.2d 112 (1962).

the penultimate reach of the police power. An ordinance was upheld where:

> The trial court found that the subject property has great value if used for rock, sand and gravel excavation . . . and . . . any suggestion that the property has economic value for any other use, including those uses for which it was zoned 'is preposterous.' [14]

Goldblatt v. Town of Hempstead [15] is frequently cited in zoning discussions, though the ordinance which resulted in the closure of a quarry was not a zoning ordinance. It might well have been a zoning ordinance, and the court sustained the regulation. While the quarry would thereby be terminated, the evidence did not show that the property had no value for other purposes.[16]

Nonconforming Uses

Natural resource extraction involves some peculiar problems with respect to the nonconforming use doctrine.[17] Most nonconforming use provisions precluded expansion of the use, though in quarrying, for example, it is obvious the pit must either be widened or deepened in order to continue operation. This is not to say that a new pit can be opened on another part of the land owned by the operator,[18] though some courts hold that once an operation is established it is a protected nonconforming use with respect to the entire deposit, at least as to that part of the deposit presently owned by the operator.[19] However, the nonconforming use right does not mean that the operator has the right to sink new wells or deepen old ones.[20] The courts have also construed nonconforming use provisions as not authorizing changes in the method of extraction involving the addition of different equipment or buildings.[21] Because the operations have near nuisance-like qualities, especially as development occurs in the area, immediate termination of the nonconforming use may be upheld by the courts.[22] Since nonconforming uses of land are frequently given less protection than nonconforming buildings or nonconforming uses of buildings,[23] rapid amortization of the nonconforming use of operations involving little or no permanent buildings is more likely to be valid than if buildings are involved.

 WESTLAW REFERENCES

sy,di(natural +3 resource /p zoned zoning /p agricultur**)
414k79

14. Id. at 519, 20 Cal.Rptr. at 640, 370 P.2d at 314.

15. 369 U.S. 590, 82 S.Ct. 987, 8 L.Ed.2d 130 (1962).

16. See generally Annot., 10 A.L.R.3d 1226 (1966).

17. See infra §§ 4.27–.36.

18. Town of Billerica v. Quinn, 320 Mass. 687, 71 N.E.2d 235 (1947).

19. McCaslin v. Monterey Park, 163 Cal.App.2d 339, 329 P.2d 522 (1958).

20. Beverly Oil Co. v. Los Angeles, 40 Cal.2d 552, 254 P.2d 865 (1953).

21. DeFelice v. Zoning Bd. of Appeals, 130 Conn. 156, 32 A.2d 635 (1943).

22. Hadacheck v. Sebastian, 239 U.S. 394, 36 S.Ct. 143, 60 L.Ed. 348 (1915); Marblehead Land Co. v. Los Angeles, 47 F.2d 528 (9th Cir.1931).

23. See infra §§ 4.27, 4.35.

Disfavored

sy,di((natural +3 resource) quarry /p nuisance)

"natural resource" quarry /s zoned zoning /p taking
    unconstitutional

Nonconforming Use

sy,di("natural resource" quarry /p nonconforming)

---

§ 4.24   Off-street Parking [1]

Parking lots may be a use of land controlled by zoning, but most of the cases dealing with off-street parking involve those ordinances which require off-street parking as a condition to the grant of a special permit, a variance or a building permit.[2] With one rather surprising exception[3] and a leading case on classification indicating that an ordinance requiring off-street parking for apartment houses but not for hotels and rooming houses is invalid,[4] off-street parking requirements are not invalid per se. They may be held invalid if the requirements for spaces is beyond any reasonable expectation of the amount of parking that will be generated by a building.[5]

Typically, the requirements are stated in terms of so many spaces per seat in a theater or a church or so many spaces per family in dwelling units or so many spaces per square foot of commercial development.[6] Ordinances generally provide for the size of required spaces and that the parking be provided within a certain distance of the use, perhaps on the same lot. Parking is typically permitted on required setbacks and yards.

 WESTLAW REFERENCES

sy,di(street +3 parking /s zoned zoning /p church)

sy,di((street +3 parking) (parking +3 lot) /s theater)

---

§ 4.25   Gasoline Service Stations

Gasoline service stations are frequently treated as a special kind of commercial use. Service stations may be a permitted use in commercial areas though they are often excluded from both residential and

---

§ 4.24

1. See also § 3.18 supra.

2. Since perhaps not a use of land itself but a matter related to the erection of a building, off-street parking requirements may be an apt subject of a building ordinance. Siller v. Board of Supervisors, 58 Cal.2d 479, 25 Cal.Rptr. 73, 375 P.2d 41 (1962).

3. City and County of Denver v. Denver Buick, Inc., 141 Colo. 121, 347 P.2d 919 (1959).

4. Ronda Realty Corp. v. Lawton, 414 Ill. 313, 111 N.E.2d 310 (1953).

5. Ridgeview Co. v. Board of Adjustment, 57 N.J.Super. 142, 154 A.2d 23 (Super.L.Div.1959).

6. For the economic effects of the imposition of a zoning requirement of one off-street parking site per apartment, see W. Smith, The Low-Rise Speculative Apartment 103 (1964).

commercial areas and such regulations are valid.[1] They are also frequently handled by special permit so as to afford greater control.[2]

Some zoning ordinances attempt to limit the number of filling stations, though direct attempts to do so may be invalid as an attempt to regulate competition, which is beyond the power of zoning.[3] Stations are often limited in terms of how proximate they can be to places of assembly such as schools and churches and these regulations are valid.[4] Regulations that require a minimum distance between stations or limit them to one per corner have been upheld on the ground of fire and traffic hazards created by bunching,[5] though some courts hold them invalid on the ground that fire hazards do not exist [6] or that the spacing limitations are really an attempt to restrict competition.[7]

WESTLAW REFERENCES

gas gasoline service filling +3 station /s zoned zoning /p limit! .
　　restrict! control prohibit*** +5 number location distance

sy,di(gas gasoline service filling +3 station /s zoned zoning /s
　　traffic)

§ 4.26 Mobile Homes and Mobile Home Courts

While residential uses are highly favored and are the "highest" use under zoning, mobile homes and their courts are not similarly favored. They are sometimes banned entirely from smaller municipalities.[1] Such a ban has been held justified because mobile home courts may not be attractive, because they are detrimental to property values and because they might retard city growth along desired lines.[2]

Clearly, the special treatment of mobile homes has historical overtones. While they do involve dense living, total exclusion from a community of multiple family apartment units producing similar densi-

§ 4.25

1. Lemir Realty Corp. v. Larkin, 11 N.Y.2d 20, 226 N.Y.S.2d 374, 181 N.E.2d 407 (1962); Annot., 75 A.L.R.2d 168 (1958).

2. See generally Williams, The Numbers Game: Gasoline Service Stations and Land Use Controls, 2 Urb.L.Ann. 23 (1969).

3. See supra § 3.19.

4. Vine v. Board of Adjustment, 136 N.J.L. 416, 56 A.2d 122 (1947).

5. Food Fair Stores, Inc. v. Zoning Bd. of Appeals, 143 So.2d 58 (Fla.2d D.C.A.1962), cert. denied 148 So.2d 280 (1962), appeal dismissed 373 U.S. 541, 83 S.Ct. 1537, 10 L.Ed.2d 687 (1963).

6. Filling stations have better than average safety records. Mosher, Proximity Regulation of the Modern Service Station, 17 Syracuse L.Rev. 1 (1965).

7. Chicago Title & Trust Co. v. Village of Lombard, 19 Ill.2d 98, 166 N.E.2d 41 (1960); Mosher, supra note 6.

§ 4.26

1. Vickers v. Township Comm., 37 N.J. 232, 181 A.2d 129 (1962), appeal dismissed, cert. denied 371 U.S. 233, 83 S.Ct. 326, 9 L.Ed.2d 495 (1963), with vigorous dissent, overruled by Southern Burlington County N.A.A.C.P. v. Township of Mount Laurel, 92 N.J. 158, 456 A.2d 390 (1983).

2. See generally Bartke & Gage, Mobile Homes: Zoning and Taxation, 55 Cornell L.J. 491 (1970); Carter, Problems in Regulation and Taxation of Mobile Homes, 48 Iowa L.Rev. 16 (1962); Note, Regulation of Mobile Homes, 13 Syracuse L.Rev. 122 (1961); Note 29 Wayne State L.Rev. 177 (1982).

ties, though perhaps valid,[3] is not as customary. While mobile home courts used to be occupied by transients who did not feel any sense of responsibility to the community, some studies have shown that movement is less in mobile home courts than is true with respect to single family homes, which is certainly a believable statistic in many suburban residential neighborhoods. Mobile homes were once trailers that were poorly constructed, were eyesores and contained space below the minimum required for healthy living. Mobile homes now can be attractive, safely constructed and large enough to meet minimums. Given the great need for low-cost housing in the country, the mobile home industry is one of the hopes for the future, if indeed the future is not already here, since about 25 percent of housing starts are mobile homes. Of course, mobile homes may not be low-cost housing despite the relatively low cost of manufacture. Compared to a single family house, interest rates are higher, down payments are higher, depreciation is more rapid and, due to zoning regulations limiting the development of new sites, land costs (in the form of rents) may be higher in high land cost areas. Therefore, mobile homes may be occupied mainly by young marrieds and the elderly retired and be located mainly in rural areas. They have not yet been utilized as housing by great numbers of the urban poor.

Some communities have excluded mobile home parks for the reason that they have high public service requirements while generating low tax revenues. This may be a myth because, on the average, the number of children per unit may not be high; thus the burden on schools may not be greater than for an equivalent number of units of a single family housing. Moreover, mobile homes can be taxed in a number of ways—as a motor vehicle, as property of the mobile home park owner, by local excise taxes, by the personal property tax or by the real property tax.

Mobile homes may be classified as a commercial use because the mobile home court is a commercial venture. They need not be classified as residential uses.[4] Some states authorize the regulation of mobile homes under separate, non-zoning enabling legislation.[5] Zoning ordinances which do not specifically cover mobile homes may cause difficulties of construction as to whether or not a mobile home is covered by the ordinance.[6] Mobile home parks are frequently handled on a special permit basis.[7]

---

3. Fanale v. Borough of Hashbrouck Heights, 26 N.J. 320, 139 A.2d 749 (1958); Annot., 17 A.L.R.4th 106 (1982).

4. Napierkowski v. Township of Gloucester, 29 N.J. 481, 150 A.2d 481 (1959).

5. See, e.g., Iowa Code Ann. § 358A.3. Plan. Advisory Serv., Am. Plan. Ass'n, Regulating Mobile Homes, Rep. No. 360 (1981).

6. Morin v. Zoning Bd. of Review, 102 R.I. 457, 232 A.2d 393 (1967) (trailer with permanent foundation became a structure within terms of zoning ordinance).

7. Scherrer v. Board of County Comm'rs, 201 Kan. 424, 441 P.2d 901 (1968) (denial of permit held unreasonable).

Mobile homes have been subject to exclusionary zoning by hostile courts particularly in residential areas. Sophisticated technology has increasingly made mobile homes less distinguishable from on site constructed homes and some jurisdictions now prohibit *per se* exclusionary zoning of mobile homes.[8] Others recognize them as judicially protected low income housing.[9]

While location of mobile homes is often left to local ordinances, mobile homes can be effectively prohibited if they must comply with local building codes. As a result, some states have preempted localities from controlling mobile home construction under local building codes so long as state standards are met.[10]

 WESTLAW REFERENCES

sy,di(mobile trailer +3 home house /s zoned zoning /s exclu!
   banned prohibit*** /s residential single-family)
414k83 /p prohibit*** ban banned exclu!

VII. NONCONFORMING USES

§ 4.27 In General

The Standard State Zoning Enabling Act[1] does not have any provisions for nonconforming uses. Nevertheless, nearly all zoning ordinances provide that a use may continue if it lawfully preexists the adoption of a zoning ordinance, though it would be unlawful if the use were established after the passage of the ordinance.[2] The term nonconforming use can be a generic term covering nonconforming buildings, as well as nonconforming activities. Because certain consequences concerning establishment, continuance and termination of nonconforming uses may depend on the classification, it is useful to think of four varieties of nonconforming uses: (1) nonconforming buildings, (2) conforming uses of nonconforming buildings, (3) nonconforming uses of conforming buildings, and (4) nonconforming uses of land. For example, a building erected at the front lot line is a nonconforming building after passage of an ordinance establishing a front yard. An oil refinery is a nonconforming building in a multi-family zone even though it has been abandoned as an oil refinery and is occupied by several families. If a single-family house is used for manufacturing furniture in a single-family zone, the building conforms though the use does not. Land may be used for a pig farm, with the land containing no structures rising to

---

8. Robinson Township v. Knoll, 410 Mich. 293, 302 N.W.2d 146 (1981).

9. Oak Forest Mobile Home Park, Inc. v. Oak Forest, 27 Ill.App.3d 303, 326 N.E.2d 473 (1975).

10. See, e.g., West's Ann.Cal. Health & Safety Code § 18101; California Factory-Built Housing Law, id. § 19960 et seq.

§ 4.27

1. U.S. Dep't of Commerce (rev. ed. 1926).

2. See Petti v. Richmond Heights, 5 Ohio St.3d 129, 449 N.E.2d 768 (1983).

the dignity of buildings. If located in a single-family use zone, the use would be nonconforming.

Nonconforming uses have been the subject of great concern since the beginning of zoning.[3] The doctrine that a police power regulation should not apply to preexisting uses is perhaps stronger in zoning than in any other kind of regulation, though there is a historical explanation for the phenomena. First, zoning has been considered a prospective tool for control, that is, its primary purpose is to control land as it develops and to maintain that control rather than to change existing development. Second, while Euclidian zoners were purists and wished to divide the landscape into districts having a place for everything and everything in its place, it is hard to convince pragmatists that a few nonconforming uses are totally contrary to the public health, safety and welfare. The feeling is particularly true since even the purists contemplated cumulative rather than exclusive zones.[4] For example, while a mom and pop grocery store is a nonconforming use in a single-family zone, the necessity for its termination is not compelling, particularly where single-family uses are permitted in areas zoned for commercial uses. Third, while the body politic could be convinced of the wisdom of zoning applied prospectively, the political forces against adoption of zoning, at least in the early days, would have been much stronger if it had been so applied so as to require wholesale compliance of existing uses. Fourth, the validity of zoning as a police power measure was in significant doubt in early years and the risk of unconstitutionality would have been in greater doubt if preexisting uses were not permitted to continue.[5]

Consequently, many enabling acts and zoning ordinances permit nonconforming uses to continue. Where not so allowed, some courts have held retroactive application invalid as having no substantial relation to the public health, safety and welfare,[6] or as not authorized by enabling acts,[7] or courts have construed the ordinance as permitting preexisting uses to continue in order to save the ordinance constitutionally,[8] or they have declined to issue an injunction as a discretionary remedy permitting the courts to do equity.[9] Courts have upheld zoning

3. Krause, Nonconforming Uses in Illinois, 43 Chi.-Kent L.Rev. 153 (1966); Strong, Nonconforming Uses: The Black Sheep of Zoning, 7 Inst. on Plan. & Zoning 25 (1968); Young, Regulation and Removal of Nonconforming Uses, 12 Case W.Res.L. Rev. 681 (1961); Annot. 10 A.L.R.4th 1122 (1979); Annot., 80 A.L.R.3d 630 (1974); Annot., 22 A.L.R.3d 1134 (1967).

4. See supra § 4.3.

5. Earlier cases upholding retroactive applications of zoning-like regulations which terminated preexisting uses had dealt with land uses that had nuisance or near-nuisance features. See, e.g., Hadacheck v. Sebastian, 239 U.S. 394, 36

S.Ct. 143, 60 L.Ed. 348 (1915) (brickyard in residential zone); Reinman v. Little Rock, 237 U.S. 171, 35 S.Ct. 511, 59 L.Ed. 900 (1915) (stables in commercial zone).

6. Jones v. Los Angeles, 211 Cal. 304, 295 P. 14 (1930).

7. Bane v. Township of Pontiac, 343 Mich. 481, 72 N.W.2d 134 (1955).

8. Amereihn v. Kotras, 194 Md. 591, 71 A.2d 865 (1950).

9. City of Toronto v. Hutton (1953), Ont.W.N. 205 (1952), Ontario High Court (injunction issued against nursing home in residential area, but enforcement delayed

ordinances which permitted existing uses to continue, while prohibiting the same kind of uses in the future on the ground that such a classification was valid.[10]

 WESTLAW REFERENCES
di nonconforming!

non-conforming /s residential single-family /s grocery convenience
+3 store

§ 4.28 Lawful Existence

While nonconforming uses can continue, they must be lawfully established at the time the ordinance making them nonconforming takes effect. Litigation on the matter is frequent for two reasons. First, considerable benefit can flow from a legal nonconforming use status due to the monopoly position that might be conferred. For example, to be the only flower shop permitted near a cemetery because of nonconforming status is a highly desirable state of affairs for the flower shop owner. Second, an application for a building permit frequently triggers legislative attention to an undesirable use and begins a race between the landowner to establish a use before legislation to prevent it takes effect. If the landowner wins the race, he is entitled to complete the construction applied for and maintain the use.[1]

A use cannot be established as lawful when it was permitted under an illegally issued permit, and courts are reluctant to apply estoppel against the municipality in such cases.[2] While a landowner might be able to vest a right to a nonconforming use by construction pursuant to a permit,[3] if he proceeds to construction without the permit he has not established a nonconforming use.[4]

A lawful use is not usually established by intent or plans, even if the intent has been perfected by purchasing land, arranging for finance, entering into contracts, clearing the land and so forth.[5] The use must be more substantial.[6]

A use might be lawful under a zoning ordinance but not be lawful for some other reason, in which case it may not be a preexisting lawful use for purposes of the nonconforming use provisions. For example, a building may not be a lawful one if it violates a building code.[7] On the

for 18 months because city reconsidering zoning in area).

10. Stone v. Cray, 89 N.H. 483, 200 A. 517 (1938).

§ 4.28

1. Annot., 89 A.L.R.3d 1051 (1975).

2. See infra § 5.10.

3. Harrisburg v. Pass, 372 Pa. 318, 93 A.2d 447 (1953).

4. Mang v. County of Santa Barbara, 182 Cal.App.2d 93, 5 Cal.Rptr. 724 (1960).

5. County of Saunders v. Moore, 182 Neb. 377, 155 N.W.2d 317 (1967).

6. Fredal v. Forster, 9 Mich.App. 215, 156 N.W.2d 606 (1967) (removal of 50,000 cubic yards of stone held to be substantial enough to establish quarry use). See also infra § 5.11.

7. State v. Stonybrook, Inc., 149 Conn. 492, 181 A.2d 601 (1962), appeal dismissed, cert. denied 371 U.S. 185, 83 S.Ct. 265, 9 L.Ed.2d 227 (1962).

other hand, a use has been held lawful for purposes of the nonconforming use doctrine though it violates a restrictive covenant.[8] The two cases are easily reconciled, because the violation of the restrictive covenant is of little interest to anyone but private parties. The building code, on the other hand, is a public law and is closely related to zoning.

WESTLAW REFERENCES

non-conforming /p illegal /s construction

414k323 & establish /s intent! plan! purchase finance contract

§ 4.29   Change in Use

While lawful nonconforming uses were allowed to continue, under early zoning theory they were at most tolerated, and the expectation was that the pressures for conformity would be strong enough so that eventually they would be eliminated. One of the pressures for conformity is the doctrine that the protected status is lost upon any change in the use.

More Intensive Use

While ordinances might permit some change, in the absence of a provision permitting it, a use cannot be expanded. For example, in State ex rel. Carter v. Harper[1] the owner of a nonconforming dairy product business found that his business was expanding so as to require a larger plant. His application for a permit to expand his business was denied and the denial was upheld by the court. Similarly, in State ex rel. City Ice & Fuel Co. v. Stegner[2] the court held it proper to deny a permit for ice manufacture where the premises had previously been used only for ice storage. However, some courts will allow "normal" expansion.[3] Similarly, if only part of a building is used for a nonconforming use, it may be improper to expand the use to other parts of the building.[4]

---

8. Gauthier v. Village of Larchmont, 30 A.D.2d 303, 291 N.Y.S.2d 584 (1968), appeal denied 22 N.Y.2d 1028, 295 N.Y.S.2d 1028, 242 N.E.2d 494 (1968).

§ 4.29

1. 182 Wis. 148, 196 N.W. 451 (1923).

2. 120 Ohio St. 418, 166 N.E. 226 (1929).

3. People v. Ferris, 18 Ill.App.2d 346, 152 N.E.2d 183 (1958) (expansion of trailer camp proper); Powers v. Building Inspector, 363 Mass. 648, 296 N.E.2d 491 (1973); Redfearn v. Creppel, 455 So.2d 1356 (La. 1984). But see Edmonds v. County of Los Angeles, 40 Cal.2d 642, 255 P.2d 772 (1953) (held expansion of number of trailer sites need not be allowed).

4. Weber v. Pieretti, 72 N.J.Super. 184, 178 A.2d 92 (Super.Ch.1962), affirmed mem. 77 N.J.Super. 423, 186 A.2d 702 (App.Div.1962), cert. denied 39 N.J. 236, 188 A.2d 177 (1963) (nonconforming bottling plant improperly extended to second floor). But see Central Jewish Inst. v. Toronto (1948), 2 D.L.R. 1 Ontario Supreme Court (part of building used for nursery school could be expanded to use entire building for school for older children); O'Sullivan Funeral Home Ltd. v. City of Sault Ste. Marie & Evans, 28 D.L.R.2d 1 (1961) Ontario Supreme Court (fact that part of house used for funeral parlor allowed adaptation of entire premises for funeral parlor use).

Most states apply a special rule with respect to natural resource extraction such as quarry operations.[5]

Similar or Less Intensive Use

Some ordinances provide that a nonconforming use can be changed to any use allowed in a zone where the nonconforming use would be a permitted use.[6] Absent an ordinance provision, however, the result is likely to be similar to that in Wechter v. Board of Appeals[7] where the landowner was not allowed to convert a building from a tinsmith and woodworking shop to a spray-paint business.

Some ordinances and courts allow a change of use to one of less intensity. For example, Arkam Machine & Tool Co. v. Township of Lyndhurst[8] held that a nonconforming factory for the manufacture of music boxes employing 80 people could be continued as a factory for manufacturing blades and eyeglasses, where only 15 people would be employed. On first impression it seems sensible to permit changes that move a use in the direction of conformity. However, if there is a desire to change, it might well be that economics have dictated that the present use should not be continued anyway, making it likely that it would be abandoned, thus resulting in full conformity.[9] Furthermore, if a new use is permitted that is only in the direction of conformity, the new nonconforming use is likely to prevail for a longer period of time.

 WESTLAW REFERENCES

non-conforming /s "change in use" /s expand! increase* larger
    grow
change +3 use /p non-conforming /s similar "less intensive"

§ 4.30 Repairs and Alterations

Most ordinances allow repairs to a nonconforming use.[1] If not, courts will typically permit repairs to be made. Such permission makes sense, because there is a general policy, particularly as represented by housing codes, to have buildings in a good state of repair. Ordinances sometimes permit repairs as measured by a percentage of the appraised or assessed value of the building so as to provide a standard which will permit repairs but eliminate substantial alterations. Assessed values frequently do not have any relation to market values and values may change over time, both of which can make application of the standard difficult or unfair.[2]

5. See supra § 4.23.

6. See supra § 3.23 (for meaning of permitted use).

7. 3 Ill.2d 13, 119 N.E.2d 747 (1954).

8. 73 N.J.Super. 528, 180 A.2d 348 (App.Div.1962).

9. See infra § 4.33.

§ 4.30

1. Annot., 57 A.L.R.3d 419 (1974).

2. See also infra § 4.33.

Alterations are another matter. They are usually precluded, and in Dienelt v. County of Monterey [3] the court found that replacement of a flagstone patio with a concrete slab patio was beyond mere repair. As with repairs, alterations costing up to a certain percentage of the value of the buildings are sometimes permitted. Alterations required by law are also usually permitted. For example, if the owner of a building is cited for building code violations and ordered to close open stairwells and install a sprinkling system, it is not likely that by responding to the order he risks violating the zoning ordinance and losing legal nonconforming use status.

WESTLAW REFERENCES

change /5 use /p non-conforming /s alteration

non-conforming /s repair replace! restore /5 building

§ 4.31   Conversion to Administrative Permission

The status of legal nonconforming use can be changed by obtaining a variance or by issuance of a special permit.[1] Some ordinances provide that owners of nonconforming uses should apply for and will be granted a variance or a special permit. Property owners sometimes resist applying because they think the nonconforming use status protects them indefinitely, while a special permit or a variance may be considered a matter of discretion, and the continuance of the administrative permission is always open to review. Of course, the assumption that a nonconforming use can continue indefinitely may be erroneous. As the discussion on termination indicates,[2] nonconforming uses do not have the right to continue indefinitely. Thus, in Town of Waterford v. Grabner,[3] the ordinance required an operator of a nonconforming quarry to apply for a renewable four-year permit. He declined to do so and the trial court indicated he need not do so since he had a protected nonconformity. The Supreme Court reversed indicating that the real issue was whether the possible termination of the permit after the four years would be unconstitutional as applied to the quarry—if not, the operator could be compelled to apply for the permit.

WESTLAW REFERENCES

non-conforming /s variance (special +3 permit) /s "set back"

§ 4.32   Termination: In General

A nonconforming use is not entitled to continuance in perpetuity. It may be terminated as a result of an act of God, such as a fire or a flood, which destroys it, and no permission for restoration may be

---

3. 113 Cal.App.2d 128, 247 P.2d 925 (1952).

§ 4.31

1. See infra ch. 6.

2. See infra §§ 4.34–.36.

3. 155 Conn. 431, 232 A.2d 481 (1967).

given; it may be terminated by the act of the owner, who abandons the nonconforming use; it may be terminated by the municipality through amortization or by a finding that the nonconformity constitutes a nuisance. These matters are discussed in the following sections of this chapter.

 WESTLAW REFERENCES
sy,di(termination /s non-conforming)

§ 4.33 Destruction and Abandonment

Destruction

Absent any provision in the ordinance, if a building is destroyed by an act of God, it may be held that it can be rebuilt.[1] Many ordinances expressly provide that if the nonconforming building is substantially destroyed, it cannot be rebuilt. Substantiality is often measured in terms of percentage of destruction or percentage of assessed value, replacement value or market value.[2] Thus, in Moffatt v. Forrest City[3], an ordinance provided that a building could not be rebuilt if it was 60 percent destroyed. The residential part of a building located in a residential zone was totally destroyed although the third of the building used as a meat market was not. The court held the building was over 60 percent destroyed, so that it could no longer be used for a meat market.

Such an ordinance might be held unconstitutional as applied, and the courts are somewhat sympathetic to the owners so as not to compound their calamities. For example, in O'Mara v. City Council of Newark,[4] a nonconforming duplex in a business zone was assessed at $400. After the fire, the building was assessed at $200 and the cost of repairs was $300. The city argued that there was a 75 percent destruction, $300/$400 so that reconstruction was prohibited under the ordinance. The court held that the destruction was $200/$400 or fifty percent and indicated substantial doubt about the constitutionality of the provision, since the market value of the property was $1,800. Since repairs would only cost $300, there was only 17 percent destruction, which did not seem substantial to the court. The court apparently overlooked that the expenditure of $300 could perhaps conform the building with little or no loss in market value.

Abandonment

If the owner abandons the use, the lawful nonconforming status is lost.[5] Many ordinances contain provisions for abandonment and state

§ 4.33

1. City of Las Cruces v. Neff, 65 N.M. 414, 338 P.2d 731 (1959); Annot. 57 A.L.R. 3d 419 (1974).

2. See supra § 4.30.

3. 234 Ark. 12, 350 S.W.2d 327 (1961).

4. 238 Cal.App.2d 836, 48 Cal.Rptr. 208 (1965).

5. Annot., 57 A.L.R.3d 279 (1974).

the time periods after which abandonment is presumed. In absence of such provision, abandonment for a reasonable period of time terminates the nonconforming status. The abandonment must be intended and voluntary. For example, in State ex rel. Morehouse v. Hunt [6] a fraternity house was located in an area zoned for single-family residential uses. For 2½ years it was rented as a rooming house and for five years thereafter it was rented to a family who had some servants and rented a room to some students. The zoning board of appeals concluded that the fraternity use was not abandoned, and the court agreed, indicating that the owner did not intend to permanently abandon the use but intended to sell it to a fraternity as soon as the opportunity arose. The case seems unduly generous to the landowner and is not typical. For example, in Attorney General v. Johnson [7] lawful nonconforming status was held lost. The owner wished to establish a coin-operated laundry where a grocery store use of the premises had ceased some five years earlier. The ordinance permitted a shift from one business use to another, and in the interim the premises had been used as a meeting house by a university religious club and as a real estate office. Similarly, in Inhabitants of Town of Windham v. Sprague,[8] removal of a house trailer in order to replace it with a new one terminated the nonconforming trailer use where the ordinance provided that on removal the trailer could only be located in a trailer park. A lawful nonconforming status as a tourist home was also lost where the home was rented for residential purposes during a summer, the summer being the tourist season in the community.[9]

By reading a requirement of intent plus some overt act as the basis for abandonment, the courts quite properly hold that a compelled abandonment does not terminate a nonconforming use. For example, in City of Fontana v. Atkinson [10] the county health department ordered the owner of a nonconforming dairy to rebuild corral fences. The fences were torn down temporarily to permit rebuilding and the city claimed that removal of the fences constituted an abandonment. The court found no abandonment. Similarly, abandonment will not be found if the use stops due to wartime restrictions, economic depression, death of the owner and the like—providing the property is devoted to its nonconforming use as soon as reasonably possible.

 WESTLAW REFERENCES

sy,di(non-conforming /s termination /s destruction abandon!)

414k336

---

6. 235 Wis. 358, 291 N.W. 745 (1940).

7. 355 S.W.2d 305 (Ky.1962).

8. 219 A.2d 548 (Me.1966).

9. Gayford v. Kolodziej, 19 D.L.R.2d 777 (1959).

10. 212 Cal.App.2d 499, 28 Cal.Rptr. 25 (1963).

§ 4.34 New Attempts at Termination: Amortization and Nuisances: In General

Despite all of the limitations on extension, repair and alteration and despite provisions for termination on destruction or abandonment, nonconforming uses continue to exist. Their continued existence is in part due to lack of municipal will in seeking their termination and a lack of enforcement of existing ordinances. In a few cases nonconforming uses have been terminated through purchase or condemnation, but both are thought too expensive. In the meantime, as zoning developed, the right to continue nonconforming uses rose to the dignity of a constitutional principle. While zoning could impair values in undeveloped land by limiting uses, the courts thought of such values as speculative only, as distinguished from existing values that inured in uses of improved property. Gradually, however, the distinction is being broken down. Property zoned for industrial use under cumulative zoning but not used may suffer as great a loss in value if rezoned for residential use as would a factory which was rezoned for residential use, particularly if a period of years is given to amortize the nonconforming use. Therefore, in recent years local governments have turned to amortization and termination by nuisance powers to eliminate nonconforming uses.

 WESTLAW REFERENCES
ti("billboard reputation and the first amendment")
di amortiz!

§ 4.35 Amortization

Ordinance Provisions

The amortization provisions in ordinances generally provide that at a time stated following the adoption of the amortization ordinance, all uses nonconforming at the time of the adoption of the ordinance shall terminate and thereafter shall conform.[1] Since uses can become nonconforming because of subsequent zoning changes, amortization provisions also require the termination at a period of years from the time and use becomes nonconforming. Unless this period is very long, such ordinances might be unconstitutional as applied to some uses. For example, it might be possible to terminate a sign at the end of five years, though to require conformance of a large hospital at the end of five years would likely be invalid. As a result, some ordinances establish different periods of termination. Nonconforming uses of land are typically given the shortest period, since there is no investment in buildings and, except for uses that consume the land such as quarries,[2]

§ 4.35

1. Annot., 22 A.L.R.3d 1134 (1967); Leonard, Amortization of Nonconforming Uses—What Are the Limits, 45 Tex.B.J. 1485 (1982).

2. See supra § 4.22.

the activities can assumedly locate elsewhere with a minimum of loss. Since the building could assumedly be used for conforming uses, relatively short periods of amortization also might be provided for nonconforming uses of conforming buildings. The periods are typically longest for nonconforming buildings, particularly those that are specialties, such as an oil refinery which would have a large capital investment and buildings that would be rather difficult to utilize for a conforming purpose. The period of amortization may also depend on the type of construction, so that the period would be longer for brick or concrete high-rise buildings and less for temporary, low-rise, inexpensively constructed warehouses.

Provisions for notice and recording the notice should be included in an ordinance so that prospective purchasers and mortgagees know of the application of the ordinance.

Leading Cases

While amortization was upheld as early as 1929 [3] it did not enjoy substantial utilization until the 1950's and 1960's, during which time the technique generated considerable literature.[4]

City of Los Angeles v. Gage [5] is perhaps the leading case on amortization of nonconforming uses. Gage owned two lots in Los Angeles and established his use in 1930. One lot was improved with a two-story house with the top floor rented for residential use. The lower floor was Gage's residence, with one room used as an office from which he conducted his plumbing supply business. Plumbing materials were stored both in buildings and outside of buildings on the two lots. In 1946, the property was zoned for multiple residential use and the new comprehensive ordinance also required the conformance of nonconforming uses such as the Gage uses within five years. In upholding the application of the ordinance, the court noted that the noise, disturbance and traffic caused by Gage's operation was high for a residential neighborhood, that the grant of variances and special permits in the past in similar kinds of situations was discretionary and did not give Gage the right to continue, that the preexistence of the business prior to residential development around it did not limit the power to regulate, that termination after the normal useful remaining life is proper,

3. State ex rel. Dema Realty Co. v. Jacoby, 168 La. 752, 123 So. 314 (1929).

4. Graham, Legislative Techniques for the Amortization of the Nonconforming Use: A Suggested Formula, 12 Wayne St. L.Rev. 435 (1966); Katarincic, Elimination of Non-conforming Uses, Buildings, and Structures by Amortization—Concept Versus Law, 2 Duq.U.L.Rev. 1 (1963); Moore, The Termination of Nonconforming Uses, 6 Wm. & Mary L.Rev. 1 (1965); Whitnall, Abatement of Nonconforming Uses, 2 Inst. on Plan. & Zoning 131 (1962). Comments and Notes include: Nonconforming Uses in

Iowa: The Amortization Answer, 55 Iowa L.Rev. 998 (1970). Eliminating the Nonconforming Use in Kentucky, 49 Ky.L.J. 142 (1960); Zoning—Abatement of Prior Nonconforming Uses: Nuisance Regulations and Amortization Provisions, 31 Mo. L.Rev. 280 (1966); Elimination of Nonconforming Uses: Alternatives and Adjuncts to Amortization, 14 UCLA L.Rev. 354 (1966); Annot. 22 A.L.R.3d 1134 (1968). See also 1 R. Anderson, American Law of Zoning § 6.66 (2d ed. 1976).

5. 127 Cal.App.2d 442, 274 P.2d 34 (1954).

that the ordinance here involved was a comprehensive one not selecting out a particular kind of use, that only a nonconforming use of land and of a conforming building was involved, that the property could be used for conforming use, and that uses such as Gage's tend to impair the development and stability of the comprehensive plan. The court further concluded that there is no material difference between an ordinance restricting future uses and one terminating present uses because the test in each case is the public gain relative to the private loss, and that the amortization provisions were no harsher than ordinances preventing extension, alteration and reuse after abandonment.

The court also indicated that Gage's loss would be small. The business had a large gross revenue; he could buy a suitably zoned lot for about $2,500 more than the value of his present lot; it would only cost him $2,500 to move, plus certain other costs of advertising the new location, and the loss of reestablishing his business was speculative. Moreover, the owner had time to plan, the loss was spread, Gage would enjoy a monopoly position for five more years, and property appropriately zoned was located within a half mile of Gage's property.

There are a few aspects of the case that bear comment. First, while in some cases there might be a normal useful life that can be amortized during its economic life or a period of depreciation,[6] there is in no sense a normal period of amortization for a business such as Gage's. By the time of the opinion, the use had continued for 24 years and would probably continue indefinitely. While some courts would preclude termination prior to the end of economic life,[7] the court in Gage is in effect saying that the use can be terminated whenever reasonable, and under the circumstances of this case a five-year termination period is reasonable.

While Gage was the victim of a comprehensive ordinance that theoretically was not directed specifically at him, it is true that the City of Los Angeles did not seek wholesale terminations of other uses such as Gage's. As in other cities, similar uses were allowed to continue through nonenforcement of the ordinance, or through extension of time periods and the issuance of variances or special permits as the amortization period expired. Despite the court's suggestion that there is no difference between restricting future uses and terminating present ones, ordinances for amortization simply would not exist if a city attempted to exercise its powers to eliminate nonconforming uses to the maximum. The outcry would be so substantial that the amortization ordinance would quickly be repealed.

6. For example, the outdoor advertising company in Grant v. Baltimore, 212 Md. 301, 129 A.2d 363 (1957) depreciated signs over a period of five years for tax purposes. App.2d 375, 27 Cal.Rptr. 136 (1962) the court held that a sign had an economic life of 10 years, and that termination prior to the end of that time would be invalid.

7. For example, in National Advertising Co. v. County of Monterey, 211 Cal.

Since the neighborhood had fully developed around Gage in residential uses, the court perhaps overstated the "rotten apple" effect of the nonconforming use. However, the unusual assumption is that a nonconforming use does have that effect.

Finally, the suggestion that Gage had a monopoly may not withstand analysis. Some nonconforming uses do enjoy monopoly positions because of their location,[8] but it is difficult to understand how Gage's business was any more profitable located where it was.[9] The only possible advantage to Gage might have been a property tax advantage. Assessors have great difficulty with assessments of land employed in nonconforming uses and the property may have been assessed as residential property.

Harbison v. Buffalo[10] is the first New York case to uphold the general principle of amortization of nonconforming uses. The landowner involved used his land in a residential zone to recondition steel drums, which was classified as a junkyard under the ordinance. The ordinance provided that such nonconforming uses were to be terminated in three years. The court remanded the case to determine the reasonableness of the amortization period, and indicated that the trial court should consider such factors as the nature of the business, the improvements involved, the character of the neighborhood and the detriment caused the property owner, such as the cost of relocation and the permissible areas of relocating.

The dissent in the 4-to-3 decision has some interesting observations which are repeated in many of the cases holding amortization invalid. The dissent was concerned that if zoning was to apply to the termination of existing uses, investment in buildings would be so risky that no investments would be made. There are several answers to the concern. First, shouldn't it be a legislative judgment as to whether future investments would be discouraged? Second, the risk of a building losing its economic value through enforcement of amortization provisions is not likely because zoning does not typically change that much or that frequently and because amortization provisions are seldom employed in a wholesale fashion but only against the worst offenders. Third, erection of a building involves many risks of other private or public decisions being made that will result in a loss of value. The amortization threat is only one more risk which should be considered.

The amortization provisions may have the positive effect of encouraging developers to pay more attention to future plans so as to anticipate rezoning that would make their use nonconforming. Lending

---

8. For example, a nonconforming flower shop near a cemetery which is located in a residential zone.

9. Gage had a wholesale and retail plumbing supply business. Perhaps near neighbors would find it advantageous to buy their plumbing supplies there rather than elsewhere, but it is rather unbelievable that the gains there would not be offset by location in a traffic-generating commercial center.

10. 4 N.Y.2d 553, 176 N.Y.S.2d 598, 152 N.E.2d 42 (1958).

institutions might be particularly concerned with future plans, particularly in those states, such as California, where there is no personal deficiency judgment against a money mortgage borrower.

The dissent also indicates that the amortization provisions are an attempt to engage in slum removal without payment of compensation. Perhaps so, though the police power has long been used to condemn and destroy buildings that are a threat to the public health, safety and welfare.[11] While not slum removal, however, amortization provisions may produce deterioration in buildings when the effect is to discourage building maintenance.

Harbison is an interesting case to compare with Town of Hempstead v. Romano.[12] The premises in Hempstead had been used as a junkyard since 1926 and in 1930 was zoned residential. Junkyards were to be terminated in three years under the terms of the ordinance. However, each year the junkyard owner had been given a permit to continue and it was not until 1961 that the Town attempted to terminate the use. The court held the termination provision invalid indicating that a substantial loss would be caused by the termination, partially because junkyards were zoned out of the Town, relocation would be expensive and goodwill would be lost. Some may wonder whether the case is not a classic case of enjoyment of a monopoly for many years, why 28 years (1961 less 1933) was not treated as an amortization period and why the yearly extensions were not considered illegal, which ordinarily vests no rights.[13]

There are a few cases that continue to hold amortization schemes invalid—making a constitutional principle of the right of a preexisting use to continue to exist indefinitely. For example, in Hoffmann v. Kinealy,[14] an ordinance required the termination of a nonconforming use of land for lumber storage within six years. The court rejected any distinction between terminating nonconforming uses of land and nonconforming buildings, held that immediate termination would be a taking and that a termination in six years was merely an immediate taking postponed. The court also quoted Holmes to indicate that great public need does not justify a taking without compensation.

While Holmes is correct of course, the court is just repeating half of the argument on the proper place to draw the line between a taking and an exercise of the police power. The police power is exercised in the interest of the public health, safety and welfare, and the termination of nonconforming uses is primarily seeking to reconcile neighborhood land uses or to prevent the imposition of harm on the neighbors. By terminating a nonconforming use, the public is not acquiring anything as it does when it condemns land for a highway, nor is the public

---

11. See infra ch. 8.

12. 33 Misc.2d 315, 226 N.Y.S.2d 291 (1962).

13. See supra § 4.25; infra ch. 5.

14. 389 S.W.2d 745 (Mo.1965).

at large benefited except indirectly from better conformity to zoning.[15] Therefore, great public need, i.e. need of neighborhood to be rid of incompatible uses externalizing harm, is used to justify termination of nonconforming uses without compensation.[16]

Signs have been particularly subject to amortization provision, perhaps because of the low social utility assigned to them.[17] In a First Amendment case concerning billboards, which the U.S. Supreme Court reversed,[18] the state court stated a one to four year amortization time period using the depreciated value of a billboard was reasonable.[19]

 WESTLAW REFERENCES

non-conforming /s amortization /s sign billboard

topic(414) & amortization /p useful +3 life

414k81 /p amortiz! & constitution!

§ 4.36   Immediate Termination of Nuisance

Some of the nonconforming uses for which short amortization periods are upheld have near nuisance like qualities, such as junkyards and signs. When a use is a nuisance, immediate termination can be imposed. The taking issue is avoided because one has no property right to maintain a nuisance. As a result, the courts have sustained ordinances immediately terminating obnoxious uses. In Reinman v. Little Rock [1] a regulation prohibited stables and was held valid as applied to a preexisting stable in a business area. In Hadacheck v. Sebastian,[2] an ordinance prohibited brickyards in an area designated for residential use by an ordinance, and the court held it valid as applied to an existing brickyard. While not a zoning ordinance, the ordinance in Goldblatt v. Town of Hempstead [3] was much like a zoning ordinance and was such a severe restriction on the operation of a quarry that it rendered its continued operation all but impossible. The Town had previously attempted but failed to secure immediate termination under the zoning ordinance because the use was held to be a protected nonconforming use. The court upheld the nonzoning regulation, pointing out that where a matter of health and safety is involved, the regulation can justify a large loss, as in Hadacheck where property worth $800,000 was reduced to $60,000. The court in Goldblatt also

15. See infra ch. 20.

16. See, e.g., Standard Oil Co. v. Tallahassee, 183 F.2d 410 (5th Cir.1950), cert. denied 340 U.S. 892, 71 S.Ct. 208, 95 L.Ed. 647 (1950), another leading case, upholding the termination of a gasoline station in ten years which was located near several governmental buildings.

17. Annot., 80 A.L.R.2d 360 (1961).

18. Metromedia, Inc. v. San Diego, 453 U.S. 490, 101 S.Ct. 2882, 69 L.Ed.2d 800 (1981), on remand 32 Cal.3d 180, 185 Cal. Rptr. 260, 649 P.2d 902 (1982).

19. Metromedia, Inc. v. San Diego, 26 Cal.3d 848, 164 Cal.Rptr. 510, 610 P.2d 407 (1980), cert. denied 453 U.S. 922, 101 S.Ct. 3158, 69 L.Ed.2d 1004 (1981).

§ 4.36

1. 237 U.S. 171, 35 S.Ct. 511, 59 L.Ed. 900 (1915).

2. 239 U.S. 394, 36 S.Ct. 143, 60 L.Ed. 348 (1915).

3. 369 U.S. 590, 82 S.Ct. 987, 81 L.Ed.2d 130 (1962).

noted that evidence was absent as to the value after the termination of use of a quarry. For all the court knew, alternate uses would still be permissible that would leave a high property valuation. The fact that the property was used as a quarry and that these kinds of uses are usually given special protection as nonconforming uses was not discussed by the court.[4]

If the use has near nuisance qualities and the zoning ordinance provides for immediate termination, the court is particularly likely to uphold it if the investment is insubstantial.[5] However, even the liberal California court would not uphold an immediate termination of a mental institution in a residential area.[6] The mental institution presented a clear case of a nonconforming use of a nonconforming building involving a large investment. It was not considered to be a nuisance by the court, and it obviously had important social values attached to the use even though residential users in the area might prefer to exchange the mental institution use for the stable in Reinman or the brickyard in Hadacheck.

Some jurisdictions have ordinances which provide for reasonable amortization unless the use is found to be a nuisance by an administrative or legislative determination, in which case the use can be terminated immediately. The court might respond to a non-judicial determination of a nuisance in either of two ways. The court might recite the doctrine that a legislative or administrative declaration that something is a nuisance does not necessarily make it so, and the court may hold the ordinance invalid if the court is not satisfied the use is a nuisance. Alternatively, the court may give great weight to the finding by the legislative or administrative body that there is a nuisance, not seriously reexamine the situation, and uphold the ordinance. The latter response seemed to be applied in Livingston Rock & Gravel Co. v. County of Los Angeles.[7] Plaintiff owned a cement mixing plant which it constructed for $18,000 and which was located in a heavy industrial zone. A few months after it began operation, the property was rezoned for light manufacturing, though the light manufacturing zone permitted some rather heavy uses such as assembly plants, automobile repair, blacksmiths, building material and bus storage, clay product manufacture and storage[8] and the like. Under the ordinance, the cement batching plant could continue for a twenty-year amortization period

4. See supra § 4.23.

5. People v. Miller, 304 N.Y. 105, 106 N.E.2d 34 (1952) (ordinance precluding keeping of pigeons in residential area valid as applied to preexisting uses).

6. Jones v. Los Angeles, 211 Cal. 304, 295 P. 14 (1930).

7. 43 Cal.2d 121, 272 P.2d 4 (1954). This case, along with Consolidated Rock Prods. Co. v. Los Angeles, 57 Cal.2d 515, 20 Cal.Rptr. 638, 370 P.2d 342 (1962), appeal dismissed 371 U.S. 36, 83 S.Ct. 145, 9 L.Ed. 2d 112 (1962), may well be cited as the cases illustrating the penultimate reach of the police power—Livingston as to preexisting uses, Consolidated as to prohibition of future uses.

8. Recall that in Hadacheck v. Sebastian, 239 U.S. 394, 36 S.Ct. 143, 60 L.Ed. 348 (1915), clay products manufacturer was considered a nuisance, but in a residential zone.

unless the planning commission found it to be detrimental to the public health or safety or to constitute a nuisance. A year after the plant was opened, it was determined to be a nuisance and was ordered terminated in one more year.[9] The court found that the cement batching plant complied with all air pollution control ordinances, which one would think would be the major nuisance-like effects of the use, but nevertheless upheld the determination of the planning commission.

The far-reaching precedential value of the case might be limited by two factors. First, the batching plant was semi-portable, so that some of its value could be preserved; and second, while the court did reverse the lower court which had held the termination invalid, it did not hold the termination valid. Rather, the case was sent back to the planning commission for a further determination of whether the plant was a nuisance though it complied with the air pollution ordinances.[10]

WESTLAW REFERENCES

non-conforming /s nuisance /s billboard sign

sy,di(nuisance /p non-conforming /p junk trash garbage +3
    land-fill)

---

9. While this might be considered an amortization case, the amortization period was so short as to constitute virtually an immediate termination.

10. The Superior Court ultimately ruled that the ordinance, as applied, was invalid.

Chapter 5

LIMITATIONS ON ZONING POWER

Analysis

I. INTRODUCTION

I. INTRODUCTION

§ 5.1 Introduction

Since the power to zone is often based on a state's enabling act, zoning beyond the authority granted by the act is often invalid.[1] In addition, zoning can only be exercised for certain purposes and zoning for other purposes may be invalid.[2] There are other limitations on the power to zone which are judicially created or general in nature, which are discussed in this chapter.[3]

 WESTLAW REFERENCES
di,sy(power /2 zon*** /s statut*** act)
414k5

§ 5.1

1. See supra §§ 3.6–.13.

2. See supra §§ 3.14–.22.

3. Monetary liability for the exercise of the zoning power in violation of the Federal Civil Rights Act (42 U.S.C. § 1983) and federal antitrust laws is discussed in ch. 24 of the lawyers' edition of this Hornbook.

414k151

di,sy(limit! /s authority power /2 zon***)

§ 5.2   Delegation to Administrative Bodies

Delegation of the police power from the state to localities is discussed in a previous section.[1] Once the power is available to a locality, questions remain about who should be permitted to exercise it.

Standard Act Provisions

Under the Standard State Zoning Enabling Act[2] the legislative body of a locality was empowered to zone. While local legislative bodies were not thereby forced to zone, if they did, the Act required appointment of a zoning commission to make recommendations. The commission could be a planning commission, the legislative body or a committee thereof. Since its only power was the power to recommend, the zoning commission was not delegated much real power. The Act also allowed the legislative body to establish a board of adjustment. Neither the types of persons who could constitute a board of adjustment nor the occupations of members was specified and the board could be the legislative body itself, though the Act does set forth some requirements for the board if established. For example, the Act provided that the "board . . . shall consist of five members."[3] The Act also provided that the

> board . . . shall have the following powers: 1. To hear and decide appeals [of decisions by administrative officials, e.g., a denial of a building permit by a building inspector on the grounds of noncompliance with the zoning ordinance] . . . . 2. To hear and decide special exceptions [which special exceptions are provided for in the ordinance] . . . . 3. To authorize upon appeal [variances from the terms of the ordinance under certain standards established by the Act].[4]

These provisions delegated administrative power and therefore give rise to problems over the propriety of the delegation. Furthermore, these provisions indicate that other individuals such as building inspectors would be exercising power, thus raising questions as to the propriety of delegation of power to them.

The Act also imposed other requirements, so that a board would not exercise its powers properly if: it did not adopt rules, meetings were kept closed to the public, records were not kept, public notice was not given, and a greater than majority vote was not required for certain actions. Since much of the work of the board dealt with special

---

§ 5.2

1. See supra §§ 3.6–3.13.

2. U.S. Dep't of Commerce (rev. ed. 1926).

3. Id. § 7.

4. Id.

exceptions and variances, which are discussed separately,[5] only a general discussion of delegation of powers is covered here.

Standards

Other than a determination of whether administrative powers are exercised within the scope delineated by the statute, there are two major questions; first, whether the administrative body or officer acted within the scope provided by the ordinance (to the extent the enabling statute permits a different scope of action), and, second, whether the enabling act or the local legislative body provided sufficient standards to guide the discretion of administrative bodies or officials. While courts vary with respect to the matter, in many states the very vague kind of standards tolerated in federal administrative law are not tolerated with respect to municipal administrative bodies. This may be a reflection of the reality that these local bodies often have little expertise and, unless controlled judicially, are peculiarly apt to make decisions that are arbitrary, based on improper bias, dictated by personal interest or conflicts of interest, or made because of bribery or other corrupt motives.

There have been changes in the way that governmental entities handle zoning amendments, and therefore, changes in the judicial position on the matter of delegation. Under certain circumstances a zoning administrator may be empowered to make determinations in simpler cases within the jurisdiction of a board of zoning appeals. Hearing examiners may also be employed to receive evidence and make recommendations.[6]

These changes have engendered a variety of new legal issues. If a local governing body decides a case contrary to the recommendations of its staff and planning commission, courts are split on the question whether the resulting decision is arbitrary.[7] A municipal governing body may violate its zoning enabling act by delegating excessive authority to its lay bodies,[8] or by imposing no standards to guide lay decision-making.[9] The validity of a delegation of power may depend upon the body to whom that power is transferred.[10]

5. See infra §§ 6.5–6.10.

6. See 4 R. Anderson, American Law of Zoning § 30.02 (2d ed. 1976); Note, Administrative Discretion in Zoning, 82 Harv.L. Rev. 668 (1969).

7. Compare Zenga v. Zebrowski, 170 Conn. 55, 364 A.2d 213 (1975) with Golden v. Overland Park, 224 Kan. 591, 584 P.2d 130 (1978).

8. Lutz v. Longview, 83 Wn.2d 566, 520 P.2d 1374 (1974) (designating a PUD area a rezoning cannot be delegated to planning commission).

9. People v. Perez, 214 Cal.App.2d Supp. 881, 29 Cal.Rptr. 781 (1963) (no stan-

dards, effect was power to rezone parcel by parcel at discretion of commission).

10. Appeal of Moreland, 497 P.2d 1287 (Okl.1972) (city can empower Board of Adjustment but not Planning Commission to approve cluster development plans). A Board of Adjustment has been held to be an independent agency with powers coming directly from the legislature which could not be abridged by local government. The action taken, however, was beyond the scope of the Board's legislative authority. Township of Dover v. Board of Adjustment of Dover, 158 N.J.Super. 401, 386 A.2d 421 (1978).

WESTLAW REFERENCES

di,sy(delgat*** /s "police power" /s zon***)

414k6

Standard Act Provisions

"standard state zoning enabling act"

Standards

administrative /2 power body officer /s scope /s zon*** /s
    ordinance statute act

zoning /s k612

standard /s discretion /s administrative /2 power body /s
    zoning

"american law of zoning"

zenga +2 zebrowski

414k197

414k41

§ 5.3 Delegation to Property Owners

Extraordinary Majority Requirements

The Standard Zoning Enabling Act[1] provides that zoning can be changed, however, if there is a protest filed by property owners of a certain percentage of the property in or near the area, the change can be made only by a greater than majority vote of the legislative body. Many statutes and ordinances have similar provisions applying to administrative decisions. While these provisions often involve problems of construction and interpretation,[2] they are valid.[3] The property owners are not making the decision.

Consent, Supreme Court Cases

Problems of delegation arise, however, where regulation is dependent on the property owners. Several United States Supreme Court cases[4] deal with this problem. In Eubank v. Richmond,[5] the ordinance required the municipality to establish a setback line of between 5 and 30 feet if two-thirds of the property owners abutting a street requested it. A property owner of a lot obtained a building permit to erect a house 11 feet from the street line, neighbors petitioned, and the line was established at 14 feet. The court held the delegation invalid as containing no standards and allowing property owners to act capriciously for their own interest. In Thomas Cusack Co. v. Chicago,[6] however, the ordinance prohibited the erection of signs on public streets where more than half of the buildings were used for residential purposes

§ 5.3

1. U.S. Dep't of Commerce (rev. ed. 1926).

2. See Annot., 4 A.L.R.2d 335 (1949).

3. City of Hattiesburg v. Mercer, 237 Miss. 423, 115 So.2d 165 (1959).

4. See supra § 3.2.

5. 226 U.S. 137, 33 S.Ct. 76, 57 L.Ed. 156 (1912).

6. 242 U.S. 526, 37 S.Ct. 190, 61 L.Ed. 472 (1917).

unless the consent of a majority of the owners of property on the street was obtained. The court upheld this ordinance because, unless consent was obtained, the signs were prohibited. Therefore, the owner wishing to erect a sign could not be injured by denial of the consent. Eubank was distinguished because the restriction was there imposed rather than removed by the property owners. Eubank was also distinguished by Gorieb v. Fox.[7] In Gorieb, the ordinance established a setback line for new houses based on the average distance from the street of other houses on the block. The application was automatic, did not depend on consent and was not an improper delegation. The city merely based its decision on the rational ground that a setback should be established based on de facto setbacks in the area. In State of Washington ex rel. Seattle Title Trust Co. v. Roberge,[8] the ordinance provided that an old age home could be built in an area if neighbors consented. While Cusack held an ordinance valid that prohibited a use unless neighbors consented, Roberge held an ordinance invalid where the use was permitted but only with consent. The Roberge court considered the signs in Cusack and the old folks home of Roberge to be distinguishable. Signs are near nuisances, so property owners should have some control; old age homes may be annoyances to property owners in residential areas, but no court is likely to rule them nuisances.

Consent, State Court Cases

The state courts have also dealt with these neighborhood consent cases. For example, in Valkanet v. Chicago[9] an ordinance permitted boarding houses, hotels and nursing homes in apartment areas but prohibited old age homes unless neighbors consented. The court held that these types of prohibitions were valid, but held the ordinance invalid as applied, since there was no rational distinction between old age homes and the boarding houses, hotels and nursing homes. The "prohibited without landowner consent" ordinances are sometimes held invalid by the state courts. For example, in State ex rel. Omaha Gas Co. v. Withnell[10] an ordinance prohibited a gas storage tank unless all owners within a radius of 1,000 feet consented. The court held the effect of the provision was to exclude the use. As a practical matter, the court indicated, unanimity was impossible to obtain, thus conferring power on neighbors to act arbitrarily and without relation to the public health, safety and welfare.

The matter was carefully considered by a state court in O'Brien v. Saint Paul.[11] The statute provided that property could be rezoned only after a tract study or only if the owners of two thirds of the parcels of real estate within 100 feet gave their consent. The city council rezoned

7. 274 U.S. 603, 47 S.Ct. 675, 71 L.Ed. 1228 (1927).

8. 278 U.S. 116, 49 S.Ct. 50, 73 L.Ed. 210 (1928).

9. 13 Ill.2d 268, 148 N.E.2d 767 (1958).

10. 78 Neb. 33, 110 N.W. 680 (1907).

11. 285 Minn. 378, 173 N.W.2d 462 (1969). Compare Curtis v. Board of Supervisors, 7 Cal.3d 942, 104 Cal.Rptr. 297, 501 P.2d 537 (1972).

the property from single and double family to multiple family use without either the tract study or the consent. The court ruled against the city. Citing Cusack, the court held the consent requirement valid because no restriction was imposed by the property owners, their consent was required only to waive restrictions previously established by the city. Roberge (old age home permitted but only with consent) was distinguished on the ground that while old age homes were not a near nuisance, apartments in single and double family areas were.[12] Moreover, the court pointed out that the single and double family zoning had remained intact for 46 years and that many persons had purchased in reliance of the zoning.[13]

Improper delegation to neighbors is most clear where the regulation can be imposed only on request or must be imposed if property owners request.[14] Where uses are prohibited unless consent is obtained, the ordinance so providing is more likely valid than where uses are permitted, but only on consent. In addition to improper delegation of legislative authority and delegation without standard problems, these consent provisions may also be invalid because there is no provision for them under the enabling act.

It is altogether a different matter when a rezoning is conditioned on passing by referendum. In City of Eastlake v. Forest City Enterprises,[15] the United States Supreme Court held that a referendum cannot be characterized as a delegation of power, for it is a means of allowing the people to have the final decision over the enactments of representative bodies. The standardless delegation of power to a limited group of property owners condemned (as violative of due process) in Eubank and Roberge is not the equivalent of decisionmaking by the people through the referendum process. Though the referendum is applicable to zoning matters when it complies with statutory requirements, if a referendum measure is authorized it cannot be applied to prevent uses which were approved prior to its authorization.[16] Retroactive application would violate the user's due process rights.[17]

12. Criticized in 22 Zoning Dig. 111 (1970), but as long as the use is not a nuisance, a landowner is not required to get consent from neighbors. Spies v. Board of Appeals, 337 Ill. 507, 169 N.E. 220 (1929) (store in residential area); Valkanet v. Chicago, 13 Ill.2d 268, 148 N.E.2d 767 (1958) (old folks home allowed in apartment district); Concordia Collegiate Inst. v. Miller, 301 N.Y. 189, 93 N.E.2d 632 (1950) (educational building an inoffensive use).

13. Generally, there is no right to rely on zoning staying the same. See supra § 3.16.

14. City of Stockton v. Frisbie & Latta, 93 Cal.App. 277, 270 P. 270 (1928).

15. 426 U.S. 668, 96 S.Ct. 2358, 49 L.Ed. 2d 132 (1976).

16. Wheeler v. Pleasant Grove, 664 F.2d 99 (5th Cir.1981), cert. denied 456 U.S. 973, 102 S.Ct. 2236, 72 L.Ed.2d 847 (1982), appeal after remand 746 F.2d 1437 (11th Cir.1984).

17. Other cases dealing with the referendum issue include Winter Springs v. Florida Land Co., 413 So.2d 84 (Fla. 5th D.C.A.1982); Margolis v. District Court In and For the County of Arapahoe, 638 P.2d 297 (Colo.1981); San Pedro N., Ltd. v. San Antonio, 562 S.W.2d 260 (Tex.Civ.App. 1978), cert. denied 439 U.S. 1004, 99 S.Ct. 616, 58 L.Ed.2d 680 (1978), rehearing denied 439 U.S. 1135, 99 S.Ct. 1060, 59 L.Ed. 2d 98 (1979).

WESTLAW REFERENCES
Extraordinary Majority Requirements
414k198
di,sy(change*** /s zon*** /s majority /2 vot***)

Consent, Supreme Court Cases
delegat*** /s property /2 owner
414k81
ordinance /s setback /s property /2 owner

Consent, State Court Cases
414k43
di,sy(ordinance /p "property owner" landowner /s consent)
"property owner" landowner /s rely reliance /s zon***
referendum /s rezon*** zon***

§ 5.4 Spot Zoning

To the popular mind, spot zoning means the improper permission to use an "island" of land for a more intensive use than permitted on adjacent properties. The popular definition needs several qualifications. Some courts use the term spot zoning to describe a certain set of facts so that the term is neutral with respect to validity or invalidity. Other courts use the term spot zoning to describe a set of facts where the zoning as applied is invalid.

The set of facts usually involves an "island" of more intensive use than surrounding property. When parcels around a given property are rezoned to allow for higher uses leaving an island of less intensive use, reverse spot zoning is the result. Usually the "island" is small. For example, if a square mile area were carved out of an agricultural zone and zoned industrial, it is not likely that anyone would refer to that as spot zoning. Furthermore the term is not properly applied to development permission that comes about by variance or special exception. Rather, the term refers to a legislative act, such as a rezoning, or to a situation in which the "island" is created by the original ordinance. A spot zone may exist though the change for the "island" permits only what is permitted in adjacent areas. For example, if a lot and adjacent areas were zoned residential, but by variances, special exceptions and nonconforming uses, the adjacent area was used for business uses, it might be spot zoning to zone the lot for business uses. Such zoning might not be invalid spot zoning, though the court may hold it invalid on the ground that it represents a classic case for an amendment that rezones both the lot and the adjacent areas for business purposes.

Spot zoning is invalid where some or all of the following factors are present:

1. a small parcel of land is singled out for special and privileged treatment;

2. the singling out is not in the public interest but only for the benefit of the landowner;

3. the action is not in accord with a comprehensive plan.

The list is not meant to suggest that the three tests are mutually exclusive. If spot zoning is invalid, usually all three elements are present, or said another way, the three statements may be merely nuances of one another.

Accord With Plans in General

As previously discussed,[1] the Standard State Zoning Enabling Act[2] requires that regulations (both original and amendments) be "made in accordance with a comprehensive plan." The requirement is often mentioned in spot zoning cases, but it is variously interpreted. The requirement may only mean that zoning should not be irrational or arbitrary,[3] and the zoning of an "island" different from surrounding areas may be irrational or arbitrary. The requirement may only mean that zoning is to effectuate public purposes and spot zoning may merely confer a special privilege on an individual property owner. Sometimes the court reads the requirement as directing its attention, for purposes of review, to the zoning map for the area. The map should disclose some plan for the area, and if the proposed spot zoning creates a different zone without any apparent variation in the parcel that justifies the difference, the court may conclude that there is no accord with the plan.[4] Some courts and commentators conclude that the zoning map is not the plan referred to, but rather the master plan. If the change accords with the master plan it will not be invalid spot zoning.[5] Finally, the accordance requirement may mean no more than that zoning should effectuate a consistent policy. For example, if a legislative body has spot zoned in similar situations in the past, that might be evidence of a policy that further spot zoning accords to some plan.

Every casebook author including materials on zoning will have a case or two on spot zoning. The cases are not easily reconciled, even within a state, though the courts of some states are more tolerant of it than those in other states. It is also frequently difficult to identify the court's rationale for holding spot zoning valid or invalid. Discussion of the following leading cases is organized by the apparent basis for the decision.

§ 5.4

1. See supra §§ 2.11–2.13.

2. U.S. Dep't of Commerce (rev. ed. 1926).

3. Kozesnik v. Township of Montgomery, 24 N.J. 154, 131 A.2d 1 (1957).

4. Zoning found invalid in Pumo v. Norristown Borough, 404 Pa. 475, 172 A.2d 828 (1961).

5. Of course, the planning might be invalid as spot planning. See supra § 2.13.

Arbitrary, Special Privilege

Benefit to Private Person, No Public Purpose

A parcel of land on a busy street in a fine residential area was rezoned from residential to commercial. Despite the fact that the busy street made the lot almost useless for residential purposes, mere economic gain to the owner by a rezoning did not justify it, absent a showing that there was a substantial change in the neighborhood. Therefore, the lot was selected out for special treatment, which made the action invalid spot zoning.[6] Similarly, a small parcel in a residential district was rezoned for business purposes. Adjacent owners were opposed, but owners nearby signed supportive petitions. An existing business district was located seven hundred feet away. The court held the rezoning to be spot zoning, not in accordance with any plan and singling out of one parcel for special treatment.[7]

As previously indicated, a spot zone may be created by leaving out an "island" from a rezoning of an area. For example, a 700-acre residential parcel was zoned to prohibit the raising of fur-bearing animals except for a 10-acre area which was excluded from the prohibition. The court held that the raising of fur-bearing animals had nuisance-like effects in residential neighborhoods, and under the facts, the 10-acre exception could only have been for benefit of the individual. The court found no power to act except in the public interest.[8]

Accord With Zoning Plan

In spot zoning cases, the courts frequently conclude that there is no accord with the zoning map or plan. For example, the owner of a 19-acre parcel desiring to use his property for business use obtained a rezoning from residential to industrial use. While the rezoning was large enough to be comprehensive in one sense (as previously indicated, the rezoning of large parcels is generally not considered spot zoning), there was no showing that the parcel could not be used for residential purposes. There was vacant commercially zoned property on the other side of an adjacent expressway and there was no need to zone the property industrial to use it for business purposes. Accordingly, the court held the zoning was not in accord with the comprehensive plan and was invalid spot zoning.[9] Similarly, a block in a residential area was rezoned commercial for a shopping center. The municipality was

6. Leahy v. Inspector of Bldgs., 308 Mass. 128, 31 N.E.2d 436 (1941).

7. Kuehne v. Town Council of East Hartford, 136 Conn. 452, 72 A.2d 474 (1950). But see State ex rel. Gutkoski v. Langhor, 160 Mont. 351, 502 P.2d 1142 (1972) (rezoning extended perimeter of an existing zone to include rezoning held not spot zoning).

8. See Chrobuck v. Snohomish County, 78 Wn.2d 858, 480 P.2d 489 (1971); Lee v.

District of Columbia Zoning Comm'n, 411 A.2d 635 (D.C.App. 1980); City of Rusk v. Cox, 665 S.W.2d 233 (Tex.App. 1984), error refused n.r.e.

9. Hewitt v. County Comm'rs, 220 Md. 48, 151 A.2d 144 (1959). See also City of Pharr v. Tippitt, 616 S.W.2d 173 (Tex. 1981).

primarily residential in character, but with a shopping area located a half-mile away. By looking at the zoning plan for the city, the court concluded there was an intent to have the municipality zoned residential, except for the area a half-mile away. Moreover, the rezoned parcel was on the border of the municipality and adjacent to residential areas of three other municipalities. The court held the rezoning to be spot zoning and not in accord with the comprehensive plans of the Borough or the region as a whole.[10]

Rezoning was held valid where eleven acres, bounded by railroad tracks, a school, a street and a manufacturing company were rezoned from a zone permitting residences on 12,000 square foot minimum lots to R–4 permitting garden apartments. Though such a use was not specified in the master plan, the court indicated that the plan was not rigid and it was possible for the zoning ordinance itself to be a comprehensive plan. Because of the surroundings, and because much of the area was zoned R–4 or commercial, which permitted R–4 uses, the court concluded no spot zoning was involved. The zoning was not unreasonable or arbitrary and the large size of the parcel weighed against a determination of spot zoning.[11]

Accord With Master Plan

Since the Standard Zoning Enabling Act requires accord that is most often held to mean accord with the zoning plan, as somehow exemplified in the ordinance itself, there are few illustrations where spot zoning was held valid because it accorded with the master plan or invalid because it did not. Further, when an opinion refers to a comprehensive plan, it is often difficult to tell whether the reference is to the phrase "accordance with a comprehensive plan" as in statutes based on the Zoning Enabling Act, or to a master plan.[12]

Ordinances might indicate, for example, that a rezoning should accord with the master plan.[13] If all courts held "[W]here the city . . . has no master plan . . . the zoning ordinance constitutes the . . . plan" [14] the resolution of the confusion would be easier. With

---

10. Borough of Cresskill v. Borough of Dumont, 15 N.J. 238, 104 A.2d 441 (1954). This case is important for its consideration of extraterritorial circumstances. But see Bucholz v. Omaha, 174 Neb. 862, 120 N.W.2d 270 (1963) (shopping center okay in residential area because the property was a large tract and another large parcel buffered neighboring land).

11. Cleaver v. Board of Adjustment, 414 Pa. 367, 200 A.2d 408 (1964).

12. Opinions sometimes manifest a lack of understanding over the difference between a master plan and the plan as exemplified by the zoning ordinance. The confusion is not surprising since comprehensive plan is a synonym for mas-

ter plan. See generally McBride & Babcock, The "Master Plan"—A Statutory Prerequisite to a Zoning Ordinance?, 12 Zoning Dig. 353 (1960); Mandelker, Role of Comprehensive Plan in Land Use Regulation, 74 Mich.L.Rev. 899 (1976); Cf. Krasnowiecki, Abolish Zoning, 31 Syracuse L.Rev. 751 (1981).

13. Such an ordinance might conflict with the enabling act requiring only accord with a comprehensive plan, where the comprehensive plan is interpreted to be the scheme provided in the zoning ordinance.

14. Hein v. Daly City, 165 Cal.App.2d 401, 405, 332 P.2d 120, 123 (1958). See also Taschner v. City Council of Laguna Beach, 31 Cal.App.3d 48, 107 Cal.Rptr. 214 (1973).

heavy reliance on Haar, "In accordance with a Comprehensive Plan",[15] a California Court once said:

> It is apparent that the plan is, in short, a constitution for all future developments within the city . . . . Any zoning ordinance adopted in the future would surely be interpreted in part by its fidelity to the general plan as well as by the standards of due process. Frequently it has occurred that where a general plan was adopted, and later a zoning change was made which appeared to be in accord with the plan, that fact in and of itself was some evidentiary weight in the determination as to whether the zoning ordinance was proper or otherwise. If the general plan is anything at all, it is a meaningful enactment and definitely affects the community and, among other things, changes land market values. The general plan is legislatively adopted by the council. True, it is couched in part in general terms, but there are many specifics, and once adopted it becomes very effective . . . . Any subdivision or other development would necessarily be considered in its relation to the general plan, and such consideration practically by itself would be a sufficient legislative guide to the exercise of such discretions.

> It surely cannot be contemplated that the council, in the adoption of future zoning ordinances . . . will go contrary, (in all but rare instances), to the general plan which it adopts.[16]

Unfortunately, the court was more optimistic than realistic; there frequently is no such close tie between the master plan and zoning. Even if there is no applicable plan, spot zoning is less likely to be found when the rezoning is supported by planning staff or consultants.[17]

Accord With Policy

Finally, spot zoning may be valid when it accords with a plan that exists nowhere but in the minds of the decision makers. Basing a zoning decision on vague policy grounds is fraught with the opportunity for arbitrary action and a court willing to approve general policy as a guide to zoning decisions may find that it must approve almost any rezoning. Some policy rationale can almost always be found; hardly any rezonings make absolutely no sense. Courts have approved spot zoning justified only by policy.

15. Haar, In Accordance With a Comprehensive Plan, 68 Harv.L.Rev. 1154 (1955).

16. O'Loane v. O'Rourke, 231 Cal.App. 2d 774, 782–83, 42 Cal.Rptr. 283, 288 (1965). The O'Loane case was considering whether the adoption of a general plan was an administrative or legislative act to determine whether it was a fit subject for a referendum. The court held the adoption was a legislative act, thus properly a matter of a referendum. See Fishman v. Palo Alto, 86 Cal.App.3d 506, 150 Cal.Rptr. 326 (1978) and supra § 3.12.

17. See Furtney v. Zoning Comm'n, 159 Conn. 585, 271 A.2d 319 (1970), and Goldberg v. Zoning Comm'n, 173 Conn. 23, 376 A.2d 385 (1978). See generally 1 R. Anderson, American Law of Zoning § 5.17 (2d ed. 1976).

For example, a lot in a single-family dwelling area was rezoned from a residential zone to a special business zone to permit the construction of a small shopping center for a drugstore, hardware store, grocery, bakery and beauty parlor. There were already four stores in the area which were legal nonconforming uses. The special business zone used had provisions for open yards, setbacks and off-street parking to make it more compatible, and the zone was specially designed for situations of this type. Since the planning commission had a policy of relieving traffic congestion by decentralizing business to outlying areas and there was no other shopping area within a mile, the action was deemed to conform with a comprehensive plan. A dissent indicated that there was no actual (written down) comprehensive plan, and the action constituted a clear case of invalid spot zoning.[18] Similarly, land containing gravel was rezoned from residential to permit quarrying. By rezoning, the municipality would receive more taxes and would put the land to its most appropriate use. These factors were considered by the court to evidence a comprehensive plan.[19]

WESTLAW REFERENCES

di spot zoning

"spot zoning" /s define* definition

Accord With Plans in General

414k35

"spot zoning" /s accord! /2 plan

Arbitrary, Special Privilege

"spot zoning" /s (special /2 privilege treatment) "public purpose"

"spot zoning" /s private public /2 benefit

414k38

414k101

414k162

Accord With Master Plan

414k30

di,sy(zoning /s comprehensive master general /3 plan)

414k159

Accord With Policy

rezon*** zon*** /s accord! /s policy

---

§ 5.5   Contract Zoning

In General

Contract zoning and floating zones [1] are sometimes considered to be varieties of spot zoning. Using the term in the generic sense, contract zoning arises when property is rezoned, frequently in circumstances

---

18. Bartram v. Zoning Comm'n, 136 Conn. 89, 68 A.2d 308 (1949).

(rezoning held invalid, but for certain technical reasons).

19. See Kozesnik v. Township of Montgomery, 24 N.J. 154, 131 A.2d 1 (1957)

§ 5.5

1. See supra § 4.10.

that would constitute spot zoning, but the use of the property is restricted in some manner which effectively zones it differently than other property in the same type zone.[2] For example, one hundred fifty-four acres were rezoned limited manufacturing to permit the erection of an electronics plant. The rezoning was conditioned on imposition of deed restrictions that made the plant compatible with the adjacent residential areas. The court held such zoning valid.[3] Similarly a 210 by 230 foot corner lot was rezoned from residence to business. Certain conditions were imposed on the permitted use to make the business use compatible with the neighborhood. The lot was on a busy street, other businesses existed a block away and it was likely the entire block would someday be devoted to business uses because of population pressures. The court held the zoning valid.[4]

In invalidating contract zoning, the courts use a similar rationale as in spot zoning cases. For example, a lot zoned residential was rezoned commercial after the owner agreed to use it only for a funeral parlor. The court held this rezoning invalid as contract zoning because of violation of uniformity requirements.[5] It also determined the action to be spot zoning, not in accordance with a comprehensive plan, and for the benefit of the individual only.

Types of Contract Zoning

There are various forms of contract zoning. It is most clearly invalid where, in effect, the zoning ordinance provides that for and in consideration of a property owner recording a deed restriction limiting the use of his property to a particular use (e.g., a funeral home), the property shall be zoned commercial and shall forever remain so zoned. Courts will declare such zoning invalid on the theory that government cannot contract away its future right to exercise the police power. Moreover, even if the government does not bind itself in perpetuity, the police power should not be exercised in situations in which the government binds itself to rezone if the property owner does what the government requests. In such a situation, the police power exercised for a different reason than to promote the public health, safety and welfare. There has been some erosion of the prohibition on contract zoning in more recent cases.[6] Often, to avoid appearing to sanction

2. The practice is to be distinguished from situations where permission to use property is obtained by the issuance of a variance or special exception, which can legitimately be tailored to a particular use. See infra §§ 6.5–6.13.

3. Sylvania Elec. Prods., Inc. v. Newton, 344 Mass. 428, 183 N.E.2d 118 (1962), Bowers v. Board of Appeals of Marshfield, 16 Mass.App.Ct. 29, 448 N.E.2d 1293 (1983), review denied 451 N.E.2d 1167 (1983), Scrutton v. County of Sacramento, 275 Cal. App.2d 412, 79 Cal.Rptr. 872 (1969).

4. Church v. Town of Islip, 8 N.Y.2d 254, 203 N.Y.S.2d 866, 168 N.E.2d 680 (1960).

5. Baylis v. Baltimore, 219 Md. 164, 148 A.2d 429 (1959). See infra § 5.7.

6. E.g., Church v. Town of Islip, supra n. 4, State ex rel. Myhre v. Spokane, 70 Wn.2d 207, 422 P.2d 790 (1967), Goffinet v. Christian County, 65 Ill.2d 40, 2 Ill.Dec. 275, 357 N.E.2d 442 (1976).

contract zoning, courts may refer to it as conditional zoning and hold such agreements valid.[7]

The kinds of situations just described involve bilateral obligations, and are contract zoning in a strict rather than generic sense. Where no reciprocal obligations are created, conditional zoning is the more precise term.

Conditional zoning arises where, without committing itself, the governmental body secures a property owner's agreement to limit the use of his property to a particular use, to dedicate property, to place the buildings in a certain way or to limit the rezoning in some similar manner. While future exercise of the police power is not bargained away by conditional zoning and the governmental body has not promised to do anything, courts might still hold it invalid as spot zoning or as providing an improper inducement to exercise of power. For example, a village was asked to rezone property for a business use to permit the erection of a nursing home. It was expected that the state might exempt nursing homes from property taxation, and the village considered conditioning its rezoning on the agreement by the nursing home owner not to file a property taxation exemption claim. The village attorney concluded the arrangement would be invalid.[8] In practical effect, the Village Board was being induced to exercise its zoning power to preserve its tax base. While preservation of tax base is sometimes a legitimate purpose of zoning,[9] in this instance the zoning body was being induced to make a decision to maintain taxes, rather than one which made good planning sense.

Conditional zoning might also be held to violate the uniformity clause.[10] Technically this may not be so because the zoning itself may remain uniform, that is, it remains like zoning on other parcels of land in the same zoning classification. For example, if property is rezoned C1 after recordation of a deed restriction precluding service stations, it is the restriction, not the zoning, that limits the uses more than on other property zoned C1. Functionally, the public would be creating specialized zones. This might lead to bargaining; to inability to rely on zoning maps, since some agreements may not be recorded; and to the demise of "comprehensive" zoning. Nevertheless, some courts approve this kind of zoning. The Wisconsin Supreme Court, however, upheld conditional zoning on the grounds that there was no agreement made with the city.[11] The court reasoned that allowing private agreements to underly zoning gave a municipality greater flexibility and control of

---

7. Goffinet, supra n. 6. See also King's Mill Homeowners Ass'n v. Westminster, 192 Colo. 305, 557 P.2d 1186 (1976); Collard v. Incorporated Village of Flower Hill, 52 N.Y.2d 594, 439 N.Y.S.2d 326, 421 N.E.2d 818 (1981); Martin v. Hatfield, 251 Ga. 638, 308 S.E.2d 833 (1983). See generally Kramer, Contract Zoning—Old Myths and New Realities, 34 Land Use L. & Zoning Dig., No. 8, at 4 (1982).

8. Letter from Alvin R. Meyer, Village Attorney to Village of Shorewood, Wis. Board, Aug. 21 (1968).

9. See supra § 3.21.

10. "All . . . . regulations shall be uniform . . . ." Standard Zoning Enabling Act, § 2. See also infra § 5.7.

11. State ex rel. Zupancic v. Schimenz, 46 Wis.2d 22, 174 N.W.2d 533 (1970); see

development in a rapidly changing area. The agreement under review was between landowners and the developer. Arguments that the city was contracting away its police power were irrelevant, and the agreed upon use was allowed.

If shortly before, at, or after the rezoning, the property owner restricts his property, and there is no disclosure of his act in the record of the rezoning proceedings, some courts will hold the rezoning valid.[12] Others will take notice of the proximity of the events, conclude that it is still conditional zoning, and hold it invalid if conditional zoning is considered improper.[13]

The court in one state has approved conditional zoning when the conditions were imposed by the planning commission as its price for recommending the change. Theoretically, the conditions were not imposed by the legislative body, so the rezoning itself was held valid.[14]

 WESTLAW REFERENCES

In General

"contract zoning" "floating zones" /s define* definition

"contract zoning" /s invalid illegal

Types of Contract Zoning

goffinet +2 christian

"conditional zoning" /s invalid illegal

414k160

"conditional zoning" /s uniformity

§ 5.6 Piecemeal or Partial Zoning

Zoning ordinances have sometimes been held invalid because they are only piecemeal or partial zoning, and hence are not comprehensive. A piecemeal ordinance could be one of five types: one that (1) zones only part of the municipality, (2) is only temporary, (3) regulates fewer than the three usual elements, i.e., height, area, and use, (4) one or more of the three basic uses, residence, commercial and industrial are not provided for, or (5) does not cover all subjects it could cover.[1] In

also Nicholson v. Tourtellotte, 110 R.I. 411, 293 A.3d 909 (1972).

12. See, e.g., Gladwyne Colony, Inc. v. Lower Merion Township, 409 Pa. 441, 187 A.2d 549 (1963). Cf. Carlino v. Whitpain Investors, 499 Pa. 498, 453 A.2d 1385 (1982).

13. Hartnett v. Austin, 93 So.2d 86 (Fla. 1956). J.C. Vereen & Sons, Inc. v. Miami, 397 So.2d 979 (Fla.3d D.C.A.1981), cf. Broward County v. Griffey, 366 So.2d 869 (Fla. 4th D.C.A.1979), cert. denied 385 So.2d 757 (1980).

14. Pressman v. Baltimore, 222 Md. 330, 160 A.2d 379 (1960), City of Greenbelt v. Brealer, 248 Md. 210, 236 A.2d 1 (1967),

Goffinet v. Christian County, 30 Ill.App.3d 1089, 333 N.E.2d 731 (1975), judgment affirmed 65 Ill.2d 40, 2 Ill.Dec. 275, 357 N.E.2d 442 (1976). See generally Shapiro, The Case for Conditional Zoning, 41 Temp. L.Q. 267 (1968); Comment, Zoning and Concomitant Agreements, 3 Gonz.L.Rev. 197 (1968); Brown & Shilling, Conditional Zoning in Virginia, 16 U.Rich.L.Rev. 117 (1981); Comment, Toward A Strategy for Utilization of Contract and Conditional Zoning, 51 J.Urb.L. 94 (1973).

§ 5.6

1. The plan must be "comprehensive as to territory, public needs and time." Fairlawns Cemetery Ass'n v. Zoning

cases where piecemeal zoning is held invalid, the rationale for the decision is that such an ordinance is not comprehensive. For example, Darlington v. Board of Councilmen,[2] states a zoning ordinance must apply to the city as a whole and not only to particular streets.[3] An interim ordinance was held invalid in Kline v. Harrisburg[4] though such ordinances might be held valid if it were clear that a permanent, comprehensive ordinance is the subject of diligent effort.[5] While a failure to regulate height, area and use might constitute a noncomprehensive ordinance, separate ordinances on these matters have historically been sustained.[6] In Connor v. Township of Chanhassen the court concluded:

> [T]he term "comprehensive zoning" does not necessarily mean a plan which makes allowances for the establishment of districts to be set aside for various commercial and professional purposes . . . . The term comprehends that the ordinance shall take the place of and include within its provisions the numerous ordinances which were formerly enacted independently and included such subjects as "Tenement House Codes," "Sanitary Codes," "Fire Zone" provisions, and parts of the "Building Codes," as well as provisions with reference to codes relating to restrictions with reference to height, proportion of parcels that must be kept open, and unbuilt yard lines, etc.[7]

 WESTLAW REFERENCES

piecemeal partial /2 zoning /s invalid valid illegal legal

welch +2 swasey

§ 5.7 Uniformity, Classification

The Standard State Zoning Enabling Act[1] provides that "regulations shall be uniform for each class or kind of buildings throughout each district, but the regulations in one district may differ from those in other districts." The uniformity clause is sometimes the basis for invalidating spot zoning[2] or for justifying homogeneity requirements.[3]

Comm'n, 138 Conn. 434, 439, 86 A.2d 74, 77 (1952).

2. 282 Ky. 778, 140 S.W.2d 392 (1940).

3. But see Commissioners of Anne Arundel County v. Ward, 186 Md. 330, 46 A.2d 684 (1946); Montgomery County v. Woodward & Lothrop, 280 Md. 686, 376 A.2d 483 (1977), cert. denied 434 U.S. 1067, 98 S.Ct. 1245, 55 L.Ed.2d 769 (1978).

4. 362 Pa. 438, 68 A.2d 182 (1949). See also Silvera v. South Lake Tahoe, 3 Cal. App.3d 554, 83 Cal.Rptr. 698 (1970); CEEED v. California Coastal Zone Conservation Comm'n, 43 Cal.App.3d 306, 118 Cal.Rptr. 315 (1974).

5. Many states now authorize interim zoning by statute, thus clarifying this form of noncomprehensive zoning. See supra § 3.13.

6. See Welch v. Swasey, 214 U.S. 91, 29 S.Ct. 567, 53 L.Ed. 923 (1909) (upheld height limitations).

7. 249 Minn. 205, 213, 81 N.W.2d 789, 796 (1957).

§ 5.7

1. U.S. Dep't of Commerce, § 2 (rev. ed. 1926).

2. See supra § 5.4.

3. See supra § 3.17.

It is also used where classifications may be unreasonable, arbitrary or discriminatory.

Generally, if a court is disposed to uphold the zoning there must be some set of assumed facts that will justify any classification. Improper classification is often a convenient "hook" upon which to "hang" a decision, so cases holding classifications valid or invalid are difficult to reconcile. For example, in Kozesnik v. Township of Montgomery,[4] a special permit for a quarry was issued conditioned on the ground that it would not be operated within 400 feet of any existing dwelling. The court held the classification invalid since surrounding undeveloped property also should have had the protection of the condition. In Pierro v. Baxendale,[5] however, the court upheld an ordinance permitting boarding houses but excluding hotels and motels on the ground that the latter appealed to transients as distinguished from the boarding houses. The court in Kelly v. Mahoney[6] upheld an ordinance permitting turkey ranches only if dust control methods were employed but permitted chicken ranches without such control. The court did not bother to explain upon what basis the classification could be justified.

Sometimes the municipality may be able to offer a good reason for classification, for example, where parochial schools are excluded but public schools are permitted. Public schools serve everyone in the community whereas religious schools can limit their attendance. Nevertheless, because of considerations involving free exercise of religion, the classification may be held invalid.[7]

The drawing of zone lines also involves a matter of classification. Zone lines must be drawn somewhere, but they may be drawn in an unreasonable place if they have no relation to street or property lines.[8] Similarly, parcels may be held to be misclassified when the so-called highest use zone, single family residential, is located next to the so-

---

4. 24 N.J. 154, 131 A.2d 1 (1957), Johnson v. Township of Montville, 109 N.J. Super. 511, 264 A.2d 75 (1970), cf. 801 Avenue C, Inc. v. Bayonne, 127 N.J.Super. 128, 316 A.2d 694 (1974), Tulsa Rock Co. v. Board of County Comm'rs of Rogers County, 531 P.2d 351 (Okl.App.1974).

5. 20 N.J. 17, 118 A.2d 401 (1955). But see Southern Burlington County N.A. A.C.P. v. Township of Mt. Laurel, 67 N.J. 151, 336 A.2d 713 (1975) (Mt. Laurel I), appeal dismissed, cert. denied 423 U.S. 808, 96 S.Ct. 18, 46 L.Ed.2d 28 (1975). Mt. Laurel cites older cases which validated restrictive zoning measures but simultaneously warned of the inevitability of future change in judicial approach because of societal needs. See also Taxpayers Association of Weymouth Township v. Weymouth Township, 80 N.J. 6, 364 A.2d 1016 (1976), cert. denied 430 U.S. 977, 97 S.Ct. 1672, 52 L.Ed.2d 373 (1977); Rives v. Clarksville,

618 S.W.2d 502 (Tenn.App.1981) (police power can be used to zone for public convenience and general prosperity as well as for promotion of general welfare).

6. 185 Cal.App.2d 799, 8 Cal.Rptr. 521 (1960).

7. Roman Catholic Welfare Corp. v. Piedmont, 45 Cal.2d 325, 289 P.2d 438 (1955), but see discussion in Town of Los Altos Hills v. Adobe Creek Properties, Inc., 32 Cal.App.3d 488, 108 Cal.Rptr. 271, 290 (1973). See generally Comment, Zoning the Church; Toward a Concept of Reasonableness, 12 Conn.L.Rev. 571 (1980), and supra, § 4.17.

8. Cordts v. Hutton Co., 146 Misc. 10, 262 N.Y.S. 539 (1932), affirmed mem. 241 A.D. 648, 269 N.Y.S. 936 (1934), affirmed mem. 266 N.Y. 399, 195 N.E. 124 (1934), see also City of Utica v. Paternoster, 64 Misc.2d 749, 315 N.Y.S.2d 418 (1970).

called lowest use zone, such as heavy industry, and the zoning may be found invalid.[9] Ordinarily, however, and particularly in recent cases, the close proximity of land to an industrial zone does not mean that it must also be zoned industrial, particularly when it is adjacent to residential zones on other sides.[10]

 WESTLAW REFERENCES

uniform*** /s building /2 class kind

di,sy(zon*** /p classification /s invalid valid)

414k650

di,sy (zon*** /p "police power" /s "public convenience" general
   /2 welfare prosperity)

414k27

"zone lines" /s draw***

§ 5.8 Exclusion From Entire Community

Since every or almost every use of land is a legitimate use somewhere, if no place is provided for a use within boundaries for which a governmental body is authorized to zone, such exclusion might be unreasonable and hence void under the police power. Clearly, however, there are many cities which are exclusively or almost exclusively zoned for one type of use or another, and it would be difficult to understand how these clutches of residential, commercial, industrial or agricultural uses could be maintained if every city had to provide a place for every use of land legitimately located somewhere in a metropolitan area.[1]

Even larger cities frequently attempt to entirely exclude particular kinds of uses such as junkyards, dumps, outdoor movies, motels, mobile home parks, hog farms or cemeteries. Obviously, the size of the city is relevant to a judicial decision upholding[2] or invalidating[3] such exclu-

9. Reschke v. Village of Winnetka, 363 Ill. 478, 2 N.E.2d 718 (1936).

10. Williams v. Village of Schiller Park, 9 Ill.2d 596, 138 N.E.2d 500 (1956), Reskin v. Northlake, 55 Ill.App.2d 184, 204 N.E.2d 600, 605 (1965).

§ 5.8

1. For example, in the Los Angeles metropolitan area, the City of Bradbury had a population of 869 persons, but there were only 9 taxable transactions in Bradbury under the California retail sales tax law. Property in the city was assessed at $3,567,240. The City of Vernon had a population of 229 persons. It had 66,052 taxable transactions generating $2,720,731 of local sales taxes and had taxable property assessed at $245,125,230. Comparatively, the City of Santa Monica had a population of 88,900; 67,366 taxable transactions generating $2,427,462 of local sales taxes; and

assessed property of $277,921,775. Obviously, Bradbury was almost totally residential, Vernon was almost totally commercial-industrial and Santa Monica was a balanced community of residences and commercial-industrial areas. Data from 1966–67 Annual Report of State Controller, Financial Transactions Concerning Cities of California; 89th State Board of Equalization Quarterly Report, Trade Outlets and Taxable Retail Sales in California (Dec. 15, 1969). As to exclusive agricultural uses, the City of Orange, California, was originally incorporated to permit the inhabitants to resist subdivision and perpetuate the orange groves by zoning.

2. Vickers v. Township Comm., 37 N.J. 232, 181 A.2d 129 (1962), cert. denied 371

3. See note 3 on page 148.

sionary ordinances. A smaller community may perhaps more legitimately claim it need not make a space available for every use, including the most obnoxious. Excluding certain uses may not be justifiable based solely on the size of a community, if the exclusive use infringes on a protected right.

The United States Supreme Court, in Schad v. Borough of Mt. Ephraim,[4] held that an ordinance banning live entertainment from the borough was invalid. Entertainment (expression) as well as political speech is protected by the first amendment.[5] When zoning interferes with a protected liberty it must be narrowly drawn and must further a sufficiently substantial government interest to be found valid.[6] The Court determined that the Borough's goal of maintaining a commercial area catering only to the immediate needs of the community was not sufficient justification for the total exclusion called for by the ordinance, nor was the limitation a reasonable time, place and manner restriction which left adequate alternative channels open for communication.[7]

Two years earlier, in Young v. American Mini-Theatres,[8] the Court held restrictions which required porno theatres be no closer together than a specified minimum distance to be valid. The restrictions amended an existing anti-skid row ordinance, adopted by Detroit in 1962, at which time the city council had found that some uses of property were especially injurious to a neighborhood when concentrated in limited areas. The ordinance provided for a waiver of the restriction if certain findings were made by the zoning commission.[9] Even though the restriction impinged on a first amendment right, because the governmental interest served was sufficiently substantial,

U.S. 233, 83 S.Ct. 326, 9 L.Ed.2d 495 (1963) (excluding trailer parks), overruled Southern Burlington County N.A.A.C.P. v. Township of Mt. Laurel, 92 N.J. 158, 456 A.2d 390 (1983); Duffcon Concrete Prods. v. Borough of Cresskill, 1 N.J. 509, 64 A.2d 347 (1949) (excluding industry); Garden State Farms v. Bay, 136 N.J.Super. 1, 343 A.2d 832 (1975), judgment reversed 146 N.J. Super. 438, 370 A.2d 37 (1977), judgment affirmed 77 N.J. 439, 390 A.2d 1177 (1978) (excluding airports); Township of Washington v. Central Bergen County Mental Health Center, Inc., 156 N.J.Super. 388, 383 A.2d 1194 (1978) (excluding Transition centers). Vickers, overruled in Mt. Laurel II, explicitly recognized that changed circumstances could require a different result (than exclusion). Mt. Laurel II indicates that the time has come and circumstances have changed. Cf. Town of Stonewood v. Bell, 165 W.Va. 653, 270 S.E.2d 787 (1980).

3. People ex rel. Trust Co. v. Village of Skokie, 408 Ill. 397, 97 N.E.2d 310 (1951) (excluding outdoor theater); Pierro v. Bax-

endale, 20 N.J. 17, 118 A.2d 401 (1955) (excluding motels); Robinson Township v. Knoll, 410 Mich.App. 293, 302 N.W.2d 146 (1981) (excluding mobile homes); Dolson Outdoor Adv'g Co. v. Macomb, 46 Ill.App. 3d 116, 4 Ill.Dec. 692, 360 N.E.2d 805 (1977).

4. 452 U.S. 61, 101 S.Ct. 2176, 61 L.Ed. 2d 671 (1981).

5. Id. at 66, 101 S.Ct. at 2181.

6. Id. at 68, 101 S.Ct. at 2182.

7. Id. at 74, 75, 101 S.Ct. at 2186. The case was remanded and the convictions under the statute were reversed. The court found no justification for the ban in the ordinance but did not expressly overturn it as that issue was not directly before the court.

8. 427 U.S. 50, 96 S.Ct. 2440, 49 L.Ed.2d 310 (1976), rehearing denied 429 U.S. 873, 97 S.Ct. 191, 50 L.Ed.2d 155 (1976).

9. Id. at 53, 96 S.Ct. at 2444.

the ordinance narrowly drawn and included a waiver provision, it was valid.

Another example of an invalid attempt by a municipality to exclude an unpopular use is Metromedia, Inc. v. San Diego.[10] In that case, the City attempted to ban all off-site billboards with twelve exceptions, and allow only onsite advertising. The ordinance as drawn was overinclusive, and prohibited not only commercial speech, but noncommercial speech as well. The United States Supreme Court held that the City could not favor a lesser-protected speech over one accorded greater protection but must regulate evenhandedly. The ordinance was stricken.[11]

 WESTLAW REFERENCES

414k76

zon*** /s exclu! limit*** forbid*** /s junkyard dump "outdoor movie" motel "mobile home park" "hog farm" cemetery

414k83

schad +2 "borough of mt. ephraim"

zon*** /s adult porno! /2 theatre movie

zon*** /s off-site /2 billboard /s speech "1st amendment"

---

§ 5.9   Extraterritorial Factors

The proper relationship between local zoning and the regional effects thereof is present in several situations. Snob zoning, often referred to as exclusionary zoning, is a lack of recognition of regional responsibilities.

The landmark case of Southern Burlington County N.A.A.C.P. v. Township of Mt. Laurel[1] set forth for the first time the doctrine requiring that a municipality's land use regulations provide a realistic opportunity for low and moderate income housing. Local zoning cannot foreclose the opportunity for low and moderate income families to obtain housing, and regulations must affirmatively afford that opportunity, at least to the extent of the municipality's fair share of present and prospective need. The municipality could avoid its duty only by sustaining the heavy burden of demonstrating particular circumstances to justify why it should not be required to bear its fair share.[2] The New Jersey Supreme Court determined that Mt. Laurel had failed to carry the burden and the trial court decision was modified to comply with the higher court opinion.

10. 453 U.S. 490, 101 S.Ct. 2882, 69 L.Ed.2d 800 (1981), on remand 32 Cal.3d 180, 185 Cal.Rptr. 260, 649 P.2d 902 (1982).

11. Id. at 513, 101 S.Ct. at 2895. For further discussion of Metromedia, see infra § 14.4.

§ 5.9

1. 67 N.J. 151, 336 A.2d 713 (1975) (Mt. Laurel I), appeal dismissed, cert. denied 423 U.S. 808, 96 S.Ct. 18, 46 L.Ed.2d 28 (1975). See also supra § 3.20.

2. 67 N.J. 151, 336 A.2d 713, 724 (1975).

Later decisions [3] watered down the Mt. Laurel doctrine, and as Mt. Laurel II began to work its way through the New Jersey court system, it appeared that the pronouncements of community responsibility espoused in Mt. Laurel I had been effectively undermined. When Mt. Laurel II reached the New Jersey supreme court,[4] it unanimously reaffirmed its original position and determined to put some steel into the original holding. The case was accompanied by five others involving questions arising from the Mt. Laurel doctrine. The court set out certain procedures for review of "Mt. Laurel" cases in an attempt to assure uniformity in future decisions, and enumerated criteria by which developing communities might determine their "fair share." By enunciating these steps the court intended for communities to comply with their "Mt. Laurel obligation." Once that obligation is met, the doctrine would not restrict the use of other zoning measures to maintain its beauty and communal character. The court specifically held that where the obligation could not be satisfied by removal of restrictive barriers, inclusionary devices such as density bonuses and mandatory set asides were constitutional and within the zoning power of a municipality. Though it preferred legislative to judicial action in this field, the court emphasized that it would continue, until the legislature acted, to uphold the constitutional obligation underlying the Mt. Laurel doctrine.

Excluding unpopular uses is another method through which municipalities shift bothersome but legitimate activities to other communities. Nonprofit and tax exempt uses are sometimes excluded though many perform valuable functions for society.[5] Overzoning for industrial and commercial areas in the hope of attracting tax base disrupts optimal land use patterns. This is being done with government sanction in some locations, however, in an attempt to revitalize deteriorated urban areas.[6]

Extraterritorial zoning power [7] is a recognition of the need to control land use beyond local borders. Lack of control by one government of extraterritorial facilities of other governments permits the intrusion of governmental uses that may be more inimical to an area

3. E.g., Pascack Ass'n, Ltd. v. Mayor & Council of Washington Tp., 74 N.J. 470, 379 A.2d 6 (1977); Southern Burlington County NAACP v. Township of Mt. Laurel (Mt. Laurel II), 161 N.J.Super. 317, 391 A.2d 935 (Law Div.1978).

4. Mt. Laurel II ultimately reached the New Jersey Supreme Court in 1980 and was decided in 1983. 92 N.J. 158, 456 A.2d 390 (1983), on remand ___ N.J.Super. ___, ___ A.2d ___ (1984).

5. E.g., in Town of Los Altos Hills v. Adobe Creek Properties, 32 Cal.App.3d 488, 108 Cal.Rptr. 271 (1973), the court explained that it might be within the scope of a municipality's police power to exclude religious schools if sites were available in nearby communities, inferring that such exclusion would not be possible if no such sites were available. See also, Roman Catholic Diocese of Newark v. Ho-Ho-Kus Borough, 47 N.J. 211, 220 A.2d 97 (1966), Grosz v. Miami Beach, 721 F.2d 729 (11th Cir.1983), rehearing denied 727 F.2d 1116 (11th Cir.1984), cert. denied ___ U.S. ___, 105 S.Ct. 108, 83 L.Ed.2d 52 (1984), and supra §§ 3.19–3.20.

6. See infra § 17.8 for discussion of enterprize zones in downtown revitalization.

7. See supra § 3.13.

than many private uses.[8] The right of a locality to control utilities, transmission lines, railroads and the like involves difficult problems of determining the appropriate level of government for decision making.[9] The right to control zoning is a major reason why areas incorporate as municipalities.

The subject of extraterritorial zoning raises, in various contexts, the basic question of whether zoning should be a local rather than regional matter. The matter has been discussed frequently in the literature.[10]

There is an essential conflict between the assumption that zoning is a local matter and the fact that in metropolitan areas, governmental boundaries are of almost no socioeconomic significance. Perhaps a simple solution would be to amend the enabling acts to provide that zoning should not only accord with intramunicipal zoning, plans and policies, but with regional considerations as well.[11] Absent such direction, there are only a few significant cases where the court squarely faced the issue of regionalism and concluded that a municipality had to zone with sensitivity toward its neighbors. The leading case is Cresskill v. Borough of Dumont,[12] in which the court not only held that property owners outside a municipal boundary could intervene in a decision to spot zone for a shopping center, but also that such zoning would be incompatible with the zoning, plans and policies of the neighboring municipality and was therefore invalid.[13]

 WESTLAW REFERENCES

snob exclusionary /2 zon***

naacp +2 "township of mt. laurel"

414k508

414k489

"extraterritorial zoning"

268k18 & zoning

---

8. See supra §§ 4.15, 4.16.

9. See supra § 4.18.

10. R. Babcock, The Zoning Game (1966); Note, Regional Development and the Courts, 16 Syracuse L.Rev. 600 (1965); Note, Zoning: Looking Beyond Municipal Borders, 1965 Wash.U.L.Q. 107; Comment, Regional Impact of Zoning: A Suggested Approach, 114 U.Pa.L.Rev. 1251 (1966); Note, Zoning: Jurisdictional Enforcement of Duty to Serve Regional Welfare, 55 Wash.L.Rev. 485 (1980). See also supra § 3.7.

11. Hagman, Book Review, 34 U.Chi.L. Rev. 469 (1967).

12. 15 N.J. 238, 104 A.2d 441 (1954).

13. See also Scott v. Indian Wells, 6 Cal.3d 541, 99 Cal.Rptr. 745, 492 P.2d 1137 (1972); Wittingham v. Village of Woodridge, 111 Ill.App.2d 147, 249 N.E.2d 332 (1969); Board of County Comm'rs of County of Adams v. Thornton, 629 P.2d 605 (Colo.1981, en banc); Village of Barrington Hills v. Village of Hoffman Estates, 81 Ill. 2d 392, 43 Ill.Dec. 37, 410 N.E.2d 37 (1980), cert. denied 449 U.S. 1126, 101 S.Ct. 943, 67 L.Ed.2d 112 (1981); Shepard v. Woodland Township Committee, 71 N.J. 230, 364 A.2d 1005 (1976); Borough of Allendale v. Township Committee, 169 N.J.Super. 34, 404 A.2d 50 (1979), judgment affirmed 177 N.J.Super. 230, 426 A.2d 73 (1981).

§ 5.10   Vesting Rights—Estoppel

It is usually difficult to successfully assert estoppel against exercises of the police power. When the public health, safety and welfare are at stake, courts are reluctant to interfere in the exercise of the police power because of some error by the governmental body. Therefore, in order to win a case against a governmental body on an estoppel theory it is necessary to meet a stringent test. The test is stated in a variety of ways, such as the following: the municipality must act affirmitively; the property owner must be unaware of the illegality of the act; the municipality must have intended or known that its conduct would be acted upon by the property owner; and the property owner must be prejudiced by his action in reliance.

In Crow v. Board of Adjustment of Iowa City,[1] for example, after receiving an opinion from the city attorney, the building inspector issued a permit to a property owner to erect a veterinary hospital in a district that permitted hospitals. The property owner purchased a lot, demolished a house on it, began excavating, purchased materials and entered into contracts. Objecting citizens appealed the issuance of the permit to the Board of Adjustment, which ruled that hospitals did not include veterinary hospitals. The court held that the ordinance was ambiguous and that in such a case the issuance of the permit was valid where the permittee had materially changed his position.

Similarly, the necessary elements of estoppel were present in Township of Pittsfield v. Malcolm,[2] where a permit was issued for a dog kennel on the ground that it was a use similar in character to other uses permitted in the zone by the ordinance, and the ordinance provided that uses similar in character could be permitted. The court held that a dog kennel was clearly not similar to other uses permitted by the ordinance, however, the kennel had been built and $45,000 had been spent. Notice that the kennel was to be built had been published, parties inclined to oppose had been informed by the nature of the construction that a kennel was being built and the building was a specialty. Therefore, the court refused to enjoin operation of the kennel.

In the above two cases, there was some ambiguity as to whether the permit had been illegally issued. Where the development is clearly illegal, the courts are not inclined to estop governmental action. For example, in City of Raleigh v. Fisher,[3] the City had allowed the defendant to conduct a business of a bakery in a home for several years. The building inspector had issued several permits for additions and

§ 5.10

1. 227 Iowa 324, 288 N.W. 145 (1939).

2. 375 Mich. 135, 134 N.W.2d 166 (1965), see also, Grand Haven Township v. Brummel, 87 Mich.App. 442, 274 N.W.2d 814 (1978), Cf. Harrell v. Lewiston, 95 Idaho 243, 506 P.2d 470 (1973).

3. 232 N.C. 629, 61 S.E.2d 897 (1950), Winston-Salem v. Hoots Concrete Co., 47 N.C.App. 405, 267 S.E.2d 569 (1980), review denied 301 N.C. 234, 283 S.E.2d 131 (1980), Board of County Comm'rs v. Echternacht, 194 Colo. 311, 572 P.2d 143 (1977), Harrell v. Lewiston, supra, n. 2.

improvements with knowledge that the use violated the zoning ordinance. The City had also collected a privilege license tax for eight years. When the City decided to enforce its ordinance the court upheld the City. If the result were otherwise, an employee of the City could deliberately misconstrue the law and be allowed to frustrate public policy.

Even where development would be otherwise legal, there are instances when a developer's reliance on preliminary approval and subsequent change of position do not outweigh a superseding statutory determination. In Avco Community Development, Inc. v. South Coast Regional Comm.,[4] the developer had acquired several thousand acres upon which it planned to construct a planned community. A final map was approved for multiple family uses on the parcel in question. By the date that the provision in California Coastal Zone Conservation Act requiring a permit from the Commission for development within a coastal zone became effective, however, Avco had not obtained a building permit. It was therefore unable to complete construction on the coastal portion of its development. The court found that claims by the company that expenditures of substantial sums entitled it to a building permit were unsound.

Many factors are weighed in the decisions of courts in these cases, and usually no one fact is determinative, but good faith and ambiguity as to legality plus substantial expenditure in reliance weigh heavily in favor of estoppel. If there is a hint of fraud, misrepresentation or concealment, realization by the party seeking to assert estoppel that the permission was illegally given, or that permission was clearly illegal and a mistake, estoppel is not likely to be a successful defense.

WESTLAW REFERENCES

di,sy("police power" /s exercis*** /s estop***)

ordinance /s ambiguous /s permit /s valid invalid

di,sy(ordinance /s permit*** /s same similar /3 use)

414k322

414k327

di,sy(permit /s violat*** /s zon***)

building /2 permit /s expend! spend /s money sum fund

§ 5.11 Vesting Under Building Permits

In some situations a landowner may have a right to a building permit or a right to complete a building under the permit. The right is

---

4. 17 Cal.3d 785, 132 Cal.Rptr. 386, 553 P.2d 546 (1976), appeal dismissed, cert. denied 429 U.S. 1083, 97 S.Ct. 1089, 51 L.Ed. 2d 529 (1977). Carty v. Ojai, 77 Cal.App.3d 329, 143 Cal.Rptr. 506 (1978), Colonial Investment Co. v. Leawood, 7 Kan.App.2d 660, 646 P.2d 1149 (1982). See generally Hagman, The Vesting Issue: Rights of Fetal Development vis-a-vis Abortions of Public Whimsey, 7 Envt'l.L. 519 (1977).

based on his establishment of a protected nonconforming use [1] or on a more general estoppel theory.[2]

Right to Obtain Permit

The time sequence of various events can change the result of litigation brought by a property owner who is attempting to obtain a building permit. For example, if a property owner purchases land to erect an industrial plant, it is rezoned for residential use on the day following purchase, and he applies for a permit to build the industrial plant on the third day, the court is not likely to order issuance of the permit. At the time of application for the permit the property was improperly zoned. The property owner may not only have his plans frustrated by such an action, but his property may be worth much less than the purchase price.

If the zoning is proper as of the time of application for a permit, various events may occur before issuance of the permit: e.g., permanent zoning is changed shortly after application for permit, permit is denied on basis that the application does not comply with zoning; [3] application is held for long period of time to permit change in zoning, permanent changes made, permit then denied; application is received, zoning changed by interim zoning, permit denied; application is denied on basis that change in zoning for area under study. Gibson v. Oberlin [4] illustrates a clear and simple rule for handling the matter. A property owner applied for a permit to build a twelve unit apartment building. The building inspector refused to issue the permit, the Board of Appeals ordered the issuance of the permit, and the City Council reversed the Board. After the property owner appealed to the court for an order directing the issuance of the permit, the City Council amended the ordinance so that apartment buildings clearly would not be permitted. The court held that since the applicant had complied with all requirements for the issuance as of the date of application, the permit must be issued, and subsequent legislation had no effect. Both the state and the property owner were held bound by regulations existing at the time of application. Under this case, a showing of expenditures in reliance on the permit is apparently not required.

Most courts hold that there is no right to a permit merely because zoning is proper as of the time of application for the permit. Therefore, if the permit is denied because of a post-application change in zoning,

§ 5.11

1. See supra §§ 4.27–4.28.

2. See supra § 5.10.

3. Hull v. Hunt, 53 Wn.2d 125, 331 P.2d 856 (1958) (denial held invalid); Eastlake Community Council v. Roanoke Associates, Inc., 82 Wn.2d 475, 513 P.2d 36 (1973).

4. 171 Ohio St. 1, 167 N.E.2d 651 (1960). Accord State ex rel. Mumma v. Stansberry, 5 Ohio App.2d 191, 214 N.E.2d 684 (1964), and see Union Oil Company of California v. Worthington, 62 Ohio St.2d 263, 405 N.E.2d 277 (1980), Dade County v. Jason, 278 So.2d 311 (Fla.3d D.C.A.1973).

the courts will not order issuance of the permit unless the zoning change was invalid.[5]

There is more reluctance to uphold denial of a permit on the basis of proposed ordinances.[6] Therefore, when a permit is denied on the basis that municipal plans for an area are not finalized, the court may order the issuance of the permit, even though the municipality places a "freeze" on the area by interim ordinance.[7] On the other hand, if the matter is under study, and the matter is to be resolved shortly, some courts will uphold denial. After the matter is resolved, permission may be granted, in which case the applicant only suffers delay. If the conclusion of the study results in a change that precludes the permit, the wisdom of the proposed change tends to be established, thus justifying the initial denial.[8]

Rights Under Permit

Once a permit is obtained, it might be revoked if the zoning changes prior to the exercise of the permit. Courts will usually uphold such a revocation unless expenditures have been made in reliance on the permit. Expenditures made prior to issuance of the permit are not usually counted to interdict revocation because they are not made in reliance on the permit.[9] Usually, the expenditures must be in the form of actual construction, though demolition of existing buildings or excavation may be insufficient. The expenditures must also be made in good faith,[10] and when bad faith is proven, decisions generally go against the permittee.[11]

Other cases illustrating the rule that the property owner must be injured, must have changed his position or have made expenditures in reliance on the permit include Rodee v. Lee.[12] In that case, while applications for building permits were pending, the ordinance was changed to require 100 rather than 50 foot widths for lots in the area. Because of the shape of the property involved, the developer would thus be able to develop only 4 rather than 11 house sites. The property

---

5. See, e.g., Smith v. Winhall Planning Commission, 140 Vt. 178, 436 A.2d 760 (1981).

6. Annot., 30 A.L.R.3d 1196 (1970).

7. See, e.g., Olympic View-Mukilteo Action Group v. Mukilteo, 97 Wn.2d 707, 649 P.2d 116 (1982).

8. West Coast Advertising Co. v. City & County of San Francisco, 256 Cal.App.2d 357, 64 Cal.Rptr. 94 (1967). Atlantic Richfield Co. v. Board of Supervisors of County of Sacramento, 40 Cal.App.3d 1059, 115 Cal.Rptr. 731 (1974).

9. Anderson v. City Council of Pleasant Hill, 229 Cal.App.2d 79, 40 Cal.Rptr. 41 (1964). Avco Community Developers, Inc. v. South Coast Regional Commission, 17 Cal.3d 785, 132 Cal.Rptr. 386, 553 P.2d 546

(1976), appeal dismissed, cert. denied 429 U.S. 1083, 97 S.Ct. 1089, 51 L.Ed.2d 529 (1977), County of Kauai v. Pacific Standard Life Ins. Co., 65 Hawaii 318, 653 P.2d 766 (1982), appeal dismissed 460 U.S. 1077, 103 S.Ct. 1762, 76 L.Ed.2d 338 (1983) (upholding denial after referendum process initiated).

10. Sakolsky v. Coral Gables, 151 So.2d 433 (Fla.1963). See also Hollywood Beach Hotel Co. v. Hollywood, 329 So.2d 10 (Fla. 1976).

11. Miami Shores Village v. Wm. N. Brockway Post No. 124, 156 Fla. 673, 24 So. 2d 33 (1945).

12. 14 N.J.Super. 188, 81 A.2d 517 (1951).

owner showed no hardship greater than anyone else in having his plans disrupted by the new ordinance, however, and he was held bound by it.

In Town of Largo v. Imperial Homes Corp.,[13] the developer bought two parcels of property relying on assurances that the town would rezone to allow construction of multi-family dwellings including a high rise apartment building. The requested zoning was for the highest allowable density, but because of resident objections, the parcels were ultimately zoned for the most restrictive single family use. The Town argued that the developer had not obtained a building permit thus no rights had vested. The Florida Supreme Court found no merit in that contention and held that builders had a right to rely on actions of the current governing body regardless of public protest. The permit was ordered.

People ex rel. Nat'l Bank of Austin v. County of Cook [14] illustrates the kind of expenditures that are necessary. The developer obtained permission to construct multi-family dwellings. Construction was delayed because of a tight money market. Because of local opposition, the property was then rezoned for single family dwellings. The evidence showed that employees of the developer spent considerable time thinking about the development of the apartment complex, but the court held that such evidence did not show the expenditure of substantial sums or the incurrence of substantial obligations and did not show reliance on the permits.[15]

Substantial reliance can be measured in various ways. Many courts hold that a landowner must have invested a certain amount of money in the project. To avoid difficulty in setting an arbitrary amount, some courts adopt a ratio approach, and require that expenditures already made be substantial relative to the total project cost. In Clackamas County v. Holmes,[16] however, the court stated that though substantial costs toward completion of the job must have been incurred, vesting of rights should not be based solely on the ratio of expenditures to total cost of the project. The defendants had taken actions to ready the property for chicken farming, and the county rezoned the property to residential use before they could secure a building permit. The Court found that other factors should be considered, such as type of preparations made by a property owner prior to putting his property to a certain use. It concluded that the defendants had acted in good faith,

13. 309 So.2d 571 (Fla.App.1975), Jones v. U.S. Steel Credit Corp., 382 So.2d 48 (Fla.2d D.C.A.1979), cert. denied 389 So.2d 1111 (1980), Cf. Pasco County v. Tampa Development Corp., 364 So.2d 850 (Fla.2d D.C.A.1978), and Town of West Hartford v. Rechel, 190 Conn. 114, 459 A.2d 1015 (1983).

14. 56 Ill.App.2d 436, 206 N.E.2d 441 (1965). O'Hare Internat'l Bank v. Zoning Bd. of Appeals, 37 Ill.App.3d 1037, 347 N.E.2d 440 (1976).

15. Cf. Town of Hillsborough v. Smith, 276 N.C. 48, 170 S.E.2d 904 (1969). Application of Campsites Unlimited, 287 N.C. 493, 215 S.E.2d 73 (1975).

16. 265 Or. 193, 508 P.2d 190 (1973). Cf. Webber v. County of Clackamas, 42 Or. App. 151, 600 P.2d 448 (1979).

the expenses incurred were substantial and directly related to its intended uses, thus rights had vested.

Zoning Change Invalid

In addition to applying an equitable estoppel theory, a court dealing with a vesting of rights to a building permit issue can often preserve the rights of the permittee by holding the rezoning invalid as applied. Therefore, a rezoning that would ordinarily be held valid may be held invalid as applied to property of a person who has a pending building permit application or one who has been issued a permit.[17]

Courts tend to uphold the governmental decision resulting in a denial or revocation of a building permit if the change in law is adopted for some general purpose and not just to thwart the plans of the applicant. In Anderson v. City Council of City of Pleasant Hill [18] the applicant had obtained a rezoning from the county, but prior to erecting a filling station, the property became part of a newly incorporated city. The new city adopted an ordinance to enable proper planning for the entire city. While the ordinance prevented the applicant from vesting a right under a building permit, it was not specifically directed against him.

Reconciling the Cases

The cases on the matter of vesting rights in building permits are confusing and difficult to reconcile. Perhaps a certain rule is preferable, such as the rule that requires the issuance of a permit if it meets the test of the applicable ordinances at the time of application. The case-by-case, equitable determination results in great uncertainty. On the other hand, there are many situations where issuance of the permit would clearly be a bad planning decision. Though planning should anticipate the situations and foreclose the issuance of the permit in advance, planning is often inadequate and the ill-advised nature of the present controls only comes to the attention of governmental decision makers when someone applies for developmental permission. Perhaps government should have a chance to correct its mistake by changing the rules and then denying the developmental permission.

Once the permit has been issued, there are situations where clearly the government should be allowed to change its mind. For example, one holding an unutilized building permit should not have a vested right to use it forever. On the other hand, the permittee should have a reasonable time period to rely on the permission. Absent fraud, once the governmental body makes a decision, it should not be changed

17. Gruber v. Township of Raritan, 39 N.J. 1, 186 A.2d 489 (1962). The intermediate appellate court had held the industrial only zoning invalid on due process grounds—that it was unreasonable, arbitrary and confiscatory. Gruber v. Township of Raritan, 73 N.J.Super. 120, 179 A.2d 145 (App.Div.1962).

18. 229 Cal.App.2d 79, 40 Cal.Rptr. 41 (1964).

primarily because of political pressures brought by objecting persons rather than because of some change in facts.

Ordinances

Absent any clear judicial guidelines in most states, the question of vesting of rights is an appropriate subject for ordinances. An ordinance might provide that a decision on a building permit should be made on the basis of ordinances that are in effect on the date of application. Alternatively, an ordinance might provide that no permit can be issued if a rezoning is under consideration, as in San Francisco,[19] though perhaps the ordinance should define how advanced the consideration must be. Where a building permit has been issued, some zoning ordinances provide that it cannot be revoked for a period of time providing construction is begun within that time and is pursued diligently to completion.[20]

In some states, developers may acquire rights to complete projects from statute or ordinances. In Massachusetts, the holder of a building permit may complete construction if the permit was granted before notice of hearing on subsequent zoning change was made, construction commenced within six months of issuance of permit, and construction proceeded in good faith, continuously to completion.[21]

A California statute [22] requires enforcement of a contract between a city and landowner if the contract states that the landowner has a right to proceed according to policies effective when the agreement was made.

In New York City, an ordinance vests rights under building permits once the foundation of a structure is completed.[23]

 WESTLAW REFERENCES

di,sy(landowner property /2 owner /s right /3 permit)

414k465

Right to Obtain Permit

gibson +2 "city of oberlin"

414k376

permit /s deny denied denial /s proposed interim /2 ordinance

19. See Fisher, Land Use Control Through Zoning: The San Francisco Experience, 13 Hastings L.J. 322, 342 n. 32 (1962).

20. NIMLO Model Ord. § 11–209(5) (1969). For other discussions of rights on application for or rights after issuance of building permits, see Hagman, Estoppel and Vesting in the Age of Multi-Land Use Permits, 11 S.W.U.L.Rev. 545 (1979); Comment, The Building Permit and Reliance Thereon in South Carolina, 21 S.C.L.Rev.

70 (1968); Comment, The Effect of Pending Legislation on Applications for Building Permits in California, 3 U.S.F.L.Rev. 124 (1968).

21. Mass.Gen.Laws Ann. c. 40A. § 6.

22. West's Ann.Cal. Gov't Code § 65864ff.

23. City of New York Zoning Reg. § 11–83, cited in Temkin v. Karagheuzoff, 34 N.Y.2d 324, 357 N.Y.S.2d 470, 313 N.E.2d 770 (1974).

Rights Under Permit

permit /2 obtain*** /s revoke* revocation /s zon***

di,sy("property owner" landowner /s rely reliance expend! /s permit

Zoning Change Invalid

di,sy(rezoning zoning /s valid invalid /4 applied)

Reconciling the Cases

"building permit" /s "reasonable time" /s rely reliance

Ordinances

find 357 n.y.s.2d 470

---

§ 5.12   Weight of Precedent

A zoning decision may not have much value as precedent. Frequently, a case only decides that zoning as applied to a particular parcel is invalid.[1] Courts seldom order a particular kind of zoning.[2] A municipality has the power to ignore the spirit of the decision. For example, if a court decided that 50 acre minimum zoning was invalid as applied to a parcel, the municipality could apply a 49 acre minimum to the parcel and force relitigation of the issue. By a series of such acts, the property owner could be exhausted by litigation. Similarly, where zoning is held invalid as applied to a parcel, a municipality is not required to change the zoning that is similarly invalid as applied to other parcels.

A landowner is also not bound by precedent. By arguing some change of circumstances, he can seek to relitigate a decision holding zoning as applied to be valid.[3]

In most states, the zoning ordinance can be amended though the same or a similar previous amendment was rejected by the legislative body.[4] There is only a limited number of states which preclude a change unless circumstances have changed.[5] If an amendment is rejected, the rejection does not usually bar an application for a variance or a special permit, or vice versa.

While precedent may have some role before administrative bodies,[6] typically a variance or a special permit cannot be obtained merely by showing that they have been granted to others in similar circumstances in the past.[7]

§ 5.12

1. First Nat'l Bank & Trust Co. v. Evanston, 30 Ill.2d 479, 197 N.E.2d 705 (1964).

2. But see Hamer v. Town of Ross, 59 Cal.2d 776, 382 P.2d 375, 31 Cal.Rptr. 335 (1963). This is a very unusual case because the court appears to order a particular kind of zoning.

3. Louisville Timber & Wooden Prods. Co. v. Beechwood Village, 376 S.W.2d 690 (Ky.1964).

4. Tarasovic v. Zoning Comm'n, 147 Conn. 65, 157 A.2d 103 (1959).

5. See supra § 3.16.

6. Corsino v. Grover, 148 Conn. 299, 170 A.2d 267 (1961).

7. County of San Diego v. McClurken, 37 Cal.2d 683, 234 P.2d 972 (1951). Contra, Redwood City Co. of Jehovah's Witnesses v. Menlo Park, 167 Cal.App.2d 686, 335 P.2d 195 (1959).

WESTLAW REFERENCES
di,sy(variance special /2 permit /s grant*** /s similar same)
414k377

§ 5.13 Zoning to Lower Condemnation Costs

Where zoning limits the use of land to fewer uses than those for which the market creates a demand, the value of the land is reduced. The effect of zoning on land is taken into account in determining just compensation in eminent domain proceedings.[1] Therefore, governmental condemnors sometimes yield to the temptation of zoning to reduce prices.

Official maps, which restrict the right to build in planned streets, parks and other public sites, and setback provisions [2] which are imposed so that streets can be widened without the necessity of paying for buildings, are examples of other regulations that have been approved as a way of limiting costs of acquisition in some circumstances.

Frequently, however, zoning is employed. For example, if the purpose of zoning land residential in the heart of an industrial area is to depress value to lower future condemnation costs, the zoning will be held invalid.[3] Since courts do not generally inquire into motives, the circumstances surrounding the zoning must be considered before concluding that the purpose of zoning was to lower values rather than for some legitimate purpose. An improper purpose may be evidenced when land that is rezoned is coextensive with land to be condemned, as distinguished from zoning that affects a large number of landowners or is part of a comprehensive rezoning.[4] Similarly, if zoning and condemnation proceedings are substantially concurrent, this factor may evidence an improper purpose. Whenever the court suspects that zoning is being used to depress values, it may hold the zoning invalid on other grounds without giving the real basis for its decision. For example, if an "island" is rezoned for agricultural uses in an area the government intends to acquire as an airport, the court may hold it to be invalid spot zoning. Of course, condemnors know the rules as well as anyone else and are often sophisticated enough to arrange the circumstances in such manner that an improper purpose is not disclosed.

§ 5.13

1. See infra § 20.10.

2. See supra § 4.8.

3. State ex rel. Tingley v. Gurda, 209 Wis. 63, 243 N.W. 317 (1932); Board of Com'rs of State Inst. v. Tallahassee B. & T. Co., 108 So.2d 74 (Fla. 1st D.C.A. 1958), quashed 116 So.2d 762 (1959); Ventures in Property I v. Wichita, 225 Kan. 698, 594 P.2d 671 (1979).

4. Kissinger v. Los Angeles, 161 Cal. App.2d 454, 327 P.2d 10 (1958); Eldridge v. Palo Alto, 57 Cal.App.3d 613, 129 Cal.Rptr. 575 (1976).

WESTLAW REFERENCES

di,sy(set back /s zoning)

zoning /s residential /s industrial /2 park

zon*** /s condemn! /s coextensive concurrent same /s
   improper invalid

Chapter 6

TYPES OF ZONING RELIEF

Analysis

I. INTRODUCTION

Sec.

6.1 Zoning "Forms of Action".

II. LEGISLATIVE AND ADMINISTRATIVE RELIEF: IN GENERAL

6.2 Amendments.

6.3 Administrative Relief: In General.

6.4 Rezoning: Legislative or Adjudicative Action.

III. VARIANCES

6.5 Variances: In General.

6.6 Effect on Public.

6.7 Effect on Neighborhood.

6.8 Characteristics of Property.

6.9 Unnecessary Hardship.

6.10 Large Parcel Use Variances.

IV. SPECIAL PERMITS

6.11 Special Permits: In General.

6.12 Standards.

6.13 Conditions.

I. INTRODUCTION

§ 6.1 Zoning "Forms of Action"

When an owner wishes to use his property in a manner that would be improper as it is presently zoned, there may be more than one way by which he can obtain permission. He might seek a legislative change through a textual or zoning map amendment, he might proceed administratively and seek a variance or special permit, he might go to court and seek a judicial declaration that the land is improperly or unconstitutionally zoned, or he might seek to qualify the property for an exception or as a nonconforming use.

More than one approach may be appropriate [1] and each is peculiar in requirements and procedure, so that they may be described as "zoning forms of action." As with common law forms of action, choice of form dictates the allegations to be made, decision makers involved, subject matter jurisdiction, evidence to be presented, standing requirements of the parties, kinds of relief allowed and availability of the appeal process. Res judicata-like effects may differ, as will opportunities to merge or split "causes of action" or "plead in the alternative," what advocates can be used (for example, lawyers or laymen) and so forth. Depending on the needs of the property owner, one zoning form of action may be preferable to another when alternatives are available.

This chapter considers the substantive details of the various forms of action, except for the nonconforming use, which is separately considered.[2]

 WESTLAW REFERENCES
268k621 /p exception variance

---

§ 6.1

1. For example, in Application of Devereux Foundation, Inc., 351 Pa. 478, 41 A.2d 744 (1945), appeal dismissed 326 U.S. 686, 66 S.Ct. 89, 90 L.Ed. 403 (1945), the board granted a special exception to permit the use of a building as a dormitory for mentally deficient children. The court concluded that such a use was not a "dormitory of an educational institution" which was permitted in the zone, that it was not a special use since there were not provisions for permitting such a use on conditions set forth in the ordinance, and it was not a variance since there was no showing of hardship or absence of adverse effect on the public interest of owners and occupants of neighboring properties.

2. See §§ 4.27–4.36 supra.

II. LEGISLATIVE AND ADMINISTRATIVE
RELIEF: IN GENERAL

§ 6.2 Amendments

Kinds of Amendments

Section 5 of the Standard State Zoning Enabling Act [1] provides that "regulations, restrictions, and boundaries may from time to time be amended, supplemented, changed, modified, or repealed." Amendments are made by ordinance by the legislative body of the local government. Proper subjects for amendment may be either procedural or substantive provisions of the ordinance. Substantive amendments include: (1) rezonings, or zoning map amendments, that is, a change of the zone that applies to a parcel of land; (2) zoning text amendments, that is, a change in use permitted within a given zone. The amendment can be initiated by either the legislative body, a governmental official or a property owner.

The vast bulk of amendments are rezonings. For example, the owner of land zoned residential may apply to have it rezoned commercial. Many property owners overlook the possibility of having the zoning text amended to change the permitted uses within a zone. Suppose a property owner wishes to construct a laundromat, which is not permitted in the light commercial zone presently applied to the property, but which is expressly permitted in a heavy commercial zone. The property owner might apply for a rezoning to a heavy commercial zone. However, such rezoning might constitute invalid spot zoning or may permit other uses, which might render it improper, or the legislative body may not be willing to grant it.[2] Alternatively, the legislative body may be willing to reconsider whether a laundromat is unintensive enough a use to be included in the list of permitted uses in the light commercial zone.

Rezoning (Zoning Map Amendments)

Rezonings should be relatively easy to obtain under certain circumstances. If the comprehensive plan for the area has designated a use which differs from the existing zoning, the decision makers theoretically need only be shown that the future contemplated by the plan has arrived and the property should be rezoned as planned.[3] If the area has not been permanently zoned but is in an interim [4] or hold [5] zone, the fact that a property owner has a definite use in mind which demonstrates a market for the property might stimulate permanent zoning of some kind, though perhaps not the kind the property owner

§ 6.2

1. U.S. Dept. of Commerce (rev. ed. 1926).

2. See § 4.14 supra.

3. See §§ 2.11–2.13 supra.

4. See § 3.13 supra.

5. See § 4.12 supra.

wishes.[6] If there is a considerable amount of vacant property in the area and property adjacent to the property to be rezoned is zoned for the use desired, it should be relatively easy to change the boundaries of the adjacent zone to incorporate the owner's property.

If an area has developed by way of nonconforming uses, special uses and variances, a rezoning which would make the uses permitted uses is highly appropriate.[7]

Of course, one should not rely on judicial opinions as a conclusive basis for an argument that a rezoning is a desirable or undesirable governmental act. A judicial opinion, affirming a rezoning that is "on all fours" with the situation affecting another parcel, does not assure that a rezoning can be obtained for the different parcel.

Change in Circumstances

If none of the circumstances suggesting the propriety of an amendment clearly exist, the property owner may also argue that conditions have changed since the last zoning and that a rezoning would be in the public interest. Legislative bodies may be convinced by an argument that a rezoning should occur because the property owner can then increase the economic value of his parcel, but if that is the only argument, and the existing restriction is not unreasonably burdensome, the zoning should not be changed. Changes should be made only if it benefits the public health, safety and welfare. As population increases in an area, some property should be rezoned to permit more intensive uses. Such changes should be based on some rational policy or plan. If it is in the public interest, the rezoning will be upheld over claims of neighbors that they have a vested right to rely on existing zoning. There is no such right.[8]

There are many changes of circumstances which logically support an argument for a change in zoning. A major highway may be built through an area zoned for agricultural purposes, which may well justify rezoning to permit residential, commercial or industrial uses. Furthermore, zoning concepts may change. For example, while strip commercial zoning had been regarded as desirable at one time (a strip commercial zone is one where only the first tier of lots along one or both sides of a busy thoroughfare are zoned commercial), the public interest may be better served by area rezoning for shopping centers, which among other advantages helps avoid problems associated with on-the-street parking.[9]

6. MacDonald v. Board of Comm'rs for Prince George's County, 238 Md. 549, 210 A.2d 325 (1965) (dissenting opinion).

7. See § 4.2 supra on Permitted uses.

8. Objecting neighbors almost always claim a reliance right to maintenance of the status quo despite the absence of such a right. Compare, however, O'Brien v. St. Paul, 285 Minn. 378, 173 N.W.2d 462, 467 (1969) where the court refused to invalidate a statute requiring neighborhood consent to a rezoning in part because "numberless homeowners have purchased and improved property relying on the protection of the statute." See supra § 3.16.

9. For an excellent recitation of facts supporting a need for rezoning, see Robinson v. Los Angeles, 146 Cal.App.2d 810, 304

In some states by statute, or by judicial lawmaking [10] a showing that a change of circumstances has occurred not only constitutes a basis for argument before a legislative body but is required, or the rezoning will be invalidated by a court if there has been no change since the original zoning.[11] As with original zoning, amendments should be made in "accordance with a comprehensive plan." [12]

WESTLAW REFERENCES

Kinds of Amendments

di,sy(amendment /s zon*** rezon*** /s permit*** /2 use)

Rezoning (Zoning Map Amendments)

interim stop-gap /2 zon*** /s rezon***

di,sy(special variance nonconform*** /2 use /s permit*** /2 use)

414k684

Change in Circumstances

di,sy(chang*** /3 circumstance condition /s zon*** rezon***)

414k465

di,sy(rest*** /2 right /s rely reliance /s zon***)

§ 6.3   Administrative Relief: In General

Section 7 of the Standard State Zoning Enabling Act provides for a board of adjustment which

> [m]ay, in appropriate cases and subject to appropriate conditions and safeguards, make special exceptions to the terms of the ordinance in harmony with its general purpose and intent and in accordance with general or specific rules therein contained.

It further provides that

> [t]he board of adjustments shall have the following powers:
>
> 1. To hear and decide appeals where it is alleged there is error in any order, requirement, decision, or determination made by an administrative official in the enforcement of this act or of any ordinance adopted pursuant thereto.
>
> 2. To hear and decide special exceptions to the terms of the ordinance upon which such board is required to pass under such ordinance.

P.2d 814 (1956). See also Arnebergh, Criteria for Rezoning: Valid Reasons, 5 Institute on Planning & Zoning 45 (1964).

10. MacDonald v. Board of Comm'rs for Prince George's County, supra note 6. The dissent indicates that the requirements of the change or mistake doctrine are judicial gloss not authorized by statute.

11. Compare, on change of circumstances, Harris Trust & Sav. Bank v. Chicago, 107 Ill.App.2d 113, 245 N.E.2d 889 (1969), with LaSalle Nat. Bank v. Village of

Skokie, 107 Ill.App.2d 104, 246 N.E.2d 105 (1969). An editorial note, 21 Zoning Digest 162 (1969) indicates "It is hard to believe [these cases] . . . were decided by the same court on the same day with opinions written by the same judge. The inconsistencies between the two cases are staggering." See also supra § 3.16.

12. See supra §§ 2.1–2.13, 5.4. Town of Somerset v. County Council, 229 Md. 42, 181 A.2d 671 (1962).

3. To authorize upon appeal in specific cases such variance from the terms of the ordinance as will not be contrary to the public interest, where, owing to special conditions, a literal enforcement of the provisions of the ordinance will result in unnecessary hardship, and so that the spirit of the ordinance shall be observed and substantial justice done.

Most states have similar provisions in their state enabling acts, though the board is frequently called a board of appeals. There is considerable confusion regarding the terminology used to describe the relief which the board of adjustment may grant. A board may grant three kinds of relief: (1) it may reverse or modify the decision of an administrative officer under subsection 1; (2) it may grant what is described by the Standard Act as a "special exception" under subsection 2 but which is more commonly known as a conditional or special use permit; and (3) it may grant a variance under subsection 3. Unfortunately, laymen, most lawyers, and many courts use the term "special exception" to refer to all three forms of relief. This confusion stems from the wording of the Standard Act.

The first sentence of Section 7 apparently uses the term special exception in a generic sense to describe all the forms of relief which the board may grant, while subsection 2 uses the term to describe a specific form of relief.

The special exceptions provided for in item 2 are conditional or special uses which are permitted in a zone if the terms of the ordinance are met. If they are, the board will issue a special permit, special use permit, conditional use permit or a special exception, all of which are synonymous.[1] (The term special permit will be used in this chapter.)

The term "exception" is also used to describe one aspect of the authority of an administrative officer which may be reviewed by the board under subsection 1. The use of the word exception in this situation has a specific, accepted meaning. One provision of an ordinance may provide for setbacks in the commercial zones while another provision modifies the setback if the commercial zone is also a transition zone.[2] An exception in this sense is a provision which modifies (or provides exceptions to) the general provisions of the ordinance for particular circumstances. The matter falls under subsection 1, because whether the exception applies is determined by an administrative officer.[3]

§ 6.3

1. See supra § 4.2, infra §§ 6.11–6.13.

2. See supra § 4.13.

3. Obviously, administrative officials pass on other matters, such as whether a laundromat can be permitted in a zone providing that a laundry is a permitted use. The determination by the administrative official that a laundromat is or is not a laundry may be appealed to the board of adjustment. See e.g., Crow v. Board of Adjustment of Iowa City, 227 Iowa 324, 288 N.W. 145 (1939), where building inspector concluded a veterinary hospital was a hospital, which determination was reversed by the board.

Subsection 3 authorizes the issuance of variances. While a special exception is a permitted use if the conditions are met, a variance is permitted only by sufferance, that is, it is granted only when because of "special conditions" the property owner suffers "unnecessary hardship" beyond the "spirit of the ordinance," so that "substantial justice" is not done.

The variance and the special permit provisions have generated a vast body of law, probably for four major reasons: first, the grant or denial of permission can frequently have substantial economic consequences and is a matter worth fighting over; second, thousands of administrative bodies make decisions; third, these bodies are frequently composed of men with greater political, economic and practical sense than technical expertise, but frequently overstep the bounds of their quasi-judicial functions; and, fourth, recognizing the inadequacies of the boards, courts are not as willing to defer to their judgments as they are to more expert administrative bodies, and lack of deference invites a judicial rehash of the issues involved.[4]

To have standing to pursue a variance, petitioners were required to have a legally cognizable interest in the subject property. The interest held by a lessee,[5] assignee [6] or agent [7] has been deemed sufficient to confer standing. Some jurisdictions do not require a petitioner to have any legal interest in the property for which a variance is sought. It has been suggested that the latter view is probably the better one.[8] Courts have become more liberal in granting standing in recent land use lawsuits, allowing "aggrieved" or "interested" parties to maintain actions, though as distance from the property involved increases it is less likely that a neighbor will be "aggrieved." [9]

Before a protest can be brought before the courts, jurisdictions require that plaintiffs exhaust their administrative remedies.[10] Futile remedies, for obvious reasons, need not be exhausted if there are certain legislative remedies available, those should be pursued.[11]

---

4. See Green, Are "Special Use" Procedures in Trouble?, 12 Zoning Digest 73 (1960); Notes, Administrative Discretion in Zoning, 82 Harv.L.Rev. 668 (1969); The Effect of Statutory Prerequisites on Decisions of Boards of Zoning Appeals, 1 Ind. Legal Forum 398 (1968).

5. Poster Advertising v. Zoning Bd. of Adjustment, 408 Pa. 248, 182 A.2d 521 (1962).

6. Cohn v. County Bd. of Supervisors, 135 Cal.App.2d 180, 286 P.2d 836 (1955).

7. Stout v. Jenkins, 268 S.W.2d 643 (Ky. 1954).

8. Board of Zoning Appeals v. Moyer, 108 Ind.App. 198, 27 N.E.2d 905 (1940);

Tramonti v. Zoning Bd. of Rev., 93 R. 1, 131, 172 A.2d 93 (1961), see generally, 4 R. Anderson, American Law of Zoning §§ 25.09–.20 (2d ed. 1977).

9. E.G. Loichot v. Allstate Development Corp., 33 Ohio App.2d 121, 292 N.E.2d 923 (1963); Renard v. Dade Co., 261 So.2d 832 (Fla.1972) (Neighbor standing).

10. Northwestern University v. Evanston, 74 Ill.2d 80, 23 Ill.Dec. 93, 383 N.E.2d 964 (1978); Fifth Avenue Corp. v. Washington County, 282 Or. 591, 581 P.2d 50 (1978).

11. Note, Exhausting Administrative and Legislative Remedies in Zoning Cases, 48 Tulane L.Rev. 665 (1974).

WESTLAW REFERENCES

di,sy(board　/2　adjustment　/s　"special exception" conditional
　　special　/2　use)

di,sy(board　/2　adjustment　/s　variance)

standing　/s　variance　/s　zon***

414k571　/p　standing

414k23

di,sy(exhaust***　/2　administrative legislative　/2　remedy　/s
　　zon***)

414k562

§ 6.4　Rezoning: Legislative or Adjudicative Action?

Judicial review of rezoning cases has historically been fairly deferrential. The majority of states treat such zoning changes with regard to one parcel as legislative acts, and accord them a presumption of validity.[1] A court will usually allow a rezoning to stand unless it can be shown that the decision had been an arbitrary and capricious one.

One judicial construct which is used in some states to control zoning changes is the "change or mistake rule." This rule required that a proponent of a rezoning show that there has been a change of physical circumstances in the neighborhood or mistake in the original zoning to justify a land use reclassification.[2] The result is that the burden of proof shifts to the one proposing the zoning change.[3]

If the original zoning were a mistake from the beginning, and clearly recognized as such, an application for a rezoning should be favorably regarded. In Eggebeen v. Sonnenburg[4] an area was zoned for single family dwellings and the property owner applied for multiple family zoning, which was granted. A major reason for the rezoning was that the soils in the area were unstable and the floating foundations required could be economically justified only if the more intensive use were permitted. Had the nature of the soils been known when the property was originally zoned, it probably would not have been zoned for single family dwellings. The original zoning constituted a mistake which essentially precluded all development. Such zoning was held unreasonable, because the court found the public interest would not be adversely affected by the rezoning.[5]

§ 6.4

1. Robinson v. Bloomfield Hills, 350 Mich. 425, 86 N.W.2d 166 (1957); Wait v. Scottsdale, 127 Ariz. 107, 618 P.2d 601 (1980); Pemberton v. Montgomery County, 275 Md. 363, 340 A.2d 240 (1975).

2. MacDonald v. Board of County Comm'rs for Prince George's County, 238 Md. 549, 210 A.2d 325 (1965), and Offutt v. Board of Zoning Appeals, 204 Md. 551, 105 A.2d 219 (1954). See generally, Burke,

Change or Mistake Rule in Maryland, 125 Am.U.L.Rev. 631 (1976).

3. Pattey v. Board of County Comm'rs, 271 Md. 352, 317 A.2d 142 (1974), Hughes v. Mayor & Comm'rs of City of Jackson, 296 So.2d 689 (Miss.1974); Roseta v. County of Washington, 254 Or. 161, 458 P.2d 405 (1969).

4. 239 Wis. 213, 1 N.W.2d 84 (1941).

5. Cf. MacDonald, supra n. 2, Barnes, J., dissenting. See also supra § 3.16.

A rezoning may also be proper when the existing zoning unreasonably burdens the property and is not necessary to safeguard the public interest. The court in Oka v. Cole [6] upheld a rezoning of property from single family to multiple residential when the property was located in an area where land costs rendered single family use economically undesirable and the public interest was not adversely affected by the change.

In recent years there has been some question whether a rezoning applied to a particular parcel is a legislative or an adjudicative action. Dissatisfaction with the results of judicial deference spread, and courts began looking into zoning decisions by local officials in greater detail. Some commentators have questioned the conventional wisdom of deferring to local legislative bodies and suggested that zoning amendments be treated as a series of administrative adjudications rather than general legislative actions.[7]

Fasano v. Board of County Commissioners,[8] a landmark Oregon case, incorporated the idea that the quasi-judicial nature of a rezoning places the burden on the challenger to show why the comprehensive plan should be changed.[9] Although the statutory posture of the case differs from those in other states, nevertheless, the Fasano rationale has been adopted in several jurisdictions.[10]

In Fasano, a statutorily mandated comprehensive plan was effective for the county, but the commissioners had approved a zoning change which would allow mobile homes in an area zoned single family residential. The plaintiffs in the case were homeowners who opposed the rezoning. The Oregon Supreme Court indicated that ordinances setting down general policies without regard for a specific parcel were usually exercises of legislative authority and subject to limited review, such as the county's comprehensive plan. It then stated that determination whether the permissible use of a specific piece of property should be changed was an exercise of judicial authority, subject to a different test. The court reasoned that local authorities were not the equivalent of state or national legislatures, thus not entitled to the "shield" of the separation of powers doctrine.[11] Individual ordinances

---

6. 145 So.2d 233 (Fla.1962), opinion conformed 145 So.2d 900 (1962).

7. E.g. Krasnowiecki, Basic System of Land Use Control, in the New Zoning 3 (N. Marcus & M. Groves, ed. 1970).

8. 264 Or. 574, 507 P.2d 23 (1973).

9. Id. at 586, 507 P.2d at 28.

10. Washington, Parkridge v. Seattle, 89 Wn.2d 454, 573 P.2d 359 (1978); Colorado, Snyder v. Lakewood, 189 Colo. 421, 543 P.2d 371 (1975); Margolis v. District Ct., In and For the County of Arapahoe, 638 P.2d 297 (Colo. 1981) (rejecting Fasano classification for referenda); Montana, Lowe v. Missoula, 165 Mont. 38, 525 P.2d 551 (1974); Nevada,

Forman v. Eagle Thrifty Drugs & Markets, Inc., 89 Nev. 533, 516 P.2d 1234 (1973); Cooper v. Board of County Comm'rs, 101 Idaho 407, 614 P.2d 947 (1980); Woodland Hills Conservation Ass'n v. Jackson, 443 So.2d 1173 (Miss. 1983). See also Kropf v. Sterling Heights, 391 Mich. 139, 215 N.W.2d 179 (1974) (Levin, J., concurring). For courts rejecting Fasano, see Arnel Dev. Co. v. Costa Mesa, 28 Cal.3d 511, 169 Cal.Rptr. 904, 620 P.2d 565 (1980); Quinn v. Town of Dodgeville, 120 Wis.2d 304, 354 N.W.2d 747 (App. 1984), affirmed 122 Wis.2d 570, 364 N.W.2d 149 (1985).

11. 264 Or. 574, 580, 507 P.2d 23, 26 (1973). See Menges v. Board of County

applied by administrative decision to specific situations were analogous to judicial decisions which applied statutes to each unique set of facts, rendering them quasi-judicial decisions from which an aggrieved party might appeal.[12]

Problems with Fasano stem from the fact that it is difficult to draw a line between legislative action and quasi-judicial determination. Recently in Neuburger v. Portland,[13] the Oregon Supreme Court attempted to deal with the issue when the city rezoned a 601-acre tract to a more intensive single family residential density. Land use decisions were found to be quasi-judicial when a particular action by local government is aimed at a relatively small number of persons regardless of parcel size, and when that action also involves the application of existing policy to a specific set of facts with a decision as the result.[14]

Neuburger [15] also revised Fasano by abandoning the requirement that a challenger show that other properties were not as suitable as his own for the proposed development. Consistency with the comprehensive plan is still required.[16]

Fasano cites with approval a line of Washington state cases which use the doctrine of "appearance of fairness" in zoning appeals cases. In Fleming v. Tacoma,[17] the state supreme court reasoned that because a rezoning decision balances the rights of both proponents and opponents of a zoning change, the process was basically adjudicatory. This justified an exception to the rule proscribing court intervention into legislative matters. Zoning decisions must not only be fair but *appear* to be fair, as well.[18] To give courts more specific guidelines for structuring their review of rezonings, the Oregon attorney general issued an opinion summarizing procedural requirements.[19] These generally parallel procedures for review of administrative decisions by appropriate courts.[20]

Commissioners of Jackson County, 606 P.2d 681 (Or.App. 1980).

12. Id. at 580, 507 P.2d at 27. Compare with Kropf, supra n. 10, (Levin, J., concurring).

13. 288 Or. 155, 603 P.2d 771 (1979), rehearing denied 288 Or. 585, 607 P.2d 722 (1980).

14. Id. at 161, 603 P.2d at 775.

15. 288 Or. 155, 603 P.2d 771 (1979), rehearing denied 288 Or. 585, 607 P.2d 722 (1980).

16. Id. at 170, 603 P.2d at 779. The other two requirements of the test are: (2) conformity to standards for planning and land-use regulation of the enabling legislation and (3) showing of public need for the change in question. Fasano, 507 P.2d at 27–29.

17. 81 Wn.2d 292, 502 P.2d 327 (1972). Compare Quinn v. Town of Dodgeville, 120 Wis.2d 304, 354 N.W.2d 747 (App. 1984), affirmed 122 Wis.2d 570, 364 N.W.2d 149 (1985).

18. Id. at 299, 502 P.2d at 331. (Emphasis supplied).

19. Oregon Attorney General Opinion, no. 7062 (Mar. 26, 1974). See also Note, Land Use: Standard for Amendments, 57 Ore.L.Rev. 463 (1978).

20. Compare, e.g. 5 U.S.C.A. § 551 et seq. (Federal Administrative Procedure Act).

The Fasano doctrine was adopted by the American Law Institute's Model Land Development Code,[21] and some states have followed Oregon's lead in the rethinking of the manner in which rezonings are viewed.[22] For example, in Golden v. Overland Park,[23] the court adopted the theory that although zoning was largely a matter of policy (in Kansas), when it involved a single tract of land, the decision to change zoning involved the same kinds of determinations as in judicial resolution of issues of law and fact. It then used certain criteria to determine the reasonableness of zoning decisions.[24] It is interesting to note that in this decision, zoning was considered a matter of policy whereas in Fasano a comprehensive zoning plan was in effect and any change was required to be consistent with the plan.

Fasano may be criticized as being anti-growth or simply as rationalization for judicial infringement into legislative prerogative. After having weighed the dangers of making desirable change more difficult against the dangers of almost irresistable pressures that can be asserted by private economic interests on local government, however, the court concluded that the latter dangers were more to be feared. The Fasano doctrine is not the majority rule in this country and is not widely followed, but it raises important issues which will have to be addressed in the future as more states adopt comprehensive planning and feel development pressure begin to affect the zoning process.

 WESTLAW REFERENCES
presumption /2 valid*** /s rezon***
change mistake /2 rule /s rezon***
fasano +s "board of county commissioner"
414k194 /p "burden of proof"
zon*** rezon*** /s appear! /2 fair

III. VARIANCES

§ 6.5 Variances: In General

Perhaps variances are more often used and misused than the other types of administrative relief. They are intended to alleviate a situation in which for no public reason, zoning for an area more stringently burdens one parcel of land than others. It also provides a "relief valve," so that zoning, which would otherwise be unconstitutional as applied, can be made constitutional. Sometimes it is used to avoid the evils of spot zoning. Strictly construed, the classic formulation of the statute enabling the granting of variances [1] does not include the latter two rationales, that zoning can be unconstitutionally applied without

21. A.L.I. Model Land Development Code, § 2–312(2) and notes (1975).

22. See supra note 10.

23. 224 Kan. 591, 584 P.2d 130 (1978).

24. Id. at 601, 584 P.2d at 138.

§ 6.5

1. See, supra § 6.3.

necessarily qualifying the land for a variance, and, while spot zoning may be invalid, a variance may not be the appropriate solution.[2]

Variances are generally of two kinds: bulk or area variances which include those granted for height and minor departures from the ordinance, and use variances, which usually involve more substantial changes. The typical enabling act does not separately authorize two different kinds of variances, though some statutes, ordinances and courts do not allow use variances, particularly for large sized parcels.[3]

The criteria for obtaining a variance are rigorous.[4] If the courts really superintended their issuance, more than ninety percent of the variances granted would probably be found invalid. When courts supervise their issuance administrative bodies may eventually limit the issuance of variances, but the educational effort involved is considerable when there are hundreds of boards in a state and the boards are composed of a changing body of laymen. Where the courts do not superintend the issuance of variances, one would expect many to be granted illegally, so that an attorney should seek one for a client if practice dictates it will be approved, regardless of the law. For example until Cow Hollow Improvement Club v. Board of Permit Appeals,[5] a case decided late in 1966, neither courts[6] nor commentators[7] could find a California appellate case which overturned the issuance of a variance. Illegal issuance is a widespread phenomenon nationwide.[8]

The precise formulation of the standards that must be met before a variance is issued vary among the enabling acts and ordinances, though most formulations are similar to provisions in the Standard Act.[9] The standards generally fall into three groups. A variance is proper only if there is: 1) no adverse effect on public, 2) no adverse effect on neighbors, and 3) the property has unique characteristics which make it

2. See, Bryden, Zoning: Rigid, Flexible or Fluid? 44 J.Urb.L. 287 (1966); Ford, Guidelines for Judicial Review in Zoning Variance Cases, 58 Mass.I.Q. 15 (1973); Rosenzweig, From Euclid to Eastlake: Toward a Unified Approach to Zoning Change Requests, 82 Dick.L.Rev. 59 (1977); Shapiro, The Zoning Variance Power: Constructive in Theory, Destructive in Practice, 29 Md.L.Rev. 3 (1969); Comment, Variances and Parcel Rezoning, 60 Neb.L.Rev. 81 (1981).

3. See infra § 6.10.

4. Criteria may be rigorous but not always adhered to. See generally Newbern, Zoning Flexibility: Bored of Adjustment, 30 Ark.L.Rev. 491 (1976).

5. 245 Cal.App.2d 160, 53 Cal.Rptr. 610 (1966).

6. Allen v. Humboldt County Bd. of Supervisors, 241 Cal.App.2d 158, 50 Cal.Rptr. 444 (1966).

7. D. Hagman, J. Larson & C. Martin, California Zoning Practice § 7.54 (1969); Gaylord, Zoning: Variances, Exceptions and Conditional Use Permits in California, 5 U.C.L.A.L.Rev. 181 (1958).

8. Dukeminier & Stapleton, The Zoning Board of Adjustment: A Case Study in Misrule, 50 Ky.L.J. 273 (1962); Shapiro, The Zoning Variance Power supra n. 2, Comment, Zoning: Variances Administration in Alameda County, 50 Calif.L.Rev. 101 (1962); Note, The Effect of Statutory Prerequisites on Decisions of Boards of Zoning Appeals, 1 Ind.Legal Forum 398 (1968); Comment, The Legislative-Adjudicative Distinction in California Land Use Regulation: A Suggested Response to Arnel Development Co. v. City of Costa Mesa, 34 Hastings L.J. 425 (1982); Note, Zoning Variation Administration in Vermont, 8 Vt L.Rev. 371 (1983).

9. See § 6.3 supra.

eligible for a variance. All standards must be met.[10] Courts are beginning to require that findings be made by the board of adjustment (or other governmental group charged with authority to grant variances) supporting their decisions.[11] The reviewing court must determine whether substantial evidence supports the findings, and ultimately, the conclusion that requirements for a variance have been satisfied.[12] Some courts have taken the position that in land use regulation the burden of proof shifts to the party attempting to retain zoning consistent with the comprehensive plan or existing zoning classification of the area.[13]

 WESTLAW REFERENCES

variance /s illegal /s issuance grant!

variance /s "unique characteristic" (adverse* * /2 neighbor
        public)

§ 6.6 Effect on Public

Enabling acts and ordinances often require that the variance not be issued if issuance would be contrary to the public interest, safety, health and welfare; would contravene the intent or spirit of the ordinance; or would have an adverse effect on the master plan. These provisions have overlapping meanings, and may be little more than a restatement of the general rule that granting of zoning variances, like other aspects of zoning, must be in the public interest. Sometimes the public interest test can be met by showing that the proposed use would be advantageous to the public, such as the convenience of a shopping center to an area.[1] It may also be met in cases in which a nonconforming use can be changed to a more nearly conforming use if a variance is given.[2] The public interest test may be met by a finding that the property taxes will increase. Generally, there need be no showing of an affirmative benefit to the public, but as the language of an ordinance usually indicates, only a showing that the public is not harmed by the variance.

It is not within the spirit or intent of a zoning ordinance to grant variances in a wholesale manner, or to permit one variance which may lead to another, eventually debilitating the entire zoning plan.[3]

10. Cow Hollow Improvement Club v. Board of Permit Appeals, 245 Cal.App.2d 160, 53 Cal.Rptr. 610 (1966).

11. See, e.g. Topanga Ass'n for a Scenic Community v. County of Los Angeles, 11 Cal.3d 506, 113 Cal.Rptr. 836, 522 P.2d 12 (1974); Fleming v. Tacoma, 81 Wn.2d 292, 502 P.2d 327 (1972) (appearance of fairness requires findings on the record.)

12. See also supra § 6.4.

13. See Board of Supervisors v. Snell Construction Corp., 214 Va. 655, 202 S.E.2d 889 (1974), accord, DeKalb County v.

Flynn, 243 Ga. 679, 256 S.E.2d 362 (1979) (a variant of the change or mistake rule; in these two cases it works to the benefit of the developer.) See also Comment, Burden of Proof in Land Use Regulations, 8 Fla. State U.L.Rev. 499 (1980).

§ 6.6

1. Ward v. Scott, 16 N.J. 16, 105 A.2d 851 (1954).

2. See supra § 4.31.

3. Heller v. Zoning Bd. of Adjustment, 404 Pa. 8, 171 A.2d 44 (1961).

Neither should a zoning ordinance permit commercial intrusions into residential areas by variance,[4] for that might violate the requirement that neighboring property not be adversely affected.

 WESTLAW REFERENCES

di,sy(variance /s "public interest" safety health welfare)

414k490

find 105 a.2d 851

variance /s "continuing right"

§ 6.7   Effect on Neighborhood

Even if there is no adverse effect on the public, or even if there is a public benefit, neighboring property may be adversely affected by a variance. If so, the variance should not be issued.[1] As a matter of practical administration, variances are seldom issued when a large number of neighbors appear and vigorously oppose, though the number of protestors and the intensity of the objections should not dictate the results.[2] Some statutes and ordinances provide that if neighbors protest, a variance can be granted only by an extraordinary majority vote of the board.[3]

A typical ordinance might provide that a variance should not be granted if it would "alter the essential character of the neighborhood." The test might not be met if, for example, a commercial use were permitted in a residential zone,[4] however, a residential zone will not be altered by a commercial variance if, because of previous commercial nonconforming uses, variances or special uses, the neighborhood is no longer totally residential in character.[5] The test may not be met if the variance would result in depreciation of property values in a given neighborhood.[6] A variance permitting a use that generates an increase in traffic may not meet the neighborhood test.[7] The neighborhood test is usually stated in terms of the effect on property, though the standard sometimes provides that issuance of a variance should not adversely affect the health or safety of persons residing in or working in the neighborhood.

The purpose of a variance is not to confer special privileges on an individual property owner, that is, it is employed to relieve hardship,

4. Cary v. Board of Appeals of Worcester, 340 Mass. 748, 166 N.E.2d 690 (1960).

§ 6.7

1. Anon v. Coral Gables, 336 So.2d 420 (Fla. 3d D.C.A. 1976).

2. Minney v. Azusa, 164 Cal.App.2d 12, 330 P.2d 255 (1958), appeal dismissed 359 U.S. 436, 79 S.Ct. 941, 3 L.Ed.2d 932 (1959).

3. See § 5.3 supra.

4. Wilson v. Borough of Mountainside, 42 N.J. 426, 201 A.2d 540 (1964); Dubin v. Wich, 120 N.J.L. 469, 200 A. 751 (Sup.Ct.

1938); Otto v. Steinhilber, 282 N.Y. 71, 24 N.E.2d 851 (1939), reargument denied 282 N.Y. 681, 26 N.E.2d 811 (1940); Bellamy v. Board of Appeals of City of Rochester, 32 Misc.2d 520, 223 N.Y.S.2d 1017 (1962).

5. Nelson v. Board of Zoning Appeals, 240 Ind. 212, 162 N.E.2d 449 (1959).

6. Greenwich Gas Co. v. Tuthill, 113 Conn. 684, 155 A. 850 (1931).

7. Corbett v. Zoning Board of Appeals, 283 App.Div. 282, 128 N.Y.S.2d 12 (1954).

not to confer benefits not enjoyed by neighboring property. For example, property zoned large lot single family is not entitled to a variance for multiple family use but only to a variance for a small lot single family use, that being the zoning in the area.[8]

Conditions

As distinguished from a rezoning, in which the legislative body may be forced to either grant or deny the application, and may not choose to limit the rezoning by contract or imposition of conditions,[9] the variance can be granted with imposition of conditions designed to remove any special privilege or adverse effect on the public or the neighborhood. To that end, the Standard Act provides that a board "may . . . subject to appropriate conditions and safeguards, make special exceptions to the terms of the ordinance in harmony with its general purpose and intent . . . ."[10] Even where the statute and ordinance do not confer such authority, the power to condition variances may be implied. The issuance of a variance is largely discretionary, and the power to grant variances is not limited to what the applicant requests.[11] Conversely, when standards are clearly met, there may be a right to a variance, or at least to some relief under one of the "zoning forms of action."[12] Conditions that are irrelevant to zoning or do not relieve the hardship may be invalid.[13]

Time conditions may be imposed on a variance. One kind is primarily designed to force utilization of the variance. A variance is not a rezoning, may not be accurately noted in zoning records and should not be granted prematurely, so if the variance is not immediately utilized, it makes sense to have it terminate after a period of time, e.g., six months.[14] Since conditions may change in the future such that a variance is no longer necessary or appropriate, the variance may be limited to a term of years, and then be subject to review again.[15] The term may be related to an event, for example, a variance may be issued for a commercial use in a holding zone, which use must be terminated if the surrounding area were later developed for residential uses. A variance issued on the condition that a restaurant in a residential zone be closed during certain hours of the evening has been held valid.[16]

8. Hamer v. Town of Ross, 59 Cal.2d 776, 31 Cal.Rptr. 335, 382 P.2d 375 (1963).

9. See § 5.5 supra.

10. Standard Act § 7. The term special exceptions in this portion of the Standard Act is a generic term that includes variances; see § 6.3 supra.

11. Everson Elec. Co. v. Zoning Bd. of Adjustment, 395 Pa. 168, 149 A.2d 63 (1959).

12. See § 6.1 supra.

13. See Strine, The Use of Conditions in Land-Use Control, 67 Dick.L.Rev. 109

(1963); Note, Zoning Amendments and Variances Subject to Conditions, 12 Syracuse L.Rev. 230 (1960).

14. Ambrosio v. Zoning Bd. of Appeals, 196 Misc. 1005, 96 N.Y.S.2d 380 (Sup.Ct. 1949).

15. Guenther v. Zoning Bd. of Review of City of Warwick, 85 R.I. 37, 125 A.2d 214 (1956).

16. Montgomery County v. Mossburg, 228 Md. 555, 180 A.2d 851 (1962); Annot., 99 A.L.R.2d 227 (1965).

The condition applies to the property rather than the applicant. It would be improper to issue a variance on the condition that the property remain under the applicant's ownership.[17] Such a decision is consistent with the theory that zoning relates to land not to ownership of land, and that the hardship to be relieved by the variance is hardship with respect to the property rather than to the owner.[18]

If the conditions are unrelated to exercise of the zoning power or the police power, they may be held invalid. Zoning deals with offstreet parking requirements, for example, so it would be proper to condition a variance for a funeral parlor by requiring provision of adequate on-site parking space.[19] A variance for a yard to store construction vehicles might be conditioned on the dedication of an easement for a road along the front of the property to alleviate increased traffic congestion, a matter relating to the purposes of zoning.[20] On the other hand, the zoning board may not have the power to condition the issuance of a variance for a laundromat by requiring that an attendant be present at all times. Such a requirement may be held invalid on the ground that such a regulation is a legislative matter[21] or is not a zoning matter, thus it is unauthorized.

 WESTLAW REFERENCES

variance /s neighbor /s oppos! affect*** protest*** challeng***

variance /s alter! +3 "essential character" +5 neighborhood

variance /s hardship /s self-created self-imposed

414k496

414k497

Conditions

di,sy(variance /s grant! /s condition)

414k501

ambrosio +2 "zoning board"

zoning /p variance /s condition /s invalid

§ 6.8   Characteristics of Property

While the effect on the public or on neighbors is sometimes dispositive, many cases turn on the ground that there are neither extraordinary or exceptional characteristics, nor unique problems or special conditions which create unnecessary hardship, practical difficulties or destroy property values.[1] The terms unique, special, exceptional and

---

17. Cohn v. County Bd. of Supervisors, 135 Cal.App.2d 180, 286 P.2d 836 (1955).

18. See § 6.9 infra.

19. Woodbury v. Zoning Bd. of Review of City of Warwick, 78 R.I. 319, 82 A.2d 164 (1951).

20. Bringle v. Board of Supervisors, 54 Cal.2d 86, 4 Cal.Rptr. 493, 351 P.2d 765 (1960).

21. DeVille Homes, Inc. v. Michaelis, 201 N.Y.S.2d 129 (1960).

§ 6.8

1. A finding that the characteristics of the property are not such as to qualify for a variance does not necessarily mean that the existing zoning is proper. It may only mean that the zoning should be attacked directly in court as being invalid as applied or that an amendment or a special permit

extraordinary suggest that a variance is proper only when the property is somehow different from other property, particularly adjacent property. A legislative act is the appropriate vehicle for a change which would affect a large number of properties.

If the land is physically unique, the classic circumstances for a variance exist. Setback lines on the sides of a triangular lot, which limited the useable space of a lot to 10 square feet, rendered it clearly unique, thus entitled to a variance from the setback requirements.[2] A lot crossed by a deep ravine was unique enough to justify a variance.[3] Depending on the circumstances, however, even that characteristic might not be unique enough. In Topanga Association for a Scenic Community v. County of Los Angeles,[4] the planning commission granted a variance which would allow a mobile home park on 28 acres in Topanga Canyon, already zoned light agricultural and large lot single family residential. The matter was appealed to the court and ultimately reached the California supreme court which reversed granting of the variance. Despite the fact that the plot was of rugged terrain and contained three stream beds, the developers were unable to show that the property was unlike neighboring parcels. It was not enough, either, to show that there was a need in the area for the proposed type of development or that it would provide a much needed fire break. The court concluded that the data did not constitute a sufficient showing to satisfy the statutory variance requirements, regardless of alleged community needs.[5] The court added that granting a variance for a 28-acre parcel was suspect in that it might not be sufficiently unrepresentative of the realty in the area, and approval of such requests would work a radical alteration of the zoning classification.

If a parcel is not unique but is disadvantaged by a zoning restriction equally with other property in the area, issuance of a variance is improper.[6] For example, if all property in an area were zoned residential so that a particular lot is fungible with the rest, it would not be entitled to a variance for a commercial use.[7] Just because property is adjacent to property zoned for business purposes does not constitute a unique enough circumstance to justify a variance from residential zoning if adjacent property were also zoned residential.[8] A variance was improperly granted to permit a funeral parlor in a residential district because the property was not distinguishable from other proper-

---

is the proper form of action. See § 6.1 supra.

2. Hoshour v. County of Contra Costa, 203 Cal.App.2d 602, 21 Cal.Rptr. 714 (1962). See also City of Little Rock v. Kaufman, 249 Ark. 530, 460 S.W.2d 88 (1970), Hankin v. Zoning Hearing Bd., 35 Pa.Commw. 164, 384 A.2d 1386 (1978).

3. Ferry v. Kownacki, 396 Pa. 283, 152 A.2d 456 (1959).

4. 11 Cal.3d 506, 113 Cal.Rptr. 836, 522 P.2d 12 (1974).

5. Id. at 520, 113 Cal.Rptr. at 845, 522 P.2d at 21.

6. Jasy Corp. v. Board of Adjustment, 413 Pa. 563, 198 A.2d 854 (1964).

7. Lee v. Board of Adjustment, 226 N.C. 107, 37 S.E.2d 128 (1946).

8. Bellamy v. Board of Appeals of City of Rochester, 32 Misc.2d 520, 223 N.Y.S.2d 1017 (1962).

ty residentially zoned.[9] If a lot is zoned residential, however, and all surrounding uses are commercial, the test of uniqueness may be met.[10] An apartment building may be located near several public garages justifying a variance from off-street parking requirements for the building.[11] In transitional or deteriorating areas property owners often apply for variances, the issuance of which may be upheld.[12]

WESTLAW REFERENCES

di,sy(variance /s property land parcel /5 special unique exceptional extraordinary)

414k494

variance /s setback /2 requirement /s unique

find 92 n.e.2d 903

lot parcel property land /3 residential /s use /5 surround***
/5 commercial

§ 6.9　Unnecessary Hardship

The Standard Act provides that a variance is authorized where the zoning "will result in unnecessary hardship." Countless judicial opinions have considered application of the phrase unnecessary hardship, which appears in almost all enabling statutes and ordinances. A zoning ordinance almost always constitutes some hardship because it restricts uses and sometimes reduces property values. Those are necessary hardships which must be suffered to gain the overall benefit from zoning.

There is some confusion whether hardship is a separate standard or is established when the other three standards are met. For example, if an applicant for a variance is able to show: (1) the public would not be adversely affected, (2) issuance would not adversely affect the neighbors, and (3) the property is unique, he may have established unnecessary hardship. If the three tests are met, the case is a proper one for a variance. Since the first two criteria are met, the public would not be hurt by the variance. If no one could be hurt, the present zoning is unnecessary, and regulation is justified only if necessary. On the other hand, perhaps the applicant has only shown hardship and in addition must show that the hardship is unnecessary.[1] Suppose a property

9. Clark v. Board of Zoning Appeals, 301 N.Y. 86, 92 N.E.2d 903 (1950), motion denied 301 N.Y. 681, 95 N.E.2d 44 (1950), cert. denied 340 U.S. 933, 71 S.Ct. 498, 95 L.Ed. 673 (1951).

10. City of Mobile v. Sorrell, 271 Ala. 468, 124 So.2d 463 (1960). An Amendment covering all the property may be a better "form of action" in this case. See § 6.2 supra.

11. Siller v. Board of Supervisors, 58 Cal.2d 479, 25 Cal.Rptr. 73, 375 P.2d 41 (1962).

12. Parsons v. Board of Zoning Appeals, 140 Conn. 290, 99 A.2d 149 (1953). However, some courts more properly reverse issuance on the ground that an amendment, or a direct attack in court on the constitutionality of the restriction is proper, since the problem is not unique. Reynolds v. Board of Appeals of Springfield, 335 Mass. 464, 140 N.E.2d 491 (1957).

§ 6.9

1. See, e.g., Levesque v. Hudson, 106 N.H. 470, 214 A.2d 553 (1965), overruled on other grounds by Winslow v. Town of Hold-

owner applies for a variance to make a commercial use of property zoned residential. The application meets all those criteria and might therefore be entitled to a variance. If the land as zoned could still enjoy a reasonable return if put to a residential use, however, he may not have established unnecessary hardship. He might be forced to prove that residential zoning is not a reasonable use for the property. There is language in the case law which supports a conclusion that unnecessary hardship is a separate standard to be met, but the matter is at best vague. Moreover, facts used to meet one standard often are the same as those used to meet other standards, so precision must sometimes yield to common sense. The number of separate standards may depend on the ordinance. For example, to obtain a variance in San Francisco, five standards must be met.[2]

Otto v. Steinhilber,[3] an early leading case, indicates that before a variance can be issued on the ground of unnecessary hardship it must be shown that the land as zoned cannot yield a reasonable return. The standard suggests more than an economic disadvantage or hardship must be shown. There must be hardship to the extent that no reasonable use of the property is possible or at least that adverse economic effect is substantial.[4]

Personal Hardship

One further aspect of the phrase unnecessary hardship has been added by judicial gloss, perhaps improperly. Administrative bodies and courts have sometimes personalized the variance, that is, its propriety

---

erness Planning Board, 125 N.H. 262, 480 A.2d 114 (1984).

2. San Francisco, Calif., City Planning Code § 302(d) (1964):

   1. That there are exceptional or extraordinary circumstances or conditions applying to the property involved, or to the intended use of the property, that do not apply generally to other property or uses in the same class of district;

   2. that owing to such exceptional or extraordinary circumstances the literal enforcement of specified provisions of the Code would result in practical difficulty or unnecessary hardship;

   3. that the variance is necessary for the preservation of a substantial property right of the petitioner possessed by other property in the same class of the district;

   4. that the granting of the variance will not be materially detrimental to the public welfare or materially injurious to the property or improvements in the vicinity; and

   5. that the granting of such variance will be in harmony with the general

purpose and intent of this Code and will not adversely effect the Master Plan.

3. 282 N.Y. 71, 24 N.E.2d 851 (1939), reargument denied 282 N.Y. 681, 26 N.E.2d 811 (1940). Cf. City of Coral Gables v. Geary, 383 So.2d 1127 (Fla. 3d D.C.A. 1980) (triangular lot a classic case for variance but denied because of self-created hardship.

4. Cf. Cresko Zoning Case, 400 Pa. 467, 162 A.2d 219 (1960), (hardship not substantial); Bellamy v. Board of Appeals of City of Rochester, 32 Misc.2d 520, 223 N.Y.S.2d 1017 (1962), without a variance there were still many uses for the property. Of course, a showing of no reasonable use of the property itself is not enough, for Otto v. Steinhilber also requires that the property be uniquely affected, see § 6.8 supra, and the variance will not alter the essential character of the locality. See § 6.7 supra. The public interest standard, see § 6.6 supra, is not stated as a separate test but more likely than not is subsumed under one of the other tests.

turns on the character of the owner rather than the nature of the property. Typically, ownership is not relevant to a zoning determination. Personal hardships are not usually held to entitle the owner to a variance because the hardship is unrelated to the property.

In some cases, however, the character of the owner is held to make a difference. For example, when property is purchased and the owners subsequently apply for a variance, it may be denied on the ground of self-induced hardship, which means that because the owners knew or should have known of the zoning of the property when purchased, they cannot establish unnecessary hardship.[5] Similarly, a variance has sometimes been denied to an option holder, because he cannot show any hardship other than the loss of the option price if the variance is denied.[6]

Courts which refuse to personalize the hardship or indicate some other reason for denial more consistently parallel the general rule that zoning is a regulation of property, not of personal conduct. Therefore, purchase with knowledge is not considered a bar to a variance by some courts.[7] If a court were compelled to deny the variance in such a situation, rather than find no hardship, it might hold that grant of a variance is discretionary, and one who buys with knowledge does not have the equities on his side.[8] Since one who buys property unsatisfactorily zoned may purchase for a lesser price, perhaps he should not be entitled to the windfall which might be generated by a variance.

The suggestion that equity can be the basis for denial conflicts with the theory that a variance is a matter of right if the tests are met, so the courts considering equities may be as wrong (or right) as those personalizing hardship.[9]

In one situation, personalizing the variance may be proper. When an applicant is the person who caused the condition requiring the variance, it would hardly be proper to compel the issuance of a variance if he were to build in violation of the zoning ordinance and then claim hardship entitling him to a variance. If that were the rule, persons who violate the ordinance could do so with impunity.

Many enabling acts and ordinances provide for the issuance of a variance if practical difficulty exists as well as unnecessary hardship. Most courts consider the terms to be interchangeable. The New York

---

5. Clark v. Board of Zoning Appeals, 301 N.Y. 86, 92 N.E.2d 903 (1950), motion denied 301 N.Y. 681, 95 N.E.2d 44 (1950), cert. denied 340 U.S. 933, 71 S.Ct. 498, 95 L.Ed. 673 (1951); Bellamy v. Board of Appeals of City of Rochester, 32 Misc.2d 520, 223 N.Y.S.2d 1017 (1962); see also Abel v. Zoning Bd. of Appeals, 172 Conn. 286, 374 A.2d 227 (1977); Beinz v. Dayton, 29 Or. App. 761, 566 P.2d 904 (1977).

6. Lee v. Board of Adjustment, 226 N.C. 107, 37 S.E.2d 128 (1946). The problem could be avoided by having the owner or

optionor or optionee apply. See Welch v. Nashua, 108 N.H. 92, 227 A.2d 600 (1967).

7. Wilson v. Borough of Mountainside, 42 N.J. 426, 201 A.2d 540 (1964).

8. Searles v. Darling, 46 Del. 263, 83 A.2d 96 (1951).

9. In a strict sense, one never has a right to a variance for his property except when the zoning is unconstitutional as applied and no other "form of action" is available.

courts have developed a rule that practical difficulty entitles an owner to an area variance, but unnecessary hardship must be established to obtain a use variance.[10] The elements necessary to prove practical difficulty are not well defined, though the test is clearly less rigorous than for unnecessary hardship.

WESTLAW REFERENCES

di,sy(variance /s "unnecessary hardship")

414k496

variance /s "unnecessary hardship" /s "reasonable return" "no reasonable use"

Personal Hardship

variance /s "personal hardship"

414k497

variance /s "practical difficulty"

§ 6.10   Large Parcel Use Variances

The Standard Act provides for variances, inter alia, when special conditions exist and the spirit of the ordinance can be preserved. The language may suggest that a variance is appropriate use only for minor departures from height or bulk regulations. A use variance may have almost the same consequences as a rezoning. For example, if a shopping center were permitted in a residential area by variance, the consequences are almost as significant as if the property were rezoned commercial. Therefore, some ordinances and some courts refuse to authorize use variances on the ground that an amendment should be sought instead.[1]

When use variances are not absolutely prohibited, there is a tendency not to grant them for large parcels, again on the ground that a rezoning amendment is more appropriate.[2] When large parcels are rezoned, courts are not apt to find illegal spot zoning.[3]

WESTLAW REFERENCES

find 96 so.2d 784

---

10. Village of Bronxville v. Francis, 1 A.D.2d 236, 150 N.Y.S.2d 906 (1956), order affirmed 1 N.Y.2d 839, 153 N.Y.S.2d 220, 135 N.E.2d 724 (1956); Bellamy v. Board of Appeals of the City of Rochester, 32 Misc. 2d 520, 223 N.Y.S.2d 1017 (1962). See also City & Borough of Juneau v. Thibodeau, 595 P.2d 626 (Alaska 1979).

§ 6.10

1. Josephson v. Autrey, 96 So.2d 784 (Fla.1957), accord Elwyn v. Miami, 113 So. 2d 849 (Fla. 3d D.C.A.) cert. denied 116 So. 2d 773 (Fla.1959).

2. Catholic Cemeteries Ass'n Zoning Case, 379 Pa. 516, 109 A.2d 537 (1954).

3. See § 5.4 supra.

IV.   SPECIAL PERMITS

§ 6.11   Special Permits: In General

Section 7 of the Standard State Zoning Enabling Act [1] provides that the Board of Adjustment shall have the power to "hear and decide special exceptions to the terms of the ordinance upon which such board is required to pass under such ordinance." [2] Under that kind of statutory authority, a board may issue a special permit for those uses listed in the ordinance as special or conditional, only if conditions described in the ordinance are met.

Distinguishing Features

"Special" refers primarily to the type of use rather than to the uniqueness of the property, as with a variance.[3] For example, an airport has such special characteristics that many ordinances do not list it as an absolutely permitted use in any zone but rather indicate it may be permitted in a given zone under circumstances stated in the ordinance. Other uses customarily subject to special permits include churches,[4] recreational facilities,[5] and schools, particularly private schools.[6]

Requirements for obtaining a permit as stated in an ordinance may be more specific or more general than standards used to determine the propriety of a variance, but there is no requirement that unnecessary hardship be shown.[7] Generally, however, the special permit is not issued or is conditioned such that neither the public [8] nor neighboring property owners [9] will be unduly affected in an adverse manner.

The special permit differs from a rezoning. It is issued for a particular use, e.g., a supermarket of a certain size, location, required parking, required screening, etc. A rezoning of property from residential to commercial would permit a supermarket but would also permit use of the property for any other commercial use allowed in that zone. Issuance of a special permit does not change the underlying zone classification.

§ 6.11

1. U.S. Dept. of Commerce, (rev. ed. 1926).

2. Id.

3. Mayflower Prop. v. Fort Lauderdale, 137 So.2d 849 (Fla. 2d D.C.A.1962); City of St. Petersburg v. Schweitzer, 297 So.2d 74 (Fla. 2d D.C.A.1974), cert. denied 308 So.2d 114 (1975).

4. See, e.g., State ex rel. Synod of Ohio of United Lutheran Church in America v. Joseph, 139 Ohio St. 229, 39 N.E.2d 515 (1942).

5. Kotrich v. County of Du Page, 19 Ill. 2d 181, 166 N.E.2d 601 (1960), appeal dismissed 364 U.S. 475, 81 S.Ct. 243, 5 L.Ed.2d 221 (1960), rehearing denied 365 U.S. 805, 81 S.Ct. 466, 5 L.Ed.2d 463 (1961).

6. Archbishop O'Hara's Appeal, 389 Pa. 35, 131 A.2d 587 (1957). See also §§ 4.15–4.17. Cf. L'Hote v. New Orleans, 177 U.S. 587, 20 S.Ct. 788, 44 L.Ed. 899 (1900).

7. See § 6.9 supra.

8. See § 6.6 supra.

9. See § 6.7 supra.

Growth in Use, Validity

The widespread use of special permits is one of the reasons for evolution of zoning to "nonzoning." Zoning was once called districting, which meant zones were created and applied to land in a comprehensive fashion. When an ordinance provides for numerous special permits, decisions may be made on an ad hoc, or discretionary, basis and districting becomes less evident.[10]

If almost every use were handled by special permit, courts would be likely to invalidate the scheme. In Rockhill v. Township of Chesterfield[11] a leading case, the entire township was zoned for agricultural and residential uses. No other use was possible without issuance of a special permit. The court found the ordinance to be antithetical to zoning, and beyond the scope of the enabling statute since the zoning was neither uniform nor comprehensive. It was instead piecemeal and spot zoning, lacking in standards and unconstitutional. Even the liberal California courts have held such broad use of special permits invalid.[12] A special permit is not spot zoning, technically, for there is no rezoning. If the standards are adequate and written into the ordinance, there is no reason to compel land uses to be controlled by districting rather than a case by case regulatory scheme.

The special permit may be more necessary and therefore more acceptable to the courts when used in connection with interim[13] or hold[14] zoning.[15] During times of study and decision concerning permanent zoning for an area or land unintensively used for which patterns of development have not become clear, it makes sense to use special permits for all but the least intensive uses. The special permit is also used in connection with planned unit developments which suggest a rather large scale yet intimately integrated development. Lot-by-lot Euclidian zoning may be too rigid for such development.

WESTLAW REFERENCES
"standard state zoning enabling Act" /s special /2 permit exception

10. See generally Arnebergh, The Functions and Duties of a Board of Zoning Adjustment, 1 Institute on Planning & Zoning 109 (1960); Craig, Particularized Zoning: Alterations While You Wait, 1 Institute on Planning & Zoning 153 (1960); Mandelker, Delegation of Power and Function in Zoning Administration, 1963 Wash.U.L.Q. 60; Note, The Use and Abuse of the Special Permit in Zoning Law, 35 Brooklyn L. Review 258 (1969); Nichols, Powers and Duties of the Zoning Board of Adjustment, 1975 Plan. Zoning & Eminent Domain Inst. 121; Comment, The Legislative-Adjudicative Distinction in California Land Use Regulation: A Suggested Response to Arnel Development Co. v. City of Costa Mesa, 34 Hastings L.J. 425 (1982); Note, Zoning Variation Administration in Vermont, 8 Vt.L.Rev. 371 (1983).

11. 23 N.J. 117, 128 A.2d 473 (1957).

12. People v. Perez, 214 Cal.App.2d Supp. 881, 29 Cal.Rptr. 781 (App.Dept. 1963). See also Board of Supervisors v. Southland Corp., 224 Va. 514, 297 S.E.2d 718 (1982).

13. See § 3.13 supra.

14. See § 4.12 supra.

15. See Mang v. County of Santa Barbara, 182 Cal.App.2d 93, 5 Cal.Rptr. 724 (1960).

Distinquishing Features

special /2 use permit /s church school airport "shopping center"
"special permit" /s requirement standard
"special permit" /s zon*** 12 class!

Growth in Use, Validity

rockhill +s "township of chesterfield"

§ 6.12   Standards

Since the special permit is authorized by almost all enabling acts and ordinances, use of the device is not always ultra vires. Typically, when its use is held invalid, it is due to the lack of standards for guiding administrative discretion. Standards are the terms or conditions listed in an ordinance that must be found before a permit will issue. For example, an ordinance might provide that airports are permitted only if a tract of 200 acres is available, the flight path is not over any areas zoned for multi-family use, there are no schools under the flight path and there is a heavy industrial use buffer zone around the airport.

Kotrich v. County of Du Page,[1] a leading case, demonstrates that standards can be rather vague. The ordinance in that case provided for a limited number of special uses including public outdoor recreation centers in R–2, a single family zone. The ordinance indicated that the special uses were established "for the location of special classes of uses which are deemed desirable for the public welfare within a given district or districts, but which are potentially incompatible with typical uses herein permitted within them. . . . " That language was held to constitute a sufficient standard for permitting an infrequent, beneficial use such as a not-for-profit club which included a clubhouse, swimming pool, tennis courts and parking area.[2]

In Kotrich, the legislative body allowed the permit and the court held that precise standards need not apply to legislative bodies. Even if the legislative body wore an administrative hat rather than a legislative one, the court recognized that it may amend an ordinance. Therefore, some courts review such actions with deference.[3] Guidelines in an ordinance which provide for issuance of conditional use permits as long as the use meets ". . . minimum requirements adopted to promote the health, safety, morals, comfort, prosperity and general welfare of the town . . . " have been held sufficient for issuance of permits.[4]

§ 6.12

1. 19 Ill.2d 181, 166 N.E.2d 601 (1960), appeal dismissed 364 U.S. 475, 81 S.Ct. 243, 5 L.Ed.2d 221 (1960), rehearing denied 365 U.S. 805, 81 S.Ct. 466, 5 L.Ed.2d 463 (1961).

2. See also, Tullo v. Township of Millburn, 54 N.J.Super. 483, 149 A.2d 620 (App.Div.1959); Mandelker, Delegation of

Power and Function in Zoning Administration, 1963 Wash.U.L.Q. 60.

3. See supra § 6.4, and discussion of standards of review.

4. Town of Richmond v. Murdock, 70 Wis.2d 642, 235 N.W.2d 497 (1975) (condition to control noise within scope of police power but discretion can be limited to a

There is a natural tendency on the part of governmental bodies to retain as much flexibility as possible and to avoid the hard thinking necessary to establish precise standards which anticipate many situations. To the extent detailed standards are set, discretion is minimized. A special use is permitted if the standards in the relevant ordinance are met.

The board may also not be permitted to impose other standards. In Archbishop O'Hara's Appeal,[5] for example, the board was not allowed to deny the permit on the ground that traffic increased, because it was not a listed criterion in the ordinance. Every special use, especially schools, would increase traffic. The board was also unable to deny the permit based on the adverse effect on neighboring homes because the homeowners knew or were presumed to know that the ordinance permitted a school in the area. That the city would have to provide sidewalks and streetlights was an expense the city would have to incur, for any use. Similarly, the board denied a permit in State ex rel. Synod of Ohio of United Lutheran Church in America v. Joseph.[6] It was denied due to a "policy" of the board not to allow churches in residential zones if property in a business zone were available for such purposes. The court held that the ordinance provided for churches as a special use in residential zones, that the standards had been met and that the permit should issue.

WESTLAW REFERENCES

standard term condition guideline /s "special permit" /s airport club

deny denied denial /s "special permit" /s traffic

414k42

§ 6.13 Conditions

As with variances, special permits can be conditioned. Sometimes the specific conditions may be listed in the ordinance. The authority to impose conditions may be expressly conferred under more general language, or the authority to impose conditions may be implied from the nature of the special permit.[1] As with variances,[2] the conditions must relate to the zoning power or, at minimum to the police power.[3]

For example, in Montgomery County v. Mossburg,[4] the court upheld a condition requiring an early closing on a special permit to expand a nonconforming restaurant. The court considered the special

determination of whether the standards have been satisfied), City of Miami Beach v. Mr. Samuels Inc., 351 So.2d 719 (Fla. 1977).

5. 389 Pa. 35, 131 A.2d 587 (1957). See also City of Naples v. Central Plaza of Naples, 303 So.2d 423 (Fla. 2d D.C.A.1974). (Standards must be specified or they can not be applied).

6. 139 Ohio St. 229, 39 N.E.2d 515 (1942).

§ 6.13

1. Pearson v. Shoemaker, 25 Misc.2d 591, 202 N.Y.S.2d 779 (1960).

2. See § 6.7 supra.

3. Annot. 99 A.L.R.2d 227 (1965).

4. 228 Md. 555, 180 A.2d 851 (1962).

permit to be a privilege to which the Board could attach conditions. The ordinance allowed special permits if the use was compatible with the general development plan for the neighborhood, would not adversely affect the health and safety of residents and workers in the area and would not be detrimental to development of adjacent properties or the general neighborhood. Such language was held sufficient to justify the condition.

Not every condition is valid. For example, in Soho Park & Land Co. v. Board of Adjustment of Town of Belleville,[5] the board issued a permit for a wire factory, but conditioned it so that: (1) only the applicant wire company could use the premises, (2) nothing but a wire factory use could be made, (3) facades had to be brick with stone facing, (4) large trees had to be planted, (5) part of the tract had to be retained for residential uses. While the case is an older one, some of the conditions might be held invalid today on the same grounds as they were held invalid then. The first two were invalidated as improper restraints on alienation.[6] The 3rd and 4th conditions may or may not be invalid, depending upon the jurisdiction, and the same may be true of the latter condition.[7]

The board not only has the power to impose conditions, but it may be required to impose conditions. For example, in Chambers v. Zoning Bd. of Adjustment,[8] the property owner applied for a permit to construct a housing project which the ordinance indicated could be issued in an R–2 zone if there were provision for an on-site garage or other satisfactory auto storage space. The board waived the condition on the ground that street parking was adequate, but the court held the waiver to be improper since the ordinance gave the board no discretion to waive the condition.

To a limited extent, issuance of a permit is a privilege rather than a right and involves some discretion by the deciding body. As a result, even if the validity of conditions is doubtful, if the special permit is accepted with conditions, the permittee may be estopped from a later attack on the conditions.[9]

Some requirements that must be met before special permits will be issued may be found invalid if they operate in a discriminatory manner. Two federal courts invalidated requirements which restricted group homes for mentally handicapped persons as being unconstitutional, indicating that courts are beginning to view mentally ill and mentally

5. 6 N.J.Misc. 686, 142 A. 548 (Sup.Ct. 1928).

6. As with variances, § 6.7 supra, conditions run to the use of property not to ownership.

7. Developmental permission today might be conditioned on dedication of property for parks, though, as distinguished from a residential subdivision which would benefit from the park, burdening development permission for a factory with the requirement of a park dedication might well be invalid. See § 7.8 infra.

8. 250 N.C. 194, 108 S.E.2d 211 (1959).

9. Convent of Sisters of St. Joseph v. Winston-Salem, 243 N.C. 316, 90 S.E.2d 879 (1956).

retarded persons as belonging to groups which need protection from discriminatory legislative action.

Plaintiffs in J.W. v. Tacoma,[10] were the owner and residents of a group home for persons recently released from mental institutions. Under the applicable zoning classification, operation of such a home required a special permit, whereas other types of group homes did not. When a permit was applied for, the city denied it, and plaintiffs pursued the matter in federal court. The Ninth Circuit scrutinized the ordinance, and found it highly likely that the distinction between types of group homes was based on stereotypic fears about former mental patients. Review of the record indicated that the permit had been denied primarily because of neighborhood opposition to the home, rather than being related to any substantial zoning interest. The court held the decision to be arbitrary and violative of due process. A permit was ordered to be issued.[11]

Relief from burdensome zoning may be obtained through legislative or administrative mechanisms, and sometimes through the judicial system. Variances and special permits provide needed flexibility within a comprehensive scheme of zoning classifications. It is beneficial for both exceptions to be strictly construed and stingily granted in the sense that to do otherwise would render comprehensive planning meaningless. By the same token, both are necessary to the regulation of property ownership and enjoyment and help maintain constitutionality of the regulation.

WESTLAW REFERENCES

"special permit"   /s   condition   /p   police zon***   /2   power
414k501
"special permit"   /s   condition   /s   invalid
adjustment zoning   /3   board   /s   waive*   /s   condition
find 720 f.2d 1126

---

10.   720 F.2d 1126 (9th Cir.1983).

11.   The other case is Cleburne Living Center, Inc. v. Cleburne, 726 F.2d 191 (5th Cir.1984), rehearing denied 735 F.2d 832 (5th Cir.1984), affirmed in part, vacated in part ___ U.S. ___, 105 S.Ct. 3249, 87 L.Ed. 2d 313 (1985). The court closely followed the *JW* equal protection analysis, rejecting strict scrutiny because the plaintiffs were part of a class that was only "quasi-suspect." The city could not adequately support its specific reasons for denying the special use permit, nor did the provision appear to serve important government interests. The ordinance was found to be invalid.

Chapter 7

SUBDIVISION CONTROL LAW

Analysis

I. INTRODUCTION

Sec.

7.1 Types of Subdivision Controls: In General.

II. SUBDIVISION REGULATIONS

7.2 Introduction and History.

7.3 Relation to Planning.

7.4 Relation to Zoning.

7.5 Definition of Subdivision.

7.6 The Subdivision Approval Process.

7.7 Enforcement Methods, Sanctions and Required Improvement Guarantees.

7.8 Exactions on Subdivision Approval.

III. MAPPING FOR FUTURE STREETS AND OTHER PUBLIC IMPROVEMENTS

7.9 In General.

7.10 Relation to Master Plan and Planning.

7.11 Relation to Zoning, Setbacks.

7.12 Relation to Subdivision Control.

7.13 Constitutionality.

7.14 Effect of Official Map on Marketability of Title.

IV. PLANNED UNIT DEVELOPMENTS

7.15 Definition and History.

7.16 Relationship to Zoning.

7.17 Legal Status of PUD's.

7.18 Planned Unit Development Approval Process.

7.19 Private Restrictions.

V. SUBDIVIDED LAND SALES

I. INTRODUCTION

§ 7.1 Types of Subdivision Controls: In General

With the exception of zoning [1] which regulates the use of land, and building and housing codes [2] which regulate construction, the land development control law system at the local level [3] consists of regulatory techniques that focus primarily on residential development. Subdivision regulations, maps for future streets and public improvements, planned unit development and subdivided land sales regulations are examples of these residential regulatory techniques.

Subdivision regulation generally refers to controls implemented during the land subdividing stage of the development process and includes such measures as platting procedures and controls, design regulation, improvement requirements, dedication requirements, in-lieu fees, performance bonds and the like. Official mapping is another kind of land use control which implements planning by giving precise locations of future streets, parks and sites for other public facilities within a local jurisdiction. Planned unit developments are residential developments that include multifamily and single-family housing and that may also include commercial development. Subdivided land sales regulations, although often implemented through state and federal statutes, are designed to regulate local and interstate real estate sales, particularly the sale of subdivided lands or lots.

In developing an understanding of the land development regulatory techniques discussed in this chapter, it is important to keep their primary residential focus in perspective. While primarily directed toward residential development, they are often cross-matched with complimentary techniques and integrated into the overall land development control law system. For example, although subdivision regulations are generally independent of zoning regulations, planned unit developments, which often include commercial uses, are often found within zoning regulations and are increasingly found in subdivision regulation ordinances.

§ 7.1

1. See Chapters 3–6 supra.

2. See Chapter 8 infra.

3. For a discussion of state and regional land development control law techniques see supra § 3.7.

WESTLAW REFERENCES

di,sy(subdivision /2 regulation control)

II. SUBDIVISION REGULATIONS

§ 7.2 Introduction and History

Subdivision regulation is a land use control based on the police power and is second in importance only to zoning as a land use control device. Unlike zoning which controls the use of land and remains important before, during and after development, subdivision regulation generally refers to controls implemented during the development process. Once land is subdivided, subdivision regulations have little or no application until redevelopment, at which time resubdivision may or may not be necessary. Although the subdivision of land occurs early in the development process, its impact on the community is lasting because "[t]he pattern of a subdivision becomes the pattern of a community, which in turn may influence the character of an entire city."[1]

Modern subdivision regulations include such measures as platting procedures and controls; design regulations including such items as layout of streets, street width, street grading and surfacing, drainage, sidewalks, sewers, water mains, lot size and screen plantings; improvement, reservation and dedication requirements; in-lieu fees; performance bonds and the like.

Prior to the 1920's the primary purpose of subdivision regulations was to provide a more efficient method of selling and conveying land. Early subdivision statutes required that maps or "plats" of the subdivision be recorded in the local records office. The plat was required to show roads, parks, lots and blocks and the surveyed dimensions of these features.[2] Once recorded, land within the subdivision could be conveyed by reference to the lot, block and plat name rather than by metes and bounds descriptions. The impetus for such statutes was the desire to create a system which would permit land conveyance and title recordation without overlapping of titles and the confusion attendant on metes and bounds descriptions. Most states still have platting statutes, often separate from the statutes authorizing subdivision control.[3]

The second period of subdivision regulation evolved from a recognition that subdivision regulations could be expanded to accomplish the substantive objective of controlling urban development.[4] As a result of

---

§ 7.2

1. R. Freilich and P. Levi, Model Subdivision Regulations: Text and Commentary 1 (Amer. Soc'y of Planning Officials, 1975).

2. See, e.g., Law of Mar. 31, 1885, SB 125 (1885) Colo.Laws; Colo.Rev.Stat. § 6603–21 (1908).

3. For references to and capsule analyses of the subdivision and platting statutes of each of the 50 states see E. Yokley, The Law of Subdivisions, Ch. 14 (2d ed. 1981).

4. For a thorough discussion of the four historical periods of subdivision regulation see R. Freilich and P. Levi, Model Subdivision Regulations, supra note 1, at 1–8.

land speculation in the 1920's, millions of vacant platted lots of such unusable sizes as 20 by 80 feet existed. Lots in these subdivisions were often undeveloped and had different owners. The diverse ownership and partial development prevented effective replatting though many of the lots were tax delinquent and hence in public ownership. New suburban development "jumped" these unusable, close-in subdivisions and left "slums" of vacant lands. Some of these "slums" could be removed only by condemnation and urban renewal.[5] Some of this platted land was also improved with streets and utilities. Through the 1920's, local governments often provided these improvements from public funds or by special assessment. During the 1930's many of these special assessment bonds were in default.

In response to the problems created by land speculation and premature development, the Department of Commerce published the Standard City Planning Enabling Act in 1928 which contained provisions on subdivision control.[6] This act[7] shifted the emphasis of subdivision regulations from a device for selling and conveying land to one of providing a means to implement community comprehensive planning. In addition to recognizing the need for a method to transfer lots by reference to a plat, the act also emphasized the need for a method to require internal improvements within the subdivision. The model statute included provisions concerning the "arrangement of streets in relation to other existing or planned streets and to the master plan, for adequate and convenient open spaces of traffic, utilities, access of fire fighting apparatus, recreation, light, and air, and for avoidance of congestion of population, including minimum width and area of lots."[8] Following the adoption of state enabling acts patterned after the model statutes, state courts upheld local government use of subdivision regulations as a land use control device to shape the growth of the entire community.[9]

The third period of subdivision regulation began in the late 40's when the pent up demand for housing generated the postwar building boom that became known as "urban sprawl."[10] This period was

5. See, e.g., People ex rel. Gutknecht v. Chicago, 414 Ill. 600, 111 N.E.2d 626 (1953) (state urban renewal legislation could be used to condemn and reassemble vacant "slum" lands).

6. Standard City Planning Enabling Act, U.S. Dep't of Commerce (1928) (hereinafter referred to as "SPEA"). Title II of SPEA, Subdivision Control, is reprinted in the American Law Institute, a Model Land Development Code, Tentative Draft No. 1, 224, 244–253 (1968).

7. In addition to the SPEA, many states base modern subdivision enabling legislation on two other model acts: the Municipal Planning Enabling Act and the Municipal Subdivision Regulation Act. The latter

two acts are reprinted in E. Bassett, F. Williams, A. Bettman and R. Whitten, Model Laws for Planning Cities, Counties and States (1935).

8. SPEA § 14 (1928).

9. See, e.g., Mansfield & Swett, Inc. v. Town of West Orange, 120 N.J.L. 145, 198 A. 225 (1938).

10. For a major governmental report focusing on the need to control urban sprawl as the number one priority in land-use planning see National Commission on Urban Problems (Douglas Commission), Alternatives to Urban Sprawl, Research Report No. 15 (1968).

marked by an increasing awareness of the demands that rapidly expanding suburban areas placed on local government facilities and services. Concern was focused on the needs of the new subdivision residents for parks, recreation facilities and adequate roads. Many local governments experienced great economic pressure to provide these facilities and services to the new development. At the same time local officials remembered the financial difficulties that were created in the 30's by excessive reliance on special assessments to fund various subdivision improvements.[11] Subdivision regulations were amended to include provisions which required developers to dedicate park and school sites,[12] on-site roads,[13] widen off-site streets,[14] and contribute funds where the need for such facilities was in areas other than the subdivision but within the general vicinity.[15] In response to the demand for control of urban sprawl, subdivision regulations have been modified to incorporate new techniques which go far beyond the needs of residents within the subdivision. Subdivision regulations are more frequently being used to delay or deny development where it can be shown that the subdivision will cause serious off-site drainage problems and flooding, reduce environmental quality, or contribute to existing problems of inadequate local government facilities.[16]

The fourth and most recent period of subdivision regulation emphasizes the relationship of the individual subdivision to its external community environment through the local government comprehensive planning process. Current emphasis is being placed on the rate of subdivision development activity. This period of the history of subdivision regulation is marked by attempts to integrate regulations into a comprehensive growth management and planning program [17] with the objective of phasing in new development in coordination with the orderly provision of adequate public facilities.[18]

11. In the 1930's many local governments faced bankruptcy when the economy collapsed and revenues which secured special assessment bonds disappeared. Most local governments assumed that increased property taxes resulting from new development would generate sufficient revenue for maintaining public facilities. The collapse of the development market in the late 1920's demonstrated the uncertainty of the assumption. See C.M. Haar, Land Use Planning 443 (2d ed. 1976).

12. See, e.g., Rosen v. Village of Downers Grove, 19 Ill.2d 448, 167 N.E.2d 230 (1960) (dedication of public school site).

13. See, e.g., Brous v. Smith, 304 N.Y. 164, 106 N.E.2d 503 (1952) (dedication of roads internal to subdivision).

14. See, e.g., Ayres v. City of Los Angeles, 34 Cal.2d 31, 207 P.2d 1 (1949) (dedication of perimeter streets bordering subdivision).

15. See, e.g., Jenad, Inc. v. Village of Scarsdale, 18 N.Y.2d 78, 271 N.Y.S.2d 955, 218 N.E.2d 673 (1966) (in lieu fee for recreational purposes upheld); Associated Home Builders v. Walnut Creek, Inc., 4 Cal.3d 633, 94 Cal.Rptr. 630, 484 P.2d 606 (1971), appeal dismissed 404 U.S. 878, 92 S.Ct. 202, 30 L.Ed.2d 159 (1971) (in lieu fee for recreation and open space upheld).

16. See, e.g., Eschette v. New Orleans, 258 La. 133, 245 So.2d 383 (1971) (drainage); Pearson Kent Corp. v. Bear, 28 N.Y.2d 396, 322 N.Y.S.2d 235, 271 N.E.2d 218 (1971) (adequate off-site roads); Salamar Builders, Inc. v. Tuttle, 29 N.Y.2d 221, 325 N.Y.S.2d 933, 275 N.E.2d 585 (1971) (environmental protection of off-site water resources).

17. See ch. 9 infra.

18. See, e.g., Golden v. Planning Board of Town of Ramapo, 30 N.Y.2d 359, 334 N.Y.S.2d 138, 285 N.E.2d 291 (1972), appeal

WESTLAW REFERENCES

"subdivision regulation" /s purpose history statut*** law

urban /2 renewal /s condemn! /s slum vacant /3 land

"standard city planning enabling act"

develop! /s dedicat! /s "school site" "on-site road" park street

subdivision /s delay*** deny denied /s drainage flood***
     environment** traffic parking

find 285 n.e.2d 291

§ 7.3 Relation to Planning

As with zoning, subdivision regulation is a land use control that implements comprehensive planning.[1] The relationship between planning and subdivision control, however, has historically been viewed as closer than in zoning.[2] This is for two reasons. First, in the zoning process the legislative body and the board of zoning adjustment often have major roles to play while the planning commission acts only in an advisory capacity. In the subdivision control process, however, the planning commission is often given authority to either draft and recommend or adopt the comprehensive plan. The planning commission is also usually given the authority to promulgate subdivision regulations and approve or deny plats submitted to it.

Second, while in many states there is no necessary relation between either zoning or subdivision controls and the comprehensive plan,[3] the statutes of many states require a master plan or at least a master plan having a major street element before the planning commission can regulate subdivisions.[4] In other states an official map is required as a prerequisite to subdivision regulations and the planning commission usually makes recommendations on the official map. In some jurisdictions the statutes specifically require that the subdivision review process include findings as to the compatibility of the subdivision plat with the plan or map.[5] In imposing these planning require-

dismissed 409 U.S. 1003, 93 S.Ct. 440, 34 L.Ed.2d 294 (1972) (constitutionality of subdivision development timing ordinance upheld); see Freilich, Golden v. Town of Ramapo, Establishing a New Dimension in American Planning Law, 4 Urb.Law ix (Summer 1972); cf. Bosselman, Can the Town of Ramapo Pass a Law to Bind the Rights of the Whole World?, 1 Fla.St.U.L. Rev. 234 (1973).

§ 7.3

1. See Cunningham, Land-Use Control—The State and Local Programs, 50 Iowa L.Rev. 367, 435 (1965) ("Ideally, both zoning and subdivision controls are tools for effectuating comprehensive land-use plans.").

2. Id. at 417.

3. See R. Freilich and P. Levi, Model Subdivision Regulations: Text and Commentary, supra § 7.2 n. 1, at 2 ("Just as the zoning requirement contained in the Standard Zoning Enabling Act . . . that zoning 'be in accordance with a comprehensive plan' has never been interpreted to require that a master plan precede adoption of a zoning ordinance . . . a master plan generally has been held not to be required in order to adopt valid subdivision regulations . . . ").

4. See, e.g., Colo.Rev.Stat. 31–23–213; Utah Code Ann. 1953, 10–9–25.

5. See, e.g., Ill.—S.H.A. Ch. 24 ¶ 11–12–8 ("the municipality shall determine whether a proposed plat of subdivision or resubdivision complies with the official map.)

ments, the statutes generally follow the guidance of one or more of the model or standard acts.[6] At least one court has held that a planning board could rely on a comprehensive plan to disapprove a subdivision plat even though the master plan had not been formally adopted.[7]

While necessary conformity between planning and subdivision control is somewhat greater than the conformity between planning and zoning, the matter is relative. Much subdivision regulation takes place without reference to the master plan.[8] In most jurisdictions, the plan is only a general guide, it is often not legislatively adopted, and property owners may not be afforded a hearing on the plan. In such circumstances subdivision denial based on non-compliance with the plan may be beyond the authority of the plat reviewing agency.[9] Other states have gone further, however, and given comprehensive planning a legal status by requiring that subdivisions be consistent with the comprehensive plan.[10]

WESTLAW REFERENCES

"master plan" /s subdivision /2 regulat!

subdivision /s plan planning /s require!

di,sy(subdivision /s consistent conform! compli! /s plan planning)

§ 7.4　Relation to Zoning

In order to develop, it is generally necessary to comply with both zoning and subdivision regulations. Although the two types of controls are intended to complement each other within the development process, they are often administered by different agencies. They are also often subject to separate enabling statutes each with its own particular requirements. As a consequence, subdivision regulations and zoning are often administered so as to appear to be working at cross-purposes. Some jurisdictions have integrated the two types of controls into a local development code which provides a consolidated procedure for considering both the zoning change and the subdivision proposal.

While the authority to approve subdivisions and the power to zone are usually authorized by separate statutes,[1] some subdivision control legislation requires that a plat conform to zoning regulations.[2] Courts have also held that local government authority to require conformance

---

6. On master plans see § 2.6 supra; on official maps see §§ 7.9–7.14 infra.

7. Neiderhofer v. Gustafson, 45 A.D.2d 812, 357 N.Y.S.2d 196 (3d Dep't 1974); cf. Lordship Park Ass'n v. Board of Zoning Appeals, 137 Conn. 84, 75 A.2d 379 (1950).

8. See Nelson, The Master Plan and Subdivision Control, 16 Me.L.Rev. 107 (1964).

9. Lordship Park Ass'n v. Board of Zoning Appeals, 137 Conn. 84, 75 A.2d 379 (1950). But see Krieger v. Planning

Comm'n of Howard County, 224 Md. 320, 167 A.2d 885 (1961).

10. See, e.g., West's Ann.Cal.Gov't Code § 66474(a); West's Fla.Stat.Ann. § 163.3202; Ill.—S.H.A. Ch. 24, ¶ 11–12–8; Board of County Comm'rs v. Gaster, 285 Md. 233, 401 A.2d 666 (1979).

§ 7.4

1. For a discussion of zoning enabling acts see ch. 3 supra.

2. See, e.g., N.J.Stat.Ann. 40:55D–38; Utah Code Ann. 1953, 10–9–26.

may be inferred from the general purposes to be served by subdivision control regulation.[3] Where the enabling legislation is silent on the relationship between the two types of controls, the local regulations often require that plats comply with local zoning.

Courts have also held that subdivision proposals may be rejected where they do not conform to zoning regulations.[4] Some courts have held that subdivision review may not be used so as to amend zoning because the exercise of such a power would effectively amount to a usurpation of the authority of the local zoning board.[5] Where the subdivision control ordinance imposes additional requirements, however, courts have held that mere compliance with the zoning ordinance is not sufficient.[6]

If an approved subdivision exists and a zoning ordinance is subsequently passed which would prevent the lots from being used as subdivided, the subdivider has no vested right to develop the subdivision.[7] Similarly, where the owner of unsold lots requests a variance, an old subdivision can be forced to comply with new subdivision regulations.[8] On the other hand, vested rights in nonconforming lots are sometimes recognized, particularly where houses have been built on some lots or sewers and waterlines installed.[9] Some statutes and ordinances provide that once a subdivision is approved, the municipality is precluded from exercising its powers inconsistent with the approval for a period of time.[10] These statutes have been interpreted, however, to apply to changes in local but not state land use regulations.[11]

 WESTLAW REFERENCES
regulation /s plat /s compli! /s zon***
414k381.5

3. See, e.g., Benny v. Alameda, 105 Cal. App.3d 1006, 164 Cal.Rptr. 776 (1980).

4. See, e.g., People v. Park Ridge, 25 Ill. App.2d 424, 166 N.E.2d 635 (1960); Durland v. Maresco, 53 A.D.2d 643, 384 N.Y.S.2d 503 (2d Dep't 1976).

5. See, e.g., Shapiro v. Town of Oyster Bay, 27 Misc.2d 844, 211 N.Y.S.2d 414 (1961), affirmed 20 A.D.2d 850, 249 N.Y.S.2d 663 (1964); Goodman v. Board of Comm'rs, 49 Pa.Cmwlth. 35, 411 A.2d 838 (1980); Snyder v. Zoning Bd., 98 R.I. 139, 200 A.2d 222 (1964).

6. See e.g., Shoptaugh v. Board of County Comm'rs, 37 Colo.App. 39, 543 P.2d 524 (1975); Popular Refreshments, Inc. v. Fuller's Milk Bar, Inc., 85 N.J.Super. 528, 205 A.2d 445 (App.Div.1964), certification denied 44 N.J. 409, 209 A.2d 143 (1965).

7. See, e.g., Lake Intervale Homes, Inc. v. Parsippany-Troy Hills Township, 28 N.J. 423, 147 A.2d 28 (1958); York Township Zoning Bd. of Adjustment v. Brown, 407 Pa. 649, 182 A.2d 706 (1962); Kapadahl v.

Alcan Pacific Co., 222 Cal.App.2d 626, 35 Cal.Rptr. 354 (1963). Smith v. Winhall Planning Comm'n, 140 Vt. 178, 436 A.2d 760 (1981).

8. See, e.g., Blevens v. Manchester, 103 N.H. 284, 170 A.2d 121 (1961).

9. Gruber v. Mayor and Township Comm. of Raritan Township, 39 N.J. 1, 186 A.2d 489 (1962); Wood v. North Salt Lake, 15 Utah 2d 245, 390 P.2d 858 (1964); Western Lands Equities, Inc. v. Logan, 617 P.2d 388 (Utah 1980); Smith v. Winhall Planning Comm'n, 140 Vt. 178, 436 A.2d 760 (1981).

10. See, e.g., Pa.Stat.Ann.Tit. 53, § 10508(4) (3 years); Conn.Gen.Stat.Ann. § 8–26a (5 years); Mass.Gen.Laws Ch. 40, § 7A (7 years).

11. Island Properties, Inc. v. Martha's Vineyard Comm'n, 372 Mass. 216, 361 N.E.2d 385 (1977); Ocean Acres v. State, 168 N.J.Super. 597, 403 A.2d 967 (App.Div. 1979), certification denied 81 N.J. 352, 407 A.2d 1226 (1979).

subdivision /s amend** change* /s zon***
subdivider /s vested /2 right % "rent control"
find 186 a.2d 489

§ 7.5   Definition of Subdivision

The Standard City Planning Enabling Act did not define the term "subdivision." As a result, the definition of subdivision in statutes and ordinances varies and is unclear in many states. Most broadly it is the division of one parcel of land into more than one parcel.[1] Many state statutes, however, define the term as a division of land into a minimum number of parcels.[2] Where a definition is omitted from the statute, courts have generally construed the statute to authorize each local government to define the term.[3] Local ordinances, however, may not generally expand the statutory definition.[4]

In general, the term subdivision is defined so as to require that the division be for the purpose of sale, lease or building development.[5] Division for other purposes may not constitute a subdivision.[6] Condominium development has been held not to be a subdivision.[7] In some statutes the number of divisions may be given a time horizon, so that property is not considered subdivided if not more than 3 lots are created within any five year period.[8] Some statutes also expressly exempt subdivisions which do not involve creation of new streets[9] or the extension of existing streets,[10] which divide land among family members,[11] or which are the result of petition actions or testamentary divisions of real property.[12]

In many states there are loopholes, and subdividers engage in elaborate schemes to divide in a way which is not a "subdivision."

§ 7.5

1. See, e.g., Mass.Gen.Laws c. 41, § 81L (two or more).

2. See, e.g., Conn.Gen.Stat.Ann. § 8–18 (three or more); West's Rev.Code Wash. Ann. 58.17.020 (five or more).

3. See, e.g., Delaware Midland Corp. v. Westhampton Beach, 79 Misc.2d 438, 359 N.Y.S.2d 944, 946 (1974), affirmed 39 N.Y.2d 1029, 387 N.Y.S.2d 248, 355 N.E.2d 302 (1976).

4. See, e.g., Peninsula Corp. v. Planning and Zoning Comm'n, 151 Conn. 450, 199 A.2d 1 (1964); Dearborn v. Town of Milford, 120 N.H. 82, 411 A.2d 1132 (1980); Martorano v. Board of Comm'rs, 51 Pa. Cmwlth. 202, 414 A.2d 411 (1980).

5. See, e.g., Pa.Stat. Title 53, § 10201(21).

6. See, e.g., Pa.Stat. Title 53, § 10201(21) (subdivision for agricultural purposes exempted); N.J.Stat.Ann.

40:55D–7 (subdivision over five acres for agricultural use); Conn.G.Stat.Ann. § 8–18 (subdivision for municipal, conservation or agricultural purposes exempted).

7. See, e.g., Gerber v. Town of Clarkstown, 78 Misc.2d 221, 356 N.Y.S.2d 926 (1974); but see N.H.Rev.Stat.Ann. 36.1, VIII (condominium development included); Colo.Rev.Stat. 30–28–101.

8. See, e.g., 30 Me.Rev.Stat.Ann. § 4956.

9. See, e.g., Stoker v. Irvington, 71 N.J. Super. 370, 177 A.2d 61 (1961); Donovan v. New Brunswick, 50 N.J.Super. 102, 141 A.2d 134 (1958).

10. See, e.g., Dube v. Senter, 107 N.H. 191, 219 A.2d 456 (1966).

11. See, e.g., Kiska v. Skrensky, 145 Conn. 28, 138 A.2d 523 (1958).

12. See, e.g., N.J.Stat.Ann. 40:55D–1 et seq; Metzdorf v. Rumson, 67 N.J.Super. 121, 170 A.2d 249 (1961).

They thereby avoid the required approval and thus may avoid the imposition of subdivision exactions.[13]　Avoidance is more common where there are no statutes or ordinances that are designed to cover less significant subdivisions.　For example, in Pratt v. Adams [14] the court voided a scheme where one parcel was conveyed to several persons in joint tenancy and the persons then "suffered" the creation of 12 parcels through a partition action, the referee setting up an elaborate scheme for roads, easements, buildings restrictions etc. as part of the partition order.

WESTLAW REFERENCES

di,sy(zoning　/s　regulation　/s　defin!　/s　subdivision)

di,sy(planning　/p　subdivision　/s　sale lease building)

283k43

di,sy(condominium　/4　subdivision)

find 219 a.2d 456

kiska　+2　skrensky

§ 7.6　The Subdivision Approval Process

The imposition of subdivision improvement requirements occurs during the subdivision approval process.　Although many variations exist in the subdivision approval process from state to state, generalizations about the process can be made.　The essential requirement of subdivision control is that a subdivider cannot convey his subdivided lands without a recorded subdivision plat.[1]　The subdivider is prohibited from recording the plat until the approval of the local subdivision approval agency has been obtained.[2]

While most state enabling acts provide for a two-step approval process,[3] some local governments include an additional preliminary step referred to as a preapplication conference.　At the conference the local agency or its staff will familiarize the applicant with the subdivision regulations and answer general questions.　At the same time the applicant will provide the agency with the basic idea of the proposal.

The submission of a "preliminary plat" follows and constitutes the first formal step in the subdivision approval process.　The regulations usually require that the applicant submit a detailed drawing of the proposed subdivision.　Included on the drawing are the necessary improvements and indications of which improvements will be dedicated to public use.　The local agency may then approve, disapprove, or conditionally approve the preliminary plat, usually after a properly

---

13.　See § 7.8 infra.

14.　229 Cal.App.2d 602, 40 Cal.Rptr. 505 (1964).

§ 7.6

1.　One court has held, however, that such a mandatory recordation requirement

results in an unconstitutional restraint an alienation.　Kass v. Lewin, 104 So.2d 572 (Fla.1958).

2.　See 4 R. Anderson, American Law of Zoning § 23.05 (2d ed. 1976).

3.　Id. at § 23.11.

noticed hearing.[4] In some states the right to subdivide may vest following approval of the preliminary plat.[5] Reasons for disapproval are usually required to be recorded and the final decision is subject to judicial review.[6] Preliminary plat approval usually authorizes the subdivider to begin construction of the improvements provided a surety bond for their completion is posted.[7]

After preliminary plat approval, the subdivider usually has one year within which to submit a final plat for approval.[8] Before the final plat is approved the subdivider must demonstrate substantial conformance to the preliminary plat and any conditions that the local agency has imposed. Some statutes require approval of the final plat if all requirements imposed on approval of the preliminary plat are satisfied.[9] Courts often construe such provisions so as to make approval of the final plat a ministerial as opposed to a discretionary act.[10] Once the final plat is approved, the subdivider may record the plat and legally convey lots within the subdivision.

Many states set time limits within which the local agency must act on either preliminary or final plats.[11] If the agency takes no action within this period, the plat is deemed approved.[12] Approval of the preliminary or final plat, however, does not constitute acceptance by the local government of the dedicated improvements. Such acceptance, and the responsibility for maintaining the improvements, occurs when the local government makes a formal decision to accept.

The subdivision control process may also include devices designed to achieve sufficient flexibility for the modification of subdivision control requirements.[13] Enabling statutes often authorize administrative relief in the form of variances where a strict application of the regulations would cause unusual and unnecessary hardship on the subdivider.[14] However, unlike zoning variances which are usually granted by the board of adjustment upon appeal from the decision of an administrative agency,[15] variance relief from subdivision regulations is usually

---

4. Id. at § 23.12.

5. See, e.g., Western Land Equities v. Logan, 617 P.2d 388 (Utah 1980).

6. See, e.g., West's Rev.Code Wash.Ann. 58.17.180.

7. See SPEA, § 14.

8. See, e.g., Nev.Rev.Stat. 278.360(1) (permitting, however, a one year extension).

9. See, e.g., West's Ann.Cal.Gov't Code § 66458; Pa.Stat. Tit. 53, § 10508(4).

10. See, e.g., Youngblood v. Board of Supervisors, 22 Cal.3d 644, 150 Rptr. 242, 586 P.2d 556 (1978); Hakim v. Board of Comm'rs, 27 Pa.Cmwlth. 405, 366 A.2d 1306 (1976).

11. See, e.g., Ill.—S.H.A. ch. 24, ¶ 11–12–8; N.J.Stat.Ann. 40:55D–1 et seq.

12. Id. It has been suggested, however, that it is doubtful that a court will permit a subdivision project to proceed if it will seriously jeopardize public health and safety. See Schultz & Kelley, Subdivision Improvement Requirements and Guarantees: A Primer, 28 Wash.U.J.Urb. & Contemp.L. 3, n. 183 at 38 (1985).

13. See, e.g., Canter v. Planning Bd., 7 Mass.App.Ct. 805, 390 N.E.2d 1128 (1979); Blevens v. Manchester, 103 N.H. 284, 170 A.2d 121, 124 (1961).

14. See, e.g., N.J.Stat.Ann. 40:55D–51(a).

15. For a detailed discussion of zoning variances and the board of adjustment, see §§ 6.5–6.10 supra.

granted by the same agency which originally reviewed the subdivision proposal. Absent a provision authorizing the zoning board of adjustment to grant variances from subdivision regulations, such board has been held without power to do so.[16] When a local agency has authority to vary the strict application of a subdivision ordinance, courts have held it can only do so by making findings of fact supported by evidence.[17]

WESTLAW REFERENCES

subdivider /s convey! /s record***

di,sy(zoning planning /p subdivision /s approv** disapprov** unapprov**)

414k465 /p subdivision

414k235 /p subdivision

414k432 /p subdivision

preliminary final /2 plat /s approv** disapprov**

subdivision /2 regulation /s variance

§ 7.7 Enforcement Methods, Sanctions and Required Improvement Guarantees

The effectiveness of subdivision regulations, like all land use control devices, depends upon the presence of fair and efficient enforcement methods, sanctions and required improvement guarantees.[1] One of the model enabling statutes provides:

> Whoever . . . sells . . . any land by reference to or exhibition of or by other use of a plat of a subdivision, before such plat has been approved . . . and recorded . . . shall . . . pay a penalty of $100 for each lot . . . . The municipal corporation may enjoin such transfer . . . or may recover the said penalty.[2]

In addition to the sanction of civil fine and injunction, statutes in various states provide other sanctions. Sometimes the sale of a lot in an unapproved subdivision is made a criminal act resulting in the imposition of a fine or imprisonment.[3] A local government or purchaser may set aside the conveyance under some statutes.[4] Generally, the

---

16. See Noonan v. Zoning Bd. of Review, 90 R.I. 466, 159 A.2d 606 (1960).

17. See, e.g., Smith v. Township Comm. of Twp. of Morris, 101 N.J.Super. 271, 244 A.2d 145 (1968).

§ 7.7

1. For a detailed discussion of enforcement methods and improvement guarantees see R. Freilich & P. Levi, Model Subdivision Regulations: Text and Commentary 30–31, 62–65 (Amer.Soc'y of Planning Officials, 1975); B. Royal, Subdivision Improvement Guarantees (Am.Soc'y of Planning Officials, Planning Advisory Serv. Report No. 298, January 1974); Schultz & Kelley,

Subdivision Improvement Requirements and Guarantees: A Primer, 28 Wash.U.J. Urb. & Contemp.L. 1 at 38–106 (1985); Yearwood, Performance Bonding for Subdivision Improvements, 46 J.Urban L. 67 (1968); Note, Prevention of Subdivision Control Evasion in Indiana, 40 Ind.L.J. 445 (1964–65).

2. Dep't of Commerce, Standard City Planning Enabling Act § 16 (1928).

3. See, e.g., N.M.Stat.Ann. 1978, § 3–26–14; Wyo.Stat. 1977, § 15–1–511.

4. See, e.g., West's Ann.Cal.Gov't Code § 66499.32; Gen.L.R.I.1956, § 45–23–13; Wis.Stat.Ann. 236.31(3).

option of using a metes and bounds provision is not available if the land involved is covered by the subdivision statute because the statute makes a circumventing conveyance by such a description illegal. As a result, if land is sold that is within the definition of a required subdivision, the statute has been violated.[5] The statute may also preclude the issuance of building permits in lands that should be but have not been submitted for subdivision approval.[6] This sanction is the most controversial because it places the penalty not upon the subdivider but upon the buyer of a lot in an unapproved subdivision. Courts have refused to uphold this type of sanction.[7]

In addition to enforcement methods and sanctions, local governments also utilize performance bonds which protect both the governmental entity and the public against uncompleted improvements required by subdivision regulations. This is appropriate because although subdivision regulations are utilized to implement local planning and as a means of placing the burden of public improvements on the subdivider, local governments are also interested in the livability of the subdivision for prospective buyers who have often been left remediless. For example, in Hocking v. Title Ins. & Trust Co.,[8] the buyer sought damages from a title insurance company insuring her lot on the ground that the lot had no access because streets required by ordinance were not built and this constituted a defect in title. Under the ordinance, the city was to have obtained a bond from the subdivider to insure the improvement of streets, but failed to do so. Despite its neglect the city would not issue a building permit. The court concluded that the problem was not one of title. A properly required performance bond, however, would have provided funds to build the street.

The performance bond mechanism also allows the subdivider to obtain building permits and begin the construction and sale of lots so as to develop an income stream that enables him to pay for improvements. Once the reviewing local government has approved the plat, however, such performance bonding requirements may not be imposed.[9] Alternatively, if the final plat is not approved by the local government, a subdivider who has posted a performance bond or deposited money to insure the completion of plat improvements, may recover the bond or deposit.[10] Since performance bonds generally name the local government as obligee, only such local government may initiate an action to enforce the bond.[11] Neither purchasers of land in the subdivision who are seeking to have the improvements installed nor contractors seeking

5. See § 7.5 supra.

6. See, e.g., West's Rev.Code Wash.Ann. 58.17.210.

7. See, e.g., Keizer v. Adams, 2 Cal.3d 976, 88 Cal.Rptr. 183, 471 P.2d 983 (1970); State ex rel. Craven v. Tacoma, 63 Wn.2d 23, 385 P.2d 372 (1963).

8. 37 Cal.2d 644, 234 P.2d 625 (1951).

9. See, e.g., McKenzie v. Arthur T. McIntosh Co., 50 Ill.App.2d 370, 200 N.E.2d 138 (1964).

10. See, e.g., Cammarano v. Borough Allendale, 65 N.J.Super. 240, 167 A.2d 431 (1961).

11. See, e.g., Town of Stoneham v. Savelo, 341 Mass. 456, 170 N.E.2d 417 (1960); Pacific County v. Sherwood Pacific, Inc., 17 Wash.App. 790, 567 P.2d 642 (1977).

monies due for construction work rendered in the proposed subdivision may bring such enforcement actions.[12]

 WESTLAW REFERENCES

sale sell /s unapprov** approv** /2 subdivision /s fine penalty
    injunction enjoin***

subdivision /s approv** /p "building permit" /s deny denied /
    s purchaser buyer

hocking +2 "title insurance"

plat /2 approv** /s "performance bond"

"subdivision developer" subdivider /p performance /2 surety
    bond /s contractor purchaser "property owner"

§ 7.8   Exactions on Subdivision Approval

As a result of the rapid suburbanization of the United States, there has been a growing acceptance of the use of land use regulations to both accommodate suburban growth and maintain the quality of governmental services. The influx of new residents into suburban areas has forced local governments to provide new streets, water and sewer lines, recreational and educational facilities, police and fire buildings and open space. The increased demand for these local government services in turn raises the difficult question of how a community should finance such services and programs without overburdening either the already strained property tax base or existing local residents who have already contributed to the financing of existing improvements.

Many local governments have chosen to cope with growth-induced financial difficulties by employing a variety of means, including subdivision exactions, to shift the cost of providing capital improvements to the new residents who create the need for them. A subdivision exaction has been defined as "one form of subdivision control, which requires that developers provide certain public improvements at their own expense."[1] No aspect of subdivision control law has interested the casebook authors and the law review article writers more than the question of what kinds of conditions, required dedications, payment of fees and improvements can be imposed for subdivision approval.[2] This

---

12. See, e.g., Gordon v. Robinson Homes, Inc., 342 Mass. 529, 174 N.E.2d 381 (1961) (purchasers); City of University City ex rel. Mackey v. Frank Miceli & Sons Realty & Bldg. Co., 347 S.W.2d 131 (Mo. 1961) (adjoining property owners); Weber v. Pacific Indemnity Co., 204 Cal.App.2d 334, 22 Cal.Rptr. 366 (1962) (unpaid contractor).

§ 7.8

1. Pavelko, Subdivision Exactions: A Review of Judicial Standards, Wash.U.J. Urb. & Contemp.L. 269, 270 (1983).

2. A partial list of law review materials includes: Adelstein & Edelson, Subdivision

Exactions and Congestion Externalities, 5 J.Legal Stud. 174 (1976); Bosselman & Stroud, Mandatory Tithes: The Legality of Land Development Linkage, 9 Nova L.J. 381 (1985); Bosselman & Stroud, Pariah to Paragon: Developer Exactions in Florida 1975–85, 14 Stetson L.Rev. 527 (1985); Burchell, Edelstein & Listokin, Fiscal Impact Analysis as a Tool for Land Use Regulation, 7 Real Est.L.J. 132 (1978); Currier, Impact Fees: Some Fundamental Issues, 12 Policy Studies J. 521 (1984); Currier, Legal and Practical Problems Associated with Drafting Impact Fee Ordinances, 1984 Inst. on Plan. Zoning and Eminent Domain 273; Cutler, Legal and Illegal Methods for

emphasis reflects the fact that most subdivision litigation concerns exactions.

(A) Historical Perspective on the Types of Exactions

Exactions usually take the form of land dedications, fees in lieu of land or impact fees. The modern use of these various types of cost shifting devices is best understood in terms of the historical context within which they evolved. With this historical perspective in mind a clearer understanding of contemporary judicial criteria for assessing the constitutionality of exactions is possible.

The first land use regulation developed to shift the capital expense burden to the developer and new residents was the required dedication. Dedication involves a conveyance of an interest in land to the government for a public purpose.[3] Dedications required under subdivision

Controlling Growth on the Urban Fringe, 1961 Wis.L.Rev. 370; Ellickson, Suburban Growth Controls: An Economic and Legal Analysis, 86 Yale L.J. 385 (1977); Feldman, The Constitutionality of Subdivision Exactions for Educational Purposes, 76 Dick.L.Rev. 651 (1972); Ferguson & Rasnic, Judicial Limitations on Mandatory Subdivision Dedications, 13 Real Est.L.J. 250 (1985); Hanna, Subdivisions: Conditions Imposed by Local Government, 6 Santa Clara Lawyer 172 (1966); Heyman and Gilhool, The Constitutionality of Imposing Increased Community Costs on New Subdivision Residents Through Subdivision Exactions, 73 Yale L.J. 1119 (1964); Jacobsen & Redding, Impact Taxes: Making Development Pay its Way, 55 N.C.L.Rev. 407 (1977); Johnston, Constitutionality of Subdivision Control Exactions: The Quest for a Rationale, 52 Cornell L.Q. 871 (1967); Juergensmeyer, Drafting Impact Fees to Alleviate Florida's Pre-Platted Lands Dilemma, 7 Fla.Envt'l & Urb.Issues 7 (Apr. 1980); Juergensmeyer and Blake, Impact Fees: An Answer to Local Governments' Capital Funding Dilemma, 9 Fla.St.U.L. Rev. 415 (1981); Karp, Subdivision Exactions for Park and Open Space Needs, 16 Am.Bus.L.J. 277 (1979); Marcus, A Comparative Look at TDR, Subdivision Exactions, and Zoning as Environmental Preservation Panaceas: The Search for Dr. Jekyll Without Mr. Hyde, 20 Urban L.Ann. 3 (1980); Pavelko, Subdivision Exactions: A Review of Judicial Standards, supra note 1; Platt, and Maloney-Merkle, Municipal Improvisation: Open Space Exactions in the Land of Pioneer Trust, 5 Urb.Law 706 (1973); Rhodes, Impact Fees: The Cost Benefit Dilemma in Florida, 27 Land Use Law & Zoning Digest, No. 10, 7 (1975); Reps & Smith, Control of Urban Land Subdivision, 14 Syracuse L.Rev. 405 (1963);

Trichelo, Subdivision Exactions: Virginia Constitutional Problems, 11 U.Rich.L.Rev. 21 (1976); Yearwood, Subdivision Law: Timing and Location Control, 44 J.Urban L. 585 (1967); Comment, The Permissible Scope of Compulsory Requirements for Land Development in Colorado, 54 Colo.L. Rev. 447 (1983); Note, Municipalities: Validity of Subdivision Fees for Schools and Parks, 66 Colum.L.Rev. 974 (1966); Note, Techniques for Preserving Open Spaces, 75 Harv.L.Rev. 1622 (1962); Note, Subdivision Exactions: Where is the Limit? 42 Notre Dame Law 400 (1967); Note, Impact Fees: National Perspective to Florida Practice, 4 Nova L.J. 137 (1980); Note, Subdivision Land Dedication: Objectives and Objections, 27 Stan.L.Rev. 419 (1975); Note, Municipal Ordinance Requiring Parkland Dedication as a Condition to Subdivision Plat Approval Held Not Unconstitutional Per Se, 16 Tex.Tech.L.Rev. 1015 (1985); Note, Development Fees: Standards to Determine Their Reasonableness, 1982 Utah L.Rev. 549; Note, Mandatory Dedication of Land by Land Developers, 26 U.Fla.L.Rev. 41 (1973); Comment, Allocating the Burden of Increased Community Costs Caused by New Developments, 1967 U.Ill.L.F. 318; Note, Money Payment Requirements as Conditions to the Approval of Subdivision Maps: Analysis and Prognosis, 9 Vill.L.R. 294 (1964); Comment, Subdivision Exactions: The Constitutional Issues, the Judicial Response, and the Pennsylvania Situation, 19 Vill.L.Rev. 782 (1974); Comment, Subdivision Exactions in Washington: The Controversy Over Imposing Fees on Developers, 59 Wash.L.Rev. 289 (1984).

3. P. Rohan, Zoning and Land Use Controls § 45.04[2] (1982). The dedicated interest may be an easement or a fee entitle-

regulations should be distinguished from common law dedications. Common law dedication involves an offer to dedicate and a corresponding acceptance by a local government. Under common law dedication a developer is estopped from later questioning the acceptance. In subdivision regulation dedication, however, questions of legislative authority and constitutionality arise.[4]

Early subdivision enabling statutes authorized local governments to adopt subdivision regulations that required developers to provide and dedicate such improvements as streets and other facilities.[5] These early statutes were designed to eliminate the confusion of disconnected street systems resulting from earlier voluntary dedications and to avoid future public debt like that incurred as a result of subdivisions made defunct by the real estate cash of the 1920's.[6] Courts often upheld these early mandatory dedications on the "privilege" theory that:

> The owner of a subdivision voluntarily dedicates sufficient land for streets in return for the advantage and privilege of having his plat recorded.[7]

During the post-World War II land development boom, many local governments began experiencing severe political and economic pressure from the need to provide facilities and services to new development. Increasingly, subdivision regulations were amended to impose new requirements that developers dedicate park and school sites, widen off-site streets, or contribute funds for a wide variety of purposes.[8] During this period the "in lieu" fee developed as a refinement of required dedications.[9] For example, to require each subdivision to dedicate land to educational purposes would not solve the problem of providing school facilities for developing suburban areas because the sites would often be inadequate in size and imperfectly located.[10] The in-lieu fee solves this problem by substituting a money payment for dedication when the local government determines the latter is not feasible.

ment. See Generally 23 Am.Jur.2d Dedications (1965).

4. See Pavelko, supra note 1, n. 9 at 270; 4 R. Anderson, American Law of Zoning § 23.26 (2d ed. 1976).

5. See Melli, Subdivision Control in Wisconsin, 1953 Wis.L.Rev. 389, 455; Note, An Analysis of Subdivision Control Legislation, supra note 2, at 554; R. Freilich and P. Levi, Model Subdivision Regulations: Text and Commentary 3 (Amer.Soc'y of Planning Officials, 1975).

6. See Note, Money Payment Requirements as Conditions to the Approval of Subdivision Maps: Analysis and Prognosis, supra note 2, at 296; see generally § 7.2 supra.

7. Ridgefield Land Co. v. Detroit, 241 Mich. 468, 217 N.W. 48 (1928). See also

Brous v. Smith, 304 N.Y. 164, 106 N.E.2d 503 (1952); Ayres v. City Council of Los Angeles, 34 Cal.2d 31, 207 P.2d 1 (1949); Garvin v. Baker, 59 So.2d 360 (Fla.1952); Pavelko, supra note 2, at 283.

8. See, e.g., Blevens v. Manchester, 103 N.H. 284, 170 A.2d 121 (1961); City of Buena Park v. Boyar, 186 Cal.App.2d 61, 8 Cal.Rptr. 674 (1960); R.M. Yearwood, The Law and Administration of Subdivision Regulation: A Study in Land Use Control 40, 152–62 (1966).

9. Juergensmeyer and Blake, supra note 2, at 418.

10. R. Anderson, supra note 4, at § 19.42.

Also during the 1950's, the "privilege" theory of granting governmental benefits and permits came under intense criticism.[11] In response to this criticism the Supreme Court began to enlarge the concept
of "property" to include the reasonable expectation of government
grants, permits and benefits.[12] Therefore, at the very time that local
governments were expanding their use of exactions the privilege theory
rationale for mandatory dedication appeared destined for obsolescence
as the subdivision of property began to seem more like a right than a
privilege.[13]

As a result of increased demands by local governments for more
contributions, and increased reluctance to characterize governmental
permits as privileges, courts began to draw back from the approval
previously given to principles of mandatory dedication.[14] Based on this
retrenchment, some commentators suggested that exactions should be
permissible only for facilities that are of exclusive benefit to the new
subdivision, such as internal subdivision streets, sewers and neighborhood parks.[15] They concluded that facilities whose benefit extends
beyond a subdivision, such as arterial roads and regional parks, were
not appropriate subjects for exactions even if the facilities were of
substantial benefit to the residents of the subdivision as well.[16]

In contrast to the exclusive benefit theory, in 1964, cost-accounting
was advocated as a method for evaluating cost-shifting devices in an
article published in the Yale Law Journal by Ira Michael Heyman and
Thomas K. Gilhool.[17] This article proposed a new way of evaluating
the validity of subdivision exactions. "Given a proper cost-accounting
approach," said the authors, "it is possible to determine the costs
generated by new residents and thus to avoid charging the newcomers
more than a proportionate share." The fact that the general public
would also benefit from the exaction is immaterial "so long as there is a
rational nexus between the exaction and the costs generated by the
creation of the subdivision." [18]

11. See Reich, The New Property, 73
Yale L.J. 733 (1964).

12. See, e.g., Speiser v. Randall, 357
U.S. 513, 78 S.Ct. 1352, 2 L.Ed.2d 1460
(1958); Flemming v. Nestor, 363 U.S. 603,
80 S.Ct. 1367, 4 L.Ed.2d 1435 (1960), rehearing denied 364 U.S. 854, 81 S.Ct. 29, 5
L.Ed.2d 77 (1960); Sherbert v. Verner, 374
U.S. 398, 83 S.Ct. 1790, 10 L.Ed.2d 965
(1963); Shapiro v. Thompson, 394 U.S. 618,
89 S.Ct. 1322, 22 L.Ed.2d 600 (1969); Goldberg v. Kelly, 397 U.S. 254, 90 S.Ct. 1011,
25 L.Ed.2d 287 (1970); Bell v. Burson, 402
U.S. 535, 91 S.Ct. 1586, 29 L.Ed.2d 90
(1971), conformed 124 Ga.App. 220, 183
S.E.2d 416 (1971).

13. See Bosselman & Stroud, Pariah to
Paragon: Developer Exactions in Florida
1975–85, supra note 2, at 529.

14. Id.

15. See Reps & Smith, supra note 2, at
405.

16. Id. Cases consistent with the "exclusive benefit" or "special benefit" test
include State ex rel. Noland v. St. Louis
County, 478 S.W.2d 363 (Mo.1972); Mc-
Kain v. Toledo City Planning Commission,
26 Ohio App.2d 171, 270 N.E.2d 370 (1971);
Pioneer Trust & Savings Bank v. Village of
Mount Prospect, 22 Ill.2d 375, 176 N.E.2d
799 (1961).

17. See Heyman & Gilhool, supra note
2, at 1118.

18. Id. at 1137.

The great appeal of this theory lay in its common sense approach. The transaction between developer and municipality was to be evaluated from an accounting standpoint in the same manner as any other business transaction. If it appeared that the costs were fairly apportioned between the affected parties the transaction should survive judicial scrutiny. Such a theory liberated the developers from the fiction that they were obtaining some sort of privilege, but it also provided local government with a flexible theory that could justify demands for payment of money as easily as for dedication of land. Because the theory was not tied to the financing of any particular type of government facility or service, it could be broadly applied across the whole range of government activities.

Out of this theory has evolved impact analysis and the use of impact fees as the most recent answer to local governments' capital funding dilemma.[19] The impact fee [20] is functionally and conceptually similar to the in lieu fee in that both are required payments for capital facilities. In fact, in certain situations the terms can be used virtually interchangeably. The impact fee concept, however, is a much more flexible cost shifting tool. Because in lieu fees are predicated on dedication requirements, they can only be used where required dedications can be appropriately utilized. In the case of sewer and water facilities, public safety facilities, and similar capital outlays, required dedications are not an appropriate device to shift a portion of the capital costs to the development because one facility (and parcel of land) can service a very wide area and there is little need for additional land in extending these services.

(B) Constitutional Challenges to Exactions

The validity of exactions is generally subject to a two-tiered constitutional attack. The preliminary and often dispositive objection to required payments by developers for capital expenses is that they are not authorized by state statute or constitution [21] and therefore are void as ultra vires.[22] If statutory authority is found, the local ordinance is alternatively challenged as an unreasonable regulation exceeding the state's police power or as a disguised tax which violates various state constitutional strictures.[23]

---

19. See Juergensmeyer & Blake, supra note 2.

20. For a discussion of impact fees in general including the advantages of impact fees over in-lieu fees see § 9.3 infra.

21. See, e.g., City of Montgomery v. Crossroads Land Co., 355 So.2d 363 (Ala. 1978) (in lieu fees for recreational purposes not authorized by state statute); Admiral Dev. Corp. v. Maitland, 267 So.2d 860 (Fla. 4th D.C.A.1972) (dedication and in lieu fees for park and recreational purposes not authorized by city charter). See also Heyman & Gilhool, supra note 2, at 1134, n. 66

(citing cases where issue of statutory authority was dispositive).

22. The power of a local government to exercise various subdivision controls, including impact fees, is derived from general state statutes, private acts, and municipal charters. E. Yokley, The Law of Subdivisions 7 (1963).

23. See, e.g., Call v. West Jordan, 606 P.2d 217 (Utah 1979), on rehearing 614 P.2d 1257 (1980) (in lieu fees for flood control, park, and recreational purposes attacked as ultra vires, an unreasonable regulation, and as an unconstitutional tax);

A review of recent constitutional challenges to exactions discloses a changing judicial attitude towards these cost-shifting devices.[24] Despite earlier negative reaction to such payment requirements, based on the exclusive benefit theory, state courts currently tend to validate them as a proper and reasonable exercise of police power.[25] These decisions, however, have utilized different and inconsistent legal theories to circumvent the restrictive standards initially established.[26] The courts' reluctance to clearly characterize these payments as either land use regulations or taxes has aggravated the confusion.[27]

1. In-lieu and Impact Fees: Land Use Regulations or Taxes

The characterization of in-lieu and impact fees as land use regulations or taxes presents a complex problem. Required dedications, which serve the same purpose as impact fees, are an acknowledged police power regulation. Because fees are functionally similar to dedications and to other land use planning and growth management tools, the regulation tag appears appropriate. Although commentators have generally adopted the regulation characterization,[28] the taxation rubric theoretically is equally appropriate, particularly when the positive nature of fees and hornbook distinctions between a tax and a regulation are considered.[29]

Jordan v. Village of Menomonee Falls, 28 Wis.2d 608, 137 N.W.2d 442 (1965), appeal dismissed 385 U.S. 4, 87 S.Ct. 36, 17 L.Ed. 2d 3 (1966) (in lieu fees for school, park, and recreational purposes attacked as ultra vires, an unreasonable regulation and as an unconstitutional tax), cert. dismissed, 385 U.S. 4 (1966). See generally Heyman & Gilhool, supra note 2, at 1122, 1146.

24. See, e.g., Associated Home Builders, Inc. v. Walnut Creek, 4 Cal.3d 633, 94 Cal. Rptr. 630, 484 P.2d 606 (1971) (subdivision fees for recreation purposes approved), cert. dismissed 404 U.S. 878, 92 S.Ct. 202, 30 L.Ed.2d 159 (1971), Billings Properties, Inc. v. Yellowstone County, 144 Mont. 25, 394 P.2d 182 (1964) (required dedication for recreational purposes upheld); Jenad, Inc. v. Village of Scarsdale, 18 N.Y.2d 78, 271 N.Y.S.2d 955, 218 N.E.2d 673 (1966) (in lieu fees for recreational purposes upheld); Call v. West Jordan, 606 P.2d 217 (Utah 1979), on rehearing 614 P.2d 1257 (1980) (in lieu fee for flood control, park, and recreational purposes upheld); Jordan v. Village of Menomonee Falls, 28 Wis.2d 608, 137 N.W.2d 442 (1965), appeal dismissed 385 U.S. 4, 87 S.Ct. 36, 17 L.Ed.2d 3 (in lieu fee for school, park, and recreational purposes upheld).

25. See note 24 supra. In the beach access context the California courts have held that exactions as conditions of approv-al for new development are not required to directly or indirectly benefit the development. See Georgia-Pacific Corp. v. California Coastal Com., 132 Cal.App.3d 678, 183 Cal.Rptr. 395 (1982); Grupe v. California Coastal Com., 166 Cal.App.3d 148, 212 Cal. Rptr. 578 (1 Dist.1985).

26. Johnston, supra note 2, at 913–14; Comment, supra note 2, at 799–802.

27. See Jordan v. Village of Menomonee Falls, 28 Wis.2d 608, 137 N.W.2d 442, 450 (1965), appeal dismissed 385 U.S. 4, 87 S.Ct. 36, 17 L.Ed.2d 3 (1966) (court admitted it was unable to decide whether in lieu fee was a regulation or an excise tax).

28. See, e.g., Heyman & Gilhool, supra note 2, at 1134; Johnson, supra note 2, at 917.

29. According to Professor Cooley, a demand for money can be upheld under the police power only if its primary purpose is regulation. If its primary purpose is revenue, it is an exercise of the taxing power. 4 T. Cooley, The Law of Taxation § 1784 (1924). According to those who argue that impact fees are taxes, such fees are primarily a revenue raising device regardless of whether they are spent inside or outside the development. See Note, supra note 2, at 408–09.

The label applied in a particular case will depend on the specificity and clarity of the enabling statute. Either label could be effectively employed by state legislatures to delegate authority to impose properly constituted fees for extradevelopment funding; however, in most cases neither the statutory authorization relied upon nor the local ordinance provides a clear guide to characterization by the courts.

The choice a court makes in tagging the fee will often be determinative of its validity. If the tax label is adopted, the fee will be invalidated unless express and specific statutory authorization for the tax exists.[30] Even if statutory authorization is present, constitutional limitations on taxation may still invalidate the statute.[31] Alternatively, if the fee is construed as a police power regulation, very broad legislative delegation will suffice.[32] Once past this statutory hurdle, the clear trend among state courts is to validate such extradevelopment capital funding payment requirements as a valid exercise of the police power.[33] Not surprisingly, therefore, most state courts have summarily labeled extradevelopment fees as either a tax or regulation in a result-oriented fashion that avoids an adequate theoretical or policy-directed explanation.[34]

Recent decisions indicate that judicial conceptions of public policy favor a regulation characterization of fee requirements for extradevelopment capital funding. In the absence of specific enabling legislation determinations must be made on an individual basis. The massive financial problems created by suburban growth, combined with broad legislative delegations of authority in land use regulation favor the characterization, their validity should be determined under the police power.

30. See, e.g., City of Montgomery v. Crossroads Land Co., 355 So.2d 363 (Ala. 1978) (in lieu fee is a tax and thus must have specific statutory authorization).

31. Many state constitutions contain prohibitions against uneven property taxation. See, e.g., West's Fla.St.Ann. Const. Art. 7, § 2. Therefore, if impact fees are characterized as property taxes they would be invalidated by such provisions. See Venditti-Siravo, Inc. v. Hollywood, 39 Fla. Supp. 121, 122–23 (17th Cir.Ct.1973) (impact fee is an invalid property tax). If impact fees are to be considered taxes, however, they are more properly characterized as excise taxes.

32. See Contractors & Builders Ass'n v. Dunedin, 329 So.2d 314, 317–20 (Fla.1976), cert. denied 444 U.S. 867, 100 S.Ct. 140, 62 L.Ed.2d 91 (1979). (If fee is characterized as a tax then it is void for lack of specific statutory authorization, but because it is a regulation, the broader delegation will suffice).

33. See, e.g., Contractors & Builders Ass'n v. Dunedin, 329 So.2d 314 (Fla.1976), cert. denied 444 U.S. 867, 100 S.Ct. 140, 62 L.Ed.2d 91 (1979) (Impact fee a regulation, valid if proper limitations placed on amounts collected); Billings Properties, Inc. v. Yellowstone County, 144 Mont. 25, 394 P.2d 182 (1964) (in lieu fee is a regulation which is valid under the police power); Jenad, Inc. v. Village of Scarsdale, 18 N.Y.2d 78, 271 N.Y.S.2d 955, 218 N.E.2d 673 (1966) (in lieu fee is a regulation held valid under the police power).

34. See generally Juergensmeyer & Blake, supra note 2, at 422–27.

2. Judicial Criteria for Assessing the Constitutionality of Exactions: Early Restrictions

Two landmark decisions placed an almost insurmountable burden on local governments seeking money payments for extradevelopment capital spending from developers whose activities necessitated such expenditures. In Pioneer Trust & Savings Bank v. Village of Mount Prospect,[35] a developer challenged the validity of an ordinance requiring subdividers to dedicate one acre per sixty residential lots for schools, parks, and other public purposes. In determining whether required dedications or money payments for recreational or educational purposes represented a valid exercise of the police power, the Illinois Supreme Court propounded the "specifically and uniquely attributable" test. The court focused on the origin of the need for the new facilities and held that unless the village could prove that the demand for additional facilities was "specifically and uniquely attributable" to the particular subdivision, such requirements were an unreasonable regulation not authorized by the police power. Thus, where schools had become overcrowded because of the "total development of the community" the subdivider could not be compelled to help fund new facilities which his activity would necessitate.

A related and equally restrictive test was delinated by the New York court in Gulest Associations, Inc. v. Town of Newburgh.[36] In that case developers attacked an ordinance which charged in lieu fees for recreational purposes. The amounts collected were to be used by the town for "neighborhood park, playground or recreation purposes including the acquisition of property."[37] The court held that the money payment requirement was an unreasonable regulation tantamount to an unconstitutional taking because the funds collected were not used solely for the benefit of the residents of the particular subdivision charged, but rather could be used in any section of town for any recreational purposes. In essence, the Gulest "direct benefit" test required that funds collected from required payments for capital expenditures be specifically tied to a benefit directly conferred on the homeowners in the subdivision which was charged. If recreational fees were used to purchase a park outside the subdivision, the direct benefit test was not met and the ordinance was invalid.

Perhaps the reason behind this initial restrictive approach was an underlying judicial suspicion that payment requirements for extradevelopment capital expenditures were in reality a tax. Unlike zoning, payment requirements did not fit neatly into traditional conceptions of police power regulations. By applying the restrictive Pioneer Trust and Gulest tests, courts imposed the substantial requirements of a special assessment on such payment requirements. This was consis-

---

35. 22 Ill.2d 375, 176 N.E.2d 799 (1961).

36. 25 Misc.2d 1004, 209 N.Y.S.2d 729 (1960), affirmed 15 A.D.2d 815, 225 N.Y.S.2d 538 (1962). The Gulest decision was overruled in Jenad, Inc. v. Village of Scarsdale, 18 N.Y.2d 78, 271 N.Y.2d 955, 957 (1966).

37. 209 N.Y.S.2d at 732.

tent with perceiving them as a tax. Unfortunately, it effectively precluded their use for most extradevelopment capital funding purposes, particularly for educational facilities.

Despite this early trend, the Pioneer Trust and Gulest tests became difficult to reconcile with the planning and funding problems imposed on local governments by the constant acceleration of suburban growth. This restrictiveness also became difficult to rationalize with the judicial view of zoning ordinances as presumptively valid. Consequently, courts were not convinced of the practical or legal necessity of such stringent standards for the validation of required payments for extradevelopment capital funding.

3. Recent Decisional Criteria Favoring the Police Power Validity of Exactions

In turning away from the restrictive standards of Gulest and Pioneer Trust, state courts developed divergent and conflicting police power criteria for assessing the constitutional validity of extradevelopment capital funding fees. Some courts nominally retained the Pioneer Trust test but reached patently contrary results without any explanation of the discrepancy. Other courts adopted a privilege theory, under which granting the privilege to subdivide entitles local governments to require payments for extradevelopment capital spending in return. The imposition of these payment requirements is viewed more as part of a transaction than as an exercise of the police power. Still other courts have deferred to legislative judgments and eschewed constitutional analysis of such payment requirements.[38] Both the disparity between test and result and the inconsistent scrutiny applied to these ordinances have been frequently criticized by commentators.[39]

In contrast to these result oriented techniques, a more disciplined constitutional standard was suggested by the Wisconsin Supreme Court in Jordan v. Village of Menomonee Falls.[40] A two part "rational nexus" test of reasonableness for judging the validity of extradevelopment impact and in lieu fees can be discerned in the decision. In response to a developer's attack upon the ordinance as both unauthorized by statute and as an unconstitutional taking without just compensation, the Jordan court addressed the constitutionality of in lieu fees for educational and recreational purposes. After concluding that the fee payments were statutorily authorized, the court focused first on the Pioneer Trust "specifically and uniquely attributable" test.

The Wisconsin Supreme Court expressed concern that it was virtually impossible for a municipality to prove that money payment or land dedication requirements were assessed to meet a need *solely* generated

---

38. See Jenad, Inc. v. Village of Scarsdale, 18 N.Y.2d 78, 271 N.Y.S.2d 955 (1966) (overruling Gulest).

39. See Johnston, supra note 2, at 913–21.

40. 28 Wis.2d 608, 137 N.W.2d 442 (1965), appeal dismissed 385 U.S. 4, 87 S.Ct. 36, 17 L.Ed.2d 3 (1966).

by a particular subdivision. Suggesting a substitute test, the court held that money payment and dedication requirements for educational and recreational purposes were a valid exercise of the police power if there was a "reasonable connection" between the need for additional facilities and the growth generated by the subdivision. This first "rational nexus" was sufficiently established if the local government could demonstrate that a series of subdivisions had generated the need to provide educational and recreational facilities for the benefit of this stream of new residents. In the absence of contrary evidence, such proof showed that the need for the facilities was sufficiently attributable to the activity of the particular developer to permit the collection of fees for financing required improvements.[41]

The Jordan court also rejected the Gulest direct benefit requirement, declining to treat the fees as a special assessment. Therefore, it imposed no requirement that the ordinance restrict the funds to the purchase of school and park facilities that would directly benefit the assessed subdivision. Instead, the court concluded that the relationship between the expenditure of funds and the benefits accruing to the subdivision providing the funds was a fact issue pertinent to the reasonableness of the payment requirement under the police power.

The Jordan court did not expressly define the "reasonableness" required in the expenditure of extradevelopment capital funds; however, a second "rational nexus" was impliedly required between the expenditure of the funds and benefits accruing to the subdivision. The court concluded that this second "rational nexus" was met where the fees were to be used exclusively for site acquisition and the amount spent by the village in constructing additional school facilities was greater than the amounts collected from the developments creating the need for additional facilities.

This second "rational nexus" requirement inferred from Jordan, therefore, is met if a local government can demonstrate that its actual or projected extradevelopment capital expenditures earmarked for the substantial benefit of a series of developments are greater than the capital payments required of those developments. Such proof establishes a sufficient benefit to a particular subdivision in the stream of residential growth such that the extradevelopment payment requirements may be deemed to be reasonable under the police power. Although most commentators have overlooked the requirement of a "sufficient benefit" nexus in analyzing the Jordan decision, the concept of benefits received is clearly distinct from the concept of needs attributable. As the Jordan court recognized, the benefit accruing to the subdivision, although it need not be direct, is a necessary factor in analyzing the reasonableness of payment requirements for extradevelopment capital funding.[42]

41. Id.   42. Id. at 450.

The dual "rational nexus" requirements deducible from Jordan provide a balanced, judicially consistent and realistic test of money payment requirements for extradevelopment capital funding. This test properly focuses on and balances the legitimate interests of the developer and the general welfare concerns and power of the municipality. In addition, the "sufficiently attributable" and "sufficient benefit" proof requirements can be accurately and realistically met by local governments through the use of modern cost accounting techniques. Finally, once these "rational nexi" are established, the burden to disprove the reasonableness of the payment requirement shifts to the developer, according the local government a semblance of the presumption of validity it enjoys in zoning and other land use regulation matters.

The sophistication and evolving complexity of rational nexus analysis has been demonstrated recently by the Supreme Court of Utah in Banberry Dev. Corp. v. South Jordan City.[43] In Banberry the court further developed the "reasonableness" issue raised by the Supreme Court of Wisconsin in Jordan. The specificity and clarity of the court's language gives considerable aid to local governments in formulating step-by-step in-lieu and impact fee implementation programs:

"[To] comply with the standard of reasonableness, a municipal fee related to services like water and sewer must not require newly developed properties to bear more than their equitable share of the capital costs in relation to benefits conferred.

To determine the equitable share of the capital costs to be borne by newly developed properties, a municipality should determine the relative burdens previously borne and yet to be borne by those properties in comparison with the other properties in the municipality as a whole; the fee in question should not exceed the amount sufficient to equalize the relative burdens of newly developed and other properties.

Among the most important factors the municipality should consider in determining the relative burden already borne and yet to be borne by newly developed properties and other properties are the following, suggested by the well-reasoned authorities cited below: (1) the cost of existing capital facilities; (2) the manner of financing existing capital facilities (such as user charges, special assessments, bonded indebtedness, general taxes, or federal grants); (3) the relative extent to which the newly developed properties and the other properties in the municipality have already contributed to the cost of existing facilities (by means such as user charges, special assessments, or payments from proceeds of general taxes); (4) the relative extent to which the newly developed and the other properties in the municipality will contribute to the cost of existing capital facilities in the future; (5) the extent to which the newly developed properties are entitled to a credit . . . ."[44]

43. 631 P.2d 899 (Utah 1981).

44. Id. at 903–04. In Lafferty v. Payson City, 642 P.2d 376 (Utah 1982), the Utah Supreme Court remanded a trial court's invalidation of connection fees for sewer, water and electrical services because not

WESTLAW REFERENCES
di,sy(subdivision /s exaction)
414k382.2 /p exaction

A. Historical Perspective on the Types of Exactions
subdivision /2 regulation /s dedication
"common law dedication"
brous +2 smith
subdivision /s dedicat*** /s lieu /2 fee
speiser +2 randall /p privilege
subdivision & exaction /s exclusive special /2 benefit
subdivision /p "impact fee"

B. Constitutional Challenges to Exactions
subdivision /p exaction /s unauthoriz** authoriz! /s statut***
    constitution
exaction /s unreasonable reasonable /s "police power"
di,sy(zoning subdivision /p exaction /s regulation tax)

    1. In-lieu and Impact Fees: Land Use Regulations or Taxes
lieu impact /2 fee /s regulation tax /s "police power"

    2. Judicial Criteria for Assessing the Constitutionality of Ex-
       actions: Early Restrictions
"pioneer trust" /s "mount prospect"
268k43 /p exaction fee dedicat***
gulest /s newburgh
92k63 /p delegat*** /s subdivision

    3. Recent Decisional Criteria Favoring the Police Power Valid-
       ity of Exactions
subdivision /p "rational nexus" /s impact lieu /2 fee
414k382.4
dedicat*** fee /s "police power" /s "reasonable connection"
    "rational nexus"
jordan /s menomenee

III. MAPPING FOR FUTURE STREETS AND OTHER PUBLIC IMPROVEMENTS

§ 7.9 In General [1]

Official mapping provisions are another kind of land use control that implements planning. An official map gives precise locations of

all of the five Banberry factors had been considered.

§ 7.9

1. For a comprehensive discussion of official maps see 4 R. Anderson, American Law of Zoning §§ 24.01–24.16 (2d ed. (1976); see also Rohan, Zoning and Land Use Controls §§ 46.01–.04 (1984); Brown, Reservation of Highway and Street Rights-of-Way by Official Maps, 66 W.Va.L.Rev. 73 (1964); Waite, The Official Map and the Constitution in Maine, 15 Maine L.Rev. 3 (1963); Comment, Date of Validation in Eminent Domain: Irreverence for Unconstitutional Practice, 30 U.Chi.L.Rev. 319 (1963); Note, Problems of Advance Land Acquisition, 52 Minn.L.Rev. 1175 (1968); Note, Municipal Street Control v. Private Property Rights, 14 Syracuse L.Rev. 70 (1963).

future streets within and sometimes without a municipality and sometimes also includes sites for parks and other public improvements. The basis for the regulation is that there is hardly any determinant of future land development as important as the location of future streets. If buildings are placed that interfere with the logical extension of streets, the public authorities are put in the unenviable position of placing major streets around scattered existing development or acquiring improvements at great cost.

The Standard City Planning Enabling Act [2] provided that a plat of an area could be adopted showing streets for future acquisition. Adoption of the plat was a reservation of the indicated streets but was neither the opening of a street nor the taking of land. The Standard Act provision was not widely adopted. The means were too expensive, since compensation was paid for the reservation for whatever period of time land was reserved. When the street itself was opened, the Act provided that additional compensation would be paid, except for buildings erected in contravention of the easement.

In addition to adoption of a major street plat, streets could also be approved under the Standard Act if shown on the master plan, if on an approved subdivision plat or if specially approved. Unless approved in one of these ways, Section 18 of the Act provided the municipality could not accept, lay out, open, improve, grade, pave, curb or light any street, or lay or authorize water mains or sewers. In addition, buildings could not be erected nor building permits issued unless the street giving access to the building had been approved in one of the four ways.

The competitor to the street plat of the Standard Act became known as the official map because the device was so denominated in Section 4 of the Municipal Planning Enabling Act suggested by Bassett and Williams.[3] The Bassett and Williams Act relied on the police power and formed the basis for legislation in many states. Local governments under the Act could adopt an official map showing existing and future streets and parks. No permit for building in the mapped areas could be issued, unless the land affected would not yield a fair return, in which case a permit in the nature of a variance [4] could be issued to relieve the hardship [5] up to the point of permitting a fair return. Provisions were included similar to those in the Standard Act for preventing utilities in streets and for prohibiting the issuance of building permits where access streets to proposed buildings were not shown on the official map. A requirement that access streets be approved and improved as a condition for issuance of a building permit is valid.[6] The theory is that building permits can be conditioned on

2. U.S. Dep't of Commerce, § 21 (1928).

3. Reprinted in E. Bassett, F. Williams, A. Bettman & R. Whitten, Model Laws for Planning Cities, Counties, and States 40 (1935).

4. See §§ 6.5–6.10 supra.

5. See § 6.9 supra.

6. Brous v. Smith, 304 N.Y. 164, 106 N.E. 503 (1952).

reasonable requirements for streets meeting minimum planning and construction standards.

The Municipal Mapped Streets Act also served as another model.[7] Amendments to the model act's official map were automatic when streets were shown on an approved subdivision plat. Buildings could be authorized by variance for two reasons: lack of reasonable return or where the interest of the owner in the use of his property outweighed that of the municipality in preserving the integrity of the official map. As with the other models, utilities could not be placed except on approved streets and building permits could not be issued for proposed buildings which did not have access to approved streets. As with the Municipal Planning Enabling Act, the Municipal Mapped Streets Act and Williams, Bettman contemplated that compensation would be paid only if land was actually taken for a street; no compensation was paid upon adoption of the map or for buildings taken that were not permitted by variance. As a practical matter, compensation is never paid, particularly for minor streets, since they are usually obtained by dedication required as a condition for subdivision approval.[8]

A few states have statutes which, rather than authorize variances, seek to keep the restriction within the scope of the police power by limiting the period of time that it can apply. For example, under the statute in Miller v. Beaver Falls,[9] parks could be designated on a map and once designated no compensation would be paid for buildings if the site was acquired. However, the reservation was void if the site was not acquired by the local government within three years. The court held this provision invalid as beyond the scope of the police power and constituting a taking for which compensation should be paid. The court distinguished between street reservations and park reservations, admitting that the reservation would be valid as to streets because they are narrow, well-defined and absolutely necessary.

Statutes often make official map provisions available to state highway departments. Some states also have special statutes authorizing highway reservations.[10]

 WESTLAW REFERENCES

di,sy(official /2 map*** /s street park % criminal)

di,sy("building permit" /s street park /s map***)

di,sy(map /p compensat*** /s land street building /s tak***)

street park highway /2 reservation /p "police power"

---

7. Reprinted in Model Laws, supra note 3, at 89.

8. See § 7.8 supra.

9. 368 Pa. 189, 82 A.2d 34 (1951).

10. See Brown, Reservation of Highway and Street Rights-of-Way by Official Maps, 66 W.Va.L.Rev. 73 (1964); Mandelker, Planning the Freeway: Interim Controls in Highway Programs, 1964 Duke L.J. 439.

§ 7.10   Relation to Master Plan and Planning

As with zoning, official maps or something like them preceded master planning, as a historical matter.   In some colonial towns there was one proprietor who owned the land and the town was laid out by map showing dedicated public places.   The law of dedication then applied.[1]   Where many owners were involved, as in the case of L'Enfants' plan for Washington, D.C., commissioners were given authority to plat the town, owners conveyed property in trust, and a plan was adopted with dedicated areas shown.   Regulations similar to modern-day official maps protected future streets in New York City as early as 1806.   Modern official map acts sometimes require some master planning as a prerequisite to official mapping.   Acts based on the Standard Act and the Municipal Mapped Streets Act require at least a major street plan, though statutes strictly based on the Bassett and Williams model would not require any kind of plan as a prerequisite.[2]   The difference between the major street plan and the official map is that the former only gives general locations, whereas the latter specifies locations and widths to survey accuracy and has the legal effects noted in the previous section.

   WESTLAW REFERENCES
official /2 map*** /s master /2 plan****

"major street plan"

§ 7.11   Relation to Zoning, Setbacks

An official map, like zoning, restricts improvements.   Unlike zoning it does not restrict uses requiring no improvements.   Since official maps can be used to designate future street widths as well as new streets, the official map device bears some resemblance to front yard requirements in zoning.[1]   A front yard requirement under zoning is theoretically used to secure air and light, improve appearance, prevent overcrowding, mitigate problems of traffic safety on intersections and the like.   Practically, the front yard requirement can be used as an official map for the purpose of reducing costs of acquisition when streets are widened.   Improvements are in fact kept from the front yard.   The official map is also related to zoning in that front yards are often measured from the edge of the officially mapped street rather than the actual street.

§ 7.10

1. See § 7.8 supra.

§ 7.11

1. See § 4.7 supra.

2. See § 7.9 supra for descriptions of these model and standard acts.

Setback provisions,[2] which may be part of the zoning, or subdivision ordinance, or a separate ordinance, are also used to keep improvements from beds of existing but to-be-widened streets.[3]

Setback and front yard requirements under private restrictions have some of the effects of official maps, even if not motivated by a desire to ease the financial burden of acquiring street sites.

WESTLAW REFERENCES

di,sy(zon***   /s   "front yard"   setback)

official   /2   map***   /p   "front yard"   setback

§ 7.12   Relation to Subdivision Control

Streets are typically shown on subdivision plats and are often approved in conjunction with the subdivision plat approval. As with official maps, subdivision controls provide that unless a street is approved in some way, streets cannot be opened or improved or utilities placed. Likewise, as with official maps, buildings cannot be built in the streets shown on the subdivision plat and building permits cannot be issued.

Subdivisions and official maps are related in another way under statutes following the Bassett and Williams model.[1] It provides the planning commission with authority to approve subdivision plats showing new streets, highways, or freeways, or the widening thereof only after adoption of the official map. Under other statutes, a subdivision can be rejected if it does not comply with an official map. If no official map has been adopted, a major or master street plan[2] does not have that effect, and the subdivision cannot be rejected, although streets are placed differently than on the master plan.[3]

WESTLAW REFERENCES

di,sy(subdivision   /s   street   /s   approv**)

"planning commission"   /p   approv**   /s   subdivision   /s   official   /
    2   map***

§ 7.13   Constitutionality

Most of the cases on official maps discussed by the treatise writers and included in the casebooks deal with constitutional problems. This recognizes that property owners whose land is affected by mapped reservation often complain that the prohibition against development constitutes a taking. Landowners also argue that the use of official

---

2. See § 4.8 supra.

3. See generally, R. Black, Building Lines and Reservations for Future Streets (1935), which is a classic study.

§ 7.12

1. See § 7.9 note 3 supra.

2. See § 7.10 supra.

3. Lordship Park Ass'n v. Board of Zoning Appeals, 137 Conn. 84, 75 A.2d 379 (1950). But see Krieger v. Planning Comm'n of Howard County, 224 Md. 320, 167 A.2d 885 (1961).

mapping statutes constitutes an improper attempt to depress the value of mapped land until the power of eminent domain can be exercised.

While compensation is obviously and clearly due where a municipality permanently acquires a street, park or other public site, the official map statutes state they intend no taking, and a temporary reservation does not appear to be an undue burden under the police power. Support for the constitutionality of official map statutes and reservations as interim development restrictions can be found in the interim zoning cases.[1] However, courts have held official mapping statutes unconstitutional where the statute authorizes a reservation for a specific number of years.[2] Where the official map statutes operate more like zoning, imposing a restriction against improvements for an indefinite rather than a fixed time, with variances to relieve hardship, the courts are more disposed to approve. The latter kind of statute may actually be a greater burden on the property than the fixed period reservations—the time period may be longer, the landowner has to prove hardship and even if proved he is not entitled to do what he wants, he can only do what must be allowed to reduce the hardship.

Actually, official map type provisions were more constitutionally secure at an earlier period than in the nearer past. In the very early days, landowners were so delighted to have roads on their property that land could be had by the public for the asking and compensation was seldom heard of. In that tradition, In re Furman St.[3] held that the owner of a building subsequently erected in the bed of an officially mapped street in 1819 was not entitled to any compensation for the building when the street was actually opened, even though the statute did not address the question of compensation for buildings built in mapped streets. The court stated that the mapping and orderly development of the area had in effect already compensated property owners in the area due to increased values.

Forster v. Scott,[4] however, led to some doubts about the constitutionality of the official map statute. In that case an entire lot was covered by a street reservation and there was no provision for variance. It was not surprising that the court held the provision invalid, as it would today if a land use restriction makes an entire separately owned parcel virtually unusable.[5] However, the case led many to assume that official mapping was constitutionally risky without payment of compensation.

§ 7.13

1. See § 3.13 supra.

2. Miller v. Beaver Falls, 368 Pa. 189, 82 A.2d 34 (1951) (3 year reservation for parks); Urbanizadora Versalles, Inc. v. Rios, 701 F.2d 993 (1st Cir.1983) (14 year reservation for highway); Lomarch Corp. v. Mayor & Common Council, 51 N.J. 108, 237 A.2d 881 (1968) (1 year reservation for parks).

3. 17 Wend. 649 (N.Y.Sup.Ct. of Judicature 1936).

4. 136 N.Y. 577, 32 N.E. 976 (1893).

5. But see Consolidated Rock Products Co. v. Los Angeles, 57 Cal.2d 515, 20 Cal. Rptr. 638, 370 P.2d 342 (1962), appeal dismissed 371 U.S. 36, 83 S.Ct. 145, 9 L.Ed.2d 112 (1962).

In Gorieb v. Fox[6] the U.S. Supreme Court upheld the fixing of a setback line along streets. Therefore it was not a major step in Headley v. Rochester[7] for the New York court to approve an official map provision which reserved 25 feet from a large lot for a widened street. The court technically reached this result because the landowner did not apply for the variance to relieve hardship authorized by the statute, but the case is read more broadly than that because courts often do not apply an exhaustion of remedies doctrine when a constitutional issue is raised.[8] Similarly, in State ex rel. Miller v. Manders,[9] even though a substantial portion of a lot was reserved for a street, and the owner was denied a building permit, the court refused to hold the statute unconstitutional where no variance was first sought.[10]

WESTLAW REFERENCES

official /2 map*** /s constitutional*** unconstitutional***

(official /2 map***) reservation

building house home residence structure /s built erect** /s
    map*** /2 street

forster +2 scott

di,sy(lot land /s reserv** condemn** take* /s street)

§ 7.14 Effect of Official Map on Marketability of Title

Generally, a zoning ordinance is not an encumbrance on title that makes property unmarketable, except where property is improved with an illegal non-conforming building. Perhaps because the official map usually designates roads and in some respects is like an easement for roads, the general rule is different in the case of official maps. A widening line has been construed to be an encumbrance as has a future mapped street over part or all of the property (despite the likely unconstitutionality of the official map provision if enforced in the latter case). The official map is an encumbrance as to buildings illegally built in the mapped area.[1] Even where a building preexisted the mapping of the street, the mapping provision was found to be an encumbrance.[2] The difference in the cases may be that the official map provisions appear to be more like easements to the court or that buyers generally

---

6. 274 U.S. 603, 47 S.Ct. 675, 71 L.Ed. 1228 (1927).

7. 272 N.Y. 197, 5 N.E.2d 198 (1936).

8. Compare Jensen v. New York, 42 N.Y.2d 1079, 399 N.Y.S.2d 645, 369 N.E.2d 1179 (1977) (not required to seek permit) with 59 Front St. Realty Corp. v. Klaess, 6 Misc.2d 774, 160 N.Y.S.2d 265 (1957) (variance required).

9. 2 Wis.2d 365, 86 N.W.2d 469 (1957).

10. See generally Waite, The Official Map and the Constitution in Maine, 15 Me. L.Rev. 3 (1963).

§ 7.14

1. Bibber v. Weber, 199 Misc. 906, 102 N.Y.S.2d 945 (1951), affirmed mem. 278 App.Div. 973, 105 N.Y.S.2d 758 (1951). But see Lansburgh v. Market St. Ry. Co., 98 Cal.App.2d 426, 220 P.2d 423 (1950) distinguishing New York cases.

2. See generally Kucirek & Beuscher, Wisconsin's Official Map Law, 1957 Wis.L. Rev. 176, 201–11.

would not be on guard for such provisions, as they would or should be in the case of zoning.

 WESTLAW REFERENCES

zon*** /s marketab! /s title

map*** /s marketab! /s title

IV. PLANNED UNIT DEVELOPMENTS

§ 7.15 Definition and History

The planned unit development (PUD) is a recent and innovative approach to land use development. Its parentage is a union of cluster zoning [1] and subdivision platting. The definition of a PUD which is most frequently encountered is:

> 'Planned unit development' means an area of land, controlled by a landowner, to be developed as a single entity for a number of dwelling units, and commercial and industrial uses, if any, the plan for which does not correspond in lot size, bulk, or type of dwelling or commercial or industrial use, density, lot coverage and required open space to the regulations established in any one or more districts created, from time to time, under the provisions of a municipal zoning ordinance enacted pursuant to the conventional zoning enabling act of the state.[2]

A PUD which contains only residential uses is frequently called a planned unit residential development (PURD) and a purely commercial uses planned unit development is called a planned unit commercial development (PUCD). A PUD is primarily an alternative to traditional zoning since it provides a mixing of uses. The location and identification of the permitted uses are provided on the PUD map or plat which closely resembles a subdivision plat. Development approval is generally granted for the PUD at one time rather than on a lot by lot basis and in that way closely tracks the subdivision approval process.

The planned unit development concept is sometimes traced to a provision contained in Section 12 of Bassett's Model Planning Enabling Act of 1925.[3]

Under that section:

> the legislative body [could] authorize the planning board to make . . . changes upon approving subdivision plats, when the owner [submitted] a plan designating the lots on which apartment houses and local shops are to be built and indicating the maximum density

§ 7.15

1. See § 4.3.

2. U.S. Advisory Commission on Intergovernmental Relations, ACIR State Legislative Program, 1970 Cumulative Supp. 31–36–00 at 5 (1969).

3. Basset, Laws of Planning Unbuilt Areas, in Neighborhood and Community Planning, Regional Survey Vol. VII, 272–73 (1929).

of population and the minimum yard requirements per lot. Section 12 also limited the average population density and the total land area covered by buildings in the entire subdivision to that permitted in the original zoning district . . . . Upon the approval of the planning board following a public hearing with proper notice, the changes were to become part of the municipality's zoning regulations.[4]

Although available since the 1920's, planned unit development provisions were not utilized until the 1960's. The new-found popularity of planned unit developments coincides with large scale development in the post second world war era. By the early sixties the incompatibility of traditional zoning and larger residential developments was recognized, and the push for the adoption of planned unit development ordinances began.[5] Today, large mixed use developments are the rule rather than the exception, and planned unit development (PUD) regulations represent one attempt to avoid the problems of large scale development under conventional zoning notions.

Planned unit developments are basically designed to permit the development of entire neighborhoods, or in some cases even towns, based on an approved plan. The completed development usually includes a variety of residential types, common open space for recreation, parks, and in some cases, commercial or even industrial areas. Since the entire project is preplanned the completed development can be based upon a logical and coherent mixture of uses.

The PUD principle is that a land area under unified control can be designed and developed in a single operation, usually by a series of prescheduled phases, and according to an officially approved "plan." The plan does not necessarily have to correspond to the property and use regulations of the zoning district in which the development is located. As can be seen from the definition, the planned unit development concept abandons the lot by lot approach to development, and is primarily an alternative to zoning.

Cluster Development

Cluster development and planned unit development are sometimes viewed as the same thing. It is more accurate to define cluster development as a device for grouping dwellings to increase dwelling densities on some portions of the development area in order to have other portions free of buildings.[6]

4. Krasnowiecki, Planned Unit Development: A Challenge to Established Theory and Practice of Land Use Control, 114 U.Pa.L.Rev. 47, 48 (1965).

5. See, e.g., Goldston and Scheuer, Zoning of Planned Residential Developments, 73 Harv.L.Rev. 241 (1959); Symposium:

Planned Unit Development, 114 U.Pa.L. Rev. 1–170 (1965).

6. Chrinko v. South Brunswick Township Planning Bd., 77 N.J.Super. 594, 187 A.2d 221 (S.L.Div.1963) is a leading case explaining and upholding cluster zoning.

Many planned unit developments use cluster development as a technique but the notion of planned unit development concept typically encompasses more.[7]

 WESTLAW REFERENCES

di cluster zoning

"planned unit development" /5 define* definition mean!

"planned unit development" /s concept principle

cluster /2 zon*** development

§ 7.16 Relationship to Zoning

Typical Zoning and PUD Incompatibility

Under typical zoning, there is no close relation to a plan [1] and the landscape is divided "into districts . . . [and] [a]ll . . . regulations shall be uniform . . . throughout each district . . ."[2] In planned unit developments, the area is not districted. A commercial use may be next to a residential use and different types of residential uses may be mixed with no intention of placing them in districts. Special conditions and controls may apply without uniformity to some commercial uses and not to others, so as to better integrate the commercial and residential development. Spot zoning[3] (in a descriptive sense of a small parcel of property controlled differently than adjacent parcels) is or may be the rule in a PUD, rather than something to be avoided.

The PUD technique may not be compatible with a typical zoning enabling act, thus leading to difficulties in the implementation of a planned unit development. There may be no territorial districts and uniformity of use within a district under PUD. Zoning without districting and without uniformity within districts may be held invalid as it was in Rockhill v. Chesterfield Township.[4] The whole town was in effect, a single district in which residential and agricultural uses were permitted, but all other uses were permitted only by special permit under a standard of benefit to the general development of the township.[5] Similarly, floating zones have been held invalid because they are not preapplied to a particular area so as to show on a zoning map.[6] A PUD may not involve a precise zoning map. A PUD is often treated as a floating zone under local ordinances.[7] When conditions have been

7. See generally, Dyckman, Book Review 12 UCLA L.Rev. 991 (1965); Urban Land Institute, New Approaches to Residential Land Development, Tech.Bull. No. 40 chs. 1–2 (1961).

§ 7.16

1. The plan to which zoning is to accord is usually read to mean the scheme of zoning itself. See ch. 2 supra.

2. U.S. Dept of Commerce, A Standard State Zoning Enabling Act § 2 (rev. ed 1926). See § 4.1 supra.

3. See § 5.4 supra.

4. 23 N.J. 117, 128 A.2d 473 (1957).

5. See generally §§ 6.11–6.13 supra.

6. Eves v. Zoning Bd. of Adjustment, 401 Pa. 211, 164 A.2d 7 (1960). See generally § 4.10 supra.

7. A "sinking zone" may also be used. See Craig, Planned Unit Development as Seen from City Hall, 114 U.Pa.L.Rev. 127, 130 (1965); § 4.10 supra.

imposed on zoning, giving rise to so-called contract zoning, the courts have sometimes held the zoning invalid, and in a PUD, conditions are imposed that may vary from parcel to parcel.[8]

Therefore, to avoid adverse judicial decisions, to avoid the impairing effects of nonunitary development controls, and to devise schemes permitting more flexibility, PUD developers have sought routes around conventional zoning. In some cases the special use permit is used under the legal fiction that. a PUD could be viewed as a single development having such special characteristics as to be appropriate for special permit treatment. The special permit [9] is a device which allows a special use to be established subject to conditions. But more than a few courts did not see anything special about large-scale development.[10] Variances [11] have sometimes also been misused to permit planned unit developments.[12] Other PUD developers sought to accomplish PUD under subdivision enabling acts.[13] Those Acts generally had the advantage of providing more administrative than legislative control and of allowing the use of conditions. But stretching the subdivision enabling acts to cover PUDs was fraught with danger when millions of dollars were to be invested in a PUD. Therefore, pressures began to develop for special enabling legislation for PUDs.[14]

Zoning the PUD, Land Use Intensity (LUI) Zoning

The Urban Land Institute states:

Density Zoning. This is "organic zoning for planned residential developments," a new style of ordinance listing the large-scale development as a normal, permitted use, with its own standards just as traditional 'lot Zoning' established standards for the single building on the single lot. Density zoning is an outgrowth of [planned unit development obtainable on a conditional use permit basis], but is distinguishable from it in that [it] treats large-scale developments as the normal thing, while the [planned unit development obtainable on a conditional use permit basis] considers them as exceptions requiring special handling.[15]

The zoning-like provisions for the PUD are described in the model acts. For example, one of the model PUD enabling acts provides:

(a) Permitted Uses. An ordinance adopted pursuant to this Act shall set forth the uses permitted . . . .

8. See § 5.5 supra.

9. See §§ 6.11–.13 supra.

10. See Rockhill v. Chesterfield Township, supra note 4.

11. See §§ 6.5–6.10 supra.

12. See Goldston & Scheuer, Zoning of Planned Residential Developments, 73 Harv.L.Rev. 241, 250 (1959).

13. See § 7.2 supra.

14. See § 7.15 supra.

15. Density Zoning—Organic Zoning for Planned Residential Developments, Technical Bull. No. 42, at p. 8 (1961).

(b) . . . (1) An ordinance adopted pursuant to this Act shall establish standards governing the density, or intensity of land use . . . .

(2) Said standards shall take into account that the density, or intensity of land use, otherwise allowable on the site under the provisions of a zoning ordinance previously enacted pursuant to [the general zoning enabling act] may not be appropriate for a Planned Unit . . . Development . . . .[16]

As the commentary on the Act indicates, intensity of land use includes such density concepts as number of dwelling units per acre or minimum square footage of lot area per dwelling unit. But the Act uses intensity of land use more broadly to include a balancing of bulk, height, open space and dwelling units to reach a permitted concentration.

The Act also provides for other zoning-like controls:

(f) . . . An ordinance adopted pursuant to this Act shall set forth the standards and criteria by which the design, bulk and location of buildings shall be evaluated . . . .[17]

The intensity of use is often carried out by a scheme entitled land-use intensity (LUI). Even if the local ordinance does not expressly provide for LUI, a developer may want to conform to LUI in order to qualify the development for FHA insured loans.

The FHA has devised standards for PUD and it determines the appropriate LUI and assigns a number. The LUI number is based on a planning analysis and a real estate judgment regarding the proposed site, its community, and the market. For example, if the FHA should determine that the area measured in square feet can be developed at an LUI of a designated number, the developer can easily determine from charts available from FHA the proper or required:

(1) Total floor area of all buildings (floor area ratio);[18]

(2) Total open space (open space ratio);

(3) Open space not used for cars (livability space);

(4) Open space planned for active and passive recreation (recreation space);

(5) Total parking spaces for the number of planned dwelling units, some of which may be on the streets (total car ratio); and

(6) Total offstreet parking spaces (occupant car ratio).[19]

---

16. Babcock, Krasnowiecki, McBride, The Model State Statute, 114 U.Pa.L.Rev. 140, 144–145 (1965).

17. Id. at 152.

18. See § 4.7 supra.

19. Further descriptions of the FHA–LUI are in Henke, Planned Unit Develop-

ment and Land Use Intensity, 114 U.Pa.L. Rev. 15 (1965); Bair, How to Regulate Planned Unit Developments for Housing—Summary of a Regulatory Approach, 17 Zoning Digest 185 (1985).

WESTLAW REFERENCES

Typical Zoning and PUD Incompatibility

spot /2 zon*** /s "planned unit development"

414k35

find 128 a.2d 473

"floating zon***" /s "planned unit development"

"planned unit development" /s condition

"planned unit development" /s special /2 use permit

"planned unit development" /s variance

intensity density organic /2 zon***

"land use intensity"

§ 7.17　Legal Status of PUD's

PUD ordinances have been upheld even where not specially authorized by enabling legislation. The first clear-cut and still leading case upholding PUD is Cheney v. Village 2 at New Hope, Inc.[1] An Ordinance had created a PUD district and another ordinance [2] rezoned an area PUD that had previously been zoned single family. The PUD zone permitted a wide variety of residential uses as well as professional, public, recreational and commercial uses. The ordinance provided that the buildable land could be developed up to 80 percent residential and 20 percent commercial. A minimum of 20 percent of the land had to be devoted to open space. The residential density could not exceed 10 units per acre, no building could exceed 12 units and no residence could include more than two bedrooms. There were no traditional setback and side-yard requirements, though a distance of 24 feet was required between buildings. The court rejected arguments that the PUD did not accord with a previously adopted comprehensive plan by indicating that a plan can be changed by adoption of the PUD ordinance if done deliberately and thoughtfully.[3] The court also rejected the allegations that the PUD ordinances constituted spot zoning and that there was an improper delegation of legislative authority because the planning commission had to decide exactly where, within a particular PUD district, specific types of buildings should be placed.[4]

The court reviewed in detail whether the planning commission, the legislative body or the board of adjustment could most appropriately handle the details of the development and concluded that the planning commission was appropriate. The legislative body would otherwise involve itself in too much detail. The board of adjustment functions were to hear appeals, to grant variances and to issue special permits.

§ 7.17

1. 429 Pa. 626, 241 A.2d 81 (1968). See, Zuker & Wolffe, Supreme Court Legalizes PUD: New Hope from New Hope, 2 Land Use Controls No. 2, at 32 (1968). But see Lutz v. Longview, 83 Wn.2d 566, 520 P.2d 1374 (1974).

2. See § 4.10 supra on floating zones.

3. See § 5.4 supra.

4. See § 5.2 supra.

The court did not believe that any of those powers were as appropriate to implementation of PUD details as were the powers conferred on a planning commission. The court regarded final PUD detailed review as not materially different from subdivision approval, a traditional planning commission function.[5]

Cheney might not have been decided favorably to PUDs,[6] since the Pennsylvania court hardly had the reputation of approving novel approaches to land use controls. However, the Cheney decision might not be followed in all states. For example, the California court which would have been expected to uphold PUDs,[7] departed from its earlier tradition of authorizing virtually standardless delegation of authority to administrative agencies, and in Millbrae Association for Residential Survival v. Millbrae [8] established some important limitations on PUDs.

In California, as in many states, a rezoning can be accomplished only by the local legislature after notice and hearing. In order to comply with that requirement, the City of Millbrae enacted an ordinance which provided a two-step approval of PUDs. In the first step, property was rezoned as a planned development by the legislature after notice and hearing. However, this rezoning was only in the nature of a generalized plan for development.[9] The rezoning provided for only the general size, location and use of proposed buildings and structures, the location and dimensions of streets, parking areas, open areas and other public and private facilities and uses. After the rezoning, the two-step ordinance required the developer to submit a precise plan, which was in the nature of the detailed development plan. The precise plan could be approved by the planning commission alone.[10] But in the precise plan, which was approved by the planning commission without legislative actions, the developer departed from the approved generalized plan and added seven additional apartments to the high-rise buildings, reduced the size of a golf course, increased the number of parking spaces and relocated two high-rise buildings. The plaintiffs alleged that such changes constituted a rezoning which had to be accomplished legislatively. The developer argued that the changes were details that could be authorized by an administrative body as in the case of special permits or variances. The court held:

5. Something much like a PUD was approved in Bigenho v. Montgomery County Council, 248 Md. 386, 237 A.2d 53 (1968), though the legislative body rezoned particular parts of a large tract, some for local community use, some for commercial office uses, some for industrial uses and some for multiple family uses.

6. Among other cases, Eves v. Zoning Bd. of Adjustments, supra note 10 was precedent for holding the PUD invalid, see 2 Zoning Digest 178 (1968).

7. The California courts generally are more disposed to approve whatever a municipality does including approval of novel land use controls, then the courts of any other state. See e.g., §§ 4.10–4.14 supra.

8. 262 Cal.App.2d 222, 59 Cal.Rptr. 251 (1968). Compare Peachtree Dev. Co. v. Paul, 67 Ohio St.2d 345, 423 N.E.2d 1087 (1981); Mullin v. Planning Bd., 17 Mass.App.Ct. 139, 456 N.E.2d 780 (1983).

9. See discussion § 16.7 supra on generalized plans.

10. See discussion § 16.6 supra on detailed development plans.

while the change in the number of apartments in each of the high-rise buildings would properly be the subject of the precise plan under the ordinance so long as it did not increase the "general size" of the buildings as delineated in the [generalized] plan since they materially and fundamentally change the location of two of the high-rise buildings and the size of the parking areas and the open areas.[11]

In short, the court upheld the PUD technique in general, but did not permit substantial changes in the planned development plan without legislative action. The California court was thus unwilling to allow delegation to the planning commission to the extent permitted by the Pennsylvania court. The case is notice to developers that some courts will superintend what is "substantial" and not uphold whatever changes the planning commission approves. Since to be safe the developer must go to the legislative body for any "substantial" change between the generalized and the detailed plan (and presumably for any changes of the generalized plan by amendments to the detailed plan), considerable flexibility is lost.

As previously indicated,[12] when courts proved indisposed to allow PUD development under typical zoning enabling legislation, PUD developers began to look for other alternatives. A few states had adopted Bassett's model provisions [13] which appeared to authorize PUDs under subdivision-like authority. But in Hiscox v. Levine [14] the court held approval of a development by a planning commission under authority of a statute based on the Bassett model to be invalid. The developer had submitted a plan for a 100-acre subdivision which involved cluster zoning.[15] It showed one house to the half acre rather than one to the acre as called for by the zoning. However, the balance of the 100 acres was dedicated for a park. The court held that the action of the administrative board in allowing lot size reductions for such a large tract was an encroachment on legislative authority. In reviewing the history and language of the Bassett Act, Krasnowiecki concludes that the Hiscox case was improperly decided.[16]

Krasnowiecki also points to language in the subdivision sections of the Standard City Planning Enabling Act which would appear to enable planning commissions to approve in the several states that adopted the provisions. The act provides that the planning board:

shall have the power to agree with the applicant upon use, height, area or bulk requirements or restrictions governing buildings and premises within the subdivision, provided such requirements or

---

11. 262 Cal.App.2d at 245, 69 Cal.Rptr. at 267.

12. Supra § 7.16.

13. See § 7.15 supra.

14. 31 Misc.2d 151, 216 N.Y.S.2d 801 (1961).

15. See supra § 7.15.

16. Krasnowiecki, Planned Unit Development: A Challenge to Established Theory and Practice of Land Use Control, 114 U.Pa.L.Rev. 47, 80–83 (1965).

restrictions do not authorize the violation of the then effective zoning ordinance of the municipality.[17]

The Act also provided:

regulations may provide for the proper arrangement of streets . . . , for adequate and convenient open spaces for traffic, utilities, access of fire-fighting apparatus, recreation, light and air, and for the avoidance of congestion of population, including minimum width and areas of lots.[18]

The trial court in Mann v. Fort Thomas [19] upheld the constitutionality of an ordinance based on the above sections of the Standard Act and sustained a planning commission's denial of an application for a PUD.[20]

Whether PUDs can be authorized under conventional subdivision enabling acts or not, special enabling legislation for PUDs clarifies the matter, and the suggested model acts contain subdivision-like provisions. For example, the model act suggested by the ACIR defines the plan to include "a plat of subdivision . . . private streets, ways and parking facilities, common open space and public facilities . . . ," [21] all of which matters are part of typical subdivision controls. In other sections the Act calls for the development of standards on "the amount, location and proposed use of common open space," [22] provisions for municipal acceptance of "the dedication of land or any interest therein for public use and maintenance" [23] and that

The authority granted to a municipality to establish standards for the location, width, course and surfacing of public streets and highways, alleys, ways for public service facilities, curbs, gutters, sidewalks, street lights, parks, playgrounds, school grounds, storm water drainage, water supply and distribution, sanitary sewers and sewage collection and treatment, shall be vested in [the body designated to administer the ordinance enacted to implement the Act].[24]

All of the above provisions are typical of conventional subdivision or official map enabling acts and ordinances.

---

17. Standard Act § 15. Violation of the zoning ordinance could be avoided through use of a sinking zone. See Craig, Planned Unit Development as Seen from City Hall, 114 U.Pa.L.Rev. 127, 130 (1965). See also § 14.14 supra.

18. Standard Act § 14. See § 4.8 on lot size as a zoning or as a subdivision matter.

19. 437 S.W.2d 209 (Ky.1969).

20. On appeal, the court did not reach the merits of the issue due to the developer's lack of standing.

21. U.S. Advisory Commission on Intergovernmental Relations, An Act Authoriz-

ing Municipalities to Provide for Planned Unit Development, § 3(4) in 1970 Cumulative ACIR State Legislative Program 31–36–00 at 5 (1969). See Sternlieb, Burchell, Hughes & Listokin, Planned Unit Development Legislation: A Summary of Necessary Considerations, 7 Urb.L.Ann. 71 (1974).

22. Id. § 4(b)(1) at 6.

23. Id. § 34(c)(1) at 7.

24. Id. § 4(e) at 8.

§ 7.18 Planned Unit Development Approval Process

Planned unit development ordinances generally provide a comprehensive review procedure that requires the developer to submit detailed information on the project, including a concept or master plan; and also allow the municipality to condition approval on changes made in the project. Because of the flexibility of the procedure and the opportunity for negotiation between local government and prospective developers PUD ordinances have been criticized for institutionalizing the bargaining process of land development.[1] However, the flexibility of planned unit development ordinances does allow local government to have input in the development process. Furthermore, by structuring a PUD ordinance to encourage beneficial uses a municipality can develop the future to fit its image.

Most planned unit development ordinances provide for a detailed review procedure. Planned unit development ordinances generally provide for a two-step process in the approval or disapproval of a large scale development. The first step is the establishment of an overlay district or master plan.[2] Planned development districts must be developed in accordance with the officially approved plan.[3]

The application process generally begins with conferences between the developer and the local government planning department and other agencies involved in the approval process. The general purpose of the preapplication conferences is for the developer and the local government officials to assess the relationship of the proposed project to the existing community. If all goes well, the petitioners for the PCD (Planned Community District) zoning submit their application along with any required materials.[4]

The developer will then conduct prehearing conferences with the local planning and zoning commission to iron out problem areas and negotiate acceptable compromises. The planning and zoning commission generally can make written proposals for changes in either the petition or the concept plan. After appropriate public notice is given, a

§ 7.18

1. 2 Williams, American Land Planning Law, § 48.02 (1st ed. 1974).

2. See Baers, Zoning Code Revisions to Permit Mixed Use Development, 7 Zoning and Planning L.Rep., 81, 85 (1984).

3. See note 4, supra. A concept plan is a professionally prepared overall concept of the project. See Aloi, Implementation of a Planned Unit Development, 2 Real Est.L.J. 523, 525 (1974).

4. For a typical listing of required documents, see Palm Beach Gardens, Fl., Zoning Code, Art. VII, § 16.7 (1983).

public hearing is held before the planning and zoning commission. The planning and zoning commission then makes its official findings and recommends either approval, conditional approval or disapproval.[5]

The final step in the initial application process is approval by the local government legislative body. Upon receiving the planning and zoning commission's recommendation, the legislative body holds a public hearing on the application, and may either grant the proposed rezoning to PCD; deny it; or grant the rezoning with conditions or modifications. If the legislative body approves the proposed application for rezoning, the concept plan of development is adopted as an amendment to the zoning code.

After a concept plan has been approved it establishes a master plan of usages. Any area development within the planned community district is a planned unit development. The second step of the large scale development is approval of the individual planned unit developments. Planned unit developments can be rezoned by resolution, after the master development plan has been adopted, since they are now in accordance with the amended zoning code.

The planned unit development procedure offers a number of benefits. First, the local government's polestar in evaluating a project is whether it is in accordance with the planning and development objectives of the jurisdiction. Second, by providing a detailed application procedure and requiring a concept plan, the local government is in a better position to evaluate the project. Third, the multistep process affords many opportunities for input from the local government's various planning, zoning and architectural commissions, thus allowing the municipality to structure future developments to conform with its growth plans.

Planned unit development regulations contain substantive standards to ensure that a project will be developed in accordance with the long range development plans. These standards can solve a number of problems. For instance, what assurance does a local government have that the developer will complete the project as it proposed in the plan? Fortunately, most PUD regulations contemplate that most projects will be staged developments. Most PUD ordinances provide safeguards to guarantee the different stages of the project will be completed. First, since the local government's legislative body still must approve individual PUDs by resolution, it retains some leverage over the developer. Second, most regulations establish timing controls as to when certain facilities must be built, thereby insuring the entire community will be completed.[6] For example, a regulation may require a park to be built

5. Id. § 16.8. By keeping the planning board in an advisory capacity and deferring the decision to the city council a local government may avoid a delegation of authority challenge. See Aloi, Implementation of a Planned Unit Development, 2 Real Est.L.J. 523, 532 (1974); see also Hiscox v. Levine, supra § 7.17, note 14 and accompanying text.

6. See Palm Beach Gardens, Fl., Zoning Code, Art. VII § 16.12 (1983).

before high density, high profit housing can be developed. Finally, the local government may require an annual report from the developer appraising the project's progress.

Many PUD regulations have substantive provisions which can encourage creative and beneficial developments. Generally, the entire project cannot exceed a certain density level. However, individual planned unit developments may have much higher densities. Also, restrictions may allow the developer to transfer excess PUD densities from one parcel to another as long as the density for the whole project must remain the same.[7]

Most PUD ordinances require a computed amount of common open space. Since open space reduces the total lot count, it is seldom utilized under traditional zoning regulations. Ordinances may provide the PUD developer with a number of ways to satisfy the open space computation. For example, the computation may prefer areas left in or restored to their natural habitat, than areas such as golf courses.[8] Accordingly, the percentage of space which would count as open space would be greater for natural habitat than that for golf courses. This type of incentive zoning allows a city to encourage beneficial uses in the ordinance and preserve those areas for the future.

 WESTLAW REFERENCES
planned /2 development /s application /s approv** disapprov**
"planned unit development" /s standard safeguard "annual report"
"planned unit development" /s density

§ 7.19 Private Restrictions

PUDs typically utilize commonly owned facilities and space to a much greater extent than the conventional development. As a result, complicated restrictions and covenants are necessary. The restrictions and covenants are private matters, though the public has an interest in them. Therefore, as with conventional subdivisions, the restrictions and covenants utilized in PUDs are subject to review under some subdivided land sales acts.[1]

The model acts for PUDs [2] also have provisions to protect the public interest in private restrictions. One model act [3] provides that the common open space need not be dedicated to the public but that the local government is authorized to require establishment of an organization to own and maintain the common open space. If the open space is

---

7. Id. § 16.16(1) (Sample Density Computations).

8. Id. § 16.16(2) (Sample open space computation).

§ 7.19

1. See §§ 7.20–7.22 infra.

2. See text § 7.17 at notes 21–24 supra, and accompanying text.

3. See Babcock, Krasnowiecki & McBride, The Model State Statute, 114 U.Pa. L.Rev. 140, 146–150 (1965).

not properly maintained, the Act authorizes the local government to maintain the space and to assess the lot owners.[4]

The elaborate negative and affirmative restrictions, covenants, conditions and easements are typically so extensive that an association or a corporation must be established as the organization to administer the provisions. The powers of the organization may include many of the functions typically performed by the government, so that the organizations created, typically a homes association, have been called private government.[5]

Suggested Legal Documents for Planned-Unit Development [6] contains recommended forms for a declaration of covenants, conditions and restrictions and articles of incorporation and by-laws for a homes association. The declaration provides that the easements, restrictions, covenants, and conditions run with the land described in the declaration and bind and benefit the owner of each parcel of property. The declaration deals with annexation of additional properties; confers membership in the association to the owner of property subject to assessment by the association; provides for voting rights in the association with suggestions for division of power between the developer and the lot owners; states the rights of the association and the lot owners to use property; provides for maintenance assessments; states the rules applying to party walls (which may be present because of cluster zoning and condominium development); establishes standards; provides that the association will maintain and repair the privately owned buildings and trees, shrubs, grass and the like; states the use restrictions; provides easements and contains general provisions dealing with enforcement, severability and amendment.

As with conventional subdivisions, the complicated covenants and restrictions in PUDs are the source of litigation. For example, in Mount Springs Association of New Jersey Inc. v. Wilson [7] the covenants provided that land could be sold only with consent of the association or to a member of the association. The defendant's grantor sold without complying with provision. The defendant grantee was willing to join the association but was not willing to pay dues for water and garbage collection. The association sued to compel the defendant to pay full dues or to reconvey the land. The court held the covenant was unenforceable as restricting free alienation and conferring unconscionable power to the association over prospective purchasers.

4. See § 12.8 infra.

5. See § 233 supra. On private control and management; see also U.S. Dep't Housing and Urban Development, FHA, Planned-Unit Development with a Homes Association, Land Planning Bull. No. 6 Jan. (1970); Urban Land Institute, The Homes Association Handbook, Technical Bull. No. 50 at 304–361 (1964).

6. U.S. Dep't of Housing and Urban Development, Federal Housing Administration and Veterans Administration, FHA Form 1400, VA 26–8200 (Rev.1973).

7. 81 N.J.Super. 564, 196 A.2d 270 (Ch. 1963).

The lengthy articles of incorporation and by-laws that are contained in the suggested form establish the institution for accomplishing the matters controlled by the declaration and provide for directors, officers, committees, finances and the like.

The amount of powers and responsibility given to the private government, of course, varies from new town to new town and from PUD to PUD. For example, the association may not have the responsibility to maintain and repair individually owned properties. That may be the responsibility of the individual owner. Moreover, public government may exercise some of the functions, such as architectural control under a zoning or PUD ordinance. Special districts or special assessment districts may be used as an alternative to provision of water and sewage services by the association.[8]

 WESTLAW REFERENCES

"planned unite development" /s covenant restriction easement

"home association" /s article bylaw

condominium /p association /p "private government"

"home association" /s "voting right" maintenance "party wall"

association /p land /s sell sale sold /s consent /s member

V. SUBDIVIDED LAND SALES

§ 7.20   In General

Local subdivision regulations which require platting, recordation, dedication and the like are to be distinguished from state and federal acts which are designed to regulate real estate sales, particularly the sale of subdivided lands. These acts police the practice of sales of lots or parcels within large scale developments to minimize possible fraud on potential purchasers or lessees, either through misrepresentation or nonrepresentation of the terms and conditions of sale, the financing arrangements, the condition of the property, or restrictions on use. At least 17 states have enacted new laws or revised existing laws since 1953 to impose varying degrees of control over the sale of subdivided lands.[1] A Uniform Land Sales Practice Act has been promulgated by the National Conference of Commissioners on Uniform State Laws.[2]

8. For an example of a special district created to maintain open space see West's Ann.Cal. Gov't Code §§ 50575–50628. See also Volpert, Creation and Maintenance of Open Spaces in Subdivisions: Another Approach, 12 U.C.L.A.L.Rev. 830 (1965).

§ 7.20

1. See G. Lefcoe, Land Development Law 426 n. 58 (1966).

2. Model Land Sales Practice Act, 7A U.L.A. 669 (1969). Ten jurisdictions have

adopted the Model Act: Alaska Stat. 34.55.004–34.55.046; Conn.Gen.Stat.Ann. §§ 20–329a to 20–329m; West's Fla.Stat. Ann. §§ 498.001–498.063; Hawaii Rev. Stat. §§ 484–1 to 484–22; Idaho Code §§ 55–1801 to 55–1823; Kan.Stat.Ann. 58–3301 to 58–3323; Minn.Stat.Ann. §§ 83.20–83.42; Mont.Code Ann. 76–4–1201 to 76–4–1251; S.C.Code 1976, §§ 27–29–10 to 27–29–210; Utah Code Ann.1953, 57–11–1 to 57–11–21.

And the federal government has enacted an Interstate Land Sales Full Disclosure Act.[3]

 WESTLAW REFERENCES
ordinance statut*** law /s sale sell /s subdivided /2 land lot
"uniform land sales practice act"

§ 7.21 State Regulation

State regulation has basically taken two forms. A number of states have enacted subdivided land acts, authorizing a special agency to supervise the sale of subdivided lands.[1] In other states, the agency which polices the sale of securities has been given jurisdiction over some real estate sales. In both cases, jurisdiction over land sales may be restricted in some way, for example, to sales of out-of-state lands,[2] to all sales of subdivided in-state land,[3] or to the installment sales of both out-of-state and in-state subdivided lands.[4]

Subdivided Lands Acts

California continues to have among the broadest of the state subdivided land statutes. It applies to improved as well as unimproved land, to land divided for financing as well as for lease or sale, and whenever 5 or more lots are involved unless the lots are larger than 160 acres.[5] Offerings in planned unit developments, condominiums, cooperative apartments, and time-share estates as well as subdivisions are covered.[6]

Before subdivided land may be offered for sale or lease by any person, such person shall notify the Department of Real Estate of their intention to sell or lease and shall file with the department an application for public report including: a statement of the condition of the title to the land; a statement of all terms and conditions upon which it is intended to dispose of the land together with copies of any contracts intended to be used; a statement of the provisions which have been made for public utilities; a statement of the use or uses for which the subdivision will be offered; a statement of any provisions which limit the use or occupancy of the parcels in the subdivision; a statement of the amount of indebtedness which is a lien upon the subdivision and which is incurred to pay for the construction of any onsite or offsite improvement, or any community or recreational facility including the amount of indebtedness to be incurred by any special district, entity,

3. See § 7.22 infra.

§ 7.21

1. A parallel set of law exist in many of these states regulating the sale of real estate securities, e.g., McKinney's N.Y.—Gen.Bus.Law §§ 352e–352j. See generally G. Lefcoe, Land Finance Law 1121–45 (1969).

2. Ohio Rev.Code § 1707.01(B).

3. N.Y.—McKinney's Real Prop.Law § 337(1).

4. West's Fla.Stat.Ann. §§ 498.001–498.063.

5. West's Ann.Cal.Bus. & Prof.Code § 11000.

6. Id. § 11004.5

taxing area or assessment district within the boundaries of which the subdivision is located.[7]

After receiving all the required information, the Real Estate Commissioner is to make an examination of the subdivision, and unless there are grounds for denial, issue a public report authorizing the sale or lease of lots in the subdivision.[8] The report is to contain the data furnished the Commissioner and which the Commissioner determines is necessary to implement the purposes of the Act.[9] A copy of the public report must be given to every prospective purchaser by the owner, subdivider or agent prior to the execution of a binding contract or agreement for the sale or lease of any lot in the subdivision.[10]

Grounds for denying a public report include: failure to provide in the contract or other writing the use or uses for which the parcels are offered together with any covenants or conditions relative thereto; that sale or lease would constitute misrepresentation to or deceit or fraud of the purchasers or lessees; inability to deliver title or other interest contracted for; inability to demonstrate that adequate financial arrangements have been made for all offsite improvements or any community, recreational or other facilities included in the offering; failure to make a showing that the parcels can be used for the purpose for which they are offered; inadequacy of agreements or bylaws to provide for management or other services pertaining to common facilities; and failure to demonstrate adequate financial arrangements have been made for any guarantee or warranty included in the offering.[11]

The California scheme goes farther than most subdivided lands acts by, for example, requiring the real estate commissioner to find that reasonable arrangements have been made to assure completion of the subdivision and all offsite improvements included in the offering.[12] Most subdivided lands acts merely require full disclosure of the basic data of interest to a prospective purchaser. Some states reach only misstatements and not omissions by merely requiring, for example, that the advertising to be used by the subdivider be furnished to a state agency for a review of its accuracy.

Application of Basic Securities Law

A number of states have expanded their basic securities regulation laws to specifically cover real estate sales.[13] As with subdivided land sales laws, these statutes generally apply to the sale of subdivided lands; isolated sales are generally exempt transactions. The application of blue sky laws to land sales is usually designed to do no more than insure full disclosure, like most subdivided lands acts. However,

7. Id. § 11010.

8. Id. § 11018.

9. Id.

10. Id. § 11018.1

11. Id. § 11018; see also Id. § 11018.5.

12. Id. § 11018.5(a)(1).

13. See, e.g., Me.Rev.Stat.Ann. tit. 32, § 751.

at least one state requires that the proposed sale be found "not on grossly unfair terms." [14]

Whether the general corporate securities law can be used when it does not by its terms encompass real estate sales depends on the statute itself, how broadly the corporation commissioner construes his authority, and whether the court will uphold a broad interpretation of "security." [15]

For example, in State v. Silberberg [16] before sales of real estate were specifically covered by the corporate security law, occupiers of a cooperative housing corporation purchased shares in the corporation and occupied a unit of the building. Upon payment of the full purchase price, the occupier received a deed for the space he occupied. The court ruled that the transaction constituted a sale of real estate which was not a security within the meaning of the Ohio Securities Act. On the other hand, before jurisdiction over such transactions was transferred to the real estate commission, several persons in California attempted to form a country club and sold memberships. The court considered the memberships to be within the statutory definition of security which included "any beneficial interest in title to property" and within the regulatory purpose of the corporate securities act, even though memberships were purchased for use and enjoyment rather than as an investment on which a return of capital was expected.[17]

In California, before authority over the sale of subdivided lands was transferred to the real estate commissioner, the sale of subdivided lands was frequently considered to be the sale of a security because of the broad statutory definition of "security" and because the corporation commissioner was aggressive in so classifying interests in title to property. Under the corporate securities law, the corporation commissioner applied a "fair, just and equitable" test before permitting the sale. Thus, application of the general corporate securities law in California to the sale of subdivided lands resulted in more rigorous scrutiny than the subdivided land act now requires. However, as stated above, some of the real estate commissioner's required findings approach a "fair, just and equitable" test.

 WESTLAW REFERENCES
"subdivided land" /2 act statute

Subdivided Land Acts
statute /s offering /s "planned unit development" condominium
    cooperative

14. Ohio Rev.Code § 1707.33(G).

15. Ordinarily, if there is no tangible title or interest to realty conveyed but only a right to share in profits or distribution of assets, the interest is considered a security. 1 CCH Blue Sky L.Rep. 1641 (1954).

16. 166 Ohio St. 101, 139 N.E.2d 342 (1956).

17. Silver Hills Country Club v. Sobieski, 55 Cal.2d 811, 13 Cal.Rptr. 186, 361 P.2d 906 (1961).

Application of Basic Securities Law
di,sy("blue sky"　/s　"real estate"　"land sale")

§ 7.22　Federal Regulation

On the federal level, beginning in 1962, the Federal Trade Commission attempted to exert some control over interstate land sales under its authority to prevent unfair or deceptive acts or practices in commerce. The FTC program was abated in deference to the Post Office department which exercised jurisdiction under authority to prosecute for the use of the mails to execute a fraudulent scheme. Federal legislation specifically dealing with the problem of land sales was originally proposed to place the matter under SEC jurisdiction, but the U.S. Department of Housing and Urban Development (HUD) was eventually given jurisdiction. The federal provisions are contained in the Interstate Land Sales Full Disclosure Act (ILSFDA), enacted in 1968.[1]

The purpose of the ILSFDA is to "deter or prohibit the sale of land by use of the mails or other channels of interstate commerce through misrepresentation of material facts relating to the property."[2] As

§ 7.22

1. 15 U.S.C.A. §§ 1700–1720. The following lists the major scholarly analysis of the ILSFDA: Coffey & Welch, Federal Regulation of Land Sales: Full Disclosure Comes Down to Earth, 21 Case W.Res. 5 (1969); Feferman, Interstate Land Sales Full Disclosure Act, 33 Tex.B.J. 625 (1970); Freidman, Regulation of Interstate Land Sales: Is Full Disclosure Sufficient? 20 Urb.L.Ann. 137 (1980); Gandal, General Outline of the Interstate Land Sales Full Disclosure Act, 3 Real Est.L.J. 3 (1974); Gose, Interstate Land Sales, 9 Real Prop. Prob. & Tr.J. 7 (1974); Krechter, LS–MFD: Land Sales Mean Full Disclosure, 4 Real Prop.Prob. & Tr.J. 1 (1969); Krechter, Federal Regulation of Interstate Land Sales, 4 Real Prop.Prob. & Tr.J. 327 (1969); Malloy, The Interstate Land Sales Full Disclosure Act: Its Requirements, Consequences, and Implications for Persons Participating in Real Estate Development, 24 B.C.L.Rev. 1187 (1983); Morris, The Interstate Land Sales Full Disclosure Act: Analysis and Evaluation, 24 S.C.L.Rev. 331 (1972); Peretz, Rescission under the Interstate Land Sales Full Disclosure Act, 58 Fla.B.J. 297 (1984); Pridgen, The Interstate Land Sales Full Disclosure Act: The Practitioner's Problems and Suggestions for Improvement, 4 Real Est.L.J. 127 (1975); Walsh, Consumer Protection in Land Development Sales, 42 Pa.B.A.Q. 38 (1970); Walsh, The Role of the Federal Government in Land Development Sales, 47 Notre Dame Law.

267 (1971); Whitney, Standing and Remedies Available to the Department of Housing and Urban Development Under the Interstate Land Sales Full Disclosure Act, 6 GMU.L.Rev. 171 (1983); Young, Land Sales and Development: Some Legal and Conceptual Considerations, 3 Real Est.L.J. 44 (1974); Comment, A Handbook to the Interstate Land Sales Full Disclosure Act, 27 Ark.L.Rev. 65 (1973); Comment, The Interstate Land Sales Full Disclosure Act: An Analysis of Administrative Policies Implemented in the Years 1968–75, 26 Cath. U.L.Rev. 348 (1977); Note Regulating the Subdivided Land Market, 81 Harv.L.Rev. 1528 (1968); Note, "Rainbow City"—The Need for Federal Control in the Sale of Undeveloped Land, 46 Notre Dame Law. 733 (1971); Comment, Applying the Interstate Land Sales Full Disclosure Act, 51 Or.L.Rev. 381 (1972); Note, Exemptions from the Registration Requirements in the Interstate Land Sales Full Disclosure Act, 15 Real Prop.Prob. & Tr.J. 334 (1980); Note, Consumer Protection and the Interstate Land Sales Full Disclosure Act, 48 St. John's L.Rev. 947 (1974); Note, Regulation of Interstate Land Sales, 25 Sta.L.Rev. 605 (1973); Note, Interstate Land Sales Regulation, 1974 Wash.U.L.Q. 123; Comment, Protecting the Buyer: New Regulations Under the Interstate Land Sales Full Disclosure Act, 1974 Wis.L.Rev. 558.

2. Conf.Rep. No. 1785, 90th Cong., 2d Sess. 161 (1968), reprinted in 1968 U.S. Code Cong. & Ad.News 3053, 3066.

originally adopted, the ILSFDA emphasized disclosure and registration of real estate development proposals and purchase conditions. The act was designed to protect the purchasers and leasees of property by requiring the preparation of a "Property Report" in order to disclose important information about the property and proposed improvements.[3] Through disclosure and registration requirements, purchasers were allegedly less likely to be influenced by "get rich quick promoters" because of the availability of better information.[4] The ILSFDA was amended, however, in 1979 to shift its emphasis away from the extensive paperwork and registration requirements. The amended act emphasizes anti-fraud protection, consumer rights, and enforcement against serious sales abuses by unscrupulous developers.[5]

The ILSFDA's disclosure and anti-fraud provisions are patterned after similar provisions of the Securities Act of 1933 and the Security Exchange Act of 1934.[6] The 1979 amendments added provisions for increased damages and enforcement.[7] The amendments also established contractual rights for private enforcement[8] and reduced the threshold for application of the anti-fraud provisions to subdivisions with 25 or more lots from the previous threshold of 100 or more lots.[9] Finally, the amendments were designed to reduce paperwork and compliance costs to developers by providing for state certification procedures that eliminate the need for duplicate registrations with state agencies as well as with the department.[10] The act now permits states requiring substantially similar standards for land sales and development to implement state registration requirements that also satisfy federal registration requirements.[11] At least two states with major land sales and development industries, California and Florida, have been certified under the ILSFDA's provisions.[12] While the state certification provisions eliminate wasteful duplication, registration un-

---

3. 15 U.S.C.A. § 1703(a), (b); see also Flint Ridge Development Co. v. Scenic Rivers Ass'n of Oklahoma, 426 U.S. 776, 778, 96 S.Ct. 2430, 2433, 49 L.Ed.2d 205 (1976), rehearing denied 429 U.S. 875, 97 S.Ct. 198, 50 L.Ed.2d 159 (1976) (recognizing that the purpose of the ILSFDA is to prevent false and deceptive practices in the sale of land by requiring developers to disclose information needed by potential purchasers).

4. See Cumberland Capital Corp. v. Harris, 621 F.2d 246, 250 (6th Cir.1980).

5. See generally, Dept. of Housing and Urban Development, Office of Interstate Land Sales Registration Biennial Rep. To Congress, 3–4 (March 1981). For a thorough discussion of the amended act see Malloy, supra note 20.

6. Flint Ridge Development Co. v. Scenic Rivers Ass'n of Oklahoma, 426 U.S. 776,

778, 96 S.Ct. 2430, 2433, 49 L.Ed.2d 205 (1976), rehearing denied 429 U.S. 875, 97 S.Ct. 198, 50 L.Ed.2d 159 (1976).

7. 15 U.S.C.A. §§ 1702, 1709. See generally, Biennial Rep. To Congress, supra note 5, at 4.

8. Pub.L. No. 96–153, title IV, §§ 403, 405, 93 Stat. 1127, 1130 (1979) (now codified at 15 U.S.C.A. § 1703(d)). For a discussion of the act's recission remedy see Peretz, supra note 1.

9. Pub.L. No. 96–153, title IV, § 402, 93 Stat. 1123 (1979) (now codified at 15 U.S.C.A. § 1702(a)(1)).

10. See Biennial Rep. to Congress, supra note 5, at 25.

11. 15 U.S.C.A. § 1708.

12. Biennial Rep. to Congress, supra note 5, at 21.

der a certified state plan does not exempt a person from the other provisions of the ILSFDA.

 WESTLAW REFERENCES

interstate /s land /s sale sell sold

"interstate land sales full disclosure act"

land /4 sale /s disclosure anti-fraud /3 provision

Chapter 8

BUILDING AND HOUSING CODES

Analysis

§ 8.1 In General

Building and housing codes constitute an ancient body of law, but their modern history in the U.S. begins with the adoption of the Tenement House Act for the City of New York in 1901.[1] They are not generally treated as land use control devices because land use controls are focused on land, and the relationship between buildings and land.[2] Building and housing codes generally deal with matters of construction and maintenance, that is, with matters inward from the outside skin of a building.

Building codes are primarily derived from structural safety laws and are generally enforced against new construction. Attention to existing properties is usually given only to those which have been severely damaged or have such serious deficiencies as to render them dangerous. Housing Codes were originally authorized by environmental health laws, and deal primarily with conditions which must be maintained in existing residential buildings to protect the public health, safety and welfare.[3] Post-construction maintenance of commer-

---

§ 8.1

1. For an historical treatment of the development of housing code standards in the United States, see Public Health Service, U.S. Dep't of Health, Education & Welfare, Basic Housing Inspection 1–3 (1976); The National Commission on Urban Problems, Housing Code Standards: Three Critical Studies 6–12 (1969).

2. See infra § 8.3. See generally Proceedings of the 1969 Conference on Code Enforcement, Bureau of Government Research, Rutgers University; Bosselman, The Legal Framework of Building and Housing Ordinances, (pts. 1 & 2) II, The Mun. Att'y 39, 67 (1970).

3. Code Enforcement: The Federal Role, 14 Urb.Law. 1, 2 (1982). A statutory

cial and state-owned buildings is governed by several codes such as electrical codes, fire codes, mechanical codes, plumbing codes and others.[4]

Building code standards are classified as belonging to one of two types: (1) specification or (2) performance. Most codes rely heavily on standards of the specification or prescriptive type. That is, the code will require the use of a specific type or grade of material to achieve the desired result. Architects are generally opposed to this sort of code, because they believe it stifles innovation and can be counterproductive in some situations.[5] These codes are usually compiled from specifications developed by various building industry trade associations. Performance standards, on the other hand, permit the use of any material that is able to meet a performance standard. Development of performance standards was required as part of the Energy Conservation Standards for New Building Act of 1976.[6] Though performance standards are favored by architects, they are sometimes impractical to use, expensive to administer and tend to centralize the related administrative functions.[7]

Building codes frequently have land use control consequences even though that is not their primary purpose.[8] The relation of buildings to one another is an important aspect of urban land use control and many key tenets of urban design regulation such as setback provisions were first found in building codes.[9] Height limits were also originally imposed in building codes rather than in zoning codes.[10]

Another land use control aspect of building codes is the requirement frequently contained in them for building permits and certificates

definition of housing codes reads as follows: ". . . any code or rule intending post construction regulation of structures which would include but not be limited to standards of maintenance, condition of facilities, condition of systems and components, living conditions, occupancy, use and room sizes. Fla.Stat. § 553.71(5) (1983).

4. See, e.g., Fla.Stat.Ann. § 553.19, § 663.557, § 553.06, "Thermal Efficiency Code," § 553.900.

5. See, e.g., Energy Building Regulations: The Effect of the Federal Performance Standards on Building Code Administration and Conservation of Energy in New Buildings, 13 U.C.D.L.Rev. 330, 336–7 nn. 32–35 (1980) [hereinafter cited as Energy Building Regulations].

6. Pub.L. No. 94–385, 90 Stat. 1144, 42 U.S.C.A. §§ 6831–40.

7. Conservation and Efficient Use of Energy: Hearings Before a Subcomm. of the House Comm. on Government Operations, 93rd Cong., 1st Sess. 33–35 (1973). Though prescriptive standards are easily

understood, they lead to centralization of the administration of energy regulations and increased expense. Performance standards are also regularly used in the U.S. National Conf. of States on Building Costs & Standards, Inc., Survey on Utilization of Systems Analysis Designs in State Energy Conservation Codes, (1979).

8. An interesting example of these "consequences" is reflected in Florida's recent strengthening of its coastal construction building standards. See Sections 161.54–161.56, Florida Statutes, as created by Chapter 85–55, Laws of Florida. These provisions establish minimum state building codes for coastal construction, require local implementation, and also establish state overview and sanctions.

9. See, e.g., Klinger v. Bicket, 117 Pa. 326, 11 A. 555 (1887) (upholding prohibition of wood building in fire zone).

10. See Welch v. Swasey, 214 U.S. 91, 29 S.Ct. 567, 53 L.Ed. 923 (1909) (allowing regulation of building height).

of occupancy. The issuance of a building permit is usually the last point at which the local government can exercise leverage regarding the type of development that will be permitted on the land, and the certificate of occupancy is the last permission needed to use the new improvements. Consequently, land use control authorities use these permits to check whether or not there has been compliance with various land use controls.[11] Local governments can also use the issuance of these permits as the point at which to assess and collect payments for capital facilities required to service the new development.[12]

Housing codes also have an indirect impact on land use to the extent that the degree of code enforcement in areas of deteriorating housing may effect the degree of abandonment of residential use. The courts have held that overenthusiastic enforcement of building and housing codes, motivated by a desire to encourage abandonment can result in a taking without just compensation.[13]

 WESTLAW REFERENCES

"tenement house act"

di building code

di,sy("building code" /s   standard)

199k32 /p "building code"

di,sy("building code" /s   specification)

di,sy("building code" /s   performance)

"building code" /s height /3 limit!

di,sy("building code" /s permit (certificate /2 occupancy))

"housing code" /s abandonment

§ 8.2 Model Codes

After passage of the Housing Act of 1954, local governments were expected to develop and implement both housing and building codes to qualify for federal urban renewal and public housing programs. Qualification for these programs required that the city submit a "workable program" to the administrator, and as a result, between 1955 and 1968, housing code adoption increased 100%, nationally.[1]

11. See Avco Community Developers, Inc. v. South Coast Regional Comm., 17 Cal.3d 785, 132 Cal.Rptr. 386 (1976), appeal dismissed, cert. denied 429 U.S. 1083, 97 S.Ct. 1089, 51 L.Ed.2d 529 (1977); City of Boynton Beach v. V.S.H. Realty, Inc., 443 So.2d 452 (Fla.App.1984); Friends of Mammoth v. Board of Supervisors, 8 Cal.3d 247, 104 Cal.Rptr. 761, 502 P.2d 1049 (1972); Polygon Corp. v. Seattle, 90 Wn.2d 59, 578 P.2d 1309 (1978); City of Houston v. Walker, 615 S.W.2d 831 (Tex.Civ.App.1981), error refused n.r.e. see also infra, § 8.6.

12. See § 9.8.

13. Amen v. Dearborn, 718 F.2d 789 (6th Cir.1983), cert. denied 465 U.S. 1101, 104 S.Ct. 1596, 80 L.Ed.2d 127 (1984).

§ 8.2

1. U.S. Nat'l Comm'n on Urban Problems, Building the American City, 227 (1968). The workable program requirement was repealed in 1974 with passage of the Housing and Community Development Act of 1974, 42 U.S.C.A. §§ 5301–5308.

A number of model building codes have been developed. They include the National Building Code of the American Insurance Association, the Uniform Building Code of the International Conference of Building Officials, the Southern Standard Building Code of the Southern Building Code Conference and the Basic Building Code of the Building Officials Conference of America.

The latter three codes are regional in effect, though to delineate those boundaries one would need to refer to individual state and local laws. The Southern Standard Building Code is generally used in Florida, Georgia, Alabama, South Carolina, North Carolina, Virginia, Tennessee, Mississippi, Texas, and the Uniform Building Code sponsored by International Conference of Building Officials is used in California, for example.

State and local building codes are increasingly based on one of the four nationally recognized codes, since most jurisdictions can not afford to write and keep up-to-date their own codes. Three of these model code organizations are comprised of state and local building officials,[2] and the fourth is an insurance trade association.

Model codes generally reflect the state of the art of building rather than scientific engineering data and are therefore easily amended by localities with differing views. The organizations which promulgate the model codes for the most part lack funds to support all their provisions with sound engineering data, and in some cases even urge local deviations. Often, instead of accepting these model codes intact, local governments make revisions, additions, deletions, and amendments, which in an overwhelming majority of cases are more restrictive in nature.[3] This has resulted in considerable variety in codes from one locale to another.

For example, an ordinance providing that a house trailer used for living or sleeping for more than 30 days in one year was subject to the local building code had been upheld.[4] Now, however, localities in some states are preempted from exercising such power.[5] As a result of local variations, Congress enacted the National Mobile Home Construction

2. The three groups are the Building Officials and Code Administrators (BOCA), International Conference of Building Officials (ICBO), and the Southern Building Code Congress International (SBCCI).

3. U.S. Dep't of Housing & Urban Dev., Final Report of the Task Force on Housing Costs 35 (May 1978).

4. Lower Merion Township v. Gallup, 158 Pa.Super. 572, 46 A.2d 35 (1946), appeal dismissed 329 U.S. 669, 67 S.Ct. 92, 91 L.Ed. 591 (1946), Duckworth v. Bonney Lake, 91 Wn.2d 19, 586 P.2d 860 (1978),

Duggins v. Town of Walnut Cove, 63 N.C. App. 684, 306 S.E.2d 186 (1983), review denied 309 N.C. 819, 310 S.E.2d 348 (1983), appeal dismissed 466 U.S. 946, 104 S.Ct. 2145, 80 L.Ed.2d 532 (1984), but see Derry Borough v. Shomo, 5 Pa.Cmwlth. 216, 289 A.2d 513 (1972).

5. E.g., West's Ann.Cal. Health & Safety Code §§ 18000–18124.5. See also California Factory-Built Housing Law, West's Ann.Cal. Health & Safety Code §§ 19960–19997.

and Safety Standards Act of 1974.[6] This set national standards so that industrialized home building became much more feasible.[7]

Not only do the model building codes vary in terms of general construction requirements, but they vary in scope, so that they may or may not include provisions for setbacks from other buildings and streets, multiple dwelling laws (which apply to apartment houses and boarding houses), health codes that deal with plumbing, sewerage, drainage, light and ventilation, house trailer codes and fire codes. If these kinds of provisions are not in the basic building code they are usually covered by separate local ordinances. In addition, there are sometimes separate boiler codes, electrical codes, elevator codes, heating codes and mechanical codes. These codes may be either promulgated by the state or drawn from specifications and standards set by the respective trade or professional associations.

The model codes are comprehensive and very detailed, and include sections on administration of the code, permitting, fees, inspection, fire district restrictions, classification of buildings by construction, fire protection within the building itself, and minimum safety requirements or characteristics for materials used in construction. Reference is also made in the codes to standards adopted by the individual industrial trade associations for their particular product.[8]

Although most promulgation and enforcement of building and housing codes has been done at the local level, state and federal governments, through legislation and responsible administrative bodies, have played a role in causing the marked increase in the number of building and housing codes enacted by city governments.[9]

 WESTLAW REFERENCES

"national building code of the american insurance association"

"southern standard building code"

"uniform building code"

find 586 p.2d 860

§ 8.3 Relation to Zoning and Urban Renewal

Some provisions of the building and housing codes and related laws were incorporated into modern zoning ordinances, though it is common to find similar provisions either in building codes or zoning codes or both. For example, fire limit ordinances which prohibited wooden buildings in certain areas of the city were a kind of precursor to zoning

---

6. 42 U.S.C.A. § 5401–26, and a portion of the Housing and Community Development Act of 1980, 94 Stat. 1640, 42 U.S. C.A. §§ 5401, 5402.

7. See infra § 8.5 for discussion of preemption.

8. See, e.g., Southern Standard Building Code, 1979.

9. See Code Enforcement, the Federal Role, 14 Urb.Law. 1, 2 (1982). See also West's Fla.Stat.Ann. §§ 161.54–161.56 (establishing minimum state building codes for coastal construction to be implemented locally).

which excludes buildings used for certain purposes, such as commercial or industrial, from parts of a city for reasons of public health, safety or welfare. The yard requirements of modern zoning ordinances are similar to the setback requirements under some fire and building codes. Heights of buildings are controlled under zoning though at an earlier time and sometimes even today, they are controlled under building codes, including "zoned" building codes that provide for different heights in different areas of the city.[1] Zoning bulk regulations dealing with portion of yard covered and density of population overlap housing code matters. A building permit frequently can be issued only after compliance with building and zoning ordinances and other ordinances as well.

It is important to distinguish between building code ordinances and zoning ordinances. In Florida, a zoning ordinance is invalid if notice requirements are not complied with, whereas building regulations are not held to such strict prerequisites to be valid. The court, in Fountain v. Jacksonville,[2] held an ordinance which required structural modifications on buildings located near air installations to reduce internal noise invalid, because procedural requirements in promulgating the ordinance were not followed. The city's argument that the standard was more akin to a building code than a zoning amendment met with little success.[3] Because the court construed an off-street parking requirement to be a building rather than a zoning ordinance matter,[4] the court upheld a variance that did not otherwise meet the criteria for a zoning variance.

Urban Renewal

Since housing codes apply to existing housing, the adoption of a minimum housing code provides a means under the police power of upgrading older housing to comply with new standards. If housing is bad enough, the owner can be required to demolish the housing under the housing code, which is based on the police power and the interests of promoting the public health, safety, and welfare. Under urban renewal, dilapidated housing was usually acquired by paying compensation, however, the current statutes have returned control of urban renewal to individual states and metropolitan areas. They are given the authority to implement redevelopment and revitalization according to the priorities and procedures utilized by a given locale. Federal involvement in urban renewal is limited to approval of grant proposals and release of funds. Thus, whether housing code violations which trigger condemnation proceedings or eminent domain is used to obtain

§ 8.3

1. Brougher v. Board of Pub. Works, 107 Cal.App. 15, 290 P. 140 (1930).

2. Fountain v. Jacksonville, 447 So.2d 353 (Fla. 1st D.C.A.1984).

3. Id. at 354.

4. Siller v. Board of Supervisors, 58 Cal. 2d 479, 25 Cal.Rptr. 73, 375 P.2d 41 (1962); cf. Off-Shore Rest. Corp. v. Linden, 30 N.Y.2d 160, 331 N.Y.S.2d 397, 282 N.E.2d 299 (1972).

property for urban renewal purposes depends largely on the authority of the relevant governmental entity, and the manner in which that authority is utilized.[5]

 WESTLAW REFERENCES
fountain +2 "city of jacksonville"

Urban Renewal
di urban renewal
di,sy("urban renewal" /s condemn! "eminent domain")

§ 8.4 Unauthorized and Unconstitutional Applications of Codes

As with other regulations, the two major routes for attacking the application of a building or housing code are to allege that the regulation is not authorized by a statute or home rule power or that it is unconstitutional. For example in Safer v. Jacksonville,[1] a Florida district court of appeal held that enabling legislation behind the housing code was valid, but that the specific code provisions (one requiring each dwelling unit to contain a sink, lavatory, tub or shower connected with potable hot water, and another code provision requiring at least two conveniently located electrical outlets per habitable room) were not demonstrably related to the health or safety of tenants, generally. The court concluded that the provisions were not authorized by the statute. Challenges to the position taken by the court in Safer, both in Florida and other jurisdictions, have failed and the requirement that specific provisions be demonstrably related to health and safety remains intact.[2]

Regulations can also be challenged as unreasonable and therefore unconstitutional. The issue has most often been raised when the codes are applied to older buildings. The property owner often loses these battles as he did in Queenside Hills Realty Co. v. Saxl,[3] a leading case. While the lodging house involved in the case met the standards of the codes when it was built, it did not have the wet pipe sprinkling system required by a new code. The court upheld the requirement, indicating that the legislature had to decide the level of protection required for safety from fire, that a hazard clearly existed and that the requirement

---

5. See infra §§ 17.7–17.8. If building code or housing code provisions are misused or the governing body regulates in a discriminatory fashion, however, such actions may result in a taking. See, e.g., Amen v. Dearborn, 718 F.2d 789 (6th Cir. 1983), cert. denied ___ U.S. ___, 104 S.Ct. 1596, 80 L.Ed.2d 127 (1984); Espanola Way Corp. v. Meyerson, 690 F.2d 827 (11th Cir. 1982), cert. denied 460 U.S. 1039, 103 S.Ct. 1431, 75 L.Ed.2d 791 (1983).

§ 8.4

1. 237 So.2d 8 (Fla. 1st D.C.A.1970). See also Early Estates, Inc. v. Housing Bd. of Review, 93 R.I. 227, 174 A.2d 117 (1961).

2. E.g., Stallings v. Jacksonville, 333 So. 2d 70 (Fla. 1st D.C.A.1976), City of St. Louis v. Brune, 515 S.W.2d 471 (Mo.1974).

3. 328 U.S. 80, 66 S.Ct. 850, 90 L.Ed. 1096 (1946). See also McCallin v. Walsh, 64 A.D.2d 46, 407 N.Y.S.2d 852 (1978), order affirmed 46 N.Y.2d 808, 413 N.Y.S.2d 922, 386 N.E.2d 833 (1978).

was not clearly unreasonable. If a building is unsafe, it must be made safe, whatever the cost, or closed, despite loss of value. While the case also involved an equal protection issue, since the sprinkling system was only applied to pre-1944 lodging houses, drawing such lines was held proper, because the risk in older buildings is greater.[4]

While the courts often compare the cost of compliance with the value of the building, a more relevant consideration might be the cost of compliance as compared to the value of the building after compliance. For example, if a sprinkling system cost $25,000 in a building worth $30,000 and after compliance the building would still be worth only $30,000, the court might more carefully consider whether the benefit to the public is slight or doubtful. If it is slight the court might hold the requirement unreasonable. On the other hand, if the building is worth $50,000 after compliance, a court might be much more disposed to uphold the regulation.

Courts often hold zoning ordinances that operate retroactively on nonconforming buildings unconstitutional and typically come to a contrary conclusion on housing codes. There are several possible reasons for the difference. Zoning was primarily adopted to control prospective development and nonconformities were typically protected under early zoning ordinances because of a fear that zoning would be held unconstitutional if applied retroactively. Courts began to believe that themselves, and some still do.[5] Housing codes, on the other hand, regulate the minimum conditions for occupancy, not development, and are applied retroactively to rid buildings of nonconformities caused by deterioration, obsolescence or changes in minimum housing requirements.

Moreover, most housing code standards are directly related to the public health and safety. Suppose the Court in Queenside Hills Realty had held the statute violated the due process clause as applied, and subsequently a fire occurred which could have been prevented by elimination of the nonconformity. The courts are reluctant to risk such results. Many zoning standards are less directly grounded on health and safety concerns. Substantial personal injury is unlikely if a building were built two feet closer than a newly imposed setback line permitted. The property owner often loses his attack on the housing code provisions,[6] unless the requirements deal with peripheral matters rather than matters basic to health and safety.[7]

---

4. The fact that a pre-1944 lodging house had burned in a disastrous fire only underscored the logic of the classification.

5. See supra §§ 4.27–4.36 (nonconforming uses).

6. Kaukas v. Chicago, 27 Ill.2d 197, 188 N.E.2d 700 (1963), appeal dismissed 375 U.S. 8, 84 S.Ct. 67, 11 L.Ed.2d 40 (1963);

City of Chicago v. Sheridan, 40 Ill.App.3d 886, 353 N.E.2d 270 (1976); Adamec v. Post, 273 N.Y. 250, 7 N.E.2d 120 (1937); Miller v. Foster, 244 Wis. 99, 11 N.W.2d 674 (1943).

7. City of Columbus v. Stubbs, 223 Ga. 765, 158 S.E.2d 392 (1967); Barrett v. Hamby, 235 Ga. 262, 219 S.E.2d 399 (1975).

If building and housing codes were "zoned," so that one code did not apply to all housing in the jurisdiction, problems of unreasonable application to older housing might be reduced. Opponents of uniform codes argue that one set of minimum standards in a normally diverse community ignores legitimate differences between neighborhoods resulting from age, structure type and socio-economic factors. Some localities are developing separate codes for historic buildings and districts.[8] Though different standards may lessen the impact of enforcing codes in the more deteriorated neighborhoods, they may be difficult to support. Zoned codes might be judicially accepted if they are based on substantial distinctions, reasonably related to the goal sought to be achieved and evenly applied.[9] Differential enforcement may be a feasible way to deal with differences in a community's housing. If it is utilized it should be acceptable as long as enforcement is uniform in the selected areas.[10] On the other hand, if enforcement of code provisions is not uniform, not based on substantial distinctions nor related to acceptable goals, a violation of equal protection may be found.[11] In Dowdell v. Apopka,[12] disparate provision of municipal services, such as paved roads, running water and sewer systems, between black and white neighborhoods led to a finding of intentional discrimination based on race. Typically, however, building and housing codes are not zoned. It has been argued that they could be, with very low jurisdiction-wide requirements, which could be variably increased on a neighborhood basis.[13]

The question whether temporary eviction can be a taking of property within the meaning of the Fifth Amendment thus entitling a tenant to compensation has also posed problems for courts. There had been some disagreement concerning regulatory takings and compensation in some jurisdictions, but the Court of Appeals, in Devines v. Maier[14] (Devines II) seems to have put the issue to rest. In Devines I,[15] the court held that a constitutional taking had occurred when the city

8. See also Aesthetic Regulation and Historic Preservation, infra ch. 14.

9. See Brennan v. Milwaukee, 265 Wis. 52, 60 N.W.2d 704 (1953) and Abbott, Housing Policy, Housing Codes and Tenant Remedies: An Integration, 56 B.U.L.Rev. 1, 105 (1976) for enumerated conditions.

10. Polaka, Housing Codes and Preservation of Urban Blight—Administrative and Enforcement Problems and Proposals, 17 Vill.L.Rev. 490, 519 (1972).

11. See Mlikotin v. Los Angeles, 643 F.2d 652 (9th Cir.1981); Village of Riverwoods v. Untermyer, 54 Ill.App.3d 816, 12 Ill.Dec. 371, 369 N.E.2d 1385 (1977). Cf. Dowdell v. Apopka, 698 F.2d 1181 (11th Cir.1983); Fairfax Countywide Citizens Association v. County of Fairfax, Va., 571 F.2d 1299 (4th Cir.1978), cert. denied 439 U.S. 1047, 99 S.Ct. 722, 58 L.Ed.2d 706 (1978); Hawkins v. Town of Shaw, 437 F.2d 1286 affirmed in banc, 461 F.2d 1171 (5th Cir.1972); Amen v. Dearborn, 718 F.2d 789 (6th Cir.1983), cert. denied 465 U.S. 1101, 104 S.Ct. 1596, 80 L.Ed.2d 127 (1984).

12. 698 F.2d 1181 (11th Cir.1983), appeal after remand 728 F.2d 876 (7th Cir. 1984), cert. denied __ U.S. __, 105 S.Ct. 130, 83 L.Ed.2d 71 (1984).

13. Babcock & Bosselman, Citizen Participation: A Suburban Suggestion for the Central City, 32 Law & Contemp. Prob. 221 (1967).

14. 728 F.2d 876 (7th Cir.1984), cert. denied __ U.S. __, 105 S.Ct. 130, 83 L.Ed. 2d 71 (1984).

15. Devines v. Maier, 665 F.2d 138 (7th Cir.1981).

ordered tenants to temporarily vacate their uninhabitable dwelling to permit repairs, pursuant to the housing code. The court reasoned that because the state had created the leasehold, its suspension resulted in the taking. The city appealed the taking question in light of intervening Supreme Court cases which cast more light on the regulatory taking issue.[16] The holding in Devines I was reversed in Devines II. The court reasoned that when the state creates a property right in the form of a possessory leasehold, and conditions possession on the continued habitability of the premises for the term of the lease, if the state later temporarily evicts a tenant because the premises are unfit for human habitation there is no taking. Housing codes are a valid exercise of the police power, and it is reasonable for a city to take measures to assure that its housing stock remains habitable. The property right is constitutionally protectible but retention of the right is subject to a reasonable condition such as continued habitability.[17]

WESTLAW REFERENCES

building housing /2 code /s authorized unauthorized /s statute

di,sy(housing building /2 code /s unconstitutional constitutional
　　reasonable unreasonable)

building housing /2 code /s compliance /s value worth

"zoning ordinance" /s retroactive** /s nonconform!

housing building /2 code /s retroactive**

housing building /2 code /s public /2 health safety

199k32

housing building /2 code /s historic /2 building district

building housing /2 code /s "equal protection" discrimination

devines +2 maien

"police power" /s habitability

§ 8.5 State and Federal Preemption

Over half of the states have adopted statewide building codes drafted by one of the three major building code organizations, most of which are mandatory.[1] In Oregon v. Troutdale,[2] the court held that the provision of the state building code permitting "single-wall" construction, did not preempt a city ordinance which required "double-wall" construction in new buildings within the city. The court determined that because the construction standards regulated builders rather than municipal government, the city could adopt building code requirements in addition to or more stringent than the statewide code, but not

---

16. Texaco, Inc. v. Short, 454 U.S. 516, 102 S.Ct. 781, 70 L.Ed.2d 738 (1982), and Loretto v. Teleprompter Manhattan CATV Corp., 484 U.S. 419, 102 S.Ct. 3164, 73 L.Ed.2d 868 (1982), on remand 58 N.Y.2d 143, 459 N.Y.S.2d 743, 446 N.E.2d 428 (1983), reargument denied 59 N.Y.2d 761, 463 N.Y.S.2d 1030, 450 N.E.2d 254 (1983).

17. Devines v. Maier, 728 F.2d 876, 883–4 (7th Cir.1984), cert. denied __ U.S. __, 105 S.Ct. 130, 83 L.Ed.2d 71 (1984).

§ 8.5

1. 5 Housing & Dev.Rep. 754 (1977).

2. 281 Or. 203, 576 P.2d 1238 (1978).

incompatible with its provisions. State regulations were to establish basic uniform standards which would reasonably safeguard health, safety, welfare and comfort. In an appropriate case, however, the need for uniformity of the law may be a sufficient basis for legislative preemption at state level.

In California, the administrative code allowed a city or county to determine changes or modifications in the state's building requirements where appropriate because of local conditions.[3] "Local conditions" had been construed rather loosely, until 1977, when the California attorney general defined local conditions as those which could be broadly labeled as geographical or topographical, excluding local political, economic or social concerns as destructive of any attempt to achieve statewide uniformity. Code uniformity reduces housing costs, increases the efficiency of the private housing construction industry and helps meet housing needs of the state. Uniform codes are generally based on professional expertise, research and testing not routinely available to local agencies.[4] Evidence of the desirability of uniformity can be seen in the development of model codes and their subsequent adoption as law by state legislatures.

Federal mobile home construction and safety standards were established by the Secretary of HUD pursuant to the National Mobile Home Construction and Safety Standards Act of 1974.[5] Whenever a federal mobile home construction and safety standard is in effect, no state or political subdivision shall have authority to enact or maintain any standard which is not identical to the federal standard.[6]

Federal preemption is much less a potential problem now than before enactment of the 1974 Housing and Community Development Act.[7] Congress was dissatisfied with code enforcement under the "workable program," and the new act entitled individual communities to decide for themselves the most appropriate building and housing standards. HUD now encourages development of more effective standards through the National Institute of Building Sciences,[8] a private organization chartered by the statute.

More recently, the federal government established the Building Energy Performance Standards (BEPS).[9] Existing building codes do not take climatic variations or energy use into account, but only regulate design and construction of buildings, principally for protecting the

---

3. West's Ann.Cal. Health & Safety Code, § 17958.5.

4. 60 Op.Att'y Gen. 234 (Cal.1977).

5. 42 U.S.C.A. § 5403(a). See § 8.2 at n. 6.

6. 42 U.S.C.A. § 5403(d). See also Title VI. Other provisions include enforcement, correction of defects, state role, prohibited acts.

7. 42 U.S.C.A. §§ 5301–5308.

8. H.R.Rep. No. 93–1279, 93rd Cong., 2d Sess. 134 (1974).

9. Building Energy Standards Act of 1976, as amended, 42 U.S.C.A. §§ 6801–6873. In 1981, these standards were made voluntary. Id.

public health and welfare.[10] Congress chose to effect energy conservation in buildings through existing codes,[11] based on the presumption that it would be more efficient and economical to use building code officials to enforce the standards rather than to develop an alternative mechanism. The department of energy was responsible for promulgating energy conservation standards for new buildings while HUD was required to formulate cost-effective "weatherization" standards for existing housing rehabilitated with federal funds.[12]

Most states had already adopted building energy conservation standards recommended in the Energy Policy and Conservation Act of 1975 [13] which made funds available to each state for development of a conservation plan meeting certain enumerated requirements.[14]

WESTLAW REFERENCES

"state building code" /s preemp*** /s "city ordinance"

"local condition" /s building /2 code requirement

building housing /2 code /s uniform*** /s purpose

"national mobile home construction"

42 +5 5403(d)

federal /s preempt*** /s state /s building housing /2
    code

building housing /2 code /s "energy conservation"

---

§ 8.6 Methods of Enforcement

Building Codes [1]

Municipal or state building codes are enforced by the commissioner of buildings or similar official under powers delegated by the city's charter (or state constitution or statutes).

The building code usually requires submission of plans for the project for approval by the building official. Forms are provided, and the application must include a description of the work and its location. For new construction or major alterations, the application must include a lot diagram showing compliance with local zoning, foundation plans,

---

10. See, e.g., Southern Standard Building Code (1979), or Uniform Building Code (1979).

11. 42 U.S.C.A. § 6831, et seq., but conservation measures may be implemented in other ways. Energy efficient buildings may be encouraged by tax credits, e.g., I.R.C. § 44c.

12. 42 U.S.C.A. § 7154. Funds have been appropriated through 1985, or until expended.

13. 89 Stat. 871, 42 U.S.C.A. § 6201.

14. These standards were based on ASHRAE guidelines—prescriptive standards which were much more easily enforced than BEPS could be. Aderman, En-

ergy Standards for New Buildings, 11 Nat. J. 1084 (1979).

§ 8.6

1. W. Correale, A Building Code Primer, xiii–xv, 1–13 (1979). The author was a consulting engineer in New York City and was familiar with the Basic Building Code, promulgated by BOCA and code administration procedures in New York. Administration and enforcement of building codes does not vary a great deal in the overall plan approval and inspection process, though codes themselves may differ from region to region to allow for variations in climatic, geological and other relevant conditions.

floor and roof plans, detailed architectural, structural and mechanical drawings. The code officials examine the plans submitted for compliance with the code, and other applicable laws and regulations. If plans comply, then they are approved in writing and notice is given to the applicant. When plans fail to comply, the application and plans will be rejected in writing with reasons clearly stated. Rejected applications may be revised and resubmitted until standards are met. Minor alterations (not affecting health, fire or structural safety of the building) and ordinary repairs (replacement or renewal of existing work during ordinary maintenance) usually do not require plan approval. Application for plan approval and the work permits are often separate processes, but may be applied for all at once.

To insure that health and safety requirements are met during the building process, the building official is authorized to enter and inspect any premises or building to check for compliance with code and other applicable laws.[2] Necessary tests are conducted at the direction of the building official, and the expense is borne by the owner or lessee of the property.

Final inspection is made upon completion of the work by a building official, and the architect, engineer or other supervisor of the work may be present also. The owner must be notified of any failures of the work to comply with code provisions. A certificate of occupancy will be issued when a building is found to substantially conform to applicable laws and regulations, and to the approved plans and code provisions.[3] A temporary certificate of occupancy can be issued for 60–90 days if occupancy of the building (or relevant portion) will not endanger public safety during that period.

Housing Codes

A violation of the housing code usually comes to the attention of local government officials when a tenant files a complaint or as the result of a survey of an area by the administrative agency of the local government. If by complaint, building officials conduct an inspection and make a report, the matter is thereafter treated as if discovered by survey, namely, the landlord is served with notice of a hearing and there is a finding that the violation exists. The administrative or judicial body having jurisdiction then typically orders repairs, a period for compliance is set, followed by a reinspection. If the repairs have not been made the compliance period is usually extended. If the repairs have still not been made (or the building is beyond repair in the first instance) the landlord can be ordered to vacate the building or to demolish it, or can be fined or imprisoned.[4] A city would be overstepping its police power, however, to require a building to be demolished

2. See, e.g., West's Fla.Stat.Ann. § 553.79(5)(a)–(c).

3. See, e.g., West's Fla.Stat.Ann. § 553.79(7)(a).

4. See, e.g., Ill.—S.H.A. ch. 38, ¶ 12–5.1. Alternatively, the list of violations and compliance date may be served first, leaving the landlord to request a hearing. See also City of Bakersfield v. Miller, 64 Cal.2d

without paying the owner compensation, if repairs could be made to the building to meet the code requirements.[5]

In some jurisdictions there are other available remedies. For example, under the New York Receivership Law [6] if a serious defect is found, the Commissioner of Real Estate can be appointed by the court as a receiver to collect rent and make repairs out of the rents.[7] The tenant is also given protection against eviction so long as violations of the housing code exist.[8] Rent strikes, a method by which tenants can petition courts to collect rent and stay eviction proceedings pending repairs, have been more symbolic than successful.[9]

In other states, statutes provide that a tenant can notify the landlord of a defect, and if it is not repaired, the tenant can repair the defect himself and deduct the expenses from the monthly rent.[10] Statutes in other states allow tenants to sue for damages if injured as a result of an injury caused by violation of the housing code.[11]

Tenants have also sought housing code compliance by arguing that rent is not due where there are housing code violations on the theory that the violation constitutes a breach of an implied warranty of habitability, which is an implied promise by the landlord that the premises are fit for human occupation and will remain so throughout the lease term.[12] This theory underlies an increasing amount of code violation cases. Javins v. First Nat'l Realty Corp.[13] presents a balanced approach to the issue. The landlord sued for possession for non-payment of rent, and the tenants countered with housing code violations as a defense. The court applied traditional contract principles to this residential rental situation and found an implied warranty of

93, 48 Cal.Rptr. 889, 410 P.2d 393 (1966), cert. denied 384 U.S. 988, 86 S.Ct. 1890, 16 L.Ed.2d 1005 (1966). Defendant was given five years to comply with city building code. When he refused, the city filed suit compelling him to comply with the code. After six years of litigation, the court finally held that the city had the power to set, define and apply standards.

5. Horton v. Gulledge, 277 N.C. 353, 177 S.E.2d 885 (1970). But see State v. Jones, 350 N.C. 520, 290 S.E.2d 675 (1982). Cf. Dickerson v. Young, 332 N.W.2d 93 (Iowa 1983).

6. N.Y.—McKinney's Mult.Dwell.Law § 309(5)(c)(1).

7. And under the Spiegel Law, also in New York, where tenant rent is paid by welfare agencies, the payments may be withheld so long as the housing code is violated. N.Y.—McKinney's Soc.Services Law § 143–b.

8. See Comment, Rent Receivership: An Evaluation of Its Effectiveness as a

Housing Code Enforcement Tool in Connecticut Cities, 2 Conn.L.Rev. 687 (1970).

9. N.Y.—McKinney's Real Prop.Acts. Law § 769 et seq. See Lipsky, Protest in City Politics: Rent Strikes, Housing and the Power of the Poor, ch. 6 & 7 (1970).

10. West's Ann.Cal.Civ. Code §§ 1941–1942; Mont.Codes Ann. 42–201 & 42–202. See Reste Realty v. Cooper, 53 N.J. 444, 251 A.2d 268 (1969) (tenant constructively evicted because of code violations).

11. La.—L.S.A.–Civ. Code arts. 2232, 2693–2695.

12. Rent abatement is a remedy frequently granted in cases based on this theory, see, e.g., Hinson v. Delis, 26 Cal.App. 3d 62, 102 Cal.Rptr. 721 (1972); Timber Ridge Town House, Inc. v. Dietz, 133 N.J. Super. 577, 338 A.2d 21 (1975). Compare Pines v. Perssion, 14 Wis.2d 590, 111 N.W.2d 409 (1961).

13. 428 F.2d 1071 (D.C.Cir.1970), cert. denied 400 U.S. 925, 91 S.Ct. 186, 27 L.Ed. 2d 185 (1970).

habitability which could be measured by the housing code requirements.

Code violations may not be sufficient to render the premises unsafe or unsanitary and make the lease contract illegal and unenforceable, but nonetheless give rise to remedies for contract breach including damages and specific performance. Violations also can be a defense to actions for possession for nonpayment of rent even if, through no fault of the tenant, they arise after the lease is signed. Statutes may vary from state to state. In Florida, for example, the applicable statute requires a tenant to deposit rent with the court when he or she sues a landlord for housing code violations.[14] The tenant is not entitled to remain on the premises during pendancy of the litigation, but the statute does protect the cause of action after vacation of the leasehold.[15]

Owners or landlords may also be liable for injuries to tenants caused by defects in the premises, though this is usually limited to situations in which the landlord knew of the defect at the time of leasing or took no action to repair after reasonable notice.[16] A landlord cannot contract out of his liability for negligence since such contracts violate public policy.[17]

There are also several legislatively established auxilliary programs such as rental assistance[18] for lower income tenants. This enables qualifying tenants to afford decent housing in the private market. Landlords can provide code-related improvements and at the same time maintain a reasonable return on their investment without creating a greater rent burden on tenants.[19]

Outright grants and loans are available to both eligible homeowners and landlords for bringing their properties into compliance with code standards. These programs can go a long way toward preventing abandonment. With the Housing and Community Development Act of 1974,[20] the federal government permitted money derived from the community development block grant program to support elimination of detrimental housing conditions through code enforcement in deteriorating or deteriorated areas, in which such enforcement may be expected to arrest the decline.[21] Technical assistance and information are available to local officials, as are funds for innovative projects dealing with

14. West's Fla.Stat.Ann. § 83.60(2).

15. K.D. Lewis Enterprises Corp., Inc. v. Smith, 445 So.2d 1032 (Fla. 5th D.C.A.1984).

16. Reitmeyer v. Sprecker, 431 Pa. 284, 243 A.2d 395 (1968) (limited by the holding in Presley v. Acme Markets, Inc., 213 Pa. Super. 265, 247 A.2d 478 (1968)).

17. Boyd v. Smith, 372 Pa. 306, 94 A.2d 44 (1953). It has been proposed that mere ownership or maintenance of a slum building should be a tort. Sax & Hiestand, "Slumlordism" as a Tort, 65 Mich.L.Rev.

869 (1967). See also Blum & Dunham, "Slumlordism" as a Tort—A Dissenting View, 66 Mich.L.Rev. 451 (1968).

18. 42 U.S.C.A. § 1473(f)(g), i.e., § 8 of the 1937 Housing Act was amended to create a rent subsidy program.

19. See, e.g., City of St. Louis v. Brune, 515 S.W.2d 471 (Mo.1974); 42 U.S.C.A. § 1473(g) and 24 C.F.R. § 882 et seq.

20. 42 U.S.C.A. §§ 5301–18.

21. Id. §§ 5301(c)(2), 5305(a)(3).

both housing and building codes.[22] Creation of other economic incentives, such as property tax abatements or downward assessments of rehabilitated properties and urban homesteading in addition to federal tax credits may help make such properties more attractive investments.

WESTLAW REFERENCES

Building Codes

di,sy("building code" /s enforce!)

building /s inspect*** /s compliance /s code

"certificate of occupancy"

Housing Codes

"housing code" /s tenant /s complain***

"police power" /s building /s demolish*** vacat***

tenant /s evict*** /s protect*** /s code /3 violation

"retaliatory eviction"

tenant /s repair /s defect /s deduct

"housing code violation" /s breach /s habitability

owner landlord /s liab! /s injur*** /s tenant /s defect

slumlordism

find 515 s.w.2d 471

42 +5 5301 /p hud

§ 8.7   Problems With Enforcement

Camara v. Municipal Court [1] and See v. Seattle [2] held that building inspectors must have either consent or a search warrant to look for violations of a housing code having criminal penalties. These cases only inconvenience administration and present no impossible barriers to enforcement. Marshall v. Barlow's, Inc.[3] although it involved an inspection by an OSHA agent of business premises, upheld the warrant requirement as established in Camara and See.

As stated above, housing code inspections are most often triggered by complaints though there are other techniques such as systematic inspection schedules or area wide inspections. Selected area inspections are more important, primarily in communities with community

---

22. See, e.g., U.S. Dep't of Hous. & Urban Dev., Rehabilitation Guidelines 1980; U.S. Dep't of Hous. & Urban Dev., Designing Rehab Programs: A Local Government Guidebook (1979); Bldg. Officials & Code Adm'rs Int'l, Inc., Code Enforcement Guidelines for Residential Rehabilitation (1975).

For example, the Department funded a 22-month innovative project conducted by the Massachusetts Department to study the degree to which existing building code requirements were an obstacle to the renovation of existing buildings and, if so,

whether or not proposed code revisions would alleviate this problem. See Mass. Executive Office of Communities & Dev., Final Report: Removing Obstacles to Building Reuse and Community Conservation at the Local Level (1980).

§ 8.7

1. 387 U.S. 523, 87 S.Ct. 1727, 18 L.Ed. 2d 930 (1967).

2. 387 U.S. 541, 87 S.Ct. 1737, 18 L.Ed. 2d 943 (1967).

3. 436 U.S. 307, 98 S.Ct. 1816, 56 L.Ed. 2d 305 (1978).

development, urban renewal or other targeted areas of preservation and rehabilitation.

Where building and housing code enforcement is primarily triggered by complaints, buildings can deteriorate rapidly if no complaints are made. Complaints may not be filed with public authorities due to the threat of retaliatory eviction. The retaliatory nature of an eviction may itself be a defense to eviction,[4] although retaliatory motive may be difficult to prove.[5] Municipal ordinances can regulate entry of inspectors, and can require inspections prior to sale or reletting, but cannot impose criminal sanctions for refusal to comply with warrantless searches.[6]

Despite a generally favorable judicial response to upholding the constitutionality of housing codes and their enforcement, enforcement problems remain. In many cities a multiplicity of agencies deal with the problem: different agencies for different parts of the code, different agencies for new buildings, for old buildings, for administration, for compliance. Inspectors are inadequate in number and frequently are not well trained.[7] Corruption is not unheard of and inspections, re-inspections, orders, extension of time to comply with orders, partial compliance being equated with good faith and the hope that compliance may be obtained short of court proceedings all delay the time prior to imposition of judicial sanctions. Once in court, problems may become moot if tenants move. Since criminal sanctions are involved, process may be difficult to serve, procedures are slow and the burden of proof difficult.

The courts have shown great reluctance to impose criminal sanctions for failure to comply with repair orders. Such penalties are neither effective nor do they create an economic incentive for the landowner to comply with the codes. As a result judicial proceedings

---

4. Edwards v. Habib, 397 F.2d 687 (D.C. Cir.1968), cert. denied 393 U.S. 1016, 89 S.Ct. 618, 21 L.Ed.2d 560 (1969); Clore v. Fredman, 59 Ill.2d 20, 319 N.E.2d 18 (1974); S.P. Growers Ass'n. v. Rodriguez, 17 Cal.3d 719, 131 Cal.Rptr. 761, 552 P.2d 1721 (1976); Voyager Village, Ltd. v. Williams, 3 Ohio App.3d 288, 444 N.E.2d 1337 (1982); Sims v. Century Kiest Apts., 567 S.W.2d 526 (Tex.Civ.App.1978). But see Hurricane v. Kanover, Ltd., 651 P.2d 1218 (Colo.1982, en banc). See also C.G.S.A. § 52–540a; Ill.—S.H.A. ch. 80, § 71.

5. Retaliatory eviction can only be used as a defense for eviction if the eviction was in retaliation for reporting violations of laws or regulations which directly affect the leasehold. For example, reporting lessor's violations of antitrust laws did not support lessee's defense of retaliatory eviction in subsequent action. Mobil Oil Corp. v. Rubenfeld, 48 A.D.2d 428, 370 N.Y.S.2d 943 (1975), order affirmed 40 N.Y.2d 936, 390 N.Y.S.2d 57, 358 N.E.2d 882 (1976), reargument denied 41 N.Y.2d 1009, 395 N.Y.S.2d 1027, 363 N.E.2d 1194 (1977).

6. See, e.g., Currier v. Pasadena City, 48 Cal.App.3d 810, 121 Cal.Rptr. 913 (1975), cert. denied 423 U.S. 1000, 96 S.Ct. 432, 46 L.Ed.2d 375 (1975); Cincinnati Bd. of Realtors, Inc. v. Cincinnati, 47 Ohio App.2d 267, 353 N.E.2d 898, 1 O.O.3d 341 (1975), judgment affirmed 46 Ohio St.2d 138, 346 N.E.2d 666 (1976); Wilson v. Cincinnati, 46 Ohio St.2d 138, 346 N.E.2d 666 (1976).

7. Howe, Code Enforcement in Three Cities: An Organizational Analysis, 13 Urb.Law. 65, 74 (1981). See also Comptroller General of the U.S., Enforcement of Housing Codes: How It Can Help Achieve the Nation's Housing Goal (1972).

are often suspended when the defendant shows some last minute efforts at compliance, sentences are suspended or fines when imposed, are small. Failure of the judiciary to impose jail sentences and the tendency to avoid stiff sanctions result in a system in which landowners include numerous petty fines in calculating their costs of doing business.[8]

While the courts are willing to broadly uphold the constitutionality of housing codes, they are not as willing to uphold convictions for violations. Courts are generally unwilling to force owners of housing to subsidize it or face criminal sanctions as the alternative.[9]

Municipalities are more frequently being held liable for negligent inspections of both new construction and existing housing, due to the erosion of sovereign immunity and the public duty doctrine.[10] In Manors of Inverrary XII Condominium Association v. Atreco-Florida, Inc.,[11] a Florida district court of appeal held that a building inspector's approval of a building permit and on-site inspections prior to issuance of a certificate of occupancy were operational, thus the sovereign immunity doctrine did not protect the municipality from liability for the negligence of the inspector in approving the plans, specifications, and construction, none of which met the requirements of the applicable building code.[12] The Wisconsin Supreme Court held a city liable for damages caused by fire because the inspector should have foreseen that his negligent inspection might result in harm.[13] After an inspection and recommendation for demolition of a building had been made but no action taken by the city or owner, when the building collapsed and two children were killed, a city in New York was found liable for failure to carry out its statutory duty.[14] The United States Supreme Court, in Block v. Neal[15] held Farmers Home Administration liable under the Tort Claims Act, for failure to properly inspect a house during construction. Defects found in the house were attributable to the negligent inspection and did not fall within the misrepresentation exception to the Act. Government can be protected from the danger of excessive damages by enacting statutes which put a ceiling on the amount of

---

8. See, e.g., Grad, New Sanctions and Remedies in Housing Code Enforcement, 3 Urb.Law. 577 (1971); Love, Landlord's Liability for Defective Premises, Caveat Lessee, Negligence or Strict Liability?, 49 Wis. L.Rev. 38 (1975).

9. See, e.g., People v. Rowen, 9 N.Y.S.2d 732, 214 N.Y.S.2d 347, 174 N.E.2d 331 (1961); Gribez & Grad, Housing Code Enforcement: Sanctions and Remedies, 66 Colum.L.Rev. 1254, 1271–72 (1966).

10. Stone & Rinker, Governmental Liability for Negligent Inspections, 57 Tul.L. Rev. 328 (1982). See Note, Municipal Liability for Negligent Building Inspection, 65 Iowa L.Rev. 1416 (1980).

11. 438 So.2d 490 (Fla.App. 4th D.C.A. 1983), petition for review dismissed 450 So. 2d 485 (1984).

12. Id. at 494.

13. Coffey v. Milwaukee, 74 Wis.2d 526, 247 N.W.2d 132 (1976).

14. Runkel v. New York, 282 App.Div. 173, 123 N.Y.S.2d 485 (1953). See also Gannon Personnel Agency, Inc. v. New York, 57 A.D.2d 535, 394 N.Y.S.2d 5 (1977); Campbell v. Bellevue, 85 Wn.2d 1, 530 P.2d 234 (1975); compare Quinn v. Nadler Bros., Inc., 92 A.D.2d 1013, 461 N.Y.S.2d 455 (1983), order affirmed 59 N.Y.2d 914, 466 N.Y.S.2d 292, 453 N.E.2d 521 (1983).

15. 460 U.S. 289, 103 S.Ct. 1089, 75 L.Ed.2d 67 (1983).

damages recoverable against it.[16] The government can also be exempted from liability for failure to inspect or negligent inspection if the property is not owned by the government.[17]

Vacation and demolition orders are also sanctions. Vacation orders inconvenience tenants, and both vacation and demolition orders can lead to a reduction of the available housing stock. Though most housing codes have provisions allowing municipalities to put teeth into enforcement through vacate orders, receivership, municipal repair, demolition or denial of tax depreciation allowances, local governments are reluctant to use these mechanisms extensively.[18] Alternatively, there are some instances in which enforcement of housing codes is undertaken in a discriminatory manner.[19] Municipalities rarely collect enough money in fines to offset enforcement costs, and because expenses for code administration and enforcement come from general revenues there is seldom enough in public coffers to support public repair of housing code violations.

 WESTLAW REFERENCES

"building inspector" /s consult warrant /s code /3 violation

marshall +2 barlow

"retaliatory eviction" /s defense /s report***

wilson +2 "city of cincinnati"

"housing code" /s enforce! /s criminal /2 sanction penalty fine
    sentence

municipality city town /s liab! inspection /3 negligen**

block +2 neal

vacat*** /2 order /s "housing code"

demoli! /2 order /s "housing code"

find 690 f.2d 827

---

16. See, e.g., West's Fla.Stat.Ann. § 768.28(5); Ill.—S.H.A. ch. 85, ¶ 2–102; Mont.Code Ann. 82–4332 to 82–4334; Or. Rev.Stat. 30.270; Utah Code Ann. 1953, §§ 63–30–22 & 63–30–34; Wis.Stat.Ann. 893.808(3).

17. West's Ann.Cal. Gov't Code § 818.6; Ill.—S.H.A. ch. 85, ¶¶ 2–105 & 2–207; West's Ann.Ind. Code 34–4–16.5–3(11); Nev.Rev.Stat. 41.033; N.J.Stat.Ann. 59:2–6; Utah Code Ann.1953, § 63–30–10(4).

18. J. Hartman, Housing and Social Policy 67 (1975). But see Devines v. Maier, 728 F.2d 876 (7th Cir.1984), cert. denied ___

U.S. ___, 105 S.Ct. 130, 83 L.Ed.2d 71 (1984). Perhaps there will be less of a disincentive to enforce codes if a vacate order is not viewed as taking requiring compensation, and thus does not entitle tenants to relocation payments if the order is temporary in nature.

19. See, e.g., Espanola Way Corp. v. Meyerson, 690 F.2d 827 (11th Cir.1982), cert. denied 460 U.S. 1039, 103 S.Ct. 1431, 75 L.Ed.2d 791 (1983); Amen v. Dearborn, 718 F.2d 789 (6th Cir.1983), cert. denied 465 U.S. 1101, 104 S.Ct. 1596, 80 L.Ed.2d 127 (1984).

Chapter 9

GROWTH MANAGEMENT AND PLANNING

Analysis

§ 9.1 The Growth Management Concept

The traditional land use control devices—zoning and subdivision control—have always had at least a potential effect on the growth rate and patterns of those local governmental entities which employ them. For example, zoning codes which include density allocations for the permitted use zones set a theoretical maximum population figure for the jurisdiction. Subdivision control ordinances likewise affect allowable population limits and the speed at which development occurs by setting minimum lot sizes and requiring construction of capital facilities before plat approval can be obtained or before building permits will be issued. Nonetheless, controlling the maximum population of a community and the rate at which growth will occur is at best a minor goal of traditional zoning and subdivision control ordinances.

The growth management plans which came in vogue in the late 1970's and early 1980's utilized many traditional land use control techniques but for the primary purpose of regulating the pace and extent of growth.[1]

§ 9.1

1. An extensive overview and analysis of these programs and their legal implica-tions are found in the Urban Land Institute's Management and Control of Growth Series, to wit: Urban Land Institute, Man-

259

The decision of various communities to manage growth has been prompted by a variety of interrelated factors—many laudable and some suspect.   Key factors include concern for the effects of growth on environmentally sensitive areas and scarce environmental resources, crowding of public facilities, the economic and social effects of the energy crisis of the 1970's, the decrease of federal money allocations to local and state governments for a wide variety of land use and public facilities programs, the high unemployment rate in the late 1970's and early 1980's, and an acceleration of the rate of growth in the so-called "sunbelt" states.   However one evaluates these factors, the growth management movement of recent years has had the effect of making land use planning and control law a more popular and controversial topic at the grass roots level than it has ever been before.   "Manage Growth", "Stop Growth", "Make Growth Pay For Itself", and "Support the Population Cap" have become familiar bumper sticker slogans. There is little if any doubt that exclusionary motives including even racial and economic discrimination lurk behind some of the proposals [2] but at the very least the controversies which envelope nearly all growth control proposals have brought much needed public interest and attention to the land use planning and control process.   In fact, it seems quite possible that growth management provides the primary theme and coherence for land use regulation and environmental protection for the remainder of the twentieth century.[3]

 WESTLAW REFERENCES
zon*** "subdivision control"   /s   limit! maximum dens!   /6
   population

§ 9.2   Growth Management Tools and Programs

Land use control planners and attorneys are still searching for effective and permissible ways of formulating and implementing growth management programs.   Several patterns are emerging.   The most important of these is that "timed" or "phased" growth control measures are more palatable for courts and the electorate than population caps.

The first major victory before the courts for pro-growth management forces occurred in litigation contesting the phased growth plan developed by Ramapo, New York.   This plan used a residential development timing technique for the avowed purpose of eliminating premature subdivision, urban sprawl, and development without adequate municipal facilities and services.   The plan did not rezone or reclassify

agement and Control of Growth Vol. I (1975), Vol. II (1975), Vol. III (1975), Vol. IV (1978); Urban Land Institute, The Permit Explosion: Coordination of the Proliferation (1976). Urban Land Institute, Growth and Change in Rural America (1979).

2. The "wolf of exclusionary zoning hides under the environmental sheepskin

worn by the stop-growth movement." Bosselman, Can the Town of Ramapo Pass a Law to Bind the Rights of the Whole World?, 1 Fla.St.U.L.Rev. 234, 249 (1973). See D. Godschalk et al, Constitutional Issues of Growth Management, ch. 6 (1979).

3. See § 1.3 supra.

any land into different residential or use districts but provided that any person engaged in residential development must obtain a special permit.

> "The standards for the issuance of special permits are framed in terms of the availability to the proposed subdivision plat of five essential facilities or services, specifically: (1) public sanitary sewers or approved substitutes; (2) drainage facilities; (3) improved public parks or recreation facilities, including public schools; (4) state, county, or town roads—major, secondary, or collector; and (5) firehouses. No special permit shall issue unless the proposed residential development has accumulated 15 development points, to be computed on a sliding scale of values assigned to the specified improvements under the statute." [1]

A developer, by agreeing to provide those improvements that would bring the proposed plat within the number of development points needed could advance the date of subdivision approval. Also applications to the "Development Easement Acquisition Commission" for a reduction in assessed valuation were authorized.

In essence the "timed" or "phased" growth programs generally limit the number of residential and/or commercial units which can be built in a specified period of time. The prototypes for this approach were developed in New York, and Florida,[2] and Colorado.[3] These programs are generally tied to the availability of public services and capital improvements. Sometimes a point system is established according to which a developer or the parcel of land sought to be developed must have a certain number of points before development is allowed. Points are earned or awarded on the basis of availability of public services and/or design criteria.[4]

A second type of growth management program is the "population cap." Under the population cap approach the local government entity sets the maximum number of dwelling units which will be allowed to be built in the jurisdiction. Perhaps the most famous of these is the Boca

§ 9.2

1. Golden v. Planning Board of Town of Ramapo, 30 N.Y.2d 359, 334 N.Y.S.2d 138, 285 N.E.2d 291 (1972), appeal dismissed 409 U.S. 1003, 93 S.Ct. 436, 34 L.Ed.2d 294 (1972). See Bosselman, Can the Town of Ramapo Pass a Law to Bind the Rights of the Whole World?, 1 Fla.St.U.L.Rev. 234 (1973).

Representative "anti" and "pro" Ramapo articles are contained in Urban Land Institute, Management and Control of Growth, Vol. II (1975). In addition to the Bosselman article, they include The Ramapo Case: Five ZD Commentaries," Id. at 32; Silverman, A Return to the Walled Cities: Ramapo As an Imperium in Imperio, Id. at

52; and Franklin, Controlling Urban Growth: But for Whom? Id. at 78.

2. See, Juergensmeyer and Wadley, Florida Land Use Restrictions, ch. 19 (Looseleaf); Godschalk et al, Constitutional Issues of Growth Management, ch. 20 (Sanibel, FL) (1979).

3. See, Godschalk et al, supra note 2, ch. 18 (Boulder, CO). See Robinson v. Boulder, 190 Colo. 357, 547 P.2d 228 (1976).

4. The refinement of the "point system" is usually attributed to Boulder, Colorado attorney Kirk Wickersham, Jr. See Wickersham, The Permit System of Managing Land Use and Growth, Urban Land Institute, Management and Control of Growth, Vol. IV (1978).

Raton plan in Florida.[5] An equally famous, though somewhat different, one is the Petaluma plan in California, [6] which set a cap on the number of dwelling units that could be built within a five-year period.

A third and more widespread approach to growth control is to forego the establishment of ultimate or periodic numbers but to avoid, deter, or overcome many problems associated with growth by conditioning the issuance of building permits or plat approval on the existence of public improvements and capital facilities or requiring that developers pay fees which will be used by the proper governmental authority to provide the roads, schools, parks, sewer and water facilities, and/or police protection which will be needed because of the new development.[7] Closely related to this approach are impact fees and impact analysis.[8]

Developing along with these various approaches to growth management are the increased usage of the so-called "temporary" growth control measures such as development moratoria and withheld municipal services.[9]

Practically all of the land use regulation and control concepts discussed in this Hornbook can be used as growth management tools. Perhaps the largest list ever made of such tools is contained in the Urban Land Institute's *Management & Control of Growth*,[10] to wit:

Action Planning	Compensable Regulations
Administrative Delays	Comprehensive Planning
Aesthetic Controls	Conditional Zoning
Agricultural Zoning	Conservation Zoning
ALI Proposals	Construction Taxes
Amenities Requirements	Contract Zoning
Annexation Policies	Covenants Restrictions
Building Codes	Critical Areas
Building Permits	Dedication/Fees
Capital Budget	Development Rights Transfer
Capital Programming	Districts-Tiered
Carrying Capacities	Down-Zoning

5. See City of Boca Raton v. Boca Villas, 371 So.2d 154 (Fla. 4th D.C.A.1979), cert. denied 381 So.2d 765 (Fla.1980). Juergensmeyer and Wadley, Florida Land Use Restrictions § 19.09, Godschalk et al supra note 2, ch. 19 (Boca Raton, FL).

6. See Construction Industry Association of Sonoma Co. v. Petaluma, 375 F.Supp. 574 (N.D.Calif.1974), reversed 522 F.2d 897 (9th Cir.1975), cert. denied 424 U.S. 934, 96 S.Ct. 1148, 47 L.Ed.2d 342 (1976); Godschalk et al supra note 2, ch. 17 (Petaluma, CA).

Representative "anti" and "pro" Petaluma articles are collected in Urban Land Institute, Management and Control of Growth, Vol. II (1975). They include Hart, The Petaluma Case, Id. at 127; Gray, The City of Petaluma: Residential Development Control, Id. at 149; Gruen, The Economics of Petaluma: Unconstitutional Regional Socio-Economic Impacts, Id. at 173; Misuraca, Petaluma v. The T.J. Hooper: Must the Suburbs be Seaworthy?, Id. at 187.

7. See §§ 9.5, 9.6, 9.7 infra.

8. See § 9.8 infra.

9. See §§ 9.5 and 9.6 infra.

10. Urban Land Institute, Management and Control of Growth, Vol. I, 24–31 (1975).

Easements	Multifamily Prohibitions
Eminent Domain	Negotiation-Administrative
Energy Siting	Official Maps
Environmental Controls	Open Space
Environmental Reviews	Over-Zoning
Environmental Standards	Parking Requirements
Excess Condemnation	Performance Standards
Exclusive Districts	Permit Review
Extraterritorial Powers	Point Systems
Facility Adequacy	Pollution Regulations
Fair Share	Population Caps
Federal Taxation	Preferential Assessment
Fiscal Analysis	Preferred Use
Floating Zones	Ramapo System
Greenbelts	Rationing Methods
Height Restrictions	Regional Taxation
Highway/Roads	Rezonings
Historic Districts	School Capacity
Holding Zones	Service Areas
Impact Zoning	Sewer Facilities
Incentive Zones	Social Analysis
Industrial Recruitment	Special Districts
Initiative Method	Special Permits
Land Banking	State Planning
Large-Lot Zoning	State Assistance
Mandatory Housing Requirements	Subdivision Control
Maximum Bedrooms	Taxation Methods
Minimum Floor Space	Timing/Phasing
Mobile Homes	Urban Renewal/Rehabs
Moratoria-Building/Planning	User Fees
Moratoria-Sewers	Zoning

Although many entries on the list overlap and are "buzz words" rather than "tools" or concepts, the list does indicate the great diversity of approaches to growth management. As consulting the index will indicate, most items are explored at length throughout this Hornbook. Moratoria, withheld or delayed governmental services, infrastructure financing, impact fees, and carrying capacity and impact analysis will be highlighted in this chapter.

 WESTLAW REFERENCES

timed phased /p growth /p control program

"building permit" /s improvement /s fee /p zon!

§ 9.3 Power of Local Government to Establish Growth Management Programs

To the extent that a unit of local government uses traditional land use control measures such as zoning or subdivision control or minor variations thereof, the "power" issue is no different nor more difficult than that encountered by local governments in other land use planning and control activities. The police power automatically possessed by the local government on home rule power theories or specifically delegated to it pursuant to zoning enabling acts suffices.[1]

Many growth management programs and devices, however, involve new, controversial or relatively untested approaches and tools. The lack of litigation or at least the lack or small number of discussions on point emanating from the courts of last resort in most jurisdictions and very little guidance on some of the most basic federal constitutional issues from the Supreme Court of the United States leave planners and attorneys with relatively little guidance.[2]

The lack or sparsity of clear judicial precedent has led many local governments to seek special legislative delegation or approval from their state legislatures. Still another approach employed by units of local government to buttress the legal status of their growth management activities is to submit their growth management plans or policies to the referendum by the electorate.[3]

The use of a referendum in this area seems to stem from the decision of the Supreme Court of the United States in James v. Valtierra.[4] In this 1971 decision, the Supreme Court reversed a three-judge panel's holding that article 34 of the California Constitution which required voter approval of proposed low rent housing projects violated equal protection principles. The Court refused to impose the compelling state interest criteria because it found that article 34 made no distinction based on race, and declined to extend the compelling state interest test to classifications based on wealth. The Court placed great stress on the referendum as a procedure for democratic decision-making, saying, "[R]eferendums demonstrate devotion to democracy, not to bias, discrimination, or prejudice."[5]

Taking the lead from this statement, the idea is in current vogue that submission of a growth management program to referendum and voter approval helps insulate such programs from equal protection, "exclusionary", discriminatory and related attacks. The Petaluma, Sanibel and Boca Raton plans were submitted to referendum and

§ 9.3

1. See generally, ch. 3 supra; Juergensmeyer and Gragg, Limiting Population Growth in Florida and the Nation: The Constitutional Issues, 26 U.Fla.L.Rev. 758 (1974).

2. See Godschalk et al, Constitutional Issues of Growth Management (1979).

3. See Juergensmeyer and Gragg, supra note 1.

4. 402 U.S. 137, 91 S.Ct. 1331, 28 L.Ed. 2d 678 (1971).

5. Id. at 143.

approved by the electorate. The first two have survived attack in the courts and the third has not.[6]

Another source of power for local governments to practice growth management stems from state legislative and constitutional environmental protection provisions. Florida, Illinois, Massachusetts, Michigan, Montana, New Mexico, New York, North Carolina, Pennsylvania, Rhode Island and Virginia have provisions in their state constitution guaranteeing their citizens a healthful environment.[7] Arguably a local government is required by such constitutional provisions or the state statutes implementing them to exercise their land use control powers in such a way as to protect environmentally sensitive land or endangered resources. This "duty" might be used as a justification of at least some elements of a growth management program. The court decisions at this point are sparse and indecisive.

A final justification for growth management by a unit of local government may be founded on mandated local government planning. As discussed elsewhere,[8] Florida's local governments are required to engage in comprehensive planning. The elements required to be included in the comprehensive plans inevitably raise growth management issues. A Florida court has held that the Local Government Comprehensive Planning Act which mandates the comprehensive planning also constitutes a source of power for local governments since all of their actions must be consistent with their plans.[9]

 WESTLAW REFERENCES

local /s zon! /s "police power"

james /s valtierra /p referendum

state local! /s constitution! /s land /s use /s control

state local /s constitution! legislat! /s environment! /s protection /s provision provid***

grow! /s population /s finance! money revenue /s govern! regulat!

§ 9.4 Limitations on the Power of Local Governments to Establish Growth Management Programs

The leading publication dealing with constitutional issues and growth control lists the following federal constitutional challenges to growth management programs: (1) the general due process challenge, (2) the taking challenge, (3) the regional welfare challenge, (4) the equal protection challenge, (5) the right to travel challenges.[1]

---

6. See § 9.2 supra.

7. See generally Godschalk supra note 2, ch. 8.

8. See §§ 2.12–2.13, supra

9. Home Builders Association v. Board of County Commissioners of Palm Beach County, 446 So.2d 140 (Fla. 4th

D.C.A.1983), cert. denied 451 So.2d 848 (Fla.1984).

§ 9.4

1. The following, slightly more comprehensive list which also includes potential state constitutional issues is found in Ju-

Growth management programs are land use planning and control activities and are therefore exercises of the police power just as much as is zoning or subdivision control. The general limitations which apply to all exercises of the police power apply to growth management. There is an especially close parallel between the limitations placed upon exclusionary zoning activities and the potential limitations placed on growth management programs. These general and specific limitations are discussed elsewhere.[2]

There are, however, several constitutional hurdles which growth management programs must survive that manifest themselves a bit differently in a growth control controversy than in a regular zoning dispute. They are the arguments that growth control measures constitute denials of substantive due process, equal protection, and/or the right to travel. They are discussed elsewhere.[3]

 WESTLAW REFERENCES
unconstitutional constitutional! & "growth management"

§ 9.5 Moratoria

The adoption of a building permit or development approval moratorium is an increasingly frequently used approach by local governments to halt or slow growth until new growth management programs, new comprehensive plans and/or new zoning ordinances can be adopted and implemented. At times, an interim zoning ordinance is also adopted.[1]

The "power" of local governments to adopt moratoria is far from settled. Some cases focus on the precise delegation of zoning power to the local government and the related issue of whether a moratorium must be enacted in the same manner (procedure, notice, hearings, etc.) as zoning ordinances. Other cases approach the validity and power issues from the exercise of the police power point of view.[2]

ergensmeyer and Wadley, Florida Land Use Restrictions § 19.01:

1. Violation of constitutional home rule power.

2. Violation of substantive due process under the federal constitution.

3. Violation of police power as a taking of property.

4. Violation of equal protection.

5. Violation of right to travel.

2. See § 10.2–10.3, infra.

3. See ch. 10, infra. See generally, Juergensmeyer and Gragg, Limiting Population Growth in Florida and the Nation: The Constitutional Issues, 26 U.Fla.L.Rev. 758 (1974).

§ 9.5

1. See § 4.14, supra. See generally, Freilich, Interim Development Controls: Essential Tools for Implementing Flexible Planning and Zoning, 49 Jr. of Urban Law 65 (1971); Freilich, Development Timing, Moratoria, and Controlling Growth, Urban Land Institute, Management and Control of Growth, Vol. II, 361 (1975); Heeter, Interim Zoning Controls: Some Thoughts on Their Abuses, Id. at 409; Juergensmeyer and Wadley, Florida Land Use Restrictions, Ch. 20; Urbanczyk, Phased Zoning: Regulation of the Tempo and Sequence of Land Development, 26 Stanford L.Rev. 585 (1974).

2. See § 9.3 supra. The leading cases discussing the governmental power issue include Collura v. Arlington, 367 Mass. 881, 329 N.E.2d 733 (1975); City of Sanibel v. Buntrock, 409 So.2d 1073 (Fla.2d

In spite of much recent litigation, the best summary of the requirements for a valid moratorium can be found in the 1976 decision of the Supreme Court of Minnesota in Almquist v. Town of Marshan.[3] That court opined that a moratorium on building permits is valid if:

(1) It is adopted by the local government in good faith

(2) It is not discriminatory

(3) It is of limited duration

(4) It is for the purpose of the development of a comprehensive zoning plan, and

(5) The local government acts promptly to adopt such a plan.

 WESTLAW REFERENCES

power /p local! /p govern! /p moratori**

§ 9.6   Withheld or Delayed Governmental Services [1]

As discussed earlier,[2] a potentially effective growth management approach is the use of the timing and location of public facilities to

D.C.A.1981), review denied, 417 So.2d 328 (Fla.1982); Schrader v. Guilford Planning and Zoning Comm., 36 Conn.Supp. 281, 418 A.2d 93 (1980); Fletcher v. Porter, 203 Cal. App.2d 313, 21 Cal.Rptr. 452 (1962); Board of Supervisors v. Horne; Matthews v. Board of Zoning Appeals, 218 Va. 270, 237 S.E.2d 128 (1977); Jason v. Dade County, 37 Fla.Supp. 190 (Cir.Ct. Dade County 1972); Metropolitan Dade County v. Rosell Construction Corp., 297 So.2d 46 (Fla.3d D.C.A.1974); Alexander v. City of Minneapolis, 267 Minn. 155, 125 N.W.2d 583 (1963).

3. 308 Minn. 52, 245 N.W.2d 819 (1976).

Leading cases discussing each of the requirements are as follows: (1) Good faith: Lake Illyria Corp. v. Gardiner, 43 A.D.2d 386, 352 N.Y.S.2d 54 (1974); Campana v. Clark, 82 N.J.Super. 392, 197 A.2d 711 (1964); Mayer Built Homes, Inc. v. Steilacoom, 17 Wn.App. 558, 564 P.2d 1170 (1977); (2) Not discriminatory: Ogo Associates v. Torrance, 37 Cal.App.3d 830, 112 Cal.Rptr. 761 (1974); Almquist v. Marshan, 308 Minn. 52, 245 N.W.2d 819 (1976); Morales v. Haines, 349 F.Supp. 684 (N.D. Ill.1972), judgment affirmed in part, vacated in part 486 F.2d 880 (7th Cir.1973); (3) Limited duration: Almquist, supra; Lake Illyria, supra; Campana, supra; Deal Gardens, Inc. v. Board of Trustees of the Village of Loch Arbour, 48 N.J. 492, 226 A.2d 607 (1967); (4) and (5) Development of Comprehensive Plan and its Prompt Adoption: Almquist, supra; Alexander, supra: Ogo, supra; Campana, supra; Meadowland

Regional Dev. Agency v. Hackensack Meadowlands Dev. Comm., 119 N.J.Super. 572, 293 A.2d 192 (1972), cert. denied 62 N.J. 72, 299 A.2d 69 (1972); Walworth Co. v. Elkhorn, 27 Wis.2d 30, 133 N.W.2d 257 (1965).

§ 9.6

1. The text of this section is excerpted from Roberts, Funding Public Capital Facilities: How Community Planning Can Help, ch. 1 of The Changing Structure of Infrastructure Finance (J.Nicholas ed.1985). Excerpted with permission of Thomas H. Roberts.

2. See § 9.2, supra.

Even though withholding or delaying governmental services is a frequently used growth management approach, relatively few reported cases analyze them. Leading cases include Associated Home Builders v. Livermore, 18 Cal.3d 582, 135 Cal.Rptr. 41, 557 P.2d 473 (1976); Smoke Rise, Inc. v. Washington Suburban Sanitary Comm., 400 F.Supp. 1369 (D.Md.1975); Robinson v. Boulder, 190 Colo. 357, 547 P.2d 228 (1976). See also Harris, Environmental Regulations, Zonings and Withheld Municipal Services: Takings of Property as Multigovernment Actions, 25 U.Fla.L.Rev. 635 (1973); Ramsay, Control of the Timing and Location of Government Utility Extensions, 26 Stanford L.Rev. 945 (1974); Forestell, and Seeger, Water Facilities and Growth Planning, Urban Land Institute, Management and Control of Growth, Vol. II 457 (1975); Hirst and Hirst, Capital Fa-

guide and shape a community's development. By deciding where to put water lines, sewers, roads, and other public facilities, and by deciding when to put them there, a community is not only making public investment decisions but, more important, is setting a pattern and establishing a framework for the much larger amount of private development that will be influenced by these public decisions. By consciously locating and timing such investments not only in response to present needs but also as a catalyst for future growth and change, a community can exercise a great deal of leverage on its development pattern. Planners generally refer to this approach as Capital Improvement Programming.

A Capital Improvement Program (CIP) is an annually compiled schedule of public construction activity covering the next five or six years, stating what public improvements will be built, where they will be built, and when, along with costs, sources of funding, and other pertinent information. It is an organized way for a community to discuss what it wants to do, what it can afford to do, what its priorities are, and how the projects will be coordinated.

The idea of capital improvements programming has been around for a long time. In fact, it evolved at about the same time in the history of American urban planning as land use regulation. In older cities such as Baltimore, Philadelphia, Pittsburgh, and Cleveland, the capital improvements program became the centerpiece of the planning program. In most places, however, communities moved more readily into the regulatory side of planning than they did into orderly fiscal planning, budgeting, and public investment programming. Urban planning in the United States today would certainly be much stronger if both the public regulatory and public investment sides of the coin had evolved together. In recent years, with the stress that has been placed first on growth management and now on managing scarce fiscal resources, the time has become ripe for public capital investment planning to blossom.

Hence, even though capital improvements planning is an old idea, its widespread and institutionalized use as part of the comprehensive planning process would really be a long overdue innovation in most cities and counties. Moreover, the imaginative combination of regulatory and investment concepts, such as through the imposition of impact fees as a form of development regulation, is an even more innovative aspect of community planning.

Each year the first year of a multiyear capital improvements program can become the basis for the capital improvements portion of the annual operating budget. Also each year the capital improvements program is recompiled, dropping the first year and adding a new fifth (or sixth) year. Hence, a capital improvements program can serve as a

cilities Planning as a Growth Control Tool,
Id. at 461; Rivkin, Sewer Moratoria as a
Growth Control Technique, Id. at 473.

policy implementation link between a long-range plan such as the comprehensive plan or one of the functional components thereof, and the actual line-item budgeting of funds for carrying out the plan.

Included among the many benefits of capital improvements programming are the following:

1. It can insure that plans for needed community facilities will actually be carried out by translating them into "bite-sized" chunks.

2. It allows various capital improvement proposals to be tested against sets of policies. Certain proposed projects may be someone's pet ideas but may not survive the tests of relevance, feasibility, or need.

3. It permits the multiyear scheduling of capital improvements that require more than one year to construct.

4. It provides an opportunity to acquire future public sites and rights-of-way before the costs go up.

5. It provides an opportunity for long-range financial planning and management.

6. It stabilizes tax rates through debt management.

7. It avoids costly and embarrassing instances of poor timing and noncoordination, such as paving a street and then tearing it up to install a sewer, or completing a school building before the water line reaches it.

8. It provides an opportunity for citizen participation and the involvement of specific interest groups in public matters that affect them.

9. It fosters better overall management of city or county affairs.

With regard to the last two points in particular, the city of Charlotte, North Carolina, a few years ago set up a special permanent exhibit in a City Hall conference room, whose walls were lined with charts on which movable tokens were placed that represented the type, cost, and schedule status of various capital improvements that were programmed or under way at any given time. Such an arrangement can be a useful coordinating mechanism for technical, administrative, and policymaking officials, as well as a learning tool and graphic demonstration of efficient public management for citizen and interest groups.

In a broader sense, capital improvements programming can also help a community establish the maximum amount of debt that it wishes to incur. It can focus on the various types of financing devices that can or should be resorted to, including traditional ones such as revenue bonds and special assessments, or some of the newer, innovative ones such as tax increment financing or impact fees.

Capital improvements programming can help determine the availability and applicability of state and federal financial participation. And perhaps most important, at least from a community planning point of view, capital improvements programming can enable a community to focus on, and select among, community objectives such as economic development in general, industrial development in particular, tourism, downtown redevelopment, neighborhood revitalization, and environmental protection.

Capital improvement programming is also an invaluable growth management tool. It can help determine whether, where, and how various parts of the community will develop. It can set priorities—for example, between the extension of public services into the urban fringe and the filling in and strengthening of services within substantially developed areas.

The planning agency should play a major role in developing its community's capital improvements program. If possible, the planning staff (and possibly the planning commission) should be designated the official body in charge of annually compiling and analyzing the various departmental needs, estimating the amount of funds available over the period of time involved, relating the departmental needs to the community's plans and to the amount of funds available, negotiating the priorities and differences among the various parties, and recommending a final program for public hearings and adoption by the governing body. The planner's actual role will depend upon the laws, customs, and structure of its particular local government and the extent to which these can be changed. In some cases the finance or budget officer or an interdepartmental committee may play a central role. At a minimum, however, the planning agency should be given ample opportunity to participate in the early stages and not simply react toward the end of the process.

 WESTLAW REFERENCES
"capital improvement plan"

§ 9.7 Infrastructure Funding [1]

Traditionally the responsibility to provide so-called "infrastructure" has fallen to local government. Potable water, waste water collection and treatment, solid waste collection and disposal, streets, parks, and public schools generally fall into the category of "infrastructure." These services are required for the community to function in a manner that the public health, safety and welfare are protected. There is no doubt that growing communities require expanded water and

§ 9.7

1. The text of this section is excerpted from Roberts, Funding Public Capital Facilities: How Community Planning Can Help, ch. 1 of The Changing Structure of

Infrastructure Finance (J. Nicholas ed.1985). Permission has been granted by Thomas H. Roberts, President, Thomas H. Roberts and Associates, Atlanta, GA.

waste water facilities, new schools additional fire stations and the like. The issue which has arisen is how are these services to be paid for?

Financial Capital Facilities Associated With New Development

It might seem that when a community experiences population growth, it would be a financial boon to all concerned—more people, more jobs, more trade, and more dollars being imported into the county and recirculated within the county. This, then, should lead to a larger tax base, more tax revenues, and more opportunity for local government to provide and pay for the public facilities that people want and need, possibly even more efficiently and at a higher level of quality than before.

Unfortunately, it doesn't usually happen that way. It is true that new outside money comes in, in the form of payroll, investments, and purchases. It is also true that the level of county government activity increases: there is more development to regulate, more public facilities to build, more community services to provide, and more taxes to collect. But generally the public revenues don't come in fast enough or in the right way to cover growing public costs. So things get out of joint: public costs go up, the availability and quality of public services go down, and the burden of additional costs is unfairly distributed, or at least that is how it is perceived by the citizenry.

Typically, there are four kinds of money shortage problems that arise in a local government experiencing growth, particularly rapid growth:

1. Not enough increased revenue to cover increased expenses.

2. Not enough revenues early enough to cover front-end costs of new public facilities (negative cash flow).

3. Not enough revenue available in the right places or for the right purposes.

4. Inequitable distribution of the cost burden.

Problem 1, not enough increased revenue to cover increased expenses, can be caused by (1) inelastic revenue sources, (2) undependability of grant sources, or (3) the voters' refusal to countenance higher taxes.

An inelastic revenue source is one that does not grow fast enough to compensate for the offsetting effects of increased service demands or inflation. A sales tax, for example, is a fairly elastic response to the effects of inflation, because it grows in direct proportion to sales receipts, which in turn grow in direct proportion to inflation. In contrast per-gallon fuel taxes are a good example of inelastic taxes, because the revenue they produce does not increase as the cost of fuel increases, nor does it increase as fuel efficiency (that is, mileage per gallon) increases. Typical local governmental revenues, such as the ad valorem real property tax [2] or business licenses and fees, may or may not be elastic, depending upon how careful local government officials are to see that property assessments and other components of revenue are periodically updated. Inasmuch as various types of development (such as residential, commercial, and industrial development) rarely produce real estate tax revenues in direct proportion to the services they consume, it is also important that local government constantly keep a close watch on the relative amounts of the various types of development it is experiencing (or permitting or encouraging) and also on the total mixture of revenues (that is, general property taxes, special assessments, user charges, business licenses, and other fees) that each type of development is producing.

Undependability of grant sources can be a serious cause of revenue shortages in local government. Federal and state funding policies can change quickly; and although federal aid can be a useful source of funding, it can also lead a local government to overcommit itself, only to find that the grants it anticipated are not forthcoming because of a change in the political or fiscal climate, leading to a change in the law or in authorization or appropriation levels. If the grants are forthcoming, they may not come when they were supposed to, or the amount may be computed conservatively or inequitably.[3]

A third typical cause of revenue shortages in growing localities is voters' opposition to higher taxes. "Taxpayer revolts" can be caused by general economic conditions or by specific dissatisfaction with the effects of growth, and they can result in the defeat of bond issues, pressure on public officials to keep taxes low, or replacement of officials at the polls with new ones who say they will keep taxes down. In any case, the result is less revenue to meet mounting expenses.

Problem 2, cash flow problems—that is, not having money in hand early enough to cover front-end costs—are the bane of any growing community, and particularly local governments confronted with rapid growth and development. Although new real estate development adds value to the tax roll, which will eventually produce more tax revenue for the city or county, these funds are not available ahead of time when they are needed to provide new public facilities. The traditional answer to this timing problem is to borrow the money by issuing bonds and paying them off over the life of a facility, usually several decades. There are limitations on this procedure, including legal debt limits, refusal by the voters or the elected officials to incur the debt, lack of identifiable or predictable future revenues to pledge (as in the case of revenue bonds), and a reluctance to charge all taxpayers for growth costs inflicted by new growth (as in the case of general obligation bonds). In addition, the currently high level of interest rates makes public borrowing more expensive than ever.

2. See infra §§ 12.2–12.5.   3. See infra §§ 17.1–17.8.

Problem 3, not enough revenue available in the right places or for the right purposes, is another funding problem typically experienced by a locality faced with new growth. In this case the amount of available funds grows, but not in such a way as to make funds available for specific purposes. One example is the revenue produced by user charges within a special taxing district or public service district, which cannot be drained off and used for some other purpose—nor should it be, however meritorious the other purpose.

Other examples include various federal and state assistance programs which make funding available only for certain projects or categories. Not only are such limitations unresponsive to local needs and priorities, but they can also tempt local governments into compounding their financial problems, for example by accepting a grant to construct a capital facility, without paying adequate attention to the true life-cycle cost of the facility, including long-term operating and maintenance costs.

Problem 4 is the inequitable distribution of the cost burden. It is common for taxpayers to feel that they are being unfairly treated in one way or another, and this feeling is almost always exacerbated in a growing area, where residents may feel that they are being made to pay not only for their own services but for the expense of accommodating newcomers as well. Sometimes this situation is brought on by the high front-end cost of new development, discussed as problem 2 above. Sometimes it is caused by the fact that the new residents demand and receive a higher level or quality of services than was provided before, such as more libraries or better garbage collection, and the higher costs of these improved services are shared by all. Sometimes taxes rise simply because of an increase in per capita costs brought on by higher densities or a larger or more complex population, as in the case of police protection costs.

Inequitable tax burdens can also occur in a growing area when one unit of government provides services to another unit of government or to the citizens of another unit. An example is the provision of sewer or water service by a municipality to the surrounding area. There is always a strong risk that the providing government may charge too much or too little for the service, creating an inequity in either case. The most common situation is for the providing government to charge enough to cover the direct costs of the service but not enough to cover the full range of indirect costs of urban impacts that go along with it. Conflicting interpretations of these complex fiscal interrelationships can easily lead to public disagreements about who is subsidizing whom.

Whenever citywide or county-wide revenue sources are used to pay for the impact of new development, such as by paying off general obligation bonds or by covering increased annual operating costs, the original residents often feel that their taxes are being raised to pay for the costs of new development; and sometimes they are. (It is also often true, however, that much of the original residential development is subsidized by commercial and industrial property tax to begin with.) Although these same residents may often benefit financially from the new growth as a result of increased economic activity in the area (new jobs, more trade, new markets for services), these benefits are not proportionally distributed. Thus a retiree or a farmer, for example, may benefit less than a merchant or insurance agent, but his taxes go up nevertheless.

As often as not, these four types of revenue shortage problems occur in combined and overlapping fashion or with additional complications. For instance, the demand for a particular public service may grow evenly in proportion to the growth rate, whereas the provision of the service may have to grow in periodic increments. Fire protection is a common example: once a fire station is constructed, equipped, and manned, it can service a certain number of additional residences that are built within its service radius without a corresponding increase in cost. However, at some point a second station or additional equipment must be provided to handle additional demand beyond the capacity or reach of the original station. Hence, while the growth may occur evenly, the public cost of servicing that growth occurs in periodic jumps, making it more difficult to allocate costs and raise revenues in a manner that is viewed as equitable by all concerned. In short, new development often brings surprises in the form of unanticipated public costs.

New development produces additional capital costs, and it also produces increased operating and maintenance costs. This discussion deals with capital costs because they constitute the large, conspicuous, early expenditures that are most directly associated with new development, whereas operating and maintenance costs tend to be absorbed into government-wide operations and funded by the locality-at-large for the benefit of the locality-at-large. However, as discussed above, new development can also increase public service costs for current and new residents alike, and this should not be overlooked in an examination of the total effects of new development.

Two distinct types of capital facility impact costs resulting from new development can be identified, as well as a third, somewhat vaguer "in-between" category. The two types are on-site (or intradevelopment) costs and off-site (or extradevelopment) costs.

On-site costs are the regular capital costs that occur within a development or that are intimately and directly related to a development. In the typical case of a residential subdivision these include, at a minimum, local streets and drainage. As the density or size of a subdivision increases, sanitary sewers, water lines, more substantial drainage facilities and related rights-of-way, and neighborhood park and playground facilities become customary on-site improvements. In addition, street lights and sidewalks may be viewed as normal improvement costs, depending upon conditions. In short, whatever it takes to convert raw land into fully groomed, finished building sites, according to whatever standards the local government seeks to attain for its people, should be viewed as on-site costs and should be funded as such. Off-site costs are those that affect the community at large with no direct connection to new development, exclusively.

"In-between" costs are those which, no matter how neatly other costs are apportioned, can be viewed as falling between on-site and off-site costs. They include costs which might be viewed as extradevelopmental for a small development but intradevelopmental for a large development. Schools are one example: a school could hardly be said to be an on-site cost for a ten-lot subdivision, but it certainly could be viewed as such for a 5,000-lot subdivision. Equity suggests, though, that a 5,000-lot developer should not be charged with providing a public school site unless 500 ten-lot developers are similarly charged. However, a large development has a greater collective impact than several small ones, and a large developer is often willing or even eager to provide such "contributions" in order to protect his relatively large stake, improve his marketability, or expedite the approval of his plans.

Another example of an "in-between" costs is that of a road needed to connect a development to the nearest paved highway. The paving of such a connector road is not really an intradevelopment cost, but its need, or at least the timing of its need, is triggered by one development in particular, so its cost tends to be associated with that development.

Because of the nature of these in-between costs, there is not always a single, obvious policy for funding them, and they can easily be overlooked, minimized, or rationalized by public officials, which means that somewhere along the way their cost will be picked up by the taxpayer. They can be an appropriate subject for either (1) ad hoc negotiations or (2) developing more formal ways to make the developer pay for them. Failure to do one or the other is very costly.

Paying for Infrastructure Costs

Six of the most popular approaches to paying for development can be identified as follows:

    (1) Required subdivision improvements

    (2) Special assessments and service districts

    (3) General revenues

    (4) Ad hoc negotiations

    (5) Impact fees

They are examined in considerable detail elsewhere in this Hornbook.[4]

4. See supra §§ 5.5, 7.7–7.8, infra § 12.8.

WESTLAW REFERENCES

infrastructure /s fund! financ!

Financial Capital Facilities Associated With New Development

increas! /p revenue /p expense /p city town! community
county /p develop! grow /p population

financ! /s capital /s facility /s city town! community county
public /s develop! grow!

inelastic /p revenue cash financ! income /p demand! inflation

federal state /p aid grant /p fund! revenue /p city town!
community county /p shortage

"taxpayer revolt"

defeat! /p "bond issue" /p revenue

"user charge" /p revenue

federal state /p assist! /p program /p fund! /p project /p
local /p facility

"cost burden" /p service facility

sewer water /5 service /p inequit! /p municipal!

"general obligation bond" /p new /p service facility /p resident
taxpayer

demand /s public /s service /s increas! grow! /s fire police
garbage

capital /s cost /s new /s develop!

residen! /s street drainage /s capital

off-site +5 cost

school /s develop! /s cost /s subdivi!

cost /s road /s connect! /s pav*****

Paying For Infrastructure Costs

pay**** /s develop! /s cost /s "special assessment"

§ 9.8 Impact Fees

The Legal Context

A common concern of most growth management programs is the
availability and financing of public facilities. An ever increasing
number of local governments—even those without full scale growth
management programs—have adopted policies and programs designed
to make new development and not existing residents bear the cost of
new capital improvements such as schools, roads, parks, and sewer and
water treatment facilities necessitated by the new development.[1]

---

§ 9.8

1. Infrastructure funding in general is
discussed in § 9.7 supra.

The analysis of impact fees in this sec-
tion parallels in many regards the follow-
ing publications: Juergensmeyer and
Blake, Impact Fees: An Answer to Local
Governments Capital Funding Dilemma, 9
Fla.St.U.L.Rev. 415 (1981); Juergensmeyer,
Drafting Impact Fees to Alleviate Florida's

Pre-Platted Lands Dilemma, 7 Fla.Envt'l
and Urb.Issues 7 (Apr.1980). Juergensmeyer, Funding Infrastructure: Paying
the Costs of Growth Through Impact Fees
and other Land Regulation Charges, Chpt.
2 of The Changing Structure of Infrastructure Finance (J. Nicholas ed. 1985); Juergensmeyer and Wadley, ch. 17, Florida
Land Use Restrictions (looseleaf).

Impact fees are charges levied by local governments against new development in order to generate revenue for capital funding necessitated by the new development. These fees are playing an increasing role in the efforts of local governments to cope with the economic burdens of population growth such as the parks, and sewer and water treatment facilities.

The first land use regulation developed to shift the capital expense burden to the developer and new residents was the required dedication. Local governments conditioned their approval of a subdivision plat upon the developer's agreement to provide and dedicate such improvements as streets and drainage ways. Required dedications for these intradevelopment capital improvements is now a well accepted part of subdivision regulation and is generally approved by the courts.[2]

The "in lieu" fee developed as a refinement of required dedications.[3] For example, to require each subdivision to dedicate land to educational purposes would not solve the problem of providing school facilities for developing suburban areas, because the sites would often be inadequate in size and inappropriately located. The in lieu fee solves this problem by substituting a money payment for dedication when the local government determines the latter is not feasible.

The impact fee is functionally and conceptually similar to the in lieu fee in that both are required payments for capital facilities. In fact, in certain situations the terms can be used virtually interchangeably. The impact fee concept, however, is a much more flexible cost shifting tool. Because in lieu fees are predicated on dedication requirements, they can only be used where required dedications can be appropriately utilized. In the case of sewer and water facilities, public safety facilities, and similar capital outlays, required dedications are not always an appropriate device to shift a portion of the capital costs to the development, because one facility (and parcel of land) can service a very wide area and there is little need for additional land in extending these services.

The distinction between in lieu fees and impact fees results in several decided advantages for impact fees. First, impact fees can be used to fund types of facilities and capital expenses which are not normally the subject of dedication requirements and in lieu fees, and can more easily be applied to facilities to be constructed outside the development (extradevelopment) as well as those inside the development (intradevelopment). Second, impact fees can be applied to developments platted before the advent of required dedications or in lieu fees and thus impose on incoming residents their fair share of these capital costs. A third advantage is that impact fees can be applied to condominium, apartment, and commercial developments which create the need for extradevelopment capital expenditures, but generally escape dedication or in lieu fee requirements because of the small land area

2. See § 7.8, supra.   3. Id.

involved or the inapplicability of subdivision regulations. Finally, impact fees can be collected at the time building permits or certificates of occupancy are issued and when growth creating a need for new services occurs, rather than at the time of platting.[4]

The validity of impact fees is generally subject to a two-tiered constitutional attack. The preliminary and often dispositive objection to required payments by developers for capital expenses is that they are not authorized by state statute or constitution and therefore are void as *ultra vires*. If statutory authority is found, the local ordinance is alternatively challenged as an unreasonable regulation exceeding the state's police power or as a disguised tax which violates various state constitutional strictures.

A review of recent constitutional challenges to impact and in lieu fees discloses a changing judicial attitude towards these cost-shifting devices. Despite earlier negative reaction to such payment requirements, state courts currently tend to validate them as a proper and reasonable exercise of police power. These decisions, however, have utilized different and inconsistent legal theories to circumvent the restrictive standards initially established. The courts' reluctance to clearly characterize these payments as either land use regulations or taxes has aggravated the confusion.

The characterization of impact fees as land use regulations or taxes presents a complex problem. Required dedications, which serve the same purpose as impact fees, are an acknowledged police power regulation. Because impact fees are functionally similar to dedications and to other land use planning and growth management tools, the regulation tag appears appropriate. Although commentators have generally adopted the regulation characterization, the taxation rubric theoretically is appropriate.

The choice a court makes in tagging the impact fee will often be determinative of its validity.[5] If the tax label is adopted, the impact fee will be invalidated unless express and specific statutory authorization

---

4. Thus, the so-called pre-platted lands problem can be avoided. The "pre-platted lands" problem refers to the situation, especially prevalent in various sunbelt states, in which thousands and thousands of acres of land were platted during the land booms in the earlier part of this century before required dedications and exactions were standard. Those lands can frequently be sold and developed without the local government having any way of obtaining the dedications exactions or in lieu fees that would be obtained if the land were being platted today. See Juergensmeyer, Drafting Impact Fees to Alleviate Florida's Pre-platted Lands Dilemma, 7 Fla.Envt'l and Urban Issues 7 (April 1980); Schnidman and Baker, Planning for Platted Lands: Land Use Remedies for Lot

Sale Subdivisions, 11 Fla.State Univ.L.Rev. 505 (1983).

Impact fees are also collected at one or more of the following stages of development: (1) Rezoning, (2) Platting, (3) Development order issuance, (4) building permit issuance, and (5) certificate of occupancy issuance. Collecting them late in the development process is best for the developer since he has no (or low) finance charges to pay on the impact fee amount. Local governments prefer collecting the fee as early as possible in the development process so that funds will be available to start construction in time to provide infrastructure when the development is completed.

5. See Heyman and Gilhool, The Constitutionality of Imposing Increased Com-

for the tax exists. Even if statutory authorization is present, constitutional limitations on taxation may still invalidate the statute. Alternatively, if the impact fee is construed as a police power regulation, very broad legislative delegation will suffice. Once past this statutory hurdle, the clear trend among state courts is to validate such extradevelopment capital funding payment requirements as a valid exercise of the police power. Not surprisingly, therefore, most state courts have summarily labeled extradevelopment impact fees as either a tax or regulation in a result-oriented fashion that avoids an adequate theoretical or policy-directed explanation.[6]

There are two rationales either implicit or expressly cited in those decisions which apply the tax label to extradevelopment impact fees. The first is a simplistic observation that impact fees are a positive exaction of funds and are therefore a tax. This criterion is an untenable basis for distinction because it exalts form over function. It ignores similar police power regulations which mandate that the developer expend great amounts of funds for streets, sewers, and other capital improvements within the development. Any distinction between impact fees and similar police power regulations made on the basis that impact fees are imposed prior to the issuance of building permits rather than after the approval of plats is a distinction without a difference. In either case, funds must be expended by the developer prior to the development of the subdivision.[7]

The second rationale used to label extradevelopment impact fees as taxes is the theory that funds for education, recreation, and public safety purposes cannot be raised under the police power. This assertion is based on the conviction that such facilities should be financed solely from general revenues provided by the community as a whole.

munity Costs on New Subdivision Residents Through Subdivision Exactions, 73 Yale L.J. 1119, 1146–55 (1964). Compare the following cases: Montgomery v. Crossroads Land Co., 355 So.2d 363 (Ala.1978) (in lieu fee a tax); Venditti-Siravo, Inc. v. Hollywood, 39 Fla.Supp. 121 (17th Cir.Ct. 1973) (impact fee an invalid property tax); Haugen v. Gleason, 226 Or. 99, 103, 359 P.2d 108, 110 (1961) (in lieu fee borders on tax); Montgomery v. Crossroads Land Co., 355 So.2d 363 (Ala.1978) (in lieu fee a tax); Contractors and Builders Ass'n of Pinellas County v. Dunedin, 329 So.2d 314 (Fla. 1976), on remand 330 So.2d 744 (Fla.2d D.C.A.1976) (impact fee properly earmarked not a tax); Western Heights Land Corp. v. City of Fort Collins, 146 Colo. 464, 362 P.2d 155 (1961) (not a tax because not intended to defray general municipal expenses); Home Builders Ass'n of Greater Salt Lake v. Provo City, 28 Utah 2d 402, 503 P.2d 451 (1972) (charge for services not a general revenue measure); Jenad, Inc. v. Scarsdale, 18 N.Y.2d 78, 271 N.Y.S.2d 955,

218 N.E.2d 673 (1966) (not a tax but a reasonable form of planning); Call v. West Jordan, 606 P.2d 217 (Utah 1979), on rehearing 614 P.2d 1257 (in-lieu fee not a tax but a form of planning).

6. The tax versus regulation dichotomy is not a key issue in California because the taxing power of local governments greatly exceeds that of local governments in most other states. Impact "fees" are consequently frequently labeled "taxes" even if they could satisfy the requirements for a "fee" in other jurisdictions. See Associated Homebuilders of Greater East Bay, Inc. v. Livermore, 56 Cal.2d 847, 17 Cal.Rptr. 5, 366 P.2d 448 (1961), vacating 11 Cal.Rptr. 485 (Ct.App.1961); English Manor Corp. v. Vallejo Sanitation and Flood Control Dist., 42 Cal.App.3d 996, 117 Cal.Rptr. 315 (1974).

7. The "other" funds which must be expended by the developer relate to so-called exactions which are analyzed in § 7.8 supra.

There is no constitutional mandate, however, that educational, recreational, and other facilities be underwritten by the general population rather than the new residents creating the need for the additional improvements. Furthermore, this rationale employs an unduly restrictive and inflexible conception of local regulatory power. State courts have increasingly found fees which shift the burden of capital funding for these extradevelopment facilities to be within the police power.

Constitutionality of Impact Fees: Early Regulations

Two landmark decisions placed an almost insurmountable burden on local governments seeking money payments for extradevelopment capital spending from developers whose activities necessitated such expenditures. In Pioneer Trust & Savings Bank v. Mount Prospect,[8] a developer challenged the validity of an ordinance requiring subdividers to dedicate one acre per sixty residential lots for schools, parks, and other public purposes. In determining whether required dedications or money payments for recreational or educational purposes represented a valid exercise of the police power, the Illinois Supreme Court propounded the "specifically and uniquely attributable" test. The court focused on the origin of the need for the new facilities and held that unless the village could prove that the demand for additional facilities was "specifically and uniquely attributable" to the particular subdivision, such requirements were an unreasonable regulation not authorized by the police power. Thus, where schools had become overcrowded because of the "total development of the community" the subdivider could not be compelled to help fund new facilities which his activity would necessitate.

A related and equally restrictive test was delineated by the New York court in Gulest Associates, Inc. v. Newburgh.[9] The Gulest decision was overruled in Jenad, Inc. v. Scarsdale.[10] In that case developers attacked an ordinance which charged in lieu fees for recreational purposes. The amounts collected were to be used by the town for "neighborhood park, playground or recreational purposes including the acquisition of property."[11] The court held that the money payment requirement was an unreasonable regulation tantamount to an unconstitutional taking because the funds collected were not used solely for the benefit of the residents of the particular subdivision charged, but rather could be used in any section of town for any recreational purposes. In essence, the Gulest "direct benefit" test required that funds collected from required payments for capital expenditures be specifically tied to a benefit directly conferred on the homeowners in the subdivision which was charged. If recreational fees were used to purchase a park outside the subdivision, the direct benefit test was not met and the ordinance was invalid.

8. 22 Ill.2d 375, 176 N.E.2d 799 (1961).

9. 25 Misc.2d 1004, 209 N.Y.S.2d 729 (Sup.Ct.1960), affirmed 15 A.D.2d 815, 225 N.Y.S. 538 (1962).

10. 18 N.Y.2d 78, 271 N.Y.S.2d 955, 218 N.E.2d 673 (1966).

11. Id. at 957.

Despite this early trend, the Pioneer Trust and Gulest tests became difficult to reconcile with the planning and funding problems imposed on local governments by the constant acceleration of suburban growth. This restrictiveness also became difficult to rationalize with the judicial view of zoning ordinance as presumptively valid. Consequently, courts were not convinced of the practical or legal necessity of such stringent standards for the validation of required payments for extradevelopment capital funding.

Recent Decisional Criteria Favoring the Police Power Validity of Impact Fees

In turning away from the restrictive standards of Gulest and Pioneer Trust, state courts developed divergent and conflicting police power criteria for assessing the constitutional validity of extradevelopment capital funding fees. Some courts nominally retained the Pioneer Trust test but reached patently contrary results without any explanation of the discrepancy. Other courts adopted a privilege theory, under which granting the privilege to subdivide entitles local governments to require payments for extradevelopment capital spending in return. The imposition of these payment requirements is viewed more as a part of a transaction than as an exercise of the police power. Still other courts have deferred to legislative judgments and eschewed constitutional analysis of such payment requirements.[12]

In contrast to these result oriented techniques, a more disciplined constitutional standard was suggested by the Wisconsin Supreme Court in Jordan v. Village of Menomonee Falls.[13] A two part "rational nexus" test of reasonableness for judging the validity of extradevelopment impact and in lieu fees can be discerned in the decision. In response to a developer's attack upon the ordinance as both unauthorized by state statute and as an unconstitutional taking without just compensation, the Jordan court addressed the constitutionality of in lieu fees for educational and recreational purposes. After concluding that the fee payments were statutorily authorized, the court focused first on the Pioneer Trust "specifically and uniquely attributable" test.

The Wisconsin Supreme Court expressed concern that it was virtually impossible for a municipality to prove that money payment or land dedication requirements were assessed to meet a need solely generated by a particular subdivision. Suggesting a substitute test, the court held that money payment and dedication requirements for educational and recreational purposes were a valid exercise of the police power if there was a "reasonable connection" between the need for additional facilities and the growth generated by the subdivision. This first "rational nexus" was sufficiently established if the local government could demonstrate that a series of subdivisions had generated the need to

---

12. See, Jordan v. Menomonee Falls, 28 Wis.2d 608, 137 N.W.2d 442 (1965); Call v. West Jordan, 606 P.2d 217 (Utah 1979), on rehearing 614 P.2d 1257 (1980).

13. 28 Wis.2d 608, 137 N.W.2d 442 (1965).

provide educational and recreational facilities for the benefit of this stream of new residents. In the absence of contrary evidence, such proof showed that the need for the facilities was sufficiently attributable to the activity of the particular developer to permit the collection of fees for financing required improvements.[14]

The Jordan court also rejected the Gulest direct benefit requirement, declining to treat the fees as a special assessment. Therefore, it imposed no requirement that the ordinance restrict the funds to the purchase of school and park facilities that would directly benefit the assessed subdivision. Instead, the court concluded that the relationship between the expenditure of funds and the benefits accruing to the subdivision providing the funds was a fact issue pertinent to the reasonableness of the payment requirement under the police power.

The Jordan court did not expressly define the "reasonableness" required in the expenditure of extradevelopment capital funds; however, a second "rational nexus" was impliedly required between the expenditure of the funds and benefits accruing to the subdivision. The court concluded that this second "rational nexus" was met where the fees were to be used exclusively for site acquisition and the amount spent by the village in constructing additional school facilities was greater than the amounts collected from the developments creating the need for additional facilities.

This second "rational nexus" requirement inferred from Jordan, therefore, is met if a local government can demonstrate that its actual or projected extradevelopment capital expenditures earmarked for the substantial benefit of a series of developments are greater than the capital payments required of those developments. Such proof establishes a sufficient benefit to a particular subdivision in the stream of residential growth such that the extradevelopment payment requirements may be deemed to be reasonable under the police power. The concept of benefits received is clearly distinct from the concept of needs attributable. As the Jordan court recognized, the benefit accruing to the subdivision, although it need not be direct, is a necessary factor in analyzing the reasonableness of payment requirements for extradevelopment [15] capital funding.

The dual "rational nexus" requirements deducible from Jordan provide a balanced, juridically consistent and realistic test of money payment requirements for extradevelopment capital funding. This test properly focuses on and balances the legitimate interests of the developer and the general welfare concerns and power of the municipality. In addition, the "sufficiently attributable" and "sufficient benefit" proof requirements can be accurately and realistically met by local governments through the use of modern cost accounting techniques. Finally, once these "rational nexi" are established, the burden to disprove the reasonableness of the payment requirement shifts to the developer,

14. Id. at 447.   15. Id. at 448.

according the local government a semblance of the presumption of validity it enjoys in zoning and other land use regulation matters.[16]

The Supreme Court of Utah in Banberry Dev. Corp. v. South Jordan City,[17] addressed the "reasonableness" issue raised by the Supreme Court of Wisconsin in Jordan. The specificity and clarity of the court's language gives considerable aid to local governments in formulating step-by-step impact fee implementation programs:

> [To] comply with the standard of reasonableness, a municipal fee related to services like water and sewer must not require newly developed properties to bear more than their equitable share of the capital costs in relation to benefits conferred.
>
> To determine the equitable share of the capital costs to be borne by newly developed properties, a municipality should determine the relative burdens previously borne and yet to be borne by those properties in comparison with the other properties in the municipality as a whole; the fee in question should not exceed the amount sufficient to equalize the relative burdens of newly developed and other properties.
>
> Among the most important factors the municipality should consider in determining the relative burden already borne and yet to be borne by newly developed properties and other properties are the following, suggested by the well-reasoned authorities cited below: (1) the cost of existing capital facilities; (2) the manner of financing existing capital facilities (such as user charges, special assessments, bonded indebtedness, general taxes, or federal grants); (3) the relative extent to which the newly developed properties and the other properties in the municipality have already contributed to the cost of existing facilities (by means such as user charges, special assessments, or payments from proceeds of general taxes); (4) the relative extent to which the newly developed and the other properties in the municipality will contribute to the cost of existing capital facilities in the future; (5) the extent to which the newly developed properties are entitled to a credit.[18]

Economic Analysis [19]

There has been extensive debate in some jurisdictions as to whether the economic underpinnings of impact fees are applicable to government activities other than utility type services. Those who argue for restricting the concept to utility type services base their reasoning on

16. The fairly debatable rule is discussed at § 6.4 supra.

17. 631 P.2d 899 (Utah 1981). See also Lafferty v. Payson City, 642 P.2d 376 (Utah 1982).

18. 631 P.2d at 903–04.

19. The economic analysis given below is excerpted from Nicholas, Florida's Experience With Impact Fees, ch. 3 of The Changing Structure of Infrastructure Finance (J. Nicholas ed. 1985). It is reproduced with the permission of the author, Professor James C. Nicholas, Department of Urban and Regional Planning, University of Florida.

the existence of a physical connection between the benefited unit and
the facilities to be constructed with the fees collected. Moreover, they
argue that utility type services are "closed ended" in that only those
who pay the fee and receive the service benefit from the capital
expansion as distinct from non-payers receiving a benefit. An "open
ended" system, such as a road or park, is different, they argue. In such
"open ended" systems it is either impossible or impractical to exclude
non-payers from benefiting from the capital improvement.

The reasoning on the other side is that local governments face a
host of capital expansion costs which may be reasonably anticipated
because of new development. (1) If the present system of roads or
parks has to be expanded to meet the needs of new development, (2) if
the fees imposed were no more than what the local government unit
would incur in accommodating the new users of the road or park
system, and (3) if the fees are expressly earmarked and spent for road
and park expansion, then the same economic logic applies.

There are two basic positions being argued on the matter of impact
fees. On the one hand there is the exclusiveness of benefit argument
and on the other there is what might be labeled the "but not for"
argument. Those who adhere to the exclusiveness of benefit argue that
only those facilities which can be provided for the exclusive benefit of
the individual paying the cost are fit candidates for impact fees. The
premise of their argument is that if there is a public benefit from the
expansion of a public facility, i.e., some individuals who do not pay for
the expansion may use the facility, then individual payments would
have to be classified as a tax rather than a fee. Such payments being
taxes follows from the premise that there may be benefits flowing to
individuals who have not paid for the facility. Thus, only those public
facilities which possess the capability to exclude non-payers (or free-
riders) are fit candidates for impact fees. Applying impact "fees" to
such facilities would be an act of taxation because others are not
excluded from the use of the facility.

The argument about impact fees is based, in part, on the economic
theory of externalities. An externality is an effect of an action by one
individual upon another. Externalities can be either positive or negative. If an externality is positive it is seen as a social benefit, and if it
is negative it is seen as a social cost. The majority of regulations
promulgated under the police power are attempts by government to
stop the creation of negative externalities, i.e., to stop individuals from
creating social costs. An example of such an exercise would be prohibition of excessive noise. Such a prohibition is not to benefit those who
would have to suffer the noise but rather to stop others (noise makers)
from causing harm. The opposite is where an individual is required to
create a social benefit. An example would be a municipal concert hall.
The requiring of individuals to provide, in whole or in part, a concert
hall is not for the prevention of harm to the public. Rather, it is to
benefit the public.

While there is no question that government is impowered to undertake such actions, requirements for individual financial participation in the creation of social benefits are exercises of the taxation powers of government rather than regulations under the police power. Given that a public park is not for the exclusive benefit of those who paid for it, it would follow, based upon the exclusiveness of benefit principle, that any requirement for individuals to financially contribute to a public park would be an act of taxation rather than of regulation. Returning to the theory of externalities; requirements to prohibit negative externalities (social costs) are considered to be regulatory under the police power to protect the public while requirements to create social benefits are seen as taxation to benefit the public. In this way the right and/or ability to exclude non-payers is very important to whether an assessment to expand a public facility will be seen as a regulatory fee or a tax.

Those who subscribe to the "but not for" argument take a different tack. Their premise is that if the facilities would not have to expand but for new development, then new development should be required to pay for that expansion. Use and benefit are seen differently in this position. It is not, herein, a matter of who uses or receives benefit from the particular facility but rather what (or who) caused the need for the facility. This line of reasoning views the theory of externalities differently. Take the example of a public park. If new development results in population growth that overcrowds the public parks, a social cost will have been created. This social cost is the loss of public use of the public park. A regulation to prevent the imposition of such public costs would have to be seen, therefore, as an exercise of the police power. While both sides of this argument would agree that requirements to create a public benefit would be an exercise of the taxation powers, the divergence comes in what constitutes a public cost.

The conservative position, characterized herein as the exclusive benefit argument, holds that public costs are only those direct impositions of harm such as excessive noise. The "but not for" position sees the loss of an existing public benefit as being a social cost. Thus, one side would argue that requiring impact fees for facilities such as parks would be taxation because the entire public, rather than only those who pay, will receive the benefit (use). The counter argument is that failure of park expansion will impose a public cost. Inasmuch as new development is the source of this public cost then regulations to prohibit such a cost would be exercises of the police power and a fee. These two positions can be argued an infinitum. The Florida courts have addressed this issue. In the Hollywood case,[20] the court wrote:

> . . . benefit accruing to the community generally does not adversely affect the validity of a development regulation ordinance as

20. Hollywood, Inc. v. Broward County, 431 So.2d 606, 612–613 (Fla. 4th D.C.A. 1983).

long as the fee does not exceed the cost of the improvements required by the new development and the improvements adequately benefit the development which is the source of the fee.

The Wisconsin and Utah courts have also addressed this matter. In Jordan v. Villages of Menomonee Falls,[21] the court wrote:

In most instances it would be impossible for the municipality to prove that the land required to be dedicated for a park or school site is to meet a need solely attributable to the anticipated influx of people in the community to occupy this particular subdivision. On the other hand, the municipality might well be able to establish that a group of subdivisions approved over a period of several years had been responsible for bringing into the community a considerable number of people making it necessary that the land dedications required of the subdividers be utilized for school, park and recreational purposes for the benefit of such influx. In the absence of contravening evidence this would establish a reasonable basis for finding that the need for the acquisition was occasioned by the activity of the subdivider.

The Utah court looked at the same issue in Call v. West Jordan.[22] In Call the court dealt directly with the issue of exclusiveness of benefit as a criterion to separate regulatory fees from taxes. The court wrote:

We agree that the dedication should have some reasonable relationship to the needs created by the subdivision. . . . But it is so plain as to hardly require expression that if the purpose of the ordinance is properly carried out, it will redound to the benefit of the subdivision as well as the general welfare of the whole community. The fact that it does so, rather than solely benefiting the individual subdivision, does not impair the validity of the ordinance.[23]

In these various cases the courts are saying that the fact the entire community may use or enjoy the facilities is not the important point. Rather, what is important is that the need for the facility is occasioned by new development and that new development itself benefits. But, it is clear that the new development need not be the exclusive recipient of the benefits. Thus, the courts are aligned with the "but not for" position. The message here is clear—exactions can benefit the entire community as long as the need for the exaction is reasonably related to the needs of new development and as long as new development itself benefits from that exaction.

Thus, the two main principles of impact fee assessment may be stated as (1) the cost imposed through the fee must flow reasonably from those costs to be borne by local government which are reasonably

21. 28 Wis.2d 608, 617, 137 N.W.2d 442, 447 (1965).

22. 606 P.2d 217, 219 (Utah 1979), on rehearing 614 P.2d 1257 (1980).

23. Id. at 220.

attributable to new development and (2) new development must benefit from the expenditure of the fees collected.

Impact Fees and Comprehensive Planning

The increased emphasis being placed on the need and even requirement for consistency between comprehensive plans and land use regulatory activities of local governments makes necessary or at least wise the inclusion of language in comprehensive plans which will authorize and support impact fees. The following language is suggested as the embodiment of the planning principles inherent in impact fees:

I. Land development shall not be permitted unless adequate capital facilities exist or are assured.

II. Land development shall bear a proportionate cost of the provision of the new or expanded capital facilities required by such development.

III. The imposition of impact fees and dedication requirements are the preferred methods of regulating land development in order to assure that it bears a proportionate share of the cost of capital facilities necessary to accommodate that development and to promote and protect the health, safety, and general welfare.[24]

 WESTLAW REFERENCES
grow! /s manag! /p financ! fund! /s public /s facility
"required dedication" /s develop!
lieu /2 fee /s facility /s develop!
"impact fee" /p collect! /p permit
"impact fee" /p valid! invalid! /p constitutional! unconstitutional
impact lieu +2 fee /p "police power"
"impact fee" /p tax*** taxable taxation regulat!
"impact fee" /p tax taxable taxation /p education school!
　　recreation safety

Constitutionality of Impact Fees: Early Regulations
"pioneer trust" /s "mount prospect" /p develop!
"specifically and uniquely attributable"
gulest "pioneer trust" /s test standard

Recent Decisional Criteria Favoring the Police Power Validity Of Impact Fees
meredith /s oxnard
hollywood /s broward & impact lieu /s fee
"reasonable connection" /p fee /p facility improv! develop!
jordan /s menomonee
"police power" /s subdivi! /s benefit! /s fund! financ!
　　expenditure
fee /p exclusiv! /p site /p acqui! /p facility
sufficient! /s benefit! attributable /s develop! /s municipal!
banberry /s jordan
reasonable! /p impact /5 fee

24. The impact fee "Magna Carta" language was drafted by Julian C. Juergensmeyer, James C. Nicholas, Thomas H. Roberts and is published in The Changing Structure of Infrastructure Finance 15 (J. Nicholas ed. 1985).

capital /p cost fund! financ! pay payment /p develop! /p
    municipality /p burden!

factor consider! /s municipal! /s relative! /s burden!

closed +2 ended class & constitution!

closed +2 ended class & reasonabl! /s relat!

city /3 seattle /s washington & municipal! /p constitution! /p
    fee rate

public /s utility /s texas /s water /s service

p–w /s investments /s westminster

fee tax /s exclusiv! /s benefit! /s road park facility improv! &
    ordinance

regulat! /s "police power" /s municipal! /s noise

municipal! public /4 park /s power /s tax

"public cost" /p municipal!

Impact Fees & Comprehensive Planning

impact /p fee /p comprehensive complete /p plan planning
    system

land property /s develop! /s capital /s facility

"dedication requirement" /p health safety welfare

---

§ 9.9 Carrying Capacity and Impact Analysis

The carrying capacity and impact analysis concepts are becoming more and more widely used in land use control law especially by growth management oriented jurisdictions.[1] The origin of both of these sometimes overlapping concepts is environmental law.

"Carrying capacity" is used to determine environmental criteria upon which to ground land use decisions and refers to the extent to which land in its natural or current state can be developed without destruction of the ecosystem.[2]

"Impact analysis" in its current usage is no doubt a transfer of the concepts involved in environmental impact studies conducted pursuant to environmental protection statutes.[3] Generally today, carrying capacity is just one way of evaluating the impact of development.

The seminal conceptual examination of impact analysis was done by Fred Bosselman, who defined impact analysis as "the process of examining a particular land development proposal and analyzing the impact it will have on a community."[4]

§ 9.9

1. See § 9.1 supra.

2. The term "carrying capacity" is also sometimes used to refer to the ability of the infrastructure in a given area to support new development: for example the excess or unused sewage treatment or water treatment capacity of the existing private and/or governmental facilities.

3. See §§ 13.2–.5 infra. See also, Schaenman & Muller, Land Development: Measuring the Impacts, Urban Land Institute, Management and Control of Growth,

Vol. II 494 (1975); Gruen, Gruen & Associates, The Impacts of Growth: An Analytical Framework and Fiscal Example, Id. at 512; Fiscal Impact: Methods and Issues, Id. at 534; Ashley Economic Services, The Fiscal Impact of Urban Growth, Id. at 543; Real Estate Research Corp., The Costs of Sprawl: Detailed Cost Analysis, Id. at 577.

4. Bosselman, "Linkage, Mitigation and Transfer: Will Impact Analysis Become the Universal Antidote to Land Use Complaints?" (1985).

Bosselman suggests that the acceptance of impact analysis techniques reflects two trends in government policy toward land use regulation: [5]

(1) Regulation should respond to specific development proposals: The policy that the formulation of land use controls should be delayed until the developer's intentions are known has been reflected in the weakening of legal support for the principle that a developer should be entitled to develop if his proposal is consistent with pre-established regulations adopted pursuant to a comprehensive plan.

(2) Development standards should be predictable: The policy that a greater degree of predictability ought to be found in the local process of responding to development proposals, has been reflected in the increasing uneasiness of courts toward local regulations that lack a "scientific" basis.

The use of impact analysis in regard to infrastructure funding has been previously discussed.[6] Three even newer ways of translating the impact analysis concept into land use regulation are "linkage," "mitigation," and "transfer." Again, Fred Bosselman has provided the definitions and examples:

linkage is a system by which a developer who wants to build one thing is required to also build something else; e.g., an office developer is required to build housing

mitigation is a system by which a developer who will cause some adverse environmental impact is required to counterbalance that impact by creating an equivalent benefit; e.g., a project that will destroy wetlands is required to create equivalent wetlands elsewhere

transfer is a system by which a certain type or degree of development is made conditional on the extinguishment of an equivalent right to undertake such development elsewhere; e.g., a height increase is made contingent on acquisition of air rights over a historic structure somewhere else.

Although the future course of growth management is far from certain concentration on the impact of development would seem to be an essential ingredient of any growth management program.[7]

WESTLAW REFERENCES

"carrying capacity" & to(414)
"impact analysis" & to(414)
develop /p standard criteri! regulat! /s predict! & to(414)
zon! /s regulat! ordinance! /s predict!
zon*** /s regulat! ordinanc! /s specific! /s develop! /s
        propos! /s plan plann***
wetland /p mitigat!
impact! /p develop! /p grow! /p manag!

---

5. Id. at 2.

6. See § 9.7 supra.

7. Bosselman, supra note 4 at 3.

Chapter 10

CONSTITUTIONAL LIMITATIONS ON THE LAND USE CONTROL POWER

Analysis

Sec.

§ 10.1 An Overview of the Constitutional Issues

The Property Conflict in American Society

Alexis de Tocqueville noted that "the love of property" is "keener" in the United States than it is anywhere else, and Americans therefore "display less inclination toward doctrines which in any way threaten the way property is owned."[1] This national trait results in intense conflict over the extent to which government may affect private property rights for the perceived greater good of society. The battle ground for this jurisprudential issue is the constitutional law of land use, not only in the fifth amendment takings clause, but also in the areas of due process, equal protection, free speech, and civil rights.[2]

Given that property is the oldest branch of the common law,[3] the legal fundamentals of property ownership are surprisingly underdeveloped. Any law student would feel much more comfortable defining crime, tort, or contract than property, possession, or ownership.[4] Pre-

§ 10.1

1. A. de Tocqueville, Democracy in America 614 (J. Mayer & M. Lerner, eds., 1966).

2. See infra §§ 10.2–10.7.

3. Common law property dates directly to William the Conqueror, the Norman

victor of the Battle of Hastings in 1066. C.J. Moynihan, Introduction to the Law of Real Property 2–8 (1962).

4. See generally Rose, Possession as the Origin of Property, 52 U.Chi.L.Rev. 73 (1985) (discussing the elusive nature of the concepts of ownership and property).

cise meanings for these property concepts do not in fact exist,[5] and this complicates the resolution of specific land use conflicts, those between individual property rights and the social interest. The absence of consistent standards thus has made this area susceptible to change, as different social and judicial outlooks have gained power over time; Justice Holmes' statement that "[e]very opinion tends to become a law"[6] has proved especially true in the area of constitutional land use issues.

Broadly, the endpoints on the line of opposing views in this area are a "proacquisitive position," which favors individual wealth, and a "prosocial position," which argues for supremacy of the common good.[7] Because constitutional issues concerning land use tend to turn on concepts as open as "safety, health, peace, good order and morals of the community,"[8] the reigning position, proacquisitive or prosocial, often seems to be determinative in deciding these constitutional concerns.

The "proacquisitive position is usually expressed through the use of the torts law sic utere concept that a person has the right to do whatever he wishes with his land.[9] This right is frequently alleged to be "absolute" and "inherent in human nature" or part of the "natural law" or "brooding omnipresence." The prosocial position is generally expressed by its defenders as a manifestation of the social function theory of ownership first popularized as a jurisprudential theory of ownership by the great Leon Duguit.[10] Under the social function theory, the ownership of property is not absolute or immutable but a changing concept which is constantly redefined to permit ownership of property to fill whatever role a given society assigns it at a given time.

Probably the most vital constitutional provisions regarding these land use issues are the taking and due process clauses of the Fifth Amendment: private property shall not be "taken for the public use without just compensation," nor shall anyone be deprived of property, or life or liberty, "without due process of law."[11] This creates the

---

5. See Ruckleshaus v. Monsanto Corp., ___ U.S. ___, 104 S.Ct. 2862, 2872–74, 81 L.Ed.2d 815 (1984) (discussing the difficulty of defining "property"); U.S.A. v. Dollfus Mieget Co. S.A., [1952] 1 All E.R. 572, 581 (H.L.) (stating that "the English law has never worked out a completely logical and exhaustive definition of 'possession' "); Rose, supra note 4 (discussing the evasive natures of these concepts).

6. Lochner v. New York, 198 U.S. 45, 76, 25 S.Ct. 539, 547, 49 L.Ed. 937 (1905) (Holmes, J., dissenting).

7. Rose, Mahon Reconstructed: Why the Takings Issue is Still a Muddle, 57 S.Cal.L.Rev. 561, 590–97 (1984).

8. Crowley v. Christensen, 137 U.S. 86, 11 S.Ct. 13, 34 L.Ed. 620 (1890). This litany of values is the commonly used standard for a valid exercise of the police power, and therefore appears in many Supreme Court decisions concerning land use.

9. Chapman v. Barrett, 131 Ind.App. 30, 169 N.E.2d 212, 214 (1960).

10. Lectures of Prof. M.E. Kadam of the Un. of Geneva prepared for the Faculte Internationel Pour L'Enseignement du Droit Compare entitled La Notion et les Limites de la Propriete Privee en Droit Compare. See also J. Juergensmeyer & J. Wadley, The Common Lands Concept: A "Commons" Solution to a Common Environmental Problem, 14 Nat.Res.J. 361, at 380 (1974).

11. U.S. Const. Amend. V. This language applies to the states through the Fourteenth Amendment due process re-

taking issue,[12] and the concern here often becomes one of line drawings; according to Justice Holmes, "if regulation goes too far it will be recognized as a taking." [13]

Many constitutional land use concerns, however, do not squarely fall on Holmes' Fifth Amendment scale. For example, substantive due process in land use has a slightly different focus, looking to the benefits which a regulation confers on society to decide whether the regulation is within the scope of government authority.[14] Procedural due process, by extension, looks to the administrative propriety, especially under state law, from which a regulation derives its authority.[15]

Further, equal protection serves to limit government regulation, especially when seemingly neutral statutes or ordinances affect the land use rights of different suspect classes in different ways.[16] Even constitutional protections of free speech and civil rights have important effects on limiting land use regulation. Free speech is especially relevant concerning ordinances which regulate sign control and concentrate sex-oriented businesses,[17] and § 1983 of the federal Civil Rights Act is a potential cause of action for a private person deprived of property rights under color of state law.[18]

Planning and Land Use Regulation: Techniques for Discrimination

While planning and land use controls have generally operated to aid the public health, safety and welfare, they may not have had that effect with respect to poor and minority groups. Rather, planning controls and related public powers have been used to exclude, separate and remove minorities and the poor. There have been strong pressures to have them live elsewhere than the places occupied by middle and upper class whites. Some of the prejudice has been implemented by direct governmental act; the direct purpose of the legislation or other act was to vent prejudice. Sometimes the governmental act has not been class or race motivated, but the effect has indirectly produced exclusion, separation and removal. Sometimes the government has participated only to enforce devices privately created to effectuate the prejudice. That state and local government processes have been and are being used to further racial discrimination is especially disheartening. More should be expected from government.

In an earlier era, zoning was explicitly and purposefully used to segregate races. In 1914, Louisville, Kentucky enacted an ordinance zoning some areas for white only occupancy and other areas for black only occupancy. Racial zoning was maintained by many Southern

quirement. Chicago, B. & Q. R.R. Co. v. Chicago, 166 U.S. 226, 235–41, 17 S.Ct. 581, 584–86, 41 L.Ed. 979 (1897).

12. See infra § 10.7.

13. Pennsylvania Coal v. Mahon, 260 U.S. 393, 415, 43 S.Ct. 158, 160, 67 L.Ed. 322 (1922).

14. See infra § 10.2.

15. See infra § 10.3.

16. See infra § 10.4.

17. See infra § 10.5.

18. See infra § 10.6.

cities as late as the 1950's. Meanwhile, in Northern suburban cities, ordinances were passed excluding Negroes from the city limits between such hours as 8:00 p.m. and 6:00 a.m.

Zoning by race could be a stated purpose of zoning because racial discrimination was socially acceptable. Economic discrimination, a caste system along economic class lines, has not been as socially acceptable in America. Therefore, no or few zoning ordinances will flat-out state that their purpose is to promote homogeneity along economic class lines.

Consider, however, that under most zoning ordinances, there are several residential districts varying from large lot single family zones to multiple family high-rise building zones. What is the basic reason for such a system? The statutes authorize regulations that create different residential zones, and the different types of zones effectuate the purposes of the statutes.[19] The division of land into different residential districts is also clearly constitutional as a general matter.

However, all of the regulations and purposes could be effectuated by planned unit residential developments involving a mixture of housing types and sizes. Why did the mixture not develop, and why do planned unit residential developments with economic and racial integration still not have general market acceptance?

The answer may be the general recognition that unintensive use residential zoning raises the cost of land per unit of housing and that such increases cause segregation along economic and therefore, because of the relative poverty of minorities, along racial lines.

Further, if zoning really is in the interest of the poor, how is it that the single family zone became known as the "highest use" zone, rather than multiple residential zones, which had greater densities of people? If zoning is in the interest of the poor, why is it that apartment buildings are the buffer zone between industrial-commercial zones and single family residential zones, rather than the single-family zones, with fewer people, being the neighbor of the undesirable commercial and industrial uses? If safety of pedestrian children is a major concern, how is it that the apartments housing the poor are on the major traffic

---

19. For example, Section 2 of U.S. Dep't Commerce, the Standard State Zoning Enabling Act (1928) authorizes regulation of

the height, number of stories, and size of buildings . . . the percentage of lot that may be occupied, the size of yards, courts, and other open spaces, the density of population, and the location and use of buildings, structures, and land for . . . residence . . . .

Section 3 of the Standard Act states the purposes to be

to lessen congestion in the streets; to secure safety from fire, panic, and other

dangers; . . . to provide adequate light and air; to prevent overcrowding of land; to avoid undue concentration of population; to facilitate the adequate provision of transportation, water sewerage, schools, parks, and other public requirements. Such regulations shall be made with reasonable consideration, among other things, to the character of the district and its peculiar suitability for particular uses, and with a view to conserving the value of buildings and encouraging the most appropriate use of land throughout such municipality.

arteries rather than the single family homes? If adequate light and air is provided for residents in multiple family high-rise buildings in the interests of their health, safety and welfare, how is the police power justified in providing more light and air by imposing regulations limiting land use to single family development? The several residential districts exist because most people want economic segregation.

Today, the poor and minority groups are sometimes kept out by rezoning property available for multiple income housing so as to exclude it, once plans for building low income housing are known. In other cases, rezoning is not necessary because municipalities have used their zoning power to substantially restrict lands available for multiple family housing, therefore increasing the cost of land available or have excluded multiple income housing entirely and refuse to rezone. Single family zoning may be combined with zoning requiring large minimum lot sizes or floor sizes, or, less frequently, large minimum costs for housing constructed.

The low income multiple family housing developer has also largely been excluded from the rezoning game. In that game, a developer acquires property zoned for some unintensive use, obtains its rezoning for a more intensive use and then develops the land for the more intensive use. The use of the property as developed generates an income stream which returns a high profit on the developer's original investment. If he had developed land initially zoned for intensive use, his profit might be nil or even negative. Therefore, his only profit comes from the public action of rezoning. The use of such a technique is one of the few ways low income housing can be built, because land zoned for multiple income housing is usually too expensive for the low income developer. His economic power is less than almost any other land user. But legislative bodies that routinely rezone for others, infrequently rezone for low income developers. Often as not, when the legislative body does rezone, the voters show their displeasure by petitioning for a referendum and then disapproving the rezoning.

If further evidence of the class motive behind the different types of residential districts is needed, consider that the state permits people to live in multiple family housing—indeed the state builds much of the worst of it; at the same time, the state holds the power to exclude apartment dwellers from areas occupied by single family houses—on the theory that the public, health, safety and welfare is thereby promoted. Perhaps the matter needs reexamination.

Subdivision regulation is another major tool to implement planning and, after zoning, the major tool for controlling land uses. Lot size may be controlled by subdivision regulations rather than zoning ordinances and by requiring a variety of improvements and wide streets and dedications, in addition to large lot requirements, land costs are made high, thus promoting class segregation.

If zoning and subdivision controls were not available, municipalities could still exclude the minorities and the poor through building codes. Building codes can and do require the use of materials that are more expensive, yet often do not have performance characteristics any better than alternatives that are less expensive.

In the previous sections it has been alleged that urban planning, controls and related governmental or private actions have been used to preserve income and race segregated housing and to deny access to desirable housing and locations. Since national policy is clearly against the use of law for such purposes, acts that produce such results, particularly governmental acts, cannot be tolerated. Of course, given the desire of people to preserve segregated housing, techniques to subvert the national policy will be developed. But at least the direct techniques for discrimination can be attacked and efforts to abate indirect techniques contained. Any indirect techniques are likely to be more complex, less effective and more costly. Since they are more complex, their widespread use tends to be eliminated except by those who are highly knowledgeable and sophisticated. Since they are less effective, greater reflective efforts are required on the part of persons who choose not to follow the national policy. Since they are more costly, persons are motivated to reexamine whether the expenditure to support their prejudice is worth it.

Litigants in recent years have been bringing an increasing number of lawsuits directed against laws and practices which exclude, separate and remove the poor and minority groups. When relief has been given, it has often been based on the equal protection clause, sometimes on the due process clause, and, due to its rediscovery by the courts, on the Civil Rights Act of 1871.

 WESTLAW REFERENCES

di property

holmes /s fifth v /2 amendment

fi 104 sct 2862

Planning & Land Use Regulation: Techniques For Discrimination

plan planning /s land /s use /s rac*****

government! /s discriminat! /s motivat! /s statut! law act /s
    race racially minority

zon! /s ordinance /s segregat! /s rac*****

ordinance /s discriminat! /s wealth

di,sy(planned /s unit /s residential /s development)

single /s family /s zon! /s "highest use"

apartment /s buffer /s zone

"aesthetic regulation"

wulfsohn /p single multiple /s family

to(414) /p rezon! /p restrict! /p multiple

low poor poverty /s income /s multiple /s family /s rezon!

burlington /s "mount laurel" /p zon! rezon! /p low /5
    income

> low /5 income /p housing /p rezon! /p profit!
>
> incentive /p zon! /p "low income"
>
> "mount laurel doctrine"
>
> rezon! /p vot! /p referendum /p disapprov! void! null! resci! reject!
>
> di,sy(subdivi! /p plan planning /p land /p use /p regulat! /p lot /p size)
>
> "building code" /p exclu! /p minority race racially ethnic wealth poor poverty "low income"
>
> law statut! /p "equal protection" "due process" /p poor minority /p exclu! segregat! separat! /p hous***

§ 10.2   Land Use Control and Substantive Due Process [1]

Substantive due process grew out of the natural law theories of the seventeenth and eighteenth centuries. All men were thought to be possessed of certain fundamental rights that no government should infringe. Combined with the contract clause [2] of the U.S. Constitution, substantive due process came to be associated by the courts with governmental infringement of property rights.[3]

In the land use context, substantive due process has come to mean that land use regulations must promote the public health, safety, morals, and general welfare. This is the police power concept. If a land use regulation serves these needs (especially the "general welfare"), courts will uphold the regulation as a valid police power exercise.

Substantive due process, being an amorphous concept to begin with, often merges with taking and equal protection jurisprudence.[4] Taking claims are the other side of the scale when courts weigh governmental police power defenses. Equal protection doctrine re-

---

§ 10.2

1. For a more thorough discussion of the substantive due process problem, see J. Nowak, R. Rotunda & J. Young, Constitutional Law 425–96 (2d ed. 1983).

2. U.S. Const. Art. 1, § 10 (no state is allowed to impair "the obligation of contracts").

3. E. Corwin, Liberty Against Government 72 (1948). Professor Corwin called this "the doctrine of vested rights."

4. It has been suggested that the difference between a violation of substantive due process and a taking is the following: for due process, there is a tripartite analysis. First, did the government have any public purpose in doing what it did, i.e., is it the business of government to be acting at all? If not, the action violates due process. Second, if a government can act, did it select a means which is rationally related to the public purpose it sought to achieve? If not,

the action violates due process, even though the government could act if it selected an appropriate means. Third, if government had a public purpose in acting and chose a proper means, is the resultant public benefit commensurate with the private loss caused by its action? If the private loss is greater than the public benefit, then due process is violated even if government had a public purpose and the means chosen were appropriate to achieve that public purpose.

While an action which meets those three tests does not violate due process, if the private loss resulting from the government action, as compared with the value of the property before the action (not as compared with the public benefit) is too great, then the action will constitute a taking. Haley, Balancing Private Loss Against Public Gain to Test for a Violation of Due Process or a Taking Without Just Compensation, 54 Wash.L.Rev. 315 (1979).

quires that governmental land classifications be related to proper public purposes.[5]

While substantive due process used to be a high hurdle for governmental regulations to clear,[6] the doctrine has been in a fairly steady decline since 1937,[7] the year of the court packing controversy. During the first part of this century courts gave little deference to the other branches of government. Starting with Nebbia v. New York [8] and perhaps culminating in the court packing controversy, the court abruptly turned away from substantive due process as a device to frustrate the legislative will. Courts today therefore use substantive due process in a very relaxed manner. Examples of the modern approach are examined below.

Land Use and Substantive Due Process: The Major Cases

Village of Euclid v. Ambler Realty Co.[9] was the Supreme Court's first chance to apply substantive due process to a land use regulatory scheme. The landowner involved claimed that Euclid's zoning ordinance, which prevented him from using his land for industrial purposes, was a taking and a violation of equal protection. The Court disagreed and held the zoning ordinance a legitimate police power regulation due to the public interest in segregating incompatible land uses. The four-fold dimunition in the landowner's property value was simply the unavoidable consequence of the police power function. Regrettable, perhaps, but not actionable. Euclid, quite simply, opened the doors to everything land use control law is today.

With one brief and somewhat uncertain exception,[10] the Supreme Court did not examine the constitutionality of land use controls until 1962 with Goldblatt v. Town of Hempstead.[11] There, a quarry operator sued when the Town of Hempstead amended its land use ordinances in such a way as to shut down plaintiff's operation.[12] Again the Court upheld the ordinance, this time emphasizing the presumption of validity such legislative actions have in our tripartite system of government.[13] Had less restrictive measures been available to the town, the plaintiff might have won his case. None existed and plaintiff's whole business had to be written off as a casualty of the town's legitimate police power regulation.

The Court had another chance to strike down a zoning ordinance on substantive due process grounds in Village of Belle Terre v. Boraas.[14]

---

5. For a discussion of equal protection problems in land use law, see infra § 10.4.

6. See J. Nowak, R. Rotunda & J. Young, supra note 1, at 431–42.

7. Id. at 443–51.

8. 291 U.S. 502, 54 S.Ct. 505, 78 L.Ed. 940 (1934).

9. 272 U.S. 365, 47 S.Ct. 114, 71 L.Ed. 303 (1926). See supra § 3.2.

10. Nectow v. Cambridge, 277 U.S. 183, 48 S.Ct. 447, 72 L.Ed. 842 (1928).

11. 369 U.S. 590, 82 S.Ct. 987, 8 L.Ed.2d 130 (1962).

12. Id. at 592, 82 S.Ct. at 988.

13. Id. at 594, 82 S.Ct. at 990.

14. 416 U.S. 1, 94 S.Ct. 1536, 39 L.Ed.2d 797 (1974).

The ordinance in question allowed only "families" (consisting of not more than two unrelated adults) to live in a single family home. The purpose of the ordinance was to prevent students from living together in a single house. A landowner who rented his house to six unrelated students brought suit on several grounds, among them "that social homogeneity is not a legitimate interest of government."[15] The ordinance was summarily upheld in an opinion by Justice William O. Douglas. Casting aside any substantive due process or equal protection arguments, Douglas stated:

> The regimes of boarding houses, fraternity houses and the like present urban problems. More people occupy a given space; more cars rather continuously pass by; more cars are parked; noise travels with crowds.

> A quiet place where yards are wide, people few, and motor vehicles restricted are legitimate guidelines in a land use project addressed to family needs . . . . The police power is not confined to elimination of filth, stench, and unhealthy places. It is ample to lay out zones where family values, youth values, and the blessings of quiet seclusion, and clean air make the area a sanctuary for people.[16]

Those who thought Belle Terre would signal the finish of the substantive due process review of residential zoning law must have been shocked at its phoenix-like rise in Moore v. East Cleveland, Ohio.[17] Moore is similar to Belle Terre in that both involved a regulation (here, a housing code ordinance) aimed at allowing only "single families" in single homes. The ordinance had a complex definition of family which precluded the plaintiff from living with her son and two grandsons (who were also first cousins). Grappling with the knowledge they were resurrecting substantive due process as a limit on police power regulation, the Moore plurality attempted to distinguish Belle Terre. Calling the ordinance at hand an "intrusive regulation of the family", the plurality stated that the Belle Terre ordinance "affected only unrelated individuals." Well aware of the quagmire they were stepping into, the plurality entered the "treacherous field" of substantive due process to strike down the ordinance only because the special sanctity of the family was at stake. There was simply no legitimate public purpose in "slicing deeply into the family itself" in order to reduce congestion or crime. Thus while Moore shows that substantive due process is not a derelict doctrine, it may be limited to a Moore-type family situation where no legitimate public purpose at all can be found for the regulation.

 WESTLAW REFERENCES

"substantive due process" /s "land use"

"property right" /s valid! invalid! /s zon! /s "police power"

15. Id. at 3, 94 S.Ct. at 1538.

16. Id. at 5, 94 S.Ct. at 1539.

17. 431 U.S. 494, 97 S.Ct. 1932, 52 L.Ed. 2d 531 (1977).

Land Use & Substantive Due Process: The Major Cases

euclid /s ambler /s zon! /s "police power"

goldblatt /s hempstead /p land /p use /p ordinance

"belle terre" /p moore /s cleveland /p family

---

§ 10.3   Land Use Control and Procedural Due Process

Procedural due process is based on the fifth and fourteenth amendment prohibitions against state actions depriving "any person of life, liberty or property without due process of law." If any of those interests is to be denied an individual, a certain "process" must be followed.[1] The refinement of what process is "due" for what degree of deprivation and for what personal interest has been going on for decades.[2]

The enormity of analyzing the doctrinal roots of procedural due process is tempered by its limitations in the land use field. The due process clause's procedural demands are not wholly pertinent to zoning law. Legislative decisions are not limited by procedural due process; only administrative decision making must provide that certain constitutionally required process. This is not always true at the state level, as various "sunshine" laws illustrate.[3] These laws were designed to prevent the abuse sometimes present where legislative zoning decisions were made, where ex parte contacts and alleged "deal making" behind closed doors often occur.[4]

Traditionally, such abuses are outside the scope of procedural due process. Thus there are generally no procedural requirements on legislative action regarding the zoning map. There is some indication that the traditional approach may be weakening, but it is an unclear trend at best.

In all, procedural due process in the land use context is a creature of state law. More often than not, the procedure required relates to publication of notice and right of appeal. As would be expected, those requirements are part and parcel of normal administrative procedure.

---

§ 10.3

1. For a more thorough discussion of the procedural due process problem, see J. Nowak, R. Rotunda & J. Young, Constitutional Law 526–79 (2d ed. 1983).

2. See generally Van Alstyne, Cracks In "The New Property": Adjudicative Due Process in the Administrative State, 62 Cornell L.Rev. 445 (1977). See also Perry v. Sinderman, 408 U.S. 593, 92 S.Ct. 2694, 33 L.Ed.2d 570 (1972); Board of Regents v. Roth, 408 U.S. 564, 92 S.Ct. 2701, 33 L.Ed. 2d 548 (1972).

3. See, e.g., West's Fla.Stat.Ann. § 286.011, which prohibits the "meeting" of any "board on commission of any state agency" at which "official acts are to be taken" behind closed doors of any sort. Such meetings are "declared to be public meetings open to the public at all times."

4. As examples of state effects to cure those abuses, see Fasano v. Board of County Comm'rs, 264 Or. 574, 507 P.2d 23 (1973); Roseta v. County of Washington, 254 Or. 161, 458 P.2d 405 (1969).

The evolution of procedural due process into the legislative field has simply not yet occurred on a wide scale basis.[5]

 WESTLAW REFERENCES

"sunshine law" /p zon!

"procedural due process" /p land /p use /p public*****

/p notice /p appeal

§ 10.4   Land Use Control and Equal Protection

That persons similarly situated be treated equally under the law is a primary commandment of the fourteenth amendment.[1] The equal protection clause has become of late the most important constitutional provision for the protection of basic liberties.[2] Equal protection is a concern of land use planners because land use ordinances categorize various land uses.

A landowner may attack a land use ordinance on its face for equal protection violations. Such would be the case were a landowner to object to a zoning regulation's classification of his land. Landowners may also bring equal protection actions based not on any use classification, but on the application of the zoning regulation to his land. This "as applied" attack usually occurs when a landowner's property is zoned for some use seen less profitable than another. Equal protection attacks are also common on racial, poverty, and age grounds. As will be seen, the chance of success for an equal protection attack depends on who the plaintiff is as well as to what the plaintiff objects.

If the plaintiff is a wealthy white developer who objects to a downzoning of his property from multifamily residential to agricultural, courts will use the "rational relationship" standard. Under this, the most relaxed standard of judicial review, courts uphold the land use scheme if there is any rational basis for its existence. The rational relationship test is by far the most common standard applied to land use cases and is the hardest standard under which to strike an ordinance or classification.[3]

If a zoning ordinance were to categorize permissible uses on the basis of race (which does not occur anymore, at least overtly), the court would apply the "strict scrutiny" standard which requires a compelling governmental interest for justification. Strict scrutiny is triggered whenever a "suspect class" (race, national origin, and, to a lesser extent, alienage) or a fundamental interest (privacy, right to travel,

5. See e.g. Couf v. DeBlaker, 652 F.2d 585 (5th Cir.1981), cert. denied 455 U.S. 921, 102 S.Ct. 1278, 71 L.Ed.2d 462 (1982).

§ 10.4

1. For a thorough discussion of the constitutional doctrine of Equal Protection, see J. Nowak, R. Rotunda & J. Young, Constitutional Law 585–829 (1983).

2. Id. at 585.

3. See, e.g., South Gwinnett Venture v. Pruitt, 491 F.2d 5 (5th Cir.1974), cert. denied 419 U.S. 837, 95 S.Ct. 66, 42 L.Ed.2d 64 (1974).

right to vote, or any explicit constitutional guarantee) is burdened by governmental action. Once strict scrutiny is applied courts almost always strike down the law or regulation in question.[4]

In the last decade or so the Supreme Court has occasionally used a middle ground equal protection standard,[5] rather than the compelling state interest or the rational basis test. The Court looks for a purpose "substantially related" to an "important governmental interest." [6] This "medium" standard appears most often in gender-based classification suits.

A prime example of an equal protection attack on a land use scheme case appears in Village of Belle Terre v. Boraas.[7] Albeit unsuccessful, the plaintiff's attempt to prove that the exclusion of unrelated families of more than two persons violated due process found a sympathetic ear with Justice Marshall.

Marshall's dissent stressed that because the zoning classification violated "fundamental rights of association and privacy," the "application of strict equal protection scrutiny is required." However, the rest of the court did not find that the ordinance infringed on those first and fourteenth amendment rights, and since the right to housing is not a fundamental right,[8] all the court looked for was mere rationality. The decision was, as are all "rational relationship" standard cases, a deferral to the legislative branch.

Zoning and Discrimination

Because traditional zoning laws have been immune from equal protection challenges since Euclid, the modern focus has been on discriminatory zoning practices.[9] Justice Marshall's dissent in Belle Terre focused on the discriminatory nature of the zoning law in question. If the ordinance were designed to protect neighborhood quiet,

---

4. See, e.g., United States v. Carolene Prod. Co., 304 U.S. 144, 58 S.Ct. 778, 82 L.Ed. 1234 (1938).

5. See J. Nowak, R. Rotunda & J. Young, supra note 1, at 592–93.

6. See, e.g., Craig v. Boren, 429 U.S. 190, 197, 97 S.Ct. 451, 457, 50 L.Ed.2d 397 (1976), rehearing denied 429 U.S. 1124, 97 S.Ct. 1161, 51 L.Ed.2d 574 (1977).

7. 416 U.S. 1, 94 S.Ct. 1536, 39 L.Ed.2d 797 (1974). See supra § 10.2.

8. Lindsey v. Norwet, 405 U.S. 56, 92 S.Ct. 862, 31 L.Ed.2d 36 (1972).

9. See generally M. Danielson, The Politics of Exclusion (1976); D. Moskowitz, Exclusionary Zoning Litigation (1977); Doyle, Retirement Communities: The Nature and Enforceability of Residential Segregation by Age, 76 Mich.L.Rev. 64 (1977); Mandelker, Racial Discrimination and Exclusionary Zoning: A Perspective on Ar-

lington Heights, 55 Tex.L.Rev. 1217 (1977); Mayo, Exclusionary Zoning, Remedies, and the Expansive Role of the Court in Public Law Litigation, 31 Syracuse L.Rev. 755 (1980); Rose, Myths and Misconceptions of Exclusionary Zoning Litigation, 8 Real Est. L.J. 97 (1979); Sager, Insular Majorities Unabated: Warth v. Seldin and City of Eastlake v. Forest City Enterprises, Inc., 91 Harv.L.Rev. 1373 (1978); Sager, Tight Little Islands: Exclusionary Zoning, Equal Protection, and the Indigent, 21 Stan.L. Rev. 767, 785 (1969); Sager, Questions I Wish I Had Never Asked: The Burger Court in Exclusionary Zoning, 11 S.W.U.L. Rev. 509 (1979); Travalio, Suffer the Little Children—But Not in My Neighborhood: A Constitutional View of Age-Restrictive Housing, 40 Ohio St.L.J. 295 (1979); Note, Zoning for the Elderly and Family Rights, 23 Cath.Law. 118 (1978).

he reasoned, it should be focused on the source of the disquietude, such as automobiles, rather than the number of people to a house.

While unsuccessful in Belle Terre, Justice Marshall raised a sensitive issue in modern zoning cases. Discrimination against minorities and the poor pervades in our bedroom suburban society. The techniques of discrimination include zoning for single family residential homes only (thus excluding multifamily apartments) or requiring lot sizes so large as to exclude all but the upper economic strata. Of course, a zoning ordinance which discriminates by race will be overturned; not since the Jim Crow days have communities explicitly zoned against racial minorities. Strict scrutiny would quickly dispose of such an ordinance. The same is not true, however, with ordinances which restrict on the basis of wealth.[10] Therein lies the problem.

Racial exclusion is usually practiced through poor people exclusion. Because racial minorities are disproportionately represented among lower income groups, communities can practice racial exclusion without fear of strict scrutiny review (at least on the federal level)[11] simply by zoning out housing projects which cater to those of modest means.

The ability to attack zoning ordinances restricting multifamily developments as racially exclusive was dealt a major blow by the Supreme Court in Village of Arlington Heights v. Metropolitan Housing Dev. Corp.[12] There, a developer wished to build a federally subsidized public housing project on land zoned for single family use. Arlington Heights refused to rezone the land, invoking its buffer policy which allowed single to multifamily rezoning only when a buffer zone was established between the two uses. The developer brought an equal protection attack.

The Court upheld Arlington Height's refusal to rezone, holding that the equal protection clause requires proof of discriminatory intent rather than effect in the zoning context. Intent is much harder to prove than effect. Even though the failure of Arlington Heights to rezone would clearly have a disproportionate impact on racial minorities, the Court held that this could only be used as evidence of intent, and intent to discriminate on the basis of race had to be a "motivating factor." Discriminatory intent could be proved by showing a "clear

---

10. See James v. Valtierra, 402 U.S. 137, 91 S.Ct. 1331, 28 L.Ed.2d 678 (1971). There the Court upheld a California constitutional provision requiring local referenda on low income public housing projects. The Court dismissed plaintiff's challenge to the provision, calling the poor one "of the diverse and shifting groups that make up the American people."

11. The state approach to discriminatory zoning is best seen in the two Mt. Laurel decisions. Southern Burlington County NAACP v. Township of Mt. Laurel (Mt. Laurel I), 67 N.J. 151, 336 A.2d 713, appeal dismissed and cert. denied 423 U.S. 808, 96 S.Ct. 18, 46 L.Ed.2d 28 (1975); Southern Burlington County NAACP v. Township of Mt. Laurel (Mt. Laurel II), 92 N.J. 158, 456 A.2d 390 (1983), on remand ___ N.J.Super. ___, ___ A.2d ___ (1984). These cases are discussed supra § 5.8.

12. 429 U.S. 252, 97 S.Ct. 555, 50 L.Ed. 2d 450 (1977), on remand 558 F.2d 1283 (7th Cir.1977), cert. denied 434 U.S. 1025, 98 S.Ct. 752, 54 L.Ed.2d 772 (1978), on remand 469 F.Supp. 836 (D.Ill.1979), affirmed 616 F.2d 1006 (7th Cir.1980).

pattern" of discriminatory effect even if the ordinance is neutral on its face. The usefulness of that approach must be questioned, however, since the Court seemingly ignored the "clear pattern" of Arlington Height's lily-white complexion.

A second way to prove discriminatory intent under Arlington Heights is to show "substantive departures" from established zoning policy.[13] Because Arlington Heights applied its buffer policy in a substantially uniform manner, plaintiffs could not challenge the failure to rezone on that ground. Further, the buffer policy was found to be a "zoning factor" commonly used by the village in reaching a decision in rezoning cases.[14]

Standing

As unfortunate as it is, the amorphous miasma of federal standing law must be discussed in regard to equal protection and land use law. No body of federal law is more confusing and contradictory. To make sense out of the various Supreme Court cases on the topic is beyond the range of human ingenuity. Yet it must be considered because it is a further limit on the availability of equal protection attacks on land use ordinances.[15] Two of the most important standing decisions to land use planning and control are Warth v. Seldin [16] and Arlington Heights.

In Warth the plaintiffs consisted of various Rochester, New York, residents challenging the adjacent suburban town of Penfield's zoning ordinance. Plaintiffs claimed the ordinance unconstitutionally excluded persons of low and moderate income from living in Penfield because of lot size, setback and floor area requirements.

Because none of the plaintiffs could show how they were personally injured by the ordinances in question, standing was denied. The Court needed to see a personal "injury in fact" causally linked to defendant's actions and proof that judicial relief would redress that injury. Instead, the Court found that no plaintiff had an interest in any Penfield property, none came under Penfield's zoning ordinance, none had asked for or had been denied a zoning variance, and there was no evidence that the proposed actions by third persons to build low income housing in Penfield would meet the plaintiff's needs.

The Court declared that the plaintiffs had not stated their case with sufficient specificity to show that judicial relief would alleviate their situation in any way. There must be "specific, concrete facts" proving harm to plaintiffs and plaintiffs would have to benefit from the Court's intervention. Thus all the plaintiffs, the nonprofit organization

---

13. The Court cited Kennedy Park Homes Ass'n v. Lackawanna, 436 F.2d 108 (2d Cir.1970), cert. denied 401 U.S. 1010, 91 S.Ct. 1256, 28 L.Ed.2d 546 (1971).

14. 429 U.S. at 270, 97 S.Ct. at 566.

15. For a recent and insightful analysis of the Supreme Court's evolving standing

doctrine, see Nichol, Rethinking Standing, 74 Calif.L.Rev. 68 (1984).

16. 422 U.S. 490, 95 S.Ct. 2197, 45 L.Ed. 2d 343 (1975).

dedicated to greater housing opportunities, the home builder's organization, and the low income racial minorities were denied access to the courtroom door.

The Arlington Heights standing problem came also in a rezoning context. There, another federally subsidized housing project developer challenged the denial of a necessary rezoning. The developer was granted standing on the basis of his preliminary expenditures on the project and his "interest in making suitable lowcost housing available in areas where such housing is scarce."

One additional plaintiff was given standing in Arlington Heights. A black employee of a nearby plant alleged that he was unable to find affordable housing near his place of work. Because his claim was based on a particular project and not speculation as to possible future projects (as in Warth), the black plaintiff proved an "injury in fact." This was so even though he might not be able to obtain housing in that particular project.

Inclusionary Planning and Zoning

The difficulty, just discussed, which the poor have encountered in federal and many state courts when they have sought relief from discriminatory exclusionary zoning has led several states to seek to alleviate the problem through inclusionary planning and zoning programs. The "inclusionary" planning technique consists of requiring planning authorities to plan for low and moderate income housing and/or housing for specific disadvantaged groups. Inclusionary zoning consists of requiring residential developments of specified size, type or location to include low and moderate income housing.[17]

Generally speaking,

> [a]n inclusionary program is a "process intended to set aside a portion of the total number of units in a development at below-market prices in order to expand housing available to low- and moderate-income persons." While it has been applied in other contexts, inclusionary provisions typically have the objective of expanding *housing* opportunity. They usually have a *triggering* specification (e.g., development of a particular size, type, or location). The inclusionary mandate may be either *mandatory* or *optional* on the developer; in the former case, the builder must comply, in the latter he is encouraged to do so. In either case, the *inclusionary requirement* is usually stated as a share of the total new housing production, usually 10 to 25 percent. To allow or encourage the developer to comply, many inclusionary programs offer a density bonus or other *inducements* (e.g., reducing subdivi-

17. "An inclusionary program is a process intended to set aside a portion of the total number of units in a development at below-market prices in order to expand housing available to low- and moderate-income persons." State of Connecticut, De- partment of Housing, Housing and Land Use: Community Options for Lowering Housing Costs 9, quoted in Burchell, Beaton & Listokin, Mount Laurel II: Challenge and Delivery of Housing 350 (1983).

sion/parking/set-back requirements, or offering lower-cost financing). To ensure that units produced under an inclusionary program remain a low/moderate-income housing resource, as opposed to providing a windfall profit to the initial occupant, most inclusionary strategies retain some type of *affordability control*. These commonly consist of a deed restriction capping subsequent resale or rental prices and/or monitoring of future occupancy by a local housing authority or other entity.[18]

Inclusionary planning concepts can be illustrated by Florida and California planning legislation. In California, local governments are required to plan so as to provide for their fair share of regional housing needs.[19] Florida's Local Government Comprehensive Planning and Land Development Regulation Act requires local government comprehensive plans to contain a housing element consisting of standards, plans, and principles to be followed in:

    1. The provision of housing for existing residents and the anticipated population growth of the area.

    2. The elimination of substandard dwelling conditions.

    3. The structural and aesthetic improvements of existing housing.

    4. The provision of adequate sites for future housing, including housing for low-income and moderate-income families, mobile homes, and group home facilities and foster care facilities, with supporting infrastructure and public facilities.

    5. Provision for relocation housing and identification of historically significant and other housing for purposes of conservation, rehabilitation, or replacement.

    6. The formulation of housing implementation programs.[20]

Florida's consistency requirement is designed to guarantee implementation of these inclusionary goals.[21]

Inclusionary zoning or the so-called "mandatory inclusionary land use ordinance" is best illustrated by the famous Mount Laurel litigation. As discussed elsewhere,[22] Mount Laurel I[23] formulated the concept of requiring local governments to meet their fair share of regional needs. Mount Laurel II[24] approved the concept of requiring municipalities to take affirmative inclusionary action such as mandatory provision of low income housing in residential developments as well as

18. Id. at 350.

19. West's Ann.Cal.Gov. Code § 65302, 65915, 65008. See Ellickson, The Irony of Inclusionary Zoning, 54 So.Calif.L.Rev. 1172 (1981).

20. West Fla.Stat.Ann. § 163.3177(6)(f).

21. Id. § 163.3194(1)(a).

22. See supra § 5.8.

23. Southern Burlington County NAACP v. Township of Mount Laurel, 67 N.J. 151, 336 A.2d 713 (1975), appeal dismissed and cert. denied 423 U.S. 808, 96 S.Ct. 18, 46 L.Ed.2d 28 (1975).

24. Southern Burlington County NAACP v. Township of Mount Laurel, 92 N.J. 158, 456 A.2d 390 (1983), on remand 207 N.J.Super. 169, 504 A.2d 66 (1984).

measures designed to facilitate the use of tax breaks and subsidies for low income housing. The court observed:

> There are several inclusionary zoning techniques that municipalities must use if they cannot otherwise assure the construction of their fair share of lower income housing. Although we will discuss some of them here, we in no way intend our list to be exhaustive; municipalities and trial courts are encouraged to create other devices and methods for meeting fair share obligations.

> The most commonly used inclusionary zoning techniques are incentive zoning and mandatory set-asides. The former involves offering economic incentives to a developer through the relaxation of various restrictions of an ordinance (typically density limits) in exchange for the construction of certain amounts of low and moderate income units. The latter, a mandatory set-aside, is basically a requirement that developers include a minimum amount of lower income housing in their projects.[25]

In spite of the enthusiasm of the Mount Laurel court and many commentators for inclusionary zoning, constitutional concepts such as the taking issue have been used to invalidate inclusionary requirements.[26]

 WESTLAW REFERENCES

    di,sy(apply applied /s zon! /s ordinance /s invalid! /s land
        /s use /s classif!)

    downzon! /p land /s use

    zon! /p permit! permissible /p use /p "strict scrutiny"
        substantial! +2 relat! /s "important governmental interest"
        /s sex gender

    "belle terre" /s "equal protection"

Zoning and Discrimination

    di,sy(discriminat! /s zon! /s practic!

    to(414) /p ordinance regulat! /s wealth income

    "arlington heights" /s single multi /s family

    "equal protection" /s discriminat! /s inten! /s zon!

    "substantive departure" /p zon!

Standing

    warth /s seldin /s zon! /s standing

    standing /s rezon!

    ordinance /p "injury in fact"

§ 10.5 Land Use Control and Free Speech

The first amendment's free speech clause typically becomes implicated in land use planning whenever billboards or sex-oriented business

25. 456 A.2d at 445.

26. See Board of Supervisors v. DeGroff Enterprises, Inc., 214 Va. 235, 198 S.E.2d 600 (1973).

("adult theatres," "strip joints") are regulated.[1] Billboard controls may be of two types for free speech purposes. Those regulating political advertisements come under the more traditional, noncommercial speech protection of the first amendment. Those regulating commercial advertisements relate to commercial speech (as do sex-business regulations). Commercial speech has been given less first amendment protection than non-commercial speech, but that distinction is narrowing.[2]

A free speech challenge to a zoning ordinance presents a special problem. Unlike most police power exercises which come clothed with a presumption of constitutionality before a court, a billboard control under a free speech challenge does not, and the presumption is reversed. Local governments then bear the burden of proving the constitutionality of the ordinance in question. Even so, zoning ordinances will be upheld if the free speech infringement is found to be merely a reasonable restriction on the time, place, and manner of the communication, and reasonable alternatives for the communication are available.

Billboard and Sign Control [3]

What would happen if a community enacted a zoning ordinance prohibiting posting "for sale" signs in the neighborhood? Suppose the reason for this ordinance was the laudatory purpose of facilitating racial integration by controlling panic selling. Would such an ordinance violate the first amendment? When faced with this problem in Linmark Assoc., Inc. v. Township of Willingboro,[4] the Supreme Court wasted no time in striking down the control as a free speech violation. The ordinance was not a mere restriction of time, place, and manner because reasonable alternatives for landowners wishing to sell were not available. Even though an example of commercial speech, the "for sale" messages were found to be vital community information.[5]

The controversy surrounding free speech challenges to billboard and sign control is seen nowhere better than in Metromedia, Inc. v. San Diego.[6] Metromedia produced five separate decisions. Because it dealt with a traditional billboard and sign control ordinance, Metromedia is to date the most important Supreme Court case on the constitutional

§ 10.5

1. For a thorough discussion of the constitutional guarantee of freedom of speech, see J. Nowak, R. Rotunda & J. Young, Constitutional Law 857–1022 (1983).

2. Id. at 923.

3. See generally Lacking, The Regulation of Outdoor Advertising: Past, Present and Future, 6 Envtl.Aff. 179 (1977); Mandelker & Reiman, The Billboard Ban: Aesthetics Comes of Age, 31 Land Use L. & Zoning Dig. 4 (1979).

4. 431 U.S. 85, 97 S.Ct. 1614, 52 L.Ed.2d 155 (1977).

5. See also Daugherty v. East Point, 447 F.Supp. 290 (N.D.Ga.1978). Where panic selling is proved, courts may uphold the ordinance. See, e.g., Barrick Realty, Inc. v. Gary, 491 F.2d 161 (7th Cir.1974).

6. 453 U.S. 490, 101 S.Ct. 2882, 69 L.Ed. 2d 800 (1981), on remand 32 Cal.3d 180, 185 Cal.Rptr. 260, 649 P.2d 902 (1982).

issues facing local governments as they wrestle with the problem of outdoor advertising.

The ordinance in Metromedia prohibited offsite billboards (billboards away from the place of business) throughout San Diego. Twelve exemptions were provided for: "government signs; signs located at public bus stops; signs manufactured, transported or stored within the city, if not used for advertising purposes; commemorative historical plaques; religious symbols; signs within shopping malls; for sale and for lease signs; signs on public and commercial vehicles; signs depicting time, temperature, and news; approved temporary, off-premises, subdivision directional signs; and 'temporary political campaign signs.' " [7]

Justice White's plurality opinion upheld the commercial speech portion of the zoning ordinance. The four-part commercial speech restriction test found in Central Hudson Gas & Electric Corp. v. Public Service Comm'n [8] was applied. To be valid, a restriction on commercial speech must (1) concern a lawful activity and not be misleading; (2) the asserted governmental interest must be substantial; if (1) and (2) are yes, (3) the regulation must directly advance the governmental interest asserted; and (4) the regulation cannot be "more extensive than is necessary to serve that interest." The plurality found all four parts satisfied.[9] In particular, the two goals furthered by the ordinance, traffic safety and aesthetic interests, were considered substantial.

The noncommercial speech aspects of San Diego's zoning law received greater scrutiny and did not fare as well. The ordinance allowed only on-site *commercial* advertising. Because it failed to provide also for on-site *noncommercial* advertising (which would be no more distracting or unattractive than commercial billboards), that portion of the law was found facially unconstitutional. This was considered impermissible content-based regulation and not a reasonable time, place, or manner restriction.

Justices Brennan and Blackmun concurred in the result but believed the ordinance actually to be a complete prohibition on all signs. They found the entire ordinance unconstitutional because neither traffic control nor aesthetic regulation was sufficiently enhanced by the San Diego law for the free speech infringement to be acceptable.[10] Nor were the alternatives to billboard advertising adequate.

The three dissenters, Justices Stevens and Rehnquist and Chief Justice Burger, would have upheld the ordinance in whole. Rehnquist

---

7. Id. at 495, 101 S.Ct. 2882 at 2886.

8. 447 U.S. 557, 100 S.Ct. 2343, 65 L.Ed. 2d 341 (1980).

9. 453 U.S. at 507, 101 S.Ct. at 2892.

10. Justice Brennan declared that San Diego had given no evidence to support the traffic safety argument and that the "commercial and industrial areas of San Diego" were not capable of being aesthetically improved through the removal of a few billboards.

thought the aesthetic purposes of the ordinance alone to be sufficient. Stevens would have upheld a law banning all billboards as well as the instant ordinance. Chief Justice Burger believed the plurality botched the issue of noncommercial signs and thought adequate alternatives were available. He considered the exemptions to be neutral and not content-related.

The final result of Metromedia is difficult to predict. Whether a total prohibition on billboards would be upheld depends on whether the dissenting or plurality view is accepted by a later Court. The dissenters would probably allow a total prohibition while the plurality would probably not. An ordinance only restricting commercial billboard use, on the other hand, would likely be upheld by a majority of the court.[11]

Regulating the Sex-Business: Erogenous Zoning [12]

Local governments who practice "erogenous zoning" face the same commercial speech concerns as do those who seek to regulate commercial billboards and signs. Such measures do not present exactly the same problem because the Court has stated that content may be considered in zoning sex businesses,[13] but the first amendment's protection of commercial speech is implicated all the same.

Erogenous zoning is usually done through either the "scattering" or "concentrating" method. The scattering method seeks to space the offending-but-protected institutions sufficiently far apart to alleviate the problems of crime, prostitution, and lowered property values that accompany them. The concentration method lumps all such businesses in one particular area, often called a "combat zone."

Because both schemes regulate speech content, the Court has applied a more rigorous type of scrutiny in sex business cases than in content neutral regulations. The scattering or deconcentration method came under this heightened brand of scrutiny in Young v. American Mini Theatres.[14] The ordinance in question there prohibited the location of adult movie theatres within 1,000 feet of each other or 10 different types of establishments.

The Young ordinance was upheld in a plurality opinion by Justice Stevens. The Court found the ordinance to be a valid exercise of the city's zoning power and not an impermissible prior restraint on free speech. The zoning law had the permissible purpose of maintaining neighborhood character and was not so stringent as to foreclose all

---

11. J. Nowak, R. Rotunda & J. Young, supra note 1, at 988.

12. See generally F. Strom, Zoning Control of Sex Businesses: The Zoning Approach to Controlling Adult Entertainment (1978); W. Toner, Regulating Sex Businesses (American Planning Ass'n, Planning Advisory Serv., Rep. No. 327, 1977); Note, Using Constitutional Zoning to Neutralize Adult Entertainment—Detroit to New York, 5 Fordham Urb.L.J. 455 (1977); Annot., 4 A.L.R.Fed. 1297 (1980).

13. Young v. American Mini Theatres, Inc., 427 U.S. 50, 70–72, 96 S.Ct. 2440, 2452–53, 49 L.Ed.2d 310 (1976), rehearing denied 429 U.S. 873, 97 S.Ct. 191, 50 L.Ed. 2d 155 (1976).

14. Id.

reasonable opportunities to that type of expression. Further, the regulation was unrelated to the suppression of ideas. In language that reflects the Court's ambiguous feelings towards erogenous zoning, Stevens declared that

> [e]ven though we recognize that the First Amendment will not tolerate the total suppression of erotic materials . . . few of us would march our sons and daughters off to war to preserve the citizen's right to see "specified sexual activities" exhibited in the theaters of our choice. Even though the First Amendment protects communication in this area from total suppression, we hold that the state may legitimately use the content of these materials as the basis for placing them in a different classification from other motion pictures.[15]

The broadest form of the scattering method of erogenous zoning is total exclusion. That type of exclusion was struck down by the Court in Schad v. Borough of Mount Ephraim.[16] The ordinance in Schad prohibited any form of "live entertainment." This included, but was not limited to, nude dancing.

After declaring that nude dancing was entitled to some degree of first amendment protection, the Court found Mount Ephraim's ordinance to be an impermissibly overbroad exclusion of entertainment of all sorts. American Mini Theatres was easily distinguished as involving only a minimal and justifiable dispersion of sex business—Schad concerned a total exclusion of any type of live entertainment.

Mount Ephraim's half-hearted justifications of parking, trash pickup and police protection problems were summarily rejected by the Court. No evidence had been presented supporting these justifications. The mere allegation that live entertainment was available outside Mount Ephraim's city limits was not sufficient to justify the zoning restriction.[17]

Schad did not address the other side of the erogenous zoning coin-"combat zone" concentration. Concentrating sex businesses will be allowed only if reasonable business opportunities for those in the erotic line of work remain. Many courts have invalidated concentration ordinances as being too restrictive, i.e., leading toward total elimination or segregation of sex businesses to the most undesirable parts of the city.[18] In general, and on the topic of erogenous zoning one can only speak in generalities, sex business concentration will be upheld only if

15. 427 U.S. at 70, 96 S.Ct. at 2452.

16. 452 U.S. 61, 101 S.Ct. 2176, 68 L.Ed. 2d 671 (1981). See supra § 5.8.

17. However, the Court did consider that this justification could work if sufficient evidence were presented along with it.

18. City of Renton v. Playtime Theatres, Inc., __ U.S. __, 106 S.Ct. 925, 89 L.Ed.2d 29 (1986). (The U.S. Supreme Court held that a city's interest in attempting to preserve the quality of urban life must be accorded high respect. Cities may regulate adult theaters by dispersing them or by effectively concentrating them. The Renton ordinance allowed for reasonable alternative avenues of communication.)

it allows for reasonable business opportunities. Municipalities can go a long way in zoning erogenously, but they must resist the temptation found in the "joy of zoning" and go too far.

 WESTLAW REFERENCES

billboard /s "first amendment"

414k81

di("commercial speech" /s protect!)

zoning /p "free speech" "first amendment" /p presum! /p
    lawful constitutional!

zoning /p free*** +2 speech /p reasonabl! /p time place
    manner

Billboard and Sign Control

"panic selling"

metromedia /s "san diego" /s billboard outdoor

central /s hudson /s gas /s public /s restrict!

non-commercial /s content

restrict! /p commerc! /p billboard /p use

Regulating the Sex Business: Erogenous Zoning

young /s american /s mini /s theatres /p content

"combat zone" /p adult bookstore theat**

scatter! concentrat! deconcentrat! dispers! /s young

§ 10.6   The Federal Civil Rights Act § 1983

Section 1983 of the Civil Rights Act of 1871[1] states:

Every person who, under color of any statute, ordinance, regulation, custom, or usage, of any state or territory, subjects or causes to be subjected, any citizen of the United States or other person within the jurisdiction thereof to the deprivation of any rights, privileges, or immunities secured by the Constitution and laws, shall be liable to the party injured in an action at law, suit in equity, or other proper proceeding for redress.[2]

Enacted as implementing legislation for the fourteenth amendment under section five, § 1983 was designed to protect the civil rights of the newly freed slaves. Far from retaining its original purpose of preventing the resubjugation of blacks, § 1983 has practically become a federal tort law.

Developers first became interested in § 1983 when the Supreme Court in 1972 extended its protective boundaries from basic constitu-

---

§ 10.6

1. For a general discussion of the Civil Rights Acts, see J. Nowak, R. Rotunda & J. Young, Constitutional Law pp. 32–54 (1983). See also C. Abernathy, Civil Rights: Cases and Materials (1980); T. Fisenberg, Civil Rights Legislation: Cases and Materials (1981); Rockwell, Constitutional Violations in Zoning: The Emerging Section 1983 Damage Remedy, 33 U.Fla.L. Rev. 168 (1981); Schnopper, Civil Rights Litigation After Monell, 79 Colum.L.Rev. 213 (1979). Section 1983 is discussed in greater detail in Hagman & Juergensmeyer, Urban Planning and Land Development Control Law, 2d ed., Practitioner's Ed., ch. 24 (1986).

2. 42 U.S.C.A. § 1983 (1976).

tional rights to include property interests.[3] In the abstract, the Court's reading seems correct in light of the fourteenth amendment's protection of "life, liberty, [and] property."[4] In practice, however, expansion of § 1983's coverage from its traditional role in protecting civil rights to protecting property rights has been accompanied by much of the same confusion that has beset the search for a bright line between a valid land use regulation and an invalid "taking."[5]

These difficulties, combined with the ingenuity of property owners who are now able to see a violation of § 1983 in almost every local government land use decision, have recently led some federal courts to complain that the lofty purposes of the statute are being trivialized[6] and to begin to formulate a variety of theories on which to dismiss § 1983 complaints based on run-of-the-mill local land use disputes.[7] However, at least for now, § 1983 remains a statute with which those involved in the land use process must be fully familiar.

§ 1983 Cause of Action

There are two "essential elements" of a § 1983 cause of action: The complained of conduct (1) must have resulted in (a) the deprivation of (b) a right, privilege or immunity secured by the constitution or laws of the United States and (2) must have been committed by a person acting "under color of state law".[8] Both intentional and negligent deprivations may be actionable, but it appears that no single standard of care will apply in all § 1983 cases; rather, the standard of care demanded will depend on the specific constitutional right under consideration.[9]

§ 1983 Immunities

While § 1983 jurisprudence dates back over a century, the history of its application in the land use context dates from only 1978. Prior to that time, local governments were not subject to § 1983 actions because Monroe v. Pape[10] had held local governments were not "persons" under § 1983 and were, therefore, absolutely immune from suit under the statute.

However, in 1978 Monroe was overruled by Monell v. New York City Dept. of Social Services.[11] Monell cheered developers eager to assault perceived deprivations of their property interests by land use ordinances, but the question of immunities still waited to be resolved. Monell said only that local governments were "persons" subject to the

---

3. Lynch v. Household Fin. Corp., 405 U.S. 538 (1972).

4. See Hagman & Juergensmeyer, Urban Planning and Land Development Control Law, 2d ed., Practitioner's Ed., ch. 24 (1986).

5. The existence *vel non* of a property right for § 1983 purposes is to be decided under state, not federal, law. Id. at §§ 24.7–.10.

6. See id.

7. See for example Baldwin v. Appalachian Power Co., 556 F.2d 241 (4th Cir. 1977).

8. Parratt v. Taylor, 451 U.S. 527, 535 (1981).

9. Id.

10. 365 U.S. 167 (1961).

11. 436 U.S. 658 (1978).

statute. It did not decide whether they might nevertheless be immune from money damages for their violations of the statute.

Immunities are a consideration under § 1983 even though the statute nowhere provides for them. The Supreme Court got around that statutory void by finding that an immunity from damages under § 1983 will be implied if such an immunity existed at common law at the time § 1983 was adopted and if implying such an immunity would be consistent with the purposes of § 1983. The court reasoned that a tradition of some immunity was so deeply rooted in our law that "congress would have specifically so provided had it wished to abolish the doctrine." [12]

That was the picture in 1980 when the Supreme Court considered Owens v. City of Independence, Mo.[13] Justice Brennen's opinion reviewed the broad range of absolute and qualified immunities available under § 1983. Judges, state and regional legislators,[14] prosecutors (when initiating and presenting the state's case) all have absolute immunity. The majority of lower federal courts also accord local legislators with an absolute immunity for their legislative acts.[15] Qualified (good faith) immunity is given executive officials, local school board members, prison officials and officers, and local police officers. This qualified immunity can be defeated only by showing malice, ill will or wanton conduct on the part of the officer or official charged.

The question of immunity for municipalities themselves is less clear. The defendant municipalities in *Owens* asserted that they were entitled to qualified (good-faith) immunity from § 1983 damages. Brennen reviewed the historical foundation for the qualified immunity and held that because no such immunity existed at common law at the time § 1983 was enacted, no qualified immunity could be implied. Some have read this holding as a broad conclusion that absolutely no municipal immunity from § 1983 exists. This may, however, read too much into Brennen's opinion. In fact, the *Owens* court acknowledged that a tradition of absolute immunity for municipal governmental and legislative acts (as opposed to qualified immunity for executive acts) was well established at common law at the time § 1983 was enacted. As the Court observed:

> To be sure, there were two doctrines that afforded municipal corporations some measure of protection from tort liability. The first sought to distinguish between a municipality's "governmental" and "proprietary" functions; as to the former, the city was held immune. Whereas in its exercise of the latter, the city was held to the same standards of liability as any private corporation. The second doctrine immunized a municipality for its "discretiona-

---

12. Id.

13. 445 U.S. 622 (1980).

14. Id.

15. Id.

ry" or "legislative" activities, but not for those which were "minis-terial" in nature.[16]

Thus, it appears that the Court is prepared to recognize immunity for legislative acts of municipalities—and that should include many of their land use decisions.[17] Indeed, any other result would appear to be inconsistent with the court's traditional deference to local legislative bodies in matters involving land use decisions.[18]

Nevertheless, the Monell-Owen couplet primed developers for an expected § 1983 field day. However, that field day never really dawn-ed. Almost as soon as those cases were decided, both the Supreme Court and lower federal courts began to back away from the spectre of having to deal with a flood of local zoning disputes as federal civil rights cases. This federal retreat has been accomplished by contracting the § 1983 cause of action, by expanding the § 1983 immunities, and by declining to exercise federal jurisdiction over § 1983 land use cases.

Limitations on § 1983 Land Use Cases

The first essential element of the § 1983 cause of action includes the requirement that there be a "deprivation" of a constitutionally protected right. In two closely related, but distinct, lines of cases, the Supreme Court and other federal courts have made it exceedingly difficult for developers to prove the required deprivation. Both of these lines of authority look to the issue of whether the alleged action has become sufficiently complete and final to constitute a deprivation. They stand generally for the proposition that the § 1983 remedy is inappropriable unless and until the challenged action has ripened into a final deprivation.

In Parratt v. Taylor [19] and in Hudson v. Palmer,[20] the Supreme Court articulated the principle that due process guarantees under the United States Constitution are not infringed where post-deprivation remedies under state law furnish the plaintiff with adequate recourse to cure the deprivation before it has become final. Parratt applied this principle where the deprivation occurred through negligent conduct, whereas Hudson expanded the principle to include cases where the deprivation occurred through intentional state actions. Under the facts of both cases, the court found that because state law furnished each plaintiff with an adequate post-deprivation remedy, federal due process requirements were satisfied and a § 1983 suit was thus fore-closed. Lower federal courts have not hesitated to apply Parratt and Hudson in cases involving disputes between disgruntled developers and local governments where the plaintiffs have sought to couch their

---

16. Id. at 644. See also Id. at 67 n. 22.

17. In determining whether a land use action is administrative or legislative, the Supreme Court has looked to state law. City of Eastlake v. Forest City Enterprises, 426 U.S. 668, 674 n. 9 (1976).

18. Village of Belle Terre v. Boraas, 416 U.S. 1 (1974); see also Berman v. Parker, 348 U.S. 26 (1954).

19. 451 U.S. 527 (1981).

20. 468 U.S. 517, 104 S.Ct. 3194, 82 L.Ed.2d 393 (1984), on remand 744 F.2d 22 (1984).

dissatisfaction with a local land use decision in terms of federal constitutional violations.[21]

Parratt and Hudson were followed by Williamson Co. Regional Planning Commission v. Hamilton Bank of Johnson City.[22] In that case, local decisions had thwarted the plaintiff in several attempts to develop its property in accordance with previously approved plans. Nevertheless, the Court held that a § 1983 claim based on a regulatory "taking" of plaintiff's property was not ripe for judicial review because the plaintiff had not pursued every possible avenue for obtaining a "final, definitive position" from the local government concerning the precise scope of development that would be allowed on the plaintiff's property. The court further held that the availability of a state court inverse condemnation remedy barred a § 1983 claim because the availability of compensation for the alleged taking precluded a finding that the Fifth Amendment prohibition against taking private property *without just compensation* had been violated.[23]

In order to establish the first element of the § 1983 cause of action, the plaintiff must also show the existence of a constitutionally protected right. In land use cases, this usually requires proof that the plaintiff has a "property right" that has been infringed. It has, however, been held that the mere denial of a request for zoning relief does not involve the denial of a protected property right.[24]

The second element of the § 1983 cause of action is that the deprivation be "under color of state law." Monell interpreted this standard to mean that municipalities would not be held liable based merely on the employment of an individual who violated the plaintiff's constitutional rights (respondeat superior liability). Rather, in order to impose municipal liability, it would be necessary to show that the deprivation resulted from the "official policy or custom" of the municipality. Monell, however, did nothing to define what would constitute such an official policy or custom. The Supreme Court has now held that a single incident will not be deemed to constitute a policy and that § 1983 plaintiffs must show a course of conduct involving a conscious choice among competing alternatives by those in a position to formulate municipal policy.[25]

The use of § 1983 as a remedy for allegedly wrongful land use decisions has also been limited by an expansion of § 1983 immunities. Shortly after opening the way for a § 1983 damage remedy against

---

21. Albery v. Reddig, 718 F.2d 245 (7th Cir.1983) (substantive due process); Scudder v. Town of Greendale, 704 F.2d 999, 103 (7th Cir.1983) (equal protection); and Chiplin Enterprises v. City of Labanon, 721 F.2d 1524, 1528 (1st Cir.1983) ("A mere bad faith refusal to follow state law in such local administrative matters simply does not amount to a deprivation of due process where state courts are available to correct the error.")

22. __ U.S. __, 105 S.Ct. 3108, 87 L.Ed. 126 (1985).

23. Id. at __, 105 S.Ct. at 3121.

24. Yale Auto Parts v. Johnson, 758 F.2d 54 (2d Cir.1985).

25. City of Oklahoma City v. Tuttle, __ U.S. __, 105 S.Ct. 2427 (1985).

municipalities in Monell and Owen, the Supreme Court held that municipalities were immune from punitive damages in such suits.[26] Furthermore, while constitutional deprivations are actionable, the court has held that such a deprivation does not automatically warrant substantial damages. Unless actual damages are proven, only nominal damages will be awarded.[27]

The scope of immunity from damages for local officials has also been expanded. As already noted, the principle of absolute immunity has been extended to regional legislators,[28] mayors acting legislatively,[29] and municipal councils or similar bodies acting in a legislative capacity.[30] Furthermore, the scope of the qualified (good faith) immunity available to local officials has been greatly expanded. When Owen was decided, good faith immunity depended on satisfying both a subjective test (did not act with malicious intent to violate constitutional rights) and an objective test (could not reasonably have known action violated constitutional rights).[31] However, two years after deciding Owen, the Supreme Court abolished the subjective test in Harlow v. Fitzgerald.[32] In Harlow, the Court stated that

> . . . government officials performing discretionary functions generally are shielded from liability for civil damages insofar as their conduct does not violate clearly established statutory or constitutional rights of which a reasonable person would have known.[33]

This revision of the test for qualified immunity is especially important because it is intended to encourage early dismissal of § 1983 cases, before local officials are subjected to the burdens and costs of litigation.[34]

The usefulness of § 1983 in land use disputes has also been limited by a noticeable tendency among federal courts to abstain from hearing such cases. Under the Pullman abstention doctrine,[35] a federal district "may, in its discretion, refrain from deciding constitutional questions which hinge on difficult state law issues, if the constitutional controversy would be terminated by resolution in state court of those issues." [36]

26. Newport v. Facts Concert, Inc., 453 U.S. 247 (1981).

27. Carey v. Phiphus, 435 U.S. 247, 98 S.Ct. 1042, 55 L.Ed.2d 252 (1978).

28. Lake Country Estates, Inc. v. Tahoe Regional Planning Agency, 440 U.S. 391 (1979).

29. Aitchison v. Raffiani, 708 F.2d 96 (3d Cir.1983); Hernandez v. City of Lafayette, 643 F.2d 1188 (5th Cir.1981), cert. denied, 455 U.S. 906 (1982); Searington Corporation v. Incorporated Village of North Hills, 575 F.Supp. 1296 (E.D.N.Y. 1981).

30. Aitchison v. Raffiani, 708 F.2d at 98; Kuzinich v. County of Santa Clara, 689 F.2d 1345 (9th Cir.1982); Hernandez v.

City of Lafayette, 643 F.2d at 1193; Gorman Towers, Inc. v. Bogoslavsky, 626 F.2d 607 (8th Cir.1980).

31. Wood v. Strickland, 420 U.S. 308 (1975).

32. 457 U.S. 800, 102 S.Ct. 2727, 73 L.Ed.2d 396 (1982).

33. Id. at 818, 102 S.Ct. at 2738.

34. Harlow v. Fitzgerald, 457 U.S. 800 (1982); Mitchell v. Forsyth, 105 S.Ct. 2806 (1985).

35. Railroad Commission of Texas v. Pullman Co., 312 U.S. 496, 61 S.Ct. 643, 85 L.Ed. 971 (1941).

36. Bank of America National Trust and Savings Association v. Summerland

Under *Burford* abstention, a federal court may decline to hear an otherwise properly brought federal case if a federal decision of the case would risk interfering with complex state regulatory schemes concerning important state policies for which expeditious and adequate judicial review is afforded in state courts.[37]

These doctrines have been applied with increasing frequency, both separately and in tandem, to dismiss § 1983 claims that federal courts considered to be little more than attempts to use § 1983 to convert the federal court into a super-zoning board.[38]

WESTLAW REFERENCES

"property interest" /p lynch /s household

"property right" /s exist! /s state federal /s law /s 1983

baldwin /s appalachian

§ 1983 Cause of Action

to(78) /p two /s "essential element" /s 1983

to(78) /p negligen! /s depriv! /s city

"civil rights" /s "standard of care"

1983 Immunities

da(aft 1977) & "civil rights" /s immun! /s monell

1983 /p "local government" /p immun! /p "money damages"

owens /s independence & 1983 /p immun!

immun! /p implement*** /s municipal! /s "civil right" 1983

to(268) /p "tort liability"

Limitations on § 1983 Land Use Cases

1983 "civil rights" /s depriv! /s ripe!

sy("due process" /p post-deprivation /p remed! /p state /p
    adequa!)

intend! intent! /s state /s action /s post-deprivation /s
    adequa!

"inverse condemnation" /p 1983 "civil rights" /p "fifth
    amendment"

yale /s auto /s parts & "property interest"

"civil rights" /p "color of state law" /p "course of conduct"

to(78) /p municipal! /p immun! /p punitive

1983 "civil rights" /p depriv! /p municipal! /p nominal actual
    /s damage

scope /p immun! /p damage /p local /p official /p 1983
    "civil rights"

harlow /s fitzgerald /s qualified /s immun! /s scope

pullman burford /s abstention /s zon!

County Water District, 767 F.2d 544, 546 (9th Cir.1985) citing Railroad Commission of Texas v. Pullman Co., 312 U.S. 496, 50001 (1941).

37. Burford v. Sun Oil Co., 319 U.S. 315 (1945).

38. See, e.g., C–Y Development Co. v. City of Redlands, 703 F.2d 375 (9th Cir. 1983); Caleb Stowe Associates v. County of Albemarle, Va., 724 F.2d 1079 (4th Cir. 1984); and Kent Island Joint Venture v. Smith, 452 F.Supp. 455 (D.Md.1978).

§ 10.7 The Taking Issue

The provision in the Fifth Amendment which prohibits the federal government, and by extension the states, from taking property without just compensation [1] is the centerpiece of constitutional land use law. Because courts have "not . . . read [the taking clause] literally" [2] to require actual possessory takings, almost any land use regulation could arguably come under the taking clause.

This section will focus on "taking" law through the line of major Supreme Court taking decisions. Treated elsewhere in this book are related topics such as zoning, eminent domain, just compensation, and the theories of compensible regulation.

Taking Cases Through the 1920's

With the important exception of three spurts of judicial activity (in the 1920's, the 1950's-early 60's, and the late 1970's–1980's), the Supreme Court has rarely decided cases under the taking clause.[3] The first major decision, Mugler v. Kansas,[4] did not appear until 1887. Mugler involved a state prohibition law which the Court held did not constitute a taking of an affected brewery even though the law had rendered it almost worthless. Read broadly, Mugler seemed to hold that regulations under the police power are immune from takings challenges unless they rise to the level of a permanent appropriation of property.[5]

If the Mugler holding was meant to be this broad, it was severely limited in the next major taking case, the 1922 decision Pennsylvania Coal v. Mahon.[6] A Pennsylvania statute had prohibited mining beneath residential areas in such a way as to cause "mine subsidence," or cave-ins. Such mining practices had then been common throughout the Pennsylvania anthracite coal region, killing people and causing severe property damage.[7] The coal company involved in Pennsylvania Coal claimed, among several entirely different arguments, that the statute was an unconstitutional taking of the company's mineral rights of the land it was mining. Years before, the company had conveyed away

§ 10.7

1. U.S. Const. amend. V; applied to the states in Chicago, B. & Q. R.R. v. Chicago, 166 U.S. 226, 235–41, 17 S.Ct. 581, 584–86, 41 L.Ed. 979 (1897). See supra § 10.1.

2. Penn Central Transportation Co. v. New York City, 438 U.S. 104, 142, 98 S.Ct. 2646, 2668, 57 L.Ed.2d 631 (1978) (Rehnquist, J., dissenting), rehearing denied 439 U.S. 883, 99 S.Ct. 226, 58 L.Ed.2d 198 (1978).

3. See generally F. Bosselman, D. Callies, J. Banta, The Taking Issue, Chap. 7 (1973).

4. 123 U.S. 623, 8 S.Ct. 273, 31 L.Ed. 205 (1887).

5. F. Bosselman, et al., supra note 3, at 120.

6. 260 U.S. 393, 43 S.Ct. 158, 67 L.Ed. 322 (1922).

7. The Pennsylvania Coal decision gives only sparse information on the facts of the case. For this background, see F. Bosselman, et al., supra note 3, at ch. 8; Rose, Mahon Reconstructed: Why the Takings Issue is Still a Muddle, 57 S.Cal.L.Rev. 561 (1984); Siemon, Of Regulatory Takings and Other Myths, 1 J. Land Use & Envtl. L. 105 (1985).

much of the land in the Pennsylvania anthracite region, and had expressly reserved title to the coal on all this property. The company argued that with contemporary technology the Pennsylvania safety statute effectively prohibited it from exercising its retained mineral rights, thereby taking its property.

The Court agreed with the coal company. The majority opinion, written by Justice Holmes, showed the strong influence of its author's pragmatic view of private contract law; that contracts, and by extension the mineral deeds which the coal company had reserved, are legal duties inextricably bound up with "the consequences of its breach." [8] To Holmes, contracts were legal relationships in which a party had simply but inextricably agreed either to perform, or else "suffer in this way or that by judgment of the court." [9]

With this outlook, the Pennsylvania Coal Fifth Amendment taking issues resolved themselves.[10] Holmes considered the police power as a "question of degree." [11] Holmes warned that "[w]e are in danger of forgetting that a strong public desire to improve the public condition is not enough to warrant achieving the desire by a shorter cut than the constitutional way of paying for the change." [12]

Pennsylvania Coal was a monumental decision which remains a vital element in contemporary taking law.[13] Much current land use scholarship deals with methods of addressing Pennsylvania Coal.[14] Some authors have suggested that the case simply was wrongly decided; [15] others have argued that the decision does not truly rest on the taking clause, but only uses its taking language metaphorically; [16] and others have argued both positions.[17] A separate thesis maintains that Pennsylvania Coal was merely a harmless private squabble since Pennsylvania itself was not a party and both litigants were private; thus, the entire discussion of the Fifth Amendment taking clause in Pennsylvania Coal may be regarded as dictum.[18]

The Supreme Court itself may have sensed the restrictive implications that Pennsylvania Coal would later have, because in only a few

8. Holmes, The Path of the Law, 10 Harv.L.Rev. 457, 458 (1897).

9. Id. See generally Pennsylvania Coal, 260 U.S. at 414–15, 43 S.Ct. at 159–60.

10. Pennsylvania Coal, 260 U.S. at 415, 43 S.Ct. at 160.

11. Id.

12. Id. at 416, 43 S.Ct. at 160.

13. Pennsylvania Coal is addressed in almost all subsequently decided taking cases. For a discussion of the present application of the decision, see Virginia Surface Mining & Reclamation Ass'n v. Andrus, 483 F.Supp. 425, 439–42 (1980), reversed on other grounds sub nom and

Hodel v. Virginia Surface Mining & Reclamation Ass'n, 452 U.S. 264, 101 S.Ct. 2352, 69 L.Ed.2d 1 (1981), judgment vacated 453 U.S. 901, 101 S.Ct. 3132, 69 L.Ed.2d 987 (1981).

14. See, e.g., Rose, supra note 7, and writings cited infra, notes 15–18.

15. See F. Bosselman, et al., supra note 3, at ch. 8.

16. See Siemon, supra note 7.

17. See Williams, Smith, Siemon, Mandleker & Babcock, The White River Junctions Manifesto, 9 Vt.L.Rev. 193, 208–14 (1984).

18. Id. at 209–10.

years it decided the landmark Euclid v. Ambler Realty Co.[19] case, holding that restrictive municipal zoning does not create a per se taking of affected private property. The Euclid decision echoes Holmes' idea that takings are a question of degree, saying that "[t]he line which in this field separates the legitimate from the illegitimate assumption of power is not capable of precise delimitation," [20] but because the Euclid holding fell on the other side of that elusive line, this passage does not seem to have sparked as much criticism as did Holmes' corresponding language in Pennsylvania Coal.

Two years after Euclid the Court retreated, apparently compromising the Euclid outlook with the Pennsylvania Coal holding. In Nectow v. Cambridge,[21] which like Euclid dealt with the validity of a zoning ordinance, the Court held there had been a taking, merely because a local magistrate had, "after a hearing and an inspection of the entire area affected," decided that the zoning ordinance in question went too far.[22]

As if weary of this line drawing, in the same year as Nectow the Court decided a taking case on grounds much more concrete, if also more limited, than the questions of degree involved in the earlier cases. In Miller v. Schoene [23] a tree disease was killing Virginia's apple trees. Cedar trees, which in Virginia served largely ornamental purposes, carried and spread this disease, but were not affected by it. Litigation arose when the state required affected cedars to be killed, in order to protect the apple industry. The Miller Court noted that the situation presented the legislature with a choice: failure to act would protect cedars as much as legislation would protect apple trees. The choice was therefore directly within the state's police power.

Taking Cases Since the 1950's

Situations like Miller are rare, and most subsequent taking decisions have dealt with the same questions of degree present in Mugler, Pennsylvania Coal, and Euclid. For example, Berman v. Parker [24] involved urban renewal legislation in Washington, D.C. In an important opinion by Justice Douglas, the Court held that the police power was broad enough to support the legislation, notwithstanding the taking claims of affected landowners. To the Court, the constitutional issue seemed almost simple: "If those who govern the District of Columbia decide that the Nation's Capital should be beautiful as well as sanitary, there is nothing in the Fifth Amendment that stands in the way." [25]

19. 272 U.S. 365, 47 S.Ct. 114, 71 L.Ed. 303 (1926).

20. Id. at 387, 47 S.Ct. at 118.

21. 277 U.S. 183, 48 S.Ct. 447, 72 L.Ed. 842 (1928).

22. Id. at 188, 48 S.Ct. at 448.

23. 276 U.S. 272, 48 S.Ct. 246, 72 L.Ed. 568 (1928).

24. 348 U.S. 26, 75 S.Ct. 98, 99 L.Ed. 27 (1954).

25. Id. at 33, 75 S.Ct. at 103.

In 1961 the Court went even farther, in Goldblatt v. Hempstead,[26] when it upheld a local ordinance which forced the closing of a mine which had been operating since 1927. The record below indicated no reason for the mine closing, so the Court simply assumed the ordinance was necessary for safety, and upheld it because of the presumption of constitutionality.[27] Goldblatt and Berman taken together seem to imply that the Court would agree with the philosophy later stated in the influential Wisconsin Supreme Court decision, Just v. Marinette County,[28] that "an owner of land has no absolute and unlimited right to change the essential natural character of his land so as to use it for a purpose for which it was unsuited in its natural state and which injures the rights of others." [29]

The Court came closest to adopting the Just view explicitly in its next important taking decision, the 1978 Penn Central Transportation Co. v. New York City.[30] In Penn Central, the owners of Grand Central Station had planned to build a 55-story office complex on top of the station, as had apparently been planned when the station was originally designed. Although New York City initially did not oppose the complex, the city ultimately came to consider the office tower an "aesthetic joke." [31] The city therefore invoked a historic preservation law to block the construction, and the station owners alleged a taking.

The Court admitted that the taking clause "has proved to be a problem of considerable difficulty," [32] and that there was no " 'set formula' for determining when 'justice and fairness' require that economic injuries caused by public action be compensated by the government, rather than remain disproportionately concentrated on a few persons." [33] In essence, the Court was faced with the same line drawing issue that Holmes had articulated in Pennsylvania v. Coal. This time, however, the Court attempted to be more concrete in its analysis. It listed three factors for consideration: (1) the economic impact on the claimant, (2) the "extent to which the regulation . . . interfered with investment-backed expectations," and (3) the character or extent of the government action.[34] In weighing these factors, the Court held that the historic preservation ordinance was not a taking, because it left the station exactly as it had been before; it did not amount to any physical invasion of the property, and it did not violate any original investment-backed expectations of the owners. Further, dictum in the decision implied that the "transferred development rights" the station owners

26. 369 U.S. 590, 82 S.Ct. 987, 8 L.Ed.2d 130 (1962).

27. Id. at 595, 82 S.Ct. at 990.

28. 56 Wis.2d 7, 201 N.W.2d 761 (1972).

29. Id. at 768. See generally Dowling, General Propositions and Concrete Cases: The Search for a Standard in the Conflict between Individual Property Rights and the Social Interest, 1 Fla.St.U.S. Land Use & Env'tl. Law 353 (1985).

30. 438 U.S. 104, 98 S.Ct. 2646, 57 L.Ed. 2d 631 (1978), rehearing denied 439 U.S. 883, 99 S.Ct. 226, 58 L.Ed.2d 198 (1978).

31. Id. at 118, 98 S.Ct. at 2656.

32. Id. at 123, 98 S.Ct. at 2659.

33. Id. at 124, 98 S.Ct. at 2659.

34. Id.

received were sufficient compensation to satisfy the Fifth Amendment.[35]

While the factors weighed in Penn Central appear well-reasoned in their context, the decision not only failed to settle the taking issue but seems to have created a spate of confusing litigation in this area. In the next year, 1979, the Court decided Andrus v. Allard,[36] which upheld a federal environmental regulation which had rendered almost valueless certain personal property, Indian artifacts made from eagle feathers, which pre-existed the legislation. However, another decision of the same year, Kaiser Aetna v. United States,[37] held that the federal government can be estopped from enforcing a ruling if a federal agency had previously led a property owner to believe that making specific changes to his property would not result in restrictive government action.

The Court distinguished Kaiser Aetna in Pruneyard Shopping Center v. Robins,[38] when it held that a government regulation allowing demonstrators to solicit support at a private shopping center did not go far enough to be a taking of shopping center property. Similarly, in Agins v. Tiburon,[39] the Court held that, on balance, a strict density zoning ordinance did not constitute a taking of unimproved land.

The Court relied on Agins in San Diego Gas & Electric Co. v. San Diego,[40] which was a relatively innocuous ruling that a zoning problem similar to that in Agins was not justiciable because there had not yet been a final judgment. The most influential part of San Diego Gas has been Justice Brennan's dissent,[41] which went to the merits of the case and argued the neo-Holmesian position that "once a court establishes that there was a regulatory 'taking,' the Constitution demands that the government entity pay just compensation for the period commencing on the date the regulation first effected the 'taking,' and ending on the date the government entity chooses to rescind or otherwise amend the regulation."[42] Brennan argued that even temporary regulatory takings should therefore be compensible,[43] and the state should bear the cost of its regulation. "After all, if a policeman must know the Constitution, then why not a planner?"[44] Although this dissent has proven persuasive in several states and in the Fifth Circuit,[45] it has

35. Id. at 137, 98 S.Ct. at 2666. Transferable development rights are discussed infra § 11.6.

36. 444 U.S. 51, 100 S.Ct. 318, 62 L.Ed. 2d 210 (1979).

37. 444 U.S. 164, 100 S.Ct. 383, 62 L.Ed. 2d 332 (1979).

38. 447 U.S. 74, 100 S.Ct. 2035, 64 L.Ed. 2d 741 (1980).

39. 447 U.S. 255, 100 S.Ct. 2138, 65 L.Ed.2d 106 (1980).

40. 450 U.S. 621, 101 S.Ct. 1287, 67 L.Ed.2d 551 (1981).

41. 450 U.S. at 636, 101 S.Ct. at 1296 (Brennan, J., dissenting).

42. Id. at 653, 101 S.Ct. at 1305 (Brennan, J., dissenting).

43. Id. at 657, 101 S.Ct. at 1307 (Brennan, J., dissenting).

44. Id. at 661 n. 26, 101 S.Ct. at 1309 n. 26 (Brennan, J., dissenting).

45. Williams, et al., supra note 17, at 193.

been denounced by those who argue that "regulatory takings" under the Fifth Amendment should not be compensable at all.[46]

The Court once again side stepped the question of whether governmental regulation can be so restrictive as to require fifth amendment just compensation in Williamson Co. Reg'l Planning Comm'n v. Hamilton Bank.[47] Although the plaintiffs passed the Agins threshhold by submitting a development plan to the county, they failed to meet the final decision requirement of Hodel[48] by not seeking variances before filing suit.[49] As such, the Penn Central factors weighing economic impact and investment backed expectations could not be applied and the case was remanded.[50]

As if to resolve the quandary to which Penn Central and the Brennan dissent in San Diego Gas have led, in the next major taking decision, Loretto v. Teleprompter Manhattan CATV Corp.,[51] the Court adopted a different standard for takings, the "permanent physical invasion" test. Loretto, together with Justice Rehnquist's dissent from the dismissal for want of substantial federal question in Fresh Pond Shopping Center v. Callahan,[52] explains this test as meaning that if an act of government amounts to a permanent physical invasion of property, even if it is as small as a television cable installed against a building owner's wishes, it is a Fifth Amendment compensable taking. This test apparently operates in the same way as the Miller v. Schoene[53] holding; it is determinative when it applies but is irrelevant to all the situations it does not directly cover.

Therefore, the "permanent physical invasion" standard may somewhat reduce the number of taking claims, but most cases which now arise are still subjected to increasingly subtle constitutional distinctions. For example, Ruckleshaus v. Monsanto[54] held that certain government controls of the pesticide industry could amount to a Fifth Amendment taking of trade secrets, but another decision from the same time, Hawaii Housing Authority v. Midkiff,[55] took an apparently looser view of the Fifth Amendment taking language in upholding a state statute allowing tenants to require that their landlords sell them fee title to their residences.

46. See Siemon, supra note 7; Williams, et al., supra note 17.

47. ___ U.S. ___, 105 S.Ct. 3108, 87 L.Ed.2d 126 (1985), on remand ___ F.2d ___ (6th Cir.1985).

48. See supra, note 13.

49. ___ U.S. at ___, 105 S.Ct. at 3117.

50. ___ U.S. at ___, 105 S.Ct. at 3119.

51. 458 U.S. 419, 102 S.Ct. 3164, 73 L.Ed.2d 868 (1982), on remand 58 N.Y.2d 143, 459 N.Y.S.2d 743, 446 N.E.2d 428 (1983), reargument denied 59 N.Y.2d 761, 463 N.Y.S.2d 1030, 450 N.E.2d 254 (1983).

52. ___ U.S. ___, 104 S.Ct. 218, 78 L.Ed. 2d 215 (1983).

53. See supra note 23.

54. ___ U.S. ___, 104 S.Ct. 2862, 81 L.Ed.2d 815 (1984).

55. ___ U.S. ___, 104 S.Ct. 2321, 81 L.Ed.2d 186 (1984), on remand 740 F.2d 15 (9th Cir.1984).

Reconciling the Taking Cases

The Supreme Court of the United States has itself recognized that it "quite simply has been unable to develop any 'set formula' " [56] for determining when there has been a taking. Commentators have referred to the taking issue as a "muddle" [57] and the regulatory taking concept as a "myth." [58] Any attempt at "understanding" the taking issue and any attempt at reconciling even the recent cases is risky at best. However, as is developed more fully elsewhere in this Hornbook,[59] the following analysis is submitted for consideration. It is premised on the assumptions, first, that the issue of whether a "taking" claim has been stated can be separated from the issue of remedy and, second, that the issue of remedy should turn, not simply on the existence of a cause of action, but on the particular facts giving rise to the cause of action.

Acceptance of these assumptions suggests the following simple solution to the taking puzzle:

(1) If a regulation "goes too far," it is a "taking" in the sense that it imposes too heavy a burden on property rights to be sustained as a police power regulation.

(2) If that is all that is involved, the regulation should be declared invalid as an abuse of the police power but it should not, by means of a damage award, be converted into an unwilling and unintentional exercise of the power of eminent domain.

(3) If, however, in addition to "going too far," the regulation seeks to appropriate the regulated property for a public use, then the government should be found to have attempted to exercise its eminent domain power imperfectly, and the Court should correct the imperfection by giving the government the choice of paying damages or abandoning the regulation.

(4) Evidence of such an imperfect attempt to appropriate should consist of more than a deprivation of all profitable private uses. It should involve a showing of physical invasion or something like it or a diversion to actual public use or a patent intent to restrict current use in order to reduce the future cost of such an invasion or diversion.

One might indeed conclude that not only should this be the law, but, if one looks at what the courts have done, it is the law.

56. Penn Central Transportation Co. v. New York City, 438 U.S. 104, 125, 98 S.Ct. 2646, 2659, 57 L.Ed.2d 631 (1978), rehearing denied 439 U.S. 883, 99 S.Ct. 226, 58 L.Ed.2d 198 (1978).

57. Rose, Mahon Reconstructed: Why the Taking Issue is Still a Muddle, 57 S.Cal.L.Rev. 561 (1984).

58. Siemon, Of Regulator Takings and Other Myths, 1 J. Land Use and Envtl.L. 105 (1985).

59. See Hagman and Juergensmeyer, Urban Planning and Land Development Control Law, 2nd edition, practitioner's ed., §§ 24.2–.6 (1986).

WESTLAW REFERENCES

implement! /p land (real +2 estate property) /p valu! /p
    captur! compens!

to(92) /p "fifth amendment" /p zon!

Taking-Cases-Through-the-1920's

mugler /s kansas /p taking /p appropriat!

coal /s mahon /p taking /p contract

nectow /s cambridge & miller /s schoene

Taking Cases Since the 1950's

berman /s partner /p renew! /s urban!

land /p zon! ordinance /p presum! /p constitutional!

historic! /p preserv! /p ordinance zon! /p taking

andrus /s allard /p kaiser /s aetna

zon! ordinance /p taking /p unimproved /p land property

regulat! /s taking /s compens!

"permanent physical invasion"

Chapter 11

WINDFALLS AND WIPEOUTS

Analysis

§ 11.1　Wipeouts Defined and Illustrated [1]

A wipeout is any decrease in the value of real estate other than one caused by the owner or by general deflation. Decreases in value caused by the owner are not wipeouts. A pyromaniac burns down his house—that's not a wipeout; a farmer wastes his land by improper cultivation—that's not a wipeout; a speculator misjudges the market and pays too much for land or sells it too low—that's not a wipeout. Nor is it a wipeout if real estate decreases in value because of general deflation, because the property is still worth the same amount in real terms.

There remain a multitude of decreases that result from other factors that enter into the pool of wipeouts. For example, there are the wipeouts resulting from land-use controls implementing the environmental and slow-growth movements. There are some who believe such wipeouts should be mitigated. If so, how about decreases caused by other types of regulations (e.g., traffic controls, prohibition of alcohol), or by planning, taxation, or government projects? The resulting decreases can be direct or indirect. For example, the opening of a new highway may indirectly decrease the value of property along the old

§ 11.1

1. This section is extracted from Windfalls for Wipeouts: Land Value Capture and Compensation, ch. 1 (D. Hagman & D. Misczynski, eds. 1978). Permission has been granted by the publisher: Planners Press, American Planning Association, Chicago, Ill.

route. These decreases may result from government action at all levels—local, regional, state, or federal.

Decreases can also be caused by natural disasters, such as by earthquake. Finally, decreases can be caused by the actions of others in the community (e.g., by a neighbor who builds a smoky factory next door), or by a change in community tastes. For example, if nobody goes skiing anymore, ski resort land would likely decrease in value. Many of these community actions and tastes are reflected in the property market as wipeouts.

Consider the following hypothetical example:

Mr. B bought a lot on Elm Street for $5,000 in 1965 which was zoned single family. He did nothing to his lot for 10 years. However, the city acquired an adjacent 20-acre site upwind of Mr. B's property for a garbage dump, which it later began using. Mr. C's property, on the sunny side of B's property, was rezoned for a 100-story skyscraper apartment which Mr. C then built. Mr. B sought a rezoning to 100-story skyscraper, too, but it was rejected by the planning commission because "it would be unhealthy to have apartment dwellers live near garbage dumps." Mr. B, however, appealed to the city council. The appeal drew attention to the property and it was discovered to be the only known habitat of the hexibilibus (a rare insect). A quickly formed Friends of the Hexibilibus Society packed the city council on the night of Mr. B's appeal and demanded that the property be placed in the CHA (conservation, historic, and antiquities) zone. Any land use can be made of the property in the CHA zone which is consistent with the reason for its designation, in this case, anything consistent with the health, safety, and welfare of hexibilibi.

The city council complied with the Friends' request and zoned CHA. In 1975, Mr. B agreed to sell the lot to the Friends of the Hexibilibus Society at its market value. The market value of hexibilibi sites downwind of garbage dumps and on the shady side of 100-story skyscrapers is $5. Five thousand dollars to $5 is a wipeout.

Note that B's wipeout could be said to be caused by government (project acquisition and use and regulation of Mr. B and Mr. C) and community action (Mr. C built his 100-story skyscraper and the market does not regard garbage dumps or high buildings as desirable neighbors).

The pervasive notion that "growth is good" and "bigger is better" has dramatically changed. The environmental decade of the 70s called forth a host of new tough wipeout-causing plans and controls. Traditional controls such as subdivision and zoning regulations became more restrictive. Planning became more pervasive and complicated. Plans took on regulatory effects as statutes were amended to require consistency with plans.[2] Where statutes were not amended, courts began to give new weight to plans, thus giving them regulatory effects. Permit systems were overlaid on traditional controls so that development was often possible only after obtaining a permit or, also likely, several permits from several different agencies. In short, nearly all land use regulations are potential progenitors of wipeouts.

 WESTLAW REFERENCES

zon! ordinance /s valueless wipeout

depress! reduc! decreas! /p value price /p (real +2 property
   estate) land /p ordinance

§ 11.2 Windfalls Defined and Illustrated [1]

A windfall is an increase in the value of real estate—other than that caused by the owner—or by general inflation. As with wipeouts, windfalls are caused by a variety of factors. Some meanings of the British term betterment are roughly synonymous with windfall; some are not.

The best-known definition for betterment is:

any increase in the value of land (including the buildings thereon) arising from central or local government action, whether positive, e.g., by the execution of public works or improvements, or negative, e.g., by the imposition of restrictions on other land.

The term [betterment] is not, however, generally understood to include enhancement in the value of property arising from general community influences, such as the growth of urban populations.[2]

Consider the following hypothetical example:

Mr. A bought a lot on Elm Street for $5,000 in 1965 that was zoned for single-family use. He did nothing with the lot for 10 years, during which there was considerable high-class private development in the area. A millionaire who owned 20 acres of land adjoining Mr. A's lot died, his will leaving the acreage to the Horticultural Society of America with an endowment to establish a formal garden. Mr. A's lot thus received the enhancement of a park-like setting. The formal garden being the diadem of the city's aesthetic resources, it decided to enhance the approaches to it by downzoning the property around the formal gardens for open space use. The downzoning did not include Mr. A's lot, which the city rezoned for 100-story commercial residential uses to serve the needs of city dwellers who came seeking quiet in the garden. To

2. See supra § 2.13.

§ 11.2

1. This section is extracted from Wind-falls for Wipeouts: Land Value Capture and Compensation, ch. 2 (D. Hagman & D. Misczynski, eds. 1978). Permission has been granted by the publisher: Planners Press, American Planning Association, Chicago, Ill.

2. English Expert Committee on Compensation and Betterment (Uthwatt Committee), Final Report, ¶ 260, Cmd. No. 6386 (1942).

minimize automobile congestion, the city also rerouted a planned subway, opening a station near the gardens and adjacent to Mr. A's lot. Mr. A sold his lot for $5,000,000 in 1975. Five thousand dollars to $5,000,000—that is a windfall, one that resulted from government regulation, a government project, and community action.

The following are reasons for recapturing windfalls:

1. Revenues would result.

2. The community is asking only for a return of wealth it creates.

3. The windfall recapture tax (charge, exaction, fee, levy, and so forth) would not raise land prices because supply is fixed.

4. When the public needs to acquire land it should not have to pay a price increased by its own activities.

5. It is a less socialistic scheme than public land ownership.

Whether sufficient support exists to make recapture of windfalls possible depends on answers to questions similar to those asked about wipeout mitigation. Some will not be supportive because windfalls from personal property are not recaptured; others will not be supportive because windfall is defined too broadly; still others will be boggled by the measurement problem or the difficulty of drawing precise lines or by other administrative concerns.

There are five additional problems. First, while the argument is not made that there is a right to risk and lose, some argue that there is a right to keep if the risk wins. Second, while some private property interests are strident in their call for wipeout mitigation, the public is not strident in its call for windfall recapture. Third, while government is often large and diverse enough to be able to distribute the cost of wipeout payments in a way that is not burdensome, especially if its accounts can be balanced by windfall recapture, the recapture of windfalls can run into resistance because of hardship. For example, if the windfall recapture technique selected is imposed on individuals and enterprises with small amounts of property and if it applies at the time there is only a paper windfall, i.e., no actual cash flow, the "little person" may have great difficulty meeting the windfall recapture payment. Fourth, windfall recapture might be most acceptable when capital gains taxes are not being used. Capital gains taxes have been in use in the United States as long as income has been taxed; capital gains have been taxed only recently in Canada and England and still are not taxed in Australia and New Zealand. With the expansion of capital gains taxes, there might be a tendency to view them as surrogate windfall recapture devices and dampen any tendency for further recapture. Fifth, there is some movement toward public land ownership as a way of keeping community-caused increments in the public treasury. England's Community Land Act, 1975, was partially so motivated and Australia and Canada are experimenting with land-banking.

§ 11.3 Implementing Land Value Capture and Compensation Programs [1]

Under a rational system of land-use controls, windfalls might roughly equal wipeouts on the theory that the price of land is largely determined by the demand for it.[2] If land-use controls prohibit a demand from finding a supply in a particular place, the demand is shunted elsewhere. Indeed, under a rational planning system that reduces imperfections in the market, planning could be wealth-creative, that is, it could lead to more windfalls than wipeouts.

However, under the "Byzantine"—to use Fred Bosselman's phrase [3]—system of land use control in America, wipeouts may exceed windfalls. Developers must spend money learning the ropes and shepherding their projects through the chambers. Windfalls (which might otherwise be recaptured) are whittled away by administrative costs. Similarly, because of the bubbling cacophony of multitudinous edicts, it is unclear where the supply is. The demand goes around searching for it, the search being another high administrative cost. In short, strong controls produce both windfalls and wipeouts in significant quantities.

Under the existing system, windfalls and wipeouts are largely left to fall where they will. Failure to recapture windfalls and mitigate wipeouts leads to several deficiencies in the planning system. First, so long as we continue to have a nonsystem of planning, who gets the goodies and who gets deprived will be perceived as arbitrary and capricious.

Even if the Mr. Wipeoutee B's of the world could be persuaded that an offending regulator's action was justified by some brooding omniplanning in the sky, they are not likely to feel that they deserved

§ 11.3

1. This section is extracted from Windfalls for Wipeouts: Land Value Capture and Compensation, ch. 3 (D. Hagman & D. Misczynski, eds. 1978). Permission has been granted by the publisher: Planners Press, American Planning Association, Chicago, Ill.

2. "The public control of the use of land . . . necessarily has the effect of shifting land values: in other words, it increases the value of some land and decreases the value of other land, but it does not destroy land values. Neither the total demand for development nor its average annual rate is materially affected, if at all, by planning

ordinances." Expert Committee on Compensation and Betterment (Uthwatt Committee), Final Report, Cmd. 6386 E 26 (London: H.M.S.O., 1942). See also R. Johnson & S. Schwartz, Public Mechanisms for Controlling Land Commission in California (Research Report, Institute of Governmental Studies, University of California, Davis); Freeman, Give and Take: Distributing Local Environmental Control Through Land Use Regulation, 60 Minn.L. Rev. 883 (1976).

3. Address by F. Bosselman, ALI–ABA Land Planning and Regulation of Development Course (Mar. 18, 1976).

their fate. And the Mr. Windfaller A's of the world are not likely to believe that they really earned theirs. Thus, even if planning is perceived to be in the public interest, the resulting windfalls and wipeouts may be regarded as arbitrary and capricious. It is another case of society pursuing otherwise laudable goals at the expense or profit of only a few of its members. If the burdened few could receive some relief, particularly if at the expense of unintended beneficiaries, one is hard disposed to understand why society doesn't go right out and do it.

Under the existing system the planner is often perceived as one who plans in the public interest without any concern for the benefits and costs to particular individuals. Indeed, there are some who fear that if the planner knew too much about the effect on individuals, planning might be inhibited. But one cannot make a positive rational case for crashing through with a plan entirely oblivious of effects on individuals. A windfalls for wipeouts system would identify the windfallers and the wipeoutees.

Further, to the extent that the planner has regard for citizen participation, the signals from the participants in the existing system may be wrong. Planners are often warmed by the support received for a plan, not realizing that the support may only be coming from those who are windfallers under the plan. Even if the plan were contrary to the overall public interest, the planner would still have their support. Similarly, the planner is often discouraged by opposition from those "special interests," the wipeoutees, who fail to be sanguine about the public interest in the face of their impending financial loss.

Under a system of windfalls for wipeouts the planner is made aware of the windfalls and wipeouts yet need not be inhibited in the face of them. That is because the windfalls are partially recaptured and the wipeouts partially mitigated.

Even if the existing system is regarded as fair, as more than a fatalistic lottery, there are still those who will struggle mightily to disrupt a good plan because there are unrecaptured windfalls to be made and unmitigated wipeouts to be avoided.

Under the existing system, where great unrecaptured windfalls and unmitigated wipeouts can occur, manipulators sometimes urge the application of land-use control not because they believe in it but merely because they know how to manipulate it better than others (sometimes benefiting from shifting values from wipeouts caused others). For example, at least in times past when members of the real estate industry dominated local planning boards, land-use controls might be urged upon the city by members of the industry, who observed that "[w]ithout zoning you can have a gas station on a corner, an expensive house down the street, and a drive-in hamburger stand around the corner."

Then, getting themselves appointed to the planning boards they so piously opined the need for, they do not resist the temptation to clothe their public duties with the private interests of themselves and their friends. No wonder then that "[i]n a zoned city, you can have a gas station on a corner, an expensive house down the street, and a drive-in hamburger stand around the corner." [4]

Under the present system, the most intense heat and participation from interested parties appears not at the comprehensive, policy-making level, but when that policy begins to affect and create windfalls or wipeouts for particular parcels. These controversies often involve the most narrow externalities problems, such as should a convenience store be permitted in this single-family residential neighborhood. Public decision-makers spend much of their time on these largely neighborhood squabble-resolving issues. Exhausted by these almost private concerns, many have little time or energy left to attend to the broader public interest.

Under some windfalls for wipeouts systems, these neighborhood externalities problems could be partially resolved by transfer payments, for example, the convenience store owner would be forced to share the windfall with those who are wiped out. There would be less incentive for making the change, less at stake if the change occurred. Neighborhood squabble resolving should therefore consume less time of public decisionmakers.

Under the present system, a city plans and zones some areas for intensive development; others for unintensive use. It places infrastructure accordingly. The result is that land prices are lower in the area scheduled for unintensive use. Where does the intensive (e.g., multiple-family) developer go to reap his windfall? He obtains a rezoning.

Thus, under the present system, planmaking invites its own destruction. Under a windfalls for wipeouts system, however, the multi-family developer will have less incentive to "break" the plan, for part of the windfall will be recaptured. Therefore, a windfalls for wipeouts system may lead to more consistent plan implementation.

Under the existing system, wipeouts are not generally mitigated, windfalls are not generally recaptured. There is now considerable pressure to pay compensation for wipeouts. When that step is considered, the first question that arises is, who will pay for it? While this seems to pose considerable difficulty, it needn't, for windfall recapture could fund wipeout mitigation. Certainly it is fair to do so. Landowners can hardly claim they should be paid for wipeouts but retain the right to keep windfalls.

There is no shortage of techniques if society has the will to apply a windfalls for wipeouts system. Some systems have already been tried.

---

4. Both quotations are taken from a cartoon appearing in Planning, Jan. 1973, at 22 (reproduced from the New York Times).

An English scheme still in effect in Australia recaptures betterment and mitigates worsenment from plans.[5] Zoning by special assessment financed eminent domain is the name for an early American scheme to pay off those damaged by zoning and assess those benefited.[6] It was used to make zoning constitutional and could still be used to make it fairer. Transferable development rights,[7] an American invention, is designed to "pay off" the wipeout from downzoning by allowing development rights to be used elsewhere. One or more of a variety of techniques could be used as a guide for wipeout mitigation, and windfall recapture. Several of these techniques are discussed in the sections which follow.

 WESTLAW REFERENCES

bosselman & land (real +2 estate property) /p regulat! control!

furey /s sacramento

windfall /s wipeout

zon! /p "special assessment"

"transferable development rights"

§ 11.4   Betterment for Worsenment—England, Canada, Australia and New Zealand as Models [1]

(A) *Betterment Recapture*

(1) England

In 1909 the English adopted the Housing, Town Planning, etc. Act of 1909. It contained a provision for recapturing increases (betterment) in land value due to adoption of a planning scheme and for paying compensation for decreases (worsenment) in land value due to the scheme. It is the closest historic parallel to the basic notion of windfall (betterment) recapture to permit compensation for wipeouts (worsenment). Both concepts were subsequently adopted in planning legislation in Australia, Canada, and New Zealand.

The 1909 Act is an intellectual relative of an obscure American practice, zoning by special assessment financed eminent domain, discussed in § 11.5, and of transferable development rights, a more recent technique described in § 11.6. All three are both windfall recapture and wipeout mitigation techniques.

5. See infra § 11.4.

6. See infra § 11.5.

7. See infra § 11.6.

§ 11.4

1. This section is extracted from Windfalls for Wipeouts: Land Value Capture and Compensation, ch. 21 (D. Hagman & D. Misczynski eds. 1978). Permission has been granted by the publisher: Planners Press, American Planning Association, Chicago, Ill.

The bill that ultimately became the 1909 Act originally provided for recapture of the entire increase in value caused by a planning scheme, with payment due when the scheme was adopted. A town planning scheme was expected to have a very powerful influence over development. Translated into American English, it was both a master plan and its implementation devices—zoning control (including provisions for termination of nonconforming uses), subdivision control, designation of lands for public facilities and for governmental purchase.

There were objections to 100 percent recapture. The argument was: previous betterment recapture flowed from a particular government project. Betterment under a planning scheme may result from future indicated government expenditure, but it also results from nongovernmental market reactions to the scheme. Rather than limit recapture to increases in land value caused by government expenditure, and purely as a compromise, the increase recaptured was limited to 50 percent.

The betterment recapture provision was brief:

> Where, by the making of any town planning scheme, any property is increased in value, the responsible authority, if they make a claim for the purpose within the time (if any) limited by the scheme . . . shall be entitled to recover from any person whose property is so increased in value one-half of the amount of that increase.[2]

The Town Planning Act 1925 consolidated previous town planning legislation but made no significant changes in the betterment recapture provision.

The betterment provisions were amended in 1932.[3] On the taking effect of any provision contained in a scheme or the execution of work under a scheme, the local authority could claim betterment up to 75 percent of the increase within 12 months of the operation or execution. Except where the landowner was requesting payment for worsenment, the claim for betterment could be deferred by the landowner until property was transferred, at which time payment was due with interest. The local authority could make a new claim for betterment upon a disposition or change of use of property within 14 years. After 14 years, a statute of limitations came into effect, and betterment could no longer be claimed.

During the 14-year period, a change of agricultural use to another agricultural use or a change in utility use would not result in a claim for payment of betterment, but a disposition of property so used would. Sums previously paid, donations of property to public use, or the provision of works by the landowner were offsettable from the claim. Betterment due could be paid in installments, for up to 30

2. See the 1909 Act, §§ 54(1), (2), 57(1), 60(1), Sch. 4.

3. Town and Country Planning Act 1932, § 21.

years, with interest. Disposition was defined to include leases of three or more years. Minor changes in use did not constitute an event on which betterment could be claimed.

Betterment recapture of the kind provided under English law from 1909 was eliminated from English law as of July 1, 1948.[4] Similar schemes were adopted at one time or another in the Australian states of New South Wales,[5] Tasmania,[6] Victoria,[7] and Western Australia,[8] and in the Canadian provinces of New Brunswick,[9] Alberta,[10] Nova Scotia,[11] Manitoba,[12] Saskatchewan [13] and Newfoundland.[14]

Evaluations and Conclusions

Perhaps the greatest failing of the English 1909 Act and its progeny was that very little betterment was recovered. In England some £1,500 was recovered in one case; £150 was recaptured in another case for the stopping up of a footpath in 1932; £1,100 was claimed for betterment by reason of construction of a new street. The latter case went to court because the land from which betterment was claimed was not within the scheme, but the Court held that not to make any difference.[15]

In Australia, only four schemes in New South Wales provided for betterment recapture, and no betterment has ever been recovered.[16] No betterment was ever recovered under the Tasmanian Act.[17] "No 'betterment' was ever collected . . ." in New Zealand.[18] While Milner indicates there is no record of any betterment ever having been recovered in Canada under 1909 Act type provisions, there was some recapture under the Newfoundland Act.[19]

4. Town and Country Planning Act 1947, § 113(2).

5. See A. Fogg, Australian Town Planning Law 514 (1974).

6. Local Government Act, 1962, §§ 738–39.

7. The Town and Country Planning Act 196K, Victoria No. 6849 Sch. 3(13).

8. The Town Planning & Development Act, 1928–1972, § 11(2).

9. The Town Planning Act, S.N.B. 1912.

10. The Town Planning Act, S. Alt. 1913, c. 18, § 5(3).

11. The Town Planning Act, S.N.S. 1915, c. 3. Section 13(5) and The Town Planning Act, S.N.S. 1912, c. 6.

12. The Town Planning Act, S. Man. 1916, c. 114, § 18(4).

13. The Town Planning and Rural Development Act, S. Sask. 1917, Sess. 2, c. 70, § 20.

14. Housing Act, 1966, No. 87, § 24.

15. R.V. Webster, ex parte Young (1932) 51 T.L.R. 201.

16. M. Wilcox, The Law of Land Development in New South Wales 297 (1967).

17. A. Fogg, supra note 5, at 519.

18. K. Robinson, Law of Town and Country Planning 6 (1968).

19. J. Milner, Community Planning 105 (1963).

There were arguably some indirect "collections" which flowed from the English Act. Some property owners who made claims for worsenment were "persuaded" to withdraw claims when local authorities threatened to collect betterment. And some property owners who were reluctant to sell property to the government were intimidated by betterment-recapture threats to be more "reasonable." On the whole, however, it must be admitted that betterment recapture failed to yield revenue. One reason for the failure to capture betterment in England was that few planning schemes were adopted. In 1942, when Uthwatt reported, the only statistics on the 1932 Act experience were in the Report for 1937–38 of the Ministry of Health. Only 25 schemes were in operation under the 1932 Act, and 16 of those had not yet been in operation a year so that the planning authority time for filing claims for betterment had not yet expired. Many of the progeny of the 1909 Act made the right to recapture betterment optional, so local governments did not even authorize themselves to collect it. But the bottom line was simply that the need to recapture betterment resulting from planning did not arouse the public conscience. The public sense of grievance over nonrecapture was minimal.

A mistake on the part of the planners may have been responsible for the failure to recapture betterment. Once betterment was charged for a scheme, it could not be charged again. Therefore, some planners may have waited until the full flowering of their planning work of art unfolded so as to maximize the betterment recapture. The trouble was the flowering never came.

Landowners resisted betterment recapture. Once a statute of limitations was imposed on recovering betterment, of course, the landowner had every incentive to resist—just a bit longer, and then keep the betterment. And according to the Memorandum prepared for Uthwatt,[20] landowners resisted betterment recapture when it stemmed from amorphous planning schemes rather than from specific projects. Also, many opposed the betterment levy on the ground that it was a property tax.

Uthwatt concluded that the 1932 Act betterment-recapture scheme was unworkable because of the difficulty of proving the increase in value that came from a planning scheme and of calculating that increase.[21] Doubts as to whether the plan increased value tended to be resolved in favor of the landowner. Further, while the increase in value was calculated from the date the scheme or one of its provisions creating betterment took effect, it was well-known that values often rose in anticipation of the scheme. Therefore, much of the value was not recapturable because the statute indicated it must be due to the "coming into operation" of a provision in the scheme.

20. Ministry of Works and Buildings, Memorandum on Betterment (1942).

21. Expert Committee on Compensation and Betterment, Final Report, Cmd. 6386 (1942). The Uthwatt Report was the third of a series of land use planning studies prepared for the British government and published before the end of World War II.

In Australia, the experience with valuation was similar. In New South Wales

> [t]he Valuer-General took the view that, although increases in value could be shown, factors other than those referred to . . . were operative in leading to that increase, e.g., inflation and the carrying out of public works by statutory authorities apart from works under the scheme. He was not able to separate such increases in value into their various components. In particular he could not fix the increase in value attributable to the scheme and so could not comply with the statutory injunction.[22]

In Victoria, similar problems arose.[23]

In New Zealand "the difficulties of calculation and collection were such that it was felt wiser to . . . " abandon betterment recapture.[24]

At least in Australia, and to a degree in New Zealand, the acceptance of English planning law was tempered by review before adoption. The Canadian provinces, however, jumped on the bandwagon early, most provinces slavishly importing and adopting the English 1909 Act before World War I. The climes in Canada and England, however, were *different*. The nonuse of the betterment recapture provisions is not surprising, for little English planning law took hold in Canada in any operational sense.

Suggestions for improvement of the betterment levy were made to Uthwatt. They included recommendations (1) that statutory undertakers (public utilities) be denied favored treatment, (2) that increases in annual rental values rather than capital values be the base for the betterment levy, (3) that local authorities be able to acquire properties not being utilized by owners who were attempting to wait out the betterment recapture time period, (4) that the increase of value should be measured from the date of decision to prepare a plan, not of its coming into operation. Others suggested that betterment recapture be limited to producing funds sufficient to pay off claims for worsenment from owners within the scheme. Still others suggested that betterment be determined on a zoned basis rather than by individual properties.

Of course, betterment recapture might be made to work if the public could be persuaded that it was desirable. But so far as one can discern, there is no more desire nowadays to recapture betterment than there ever has been, except perhaps as a source of funds for compensation for wipeouts. But at least the concept might be useful to offset claims for damages. Consider an example:

22. L. Hort, An Introduction to Land Development Contribution Law and Practice in New South Wales 23 (1972) (citing Pullen, The Betterment Levy, A.P.I.J. Apr. 1968, at 43).

23. K. Gifford, The Victorian Town Planning Handbook 327 (4th ed. 1973).

24. K. Robinson, supra note 18, at 6.

In Aaron v. Los Angeles,[25] landowners recovered for damages to their properties caused by the presence of noisy jets. They recovered even though the presence of the airport might have actually increased the value of their properties. For example, assume a parcel is worth $10,000. An airport is built in the area, and the parcel thereby enjoys betterment resulting in a value of $20,000. But because the airport becomes a noisy jetport, the value is depreciated to $18,000. The parcel owner is paid $2,000 by the government because of the noise even though, but for the airport, the property would still be worth $10,000. If betterment had been offset against worsenment, the City of Los Angeles in this case would have saved $2,000. It can hardly be claimed that it would be unjust to deny the landowner this $2,000 payment for worsenment, since he was "given" $10,000 of betterment.

Perhaps the difficulty with the 1909 Act was that betterment recapture was not made mandatory. Recapturing increases is no more popular than any kind of tax, and local governments, given the option, simply decided not to levy the tax.

There was also the problem of realization. "Realization" means that the landowner has a cash flow or the opportunity for it at the time the betterment charge is due. Realization minimizes hardship. Since realization is seldom actually present even in the case of special assessments, the charge is made a lien on the property and the landowner is given a period of time to pay off the assessment. The 1909 Act and its progeny used a similar technique and others, such as permitting deferment until a sale or change of use.

The measurement problem was also complicated by inability to clearly state that, for instance, a rezoning caused the increase. At best it just unleashed other economic forces, without which no change in value would take place. For example, the rezoning of property in the boondocks from residential to commercial might not change values at all.

The solution to the measurement problem is perhaps to define betterment to include all increases in value other than those due to inflation or to the efforts of the landowner. The adoption of the planning scheme, its implementation by regulation, or its implementation by public works need not be regarded as a tax-triggering event. Rather, the appraiser (or assessor) need merely observe periodically (e.g., annually) that property increased in value, subtract the portion caused by inflation and by the owner (both of which measurements are difficult enough), and regard the rest of the increase as unearned, recapturing part of it for the community.

25. 40 Cal.App.3d 471, 115 Cal.Rptr. 162 (1974), cert. denied 419 U.S. 1122, 95 S.Ct. 806, 42 L.Ed.2d 822 (1975).

The rate of recapture is another issue. All existing 1909 Act and progeny models used between 50 and 80 percent. If all increases (other than inflationary or owner caused) were recaptured, the rate might justifiably be less.

Both for purposes of assessment and collection, it does seem best to tie increase recapture into the property tax system. The 1909 Act and progeny models do so, and there is no evidence that such a tie-in is undesirable. Special assessments are now frequently also collected through the property tax system.

Perhaps the reason why such provisions work in the case of special assessments is tied to the problem of measurement. The special assessment proceeds on the theory that it is recovery of cost, up to the benefit received from a particular public works. The exact amount of benefit received is not always clear, but at least the assessee has a tangible improvement to contemplate. Further, the special assessment usually does not seek to measure the exact increase in value which is complicated by the fact that the increase occurs in anticipation of a betterment triggering act. In a special assessment, it is only necessary to determine whether the benefit received equals or exceeds the assessment of apportioned cost.

(B) *Worsenment Mitigation*

(1) England

In addition to recapture of betterment, England's 1909 comprehensive planning law also dealt with compensation for regulation, providing that "Any person whose property is injuriously affected by the making of a town planning scheme shall . . . be entitled to obtain compensation in respect thereof from the responsible authority." [26] Restating the statute in American English, the 1909 Act provided that compensation was payable for depreciation in property values caused by adoption of a land-use control such as zoning by a local government. Compensation was the general rule. Nonliability was the exception.

No compensation was payable for property damaged by a plan where the damage resulted to something started (e.g., the construction of a building) after the local government applied to the national government for permission to prepare a scheme. But if expenditure to comply with the scheme was rendered abortive by revocation of a scheme, compensation was payable. On the other hand, if the damage could have resulted from enforcement of a by-law (a regulation under another ordinance) rather than flowing from a planning scheme, no compensation was payable.

If the planning scheme included a provision regarded as "reasonable" to secure "the amenity of the area" such as "space about buildings or limit the number of buildings to be erected, or prescribe the height

26. Housing Town Planning etc. Act 1909, § 58(1), 9 & 10 Geo. 5, c. 35, Sch. 3.

or character of buildings," the injurious affection was not compensable. These provisions are sometimes called the good neighbor provisions. A later law made good neighbor restrictions noncompensable regardless of whether for amenity or for other purposes. Restated in American terms, if a regulation had reasonable yard requirements or reasonable limits on heights, there was no compensation. The 1909 Act also provided that if compensation was payable under some other act, an owner of injuriously affected property could neither recover twice nor could recovery be for more than permitted under the other act.

The 1909 Act provisions on compensation remained virtually unchanged through their consolidation in The Town Planning Act, 1926. The major change (in the Housing, etc. Act, 1923, § 20) was that if an award of compensation was made, the local authority had the option of changing the planning scheme.

The Town and Country Planning Act, 1932, the basic act until 1947, was a comprehensive revision of English planning law. Compensation for injurious affection was provided for "the coming into operation of any provision contained in a scheme, or by the execution of any work under a scheme." [27] The first provision might have restricted liability somewhat. While before the injurious affection flowed from the plan itself, it was now the coming into operation of one of its provisions that triggered compensation. The "execution of any work under a scheme" provision, however, may have increased the possibility of obtaining recovery. Compensation was also made available for damage to a business resulting from the injurious affection to property occupied by a business. Compensation was also available if a building of historic or architectural interest was injuriously affected by a preservation order made during the preparation of a scheme. If a scheme was so enforced that property which constituted a preexisting lawful nonconforming use was thereby damaged, compensation was payable.

Previously, only injurious affection flowing from the scheme triggered compensation. Under the 1932 Act, in awarding compensation for scheme-caused injurious affection, if the landowner had been denied permission to develop property during the preparation of the scheme, and the denial was upheld by the government on appeal, compensation was paid for the additional injurious affection caused by the denial. Compensation was not payable if an action taken prohibited advertising.

The only other major change was that the exclusions from compensation were not automatic. Rather, the planning scheme had to state what was excluded. But the list was expanded so that no compensation had to be paid for imposing temporary restrictions on development, prohibiting building permanently because of danger to health or because excessive expenditure for infrastructure would be required, prohibiting uses because of damage to health or serious detriment to

---

27. 22 & 23 Geo. 5, c. 48, § 1824.

the neighborhood, restricting use of buildings, regulating walls, fences, or hedges near bends or roads, limiting the access to roads, imposing a building line on vacant property, or requiring off-street loading and unloading of business or industrial property users. If the planning scheme contained one of those exclusions of compensation, the government on review had to find it proper, reasonable, and expedient, having regard to local circumstances, the nature, situation and existing development of the land and neighboring land and the interests of all persons.

The 1932 Act also provided for compensation in three situations *before* the plan took effect. One, already mentioned, was for the injurious affection of preservation orders. Second, if a decision to prepare a plan was revoked and a person was injuriously affected because of denial of a permission to develop during the interim or permission was conditioned and the person appealed the decision and was not given relief, compensation would be payable. Similarly if a developer complied with any conditions imposed during the plan preparation stage and the expenditure was rendered abortive by the decision not to prepare a plan, compensation was payable.

Third, if permission was conditioned and the condition upheld on appeal, the conditions were imposed in anticipation of the reservation of land for a public purpose or the execution of the works under the scheme, the developer complied with the conditions, and the reservation or works did not appear on the plan, damages were recoverable.

(2) Australia

The English compensation regulation system was abandoned in England in 1947, but by that time it had been adopted in most of the Australian states. When comprehensive town planning first came to New South Wales, the Local Government Town and Country Planning Amendment Act, 1945 [28] also contained provisions for compensation based largely on the 1932 English Act and the New Zealand Planning Act, which in turn had been based on the English model. As finally adopted, an important addition was that no compensation was paid for provisions in a scheme prohibiting or restricting the use of land unless the applicant established that some specified use of the land which was prohibited or restricted by the prescribed scheme was practicable immediately before the prescribed scheme came into operation and that there was at that time a demand for such use.

Whatever hopes landowners had for compensation for regulation and whatever the New South Wales government had in mind, the courts were not sympathetic:

> There are only three reported claims for compensation for injurious affection: all, for different reasons, failed. They are Bingham v.

___

28. No. 21, now Local Government Act, 1919.

Cumberland County Council (1954) 20 L.G.R. (N.S.W.) [1], Whittle v. Cumberland County Council (1955) 20 L.G.R. (N.S.W.) 272; Baker v. Cumberland County Council (1956) 1 L.G.R. 321. It is understood that in fact these have been the only claims determined by a court.[29]

The plaintiff in Bingham failed because it was concluded that benefits received offset damages. In Whittle the claimant lost because of a failure to file a claim on time. Both dealt with restrictions looking forward to acquisition. Baker, however, dealt with a mere regulation.

The property of the plaintiff landowner in Baker consisted of three acres improved with a cottage residence. Its use was restricted by the planning scheme to greenbelt purposes. As a result, buildings could not be erected or used for the purpose of dwelling houses without consent. The landowner claimed that prior to the application of the planning scheme, it would have been practicable to use the property for such development and claimed £650 in compensation.

The County of Cumberland argued that compensation was not payable for "zoning" as distinguished from "reservation." The judge disagreed, but focused on the good-neighbor exception. The statute provided that: "Compensation shall not be payable in the following cases: . . . (c) where an estate or interest in land is affected by any provision of the prescribed scheme which prescribes the space about buildings or limits the number of buildings to be erected, or prescribes the height, bulk, floor space, use, design, external appearance, or character of building . . . ."[30]

The judge held that the restriction prescribed the "use" of buildings. New buildings in the greenbelt could not be erected or used for the purpose of dwelling houses without consent. The restriction also prescribed the "character" of buildings: "A prescription of 'character' of buildings is . . . one which prescribes the nature, or sort, of buildings, in respects other than those of 'height,' etc., which are specifically enumerated. For example . . . a provision that . . . houses, churches, and schools may be erected, but shops and factories shall not, would be a prescription of the 'character' of buildings."[31]

While Cabinet meetings indicated that the authors of the language felt that the use and character of buildings provision had a rather narrower meaning, namely to allow decisions on building applications (permits) without drawing compensation, the Court had in effect held zoning noncompensable unless it prohibited a use of land in some way unrelated to any buildings.

These three cases were sufficient to convince landowners and lawyers that the courts would interpret the compensation provisions very narrowly. It also became widely understood at the time that if a

29. M. Wilcox, supra note 16, at 278.   31. (1956) 1 L.G.R.A. 321, 331.

30. Local Government Act, 1919, § 342AC(2).

case ever arose where compensation in substantial amount was payable, the legislature would act to close off that right.

Parliament removed any remaining doubt about whether compensation would be payable for zoning with a 1963 amendment to the planning act which excluded compensation for injurious affection flowing from any provision which specifies "the purposes for which land may be used or which prohibits, restricts, or regulates the use of land . . . ."[32] Cabinet minutes explain that this amendment was intended to

> state in clearer terms that compensation shall not be payable for zoning of land for any purpose other than a public purpose (this conforms with the judgment of the Land and Valuation Court in the case of Baker v. Cumberland County Council) nor for a restriction which could be lawfully imposed (other than on a planning scheme) without incurring any liability.[33]

In 1944, comprehensive planning legislation was first enacted in Victoria, the second most populous Australian state. Just as in New South Wales, the expectation apparently was that most injurious affection from interim development controls of planning schemes would be compensable.[34]

In the Town and Country Planning Act, 1954, however, while

> the superficial form of the legislation was not changed . . . the real emphasis was changed completely. Compensation was now provided for any loss or damage suffered . . . Loss or damage may indeed prove to be less extensive than "prejudicial affection" . . . . [T]here was a complete destruction of all compensation payable under . . . interim . . . control.[35]

The present Town and Country Planning legislation still begins with a broad provision for compensation: "Subject to this Act compensation shall be payable . . . for loss or damage suffered by or as a result of the operation of any interim development order or of any planning scheme under this Act . . . ."[36] But the exceptions are such that compensation is not available as of right now in very many situations. While one commentator indicates that local authorities could not be generous and pay compensation even if they wished to because they "have no general power to pay compensation," the law does provide that permits can contain compensation provisions.[37]

Compensation is payable in the following situations: (1) A local authority makes an error in its certificate indicating the permitted use

32. Local Government Act, 1919, § 342AC(h) added by Act No. 59, 1963, s. 72.

33. Local Government (Town and Country Planning) Amendment Act, 1962.

34. Phillips, Compensation and Planning in Victoria, 2 Melbourne U.L.Rev. 331, 344 (1960).

35. Id. at 345.

36. The Town and Country Planning Act, 1961, No. 6849, incorporating amendments up to Act No. 8380.

37. K. Gifford, supra note 23, at 352.

of property, which error leads to loss or damage by reason of operation of an interim development order or planning scheme. (2) The revocation of a permit to the extent that such revocation leads to damage from expenditures or liability therefore rendered abortive. (3) An authority forbids the continuance of a nonconforming use or requires the removal or substantial alteration of buildings or works lawfully in existence before the planning scheme takes effect.

Queensland is the third most populous Australian state. Its first comprehensive planning legislation dates back to 1934 and was based on the English 1909–32 Act model.[38] The legislation was basically revised in 1966, at which time compensation provisions were largely based on the 1945 New South Wales legislation, which, in turn, had been based on the English 1932 Act. Brisbane, Queensland's largest city, has had special town planning legislation applicable to it since 1952, but the compensation provisions are basically similar to those in the 1966 statute.[39]

Western Australia also inherited the English system. A 1951 report noted that "a satisfactory and workable solution to the joint problem of compensation and betterment is of the utmost importance if any real planning and implementation are to be achieved."[40] A 1955 report became the basis for the first town planning scheme in Western Australia.[41] Where a regulation prohibited all beneficial uses, such as in an open space zone, the report recommended that the land be publicly acquired, and that the plan show the property as being reserved rather than as zoned.

(3) New Zealand

New Zealand's Town and Country Planning Act 1953,[42] has compensation provisions that retain the English 1909–32 Act pedigree. The general rule is that compensation is payable for injurious affection resulting from the operation of any district planning scheme or of any refusal of a permit on the ground that development would be detrimental to the plan in preparation. The amount of compensation paid is equal to what would be paid if the restrictions imposed were a taking of a corresponding interest. Consequently, if the restriction is only temporary, the damages paid are only for the temporary taking of the interest. The claim is against the unit of government which requires the restriction, not against the plan-making government.

As distinguished from some Australian and English provisions, compensation is excluded if the restriction "could have been made and

---

38. City of Macay and Other Town Planning Schemes Approval Act of 1934.

39. Now City of Brisbane Town Planning Acts, 1964–1967.

40. Honorary Royal Commission on Town Planning and Development Act Amendment Bill, Report 8 (1951).

41. G. Stephenson & J. Hepburn, Plan for the Metropolitan Region: Perth and Fremantle, Western Australia (1955).

42. 3 New Zealand Statutes 2669 (1972).

enforced without liability" under some other act. The other restriction need not actually have been made. Good neighbor restrictions are not compensable. No compensation is paid for things done in contravention of a scheme or in contravention of any interim-permit-while-planning provision. As distinguished from Australian practice, no compensation is payable merely because the district scheme shows a proposed highway, a widening of a street, or the closing of a highway, or any proposed public reserve or open space.

If compensation is paid and the restriction is later removed or lapses, the landowner must return any compensation paid under the assumption of a longer application of the restriction. As with the English and some Australian statutes, if a claim is made, the local authority can change the scheme so as to avoid compensation. It must pay the landowner's costs and any expenditures rendered nugatory that were reasonably incurred as a result of the scheme or permit refused.

There has been one significant "mere" regulation case interpreting the New Zealand statute. In Allison v. Piako County,[43] the landowner claimed compensation of £1,000 because of the county's refusal to approve a subdivision creating for small lots an existing road out of a larger parcel. The reason for the refusal was that the property was zoned for rural uses. Under Section 44(3), "compensation is payable in respect to zoning." However, Section 44(6)(b)(iii) provides that compensation for "regulating the use of buildings or land" is payable only if the refusal deprives a use where the use would not "cause an extension that is not in the economic interests of the region or locality of the subdivision into lots . . . along existing highways." The Court referred to that provision as an anti-ribbon development or anti-urban sprawl provision, violation of which is prima facie undesirable and uneconomical. Therefore compensation was denied.

(4) Canada

As indicated in the betterment discussion, many Canadian provinces adopted the English 1909 Act model. All provinces eventually abolished the compensation provisions except Manitoba which revised the provision, made it incomprehensible, but retained it in a basic revision of its planning law in 1975. On June 11, 1976, however the last vestiges of the compensation and betterment provisions surviving in Canada were wiped from the statute books.[44]

(5) Evaluations and Conclusions

If the success of the 1909 Act and its progeny provisions for compensation had to be judged in terms of the amount of compensation actually paid, the worsenment provisions must be regarded as failures. Moreover, it is clear that both the courts by interpretation and the legislatures by amendment have narrowed rather than broadened the provisions over the years.

---

43. 1957 N.Z.L.R. 1214. **44.** 1976 S. Man. 1976 c. 51 § 388.

Why did the provisions fail to actually result in payment? There are many reasons. (1) In the courts, compensation for restrictions was novel and hence narrowly construed. This attitude was abetted by (2) fear that payments in even the obvious situations would be precedent for much broader recovery. In addition, there was (3) failure to recapture betterment so no money was "available" to fund worsenment payments. (4) There were few adoptions of planning schemes providing for compensation payments, (5) absence of damage in those days when plans were weak and growth was good, and (6) enormity of procedural hurdles that must be overcome in order to win an inadequate and uncertain victory. The lines between compensation and noncompensation not being clearly defined, (7) governments used noncompensatory alternatives. (8) In Australia, Canada and New Zealand the provisions were imports not related to the needs of a sparsely populated landscape. (9) Finally, the requirement of full compensation did not seem proper to some in the face of the "floating value" problem.

The Uthwatt Committee reviewed the compensation for planning provisions under the English 1932 Act.[45] It noted that since no compensation was payable for density limits, but was payable for forbidding building altogether, density limitations were being drafted to in effect preclude development. It also noted the inconsistency of compensating for the newer planning restrictions but not the older road restrictions.

Noting that the alternatives were either full or no compensation, the Committee believed it would be desirable to permit partial compensation to be paid. That was ultimately not recommended, however, because of the burdensome duties exercising such discretion would impose on the national government.

Rather than a list of restrictions which the plan could exclude from compensation, to be approved on review by the national government after considering local circumstances, Uthwatt recommended that local authorities be given general power to exclude compensation. It also recommended that the approval on review be based on regard for national as well as local circumstances.

In general, the main lesson to be learned from the attempts to specify by statute when restrictions are compensable and when they are not is that the statutes have failed to draw lines regarded as workable and fair. One might be tempted, then, to conclude either that all should be compensable in full, or that none should be, or that partial compensation should be paid in all cases. Perhaps the American pragmatic balancing approach is better than any specification by statute approach.

England's 1909 Act is surely the closest precedent for the dominant thought behind windfalls for wipeouts, namely, that windfalls should be

45. Ministry of Works and Planning, Expert Committee on Compensation and Betterment [Uthwatt Report], Final Report, Cmd. No. 6386 (1942).

recaptured, at least in part. Considered separately, both ideas were busts. Considered together, betterment for worsement was a bust.

Whether society would be interested in adopting and implementing an English 1909-type Act modified to eliminate its technical defects is open to doubt. It is interesting to note that the quantum increase these days in the harshness of regulation which has led to pleas for compensation in America had a parallel in 1909. Then, too, compensation was provided because land-use control was perceived to be a harsh new regulation. Then, too, it was thought only fair that if worsement was to be mitigated, it should be paid by recapturing from those who earned betterment.

It all seems so logical and fair. But the 1909 Act failed, perhaps because there was no will to recapture betterment and that led to a failure to compensate. The experience suggests a dilemma. Neither windfalls will be recaptured nor wipeouts mitigated unless both steps are taken at the same time. Yet, while political forces for recapturing windfalls are strong and political forces for mitigating wipeouts are strong neither is strong enough to pull its own goal by way of implemented legislation. On the other hand, both groups lose interest if both issues are addressed simultaneously.

WESTLAW REFERENCES

aaron /s "los angeles" /p compens!

increas! /p recaptur! /p property /p tax

(B) Worsement Litigation

    (1) England

pete /s united /s states /p compens!

regulat! ordinance zon! /p reasonable! /p height /p require*
    requirement requiring /p compens!

property /p nonconforming /p compens!

---

§ 11.5   Zoning by Special Assessment Financed Eminent Domain (ZSAFED) [1]

Nirvana is a mythical unspoiled island located just offshore of an expanding metropolis. Although it was zoned many years ago for single family residences, the island was never developed. The owners have recently announced plans to build on their property. Conservationists oppose the development, but the government does not have enough money to purchase the island.

A politically acceptable compromise would be to develop only the south half of the island, preserving the north half for conservation

§ 11.5

1. This section is extracted from Hagman, Zoning by Special Assessment Financed Eminent Domain (ZSAFED), 28 U.Fla.L.Rev. 655 (1976). Permission has been granted by the University of Florida Law Review. Comparable material can also be found in chapter 22 of Windfalls for Wipeouts: Land Value Capture and Compensation (D. Hagman & D. Misczynski, eds. 1978).

purposes. Accordingly, experts of zoning by special assessment financed eminent domain (ZSAFED) propose a plan to implement the compromise.[2] While the south half would be upzoned to multiple family use, the north half would be downzoned to conservation and recreation uses. The owners of the north half would be injured to the extent that their property has lost value. Under ZSAFED, damages would be paid to these owners since the right to develop the north half would be treated as if it had been taken by eminent domain. Owners of the south half would enjoy an increase in the value of their property from the change in zoning not only because the supply of property in competition for sales would shrink but also because the south half could be developed more intensively. Therefore, a special assessment would be levied against the south half property, capturing the windfall to finance payment for damages to the north half.

History of ZSAFED

ZSAFED was invented in 1893 by residents of Gladstone Boulevard in Kansas City who were attempting to preserve the residential character of their street.[3] The Gladstonians petitioned to exclude business uses within 159 feet of the boulevard and offered to pay damages or assess benefits to affected property owners. Perhaps since experts opined that boulevard property would appreciate from the restriction and no damages would be paid, some disgruntled property owners brought suit seeking to invalidate the implementing ordinance. The basic question was whether the restriction constituted a taking for public use. The court had no trouble construing this restriction as a taking and found, in addition, that the city charter, which permitted the use of eminent domain for public purposes, was sufficient to authorize the ordinance.

ZSAFED did not surface in the Missouri appellate courts again until 1966.[4] Coleman Highlands, a residential area in Kansas City, had been restricted to single family dwellings. Most of the houses contained 1 to 14 rooms and were occupied by families with children. Some houses located along a major thoroughfare had been converted to apartment units. Recalling the 1893 ordinance, the vast majority of Coleman Highlands residents asked for the applications of ZSAFED, and it was instituted.

---

2. For a discussion of alternative plans, see Carmichael, Transferable Development Rights as a Basis for Land Use Control, 2 Fla.St.U.L.Rev. 35 (1975); Costonis, Development Rights Transfer: An Exploratory Essay, 83 Yale L.J. 75 (1973); Haik, Police Power Versus Condemnation, 7 Nat.Resources L. 21 (1974); Marcus, Mandatory Development Rights Transfer and the Taking Clause: The Case of Manhattan's Tudor City Parks, 24 Buff.L.Rev. 77 (1974); Rose, Transfer of Development Rights: A Preview of an Expanding Concept, 3 Real

Estate L.J. 330 (1975); Rose, Proposal for the Separation and Marketability of Development Rights as a Technique to Preserve Open Space, 2 Real Estate L.J. 635 (1974); Note, Compensable Regulations: Outline of a New Land Use Planning Tool, 10 Willamette L.J. 451 (1974).

3. Kansas City v. Liebi, 298 Mo. 569, 252 S.W. 404 (1923).

4. Kindle v. Kansas City, 401 S.W.2d 385 (Mo.1966).

The application of ZSAFED resulted in a determination of damages of $37,588.88 and an assessment for benefits of the same amount. Most of the damages were to be paid to the landowners of apartment units located along the thoroughfare. These landowners, the primary group unhappy with the imposition of ZSAFED to enable the single family restriction to be enforced, attacked the ordinance in court.[5] Given the earlier judicial decision upholding restriction under ZSAFED,[6] proponents of the ordinance expected no trouble. However, the Missouri Supreme Court, wanting more facts, sent the matter back to the trial court for a determination of whether the ordinance was passed primarily for public or for private benefit.[7] When the case returned to the supreme court,[8] ZSAFED was sustained; the court applauded this zoning technique for its usefulness in preserving a residential neighborhood and for its method of compensating landowners for any demonstrably substantial damages that were suffered.[9] The court regarded the earlier decision as precedent, despite the fact that in the earlier case the character of property along a public street had been preserved, whereas in this decision the court sustained the use of ZSAFED to preserve a sizeable subdivision for residential use.[10]

In 1912, some residents of Minneapolis desired to live in areas undisturbed by apartment and commercial use. The city council met this demand by precluding the erection of commercial buildings and apartment houses over two and one-half stories on the exclusive Dupont Avenue South.[11] When questions were raised about the legality of a city's imposing such a restriction, the state legislature supplied the necessary authority.[12] Thus, zoning was instituted in Minnesota, and on this basis the Minneapolis building inspector began denying building permits for apartment buildings. The Minnesota courts, however, concluded that zoning was not a proper exercise of the police power.[13] In response to the invalidation of their authority, planners felt that

5. Id.

6. Kansas City v. Liebi, 298 Mo. 569, 252 S.W. 404 (1923).

7. Kindle v. Kansas City, 401 S.W.2d 385, 388 (Mo.1966).

8. Kansas City v. Kindle, 446 S.W.2d 807 (Mo.1969).

9. Id. at 816.

10. Opponents of ZSAFED in Kindle attempted to distinguish Liebi on the basis that ZSAFED had been used previously to protect the environs of a public project rather than to preserve the value of private property. Id. at 816–17. See also United States v. Gettysburg Elec. Ry. Co., 160 U.S. 668, 16 S.Ct. 427, 40 L.Ed. 576 (1896); Attorney Gen. v. Williams, 174 Mass. 476, 55 N.E. 77 (1899); Bunyan v. Commissioners, 167 App.Div. 457, 153 N.Y.S. 622 (1915).

Kindle did not clearly resolve the issue of the legitimacy of converted uses. The 1923 and 1943 restrictions were apparently of questionable validity so that zoning the property for single family development in 1963 under the police power would leave these uses as vested nonconforming uses. If the uses had been established illegally, of course, it would have been possible to make them conform to single family zoning under the police power.

11. 38 Minneapolis Council Proceedings 1154 (1912).

12. Ch. 98, § 1, [1913] Minn.Laws 102; Ch. 420, §§ 1–4, [1913] Minn.Laws 618.

13. State ex rel. Roerig v. Minneapolis, 136 Minn. 479, 162 N.W. 477 (1917); State ex rel. Lachtman v. Houghton, 134 Minn. 226, 158 N.W. 1017 (1916).

payment of compensation for the taking of the right to develop for apartment and commercial use would overcome constitutional objections. This theory was based on cases that had upheld restriction on the right to develop if compensation was paid.[14] Therefore, "in great haste and with a minimum of consultation . . . ," [15] ZSAFED came to Minnesota, authorized by state statute.[16]

The Act, which applied to Minneapolis, St. Paul, and Duluth, permitted a city council to create restricted residential districts on petition of 50 percent of the owners of real estate in an area. The city was given the power of eminent domain to acquire the right to develop for anything but residential purposes. After notice to the record title holder of the property, a visit to the property, and a hearing, appointed appraisers determined the amount of damages to each parcel from the taking. They also assessed benefits in the district. These benefits were offset against damages, leaving a net damage or net benefit to each parcel. Net benefits were specifically assessed, although the total benefits assessed in the district could not exceed the total amount of damages plus costs.[17] The last step of the procedure fell to the city council, which confirmed the determination of damages and benefits. The damages were "a charge upon the city . . . [while] assessments [for benefits were] . . . a lien and charge upon the respective lands until paid." [18] If there was a delay in payments, interest was charged on the award of damages.

Maps of the restricted region were filed to establish the boundaries of the districts. The county auditor received a copy of the maps and the assessments on each parcel and collected them along with general property taxes. If nonresidential buildings were thereafter erected on restricted property, the structures were declared to be nuisances. After operating under this system for a short time, cities found that appraisals were becoming expensive; thus, the statute was amended to make it clear that appraisal costs would be assessed to the area rather than paid by the city.[19]

Thwarted by the ordinance, the owner of a three story apartment house in one of the restricted residence districts challenged the ZSAFED system in court. In a three to two decision, the Minnesota supreme court decided in favor of the landowner.[20] The court noted eminent domain may be used only to acquire property for public use. "A condemnation against an apartment house is not for a public use." [21]

14. Attorney Gen. v. Williams, 174 Mass. 476, 55 N.E. 77 (1899).

15. Rockwood, The Minnesota Residence District Act of 1915, 1 Minn.L.Rev. 487, 490–91 (1917).

16. Ch. 128, [1915] Minn.Laws 180 (now Minn.Stat. § 462.12–.17).

17. In re Establishment of Restricted Residence Dist., 151 Minn. 115, 186 N.W. 292 (1922).

18. Ch. 128, § 3, [1915] Minn.Laws 186.

19. Ch. 297, [1919] Minn.Laws 305.

20. State ex rel. Twin City Bldg. & Inv. Co. v. Houghton, 144 Minn. 1, 174 N.W. 885 (1919).

21. Id. at 12, 174 N.W. at 888.

The court distinguished a series of other cases that had upheld the use of regulation with compensation to preserve aesthetic vistas around public facilities.[22]

As a commentator subsequently noted, the decision "seal[ed] one avenue of progress in the general program of the improvement of city life." [23] This criticism moved the court; when the case was reargued, one judge changed his mind and ZSAFED was found to be constitutional. The new majority analogized the public utilization of ZSAFED to the implementation of a drainage district and lauded the new act on policy grounds.[24]

In another application of ZSAFED, the City of St. Paul had established a restricted residence district along Summit Avenue, a distance of some four miles. A few areas were excluded, such as an area where expensive apartment buildings already existed. Other lots had also been excluded because they were part of another proceeding, later abandoned, that was attempting to establish a separate district. In a challenge to the exclusion, the court refused to invalidate the restriction because it found no gross irrationality in the scheme.[25]

In Dexner v. Houghton,[26] the plaintiff had applied for a building permit to construct a three story apartment building, although he knew a petition was being circulated to create a restricted residential district and that the building inspector had been directed to issue no building permits in the area pending the council's decision on the matter.[27] The apparent goal of the application was to increase the plaintiff's damages when the residential district was later created. His suit for the permit was unsuccessful. The court analogized the situation to one in which a property owner, who has notice of a proposed taking, builds a structure on the property in an attempt to increase the condemnation award.[28] While ideally the commencement of an eminent domain action and the payment of compensation should be concurrent, the court indicated that concurrence of these two events is a practical impossibility.[29] A temporary deprivation of the building permit does the landowner no harm. If the proceedings move reasonably expeditiously, the city may properly refuse the permit and award damages in due course.

Perhaps ZSAFED's failure to provide for a change in established restrictions had been an oversight. Alternatively, given the static

22. United States v. Gettysburg Elec. Ry. Co., 160 U.S. 668, 16 S.Ct. 427, 40 L.Ed. 576 (1896); Attorney Gen. v. Williams, 174 Mass. 476, 55 N.E. 77 (1899); Bunyan v. Commissioners, 167 A.D. 457, 153 N.Y.S. 622 (1915); In re New York, 57 App.Div. 166, 68 N.Y.S. 196 (1901).

23. Comment, The Failure of the Minnesota Residence District Act, 4 Minn.L. Rev. 50 (1919).

24. State ex rel. Twin City Bldg. & Inv. Co. v. Houghton, 144 Minn. 1, 19–20, 176 N.W. 159, 162 (1920).

25. In re Establishment of Restricted Residence Dist., 151 Minn. 115, 186 N.W. 292 (1922).

26. 153 Minn. 284, 190 N.W. 179 (1922).

27. Id. at 285, 190 N.W. at 180.

28. Id. at 288, 190 N.W. at 181. The court reaffirmed this position in State ex rel. Burton Inv. Co. v. Houghton, 153 Minn. 518, 190 N.W. 979 (1922).

29. 153 Minn. at 288, 190 N.W. at 181.

nature of zoning in its early days, it is possible that the drafters of the ZSAFED statute did not contemplate this need. In any event, not until 1923 did it become apparent that a means for undoing the application of ZSAFED to particular property was required. In that year, the Minnesota legislation was amended to provide that on petition of the owners of the real estate in a district, the restrictions could be removed by the city council with damages and benefits assessed as on the formation of the district.[30]

At the same time ZSAFED was being refined, zoning under the police power was becoming well-accepted and, in fact, Minneapolis had continued to zone without paying compensation. When ordinary zoning was challenged in 1925, the Minnesota supreme court upheld it, indicating a preference for zoning by exercise of the police power.

> [A]n award of damages to obtain a restricted residential district is largely theoretical, and, resulting in a possible incumbering of property with something akin to an easement, is practically objectionable. If restricted residential districts are to be established, there are substantial reasons why the result should be accomplished through the exercise of the police power.[31]

Fortunately, there had been enough districts established under ZSAFED by 1925 so that its merits could be subject to the crucible of experience. In one case, for example, a landowner in Duluth sold property by means of a contract calling for delivery of a deed without encumbrances.[32]

In State ex rel. Madsen v. Houghton,[33] a multiple dwelling building permit was denied to the owner of a lot that had been restricted under ZSAFED and subsequently zoned under the police power for multiple dwellings. Holding that ZSAFED restrictions were not eradicated when the property was zoned for multiple family housing, the court noted that a procedure for undoing the ZSAFED restrictions had been provided. The owner or his predecessors had been paid damages previously; therefore, he could not now reverse the restrictions except by persuading a sufficient number of the other owners to petition the city council and to accept a possible assessment when the restriction is removed.

Securing the agreement of enough owners to petition for removal of restrictions from the entire original district is difficult. Thus, pressure

---

30. Ch. 133, [1923] Minn.Laws 142.

No use has yet been made of the authority conferred by this act [the 1923 amendment], and it is likely that a simpler and more clearly defined procedure, such as was proposed in a bill in the 1927 session of the legislature, will be necessary to produce the desired ease and flexibility of change.

Anderson, Zoning in Minnesota: Eminent Domain vs. Police Power, 16 Nat'l Mun.

Rev. 624, 629 (1927). It is not known what the proposed 1927 amendment contained, because it was never enacted.

31. State *ex rel.* Beery v. Houghton, 164 Minn. 146, 148, 204 N.W. 569, 569 (1925).

32. Summers v. Midland Co., 167 Minn. 453, 209 N.W. 323 (1926).

33. 182 Minn. 77, 233 N.W. 831 (1930).

mounted to make this release process easier. In 1931 the legislature provided that 50 percent of the owners of a portion of the original district could petition for vacation of the restrictions. This portion, however, had to be on an end of the district, an entire block, or a section of a district that is adjacent to a nonresidential district. The 1931 legislation also provided that overlapping zoning under the police power should not be considered in determining the value of property on vacation of a district. Because cities were apparently no longer willing to accept the cost of abandoned proceedings to establish districts,[34] the 1931 amendments also required petitioners to deposit their probable costs.[35]

Finally, the 1931 statute amended ZSAFED to provide for notice of the commencement of proceedings for establishment or vacation of a district to the owner and mortgage rather than only to the property tax assessee.[36] The mortgagee has an obvious interest in having knowledge of these matters that might affect security.

ZSAFED was not amended again until 1943. This amendment permitted the city council to allow the conversion of buildings in restricted residential areas into fourplexes if the buildings had 1,000 or more square feet.[37] The constitutionality of such a change was questionable since it is clear that ZSAFED's purpose was to exclude apartment buildings from single and double residence districts. Nevertheless, it had been over 25 years since some restricted residential areas had been created, and these neighborhoods had changed. Despite this plea of changed circumstances, the court sustained an injunction against remodeling a single family dwelling in a restricted area into a four-plex. Today, there are still ZSAFED districts in Minnesota, some of which date back approximately 60 years.

Modernizing ZSAFED

ZSAFED was originally devised because zoning without compensation was thought to be constitutionally impermissible. The courts have since allowed governments to severely restrict usage of property through zoning under the police power without paying compensation.[38] Modern ZSAFED would be implemented for moral rather than legal reasons. First, a person whose property loses value because of government regulation would be entitled to receive payment for the damages as in an eminent domain proceeding. Second, a person whose property increases in value solely because of regulation by government should

34. See In re Establishment of Restricted Residence Dist., 151 Minn. 115, 118, 186 N.W. 292, 293–94 (1922) (the court noted that the city would bear the costs of proceedings that were abandoned before a district was established).

35. Ch. 290, § 2, [1931] Minn.Laws 339. The costs of vacating a district were also likely covered by this provision, which makes ZSAFED even more stable.

36. Ch. 290, § 3, [1931] Minn.Laws 339.

37. Ch. 246, [1943] Minn.Laws 348–50.

38. See, e.g., Consolidated Rock Prods. v. Los Angeles, 57 Cal.2d 515, 20 Cal.Rptr. 638, 370 P.2d 342 (1962), appeal dismissed 371 U.S. 36, 83 S.Ct. 145, 9 L.Ed.2d 112 (1962).

not be allowed to keep the unearned profit. To effectuate these goals in the 1980's, ZSAFED must be modernized.

The fact that ZSAFED, as originally practiced, involved appraisals by specially appointed persons increased administrative costs. Tax assessors could do appraisals in a modern system, which would avoid duplication of costs. The assessor's present job is to measure the market value of property and to reassess property affected in value by a rezoning. ZSAFED would require only a computation of the change in value.

It would not be desirable to attempt to compensate 100 percent of damages or to recapture 100 percent of benefits because assessments are incapable of precisely reflecting true value. Furthermore, total elimination of risk could lead to stagnation and lack of change. ZSAFED should only minimize risk by moderating wipeout and windfall rather than excluding them entirely. Paying damages or assessing benefits of 50 to 75 percent of the change in value would move in the direction of equity without eliminating the risk inherent in a free market system. Similarly, slight changes in value should be ignored. Before ZSAFED would operate, a substantial change—for example more than ten percent—should occur.

In most instances benefits will equal damages. If property is down-zoned, other property must become more valuable because competitive supply is reduced. ZSAFED should recapture benefit even though it is more than is necessary to pay damages from a particular change in zoning. Recapturing all ascertainable benefits would provide funds to pay damages in those instances when damages but not benefits can be determined. In addition, one goal of a modern ZSAFED should be to recapture windfalls. Sharing the benefit is the price of insurance against damage; moreover, planning may actually create wealth by imposing order.[39] Benefits should exceed damages in a community in which the planning is continually better; thus, the ZSAFED fund might show a profit. In such a case, the excess fund could be applied toward general government functions.

Whereas zoning under the police power has often been too easily changed, ZSAFED was almost impossible to change in Minnesota, but extreme rigidity is as undesirable as frequent rezoning. Under modern ZSAFED, the regulating government, landowners, or voter residents in the area should be permitted to initiate rezoning. Expanding the opportunity for change would not result in the upzoning pressures traditional to zoning under the police power since recapture eliminates much of the landowner's incentive to seek rezoning to a more intensive use.

---

39. Chicago School economists argue to the contrary that wealth generation is greatest under free market conditions and that government control either dampens the increase or causes net loss. B. Siegan, Land Use Without Zoning (1972) (author makes the most elaborate case for the Chicago School in the context of land use).

Increasingly, it is no longer the case that zoning is the only control of land use. Local governments are shifting to permit systems of control, and control may also be exercised by one or more regional, state, or federal authorities. Therefore, a rezoning alone does not trigger realization of benefit or reception of damage. ZSAFED should be expanded to accommodate the changing kinds of controls on land use. Developers must usually obtain various permits before initiating a new project. This system of multiple permits from different levels of government complicates matters. A benefit is measured as the change in values before and after, but before and after *what* is the crucial issue. If, for example, five permissions are required before development can proceed, does the assessor make a determination of assessable benefits as each is obtained? Alternatively, since the project is not viable until all permits are obtained, should the "before" value be calculated as if no permit had been obtained and the "after" value as if all permits had been obtained?

The problem is a muddle of the first order. Perhaps the solution is as follows: if there is a governmental activity after which actual development would be possible when it was not previously possible, that activity is the event that triggers the determination of benefit or damage. The solution has problems, particularly if ZSAFED is built on an assessment system because the market will anticipate the benefit-damage triggering activity. When the first permit is issued, value may rise a bit; on the second permit value would increase a little more, and so on. The increase in value between the fourth and fifth permits may also be small, but under the suggested solution, the assessor will have to determine benefit or damage as if all five permits had been obtained at once.

The manner of multiple controls raises one other issue. Under the 1931 amendment to the Minnesota ZSAFED statute, other regulations were to be disregarded for the calculation of benefits and damages when ZSAFED was undone. This would not be the case under modernized ZSAFED since all land use controls would carry compensation and recapture incidents.

Benefits and damages from governmental development projects should also be included in a modernized ZSAFED. For example, if a government built a new causeway to Nirvana, making it more accessible, the benefits should be recaptured in part. ZSAFED would thus tax the cost of improvements in the same way as traditional special assessments [40] but with the difference that large projects would be included and recapture would not be limited to costs. Similarly, if the government built a regional garbage dump on the north end of Nirva-

---

40. For a more detailed discussion of the history of special assessments, see Windfalls for Wipeouts? Land Value Gains and Losses from Planning and a Catalog of Methods for Redistributing Them, ch. 13 (D. Hagman & D. Misczynski, eds. 1978).

na, owners of property on the south end could be compensated by a modernized ZSAFED.

Under ancient ZSAFED, each restricted residential district was a distinct entity. Because damages from restricting property to low density residential use were often offset to each landowner by the benefit of having neighboring property limited to residential use, little money was exchanged within a district and none could exchange hands outside the district for the law did not cover extradistrict benefits and damages. Under modern ZSAFED, there would be no districts. Damages and benefits would be identified by changes in value wherever they occurred. For example, if property was rezoned commercial for a shopping center and resulted in more than a 10 percent increase in value, a special assessment would be levied. Neighboring property might increase or decrease in value, and ZSAFED would assess benefits and pay damages accordingly. If the damage showed up far from the rezoned site, such as the location of an older shopping center, ZSAFED would pay compensation.

Separate accounting for the damage caused and the benefit resulting from each change would add an unnecessary complication. Rather, when an assessment is made, payments would go into a common fund; damage payments would be made from the same fund. Revolving funds are customarily used for local improvements that are funded partially by special assessments and partially by government. This obviates the need to issue bonds.

It may be necessary, for constitutional reasons, to pay damages when the damaging event occurs, but it will not be possible to recapture all benefits immediately. Suppose, for example, the property of a single family homeowner increases in value from $20,000 to $40,000 as the result of a rezoning. The assessment would be $10,000, and a lien would be imposed immediately on the property for that amount. For political reasons, however, immediate payment could not be exacted. The conventional practice of accepting payments for special assessments by installments would be followed. For example, the assessee might be given 18 years to pay at $500 per year plus interest. The amount would be added to the property tax bill and collected in the same way as other special assessments.

If damage payments also could be paid by installment, then it would not be necessary to issue bonds to make such payments before the ZSAFED revolving fund had been established. Damage payments could be used to offset property taxes. In actuality, while some property may remain unaffected, other land is likely to be buffeted by damages and benefits frequently, each canceling the other in a frenzy of activity that only computers could reconcile.

The administration of ZSAFED, although complicated, is essentially the same as conventional property tax and special assessment practices. Moreover, modern ZSAFED could replace many bodies of damage mitigation law that result in high administrative costs, such as nuisance, damages in eminent domain to severed parcels, inverse condemnation for regulatory and planning blight, and invalidation of land use regulation under the "taking" clause. It could also supplement or replace special assessments for particular projects, exactions on development permissions, and impact taxes.

It is not yet clear that ZSAFED is an answer to windfalls for wipeouts problems. However, precedent certainly has established that ZSAFED is valid, and this precedent should continue as ZSAFED is modernized. Armed with early experience and improved by the theory developed in connection with transferable development rights research, ZSAFED may well have a future as well as a past.

 WESTLAW REFERENCES
History of ZSAFED
liebi kindle /s "kansas city" & zon!
(roerig /s minneapolis) (lachtman /s houghton)
"eminent domain" /p acqui! /p property /p "public use" /p
   apartment
exclu! restrict! /p district /p irrational! /p zon!

Modernizing ZSAFED
consolidated /s rock /s products /s "los angeles" /p
   compens! /p "police power"
assess! /p "market value" /p land (real +2 estate property)
   /p rezon!
downzon! & (hfh /s superior /s court /s "los angeles")
   ("san diego" /s gas /s electric /s city) (harris /s trust
   /s savings /s bank /s duggan)
vot! /p residen! /p initiat! /p rezon!
local /s govern! /s permit /s control! /s develop!
land /s use /s calculat! /s recaptur! compensat!
port /s "new york" /s authority & calculat!
assess! damage /p payment /p revolving common +1 fund
   /p improv!
constitution! /p pay paying payment paid /p damag! /p event
   /p occur! /p land (real +2 estate property)
assess! benefit! & (gamma /s realty /s "miami beach") (crowe
   /s sparata) (tocci /s "three forks")

§ 11.6 Transferable Development Rights (TDR's)

Santa Bella is a 100 acre mythical island located one-fourth mile off the coast. In 1980 the owner divided the island into 100 one acre parcels and sold them to 100 purchasers. The entire island is zoned single family residential but no development has yet occurred.

The County Commission having jurisdiction over the island is in the process of amending its comprehensive plan and rewriting its development code. In the course of this process, it is brought to the attention of the County Growth Management Department that the northern one-half of the island is environmentally sensitive land which is now a haven for birds and other wildlife. The southern one-half of the island is suitable for residential development and has a carrying capacity [1] of approximately two residential units per acre. The county planners have asked the county attorney how and if they can designate the northern one-half of the island in the County Comprehensive Plan as open space (undevelopable) land and rezone accordingly.

The county attorney, being well-versed in land use control techniques, will first warn his colleagues in the planning department that the fifty lot owners of the northern part of Santa Bella would probably have a good argument that their land has been taken without compensation since the economic value of open space in such a situation may well be zero.

After scaring the planners with a long citation of taking issue cases,[2] the county attorney should then mention that Santa Bella seems the ideal locale for the establishment of a transferable development rights (TDR) program.

The TDR concept seems to have been so named in the United States in 1961 and since then has been frequently written and commented on in law reviews, casebooks, and CLE programs.[3] Several such programs have been established and litigated so that there is now a small but impressive body of caselaw on point including the 1978 decision of the Supreme Court of the United States in Penn Central Transportation Co. v. New York.[4]

The conceptual key to TDR's is the notion established in England that the development rights in the bundle of sticks representing land ownership can be separated from the other ownership rights and made transferable to others.[5]

Another way to view the principle behind the concept is to reason that when an area of land owned by two or more individuals or entities is brought under a land use control entity or program, the development potential of all tracts is pooled. In other words, the development

§ 11.6

1. The carrying capacity concept is discussed in § 9.9.

2. See supra § 10.7.

3. See generally, Marcus, A Comparative Look at TDR, Subdivision Exactions and Zoning as Environmental Preservation Panaceas, 13 Land Use & Env.L.Rev. 231 (1982); Richards, Transferable Development Rights: Corrective, Catastrophe, or Curiosity? 12 Real Estate L.J. 26 (1983); Pedowitz, TDR (The Demise of the Fee Simple), 19 Real Prop., Prob. & Trust J. 604 (1984); Boast, Transferable Development Rights (New Zealand) 1984 N.Z.L.J. 339; Carmichael, Transferable Development Rights as a Basis for Land Use Control, 2 Fla.St.U.L.Rev. 35 (1974); Spagna, Transfer of Development Rights: The Collier County Experience, 6 Fla.Env. & Ur-

ban Issues 7 (1979); Pedowitz, Transfer of Air Rights and Development Rights, 9 Real Property, Probate and Trust J. 183 (1974); Schnidman, Transfer of Development Rights: Questions and Bibliograph, III Management and Control of Growth 127 (1975); Bozung, Transfer of Development Rights: Compensation for Owners of Restricted Property, 6 Zoning & Plan L.Rep. 129 (1983); Delaney, Kommiers & Gordon, TDR Redux: A Second Generation of Practical Legal Concerns, 15 Urb.Law 593 (1983); Note, Transferable Development Rights: An Innovative Concept Faces an Uncertain Future in South Florida, 8 Nova L.J. 201 (1983).

4. 438 U.S. 104, 99 S.Ct. 2646, 57 L.Ed. 2d 631 (1978), rehearing denied 439 U.S. 883, 99 S.Ct. 226, 58 L.Ed.2d 198 (1978).

5. See supra § 11.4.

potential of each tract is subordinated to and merged with that of all other tracts within the area. The development potential in the pool is then allocated among the individual tracts within the area as part of the planning and land use control process. The allocation of development rights is made on an equal or equitable basis to the land owners even though some land in the area may not be allowed development permission or even though some parcels of land will be permitted a greater density of development (say five units per acre) than others (say one unit per five acres). Since the development rights were allocated equally to all owners in the area, those whose land was designated for no or low density development might have more development rights than they could use on their land while other owners would need more rights than they received in order to develop their land to the full extent possible under the local development or zoning code.

If one takes an Adam Smith view of the world, the local market place would soon be crowded by landowners seeking to sell the rights they couldn't use and they would quickly encounter landowners seeking to buy the additional rights they needed. Although government land use regulation brought about this scenario, it would be solved by private market arrangements.

Returning to Santa Bella, let us see how the TDR concept might operate. Remember that there are 100 one-acre parcels but that the land use control authorities only want to allow development of the 50 parcels which constitute the southern one-half of the island. Also remember, that the land use control authorities will permit two dwelling units per parcel (i.e. per acre). If the land use control authorities simply sent a letter to the northern landowners saying "sorry, but you can not develop your land" there would almost certainly be a taking case which the county might well lose. However, the situation is arguably quite different if the county includes in the letter a stock-like certificate which is titled "One Transferable Development Right" and reads "Bearer hereof has the development permission to build one single-family dwelling on an appropriately zoned parcel." Of course a letter must also be sent to each southern lot owner saying that each of the fifty southern lots can now have two single family dwellings built on them provided that the land owner attaches one TDR certificate for each dwelling when he applies for a building permit. The southern owners will receive one TDR certificate per parcel in the mail but will rush to the market place to buy an additional one from a northern landowner.

What will be the end result? Everyone will be happy and/or prosperous. The County authorities (and of course their electorate) will be happy because the northern half of Santa Bella has been preserved for birds and other wildlife. The taxpayers are happy because the wildlife sanctuary didn't require any expenditure of public funds (except planning costs). The northern lot owners are perhaps not happy (they may have wanted to build their dream cottages on their land) but they are at least prosperous in the sense that they suffered no wipeout of economic value due to the stringent land use regulation since they were "compensated" by the money they received from selling TDR certificates to the southern landowners. They also still own their land and can use it for sunbathing, picnicking, and, of course, bird watching. The southern landowners are happy because they have been able to build and therefore make a profit from building two houses rather than one.

If you think the Santa Bella situation sounds a bit too ideal, you are right. The logistics of setting up such a system can be staggering. Difficult formulas are required to get the correct ratio between restricted land (sending areas) and the land on which the TDR can be used (receiving areas). Administration of the system and regulation of the trading of the certificates also provide many interesting challenges.[6]

Judicial scrutiny has focused primarily on whether or not TDR's constitute compensation or an acceptable substitute for compensation. The leading case is Penn Central Transportation Co. v. New York.[7] It, and other relevant cases are discussed in detail elsewhere in this Hornbook[8] and it should be remembered that although there is very pro TDR language in the Penn Central decision, it can be considered dicta since the court found no taking for which compensation was due.

In the final analysis, the judicial acceptability of TDR's seems dependent upon the creating local government's ability to demonstrate monetary value for them. The economic analysis set forth below is designed to give attorneys and students the concepts for determining economic value.[9]

A Model of TDR Value Determination

A TDR allows its owner to build something or more of something on a designated parcel of land than the normal development regulations would allow. This is typically known as increasing density. Thus, a TDR allows an increased density. The value of the TDR would then be the marginal revenue product of an increase in density.

Given that the value of a TDR will be the marginal revenue product of increasing density on a particular parcel of land, the economics can be easily worked out.

6. See Schnidman, Transferable Development Rights (TDR), Windfalls for Wipeouts, ch. 23. (D. Hagman & D. Misczynski eds. 1978); Nicholas, Transferable Development Rights in Dade and Palm Beach Counties, Florida, in Transferable Development Rights: The Perspective of a Decade (Schnidman & Roberts eds.1982).

7. Note 4 supra. See also, City of Hollywood v. Hollywood Inc., 432 So.2d 1332 (4th D.C.A.1983), petition for review denied, 441 So.2d 632 (1982); Matlack v.

Board of Chosen Freeholders, 199 N.J. Super. 236, 466 A.2d 83 (1982), judgment aff'd, 194 N.J.Super. 359, 476 A.2d 1262 (1984), certification denied 99 N.J. 191, 491 A.2d 693 (1984).

8. See supra § 10.7; infra § 14.9–.10.

9. The discussion which follows was prepared for the author by land economist Professor James Nicholas, Department of Urban & Regional Planning, University of Florida.

Assume:

$$R = PQ$$

where

R—revenue

P—price per unit

O—units sold

and further assume:

$$P = A-bDEN$$

where

A—price of the unit at the lowest density per acre

b—coefficient of price with respect to density

DEN—density per acre

On the cost side assume:

$$C = XQ$$

where:

C—total cost

X—cost per unit

and further assume that:

$$X = Y + zDEN$$

where:

Y—cost per unit at the lowest density per acre

z—coefficient of cost with respect to density.

Profit would then be:

$$PROFIT = Q [A-Y - (b-z) DEN].$$

If z > b then there will be an incremental profit from adding more units by means of increased density. The value of TDRs would be:

$$\delta PROFIT/\delta DEN = (z-b) dQ.$$

If it is assumed that dQ is one, then the value of the TDR is z–b.

The market dictates that the price of housing will tend to decline with respect to density per acre.[10] Additionally, construction costs will tend to decline with respect to density. Thus, there is a market inducement to increase densities until z = b. However, zoning tends to prevent this market adjustment. This zoning induced underallocation of density becomes the basis for value of TDRs. If a particular community is not underzoned then there will be little, if any, value for TDRs.

 WESTLAW REFERENCES
"transferable development rights"

10. W. Alonso, The Theory of Rent (1964).

''transferable development rights'' & (penn /s central /s transportation /s ''new york'')

A Model of TDR Value Determination

(wolpe /s poretsky) (park /s view /s heights /s ''black jack'') & zon! /p house housing /p dens!

Chapter 12

TAXATION AS A LAND USE CONTROL DEVICE

Analysis

I. INTRODUCTION

I. INTRODUCTION

§ 12.1 Introduction

The primary purpose of taxation is to raise revenues, although, as is illustrated by progressive income, gift, and estate taxes, wealth redistribution may be seen as another important purpose. In addition to these purposes, taxation has an effect upon land use decisions, though it is more often by default than by design.

363

For example, real property taxes based upon the market value of the land can cause farmers to sell farmlands which then become housing subdivisions. Federal income tax policy clearly shapes investment decisions by its differing treatment of similar transactions, or by simply reducing an individual's disposable income. Further, the emphasis or lack of emphasis on sales taxes in a jurisdiction can affect income and property values (based upon the corresponding fine tuning of the real property taxes).

In a seminal article, Professor Currier observed that taxes shape investment decisions, which by definition affect development patterns.[1] In many cases however, government can hardly be seen as carrying out a land use policy through the results achieved. In other words, with respect to influencing land use policy through taxation, government often acts by not acting.

Most purposeful land use policy is based upon the police power and, to a somewhat lesser extent, the power of eminent domain. This does not mean that taxation cannot be used to shape land use policy. It means simply that taxation is not used as frequently because its effectiveness as a land use control device is restricted by equal protection and uniformity requirements. Thus taxation lacks the flexibility and precision of the police power.[2] However, within the constraints of the conventional real property taxation and statutory changes to the traditional schemes, taxation can effectively be used to accomplish governmental land use purposes.[3]

 WESTLAW REFERENCES
farm! /p sell! sold /p house housing /p subdivi!
tax taxation taxing /p "land use" /s policy

II. PROPERTY TAXES

§ 12.2 Ad Valorem Taxation

Ad valorem taxation is a tax imposed upon the value of property.[1] In the real estate context, ad valorem taxation is simply called the "property tax." It is frequently the sole tax source of revenue for local

§ 12.1

1. See Currier, Exploring the Role of Taxation in the Land Use Planning Process, 51 Ind.L.J. 27 (1975).

2. Id. at 38–44 for a discussion of the legal framework of the taxing power.

3. See generally Kulkin, Impetus to an Industry—The Effect of Taxation of Real Estate and Real Estate Derived Income on Real Property Development in the United States, 17 Real Prop., Prob. & Tr.J. 450 (1982).

§ 12.2

1. Ad valorem literally means according to value. The scheme refers to a tax levied on property or an article of commerce in proportion to its value. See Callaway v. Overland Park, 211 Kan. 646, 508 P.2d 902 (1973).

government, since revenues from income, sales and documentary taxes often go to the state.[2]

Ad valorem taxation is sometimes referred to as a single tax system, because the value of the property includes in one tax its present use and its situs or development value.[3] The measure of value used is the market test, presumably based upon what the land would bring in a market transaction.

Because of the historically sensitive nature of land taxation in the United States, there are usually constitutional or other restrictions imposed in this area. Two of the most often seen restrictions are that land should be taxed uniformly and at fair market value.[4] Uniformity means that all property within a taxing district should be assessed at the same proportion of its market value and taxed at the same rate. Use of full fair market value assessment of all property in conjunction with a uniform rate results in uniform taxation.

Ad valorem taxes usually have their effects upon land use by default; the cost of the tax is often seen as decreasing the value of a piece of property to its owner or increasing the rent a lessee must pay.[5] The "by default" effect is also attributable to the restrictions on taxation; uniformity and fair market value assessment measures do not readily provide the flexibility necessary for purposeful land use policy implementation.

 WESTLAW REFERENCES

"ad valorem" /s valu! /s property % personal
"ad valorem" "property tax" /p sole** major! /s source /s
     money revenue fund*** /s local!
land real property /s tax taxation taxed /s constitution!
     unconstitution! /s uniform! /s "fair market value"

§ 12.3   Assessment Irregularity as a Land Use Control Device

Assessment irregularity occurs when property is not taxed at full fair market value.[1] It is a frequently used but not always sanctioned means of using taxation to control land use. Sometimes irregularity is caused by defects in the assessment process or a lag in reassessment, but also, built in pressures for underassessment brought about by the uniformity requirement often exist. For example, a community may wish to encourage farming or to discourage speculative holding of

---

2. See, e.g., West's Fla.Stat.Ann. Const. Art. 7, § 1(a); Ga. Const. Art. 9, § 4, para. 3; N.Y.—McKinney's Const. Art. VIII, § 12; N.C. Const. Art. 5, § 2(1, 2); Or. Const. Art. 11, § 11.

3. Berger, Controlling Urban Growth Via Tax Policy, 2 Urb.L. and Pol'y 295, 301 (1979).

4. See e.g., West's Ann.Cal. Const. Art. XIII, § 1; West's Fla. Const. Art. 7, §§ 2, 4; Ga. Const. Art. 7, § 1, para. 3; N.Y.—

McKinney's Const. Art. XVI, § 2; N.C. Const. Art. 5, § 2(1, 2); Or. Const. Art. 9, § 1.

5. See generally Currier, Exploring the Role of Taxation in the Land Use Planning Process, 51 Ind.L.J. 27 (1975).

§ 12.3

1. Full fair market value assessment is commonly required by constitution. See § 12.2, supra.

vacant lands. In such a case, the assessor may become a land use planner; land undervalued by the assessor can be retained in a non-intensive use while lands assessed at a higher proportion of value are taxed into more intensive uses to pay for the taxes.

Courts sometimes tolerate these departures from the law. For example, the Supreme Court in Sioux City Bridge Company v. Dakota County[2] dispensed with the required full value taxation in order to meet the test of uniformity within classes. Thus, for example, all farmland in an area could be assessed at 50 percent of market value without violating federal constitutional principles. Often, courts do not formally sanction underassessment schemes.[3] They exist in most cases primarily because courts are rarely willing to overturn an assessment, except in cases of gross abuse.[4] Further, individuals who might otherwise complain are often chilled by the fact that their own assessments, while not as advantageous as some others, are not at one-hundred percent of valuation. Finally, the community may benefit as a whole from the advantages granted by the assessor and this curtails complaints. The overall result is that underassessment may be the rule rather than the exception, despite its illegality or unconstitutionality.

WESTLAW REFERENCES

assess! /s irregular! /s tax taxed taxation taxing

sioux /s city /s bridge /s dakota /s county

(sacramento /s hickman) (switz /s middleman) /s assess! /s
    constitutional!

review! overturn! /p assess! /p gross! /p abus! & "ad
    valorem" "property tax"

§ 12.4   Tax Classifications as a Land Use Control Device

Tax classification systems have long existed as a means of providing special tax treatment for certain types of land uses. At least 48 states have adopted statutory or constitutional provisions allowing some form of differential taxation.[1] Unlike other forms of preferential treatment, which operate to reduce the taxpayer's burden through the

---

2. 260 U.S. 441, 43 S.Ct. 190, 67 L.Ed. 340 (1923).

3. Compare County of Sacramento v. Hickman, 66 Cal.2d 841, 59 Cal.Rptr. 609, 428 P.2d 593 (1967) where the court upheld a statute requiring assessment at 25 percent of full cash value though the state constitution requires full cash value assessment with Switz v. Township of Middletown, 23 N.J. 580, 130 A.2d 15 (1957) which upheld a writ of mandate to assess at the constitutionally required full value. The Switz case has stimulated the judiciary in many states to hold invalid taxes that depart from constitutional requirements of uniformity and full value assessment.

4. See generally Hellerstein, Judicial Review of Property Tax Assessments, 14 Tax L.Rev. 327 (1959) as to the court's varying degrees willingness to review assessments. See also Youngman, Defining and Valuing the Base of the Property Tax, 58 Wash.L.Rev. 713 (1983); Koeppel & Fenchel, Challenging Ad Valorem Real Property Assessments in Florida, 3 J.St. Tax'n 113 (Summer 1984).

§ 12.4

1. Dunford, A Survey of Property Tax Relief Programs for the Retention of Agricultural and Open Space Lands, 15 Gonz.L. Rev. 675 (1980).

application of credits and abatements, classification schemes confer their benefit before computation of tax liability. The process typically involves assessment based on some fraction of market value or on an entirely different valuation formula. When a uniform tax rate is applied to the lower assessed value, the result is a lower tax bill for the land owner to shoulder.

Two commonly cited examples of differential taxation are the agricultural and open land classifications. Under such a classification, farmland having a value of $100,000 may be assessed at $50,000 and industrial land of equivalent value may be assessed at $80,000. The financial benefits resulting from this treatment are obvious. Thus, to the extent that investment decisions can be shaped through tax incentives, differential assessments can be used to encourage or discourage certain types of land uses.

Two arguments are typically made to justify differential taxation.[2] The first is the farmland preservation theory. Agricultural land tax breaks save farmers money, making farming activities more profitable, and consequently giving an economic incentive to continue farming. This is especially important today where development is constantly encroaching on rural lands and driving the farmland values upward. Without the preferential assessment, many farmers might be forced to sell their land for development: one reason is that neighboring subdivisions increase the farmland's value and hence its tax liability; the other is that farmers may be unable to resist increasingly attractive offers to purchase the farmland by those wishing to develop it.

The second justification for treating farm and open lands differently is that those uses generally do not place the same demands on governmental services as urban land uses do.[3] The property is entitled to tax breaks because otherwise it will be paying more than its fair share of the costs of governmental services. Despite these justifications, differential taxation is a frequently debated and controversial topic.[4]

Because classification schemes can have the effect of treating similarly situated individuals differently, constitutional issues may arise. Where a rationality standard is met however, courts tend to approach classification systems with deference.[5] Although many state

---

2. See Juergensmeyer and Wadley, Agricultural Law § 4.18 (1982).

3. Id.

4. See e.g., Currier, An Analysis of Differential Uses, 30 U.Fla.L.Rev. 832 (1978); Henke, Preferential Property Tax Treatment for Farmland, 53 Ore.L.Rev. 117 (1974); Juergensmeyer, State and Local Land Use Planning and Control in the Agricultural Context, 25 S.D.L.Rev. 463 (1980); Keene, Agricultural Land Preser-

vation: Legal and Constitutional Issues, 15 Gonz.L.Rev. 621 (1980); Lapping, Bevins, & Herbers, Differential Assessment and Other Techniques to Preserve Missouri's Farmlands, 42 Mo.L.Rev. 369 (1977); Ellington, Differential Assessment and Local Government Controls to Preserve Agricultural Lands, 20 S.D.L.Rev. 548 (1975).

5. Newhouse, Constitutional Uniformity and Equality in State Taxation, Mich. Legal Studies (1959).

constitutions require uniformity of taxation, most provide specifically for this form of differential taxation.[6]

WESTLAW REFERENCES

"differential taxation"

di,sy(land /s use /s classif! /s tax taxation taxed taxing /s assess!)

"use classification" & "preferential treatment"

assess! /s "market value" /s fraction

sy(agricultur! /s classif! /s assess!)

tax taxation taxing /p incentive /p encourag! discourag! /p land property /p use

di(farm! /s preserv! /s tax)

agricultur! /s land /s tax /s prefer!

mindel /s franklin & farm!

di("farmland assessment act" /s tax)

rational /s standard test /s classif! /s land property

§ 12.5 Tax Credits, Abatements and Exemptions as Land Use Control Devices

Because a number of restrictions are placed on the use of ad valorem taxation,[1] many jurisdictions have resorted to systems of abatements, credits and exemptions to circumvent uniformity problems. The manner in which each of these systems provides tax relief is basically the same; each amounts to a deduction from the taxpayer's liability. In other words, after full fair market value assessment and application of a uniform rate, the taxpayer's bill is reduced by a specified amount. The use of a "carrot" (rather than a stick) approach is especially important to many localities; it is always politically easier to exempt or abate something from taxation than it is to secure passage of an additional tax. Thus, this positive form of taxation has been used frequently for such socially desirable goals as halting urban blight and sprawl, providing subsidized housing, and promoting preservation of historic properties.

Implementation of this type of scheme presents some difficulties. Abatement, credit, and exemption programs are always easier to establish in jurisdictions where the uniformity requirement is not strictly construed or where such schemes are specifically authorized. For example, the early federal subsidized housing program under the Roosevelt administration combined federal money with a local ordi-

---

6. See Keene, Agricultural Land Preservation: Legal and Constitutional Issues, 15 Gonz.L.Rev. 621, 657–660 (1980).

§ 12.5

1. See Berger, Controlling Urban Growth Via Tax Policy, 2 Urb.L. & Pol'y 295 (1979).

nance to exempt low income housing from property taxes for a number of years.[2]

The area of subsidized housing also contains a good example of the use of property tax abatements to direct land use. New York State's Limited Profit Housing Program, or Mitchell-Lama, was designed to meet the problem of increased property tax costs in urban areas. The specific problem in New York arose from the destruction of old buildings and the construction of new ones, causing the new buildings to be assessed much higher value than surrounding properties. This of course acted as a disincentive for urban renewal. Here higher taxes engendered by rising property values were abated and the final tax was reduced by the amount of taxes on the previously existing, destroyed or dilapidated building.

New York City's urban problems provided the impetus for another plan dealing with the renovation of older buildings. This plan, known as the J–51 plan, combined positive incentives with tax abatements to motivate the renewal.[3] Through the program, the city froze the value of property qualifying for renovations for twelve years. The owner further received an annual credit on his tax bill, based on the frozen assessment.[4] Thus, final tax liability was reduced to deal with what would otherwise be a disincentive for urban renewal.

The above are just a few examples of the use of tax policy to accomplish social goals by relaxing uniformity constraints. This can sometimes be difficult to achieve and defend. For example, New York City's tax subsidization plans evolved to include middle and upper income housing. The renovation programs came to be seen as an aid to the "haves", because historic preservation efforts improved older buildings, frequently displacing the previous "have not" occupants. Hence, the phenomena of gentrification and displacement began to occur.

Lands commonly exempted from taxation (marshlands, parks, playgrounds, and forests) may or may not be exempted for landuse policy purposes. When such exemptions are challenged, cases generally turn on an interpretation of the uniformity clause or on attempts by groups marginally covered by the exemption to qualify for it.[5]

2. See, e.g., Hermitage Co. v. Goldfogle, 204 App.Div. 710, 199 N.Y. 382 (1923), affirmed mem., 236 N.Y. 554, 142 N.E. 281 (1923) upholding exemption for new housing; Madway v. Board of Assessment & Revision of Taxes, 427 Pa. 138, 233 A.2d 273 (1967), statute provided for no increase in assessment for new housing until occupied or sold.

3. See Vorsanger, New York City's J–51 Program: Controversy and Revision, 12 Fordham Urb.L.J. 103 (1983).

4. See, Berger supra note 1, at 298.

5. See, e.g., Denison Univ. v. Board of Tax Appeals, 173 Ohio St. 429, 183 N.E.2d 773 (1962); Lawrence University v. Outagamie County, 150 Wis. 244, 136 N.W. 619 (1912), education; Jefferson Post No. 15, Am. Legion v. Louisville, 280 S.W.2d 706 (Ky.1955) and Rotary Int'l. v. Paschen, 14 Ill.2d 480, 153 N.E.2d 4 (1958), charitable and educational; Fellowship of Humanity v. County of Alameda, 153 Cal.App.2d 673, 315 P.2d 394 (1957), churches. Walz v. Tax Commission, 397 U.S. 664, 90 S.Ct. 1409, 25 L.Ed.2d 697 (1970) (exemption of churches does not violate the U.S. Constitution).

A significant problem with exemption programs is that a large amount of property in a taxing jurisdiction can become exempt. Because this decreases overall revenues, it can result in the application of higher rates to property that continues to be taxed. For example, some rural school districts in California have seen their tax base substantially eroded by the preferential assessment of agricultural lands.[6] To cure the problem, the state has authorized cities or counties in the school district area to make gifts of funds to the school district.[7] Thus it can be seen that taxation, like any other type of land use control, can cause as many problems as it sets out to prevent.

WESTLAW REFERENCES

restrict! requir! /p uniform! /p "ad valorem" /p exemption

tax taxing taxed taxation /p urban /p blight sprawl

tax taxing taxed taxation /s preserv! /s historic! /s property

hermitage /s goldfogle

exempt! /s "low income" /s house housing /s property /s tax taxing taxation taxed

"limited profit housing program" "mitchell lama" /p urban!

j–51 /s renovat!

to(371) /p social! /p goal

exempt! /s challeng! /s uniformity

denison /s board /s tax /s appeals & exempt!

§ 12.6 Valuation Schemes

Classification, credit and abatement schemes are not the only means of shaping land use policy through taxation. In addition to these, differing methods of valuation can be applied to produce preferential treatment. Many of the previously discussed methods deal with variations on the uniformity requirement. Valuation schemes, however, address the problem by manipulating the system used to determine the property's value, and hence, the amount of tax owed.

A striking illustration of the difference that a valuation scheme can make is seen in Joseph E. Seagram & Sons, Inc. v. Tax Commission of the City of New York,[1] the so-called "tax on beauty" case. In Seagram, the taxpayers had constructed a building of unusual architectural style, leaving considerable open space around it. Under one assessment scheme, the structure's total cost, $36 million, would be the assessed value. This was based upon historic cost (the actual cost at the time of building) which is a frequently used measure of assessed value, particularly when a building is recently built. Reproduction cost (what it would cost to reproduce the building exactly) was another possible means of valuation. This method produces results similar to

---

6. West's Ann.Cal.Rev. & Tax Code § 421 et seq.

7. West's Ann.Cal.Gov't.Code § 51204.

§ 12.6

1. 14 N.Y.2d 314, 251 N.Y.S.2d 460, 200 N.E.2d 447 (1964). See also Lefcoe, The Real Property Tax and Architecture; A Note on the Seagram Case, 41 Land Econ. 57 (1965).

historic cost where building costs, methods, and materials have not changed.

The taxpayer in Seagram used the capitalization of rental income method and concluded that the assessment should be about $17.8 million. The assessor used the "replacement cost (the cost to construct another building of equivalent utility) less depreciation" method and set an assessed value of $21 million.[2] Replacement cost however does not contemplate construction of exact replica, as is the case with reproduction cost. Had there been a recent arms-length sale of the building, or sales of comparable properties, such evidence could also be used as a means of fixing assessed value.[3]

Because he did not choose the method resulting in the lowest assessed value (the one presented by the taxpayer), the assessor was accused of being anti-aesthetic and of penalizing beauty. The court ultimately upheld the assessor's position on the basis that he had employed a rational method. The court noted the assessor's job is to find a fair assessed value and not one which will encourage (or discourage) the construction of beautiful buildings. The case does illustrate, however, that the method of valuation used can result in dramatic tax differences.

Another assessment difficulty occurs where property ownership is split into separate interests. Typically, separate interests in property are not separately taxed. For example, the interests of the mortgagor and mortgagee, lessor and lessee, and the interests of the holder of an easement and the owner of the servient property, are not separately assessed. Sometimes the assessor has difficulty in applying the doctrine. For example, should he assess common open space in a planned unit development separately, not assess it at all on the assumption that it is assessed as part of the building sites, or assess the open space separately as adding value to the building sites? If the latter method is chosen, some argue that double taxation will occur.[4]

Legislation is sometimes necessary to guide the assessor in these types of cases.[5] For example, New York has no personal property tax. Occupants of trailer parks in that state require the same type and amount of municipal services as do more traditional residential areas, and they can be just as much of a burden on local government. The New York legislature therefore decided to classify trailers as real

---

2. The "replacement cost" formula is what the appellate division said the city was relying on, 18 A.D.2d 109, 238 N.Y.S.2d 228 (1963). The court may have meant reproduction cost. The two terms are frequently used mistakenly or interchangeably.

3. See § 20.9 supra on use of similar valuation techniques in eminent domain.

4. See generally Schultz, The Real Property Taxation of Common Areas in Planned Unit Developments: Advocating the Rights of Homeowner Associations, 1983 Utah L.Rev. 825 (1983); Youngman, Defining and Valuing the Base of Property Tax, 58 Wash.L.Rev. 713 (1983).

5. See e.g. Unit Property Act, Pa.Stat. Ann. tit. 68, § 700.101 et seq. See also Crane-Berkley Corp. v. Lavis, 238 App.Div. 124, 263 N.Y.S. 556 (1933); People ex rel. Poor v. Wells, 139 App.Div. 83, 124 N.Y.S. 36 (1910).

property and have the value assessed to the trailer park owner. A state court upheld the law on the ground that trailers could be considered realty and their value could be assessed to the trailer park owner.[6] It analogized the situation to the value of buildings built on leasehold interests which are, of course, assessed to the owner of the fee.

 WESTLAW REFERENCES

sy(valuation /s method /s land /s tax)

seagram /s sons /s "new york" /p valu!

di(valuation /s capitalization /s income /s assessment /s tax)

assessment /s land /s own owned owning ownership /s split

separate /s interest

ti(defining /s valuing /s property)

§ 12.7 Nontraditional Taxation Schemes as Land Use Controls

Ad valorem taxation is almost universally used by local governments in the United States. As noted above, however, its usefulness as a land use control is limited by a number of constraints.[1] Although most localities favor this form of taxation (often coupled with some form of tax credit), alternative tax schemes have been suggested.

One of the favorite alternatives to traditional methods is based upon a 1911 book by Henry George.[2] George observed that blight is caused because owners have no incentive to maintain and rehabilitate their properties; if maintenance increases property value, and tax bill increases correspondingly, why continue making improvements? He continued by noting that even if this did not directly cause blight, it still led to overassessment of property to such an extent that funds available for maintenance would be curtailed.

In response to this phenomenon, a new form of taxation called "Henry George" has sprung up. Henry George taxation, also referred to as site value or land value taxation, is a favorite subject of planners interested in property taxation as a tool of land use control. Under this form of taxation, only the land is taxed and improvements to the land are not. But the Henry George tax is of only intellectual interest in the United States, as it has been tried in only a few jurisdictions.[3] The theory behind the tax is that high property taxes will force land into a more intensive use in order to pay the tax. Thus, some argue

6. New York Mobile Home Ass'n. v. Steckel, 9 N.Y.2d 533, 215 N.Y.S.2d 487, 175 N.E.2d 151 (1961), appeal dismissed 369 U.S. 150, 82 S.Ct. 685, 7 L.Ed.2d 782 (1962).

§ 12.7

1. See §§ 12.1–.2 supra.

2. H. George, Progress and Poverty (1911).

3. California, Hawaii, and Vermont have adopted variations of Henry George taxation with differing degrees of success. See generally, D. Hagman & D. Misczynski, Windfalls for Wipeouts at 411–412 (1978). Henry George taxation is in use in Australia, Canada, England, New Zealand and South Africa. Id.

that the tax will insure urban renewal.[4] It is also thought to reduce speculation in land since, under the scheme, speculators could less afford to withhold the land from use. It is further suggested that the tax would stimulate the construction industry, because those renovating buildings to comply with housing codes would not be "penalized" by the remodeling triggering a higher assessment. Finally the tax is thought to be fair because increased land values are usually caused by other public and private investment in the area, and not by the landowner's individual efforts.

Considerable doubt exists about the merits of the land value tax.[5] Opponents of Henry George taxation contend that land speculation may be desirable because it encourages assembly and withholding of land, thus preventing its premature development. Open space in the form of farms and golf courses might be taxed out of existence within urban areas. The tax might cause higher urban densities than desired. A shift to land value taxation would give some taxpayers a windfall in the value of their land at the expense of other landowners. For example, land with a high site value, such as land in a downtown business area, would experience a great tax increase. This would make the property less attractive and would lower land values. On the other hand, land with a low site value, such as residential property, would experience a great decrease in taxes, thereby increasing land values. The city core could become decentralized because, despite lower land costs, the tax cost would be so high as to discourage centralization. Moreover, the tax has no ability to discriminate between slums (undesirable) and (desirable) low income housing areas.[6]

Finally, the premise of land value taxation itself has come under attack. As one authority has pointed out, ordinary maintenance does not add to tax bills, and most improvements are not followed by reassessment.[7]

 WESTLAW REFERENCES

george /s progress /s poverty

"henry george" /p tax taxation

"land value tax"

4. Gaffney, Land Planning and the Property Tax, 35 J.Am. Institute of Planners 178 (1969). See generally, D. Setzer, Impact of the Property Tax, Research Rpt. No. 1 to the National Commission on Urban Problems (1968).

5. Clark, Site Valuation as a Base for Local Taxation, Canadian Tax Foundation, Conference Report (1961); George, Our Land and Land Policy, 9 Works of Henry George 108–12 (1898); National Commission on Urban Problems, Building the American City, 383, 388–91, 394–98 (1968); Rawson, Property Taxation and Urban De-

velopment, Urban Land Institute, Research Monograph 4 (1961); Hagman, The Single Tax and Land-Use Planning; Henry George Updated, 12 U.C.L.A.L.Rev. 702 (1965).

6. See generally Clark, supra note 5. See also Kmiec, Deregulating Land Use: An Alternative Free Enterprise Development System, 1983 Land Use & Env't L.Rev. 279, 373 (1983).

7. See generally Currier, Exploring the Role of Taxation in the Land Use Planning Process, 51 Ind.L.J. 27 (1975).

land /p prevent! /p prematur! /p develop!
"williamson act"

III. SPECIAL ASSESSMENTS AND SPECIAL TAX DISTRICTS

§ 12.8   Special Assessments and Special Tax Districts as Land Use Control Devices

The rapid, sprawling, suburban growth, experienced in recent years, has placed enormous pressure on local government's financial ability to continue providing traditional governmental services such as roads, schools, sewers and parks. In response to these fiscal crises, local governments have begun to seek alternative means of raising funds to provide such services. Two commonly used devices are special assessments and special taxing districts.[1] Although both devices are used to accomplish similar purposes, important differences exist between them.

A special assessment is a charge upon lands deriving a special benefit from some nearby capital improvement, to defray the cost of the improvement.[2] Special assessments are typically used to provide revenues for streets, sidewalks, streetlights and sewers. Their use however is limited to situations where there is some special benefit to the property assessed.[3] The charge generally cannot be for more than the benefit received nor for more than the cost of the improvement.[4]

Frequently, the assessment is apportioned on the basis of the front footage of the land. This may be justified as many improvements such as water and sewer lines, streets and sidewalks arguably do provide benefits in relation to front footage. But other apportioning measures, such as the area or value of the property benefitted, are sometimes used.

Special assessments are sometimes difficult to distinguish from property taxes. In theory, however, the two are quite different. Special assessments use the value of the property only as a rational means of measuring the benefit received and apportioning its cost. Property taxes on the other hand are applied regardless of whether the property receives a special benefit.

Planners have shown only a small interest in the use of special assessments as a land use control device, and there has been relatively

---

§ 12.8

1. Another device gaining increasing support is the impact fee. See § 9.8, supra.

2. Davies v. Lawrence, 218 Kan. 551, 545 P.2d 1115 (1976).

3. See Reynolds, A Handbook of Local Government Law § 99 (1982). See generally Diamond, Constitutional Limits on the Growth of Special Assessments, 6 Urb.L. & Pol'y 311 (1984).

4. See generally Diamond, supra note 3.

little scholarly commentary on the subject.[5] A number of reasons for the disinterest have been suggested. One explanation is that, in relative terms, special assessments do not produce large revenues. Another is that because they are not readily classified as belonging to the tax, eminent domain or police powers, special assessments are frequently overlooked by treatises on those subjects. Finally, assessments earned a bad name during the depression when millions of dollars of subdivision improvement bonds financed by special assessments went into default.

Special taxing districts perform many of the same functions that special assessments do but are generally not limited to providing a single service.[6] They are organized governmental entities, possessing a structural form, an official name and the rights to sue and be sued, to enter into contracts, to obtain and dispose of property, and to issue bonds to finance capital improvements.[7] One jurisdiction defines the special district as a "unit of special government . . . created for the purpose of performing prescribed functions, including urban services, within limited boundaries.[8] Special districts are usually run by elected officials and are subject to a high degree of accountability.[9] They have been created to provide such diverse services as road and bridge networks, drainage and irrigation systems, police and fire protection services, and recreational facilities.

As noted above, special districts differ from special assessments in a number of ways. While special assessments are limited to raising funds to defray the cost of a given improvement, taxing districts can serve a number of purposes. Special districts are in reality a separate form of local government. Many have the power to finance capital improvements by issuing bonds payable from ad valorem taxes. This is particularly important as it can serve as a strong development incentive. Taxing districts can be and have been used by developers as a self-financing means of providing the capital improvements requisite to land development. Hence the availability of special districts for such purposes provides yet another means of controlling land use through taxation.

 WESTLAW REFERENCES

di assessment

di(land /s assess! /s benefit! improv! /s defray!)

land /p assess! /p apportion! /p front /s footage

special /s tax taxing taxation /s district /s govern! /s entity

5. Some commentary does exist however. See Winter, The Special Assessment in Illinois, (1959); Dekker & Powell, Wichita Special Assessment Based on Fair Market Value of Land Upheld, 23 Mun.Att'y 3 (1982); Diamond, The Death and Transfiguration of Benefit Taxation: Special Assessments in Nineteenth Century America, 12 J.Legal Stud. 201 (1983). See also Diamond, supra note 3.

6. See Hudson, Special Taxing Districts in Florida, 10 Fla.St.U.L.Rev. 49 (1982).

7. Bollens, Special District Governments in the United States 1 (1957). See also Hudson, supra note 6.

8. West's Fla.Stat.Ann. § 218.31(5).

9. See generally Hudson, supra note 6 at 50.

di(special /s district /s bond /s financ! /s improv!)
taxing /s district /s bond /s ''ad valorem'' /s power

Chapter 13

ENVIRONMENTAL ASPECTS OF LAND USE CONTROLS

Analysis

I. INTRODUCTION

Sec.

13.1   Introduction.

II. NATIONAL ENVIRONMENTAL POLICY ACT (NEPA)

13.2   Introduction to the Statute.
13.3   Council on Environmental Quality; Report and Guidelines.

III. STATE ENVIRONMENTAL POLICY ACTS (SEPAs)

13.4   NEPA–Like State Acts.
13.5   Relation to Planning and Land Use Control.

IV. LAND USE AND THE POLLUTION LAWS—CLEAN AIR

13.6   Basic Scheme of the Clean Air Act.

I. INTRODUCTION

§ 13.1 Introduction

Scarcely a concern before the 1960's, environmental aspects of land use control have become a primary consideration of land use planners. Even during the environmental renaissance of the 1960's, land use did not receive the attention focused on air and water pollution. Air and water were viewed as public trusts to be shared by all. Land was considered a matter of private property generally out of governmental reach. That attitude has changed markedly in the last decade. Nowhere has that attitude changed more dramatically than in regard to environmental land use.[1]

It would be a mistake to attribute the new land use concern with environmental matters to a mere extension of traditional land use controls because environmental regulations are often based on subjective value judgments giving priority to ecological quality.[2] Another unique aspect of environmental land use is the major role played by federal and state governments. Although not true national planning, the National Environmental Policy Act (NEPA) and its state progeny provide for explicit environmental weighting in agency decisionmaking.

While NEPA's goals and the accompanying Clean Air and Water Act's implementing measures are primarily concerned with pollution abatement through emission and effluent standards, land use policies are factored in to a significant degree. At the very minimum, land use planners will have to consider carefully those federal acts when siting a development with possible pollution problems.

A second branch of environmental land use involves environmentally sensitive lands. Lands may be environmentally sensitive for many reasons, but the most common examples of sensitive lands are (1) wetlands, (2) coastal zones, (3) floodplains, and (4) habitat areas for endangered species. Regulations concerning these locales are closer to traditional land use controls because they deal with land as such. As with restrictive zoning, environmental land use controls are often attacked as "takings" of property prohibited by the fifth and fourteenth amendments. The modern trend is to turn down such challenges unless the regulating entity shows blatant disregard for property rights.

The basic problem in all environmental land use decisions is that land is a finite resource. There must be room not only for houses, shopping malls, and paper mills, but for wetlands, beaches, barrier islands and snail darters. Industrial and economic growth are considered desirable, but so are clean air and water. Somewhere a balance must be struck.

Development on environmentally sensitive land must be cautiously done. Both future and present needs have to be considered. While a residential subdivision in a prime aquifer recharging wetland may

§ 13.1

1. See Natural Resources Defense Council, Land Use Controls in the United States 1 (1977); Juergensmeyer, The American Legal System and Environmental Pollution, 33 U.Fla.L.Rev. 439 (1971). Environmental land use encompasses the effects of and impact on land use planning imposed by environmental protection measures emanating from state and federal constitutions, statutes and regulations, as well as from common law and statutory decisions. For general information on environmental law, see Rodgers, Environmental Law (1977).

2. D. Mandelker, Environment and Equity; A Regulatory Challenge XI (1981) (Professor Mandelker attributes this thought to Professor A. Dan Tarlock).

expand a local government's tax base, the bargain may prove faustian when drinking wells dry up.

The laws and regulations now governing that balance are the subject of this chapter. While primarily concerned with the broader federal and state controls so typical in this area, it is increasingly important to note the expanding contribution of local governments. County and municipal governments are on the rebound. From total planning control to mere benchwarmer status in the recently enacted environmental regulations, local governments are working themselves back into the forefront of land use planning of all types including environmental and sensitive lands regulation. This trend is boosted by sympathetic federal and state regulations requesting local implementation. The end result may be, and to a large extent already is, a comprehensive multi-tiered system of interlocking federal, state, and local controls in environmental land use.

The overlap in this layered regulatory interlock can lead to complicated jurisdictional problems. Of even greater concern may be the complications arising from policy conflict. Zoning development away from one environmentally sensitive area may add development pressure to another. These jurisdictional and policy conflicts are part and parcel of the approach governments at all levels have taken to the problem of environmental land use. Whether such a complicated approach really works is still, even after more than a decade of focused analysis, uncertain.

This complex, interconnected approach was perhaps best illustrated by a hypothetical developed by the prominent land use lawyer, Fred Bosselman.[3] Even though written over a decade ago, the complexity of the problems identified and the interaction of the various environmental laws remains true to the present day. With the particular pollution problems indicated in the left margin and the desired public goals on the right, consider the problems facing the "metropolitan sanitary district of Camelot."

water	The metropolitan sanitary district of Camelot has installed waste water treatment facilities to meet its National Pollutant Discharge Elimination System (NPDES) permit requirements but	metro solution clean water
solid waste odor	in so doing accumulates enormous quantities of semi-liquid sludge. State odor regulations prevent converting all	odorless air
land	sludge into a solid form. The sludge	land fill
water	could be used in Desolation County in an effort to reclaim strip-mined land but the permeability characteristics of the soil will result in polluting under-	clean water
odor	ground water (via leaching) and surface water (via runoff) contrary to the Water Pollution Control Act. Odor problems	odorless air

3. Adapted from F. Bosselman, et al., EPA Authority Affecting Land Use 142, 143, 145, 147, 148 (1974).

solid waste

air, noise

air

water

water

air

noise

air

sprawl

water

noise

air

air

also limit the amount of sludge which can be disposed of in this way. Garbage presents a similar problem. Neither the Solid Waste Disposal Act nor nearby counties and municipalities permit landfills. Sludge and garbage has to be transported great distances for disposal to those few areas such as Gotham which are both willing to have dumps in their back yard and are not so far as to make disposal there uneconomic.

The Clean Air Act's state implementation plan makes incineration difficult as Camelot's air quality does not comply with national ambient air quality standards. Although Camelot is on the ocean, it is limited in its ability to use the sea as a dump by the Marine Protection, Research and Sanctuaries Act. 33 U.S.C.A. § 1401 et seq.

Meanwhile, the federal government is expanding its employment in Camelot, which has led to considerable in-migration and a concomitant demand for housing, either new or rehabilitated.

The continuing planning process under the Water Pollution Control Act dictates location of waste water treatment plans where there is existing sewer and incidental water capacity. There is little excess capacity except in the fringe areas, where there is little existing housing to rehabilitate. Construction of new housing will increase the chance of degrading "clean" air because of the almost certain development of indirect sources, like shopping centers, which will accompany fringe residential construction. Adequate mass transit is not readily available in fringe areas so increased use of motor vehicles is inevitable.

Building or rehabilitating existing structures in older areas where bus or other mass transit systems are readily available will lessen pollution from mobile sources. And construction of a mass transit system under the National Mass Transit Act, favors dense clustering of development around stops. However, the central city is where sewage treatment capacity is limited.

The airport is too small to meet air traffic needs. Even if sufficient land were available to accommodate a jet airport in Camelot, airport noise regulations would prohibit a location so close to a high population density. However, compliance with Noise Act standards would place the airport beyond existing mass transit facilities requiring reliance on automobiles for transportation to the airport. This would mean development of a substan-

clean air, quiet

economic solution

clean air

clean water

economic growth
right to travel
good housing

use of existing
  infrastructure
clean water

clean air

clean air
low cost transit

dense develop-
ment

clean water

improved air
  service
quiet

clean air

non-degraded air

water

tial indirect source in a rural area
where the air is clean. Furthermore,
existing sewage plant capacity is not
sufficient to handle all the storm water
run-off from runways and parking lots.

clean water

air

heat

air

Fossil-fueled electric generators are not
permitted in the city limits because of
air quality problems, though electric
power demands are rising. The lack of
sufficient water and land for cooling
ponds limits the usefulness of nuclear
generating plants because of inability
to meet thermal pollution standards.
Construction of coal-fired generating facilities at coal mines outside the city is
inhibited because of the significant deterioration regulations applicable to the
clean air in the rural area of the coal
mine.

clean air

inexpensive
 electricity
cool water

clean air

WESTLAW REFERENCES

environment! /p aspect /p land /p use /p control

da(bef 1965 & aft 1955) & air water /s "public trust"

to(199) /p "national environmental policy act" n.e.p.a.
     /s environment! /s weigh!

"clean air and water act"

pollut! /s abat! /s emission effluent /s standard

land /p use /p policy /p plan**** /p develop!
     /p pollut! /p federal!

environment! /s sensitiv! /s land

ecolog! /p preserv! protect! conserv! /p taking /p constitution!
     unconstitution!

mandelker tarlock /s environment!

local /s govern! /s environment! /s regulat!

overlap! /s land /p regulat! /p jurisdiction! % nish

II. NATIONAL ENVIRONMENTAL POLICY ACT
(NEPA)

§ 13.2 Introduction to the Statute

Through the National Environmental Policy Act (NEPA),[1] Congress
hoped to insure that federal agencies would consider the environmental
effects of their actions. Thus NEPA requires that agencies develop
procedures for doing so and requires them to prepare environmental
impact statements (EISs) on major federal actions which may have a
significant impact on the environment.

§ 13.2

1. Pub.L. No. 91–190, 83 Stat. 852, codified at 42 U.S.C.A. §§ 4321–4361. For a
general review of this statute which, remarkably, has remained virtually amend-
ment-free since its enactment in 1969, see

Delogu, NEPA, 26 Land Use L. & Zoning
Dig. 5 (1974); Leaventhal, Environmental
Decisionmaking and the Courts, 122 U.Pa.
L.Rev. 509 (1974); Yost, Streamlining
NEPA—An Environmental Success Story,
9 Envtl.Aff. 507 (1981).

Many states have adopted legislation patterned on NEPA,[2] and state courts often use NEPA cases to interpret their own state acts. NEPA and its state copies are a powerful force affecting land use. As will become clear, they can be said to constitute land use controls in environmental policy clothing. Some might regard them as a threat to traditional planning and land use controls. Others might regard them as a promise of a new scheme for planning and control.

The Statute

A statement of purpose and a declaration of policy expressing a federal commitment to preserve and enhance the environment preface the heart of NEPA, Section 102.[3] That section indicates that to the fullest extent possible all federal policies, regulations and laws will be interpreted by NEPA policies. All agencies of the Federal Government are also directed to utilize systematic, interdisciplinary decisionmaking and to develop means of giving appropriate weight to environmental amenities and values. Subsection 102(c), worth quoting in full, is the core of NEPA. Federal agencies must:

> include in every recommendation or report on proposals for legislation and other major Federal actions significantly affecting the quality of the human environment, a detailed statement by the responsible official on—
>
> (i) the environmental impact of the proposed action,
>
> (ii) any adverse environmental effects which cannot be avoided should the proposal be implemented,
>
> (iii) alternatives to the proposed action,
>
> (iv) the relationship between local short-term uses of man's environment and the maintenance and enhancement of long-term productivity, and
>
> (v) any irreversible and irretrievable commitments of resources which would be involved in the proposed action should it be implemented.[4]

Subsection (c) continues with imposition of a duty to consult with and obtain comments from other specialized federal agencies having competency about a matter before making the detailed statement. The statements and the comments, including comments of state and local agencies are to be made available to the President, to the Council on Environmental Quality (CEQ) and to the public and are to accompany the proposal through the agency review process.

All agencies are also to review their statutory authority, regulations, policies and procedures to permit compliance with NEPA policy and are to recommend changes where necessary. NEPA does not affect

---

2. See infra Part III.

3. 42 U.S.C.A. § 4332. See, e.g., Friends of Mammoth v. Board of Supervi-

sors of Mono County, 8 Cal.3d 247, 104 Cal. Rptr. 761, 502 P.2d 1049 (1972).

4. 42 U.S.C.A. § 4332(c).

any duty to comply with other environmental quality requirements, nor to consult or coordinate in other non-environmental matters with any Federal or State agencies. Finally, NEPA policies and goals supplement those set forth in other authorizations of federal agencies.

 WESTLAW REFERENCES

ci(42 +5 423* 433* 434* 435* 4361 % 423 433)
sy("environmental impact statement" /s federal /s environment!)

The Statute
n.e.p.a. /s 102(c)

§ 13.3 Council on Environmental Quality; Report and Guidelines

NEPA also established the Council on Environmental Quality (CEQ).[1] The CEQ provides assistance to the President, who is required to prepare the annual Environmental Quality Report.[2] This report is like an environmental state of the union review. CEQ gathers information and conducts research on environmental issues, suggests new policies, and checks governmental actions to see if they conform with environmental goals.

Its primary duty is to watchdog the environmental review process in the agencies of the federal government. It publishes guidelines to help agencies implement NEPA, consults with each agency on acceptable methodologies, and reviews the EISs prepared by the various agencies.

Although CEQ's Guidelines[3] were originally regarded as advisory only, they have nonetheless proven to be persuasive authority in court interpretations of NEPA. The absence of formal agency regulatory status was cured by a 1977 Executive Order[4] authorizing the CEQ to adopt formal EIS regulations. Although the new regulations are not treated as controlling, they are accorded considerable weight.[5]

CEQ requires that each federal agency prepare its own guidelines.[6] Agency guidelines are to list those types of agency actions which are likely to have a significant impact on the environment and which would therefore require an EIS. The guidelines must identify the

§ 13.3

1. 42 U.S.C.A. § 4342 et seq.

2. Called "Environmental Quality," the report is published annually in the fall.

3. 43 Fed.Reg. 55,990 (1978); 40 C.F.R. Pt. 1500. See also Lynch, The 1973 CEQ Guidelines: Cautious Updating of the Environmental Impact Statement Process, 11 Cal.W.L.Rev. 297 (1975).

4. Exec.Order N. 11,990, 42 Fed.Reg. 26967, reprinted in 42 U.S.C.A.App. § 4321.

5. Andrus v. Sierra Club, 442 U.S. 347, 99 S.Ct. 2335, 60 L.Ed.2d 943 (1979). But see Sierra Club v. Sigler, 695 F.2d 957 (5th Cir.1983), rehearing denied 704 F.2d 1251 (5th Cir.1983) (holding that the 1978 CEQ regulations are controlling). See generally Mandelker, NEPA Law & Litigation §§ 2:10–13 (1984).

6. For agency guidelines, see, e.g., Nuclear Regulatory Commission, 10 C.F.R. § 11.1 et seq.; Environmental Protection Agency, 40 C.F.R. § 6.10 et seq.; Post Office, 39 C.F.R. Pt. 775 et seq.

agency officials responsible for preparing EISs and establish procedures for consulting with other agencies for providing public information on environmentally significant projects.

The CEQ Guidelines offer no further elaboration on what a major action or what a significant effect is. Each agency is to decide what types of projects are major or significant.

When the agency has decided that a proposed action is major and will have a significant impact on the environment, the CEQ Guidelines recommend that the agency prepare a draft EIS for circulation to other agencies and to the public for comment. The agency's effort must be its best, as if its product were a final EIS, but the agency is required to consider outside comments and incorporate them into the final EIS whenever appropriate.

The EIS Requirement

The CEQ guidelines provide that the EIS is to be written in plain language with appropriate graphics. Simple, clear prose is stressed, and the final result should be readily comprehensible by the public.

Strict requirements on format, page limits, and style are established. To reduce paperwork, CEQ provides that the EIS is to be analytic rather than encyclopedic. Length of discussion should be in direct correlation to importance. Only if the potential environmental problems are great or the proposed project is of an unusually large size should there be a need for an EIS of more than two hundred pages in length.

The probable impact of the proposed project should be described in reference to direct and indirect effects, as well as possible conflicts with land use policies, plans, and controls of all levels of government having jurisdiction over the project site.

Alternatives are the heart of the EIS. All reasonable alternatives are to be described and analyzed for their environmental impacts. Alternatives include abandonment of the project and delay for further study. Even those alternatives which are not within the preparing agency's powers are to be discussed.

The EIS is to describe environmental effects which cannot be avoided and actions that could mitigate adverse environmental effects. A study of the relationship between short term use of man's environment and the maintenance and enhancement of long term productivity should include a discussion of environmental trade-offs. These include the extent to which the action would foreclose future options, or cause an irreversible and irretrievable commitment of resources.

If the agency has prepared a cost-benefit analysis for the project, it should be submitted with the EIS. If it is determined that a cost benefit analysis is not necessary for the proposed action, the agency should still submit a discussion of relevant nonenvironmental considerations of a project.

Properly utilized, the EIS process achieves two goals. First, it forces agencies to consider the environmental effect of their decisions. Second, it provides a disclosure statement showing both the environmental consequences of the proposed action and the agency's decision-making process.

Environmental groups use the EIS process as a legal handle to challenge agency action. The legal issues involved depend on whether or not an EIS was prepared. If not, the plaintiff will argue the need for an EIS. Using NEPA standards, the reviewing court will examine the facts surrounding the case to see if the action has *federal* involvement, if the action is *major,* and if the action *significantly affects* the environment.[7] If so, the court will order an EIS prepared.

If an EIS was prepared, but the agency decides to proceed with its action despite adverse environmental consequences, the issue becomes whether the reviewing court will overturn the administrative decision. The plaintiff here has a heavy burden. An enormous amount of litigation has occurred regarding this last point, and the decisions are anything but uniform.[8]

 WESTLAW REFERENCES

ci(42 +3 26967)

andrus sigler /s "sierra club" /s regulat!

ci(10 40 +4 11.1 6.10)

The EIS Requirement

n.e.p.a. c.e.q. /p guideline /p "environmental impact statement"
     e.i.s. /p language

sy("environmental impact statement" e.i.s. /s impact /s project
     /s effect)

sy(environmental impact statement" e.i.s. /s alternative
     /s impact /s environment

n.e.p.a. /s requir! /s court /s federal /s action
     /s significant /s environment!

"environmental impact statement" & overturn! /p board!

III. STATE ENVIRONMENTAL POLICY ACTS
(SEPAs)

§ 13.4   NEPA–Like State Acts [1]

In General

Many states have passed "SEPAs", acts that are modeled on NEPA. Some of the states require a report similar to a NEPA environmental statement (EIS) under circumstances where state action

---

7. See J. Rose, Legal Foundations of Environmental Planning 83 (1983); Shea, The Judicial Standard for Review of Environmental Impact Statement Threshold Decisions, 9 Envtl.Aff. 63 (1980).

8. See J. Rose, supra note 5; Shea, supra note 5, at 88–99.

§ 13.4

1. See generally Council of State Governments, Environmental Impact Assess-

is similar to federal action. Other states require an EIS only for a more limited type of action. Some require local governments to file statements for their own actions, others do not, and some leave the question open. Some require or allow municipalities to prepare EISs on governmentally permitted private development.

A State of Washington NEPA-like act [2], one of the broadest, has been interpreted to confer substantive authority to the deciding agency to act on the basis of the findings disclosed.[3] This same decision found that even though Washington's Act authorizes the superintendent of buildings to deny a building permit, it is not a "zoning" law because permit allowance or rejection is based solely on environmental effects. North Carolina [4] and California,[5] in addition to the five requirements of NEPA, require a sixth EIS provision providing for "mitigation measures proposed to minimize the impact." [6]

Massachusetts [7] requires its secretary of environmental controls to approve any consultant engaged to prepare a statement. Development agencies are also required to reimburse environmental agencies for their work in reviewing EISs.

New York's State Environmental Quality Review Act [8] statutorily brings both private developers and local governments under its EIS requirement. Ministerial actions are exempt,[9] and the Act goes beyond NEPA in requiring consideration of mitigation measures, growth-inducing effects, and energy conservation.[10]

WESTLAW REFERENCES
s.e.p.a. & substantive /p authority
"mitigation measures proposed to minimize the impact"
"environmental quality review act" /p ministerial

---

ment: Policy Considerations for the States (1977); S. Hark & G. Enk, Green Goals and Greenbacks: State Level Environmental Review Programs and Their Associated Costs (1980); D. Mandelker, Environmental and Land Controls Legislation 147–68 (1976); Hagman, NEPA's Progeny Inhabit the States—Were the Genes Defective?, 1974 Urb.L.Ann. 3; McLach, The Rise and Demise of the New Mexico Environmental Quality Act, "Little NEPA," 16 Nat. Resources J. 401 (1974); Tjossem, The Environmental Policy Acts: Analysis and Application, 10 Willamette L.J. 336 (1974); Yost, NEPA's Progeny: State Environmental Policy Acts, 3 Envtl.L.Rep. 50096 (1973); Note, State Environmental Impact Statements, 15 Washburn L.J. 64 (1976).

2. State Environmental Policy Act of 1971, West's Rev.Code Wash.Ann. 43.21 C. 010–43.21C.910.

3. Polygon Corp. v. Seattle, 90 Wn.2d 59, 578 P.2d 1309 (1978).

4. North Carolina Environmental Policy Act of 1971, N.C.Gen.Stat. §§ 113A–1–113A–10.

5. Environmental Quality Act of 1970, West's Ann.Cal.Pub.Res.Code §§ 21000–21151, 1970 Reg.Sess. Ch. 1433, § 1, approved and filed Sept. 18, 1970, amended in 1972, now West's Ann.Cal.Pub.Res.Code §§ 21000–21174, 1972 Reg.Sess. Ch. 1154, §§ 1–19, effective Dec. 5, 1972.

6. Compare the five elements to be included in a federal EIS as described supra § 13.2, at note 4. The CEQ guidelines, however, ask agencies to detail mitigating actions. 38 Fed.Reg. 20,550, at 20,554.

7. Mass.Gen.Laws Ann. c. 30, §§ 61–62.

8. N.Y.—McKinney's Envtl.Conserv. Law § 8–0101 et seq.

9. Id. § 8–0105(5).

10. Id. § 8–0109(2).

§ 13.5 Relation to Planning and Land Use Control

The federal government has no central, comprehensive land use planning capability and is not likely to have any in the foreseeable future. The legislative history [1] of NEPA illustrates that Congress recognized the problem of no national planning by requiring the Council of Environmental Quality to take an overall view of the activities of the federal government and their effect on the environment:

> It is a simple fact of life that policies of agencies of the Federal Government may and do conflict; it is equally true that there are occasions where, without the benefit of policies, these [governmental agencies] may and do adopt causes that appear to conflict with the general public interest.[2]

Thus, the NEPA ordered systematic, interdisciplinary, long range, alternative-considering approach is a step toward good planning. Requiring the agencies to pay attention to environmental standards set by other agencies, securing their comment and their expertise, and requiring that one agency take the lead are progressive administrative arrangements, as are the provisions for public participation.

NEPA was needed to put environmental concerns on an equal footing with other traditional bases for decisionmaking. It has probably done that. But true planning requires examination of the whole panoply of social, engineering, and economic concerns as well as the need for a sound physical environment. While NEPA guidelines are certainly not the sole criteria for a project's development,[3] they are important if for no other reason than disregard of the NEPA mandate will surely end in costly and time consuming litigation. Thus federal agencies must incorporate NEPA early on into their plans. To provide for a more synergistic approach toward agency planning, CEQ Guidelines provide for "interdisciplinary preparation" of all EISs.[4] This planning process is furthered by CEQ's "NEPA and Agency Planning" guidelines [5] which requires each agency to:

> (a) Integrat[e] the NEPA process into early planning to insure appropriate consideration of NEPA's policies and to eliminate delay.

§ 13.5

1. U.S. Code Cong. & Ad.News, 91st Cong., 1st Sess. 2751–73 (1969).

2. Id. at 2753–54.

3. See, e.g., Strycker's Bay Neighborhood Council v. Karlen, 444 U.S. 223, 100 S.Ct. 497, 62 L.Ed.2d 433 (1980) (Department of Housing and Urban Development need only show it considered environmental and social effects of a proposed low income housing development on Manhattan's Upper West Side—final decision need not be based on those considerations); Ver-

mont Yankee Nuclear Power Corp. v. NRDC, 435 U.S. 519, 98 S.Ct. 1197, 55 L.Ed.2d 460 (1978), on remand 685 F.2d 459 (D.C.Cir.1982), judgment reversed 462 U.S. 87, 103 S.Ct. 2246, 76 L.Ed.2d 437 (1983) (NEPA guidelines essentially procedural; environmental concerns are not to be elevated over "other appropriate considerations").

4. 40 C.F.R. § 1502.6 (interdisciplinary includes social as well as environmental imput).

5. Id. § 1501.

(b) Emphasiz[e] cooperative consultation among agencies before the environmental impact statement is prepared rather than submission of adversary comments on a completed document.[6]

Federal compliance with plans, federal, state and local, combined with the requirements of the A–95 review process,[7] should give sub-national plans considerably more force, for even federal plans are usually prepared on a regional basis. The Clean Air and Water Acts [8] plans are plans for sub-national and usually sub-state areas.

The courts have provided some assistance in relating traditional land use controls to the EIS system. For example, in Maryland-National Capital Park and Planning Commission v. United States Postal Service,[9] the Post Office had an environmental assessment conducted on a proposed major facility in Prince George's County, Maryland and concluded that the environmental impact of the facility would not be significant, therefore, no EIS was prepared. In reviewing whether the district court properly denied the plaintiff a preliminary injunction, the court discussed the effect of zoning. The court indicated that if the Federal Government facility conformed to local or regional regulations of land use "there is room for the contention, and there may even be a presumption" that the incremental impact on the environment is not significant. The rationale is that NEPA goals are to be achieved in cooperation with state and local governments. On the other hand, where federal preemption leads to projects that would not comply with local plans and controls if privately built, the environmental impact is likely to be significant. Further, even if the local zoning may permit governmental uses, where the facility is massive or very different from a more typical kind of governmental use probably contemplated by the zoning ordinance, the presumption of no significant impact may be inapplicable.

A mere difference between the federal use and the zoning does not necessarily mean, however, that the impact will be significant. For example, in the Maryland-National Capital Park and Planning Commission case, the Commission had no environmental objections. The objections were socio-economic. The Commission was worried about loss of tax base and the influx of low income residents. Under such circumstances, the fact that local zoning would not permit a private

---

6. Id. § 1501.1. Other listed purposes are swift resolution of lead agency disputes, early identification of significant environmental issues, and placing time limitations on the EIS process. Id. § 1501.1(c)–(e).

7. The A–95 process established by the Office of Management and Budget (OMB) under federal statute is an omnibus attempt to secure better coordination of Federal programs. It requires applicants for federal grants to seek comment from other governmental entities through state or areawide clearinghouses. The comments include NEPA considerations but are broader, going to overall relationships.

8. These acts are described infra §§ 13.6, 13.7.

9. 159 U.S.App.D.C. 158, 487 F.2d 1029 (1973).

facility like the governmental one would not necessarily raise a presumption that the *environmental* impact was significant.[10]

Jones v. District of Columbia Redevelopment Land Agency [11] also illustrates how NEPA reinforces the traditional planning concept that environmental considerations should be present at all stages of planning. The case involved a neighborhood development program (urban renewal) under which the District of Columbia Redevelopment Land Agency proposed a program which was passed on by the National Capital Planning Commission and sent to the District of Columbia City Council to decide whether the Redevelopment Land Agency could apply to the U.S. Department of Housing & Urban Development for funds. The court held that the Redevelopment Agency, the Commission and the Department should all prepare EISs, since each of their actions were major and could have a significant effect on the environment.

These cases point in a direction and indicate a glimmer of hope. Rather than be competitive, traditional planning control and the EIS systems can be wed into an environmentally sensitive, and planning approach to major federal actions having a significant effect on the environment.

 WESTLAW REFERENCES

(strycker /s karlen) (vermont /s yankee /s nuclear /s n.r.d.c.)
    /p environment! /p elevat!

ci(40 +4 1502.6)

integrat! /p n.e.p.a. /p e.i.s. /p policy

di(land /p use /p control! /p e.i.s. "environmental impact
    statement")

environment! /s assess! /s impact! /p "environmental impact
    statement" e.i.s. /p local! /p govern!

di("environmental impact statement" e.i.s. /s major /s significant!
    /s effect /s environment)

---

10. The court cites other cases of interest in considering the effect of local plans and zoning in relation to NEPA. See, e.g., Hiram Clarke Civic Club v. Lynn, 476 F.2d 421 (5th Cir.1973); Hanly v. Kleindienst, 471 F.2d 823, 830–31 (2d Cir.1972), cert. denied 412 U.S. 908, 93 S.Ct. 2290, 36 L.Ed. 2d 974 (1973), appeal after remand 484 F.2d 448 (2d Cir.1973), cert. denied 416 U.S. 936, 94 S.Ct. 1934, 40 L.Ed.2d 286 (1974); Ely v. Velde, 451 F.2d 1130 (4th Cir.1971), on remand 363 F.Supp. 277 (D.Va.1973), judgment reversed and remanded 497 F.2d 252 (4th Cir.1974); Town of Groton v. Laird, 353 F.Supp. 344, 350 (D.Conn.1972); Goose Hollow Foothills League v. Romney, 334 F.Supp. 877, 879 (D.Or.1971). It should be noted, however, that NEPA expressly covers socio-economic impacts in the EIS process.

11. 499 F.2d 502 (D.C.Cir.1974).

IV. LAND USE AND THE POLLUTION LAWS— CLEAN AIR

§ 13.6 Basic Scheme of the Clean Air Act

The regulation and direction of new development is at the heart of land use controls. The Clean Air Act [1] makes these controls serve a clean air master. Land use planners and controllers theoretically had always been concerned with planning and controlling land uses in a way to minimize air pollution, but the levels of pollution in many major metropolitan areas were a clear indication that theory had not been translated into practice.

The Clean Air Act targets both stationary sources (e.g., industrial smokestacks, dust from grain loading docks, etc.) and mobile sources (e.g., auto and truck exhaust) of air pollution. Mobile sources are generally not of great concern to land use planners and will not be covered here.[2] Stationary sources are another matter. For instance, the siting of a major coal burning power plant could be subject to state and local land use regulation as well as EPA jurisdiction under the Clean Air Act.[3]

While the states are delegated the authority to design plans to reduce air pollution directly, the basic framework of the Clean Air Act consists of federal authority over five broad statutory areas. They are (1) creation of national ambient air quality standards, (2) creation of air quality control regions, (3) approval of State Implementation Plans, (4) emission standards for specified new sources of air pollution, and (5) emission standards for hazardous air pollutants. Each area will be discussed in turn.

National Ambient Air Quality Standards (NAAQSs)

The Clean Air Act requires the Environmental Protection Agency (EPA) to establish primary and secondary national ambient air quality standards.[4] Primary standards are those necessary to protect public health. EPA has decided that health is impared if, for example, there is more than 0.03 parts per million (p.p.m.) sulfur dioxide in the air on an average in a region or if there is more than 0.14 p.p.m. sulfur dioxide in the air more than once a year.[5] Similar standards are set for

§ 13.6

1. 42 U.S.C.A. § 7401 et seq. The Clean Air Act was substantially modified in 1977. All references reflect those amendments.

2. For a discussion of mobile sources, see J. Rose, Legal Foundations of Environmental Planning 259 (1983).

3. Existing stationary sources are controlled by the states with federal review only in regard to the state implementation plan. New construction of certain specified sources of air pollution are directly controlled by the federal government and are the topic of the following sections.

4. 42 U.S.C.A. § 7409. See, e.g., NRDC v. Train, 545 F.2d 320 (2d Cir.1976); Friends of the Earth v. Potomac Electric Power, 419 F.Supp. 528 (D.D.C.1976).

5. 40 C.F.R. § 50.4. See id. §§ 50.6–.12 for standards for other pollutants.

other pollutants. Secondary standards are those necessary to protect public welfare. According to EPA, for example, welfare is affected by sulfur dioxide if there is more than 0.5 p.p.m. as a "maximum concentration" exceeded more than once per year.

States are required to submit to EPA an implementation plan designed to maintain NAAQSs inside their borders within nine months after NAAQSs promulgation.[6] If the state implementation plan (SIP) meets EPA standards it will be approved. Once approved, the SIP is enforceable by either federal or state authorities.[7] If a state fails to promulgate an adequate SIP, the EPA Administrator himself will issue sufficient regulations to bring the recalcitrant state into line.[8]

Air Quality Control Regions

Air quality control regions are areas characterized by similar air pollution problems. Individual states are responsible for setting up these regions within their borders. However, the EPA itself must establish the precise pollution limitations in the air quality control regions themselves.

The 1977 amendments classify these regions as either nondeterioration or nonattainment areas. Nondeterioration areas[9] are those geographic areas with air considered clean under the Act. The key to these areas is the Prevention of Significant Deterioration in Air Quality (PSD) provisions of the Clean Air Act.[10] PSD areas have air quality better than NAAQS requires. They are divided into two subclasses. Large national parks and wilderness areas are Class I, where almost no air quality degradation is allowed. All other areas are Class II, which allows moderate air pollution increases, provided they do not exceed NAAQSs. State governors may reclassify Class II areas as either Class I or Class III, which allows a tradeoff of more pollution for greater industrial expansion. Again, no NAAQS may be violated.

For a "major" new source to be built in a PSD area, a permit is required. The applicant must show that no NAAQS will be violated, and that "best available control technology (BACT) will be used for *all* pollutants.

Nonattainment areas are those localities not meeting primary and secondary NAAQSs.[11] Such a label makes development of new station-

6. 42 U.S.C.A. § 7410(a)(1).

7. Id. § 7413.

8. Id. § 7410(c)(1).

9. See, e.g., Alabama Power Co. v. Costle, 606 F.2d 1068 (D.C.Cir.1979), opinion superseded, on reconsideration 636 F.2d 323 (D.C.Cir.1979); Sierra Club v. EPA, 540 F.2d 1114 (D.C.Cir.1976), cert. denied 430 U.S. 959, 97 S.Ct. 1610, 51 L.Ed. 2d 811 (1977), judgment vacated and remanded 434 U.S. 809, 98 S.Ct. 42, 54 L.Ed. 2d 66 (1977). See 42 U.S.C.A. § 7407(d)(1).

10. 42 U.S.C.A. § 7470 et seq.

11. See, e.g., PPG Industries, Inc. v. Costle, 630 F.2d 462 (6th Cir.1980); Republic Steel Corp. v. Costle, 621 F.2d 797 (6th Cir.1980); New England Legal Found. v. Costle, 475 F.Supp. 425 (D.Conn.1979), affirmed in part, jurisdiction reserved in part 632 F.2d 936 (2d Cir.1980) affirmed 666 F.2d 30 (2d Cir.1981). See also State of N.J. v. E.P.A., 626 F.2d 1038 (D.C.Cir. 1980).

ary sources of pollution very difficult. To get a permit, an applicant must comply with the "lowest achievable emission rate" (LAER) and show that "offset" requirements are met.[12] "Offset" means that for any new pollutant source, emissions from existing sources within the air quality control region must be reduced such that a net improvement in air quality occurs.[13] LAER is defined as "the most stringent emission limitation . . . contained in the implementation plan of any state." [14] Thus any proposed industrial development can only be made at great cost, since not only must the best pollution control devices be used, but the plant owners must either significantly reduce pollution at some other owned source or pay for a similar reduction at another firm's plant.

State Implementation Plans

Each state is required to develop state implementation plans (SIPs) sufficient to meet all national primary and secondary air quality standards.[15] If a sufficient SIP is not received by EPA, the EPA will impose one until the state comes through. Each SIP must contain categories showing: (1) Legal authority, (2) control strategy, (3) compliance schedules, (4) emergency episode procedures, (5) surveillance systems, (6) review of new sources, (7) resources, (8) interstate cooperation and (9) public participation.[16]

The above categories are the federal standards all states must meet. Otherwise, the joint federal/state cooperation at the heart of the Clean Air Act controls, and the individual states are pretty much left to their own in determining the exact "hows" of NAAQS attainment. An approved SIP is the carrot. The stick is two pronged: a federally imposed plan and the possible withholding of federal funds for highway, sewer, and other projects deemed pollution causing.

12. See 42 U.S.C.A. § 7501 (defining LAER) and § 7503 (establishing a permit requirements and offsets program).

13. The use of offsets within the same source is called "bubbling." Recognizing the need to address economic considerations, the EPA in 1979 adopted rules authorizing use of the bubble concept. Under the program, the EPA interpreted the NSPS definition of source to allow netting the effects of multiple emission points within a single family. Thus, the plant wide approach treats a facility as if it were covered by a bubble, applying emissions limitations to it as a single source. This interpretation was recently upheld in Chevron U.S.A., Inc. v. Natural Resources Defense Council, Inc., ___ U.S. ___, 104 S.Ct. 2778, 81 L.Ed.2d 694 (1984), rehearing denied ___ U.S. ___, 105 S.Ct. 28, 82 L.Ed.

2d 921 (1985) (where congressional intent cannot be determined, review is limited to whether agency's construction is reasonable; bubbling interpretation valid).

14. 42 U.S.C.A. § 7501(3).

15. Id. § 7410. Rules governing SIPs are listed at 40 C.F.R. Pt. 51 et seq. See also Union Electric Co. v. EPA, 427 U.S. 246, 96 S.Ct. 2518, 49 L.Ed.2d 474 (1976), rehearing denied, 429 U.S. 873, 97 S.Ct. 189, 50 L.Ed.2d 154 (1976); Train v. NRDC, 421 U.S. 60, 95 S.Ct. 1470, 43 L.Ed.2d 731 (1975), vacated in part 516 F.2d 488 (5th Cir.1975), opinion supplemented 539 F.2d 1068 (5th Cir.1976); Bunker Hill Co. v. EPA, 572 F.2d 1286 (9th Cir.1977).

16. 40 C.F.R. Pt. 51 et seq. See also J. Rose, Legal Foundations of Environmental Planning 260–63 (1983).

New Source Performance Standards (NSPS)

Section III of the Clean Air Act requires the EPA Administrator to promulgate "standards of performance" for all stationary sources not in existence as of the date of applicable regulations.[17] This is in direct contrast to the congressional mandate directing individual state action concerning existing sources. Apparently, Congress was concerned that some states would succumb to the mentality equating dirty air with more jobs.

To counter that tendency, Section III new source standards require emission controls which

> [reflect] the degree of emission reduction achievable through the application of the best system of continuous emission reduction which (taking into consideration the cost of achieving such emission reduction, and any nonair quality health and environmental impact and energy requirements) the Administrator determines has been adequately demonstrated for that category of sources.[18]

What exact standard will be used depends on whether the proposed site is a nonattainment area or prevention of significant deterioration (PSD) area.[19]

EPA has been lethargic in implementing new source performance standards.[20] In part, the reason for the alleged foot dragging is the difficulty in setting a NSPS that industry can achieve without—so they say—going broke. Intense industrial lobbying resulted not only in the slow NSPS implementation, but the 1977 Amendments themselves.[21]

There is one interesting land use consequence of the stationary new source provisions. Because the emission limits are the same throughout the nation, industry cannot "shop around" for a jurisdiction that will treat them benignly by allowing more pollution than somewhere else. Therefore, as to new stationary sources, the regulations do not determine location.

17. 42 U.S.C.A. § 7411.

18. Id. § 7411(a)(1)(C).

19. See supra note 10 and accompanying text.

20. The following cases give a good overview of the problems NSPS implementation has caused. National Lime Association v. EPA, 627 F.2d 416 (D.C.Cir.1980); Asarco, Inc. v. EPA, 578 F.2d 319 (D.C.Cir. 1978); Portland Cement Association v. Ruckelshaus, 486 F.2d 375 (D.C.Cir.1973), cert. denied 417 U.S. 921, 94 S.Ct. 2628, 41 L.Ed.2d 226 (1974), appeal after remand 513 F.2d 506 (D.C.Cir.1975), cert. denied 423 U.S. 1025, 96 S.Ct. 469, 46 L.Ed.2d 399 (1975), rehearing denied 423 U.S. 1092, 96 S.Ct. 889, 47 L.Ed.2d 104 (1976).

21. One result of this successful lobbying effort is the inclusion of § 317 in the 1977 amendments (codified at 42 U.S.C.A. § 7617). It provides that before publishing notice of any proposed rulemaking under § 111 (NSPS), the Administrator must prepare "an economic impact assessment respecting such standard or regulation." 42 U.S.C.A. § 7617(b). Even though limited by a subsequent section preventing any change in the "basis on which a standard or regulation is promulgated," id. § 7617(e), this provision gives polluting industries a good legal handle.

Hazardous Pollutants

Section 112 of the Clean Air Act covers "hazardous air pollutants," and defines as "hazardous" an air pollutant

> to which no ambient air quality standard is applicable and which in the judgment of the Administrator causes, or contributes to, air pollution which may reasonably be anticipated to result in an increase in mortality or an increase in serious irreversible, or incapacitating reversible illness.[22]

The Administrator is directed to publish a list of hazardous air pollutants and set a national emission standard providing for an "ample margin of safety to protect the public health."[23] In contrast to new source standards for such "established" pollutants as sulfur dioxide, particulate matter, and carbon monoxide, economic and technical feasibility of compliance is not a factor in setting emission standards for hazardous pollutants. Only the President is given authority to exempt a particular hazardous pollutant, and then for only two years and only if control is technologically infeasible and exemption is necessary for "national security" reasons.[24] If technologically infeasible and not subject to a presidential exemption, the Administrator may promulgate design, equipment, work practice, or operational standards such that the public health is protected with an adequate margin of safety.[25]

 WESTLAW REFERENCES

ci(42 +5 7401)

"stationary source" /p e.p.a. "environmental protection
　　agency" /p jurisdiction! /p "clean air act"

National Ambient Air Quality Standards

n.a.a.q.s. /p primary /p health

n.a.a.q.s. /p s.i.p. /p approv! /p enforc!

Air Quality Control Regions

"air quality control region" /p classif!

p.s.d. /p pollut!

permit! /p "best available control technology" b.a.c.t.

l.a.e.r. /p offset

State Implementation Plans

"state implementation plan" s.i.p. /s standard /s e.p.a.
　　"environmental protection agency"

New Source Performance Standards

n.s.p.s. /p "standards of performance"

Hazardous Pollutants

"hazardous air pollutant" /p emission standard"

---

22. Id. § 7412(a)(1).

23. Id. § 7412(b)(1)(B).

24. Id. § 7412(c)(2).

25. Id. § 7412(e)(1). For a good discussion of the problems inherent in hazardous air pollutant controls under § 112, see Adamo Wrecking Co. v. United States, 434 U.S. 275, 98 S.Ct. 566, 54 L.Ed.2d 538 (1978).

V. LAND USE AND POLLUTION CONTROL LAWS—CLEAN WATER

§ 13.7 The Clean Water Act as a Land Use Control Measure

The Federal Water Pollution Control Act [1] is the primary national statute for preventing water pollution. Substantially amended in 1972 and 1977 (when it was denominated the Clean Water Act), the Water Act along with NEPA and the Clean Air Act completes a trilogy of federal environmental juggernauts which provide considerable federal control over some forms of land use.

The Water Act is largely administered by the Environmental Protection Agency (EPA).[2] The section most pertinent to land use controls—the dredge and fill program under section 404—is an exception in that the United States Army Corps of Engineers has primary jurisdiction with EPA playing a reviewing role. Section 404 is discussed at length in this chapter in part VII.

The Water Act directs the EPA to establish research programs and provides for grants for research and development and for pollution control programs.[3] The amounts provided for such grants, however, are modest compared with the massive funds for construction of publicly owned treatment works, for which the EPA makes larger grants.[4] Conditions are imposed on eligibility for these grants, including the requirement that a facility be in accord with any applicable areawide waste treatment management plan.[5] As with the Clean Air Act, two standards for clean water must be met, emission or effluent [6] standards and ambient standards.[7] The ambient standards are set by the states and can and do vary. Much water pollution does not come out of the end of a pipe but from water runoff, and the Act addresses these non-point sources.[8] Anything that does come out of a pipe is a point source, and the Act provides control by requiring that a permit be obtained from EPA for the discharge of any pollutant.[9] As with the Clean Air Act, much of the federal power is willingly delegated to any state which is able to administer a program to the federal requirements.

Grants

As with the Clean Air Act, the Clean Water Act can encourage land use control as dictated by water quality needs through conditions on grants. Thus, in order to obtain a grant for pollution control

§ 13.7

1. 33 U.S.C.A. § 1251 et seq.
2. Id. § 1251(d).
3. Id. §§ 1254–1265.
4. Id. §§ 1281–1287.
5. Id. § 1288.
6. Id. §§ 1311, 1316.
7. Id. § 1313.
8. Id. § 1314(f).
9. Id. §§ 1341–1345. See also id. § 1362(14).

programs,[10] recipient states and other eligible governmental agencies could be required to establish land use controls. Grants for treatment works [11] are also available only if consistent with any existing areawide waste treatment management plan,[12] and with an applicable continuing planning process and only if the treatment work constitutes a priority need.[13] However powerful the grant inducements, they do not constitute direct control.

Areawide Waste Treatment Management Plans

Areawide Waste Treatment Management Plans [14] are required to be prepared according to EPA guidelines for areas where urban-industrial concentrations have produced substantial water quality control problems, but there are no sanctions if they are not prepared; and EPA has no power to impose them as is also the case under the Clean Air Act. If prepared, permits to discharge pollutants and grants for treatment works must be consistent with the plans. The plans constitute a land use control because they cover such things as indicating where future treatment works are to be located and establishment of construction priorities for treatment works. More pervasively, the areawide plans are to "regulate the location, modification, and construction of any facilities within such area which may result in any discharge in such area . . . ." [15] This could include regulations over any private or publicly owned sewage treatment plant as well as any other point source of water pollution, such as a paper mill. Additionally, "methods" (including land use requirements) are to be included "to control" non-point source pollution from agriculture and mining operations and to control pollution from construction sites.[16] These provisions, in short, require control over many land uses of an industrial, agricultural, mining or construction nature.

Standards and Deadlines

The 1972 Federal Water Pollution Control amendments aimed for a goal of "fishable and swimmable" waters by 1983 and the complete elimination of pollution discharge by 1985. Those goals were not met. Recognizing that fact when the 1977 Clean Water Act Amendments were introduced, Congress established a three-step process setting forth new standards and deadlines. Separate standards and deadlines were set for pollution from various sources and of various types. The odds for these new deadlines being met by all sources on time are, to say the least, not good. However, it is probable that substantial compliance will occur. In any event, the revised standards and deadlines are as follows.

10. Id. § 1256.

11. Id. § 1281(g).

12. Id. § 1288(d).

13. Id. § 1284.

14. Id. § 1288.

15. Id. § 1288(b)(2)(C)(ii).

16. Id. § 1288(b)(2)(F).

For municipal treatment plants, secondary treatment was to be in place by 1977 and the "best practicable waste treatment over the life of the works" by 1983.[17] However, 1981 amendments moved this date up to 1988 because of reductions in federal aid. For industries, the situation is much more complex. The 1977 standards for industries is the "best practicable control technology currently available" (BPT).[18] BPT is defined as an effluent standard based on the average performance of plants of similar types and ages within each industrial category.[19] The 1977 amendments also created three subclasses of industrial pollutants and set extended deadlines for compliance.

Conventional pollutants, defined in general to include sewage and sewage-related waste, must meet effluent standards based on the "best conventional pollutant control technology" (BCT).[20] BCT is a medium strict standard allowing economic considerations. The deadline was July 1, 1984, and no waivers are provided for.[21] However, the deadline had not been met when the FWCPA was reauthorized in 1985. Toxic pollutants, listed by the EPA (some 129-different substances were initially listed) as deserving special concern, must meet effluent standards based on the "best available technology economically achievable" (BAT).[22] BAT is the most stringent standard and is based on the best performer in any industrial class. The deadline was again July 1, 1984, with no allowance for waiver[23] or economic consideration, but was extended to 1988.[23a] Nonconventional pollutants, defined as neither conventional nor toxic, must also be controlled by BAT standards.[24] However, the deadline is more flexible, allowing implementation to wait until July 1, 1987.[25] These (and the prior 1972) standards and deadlines are responsible for a great bulk of the total litigation involving the Clean Water Act.[26] There is no reason to believe that fact will change much as the deadlines approach and pass.

Variable Emission Limitations

While the effluent limitation standards are the same nationally, special effluent limitations or other control strategies can be applied by

17. Id. § 1311.

18. Id. § 1311(b)(1)(A).

19. Id. § 1314(b)(1)(B).

20. Id. § 1311(b)(2)(E).

21. Id.

22. Id. § 1317. See also Hercules, Inc. v. EPA, 598 F.2d 91 (D.C.Cir.1978); T. Schoenbaum, Environmental Policy Law 724–26 (1982).

23. 33 U.S.C.A. § 1311(b)(2)(C).

23a. For a case illustrating judicial leniency, see Chemical Mfrs. Ass'n v. Natural Resources Defense Council, Inc., ___ U.S. ___, 105 S.Ct. 1102, 84 L.Ed.2d 90 (1985).

24. Id. § 1311(b)(2)(A).

25. Id. § 1311(b)(2)(F).

26. See generally EPA v. National Crushed Stone Association, 449 U.S. 64, 101 S.Ct. 295, 66 L.Ed.2d 268 (1980), on remand 643 F.2d 163 (4th Cir.1981); E.I. Du Pont De Nemours & Co. v. Train, 430 U.S. 112, 97 S.Ct. 965, 51 L.Ed.2d 204 (1977); Appalachian Power Co. v. EPA, 671 F.2d 801 (4th Cir.1982); California & Hawaiian Sugar Co. v. EPA, 553 F.2d 280 (2d Cir.1977); American Frozen Food Institutes v. Train, 539 F.2d 107 (D.C.Cir.1976); American Meat Institute v. EPA, 526 F.2d 442 (7th Cir.1975).

EPA to point sources discharging into particular waters.[27] These special limitations which vary by location could mean, for example, that water pollution considerations would "force" a paper mill from one location to another with all the direct and indirect land use consequences such locational decisions imply.

Continuing Planning Process

Once the standards are established, each state must identify those waters which cannot be made clean to the standard by effluent limitations alone. Maximum daily pollutant loads must be assigned such waters. Each state must have a continuing planning process, roughly the equivalent of implementation plans under the Clean Air Act, and therefore not surprisingly often referred to as the implementation plan. The implementation plan can be approved by EPA only if it provides at least for EPA set effluent limitations, incorporates areawide waste management plans, provides for maximum daily pollutant loads, includes procedures for revision of water quality standards and indicates there is available authority for intergovernmental cooperation and power to implement effluent and water quality limitations and standards.[28]

Nonpoint Sources

By definition, a nonpoint pollution source is pollution not discharged through a pipe or other "discrete conveyance." The most common nonpoint sources facing land use planning are agricultural and urban runoff. Other nonpoint pollution sources result from silviculture and mining operations.

The nonpoint source [29] problem is particularly susceptible to regulation by land use control. While municipal and industrial waste discharges require expensive treatment facilities, nonpoint sources can be controlled through changes in land use policies. The only other options are to provide a collection point so that the runoff becomes a point source or ban enough point sources from the area so that water quality standards are met.

Agricultural nonpoint source pollution results from irrigation, erosion, animal waste, fertilizer and pesticide runoff. Additionally, poor irrigation and tillage practices result in soil erosion, which depletes soil fertility as it pollutes. To control agricultural runoff, techniques such as conservation tillage, terracing, contouring, strip cropping, and drainage construction projects are used.[30]

The Water Act combats agricultural runoff through section 208 planning guidelines, with implementation left to state and local govern-

27. 33 U.S.C.A. § 1312.

28. Id. § 1313(e).

29. Id. § 1314(f).

30. National Conference of State Legislatures, Land Management: Sustaining Re-

sources Values 163 (Oct. 1983) [hereinafter cited as National Conference]. See also J. Juergensmeyer & J. Wadley, Agricultural Law § 23.4 (1982).

ments.[31] Section 208 provides for Best Management Practices (BMP), administered through state departments of agriculture and local soil and water conservation districts.[32] These BMPs use the above runoff control techniques.

Urban runoff contributes to nonpoint pollution problems by funneling oil, heavy metals, and sediment into streams and groundwater supplies. The key villain in urban runoff is construction; rainwater that used to slowly filter through earth is now met by concrete and asphalt. As with agricultural runoff, section 208 plans and Best Management Practices are the Clean Water Act's response to urban nonpoint source pollution. The BMPs used to control urban runoff include street cleaning, covering stored construction materials, and using detention basins and infiltration methods.[33] Local governments usually control these programs through zoning and building permit controls. One benefit of this approach is that a land developer can plan ahead for nonpoint source controls. Thus, the control program can be factored into the construction process allowing costs to be amortized over time.[34]

Governmental Facilities

Governmental facilities are often bad neighbors from a land use point of view but are often exempt from traditional land use controls. Not even federal government facilities are exempt under the Clean Water Act unless specifically exempted by the President, and not even the President can exempt projects from the national effluent limitations. Such facilities must comply as if owned by any other person and must comply not only with federal but with state, interstate and local requirements respecting control and abatement of pollution.[35]

Clean Lakes

While no sanction for noncompliance is indicated, each state is required to identify publicly owned fresh water lakes and to establish "methods (including land use requirements), to control sources of pollution of such lakes." [36] Grants are available to "carry out methods and procedures" approved by EPA.[37]

Permit System

Despite the previously described powerful inducements, one might quibble that they represent direct land use control. The permit system

31. 33 U.S.C.A. § 1288(b)(1)(A).

32. See T. Schoenbaum, supra note 22, at 788.

33. Id.

34. National Conference, supra note 30, at 164.

35. 33 U.S.C.A. § 1323.

36. Id. § 1324.

37. For "model" acts which provide examples of methods that might be used, see, e.g., Washington Shoreline Management Act of 1971, West's Rev.Code Wash.Ann. ch. 90.58; Wisconsin Shoreland Zoning Law, Wis.Stat.Ann. 59.971, 144.26; Tahoe Regional Planning Compact, P.L. 91–158, 83 Stat. 360, Dec. 18, 1969.

established by the FWPCA, however, clearly involves direct control. The National Pollutant Discharge Elimination System (NPDES) requires an EPA permit to discharge any pollutant into any waters of the United States. The permit can issue only if the discharger complies with all standards in the FWPCA. States can administer permits only if EPA has approved a state permit program that meets EPA standards and if a continuing planning process is in existence. No permit can be issued which conflicts with any areawide waste treatment plan.[38]

Publicly owned waste treatment plants are required to have permits. These permits can be conditioned to assure standards are met. If the conditions are violated, EPA has power to seek a court order prohibiting any further use of the treatment plant by a new source of pollution.[39] Popularly called the "sewer ban" provision, it could make new development impossible unless other alternative means of disposal were found which, of course, would also have to comply with the Water Act. Private sources of pollution must also comply and permits are denied where water quality standards or effluent limitations cannot be met.[40]

     WESTLAW REFERENCES

ci(33 +5 1251)

da(aft 10–8–77 & bef 1978) & "water pollution control act"

water /s emission effluent ambient +s standard /s "point
     source"

sy(permit /s e.p.a. /s discharg! /s pollutant)

Grants

"clean water act" /p grant /s "treatment work"

Areawide Waste Treatment Management Plans

"waste treatment management plan"

Standards and Deadlines

"best practicable control technology currently available"
     b.p.t. /s industr!

"conventional pollutant" /s b.c.t.

Variable Emission Limitations

199k25.7(16) & "point source"

Continuing Planning Process

33 +5 1313(e)

Non-Point Sources

"non point" /p defin! characteriz!

33 +5 1314(f)

runoff /p collection /s point

"water act" /s 208

38. 33 U.S.C.A. § 1342(a).

39. Id. § 1342(h).

40. Ipsen & Rasch, Enforcement Under
the Federal Water Pollution Control Act

Amendments of 1972, 9 Land & Water
L.Rev. 369 (1974).

"urban runoff"

agricultur! farm! /p "non point" runoff /p pollut!

Government Facilities

33 +5 1323 /s water

393k3 /p water

Clean Lakes

grant fund*** /p federal! /p water lake

Permit System

f.w.p.c.a. /p permit /p pollut! /p water /p sewage

state /p permit /p e.p.a. /p approv! /p standard

he(33 +8 1342(a))

360k4.13 /p pollut!

199k28 /p consistent! conflict! /p permit

270k35 /p permit

public! /s waste /s treat! /s plant /s permit /s requir!

268k838

"sewer ban"

privat! /p pollut! /p comply! compli**** /p permit /p water

VI. LAND USE AND POLLUTION CONTROL LAWS—SAFE DRINKING WATER, HAZARDOUS WASTES AND QUIETUDE

§ 13.8 The Safe Drinking Water Act

The Safe Drinking Water Act (SDWA)[1] has a land use control effect in that it seeks to ensure that public water supply systems do not endanger the public health. By setting up a two-stage procedure calling for interim and then revised national primary drinking water regulations, the SDWA reflects congressional concern for expense and feasibility. The interim regulations are to protect health only "to the extent feasible" considering cost and available technology.[2]

The revised national standards are to be set based upon a study by the National Academy of Sciences (NAS).[3] That study is to determine both the maximum contaminant level in drinking water allowable without harming health and whether there is any contaminant "the levels of which in drinking water cannot be determined but which may have an adverse effect on the health of persons."[4] EPA may, but does not have to, set secondary regulations dealing with non-hazardous unpleasantries in drinking water affecting taste, odor and appearance.

§ 13.8

1. 42 U.S.C.A. § 300f et seq. See also Environmental Defense Fund, Inc. v. Costle, 578 F.2d 337 (D.C.Cir.1978).

2. 42 U.S.C.A. § 300g–1(a)(1). The implementing regulations for the SDWA are at 40 C.F.R. Pt. 141 et seq.

3. 42 U.S.C.A. § 300g–1(e)(1).

4. Id.

As with most environmental statutes, the chief land use effect of the SDWA lies in enforcement. The states have primary authority for enforcing the national primary regulations provided they meet federal standards.[5] EPA will provide enforcement authority if a state either fails or chooses not to meet federal standards. However, EPA's enforcement authority under the SDWA is quite limited in comparison to the Clean Water Act. First, EPA has discretion in whether to bring an enforcement action or not. Second, EPA can only file a civil suit for a SDWA violation, it cannot issue administrative compliance orders.[6] The SDWA's teeth are short, and the only likelihood of their being lengthened in the near future is if a large metropolitan area's water becomes too poisonous to drink.

WESTLAW REFERENCES
"national academy of sciences" n.a.s. /p contamina!
"safe drinking water act" s.d.w.a. /p enforc!

§ 13.9 Deadly Garbage—The Resource Conservation and Recovery Act (RCRA) and the Comprehensive Environmental Response, Compensation, and Liability Act of 1980 (CERCLA/"Superfund")

Proper disposal of hazardous wastes is undoubtedly the "sexy" environmental issue for the 1980's. Spawned by tragedies such as Love Canal, public and political interest in hazardous waste disposal remains high despite recent assaults on environmental regulation—perhaps because the issue strikes so close to home since a primary risk of improper waste disposal is the poisoning of drinking water supplies.

Concern over safe disposal of hazardous materials fits easily into the land use planners' bag of worries. From decades of experience in siting private and municipal garbage dumps, land use planners can be expected to pay close attention to regulations concerning the proper disposal of the deadly garbage our technological-based society produces. Through years of neglect, federal, state and local officials have allowed the creation of some 50,000 hazardous waste dumps. More than a thousand are considered real and immediate hazards. These figures reveal the national nightmare hazardous wastes have become.

The Resource Conservation and Recovery Act (RCRA)[1] is the nation's first line of defense against the hazardous waste nightmare. RCRA is based on a "cradle to grave" system of regulation. Separate standards cover the production, transportation, and disposal of hazard-

5. Id. § 300g-2(a).

6. Id. § 300g-3(a)(1)(B). See also J. Rose, Legal Foundations of Environmental Planning 405 (1983). See generally Douglas, Safe Drinking Water Act of 1974—History and Critique, 5 Envtl.Aff. 501 (1976).

§ 13.9

1. 42 U.S.C.A. § 6901 et seq. For an excellent analysis of the enormously complicated RCRA program, see J. Quarles, Federal Regulation of Hazardous Waste: A Guide to RCRA, (Env'l Law Inst.1982).

ous wastes.[2] Hazardous wastes are identified by "taking into account toxicity, persistence, and degradability in nature, potential for accumulation in tissue, and other related factors such as flammability, corrosiveness, and other hazardous characteristics." [3]

Disposal is allowed only upon obtaining a permit.[4] Permits are issued only if the waste is covered by a manifest [5]—the ubiquitous document responsible for keeping track of the waste from production to disposal. Unlike the feeble SDWA, RCRA's fangs include civil and criminal penalties for either permit violations or document falsification.[6] Injunctive relief is also available upon a finding of an "imminent and substantial endangerment to health or the environment." [7]

Perhaps the best known of the hazardous waste statutes is the Comprehensive Environmental Response, Compensation, and Liability Act of 1980 (CERCLA) [8]. Nicknamed "superfund," CERCLA establishes a pool of money collected as a tax on toxic chemical manufacture.[9] This money is to be used for expenses entailed in the presidentially implemented "national contingency plan." [10] This plan is the basis for hazardous waste site cleanup. If federal standards are met, this responsibility can be delegated to the states.[11]

The most important, and certainly the most litigated, aspect of CERCLA is the provision requiring hazardous waste generators to pay for cleanup costs and natural resource destruction (if the resources are owned by a governmental entity).[12] Even though it is a perfect example of pollution laws paying for themselves, recovery of cleanup costs has been extremely slow.

WESTLAW REFERENCES

proper** /p dispos! /p hazard! /p waste /p land property
    /p develop!

r.c.r.a. /p "cradle to grave"

r.c.r.a. /p "hazardous waste" /p dispos! /p permit

r.c.r.a. /p criminal superfund /p toxic hazardous dangerous
    /p chemical substance waste dump

c.e.r.c.l.a. /p tax

199k25.5(5.5)

"national contingency plan" /s cleanup

---

2. Id. §§ 6922, 6923, 6924, 6925.

3. Id. § 6921(a).

4. Id. § 6925.

5. Id. § 6922(5).

6. Id. § 6928.

7. Id. § 6973(a). See also United States v. Price, 688 F.2d 204 (3d Cir.1982).

8. 42 U.S.C.A. § 9601 et seq.

9. Id. § 9611.

10. Id. §§ 9604(a), 9631, 9641.

11. Id. § 9604(c), (d).

12. Id. § 9607.

§ 13.10 Noise Control Act of 1972

The basic thrust of the Noise Control Act [1] is that EPA is required to set noise emission limits for new products that produce considerable noise. Examples are transportation vehicles, construction equipment, and other kinds of motors and engines.[2] As true with the Clean Air and Clean Water Acts, emission limitations that apply nationwide do not have many land use implications.

To be sure, if trucks are made to run more quietly, areas now inundated by noise from trucks will become more pleasant places. But that land use result hardly involves direct EPA control of land use.

EPA is also required to publish noise standards necessary to protect the public health and welfare, and to publish information on techniques for control of noise.[3] While that authority might be broad enough to permit EPA to suggest how industrial noise can be controlled, which in turn might involve such land use techniques as buffer zones or performance standards, states are not required to apply such techniques.[4]

Airport location may be affected by the EPA under the Noise Act, for it is directed to study such matters.[5] It is also to recommend regulations for control and abatement of noise to the Federal Aviation Agency, which then will promulgate appropriate regulations,[6] including those necessary to protect the public health and welfare. Under such regulations, the FAA might consider such land use matters as locations of airports, requiring large sites, airport zoning and limitations on uses around airports to include only those that are noise insensitive or are easy to insulate from noise. But as of this writing, the FAA has shown no inclination to flex any direct land use control muscle.

The EPA can also promulgate noise standards for railroad equipment and motor carriers engaged in interstate commerce.[7] But these provisions are probably not broad enough to authorize the EPA to, for example, restrict locations of railroad or truck yards or rail lines or highways.

As with the Clean Water Act, if states and localities come up with noise control programs, the federal government must play by state and local rules. Federal agencies and activities shall comply with Federal, State, interstate, and local requirements respecting control and abatement of environmental noise to the same extent that any person is

§ 13.10

1. 42 U.S.C.A. § 4901 et seq. See also Comment, Toward the Comprehensive Abatement of Noise Pollution: Recent Federal and New York City Noise Control Legislation, 4 Ecology L.Q. 109 (1974).

2. 42 U.S.C.A. § 4905(a)(1)(C).

3. Id. § 4904.

4. Some zoning ordinances already apply sophisticated performance standards, including noise emission standards, for determining whether a particular industrial use is allowable in a zone. See supra §§ 4.11, 4.13.

5. 42 U.S.C.A. § 4906.

6. 49 U.S.C.A. § 1431(c).

7. 42 U.S.C.A. §§ 4916, 4917.

subject . . . . The President may exempt . . . in the paramount interest of the United States [except in several specified situations] . . . .[8]

 WESTLAW REFERENCES

"noise control act" /p noise /p emi****** /p limit!

e.p.a. "environmental protection agency" /p publish! publication /p noise /p standard

f.a.a. "federal aviation administration" /p e.p.a. "environmental protection" /p noise

e.p.a. "environmental protection agency" /p noise /p railroad "motor carrier"

42 +5 4903(b)

VII. LAND USE AND ENVIRONMENTALLY SENSITIVE LANDS: WETLANDS

§ 13.11 Definition and Importance of Wetlands

To many people the idea of "wetlands" conjures up images of dismal, dank, mosquito-ridden, snake-infested, miasmic swamps to either be avoided or paved over. Indeed, this notion has been so prevalent in our nation's collective subconscious that we have destroyed up to forty percent of our wetland resources.[1] They were lost beneath the crunching blow of drag lines and dredges making way for subdivisions, trailer parks, agribusiness and dumps. For those with the above delusion this turn of events may seem just fine; the best swamp is a drained swamp. Yet as a nation, we are just now beginning to realize that wetlands may be the most important (economically, as well as ecologically) of all environmentally sensitive lands.

Saltwater marshes are the most biologically productive lands on earth, producing more than twice the biomass of our most fertile hayfields.[2] Such estuarine areas also serve an essential role as nurseries for seven of the ten most commercially valuable fish and shellfish consumed in this country.[3] Fresh water wetlands play an important (critical, in some areas) role in aquifer recharge, pollution control (through a remarkably efficient system of capture and filtration), flood

8. Id. § 4903(b).

§ 13.11

1. See E. Horwitz, Our Nation's Wetlands 1, 49 (1978) (Interagency Task Force Report coordinated by the Council on Environmental Quality).

2. Id. at 21.

3. McHugh, Management of Estuarine Fisheries, A Symposium on Estuarine Fish-eries, 3 Am. Fisheries Soc'y Special Publication (1966). The top ten species are shrimp, salmon, tuna, oysters, menhaden, crabs, lobsters, flounders, clams and haddock. The three exceptions to the estuarine dependent rule are tuna, lobsters, and haddock.

control, prevention of soil erosion and as wildlife habitat.[4] Absent adequate wetlands protection, there will occur a dramatic drop in fish, shellfish, wildlife, and timber production nationwide with a corresponding rise in flood damage, soil loss, fresh water depletion (accompanied by salt water intrusion in coastal areas) and general environmental degradation as pollutants concentrate.[5]

With wetlands' value identified and need for protection recognized, the first hurdle toward sensible management is definitional. There is simply no standard, all inclusive definition of a wetland that meets all needs.[6] Marshes, swamps, bogs, some types of hardwood forested areas, sloughs, wet meadows, natural ponds, potholes and river overflow areas have all been described as wetlands. Basically, the term "wetlands" is generic and refers to areas supporting vegetation capable of withstanding wet conditions. This occurs where land levels are low and ground water levels are high.

WESTLAW REFERENCES
wetland /2 defin!
wetland /s flood! /s prevent!

§ 13.12   The Federal Presence

As with other types of environmental land use control, wetlands protection is characterized by a strong federal and state regulatory presence. From a "do as you damn well please" attitude, wetlands development has become dominated by a bewildering array of state and federal regulations and permit requirements. In addition, many states with substantial wetlands acreage have local regulations tied in with the broader federal and state programs.

Because permits at all levels must be obtained before any form of development may occur in a wetland area it is important to understand the regulatory interplay in the permitting process and the federal, state, and local jurisdictions involved.

The Rivers and Harbors Act of 1899

The granddaddy of all wetland regulations was not designed to conserve wetlands at all. When President McKinley signed the Rivers and Harbors Act of 1899, his intent was to protect navigable waters to the extent they were safe for shipping.[1] Thus jurisdiction was provided

---

4. See E. Horwitz, supra note 1, at 22–25.

5. The quantifiable value of wetlands is difficult to ascertain, but the figures tentatively reached in certain localized areas are staggering. Relatively small wetland regions may have values exceeding seven figures annually. See id. at 28–29.

6. For definitional examples, see, e.g., Inst. of Water Resources, U.S. Army Corps

of Eng'rs, Wetlands Values Concepts and Methods for Wetlands Evaluations 3 (1979); U.S. Fish & Wildlife Serv., Dep't of the Interior, Wetlands of the United States Circular 393 (1971).

§ 13.12

1. 33 U.S.C.A. §§ 401–418.

over "navigable waters" alone. Nevertheless, by prohibiting the obstruction or alteration of "navigable waters of the United States" without recommendation by the Chief of Engineers and authorization by the Secretary of the Army,[2] section 10 of the Rivers and Harbors Act has become of considerable importance in wetlands regulation and conservation.

The Army Corp of Engineers defines "navigable waters" as "those waters that are subject to the ebb and flow of the tide and/or are presently used, or have been used in the past, or may be susceptible for use to transport interstate or foreign commerce."[3] Whether a waterbody comes under the above definition is a regulatory decision made by the Division Engineer based upon a report prepared at the district level.[4] The decision, as it would be considering the above definition, is based upon the past, present, or potential presence of interstate or foreign commerce and the physical capabilities of the waterbody for use by such commerce.[5]

While many environmentally sensitive wetlands are not covered by this definition, some larger areas are. Section 10's applicability to wetlands regulation was verified by the Fifth Circuit Court of Appeals in Zabel v. Tabb.[6] There, two developers applied for a permit to dredge and fill in the navigable waters of Boca Ciega Bay, near St. Petersburg, Florida, in order to build a trailer park. The project was denied the necessary permits by the Corps of Engineers. Under normal circumstances (at that time) the matter would probably have ended there. However, the permit denial was issued solely on the basis of environmental concerns—the project would neither interfere with navigation nor flood control. The developers cried foul in that they believed the Corps had no authority to deny a dredge and fill permit on purely environmental grounds,[7] and the district court agreed with them.[8] In a sweeping opinion, Judge John R. Brown reversed the district court and held that the Corps had indeed such power, and could base its permitting decisions either partially or wholly on ecological reasons.[9]

2. Id. § 403.

3. 33 C.F.R. § 329.4.

4. Id. § 329.14.

5. Id. § 329.12.

6. 430 F.2d 199 (5th Cir.1970), cert. denied 401 U.S. 910, 91 S.Ct. 873, 27 L.Ed.2d 808 (1971).

7. Actually, the Corps had broadened its jurisdiction through regulation in 1968. The regulations allowed the Corps to consider public interest and environmental factors. 33 C.F.R. § 209.120 (superseded by 42 Fed.Reg. 37,133 (1977)).

8. 430 F.2d at 201.

9. Judge Brown's decision was prefaced by an extraordinary preface which is well worth quoting in its entirety:

It is the destiny of the Fifth Circuit to be in the middle of great, oftentimes explosive issues of spectacular public importance. So it is here as we enter in depth the contemporary interest in the preservation of our environment. By an injunction requiring the issuance of a permit to fill in eleven acres of tidelands in the beautiful Boca Ciega Bay in the St. Petersburg-Tampa, Florida area for use as a commercial mobile trailer park, the District Judge held that the Secretary of the Army and his functionary, the Chief of Engineers, had no power to consider anything except interference with navigation. There being no such obstruction to navigation, they were ordered to issue a permit even though the permittees acknowledge that "there was

Section 10 Jurisdiction

Federal jurisdiction under section 10 is complicated by water level changes. Jurisdiction over tidal water extends to the mean high water line.[10] The mean high water line is calculated by using tidal cycle data. The ordinary high water mark which defines federal jurisdiction in nontidal water is not so easily determined. As defined by regulation,

> [t]he "ordinary high water mark" on nontidal rivers is the line on the shore established by the fluctuations of water and indicated by physical characteristics such as a clear, natural line impressed on the bank; shelving; changes in the character of soil; destruction of terrestrial vegetation; the presence of litter and debris; or other appropriate means that consider the characteristics of the surrounding areas.[11]

Because of the definitional complexity of section 10, setting jurisdiction in nontidal lakes and rivers (whose shore areas are often classified as wetlands) is accomplished by using eyewitness accounts, photographs, and surveys of biological and physical data.[12]

One important land use aspect of section 10 jurisdiction concerns artificial canals. Real estate developers have used these canals for more than a decade to attract buyers looking for "waterfront" property with lake or ocean access. These canals often run into section 10 problems when constructed within tidal areas.[13] Greater jurisdictional uncertainties occur when canals are constructed in inland waters not subject to tidal flow.[14]

evidence before the Corps of Engineers sufficient to justify an administrative agency finding that [the] fill would do damage to the ecology or marine life on the bottom." We hold that nothing in the statutory structure compels the Secretary to close his eyes to all that others see or think they see. The establishment was entitled, if not required, to consider ecological factors and, being persuaded by them, to deny that which might have been granted routinely five, ten, or fifteen years ago before man's explosive increase made all, including Congress, aware of civilization's potential destruction from breathing its own polluted air and drinking its own infected water and the immeasurable loss from a silent-spring-like disturbance of nature's economy. We reverse.

Id. at 200.

10. 33 C.F.R. § 329.12.

11. Id. § 329.11. Nontidal waters are subject to fluctuation based on rain fall, topography, and other factors in a complex fashion. Calculations of water levels in a tidally dominated system, on the other hand, are by no means simple but are at

least related to the mathematically predictable nature of tidal waves.

12. See, e.g., United States v. Cameron, 466 F.Supp. 1099, 1111 (M.D.Fla.1978). In examining the admissibility of extensive survey data introduced by the government, the court recognized that

> the ordinary high water line is not readily susceptible to a uniform and precise definition which will provide guidance for each and every case. Rather, the term is best regarded as a concept which denotes the point at which the bed of a lake or river ceases and the shore or fast lands begins, a point which may be capable of proof by a variety of methods depending upon the facts and circumstances of the particular case.

Among the available methods the court noted are the use of a clear natural line of changing physical characteristics, biological changes, or upon reliable water elevation data. Id.

13. See United States v. Sexton Cove Estates, 526 F.2d 1293 (5th Cir.1976).

14. See National Wildlife Federation v. Alexander, 613 F.2d 1054, 1066 (D.C.Cir.

A favorite trick of developers to escape section 10 jurisdiction is to build a series of unconnected canals.[15] Unconnected canals are not "navigable" and are thus not regulated by section 10. These canals invariably become connected, allowing ocean or lake access, through somewhat mysterious activities, usually undertaken late at night with the aid of bulldozers and draglines. Indeed, these canals are occasionally opened up by environmental officials worried about the adverse ecological effects resulting from stagnant water.

While this activity still occurs, a recent case [16] has found a section 10 violation in the washing out of an earthen plug (during a heavy storm) that separated the developer's canal from a navigable water. Because the violation occurred when the plug washed out, not in building the canal,[17] the case may not be very persuasive precedent in light of the millions of dollars to be made in selling waterfront property. It seems that to find a section 10 violation in this kind of ditch digging, it will take a court willing to find a violation based on the developer's intent. While certainly possible, intent is not an easy thing to prove.

 WESTLAW REFERENCES

wetland /s federal /s regulat! /s develop!

The Rivers and Harbors Act of 1899

"rivers and harbors act of 1899" /p protect! /p "navigable waters"

270k35 /p permit /p army

270k3 /p "rivers and harbors" /p interpret! mean meant meaning refer! scope

obstruct! /s "navigable waters" /s recommend! /s "chief of engineers"

83k82 /p "rivers and harbors"

prior /p enact! /p "refuse act"

sy(division "army corp" /2 engineer /s jurisdiction /s regulat!)

kaiser /s aetna /s navigability

270k1(3) /p navigability

"division engineer" /s report! /s district

zabel /s tabb /p 10

permit /s dredge /s fill /s deni**** deny!

Section 10 Jurisdiction

tidal /s water /s 10 /s jurisdiction!

united /s states /s sexton /s cove /p 10

canal /p 10 /p jurisdiction! /p water waterfront

1979), appeal after remand 665 F.2d 390 (D.C.Cir.1981). (§ 10 held not to apply).

15. United States v. Sexton Cove Estates, 526 F.2d 1293 (5th Cir.1976) (§ 10 jurisdiction does not include unconnected canals).

16. United States v. Hanna, 19 Env't Rep.Cas. (BNA) 1068 (D.S.C.1983).

17. Id. at 1077.

§ 13.13   Section 404 of the Clean Water Act

While section 10 gave some limited protection to certain wetlands under the "navigable waters" rubric,[1] it was not until the passage of section 404 of the Federal Water Pollution Control Act[2] in 1972 that wetlands were protected as valuable entities unto themselves.[3] Corps jurisdiction under section 404 over dredge and fill activities is extended to "waters of the United States."[4] The legislative history of the Act indicates congressional intent that the term "be given the broadest constitutional interpretation unencumbered by agency determinations which would have been made or may be made for administrative purposes."[5] The Corps defines "waters of the United States" to include:

(1) The territorial seas with respect to the discharge of fill material.

(2) Coastal and inland waters, lakes, rivers, and streams that are navigable waters of the United States and their adjacent wetlands.

(3) Tributaries to navigable waters of the United States including adjacent wetlands but not including artificial nontidal drainage and irrigation ditches excavated on dry land.

(4) Interstate waters and their tributaries including adjacent wetlands.

(5) All other waters of the United States including isolated wetlands and lakes, intermittent streams, prairie potholes, and other waters that are not part of a tributary system to interstate

§ 13.13

1. With the advent of § 404 of the Clean Water Act (discussed infra), jurisdiction under § 10 of the Rivers and Harbors Act became more limited. This is because § 404 has a much broader geographic reach. However, § 10 is still useful in situations where, for instance, a § 404 exemption applies and § 10 is the only protection left. See, e.g., Save Our Sound Fisheries Association v. Callaway, 387 F.Supp. 292, 305 (D.R.I.1974).

2. Pub.L.No. 92–500, § 404, 86 Stat. 816 (1972) (codified at 33 U.S.C.A. § 1344). Since the 1977 amendments to the F.W. P.C.A., Clean Water Act of 1977, Pub.L.No. 95–217, § 67, 91 Stat. 1566 (amending 33 U.S.C.A. § 1344), the Act has been known as the Clean Water Act. Further discussion of the Clean Water Act's impact on land use planning is discussed in § 13.7 of this chapter.

3. The latest figures indicate that § 404 has reduced the annual destruction of wet-

lands by half—from 660,000 acres per year to 330,000 acres per year in 1981. Supposedly, this reduction was accomplished without unreasonable moratoria on development. Comment, Corps Recasts § 404 Permit Program, Braces for Political, Legal Skirmishes, 13 Envtl.L.Rep. 10129 (May 1983).

4. 33 U.S.C.A. § 1344 provides the authority for the Secretary of the Army to issue permits after notice and hearing for the discharge of dredged or fill material into the "navigable waters" at specified disposal sites. However, 33 U.S.C.A. § 1362(7) defines "navigable waters" to mean "the waters of the United States including the territorial seas."

5. S.Rep.No. 92–1236, 92 Cong., 1st Sess. 144, reprinted in (1972) U.S. Code Cong. & Ad.News 3822. See also 33 C.F.R. § 323.2(a)(5) n.2.

waters or to navigable waters of the United States if the degradation or destruction of such could affect interstate commerce.[6]

Number 5 above is particularly important. It states that section 404 covers not only those water bodies suitable for navigation under section 10 of the Rivers and Harbors Act, but almost any wetland area in the nation if injury to it could "affect interstate commerce."

In the seminal case of United States v. Holland,[7] a federal court found section 404's broad definition of federally controlled waters to be within commerce clause authority. The court stated:

> Congress and the courts have become aware of the lethal effect pollution has on all organisms. Weakening of any of the life support systems bodes disaster for the rest of the interrelated life forms. To recognize this and yet hold that pollution does not affect interstate commerce unless committed in navigable waters below the mean high water line would be contrary to reason. Congress is not limited by the "navigable waters" test in its authority to control pollution under the commerce clause.[8]

To ensure enforcement of section 404's congressional mandate, the federal courts have forced the Corps of Engineers to accept and police their jurisdictional authority. The Corps had first avoided this responsibility by promulgating regulations giving it authority only over navigable waters below the mean high water line. These regulations were struck down in Natural Resources Defense Council v. Callaway,[9] where the court found the Corps' self-limitation an unlawful act in derogation of their responsibilities under section 404. Thus, the above five categories of "waters of the United States" is a judicially imposed interpretation of congressional intent factored through the Corps' rulemaking process.[10] Once implemented, these definitions were found to cover up to sixty percent of all U.S. wetlands.[11]

---

6. 33 C.F.R. § 323.2(a). For discussions of Corps jurisdiction under § 404, see Comment, Wetlands Reluctant Champion: The Corps Takes a Fresh Look at "Navigable Waters," 6 Envt'l L.Rev. 217 (1975); Comment, Wetlands Protection under the Corps of Engineers' New Dredge and Fill Jurisdiction, 28 Hastings L.J. 223 (1976). For case law interpreting these individual definitions, see, e.g., United States v. Lee Wood Contracting, Inc., 529 F.Supp. 119, 120 (E.D.Mich.1981); United States v. Tilton, 714 F.2d 642 (6th Cir.1983); United States v. Carter, 18 Env't Rep.Cas. (BNA) 1804, 1809 (S.D.Fla.1982).

7. 373 F.Supp. 665 (M.D.Fla.1974).

8. Id. at 673.

9. 392 F.Supp. 685 (D.D.C.1975).

10. The expansive jurisdiction of the Corps under § 404 is under broad attack by special interests. They claim the present jurisdiction goes beyond congressional intent and that it usurps state authority. Additionally, even though states are authorized to assume § 404 authority, 33 U.S. C.A. § 1344(g), no state has done so yet. In part, the reason for this lack of state enthusiasm is the difficulty in meeting the statutory criteria and the lack of incentive to do so; no funding is authorized. See American Bar Ass'n, Concerning the Use of Water Related Lands: Flood Hazard Areas, Mudflows and Wetlands, at J–3 (1982). Attempts were made in the 97th Congress to limit § 404 jurisdiction, but were not successful. See S. 773, H.R. 383, H.R. 393, and H.R. 3962, 97th Cong., 1st Sess. (1981).

11. See Note, The Wetlands Controversy: A Coastal Concern Washes Inland, 52 Notre Dame Law. 1015, 1017 (1977).

Upon assuming such inclusive jurisdiction, the Corps was faced with the common problem of defining wetlands. The eventually-agreed-on definition is:

> Those areas that are inundated or saturated by surface or ground water at a frequency and duration sufficient to support, and that under normal circumstances do support, a prevalence of vegetation typically adopted for life in saturated soil conditions. Wetlands generally include swamps, marshes, bogs, and similar areas.[12]

Statutory Exemptions from Section 404

Section 404 applies only to discharge of dredge or fill debris.[13] It does not cover any wastewater or pollutant discharged for waste disposal purposes.[14] Certain dredge or fill activities are specifically exempted by statute. Those include the discharge of dredged or fill material from "normal" farming, silviculture, ranching and other specified activities, usually of a temporary or emergency nature.[15]

These exceptions do not apply if the activity results in changing navigable waters to a new use or if circulation of the affected waters is changed or reduced. In Avoyelles Sportsmen's League, Inc. v. Alexander (Avoyelles I),[16] these exemptions were construed narrowly in a challenge brought under section 404 concerning an operation converting wetland forest to agricultural use. The court reasoned the exemption for farming applied only to ongoing activity and not the type of clearing operation (hardwood wetland to soybean fields) in dispute. The court concluded that the "normal farming" exemption from section 404 does not extend to projects that convert wetlands to dry lands.[17]

General Permits

One potential way around the individual permit system is the use of a general permit. General permits may be issued by the Corps of Engineers under section 404 for activities with minimal environmental

---

12. 33 C.F.R. § 323.2(c). Under present practice, both the U.S. Fish and Wildlife Service and the Corps will inspect low-lying areas to determine if contemplated activities would be sufficient to trigger § 404 permitting. For cases examining Corps wetland jurisdiction under this definition, see United States v. DeFelice, 641 F.2d 1169 (5th Cir.1981), cert. denied 454 U.S. 940, 102 S.Ct. 474, 70 L.Ed.2d 247 (1981); Bayou Des Familles Development Corp. v. United States Corps of Engineers, 541 F.Supp. 1025 (E.D.La.1982); Bayou St. John Improvement Association v. Sands, 13 ELR 20011 (E.D.La.1982); Avoyelles Sportmen's League, Inc. v. Marsh, 715 F.2d 897 (1983).

13. See 33 C.F.R. § 323.2(*l*), 323.2(k), 323.2(n) for definitions of "dredged" or

"fill" material. In general, the terms are limited, again, to material taken from or to be discharged into waters of the United States.

14. Id. § 323.2(m). Pollutant discharge is covered by § 402(a) of the Clean Water Act, discussed supra at § 13.7.

15. 33 U.S.C.A. § 1344(f).

16. 473 F.Supp. 525 (W.D.La.1979).

17. Id. at 534–35. Any type of fill or dredge material discharge, even those de minimis in nature, are subject to § 404. See id. at 532. See also Minnehaha Creek Watershed District v. Hoffman, 597 F.2d 617 (8th Cir.1979); United States v. Carter, 12 ELR 20682 (S.D.Fla.1982); J. Juergensmeyer & J. Wadley, Agricultural Law § 23.3 (1982).

effects.[18]   These permits may be issued on a state, regional, or nation-wide basis and activities so permitted generally do not require individual permits.[19]   Only if the discharge represents a threat to the wetlands ecosystem (as defined in section 404 guidelines) will an individual permit be required on top of the general permit.[20]   Whether general permits actually relax the paperwork requirement for wetlands development is problematic.[21]   It is known that the permit requirements are very expensive due to the quantity of scientific data needed.   Because of that expense, outside of large corporate interests, most developers will only estimate the effect of their activities on the wetlands environment.   They often only discover that effect when sued by the Corps for a section 404 violation.[22]

Whatever its problems, the general permit program was the focus of the ill-fated 1982 section 404 regulatory amendments.[23]   Those amendments, which provided for various exemptions [24] and broader "head water" and "isolated waters" general permits,[25] were extremely controversial.[26]   While they did reduce the clamor for statutory changes to the section 404 program, the amendments were short lived.   Challenged in a lawsuit brought by the National Wildlife Federation and fifteen other environmental organizations, the 1982 amendments were thrown out in a settlement made with the Corps.[27]   The Corps agreed to the binding effect of the section 404 guidelines, and new regulations are under consideration.[28]

The Permit Process

The individual permitting process itself is currently based on statutory and regulatory guidelines covering and promulgated by both the Corps of Engineers and the Environmental Protection Agency. When the Corps receives an application, the proposed activity is initial-

18. 33 U.S.C.A. § 1344(e).

19. Id.   Nationwide permits may be for specific discharges in any location or for discharges in a certain area.   The permits may also be subject to various conditions imposed by the Corps of Engineers.

20. 33 C.F.R. § 323.4–323.5.

21. For an opinion that general permits are now the "Jekyll and Hyde" feature of § 404, creating more confusion and uncertainty than under the strictly individual permit system, see Parish & Morgan, History, Practice and Emerging Problems of Wetlands Regulation: Reconsidering Section 404 of the Clean Water Act, 27 Land & Water Rev. 43, 57–60 (1982).

22. Id. at 59–60.

23. The 1982 rule amendments came as a result of the Reagan Administration's President's Task Force on Regulatory Relief; Administrative Reforms to the Regulatory Program Under Section 404 of the Clean Water Act and Section 10 of the Rivers and Harbors Act (May 7, 1982).

24. 33 C.F.R. §§ 325.5(c), 330.

25. Id. § 330.4(a)(1).   See also Comment, supra note 3, at 10132.

26. 33 C.F.R. § 330.4(a)(2).   One effect of these provisions was to exempt over one million acres of wetlands in the upper midwest from individual permit requirements. See Comment, supra note 3, at 10132.

27. See U.S. Agrees to Stricter Measures to Protect Wetlands, Wall St.J., Feb. 10, 1984, at 3, col. 4.

28. Id.   United States v. Riverside Bayview Homes, Inc., __ U.S. __, 106 S.Ct. 455, 88 L.Ed.2d 419 (1985), upheld a broad interpretation of section 404 wetlands.   But for a different perspective, see Habicht, Implementing Section 404: The View from the Justice Department, 16 ELR 10073 (1986).

ly reviewed to see if it is in "the public interest." [29] Factors considered include conservation, economics, aesthetics, fish and wildlife values and general environmental concerns, among others.[30] A wetlands review is then conducted by the Corps.[31] The regulatory presumption is that "wetlands are vital areas that constitute a productive and viable public resource, the unnecessary alteration and destruction of which should be discouraged as contrary to the public interest." [32] If an activity is determined by the Corps not to be in the "public interest," a permit will not be issued.[33]

Even if an activity is found not to be against the "public interest" the Corps must still follow certain permitting guidelines [34] set out by the Environmental Protection Agency as authorized by section 404(b).[35] If proposed activity would cause or contribute to "significant degradation" of waters of the United States no permit may be issued. Effects leading to a finding of significant degradation include:

> (1) Significantly adverse effects of the discharge of pollutants on human health or welfare, including but not limited to effects on municipal water supplies plankton, fish, shellfish, wildlife, and special aquatic sites.

> (2) Significant adverse effects of the discharge of pollutants on life stages of aquatic life and other wildlife dependent on aquatic ecosystems.

> (3) Significantly adverse effects of the discharge of pollutants on aquatic ecosystem diversity, productivity, and stability.

> (4) Significantly adverse effects of discharge of pollutants on recreational, aesthetic, and economic values.[36]

29. 33 C.F.R. § 320.4(a)(1).

30. Id. § 320.4(a)(2).

31. Id. § 320.4(b)(1).

32. Id. § 320.4(b)(2). Wetlands are considered vital if they:

(i) Serve important natural biological functions, including food chain production, general habitat, and nesting, spawning, rearing and resting sites for aquatic or land species;

(ii) are set aside for study of the aquatic environment or as sanctuaries or refuges;

(iii) their destruction or alteration would detrimentally affect natural drainage characteristics, sedimentation patterns, salinity distribution, flushing characteristics, current patterns, or other environmental characteristics;

(iv) are significant in shielding other areas from wave action, erosion, or storm damage;

(v) serve as valuable storage areas for storm and flood waters;

(vi) are prime natural recharge areas; and

(vii) serve to purify water through natural water filtration.

Id.

33. The Eleventh Circuit has ruled that neither § 404 of the Clean Water Act nor the due process clause requires the Corps to give an applicant a trial-type hearing before denying a dredge and fill permit. Battrey v. United States, 13 ELR 20085 (11th Cir. Nov. 8, 1982).

34. The general purpose of the EPA's guidelines is to "restore and maintain the chemical, physical, and biological integrity of waters of the United States through the control of discharges of dredged or fill material." 40 C.F.R. § 230.1(a).

35. Id. § 230.10(b), (c).

36. Id. § 230.10(c).

Furthermore, no permit may be issued where the discharge of dredged or fill material violates any state water quality standard, toxic effluent standard, jeopardizes a threatened or endangered species, or harms a marine sanctuary.[37] When reviewing a permit application possibly affecting a threatened or endangered species, the Corps will consult interested state wildlife agencies as well as the United States Fish and Wildlife Service.[38] If no exemption exists, a finding by the Secretary of the Interior concerning the discharge's impact on the species or their habitat will be considered final by the Corps.[39]

Both state and federal fish and wildlife services can be of considerable importance in dredge and fill permit applications. The Corps must give "great weight" to these agencies' determinations when wildlife may be affected by development in a wetland area.[40] While the Corps may ignore state or federal wildlife agency recommendations, the Environmental Protection Agency may block any permit authorization by the Corps.[41]

As can easily be seen, the regulatory roadblocks to wetlands alteration are formidable indeed.[42] However, only a third of the process has been completed. State and local permits must also be acquired. Individual states and localities may have stricter guidelines than those followed by the Corps. They may also be more lenient, but since one has to gather all permits, state and federal, that supposed leniency will not matter if the Corps says no.

 WESTLAW REFERENCES

ci(33 +5 1344)

"waters of the united states" /p "territorial sea" /p defin!
    /p corp

"commerce clause" /p water /p 404

natural /s resources /s callaway /s 404

Statutory Exemptions from Section 404

dredge fill /p exempt! /p 404 /p water

199k25.7(6) /p water

General Permits

nationwide +5 permit! /s corp

---

37. Id. § 230.10(b).

38. Id. § 230.10(b)(3).

39. Id. § 230.30(c).

40. 33 C.F.R. § 320.4(c). The Fish and Wildlife Coordination Act also requires the Corps to give these agencies' reports "full consideration." 16 U.S.C.A. § 662(b).

41. 33 U.S.C.A. § 1344(c). EPA Regional Administrators may deny, restrict the use of, or withdraw particular sites if they have reason to believe that an alteration is likely to result in significant loss or damage to fisheries, shellfish, wildlife habitat or recreation areas. Id.

42. For a complete analysis of the federal permitting process under § 404, see Parish & Morgan, supra note 33, at 68–73. Section 404 roadblocks may, in addition to the withdrawn 1982 amendments, be further lessened by the new memoranda of agreements (MOAs) the Corps has with the Departments of Interior, Agriculture, Commerce, Transportation and the EPA. Environmental groups and some politicians see these MOAs as removing environmental groups' input into the decisionmaking process. See Comment, supra note 3, at 10134.

The Permit Process

```
corp  /s  engineer  /p  "environmental protection agency"
e.p.a.  /p  guideline  /p  permit!  /p  apply! application
permit  /p  "significant degradation"
199k25.7(2)  /p  water
found finding  /p  secretary  /p  interior  /p  species
      habitat  /p  final!
"great weight"  /p  corp  /s  engineer  /p  fish wildlife  /s  agency
      service
33  +5  1344(c)
```

§ 13.14 State and Local Wetlands Regulation: The Basic Schemes

While state wetland programs are marked by a good deal of diversity in individual structure and jurisdictional approach, there is considerable uniformity in the desired end effect. They all seek to limit the degree and kind of development allowed in defined wetland areas. State and local regulations are generally restrictive—often times much more so than the federal section 404 program. Still, most follow the permit oriented system of section 404.[1]

Generally, state programs begin with a thorough mapping and inventory of the state's wetlands resources. Within the wetland boundaries (set usually only after extensive public hearings have been held) state and/or local agencies directly regulate all activities. Regulation is done through a permit process which contains standards and lists procedures both for application and appeal if an application is denied.[2] Before the state or local plans are implemented, it is important for interim development controls to be developed and enforced, lest those with an interest in dredging and filling get a jump on the program.

State regulatory programs often differentiate between coastal and inland wetlands. Most coastal states regulate coastal wetlands through their individual coastal zone management programs.[3] Coastal wetlands are usually better protected than inland areas due to the longer state regulatory presence in the field as well as the federal Coastal Zone Management Act's inducements for state regulatory action.[4] Few states have programs covering inland wetlands. In all, only Massachusetts,[5] Connecticut,[6] New Hampshire,[7] Rhode Island,[8] Michigan,[9] Wis-

---

§ 13.14

1. For an overview of state programs, see generally J. Kusler, Our National Wetland Heritage, Environmental Law Institute (1983). See also National Conference of State Legislatures, Land Management; Sustaining Resource Values 197–200 (Oct. 1983).

2. See generally U.S. Water Resources Council, State and Local Acquisition of Flood Plains and Wetlands (Sept. 1981).

3. See infra part VII for a discussion of coastal zone protection.

4. See Dawson, Wetlands Regulation, 6 Zoning & Planning L.Rep. 154 (1983).

5. Wetlands Protection Act, Mass.Gen. Laws Ann. 131, § 40. See also Mass.Admin.Code tit. 310, § 10.

6.–9. See notes 6–9 on page 418.

consin,[10] and New York [11] directly regulate inland wetland use. Other states, including Florida,[12] Oregon,[13] Vermont,[14] and Maine [15] regulate inland wetlands tangentially through comprehensive land use plans.[16]

Whether wetlands should be regulated by state or local governments, or both, is a topic of considerable debate.[17] Laws often overlap. The two basic schemes of wetland regulations are local administration with state oversight and state control with local input.[18] The trend toward increased home rule tends to favor local administration.[19] State control over the purse strings, on the other hand, gives state government a great advantage.[20] State regulations may preempt local ones, with the answer depending on the particular state's constitutional and legislative provisions regarding the subject.[21]

WESTLAW REFERENCES

state local /p wetland /p regulat! /p program! scheme

wetland /p inventory! /p map!

199k25.5(6) /p wetland

interim /s regulat! /s wetland water

state /p regulat! /p coastal /p zone /p manag!

regulat! /p inland /p wetland /p use

state /s regulat! /s wetland water /s preempt! /s local

(mills /s murphy) (santini /s lyons) /p wetland

6. Connecticut Inland Wetlands and Watercourses Law, Conn.Gen.Stat.Ann. §§ 22a–36 to –45.

7. N.H.Rev.Stat.Ann. ch. 438–A, §§ 1–7.

8. Freshwater Wetland Act, R.I.Gen. Laws 1956, §§ 2–1–8 to 2–1–25. Upheld against facial attack in J.M. Mills, Inc. v. Murphy, 116 R.I. 54, 352 A.2d 661 (1976); Santini v. Lyons, ___ R.I. ___, 448 A.2d 124 (1982).

9. Goemaere-Anderson Wetland Protection Act, Mich.Comp.Laws Ann. § 281.701 et seq.

10. Wis.Stat.Ann. 61.351.

11. Freshwater Wetlands Act, N.Y.—McKinney's Envtl.Conserv.Law § 24–0101 et seq.

12. Three statutes control the bulk of inland wetlands protection in Florida. The "State Land Trust Fund," West's Fla. Stat.Ann. ch. 253; the "Florida Air and Water Pollution Control Act," West's Fla. Stat.Ann. ch. 403; and the "Florida Environmental Land and Water Management Act," West's Fla.Stat.Ann. ch. 380. A bill

entitled the "Florida Wetlands Protection Act of 1984" was introduced into the Florida Legislature in January of that year. It was passed in June. The bill provides for a more comprehensive definition of what constitutes a wetland, but was heavily amended under pressure from agricultural and development special interests.

13. Or.Rev.Stat. 197.230.

14. 10 Vt.Stat.Ann. §§ 1421–1425, 6001–6089; id. tit. 24, § 4410.

15. 5 Me.Rev.Stat.Ann. §§ 3310–3314; id. tit. 12, §§ 4811–4814.

16. See Dawson, supra note 4, at 156.

17. See, e.g., id. at 154.

18. Dawson, Wetlands Regulation (pt. 11), Zoning & Plan L.Rep. 161 (Nov. 1983).

19. Id.

20. Id.

21. See, e.g., Golden v. Board of Selectmen, 358 Mass. 519, 265 N.E.2d 573 (1970) (state wetland statute did not preempt local program because local program was separate and distinct from state law).

§ 13.15   State and Local Wetlands Regulation: The Modern Case Law

While some are contra,[1] a series of modern cases have upheld the validity of state wetlands regulation. A general pattern seems to be followed in state decisions. After an initial period of caution and some resistence, the expanding public awareness of wetlands' great value eventually overcomes judicial reticence based on landowners' rights. The primary question in most cases is whether the regulation is a reasonable exercise of the state or local government's police power. The issue often boils down to a single question—are the remaining uses of the land after regulation sufficient to prevent a "taking" of property?[2]

Just v. Marinette County[3] is the landmark decision upholding stringent restrictions on development in wetland areas. There, a landowner[4] was prosecuted for filling in a lakeshore area in violation of a county ordinance. The landowner claimed an unconstitutional taking. The court applied the "harm/benefit" test, which validates those land use restrictions preventing a public harm, but overturns those which supposedly only confer a public benefit.[5] Upholding the ordinance, the court declared that

> [t]he shoreland zoning ordinance preserves nature, the environment and natural resources as they were created and to which the people have a present right. · The ordinance does not create or improve the public condition but only preserves nature from the despoilage and harm resulting from the unrestricted activities of humans.[6]

§ 13.15

1. See, e.g., State v. Johnson, 265 A.2d 711 (Me.1970) (state wetland program held unconstitutional as a taking of property); American National Bank & Trust Co. v. Village of Winfield, 1 Ill.App.3d 376, 274 N.E.2d 144 (1971) (if land cannot be developed for a profit, the regulation is unreasonable).

2. The taking defense has also been used in § 404 cases. If anything, the claim is even less successful at the federal level than it is in state courts. See generally Jentgen v. United States, 228 Ct.Cl. 527, 657 F.2d 1210 (1981), cert. denied 455 U.S. 1017, 102 S.Ct. 1711, 72 L.Ed.2d 134 (1982); Deltona v. United States, 228 Ct.Cl. 476, 657 F.2d 1184 (1981), cert. denied 455 U.S. 1017, 102 S.Ct. 1712, 72 L.Ed.2d 135 (1982); Laney v. United States, 228 Ct.Cl. 519, 661 F.2d 145, 11 Envtl.L.Rep. (Envtl.L.Inst.) 20,910 (1981). The sole § 404 case finding a taking on the merits is 1902 Atlantic Ltd. v. Hudson, 574 F.Supp 1381, 19 Env't Rep. Cas. (BNA) 1926 (E.D.Va.1983), and it was based on the fact that the filling of the borrow pit in question would have no ill environmental effects. Id. at 1938, 1946–47.

3. 56 Wis.2d 7, 201 N.W.2d 761 (1972).

4. Ronald Just was no ordinary landowner. A member to be of the John Birch Society, Mr. Just saw any governmental control over his land as anathema. For a fascinating exploration of the case and the individuals involved, see Bryden, A Phantom Doctrine: The Origins and Effects of Just v. Marinette County, 1978 Am.B. Found.Res.J. 397.

5. For a discussion of the harm/benefit test, see § 20.2. And see J. Juergensmeyer & J. Wadley, Florida Land Use Restrictions § 2.08. And see Just v. Marinette County, 56 Wis.2d 7, 201 N.W.2d 761 (1972); Graham v. Estuary Properties, Inc., 399 So.2d 1374, 1382 (Fla.1981), cert. denied 454 U.S. 1083, 102 S.Ct. 640, 70 L.Ed. 2d 618 (1981).

6. 56 Wis.2d at 23–24, 201 N.W.2d at 771.

The court's language has since become a rallying point for those seeking wetlands protection:

> Is the ownership of a parcel of land so absolute that man can change its nature to suit any of his purposes? . . . An owner of land has no absolute and unlimited right to change the essential natural character of his land so as to use it for a purpose for which it was unsuited in its natural state and which injures the rights of others. . . . The changing of wetlands and swamps to the damage of the general public by upsetting the natural environment and the natural relationship is not a reasonable use of that land which is protected from police power regulation. . . . [7]

Another in this line of wetlands protection cases is Sibson v. State.[8] There, a developer was denied a permit to fill four acres of salt marsh. Even though a house had already been built on two acres already filled, the supreme court of New Hampshire found this permit denial to be a valid police power exercise. The marsh was shown to be ecologically valuable and any proposed fill operations would destroy that value. Without fill, however, the marsh was of almost no pecuniary value to the landowner. The court could have decided the case on the ground that because a house was constructed on part of the original six acres, only speculative profit was denied.[9] The court decided to base its holding on whether there was a right to fill the remaining four acres standing alone. Holding the permit denial a prevention of public harm, the court declared the permit denial did not, in fact:

> depreciate the value of the marsh land or cause it to become "of practically no pecuniary value." Its value was the same after the denial of the permit as before and it remained as it had been for milleniums. The referee correctly found that the action of the board denied plaintiffs none of the normal traditional uses of the marsh land including wildlife observation, hunting, haying of marsh grass, clam and shellfish harvesting and aesthetic purposes. The board has not denied plaintiff's current uses of their marsh but prevented a major change in the marsh that plaintiffs seek to make for speculative profit.[10]

Building upon Just as precedent and Sibson in spirit, the Florida Supreme Court strongly upheld wetlands protection as a proper police power exercise in Graham v. Estuary Properties.[11] There, a gulf coast developer owned 6,500 acres of coastal land. Of this land, about 2,800 acres were red mangroves and 1,800 acres black mangroves. The developer wished to install 26,500 dwelling units by dredging out the

---

7. Id. at 17–18, 201 N.W.2d at 768.

8. 115 N.H. 124, 336 A.2d 239 (1975).

9. Id. at 241.

10. Id. at 243. Sibson may have been limited by the decision in Burrows v. Keene, 121 N.H. 590, 432 A.2d 15 (1981), which found a "taking" in a rezoning of land to a "conservation zone." Sibson, however, was distinguished as involving especially valuable estuarine, as opposed to freshwater, wetlands.

11. 399 So.2d 1374 (Fla.1981), cert. denied sub nom. Taylor v. Graham, 454 U.S. 1083, 102 S.Ct. 640, 70 L.Ed.2d 618 (1981).

black mangroves. Because of its size, the project was a Development of Regional Impact (DRI) under Chapter 380 of the Florida statutes. A development permit was denied by both the local government and the regional DRI authority. The trial and appellate court held for the developer. The supreme court reversed.

In finding the denial reasonable, the court said:

> Protection of environmentally sensitive areas and pollution prevention are legitimate concerns within the police power. In the instant case, . . . the proposed development would cause pollution in the surrounding bays. Such pollution would affect the economy of Lee County. Therefore the regulation at issue here promotes the welfare of the public, prevents a public harm, and has not been arbitrarily applied.[12]

The court's finding was integral to its decision that the regulation did not effect an unconstitutional taking.[13] The court found there to be no taking for several reasons. The proposed development would have severely damaged the ecology of the wetlands to the detriment of the general public. Because the developer could still build on the non-wetland portion of its property, the regulation did not completely destroy its pecuniary interest in the land. The court quoted with approval the language from Just declaring that a landowner has no absolute right to change the natural character of his land, then went on to clarify its interpretation of the harm/benefit test. The court noted the inherent fuzziness of any line between prevention of a public harm and creation of a public benefit. In fact, whenever a harm is prevented "it is a necessary result that the public benefits."[14] Further:

> It is true that the public benefits in that the bays will remain clean, but that is a benefit in the form of maintaining the status quo. Estuary is not being required to change its development plan so that public waterways will be improved. That would be the creation of a public benefit beyond the scope of the state's police power.[15]

Estuary Properties referred to an important issue in wetlands regulation: the preference of courts to examine a regulation's effect on an entire parcel of land, not just the part restricted in use. This tendency was given constitutional credence by the United States Supreme Court in Penn Central Transp. Co. v. New York City.[16] Quoting from Penn Central, the Massachusetts Supreme Court in Moskow v. Commissioner[17] upheld a strict inland wetlands regulation against a taking challenge:

12. 399 So.2d at 1381.

13. See Hamann, Commentary and Legal Analysis: A Model Flood Management Ordinance (1982) (prepared for the Southwest Florida Water Management District).

14. 399 So.2d at 1382.

15. Id.

16. 438 U.S. 104, 130–31, 98 S.Ct. 2646, 2662, 57 L.Ed.2d 631 (1978), rehearing denied 439 U.S. 883, 99 S.Ct. 226, 58 L.Ed.2d 198 (1978). For a complete discussion of Penn Central, see §§ 10.7, 11.6, 14.9, 14.10.

17. 384 Mass. 530, 427 N.E.2d 750 (1981).

" 'Taking' jurisprudence does not divide a single parcel into discreet segments and attempt to determine whether rights in a particular segment have been entirely abrogated. In deciding whether a particular governmental action has effected a taking, this court focuses rather both on the character of the action and on the nature and extent of the interference with rights in the parcel as a whole . . . ." [18]

Thus because the landowner in question could still subdivide a portion of his remaining parcel (as well as use the wetlands portion in any way consistent with its natural state) [19] the court found no taking.

 WESTLAW REFERENCES

d'annolfo candlestick brecciaroli (potomac /s maryland) sibson
marinette /p "equal protection" taking /p wetland

§ 13.16 Wetlands Protection: An Uncertain Future

Even after a decade of progress in controlling wetlands destruction the future of federal and state regulatory programs is unclear. Section 404 is under attack from both private development interests and the federal government itself.[1] Adding to the uncertainty is the Reagan Administration's decision to seek to reduce § 404's effectiveness on the one hand while introducing a bill designed to end all federal subsidies and flood insurance to wetlands development on the other.[2] While state programs are becoming more numerous,[3] federal funding cutbacks and various Proposition 13-type state revenue restrictions are making it more difficult to develop and implement state wetlands regulations.

Coastal wetlands programs have generally been more successful than inland ones.[4] Once public awareness of inland wetland values catches up with the known worth of saltwater marshes, the protection offered may balance out. Coupled with that perception problem, however, is the need to convince state and national legislatures and courts that wetlands regulation does not prevent development in the broad sense.[5] The aggravations of paperwork are certainly there, but only a

18. Id. at 753.

19. Among the uses still allowable in the landowners' wetlands area include the construction of catwalks, duckblinds, certain types of roads, underground or overhead utilities, "commercial and non-commercial outdoor recreation activities including hiking, boating[,] trapping, [and] hunting." Id. at 752.

§ 13.16

1. See Comment, Corps Recasts § 404 Permit Program, Braces for Political, Legal Skirmishes, 13 Envtl.L.Rep. 10129 (May 1983).

2. Dawson, Wetlands Regulation, 6 Zoning & Planning L.Rep. 166 (1983).

3. As of the 1983 legislative session, New Jersey was considering a "graduated institutional regulatory program" to conserve inland wetlands. The New Jersey proposal has an interesting jurisdictional provision granting municipal, county and state jurisdiction depending on the scope of the anticipated development. See National Conference of State Legislatures, Land Management; Sustaining Resource Values 198 (Oct. 1983).

4. Dawson, supra note 2, at 164.

5. Id.

minute percentage of development permits nationally are denied due to wetlands considerations.[6] Yet until public perceptions concerning wetlands changes to reflect the modern knowledge of wetlands value—and it is changing—true wetlands protection, necessarily coordinated at federal, state, and local levels, will not occur.

 WESTLAW REFERENCES
ci(47 +3 35696–01)

VIII. LAND USE AND ENVIRONMENTALLY SENSITIVE LANDS—COASTAL ZONES

§ 13.17   Coastal Zone Values

The intense population pressures exerted upon coastal areas combined with their inherent fragility make them a microcosm of land use practice and theory. All the successes and failures of land development and regulation can be found in that narrow band betwixt land and sea that comprises the coastal zone. With over half this nation's population living near the coast and more arriving every day, coastal zone management promises to be a growth industry in its own right.

Coastal zones are actually comprised of two separate types of environmentally sensitive lands. Wetlands, in the form of estuarine areas, form a substantial percentage of the coastal zone. While wetlands protection in general has already been discussed, it should be noted that many states distinguish between inland wetlands and coastal wetlands.[1] Virtually all coastal states protect estuarine wetlands through coastal zone management programs. Only a few protect inland wetlands as such.[2]

The other environmentally sensitive aspect of coastal zones is the substance most often identified with the coast—sand. Sand bars and dunes play an important role in protecting inland areas from flooding. That role, however, can only be played when sufficient vegetation is present to secure the sand from undue erosion.[3] A condominium does not a foundation make.

6. Id. Environmental interest groups contend that § 404 itself is neither unreasonably burdensome nor time consuming. In fact, the Corps' own study tends to show that wetlands regulation delays cost only 0.7% of the total price of even controversial projects. See Comment, supra note 1, at 10133.

§ 13.17

1. See, e.g., Burrows v. Keene, 121 N.H. 590, 432 A.2d 15 (1981) (distinguishes between "unique" value of saltwater marshes and all other inland wetlands). See also supra § 13.14.

2. See supra § 13.14. In part, the greater protection given coastal wetlands may be due to the fact that the commercial value of estuaries has long been recognized—the great majority of commercially valuable fish and shellfish spend part of their lives in estuarine areas. Maloney & O'Donnell, Drawing the Line at the Ocean Front: The Role of Construction Setback Lines in Regulating Development of the Coastal Zone, 30 U.Fla.L.Rev. 383, 389 (1978).

3. National Conference of State Legislatures, Land Management; Sustaining Resource Values 66 (Oct. 1983).

Thus the concern of coastal zone management is that development not unduly interfere with natural coastal processes. Where needed, moratoria are placed on building permits. More commonly, coastal setback lines and density restrictions are established. Just how and through what authority coastal zone regulation is accomplished is the subject of the following sections.

 WESTLAW REFERENCES

coast! /p zone /p wetland estuar! /p inland

coast! /p setback density /p regulat! restrict! rule

moratori! /p build! /p permit! /p coast!

§ 13.18 Legislative Responses to Coastal Management Needs: Federal Action

The National Coastal Zone Management Act of 1972 (CZMA) [1] was the nation's first attempt to develop a comprehensive coastal zone protection plan. Shoreline regulation was historically a local concern until coastal resources (such as offshore oil and gas) became economically and politically important. Such resources led to a federal/state conflict over jurisdiction and revenue collection. The CZMA was a congressional attempt to defuse the growing polarization between the federal government and the states over these resource management issues. As such, the Coastal Act relies on joint federal/state cooperation and funding.

The CZMA's genesis came from a two-year presidential commission study of maritime resources published in 1969. Commonly called the Stratton Commission, the report of the Commission on marine science, engineering and resources [2] highlighted the importance of shoreline areas. It noted that while less than ten percent of the country's land area could be considered coastal, over forty percent of the nation's population lived near the coast (at that time) with the trend toward ever greater growth. The Commission recommended a federally supported, state administered Coastal Management Act. The resulting CZMA was enacted after four years of Congressional attention on October 27, 1972.

The CZMA proceeds under a two-tiered process whereby states obtain federal financial assistance for coastal zone protection by

 1) developing a comprehensive, long-range coastal management plan meeting federal statutory criteria; and

 2) getting approval for that plan followed by state implementation. [3]

§ 13.18

1. 16 U.S.C.A. § 1451 et seq.

2. Report of the Comm'n on Marine Science, Engineering & Resources (Jan. 1969).

3. Natural Resources Defense Council, Land Use Controls in the United States 100 (Moss ed. 1977). Chapter 6, beginning on page 98, is a comprehensive and reada-

To meet the CZMA's requirements for matching funds, the state program must comply with the act's statutory coastal management program in the judgment of the Secretary of Commerce.[4] The pieces of the federal pie each coastal state seeks are the CZMA's grants covering development and implementation of state coastal programs. The program development grants (which help states devise their plans) are known as section 305 grants, and the state implementation grants (which help put the plans into practice) are called section 306 grants. Most states and territories have federally approved programs.[5] These states and territories comprise over ninety percent of the nation's coastline, including the Great Lakes.[6]

The structure and scope of coastal zone management programs vary widely from state to state. Congress intended this diversity as a means of reflecting individual state concerns. Each state plan must, however, include the following:

1) an identification of the boundaries of the coastal zone subject to the management program;

2) a definition of what shall constitute permissible land and water uses within the coastal zone which have a direct and significant impact on the coastal waters;

3) an inventory and designation of areas of particular concern within the coastal zone;

4) an identification of the means by which the state proposes to exert control over the land and water uses referred to in paragraph 2) including a listing of relevant constitutional provisions, legislative enactments, regulations and judicial decisions;

5) broad guidelines on priority of uses in particular areas, including specifically those uses of lowest priority;

6) a description of the organizational structure proposed to implement the management program, including the responsibility and interrelationships of local, areawide, state, regional, and interstate agencies in the management process;

7) a definition of the term "beach" and a planning process for the protection of, and access to, public beaches and other public coastal areas of environmental, recreational, historical, aesthetic, ecological, or cultural value;

ble discussion of the history and policies of the Coastal Zone Management Act.

4. The U.S. Secretary of Commerce is assigned the responsibility of administering the Act's provisions. That responsibility has been delegated to the National Oceanic and Atmosphere Administration (NOAA), one of the agencies of the Commerce Department. An office of Coastal Zone Management has been created within NOAA to implement the Act.

5. Under the Act, the term "coastal state" also applied to the American territories of Puerto Rico, the Virgin Islands, Guam, and American Samoa. "Coastal zone" is defined as coastal waters and adjacent shorelands of the coastal states, including "transitional and intertidal areas, salt marshes, wetlands, and beaches."

6. Nat'l Conference of State Legislatures, Land Management; Sustaining Resource Values 203 (Oct. 1983).

8) a planning process for energy facilities likely to be located in, or which may significantly affect, the coastal zone, including, but not limited to, a process for anticipating and managing the impacts from such facilities;

9) a planning process for (A) assessing the effects of shoreline erosion (however caused), and (B) studying and evaluating ways to control, or lessen the impact of, such erosion, and to restore areas adversely affected by such erosion.[7]

Importantly, state programs must have viable coordinating mechanisms with local governments and designate a specific state agency to administer the program.[8] States with approved programs are given "federal consistency" authority which assures that federal actions are consistent with state coastal management programs.[9]

Section 307 of the CZMA provides for federal/state consistency. The section requires that activities affecting the coastal zone supported or conducted by federal agencies must be consistent with approved state programs to the "maximum extent practicable." [10] Of more importance to the private developer is the subsection providing that private activities significantly affecting land and water uses in the coastal zone and which require federal licenses and permits must be consistent with the state's approved program.[11] The state must approve the applicant's

---

7. 16 U.S.C.A. § 1454(b). It is worth noting that the definition of a coastal management plan in the CZMA tracks the definition of a plan in model planning legislation adopted by the American Law Institute. See D. Mandelker, Environment and Equity 138 (1981).

8. See H.R.Rep.No. 97–628, 97th Cong., 2d Sess. 24 (1982) (report of Congressman Jones of North Carolina of the Committee on Merchant Marine and Fisheries concerning the Ocean and Coastal Resources Management and Development Block Grant Act).

9. 16 U.S.C.A. § 1456(c). Twenty-eight of the thirty-five coastal states have federally approved coastal zone management programs. Georgia, Illinois, Indiana, Minnesota, Ohio, Texas and Virginia do not. Even without those states, approximately 90% of the country's coastline is covered by the CZMA. See National Conference, supra note 6.

10. Considerable amendments to the 1972 Act were made in 1976 to clarify the applicability of the consistency provisions to Outer Continental Shelf (OCS) oil, gas and mineral exploration and exploitation activities. The final word on this subject as the Act reads now was made by the United States Supreme Court in Secretary of the Interior v. California, 464 U.S. 312, 104 S.Ct. 656, 78 L.Ed.2d 496 (1984), on

remand 729 F.2d 614 (9th Cir.1984). There, the Department of the Interior rejected California's contentions that federal sale of oil and gas leases in certain OCS tracts off California required a consistency review under § 307(c)(1) of the CZMA. The district court entered summary judgment and the court of appeals affirmed. By a 5–4 vote the Supreme Court held Interior's sale of OCS oil and gas leases do not constitute activity "directly affecting" California's coastal zone within § 307(c)(1)'s meaning. Consistency review was thus not required. Justice Stevens delivered a stinging dissent which quite clearly showed that OCS leasing was very much within the consistency domain of the CZMA. Until congressional action, however, consistency review for OCS oil and gas leasing will not be required.

11. 16 U.S.C.A. § 1456(c)(3). In American Petroleum Institute v. Knecht, 609 F.2d 1306 (9th Cir.1979), the court considered the question of just how specific state land use control policies in state coastal management programs must be. The court rejected petitioner's position that state programs must be sufficiently specific to inform those desiring to develop in coastal areas of the rules and conditions they must comply with. The court held that the CZMA does not require "detailed criteria" that private developers can rely

certification of consistency for the federal license or permit to be granted. However, a state's determination of inconsistency may be overturned by the Secretary of Commerce if he establishes that consistency does in fact exist.[12] Finally, federal agencies may not approve state or local applications for federal assistance for activities significantly affecting the coastal zone if they are inconsistent with the state's approved coastal management program.[13]

The entire CZMA was reviewed by Congress in 1980 to determine whether it should be reauthorized. The result was a series of amendments referred to as the Coastal Management Improvement Act of 1980.[14] Greater clarity in the policy behind the CZMA was made through additions in the statement of congressional findings (found in section 302). These policies again reflect a strong desire to manage and protect coastal resources through joint federal/state cooperation. The resources themselves, from fisheries to defense installation sitings, are spelled out in considerable detail.[15] The section 306 implementation grant process was revised so that each complying state must use a greater proportion of the grant money (up to thirty percent) to implement these policies spelled out by Congress in section 302. The entire program was also reauthorized for five years.[16]

The 1980 amendments included a new section of activities entitled the "Coastal Resource Improvement Program."[17] This may be the most important change made by the 1980 legislation.[18] This section assumed the states were ready to move the CZMA from planning into implementation and management. It provides states with incentives to implement their management programs in view of specific objectives and results. In general, the section gives federal assistance to states in "meeting low-cost construction, land acquisition, and shoreline stabilization costs associated with the designation of areas of preservation and restoration, the revitalization of urban waterfronts and parks, and public access to coastal acres."[19]

Section 306A(b)(1), the preservation subsection, is based on an assumption that through low-cost construction, environmentally sensitive areas could be protected and increased public access established. Such objectives could be reached by building paths through dunes (environmentally sensitive areas in themselves) to channel public access to beach areas. These paths or trails could be accompanied by

---

on without "interaction between the relevant state agencies and the user." Id. at 1312. The court quoted with approval language of the district court suggesting that the CZMA did not require a "zoning map" committing the state before it received the exact proposal of a private developer. Id.

12. 16 U.S.C.A. § 1456.

13. Id.

14. These amendments are listed in their entirety in Id. § 1451 et seq.

15. Id. § 1452(2).

16. See H.R.Rep.No. 97–628, supra note 8, at 26.

17. 16 U.S.C.A. § 1455a.

18. See H.R.Rep.No. 97–628, supra note 8, at 26.

19. Id.

signs, exhibits, and other "small scale construction programs" complementing a state's coastal zone management program.[20]

In locales already developed, section 306A(a) provides assistance in urban waterfront and port development. The program stresses public access to port areas, rehabilitation of piers, bulkhead restoration and piling removal or replacement to the extent such activities comport with the policies behind the CZMA. Grants under this section could be used to devise urban waterfront redevelopment programs not eligible for any other federal funding.

The Coastal Barrier Resources Act

The passage of the Coastal Barrier Resources Act [21] in 1982 gives additional protection to coastal zones. Coastal barriers are islands or spits consisting chiefly of sand which have the effect of protecting landward areas from direct wave action.[22] A typical example would be Cape Hatterras, North Carolina. Because they consist of unstable sediments and serve as "natural storm protection buffers," coastal barriers are particularly ill suited for development.[23] Yet by providing financial assistance in the form of subsidies and flood insurance, the federal government actively encouraged coastal barrier development for years.[24] It is the purpose of the Coastal Barrier Resources Act to restrict development through the termination of federal assistance in undeveloped coastal barriers.[25]

The Act is quite simple in its approach. It first sets up a "Coastal Barrier Resources System" consisting of all undeveloped coastal barriers located on the Atlantic and Gulf Coasts.[26] This system is carefully mapped and the boundaries set.[27] With some exceptions,[28] "no new expenditures or new financial assistance may be made available under authority of any federal law for any purpose within the Coastal Barrier Resource System." [29] Thus any state permitted development will have to pay its own way. The effectiveness of the Coastal Barrier Resources Act has yet to be determined, but the simplicity of its approach is certainly in its favor.

 WESTLAW REFERENCES

c.z.m.a. /p offshore /p oil gas

c.z.m.a. /p federal state /p fund****

20. Id. This subsection stresses the "acquisition of fee simple and other interests in land" in order to meet the listed objectives in environmentally sensitive lands.

21. 16 U.S.C.A. § 3501 et seq.

22. Id. § 3502(1)(A). For purposes of the Act, adjacent wetlands are included in the statutory coverage. Id. § 3502(1)(B).

23. Id. § 3501(a)(3).

24. Id.

25. See Dawson, Wetlands Regulation, 6 Zoning & Planning L.Rep. 154 (1983).

26. 16 U.S.C.A. § 3503.

27. Id. Boundary modification is made through § 3503(c).

28. These exceptions include energy exploration and exploitation, maintenance of existing channels and roads and necessary military activities. Id. § 3505.

29. Id. § 3504(a).

c.z.m.a. /p "secretary of commerce"

state /s plan planned planning /s requir! /s coast!

The Coastal Barrier Resources Act

"coastal barrier resources act"

---

§ 13.19 Legislative Responses to Coastal Management Needs: State Action

As mentioned earlier, state programs under the CZMA vary widely in scope and effect. Constrained only by the basic guidelines established in the act, the states were free (indeed, encouraged) to develop programs tailored to meet their special needs. Nevertheless, state coastal management programs are different from other state land use plans because they were developed with the need for federal approval in mind.[1] As examples of state programs following the CZMA's lead, the following discussion of California's and Florida's coastal management programs should give an idea of the types of approaches available.[2]

California Coastal Act

California's coastal management program was first adopted by voter initiative in 1972. This interim law set up a coastal commission along with regional commissions responsible for issuing development permits in the narrowly defined coastal area.[3] The interim law provided that a state coastal plan be developed by the regional commissions. It was completed in late 1975 and became the California Coastal Act of 1976.[4]

The act covers the same coastal zone management area as did the interim law: all land one thousand yards inland from the mean high tide mark.[5] The area varies widely in that its coverage extends from up to five miles or the "first major ridgeline paralleling the sea" in significant wetland and recreational areas to less than one thousand yards in urban areas already developed. San Francisco Bay is exempted from the act because it is covered by its own, separately approved, permit program.

§ 13.19

1. See T. Schoenbaum, Environmental Policy Law 516 (1982).

2. North Carolina's Coastal Act (N.C. Gen.Stat. § 113A–100 et seq.) is also a well established example of a state coastal plan. The Act emphasizes local planning and management with overriding state authority only in environmentally sensitive areas.

3. For a general discussion of the interim law, see R. Healy & J. Rosenberg, Land Use and the States, ch. 4 (2d ed. 1979); Ausness, Land Use Controls in Coastal Ar-

eas, 9 Cal.W.L.Rev. 391 (1973); Diamon, di Donato, Marley & Tubert, Political Reform Act: Greater Access to Initiative Process, 7 Sw.L.J. 453 (1975); Sabatier, State Review of Local Land-Use Decisions, 3 Coastal Zone Mgmt.J. 255 (1977).

4. West's Ann.Cal.Pub.Res.Code § 30000 et seq. For a useful discussion of the state act, see Offshore Oil and Gas Development: California Coastal Act of 1976, Comment, 8 Pac.L.J. 783 (1977); Symposium, 49 S.Cal. L.Rev. 710–83 (1976).

5. West's Ann.Cal.Pub.Res.Code § 30103.

The legislatively expressed goals of the act are to:

(a) Protect, maintain, and where feasible, enhance and restore the overall quality of the coastal zone environment and its natural and artificial resources.

(b) Assure orderly, balanced utilization and conservation of coastal zone resources taking into account the social and economic needs of the people of the state.

(c) Maximize public access to and along the coast and maximize public recreational opportunities in the coastal zone consistent with sound resources conservation principles and constitutionally protected rights of private property owners.

(d) Assure priority for coastal-dependent and coastal-related development over other development on the coast.

(e) Encourage state and local initiatives and cooperation in preparing procedures to implement coordinated planning and development for mutually beneficial uses, including educational uses, in the coastal zone.[6]

The act contains separate sections detailing ecological and economic "findings and declarations." After listing the environmental importance of California's coastal zone in the "ecological section," the act declares "it is necessary to protect the ecological balance of the coastal zone and prevent its deterioration and destruction."[7] This sweeping language, however, is tempered by the "economic development" section's findings which state that it may well be necessary to locate power plants, refineries, and other "coastal-dependent developments" in the coastal zone despite their "significant adverse effects on coastal resources or coastal access . . . [in] order to ensure that inland as well as coastal resources are preserved and that orderly economic development proceeds within the state."[8] Thus the competing special interests of environment and economy each made their point.

The California Act provides for special protection of environmentally sensitive areas:

(a) Environmentally sensitive habitat areas shall be protected against any significant disruption of habitat values, and only uses dependent on such resources shall be allowed within such areas.

(b) Development in areas adjacent to environmentally sensitive habitat areas and parks and recreation areas shall be sited and designed to prevent impacts which would significantly degrade such areas, and shall be compatible with the continuance of such habitat areas.[9]

---

6. Id. § 30001.5.

7. Id. § 30001(c).

8. Id. § 30001.2.

9. Id. § 30240. For an example of a denial of a real estate development applica-

tion being upheld by the courts based on this provision, see Bel Mar Estates v. California Coastal Commission, 115 Cal.App.3d 936, 171 Cal.Rptr. 773 (1981).

New development in the coastal zone is covered by a separate provision which requires that new residential, commercial, or industrial development be located as near existing developed areas as possible; if those areas are unable to accommodate the new development then the new development will be sited wherever sufficient public services exist and the development's individual or cumulative impact will not have significantly adverse effects.[10]

Implementation of the California Act is provided in chapter six, whose various articles provide for "local coastal programs."[11] These programs are to contain the local coastal plan, maps, zoning ordinances and "implementing actions."[12] "Implementing actions" are defined as the "ordinances, regulations, or programs which implement either the provisions of the certified local coastal program" or the Act's statutory policies.[13] These local coastal programs are then submitted to a regional commissioner subject to his approval.[14] If denied, the state commission may hear appeals.[15] After approval, local governments are delegated development control and the regional commissions themselves are abolished after approval is granted all local programs.[16]

Of particular interest are the California Act's provisions for the special protection of lands under the "[d]esignation of sensitive coastal resource areas."[17] Defined as "[s]pecial marine and land habitat areas, wetlands, lagoons, and estuaries,"[18] and areas having particular recreational, scenic, or archaeological value, these areas must get legislative approval before adoption.[19] In addition, state and regional commissions must approve "other implementing actions" along with all other statutory requirements.[20]

The permitting process for coastal developments in California is multi-tiered. A coastal development permit must be received from the appropriate local government as well as any additional permits required "from any state, regional, or local agency."[21] A regional commission permit is required for:

> (1) Developments between the sea and the first public road paralleling the sea or within 300 feet of the inland extent of any

10. West's Ann.Cal.Pub.Res.Code § 30250. For an argument that because this section may not require local governments in the zone to provide additional areas for development it is anti-growth, see Ellickson, Ticket to Thermidor: A Commentary on the Proposed California Coastal Plan, 46 S.Cal.L.Rev. 715, 724–32 (1976). For a response to that position, see D. Mandelker, Environmental and Land Controls Legislation 120 (1980 Supp.).

11. West's Ann.Cal.Pub.Res.Code § 30500.

12. Id. §§ 30502 & 30108.4.

13. Id.

14. Id. § 30510.

15. Id. § 30513.

16. Id. § 30519.

17. Id. § 30502.

18. Id. § 30116.

19. Id. § 30502.5.

20. Id. § 30600(a). "Development" is defined broadly to include any kind of building, discharge, disposal or use of the land resulting in any "change in the intensity of use." Id. § 30106.

21. Id. § 30601.

beach or of the mean high tide line of the sea where there is no beach, whichever is the greater distance.

(2) Developments not included within paragraph (1) located on tidelands, submerged lands, public trust lands, within 100 feet of any wetland, estuary, stream, or within 300 feet of the top of the seaward face of any coastal bluff.

(3) Any development which constitutes a major public works project or a major energy facility.[22]

Only if the proposed development "is in conformity with the certified local coastal program" will a permit be issued.[23] If a project is denied, a developer may appeal to the state commission in certain statutorily defined instances. These include the above mentioned types of developments plus those projects to be located in a "sensitive coastal resource area" or any county approved development not being the "principal permitted use under the zoning ordinance or zoning district map . . . ."[24] The grounds for an appeal of a permit denial (except for local government approval of a development meeting the standards of paragraph (1) above) are "limited to an allegation that the development does not conform to the certified local program."[25]

As can be readily seen, the California Coastal Management Act is an extremely detailed and complicated piece of legislation. Because of the joint state and local responsibilities, the Act's effectiveness depends upon the diligence of agencies at both levels. A greater burden is placed on local governments because it is up to them to take broad statutory policies and translate them into local coastal plans sufficiently precise to administer the development permit process.[26] The pre-1976 interim law, while granting permits to over ninety percent of all development applications, was at least partially successful in halting ill-planned projects. If local governments cannot or choose not to resist the siren call of economic development *über alles*, the 1976 act may be less effective than the interim law it was designed to replace.[27]

The Florida Approach

Florida's approach to the coastal planning challenge laid down by the CZMA is quite different from the California example. While California's coastal management code consists of more than one hundred pages of complex and generally turgid statutory prose, Florida's Coastal Planning and Management Act (FCMA) is the very model of

22. Id. § 30104(b).

23. Id. § 30603(a). Further restrictions are placed on grounds for appeal under paragraph (1) which reflect a need for specific adverse environmental or public impact.

24. Id. § 30603(c).

25. See D. Mandelker, supra note 10, at 123.

26. R. Healy, Land Use Law and the States 75 (1976).

27. The continued controversy over California's coastal act may lead to its eventual modification. Developers are frustrated by the Act's regulatory roadblocks and local governments are hesitant to give up their land use control power along the coast. D. Mandelker, supra note 10, at 114 (1982 Supp.).

legislative brevity.[28]   Consisting of six subsections covering less than four pages, the FCMA is more a legislative call to action than a detailed code of conduct.   In part, Florida's approach signifies the state's belief that the various previously enacted state and local coastal programs (some of which are outlined below) will be adequate to meet the threat of coastal overdevelopment.

As early as 1968, Florida proclaimed environmental protection (of which coastal planning is a, if not the, prime environmental issue in a peninsular state) as an important concern of the state.   The 1968 constitutional revision included an added section 7 to Article II stating that

> [i]t shall be the policy of the state to conserve and protect its natural resources and scenic beauty.   Adequate provision shall be made by law for the abatement of air and water pollution and of excessive and unnecessary noise.[29]

The Florida legislature built upon this constitutional bedrock in 1970 with the creation of the Coastal Coordination Council.[30]   1970 witnessed also the first coastal construction setback line [31] and an additional constitutional amendment (Article X, § 11) allowing sale of the state's sovereignty lands "only when in the public interest." [32]   The coastal setback line is part of the Beach and Shore Preservation Act.   It regulates coastal construction and provides incentives for preventing beach erosion.   The State Department of Natural Resources (DNR) has jurisdiction and sole authority for issuing permits for structures to be built on sovereignty lands below the mean high water mark in the tidal waters of the state.[33]   All riparian owners within one thousand feet of any planned construction in this zone must be given notice before a permit may be issued by DNR.   These owners have thirty days to

28. West's Fla.Stat.Ann. § 380.19 et seq.   However, the Plan itself covers nearly 1,000 pages of fine print.

29. West's Fla.Stat.Ann.Const. Art. 2, § 7.

30. Fla.Laws 1970, ch. 70–259; West's Fla.Stat.Ann. § 370.0211.   The executive directors of the Departments of Pollution Control, Department of Natural Resources and the executive director of the Board of Trustees of the Internal Improvement Trust Fund make up the Council.   The Council developed a comprehensive coastal plan comprising a series of coastal zone atlases.   These atlases detailed the physical, biological and land use information about Florida's coast needed for a comprehensive plan.   When the state's environmental agencies were reorganized in 1975, the Council was eliminated and its responsibilities shifted to the Department of Natural Resources.   Fla.Laws 1975, ch. 75–22,

§ 18.   In turn, those responsibilities were again shifted, this time to the Department of Environmental Regulation.   Fla.Laws 1977, ch. 77–366, § 4.   The detailed atlases were expressly abolished by the legislature (along with an ambitious plan to divide the coastal areas of the state into classifications of vital, conservation, and development zones) in 1978.   West's Fla.Stat.Ann. § 380.25c.

31. Beach and Shore Preservation Act, Fla.Stat. §§ 161.011–161.45.

32. West's Fla.Stat.Ann. Const. Art. 10, § 11.

33. Fla.Stat.Ann. § 161.041.   The types of projects that would typically require a permit include construction of jetties, groins, seawalls, breakwaters, beach nourishment or restoration projects, and the like.

respond, and a final hearing will be had in front of the Governor and Cabinet before a final decision is made.[34]

Before Article X was amended, state sovereignty lands could be sold to private development interests provided the sale was "not contrary to the public interest." [35] However, Florida's authority to regulate construction on sovereignty lands has been well established for decades.[36] Since that time, the state's authority has been established over beach nourishment and restoration projects, including those carried out by the United States Army Corps of Engineers.[37] Perhaps the DNR's greatest land use power is the ability to force any landowner to adjust, alter, or remove, at his expense, any nonessential structure on sovereignty land no matter when constructed and whether or not a permit had been issued.[38]

The Florida Coastal Management Act of 1978 (FCMA) was based upon a special session of the legislature authorizing the Department of Environmental Regulation (DER) to submit an application for the federal funds available under the CZMA.[39] The FCMA, as mentioned earlier, is based upon the above and other existing state programs.[40] This policy is enforced through the legislature's failure to provide authority for any new coastal management regulations.[41] However, because the FCMA's thrust is to focus and coordinate the various state programs to meet the federal CZMA criteria, all federally required aspects of coastal management are included.

A primary requirement of the CZMA is for the states to define their coastal zones.[42] As described earlier, California chose a boundary 1000 yards inland from shore in general. Florida could not choose such a simple demarcation.

With nearly 11,000 miles of marine coastal property and a combination of low land elevation and high ground water levels, Florida has a unique land/water interphase problem.[43] Just where maritime influences stop in Florida is impossible to map with any certainty. Thus

---

34. West's Fla.Stat.Ann.Admin.Code §§ 16B–24.07(3), 16B–24.07(4), 16B–24.08(1).

35. Guy, Florida's Coastal Management Program: A Critical Analysis, 11 Coastal Zone Mgmt.J. 219, 221 (1983).

36. See State v. Anna Maria Island Erosion Prevention District, 58 So.2d 845 (Fla. 1952) (court upheld legislative authority to establish beach erosion control districts with power to levy taxes); Williams v. Guthrie, 102 Fla. 1047, 137 So. 682 (1931) (state owns all submerged lands—burden on developer to show otherwise); State ex rel. Buford v. Tampa, 88 Fla. 196, 102 So. 336 (1924) (state owns marsh lands and lands subject to tidal flow).

37. Op.Att'y Gen.Fla. 074–118 (1974).

38. West's Fla.Stat.Ann. § 161.061.

39. Florida Coastal Zone Management Act of 1978 (presently codified at West's Fla.Stat.Ann. §§ 380.21–380.25) as created in ch. 28–287, Law of Florida. As an approved program, Florida is eligible to receive approximately $2.5–3.0 million annually for implementation.

40. West's Fla.Stat.Ann. § 380.22(1).

41. Id. § 380.21(2). However, additional regulatory authority may be had in the area of federal consistency. Id. § 380.23.

42. See supra § 13.18.

43. U.S. Dep't of Commerce, The Coastline of the United States, NOAA–PA 71046 (1975); Fla. Dep't of Nat. Resources, Statistical Inventory of Key Biophysical Elements in Florida's Coastal Zone (1973).

Florida, along with Delaware and Hawaii, includes the entire state in its definition of the coastal zone.[44] Because a boundary is needed for federal funding and consistency reasons, Florida created an artificial boundary consisting of coastal counties where marine vegetation dominates.[45] This gives Florida a "two-tier" plan,[46] whose only purpose is to collect federal dollars.

Another problem created by Florida's land/water interphase lies in determining just where the mean high water line is located so that the state's sovereignty land may be identified.[47] The court in Ocean Hotels, Inc. v. State of Florida, Department of Natural Resources, chose the landward-most mean water line (the winter line) as the benchmark.[48] However, DNR is authorized to set coastal construction control lines on a county by county basis.[49] Public hearings are held before the line is set and public input as well as comprehensive engineering and topographical studies are used in the decisionmaking process.[50] These control lines are kept as public records in each county and municipality affected and became effective when recorded.[51] If a riparian owner believes the control line too restrictive, it may be reviewed by DNR upon request.[52] If circumstances so warrant, variances in the control line may be established.[53]

The FCMA clearly establishes a public interest in protecting the natural, commercial, recreational, ecological, industrial, and aesthetic resources of the coastal zone.[54] By utilizing a variety of state and local regulations in a network of related laws, Florida hopes to create a comprehensive framework whose total protective effect is greater than the sum of its parts.

This network ("patchwork" may be a better term in some states) approach is used by most states.[55] California, as illustrated by the prior

44. Brindell, Coastal Zone Management, 54 Fla.B.J. 295, 298 (1980).

45. West's Fla.Stat.Ann. § 380.24.

46. Nat'l Oceanic & Atmospheric Administration (NOAA) & Fla. Dep't of Envtl. Regulation, U.S. Department of Commerce Final Environmental Impact Statement of the Proposed Coastal Management Program for the State of Florida, at 11–12 (Aug. 1981).

47. West's Fla.Stat.Ann. § 161.052 provides that no construction shall occur within 50 feet of the mean high water line on any coastal location. Bays, inlets, rivers, harbors, etc. are exempted.

48. 40 Fla.Supp. 26 (15th Cir., Palm Beach County, 1974).

49. West's Fla.Stat.Ann. § 161.053(1).

50. Id. § 161.053(2).

51. Id.

52. Id. (as amended by ch. 80–183 Laws of Fla.).

53. Id. Variance acquisition is covered by West's Fla.Stat.Ann.Admin.Code §§ 16B–25.05, 16B–25.07(3) & 16B–25.08(1). Some types of minor constructions, such as safety fences, boardwalks or viewing platforms, may get an administrative variance without approval of the Governor and cabinet. See Minutes of the Department of Natural Resources at 2 (Aug. 19, 1975) and at 4 (Dec. 7, 1976). Administrative variance procedures are detailed in West's Fla. Stat.Ann.Admin.Code § 16B–25.05.

54. West's Fla.Stat.Ann. § 380.21. Thus, if Florida needs to use its eminent domain powers to acquire land with a primary purpose at least arguably private (impermissible under Florida law), the issue of public purpose will already have been formally addressed by the legislature and the presumption favoring such power will have been enhanced. See J. Juergensmeyer & J. Wadley, Florida Land Use Restrictions § 16.14.

55. See Guy, supra note 35, at 224.

discussion of its coastal program, is a notable exception. California's Coastal Act of 1976 is in itself a comprehensive land use plan utilizing local controls restricted to the coastal zone.[56] The Act uses local plans, but requires local consistency with state policy to a greater degree than does Florida.[57] Florida's state consistency provisions are almost reversed; they require that state land and water management policies "to the maximum possible extent be implemented by local governments through existing processes for the guidance of growth and development." [58] If this provision sufficiently weakens state coastal management policies, it could be the Achilles heel of Florida's program. Too much local control provides greater potential for development interests to subvert the program at the very level where their influence is greatest.[59]

If state consistency is the microcosm of the coastal management battle, federal consistency is the macrocosm. In fact, federal consistency is covered by the longest section of the FCMA.[60] Issuance or renewal of a state license will "automatically constitute" state agreement of consistency. Likewise, a denial is automatic state agreement with a finding of inconsistency. Two particularly detailed subsections of the Florida federal consistency provision concern federal activities seaward of the state's three-mile jurisdiction.[61] States no longer have a right to challenge federal leasing of outer continental shelf (OCS) tracts for oil and mineral exploration since the Supreme Court's opinion in Secretary of the Interior v. California.[62] While oil exploration and development permits are still subject to federal/state consistency provisions under the CZMA (and thus also the coastal programs of all states including Florida's), it may prove impossible for a state to challenge oil development off its coast once the federal government has sold the leases. Hence, the continued validity of FCMA's provisions on federal/state consistency may be open to question.

Coastal Zone Regulation: An Uncertain Future

Coastal zone protection of environmentally sensitive lands is, as illustrated by the preceding discussions, a complicated process. Federal, state, and local plans, acts, policies, and laws must all be consulted before development may take place in coastal areas. Whether such a

56. Id.

57. Id. See also Finnell, Coastal Land Management in California, 2 A.B.F.Res.J. 647, 728 (Fall 1978).

58. West's Fla.Stat.Ann. § 380.21(1)(c).

59. For an in-depth discussion of the problems of Florida's Coastal Zone Management Act and possible solutions to those problems, see Guy, supra note 35, at 225–42.

60. West's Fla.Stat.Ann. § 380.23. An excellent example of how effective state/federal consistency provisions of the CZMA

and its state progeny are occurred in Cape May Greene, Inc. v. Warren, 698 F.2d 179 (3d Cir.1983). There, the federal appellate court struck down a Resigned EPA Administrator's conditions imposed on a residential development as being inconsistent with New Jersey's federally approved coastal management plan.

61. Id. § 380.23(2), (3).

62. 464 U.S. 312, 104 S.Ct. 656, 78 L.Ed. 2d 496 (1984), on remand 729 F.2d 614 (9th Cir.1984). See also supra § 13.18 n. 10.

mish-mash of competing jurisdictions can reach the desired goal of comprehensive, cohesive, and consistent management has not yet been demonstrated. With recent federal budget cutbacks of up to 80% and subversive regulatory changes out of the public's eye, future coastal management and protection will be more and more a state and local activity. That trend has the possibility of destroying more than a decade of progress in protecting sensitive coastal lands. Unless, of course, state and local governments respond to the challenge and provide the funding and expertise needed. Of even greater importance, however, is a fundamental change in attitude. Economic development through an enlarged tax base must be seen as the chimera it really is in environmentally sensitive coastal areas. A quick buck through a dredge and fill or building permit may end up costing dearly when the real interest comes due.

 WESTLAW REFERENCES

California Coastal Act

california /s coastal /s act /s 1976 /p permit /p exempt!

california /s coastal /p zone /p new** /p develop!

california /s coastal /p substantial! significant! /p advers!
/p effect! impact!

california /s coastal /p "implementing actions"

local /s coastal /s program! /p region! /p comission!

The Florida Approach

chapter +5 380 /s appeal!

constitution! /s section /s seven /s article /s ii /p "natural
resources"

199k25.5(2)

coast! /s construct! /s setback

article /s x /s section /s 11 xi /p "public interest"

chapter /s 161 /p beach!

"coastal zone protection act"

chapter +5 403 /p enforc!

"department of environmental regulation" d.e.r. /p "dredge and
fill" /p permit

sy(department /s environmental /s regulat! /p permit!
/p water coast!)

department /s environmental /s regulat! /p permit
/p sovereign! /p land

coast! /p defin! & (getty /s state /s natural /s resource)
bateman (burgess /s pine /s island) mounier

mean /s high /s water /s line /p sovereign! /p land

coast! /p construct! /p control /p line /p county
f.c.m.a.

state /p challeng! /p "outer continental shelf" o.c.s. /p oil
mineral

oil /s explor! develop! /s permit! /s consisten!

IX. LAND USE AND ENVIRONMENTALLY SENSITIVE LANDS—FLOOD PLAINS

§ 13.20 Flood Plain Use and Abuse

Flood plains are areas adjacent to rivers, streams, or other water-bodies subject to periodic flooding of some degree.[1] They form an important component of a particular geographic area's watershed. A watershed is the land's natural drainage system.[2] Over geologic time, floods are as natural as the river channel itself.[3] The river channel and flood plain combine to form the drainage pathway for each water-shed.[4]

Flood plains are of three basic types. The most common are those associated with major rivers whose flooding is characterized by slow water movement over low land gradients, such as the Mississippi and Nile.[5] Because the land is flat, a large amount of flood prone development occurs in this type of flood plain. The other flood plain types are those located in mountain valleys and coastal areas.[6]

While not all flood plain areas are environmentally sensitive, a substantial proportion (usually wetlands and coastal zones) are. Even those areas not normally noted for their environmental value have a sensitivity all their own—if you live on them without precautions they can kill you. Furthermore, every structure built on a flood plain has the effect of increasing the intensity of any given flood, often making flood damage even greater to those areas downstream. Thus, flood plain regulation is a close relative (incestuous, in the case of wetlands and coastal zones) to land use regulations in other, nonhazardous, environmentally sensitive lands.

Flood Plain Values

Flood plains serve much the same purposes as wetlands.[7] In fact, many wetlands are part of flood plains. Historically, the most important human flood plain benefit is agricultural.[8] Flood-water deposition

§ 13.20

1. National Science Foundation, A Report on Flood Hazard Mitigation, 250 (Sept. 1980).

2. Kusler & Platt, Physical Characteristics of Flood Plains and Wetlands, Conference on Local Options for Flood Plain and Wetlands Management, at I–32 (Sept. 1982). Watersheds are drainage basins formed by geologic and gravitational forces. They form the route for water flowing downhill and can be as narrow as a mountain valley or as wide as a prairie. Id. at I–31.

3. Id. at I–32.

4. Id.

5. Nat'l Conference of State Legislatures, Land Management; Sustaining Resource Values, 63 (Oct. 1983) [hereinafter cited as Nat'l Conference].

6. Id.

7. See supra § 13.11.

8. Kasler & Platt, supra note 2, at I–49.

of silt and nutrients allowed the Nile and Tigris and Euphrates Rivers to serve as "cradles of civilization."[9] Agricultural practices were designed to match the rise and fall in floodwaters. When the waters were in normal floodstage, crops were not endangered because they were not yet planted. People were not endangered because they were not so dumb as to build on land subject to yearly flooding. Today, there are almost six and one-half million homes built on flood hazard areas in this country.[10]

Development in Flood Plains

In contrast to the practices of years gone by, today's society has moved from an agricultural orientation to one divorced from the cycles of the seasons. Residential, commercial, and agricultural development is now widespread in flood plain areas. This development is often due to ignorance or nonchalance concerning flood hazards.[11] Draining, dredging, filling, diking and impoundment building are all used to create habitable land in flood plains. If done with foresight (i.e., building houses on stilts or earth embankments) and away from the most hazardous areas, some development can successfully occur in flood plains. If not, situations as ironic as that found in the Everglades region of South Florida can happen. There, a fifty mile sheet flow of floodplain water was reduced by development to a twelve foot wide spillway.[12] Because the Everglades' extremities are bordered with levees and canals to protect residential and agricultural development, the water forced through this spillway is too much for the natural absorption processes of the reduced surface area of the Everglades to accept.[13] Thus, the water management control districts involved must make the choice between destroying Everglades habitat as the water rises or opening up the levees and flooding the developed land.[14]

Flood Plain Regulation

Although closely related, flood plain protection is more readily acceptable to most courts than is wetlands regulation.[15] This is probably true because the public hazard of flooding is better understood than the detriment accruing to the public through wetlands destruction.[16] Another reason is that flood plain regulations are the oldest and most extensive of all sensitive land programs.[17]

---

9. Id. at I–50.

10. Id.

11. Id.

12. Nat'l Conference, supra note 5, at 64.

13. Id.

14. Id.

15. Dawson, Wetlands Regulation, 6 Zoning & Planning, L.Rep. (pt. II) 162 (Nov. 1983).

16. Id. This is true even though wetlands serve as one of nature's best flood protection devices.

17. J. Kusler, Regulating Sensitive Lands 22 (1980). At least twenty-four states and seventeen thousand local governments have flood plain programs, usually adopted in order to qualify for federal flood insurance. Id.

Flood plain mapping must occur before land use regulations can properly control development there. Once mapped, specific zoning laws can be applied by the appropriate local or state authorities.[18] Mapping reveals to these authorities, among other things, two flood plain areas of note for land use purposes; floodways and flood fringes. Floodways are the unobstructed stream channel and overbank areas where flooding is most common. Structural development of any sort is generally prohibited there.[19] Flood fringes are adjacent to floodways and are subject to less flooding and less damage (or potential damage) when floods do occur. A variety of land uses are permitted in flood fringe areas provided precautions such as elevation are taken.[20]

The National Flood Insurance Program [21] is a key component in flood plain development. Local governments must have a comprehensive flood plain regulatory plan in order for buildings in the flood plain to get federal flood insurance.[22] Without such insurance, lending institutions and mortgage companies will usually not finance development or support resale of property in flood prone areas.[23]

Judicial Reaction to Flood Plain Regulation

Because flood protection is a legitimate police power objective, courts have been very favorable in their reactions to flood plain land use ordinances.[24] For instance, in Turnpike Realty Co. v. Town of Dedham,[25] the court upheld a flood plain ordinance so severely restricting development that the restricted land was reduced in value from $431,000 to $53,000. In Usdin v. State,[26] a New Jersey court upheld a restrictive flood plain ordinance on ecological grounds. In examining the taking issue, the court stated that ecological principles must be balanced with the landowners' rights, and that a proper police power function of the state is to prevent serious ecological harm.[27]

Some cases, while not critical of flood plain regulations in general, have found problems with certain implementations of those regulations. If no real flood danger is proved up at the trial level, a court may be very sympathetic to a landowners' taking plea.[28] Likewise, if *all* pecuniary value of a landowners' property is lost due to flood plain

18. Id. at 23.

19. Id.

20. Id.

21. 42 U.S.C.A. § 4001 et seq.

22. Nat'l Conference, supra note 5, at 202.

23. Id.

24. See, e.g., Turner v. County of Del Norte, 24 Cal.App.3d 311, 101 Cal.Rptr. 93 (1972); Vartelas v. Water Resources Commission, 146 Conn. 650, 153 A.2d 822 (1959); Iowa Natural Resources Council v.

Van Zee, 261 Iowa 1287, 158 N.W.2d 111 (1968). See generally supra § 4.9.

25. 362 Mass. 221, 284 N.E.2d 891 (1972), cert. denied 409 U.S. 1108, 93 S.Ct. 908, 34 L.Ed.2d 689 (1973).

26. 173 N.J.Super. 311, 414 A.2d 280 (1980), affirmed 179 N.J.Super. 113, 430 A.2d 949 (1981).

27. Id. at 319, 414 A.2d at 288.

28. Sturdy Homes, Inc. v. Township of Redford, 30 Mich.App. 53, 186 N.W.2d 43 (1971).

regulations, courts will frequently find a taking.[29]   Other cases have struck down particular flood plain ordinance application where the court believes the action discriminatory [30] or unreasonable.[31]

 WESTLAW REFERENCES

"flood plain" /p adjoin! adjacent!

watershed /p natur! /p drain!

"flood plain" /p regulat! /p environment!

Flood Plain Values

di("flood plain" /s agricultur! farm! crop)

Development in Flood Plains

"flood plain /s develop! /s commercial

flood /s hazards /s plain

everglade /p flood!

Flood Plain Regulation

sy("flood plain" /s map!)

"flood plain /s protect! /s hazard

"flood plain" /s zon! /s city

floodway /p prohibit! /p building

"flood fringe"

"national flood insurance program"

Judicial Reaction to Flood Plain Regulation

"flood plain" /s regulat! /s taking

sy("flood plain" /p discriminat! unconstitution! constitution!
    unreasonabl!)

X. LAND USE AND ENVIRONMENTALLY SENSITIVE LANDS—THE ENDANGERED SPECIES ACT

§ 13.21   The Endangered Species Act as a Land Use Control

The Endangered Species Act [1] has proved to be a useful land use control tool in environmentally sensitive areas.[2] This is so even though the Act's land use-type provisions are not generally well known. To

---

29. See, e.g., Dooley v. Town Plan & Zoning Commission, 151 Conn. 304, 197 A.2d 770 (1964); Baker v. Planning Board, 353 Mass. 141, 228 N.E.2d 831 (1967); Morris County Land Township Co. v. Parsippany-Troy Hills Township, 40 N.J. 539, 193 A.2d 232 (1963).

30. City of Welch v. Mitchell, 95 W.Va. 377, 121 S.E. 165 (1924).

31. See, e.g., Kesselring v. Wakefield Realty Co., Inc., 306 Ky. 725, 209 S.W.2d 63 (1948); Sturdy Homes Inc. v. Township of

Redford, 30 Mich.App. 53, 186 N.W.2d 43 (1971).

§ 13.21

1. 16 U.S.C.A. §§ 1531–1543.

2. For an excellent discussion of the Endangered Species Act, see W. Harrington & A. Fisher, Endangered Species in Natural Resources Policy 117–48 (P. Portney ed. 1982); T. Schoenbaum, Environmental Policy Law 401–16 (1981).

most people, the Act simply forbids one from hunting bald eagles or fishing for snail darters. Its secret for success lies in its ability to alter or even halt development that threatens a plant or animal species listed by the Secretary of the Interior as endangered.[3] This ties in with the Act's stated purpose "to provide a means whereby the ecosystems upon which endangered species and threatened species depend may be conserved." [4]

The land use element in the Endangered Species Act is section 7. It authorizes the Secretary of Interior to designate areas of "critical habitat" for specified species.[5] This section reflects ecological reality; there is no use in protecting a plant or animal species if that species has no place to live.

Until the 1978 amendments to the Act, section 7 was an absolute. If a project posed a threat to an endangered species, it had to be stopped or altered. Balancing of any sort was not allowed.[6]

The 1978 Amendments [7]

In contrast to the original Act, the 1978 amendments to the Endangered Species Act provide for economic as well as ecological considerations. These amendments came primarily because of a single case—TVA v. Hill.[8] More commonly known as the snail darter case, TVA v. Hill is a perfect example of the political backlash that can follow an environmental "victory" viewed as extreme.

TVA v. Hill also illustrates the endangered species act acting as a land use control. There, plaintiffs sought an injunction to prevent completion of the Tellico Dam on the Little Tennessee River. The real reason for bringing the suit was to prevent the flooding of over 16,000 acres of land—much of it prime Tennessee farmland.[9] But until the tiny snail darter was discovered and listed as an endangered species (living only in the to-be flooded waters of the Little Tennessee River) the plaintiffs had no legal handle sturdy enough to challenge a virtually completed multi-million dollar dam project.[10]

3. The process to be followed by the Secretary in adding or subtracting a species from the act's domain is found at 16 U.S.C.A. § 1533(a), (b).

4. Id. § 1531(b).

5. Id. § 1533(a)(3).

6. W. Harrington & A. Fisher, supra note 2, at 133.

7. The Endangered Species Act Amendments of 1978, 92 Stat. 3751 (1978) (current version at 16 U.S.C.A. §§ 1531–1543).

8. 437 U.S. 153, 98 S.Ct. 2279, 57 L.Ed. 2d 117 (1978). For a comprehensive and insightful analysis of the Tellico Dam litigation authored by counsel for plaintiffs,

see Plater, Reflected in a River: Agency Accountability and the TVA Tellico Dam case, 49 Tenn.L.Rev. 747 (1982).

9. Id. at 153, 98 S.Ct. at 2279. Amicus briefs were filed by both the Eastern Board of Cherokee Indians and the East Tennessee Valley Landowners Association.

10. Previous suits, successful until 1973, were based on NEPA's EIS requirement. See, Environmental Defense Fund v. TVA, 371 F.Supp. 1004 (E.D.Tenn.1973), affirmed 492 F.2d 466 (6th Cir.1974); Environmental Defense Fund v. TVA, 339 F.Supp. 806 (E.D.Tenn.1972), affirmed 468 F.2d 1164 (6th Cir.1972).

Plaintiffs alleged that Tellico would destroy the snail darter, a prohibited act under the Endangered Species Act.[11] They claimed that no matter how much money had been spent, there could be no exceptions. Plaintiffs won, but they proved too much.

Headlines proclaiming victory for the David snail darter versus the Goliath Tennessee Valley Authority scared some congressmen who apparently did not know the extent of the bill they had voted for. The congressional response was immediate. That response consisted of amendments which limited critical habitat designations to areas "essential to the conservation of the species." [12] Before the Secretary of the Interior can make such a designation, the amendments specify that the "economic impact and any other relevant impacts" must be considered.[13] In addition, an exemption procedure was added which can, if fairly stringent safeguards are met, allow a project to continue despite its adverse effects on an endangered species.[14] It was through such an exemption that the Tellico Dam was completed.[15]

The 1982 Amendments

The 1982 Amendments to the Endangered Species Act was prompted by confrontations between developers and environmentalists over projects already approved by the pertinent authorities.[16] The amendments were designed to add flexibility to the Secretary of Interior's powers over development regulation. While giving what is perceived as at least some reduction in endangered species protection, the 1982 amendments may actually further the goal of species and habitat protection by rewarding cooperation rather than confrontation when developers and environmentalists clash over a particular project.

This cooperation is achieved through the age-old method of the quid-pro-quo. Developers sought assurances that otherwise legal projects would not be halted by the section 9 prohibitions against "taking" an endangered species. Environmentalists feared species extinction and desired legal roadblocks to halt development if it interfered with an endangered species. Thus a balance was struck with section 10(a) of the Act being amended so that certain "incidental takings" of endangered species would be authorized provided strict guidelines were met. A permit must be acquired (listing all alternatives) which shows to the secretary's satisfaction that the "incidental

11. 437 U.S. at 162, 98 S.Ct. at 2285.

12. 16 U.S.C.A. § 1532(5)(A)(ii)(I).

13. Id. at § 1533(b)(2).

14. Id. at § 1536(g).

15. The Endangered Species Committee created by the 1978 amendments as part of the exemption process voted unanimously against an exemption for the Tellico project. It took an act of Congress to override that decision and dam the Little Tennessee River. Curiously enough, the Committee

denied the exemption on economic grounds. Tellico was pure pork-barrel with few if no redeeming features. Only through the intense lobbying effects of Tennessee Senator Howard Baker—who argued that the Committee could not consider economic aspects—was Tellico exempted. See W. Harrington & A. Fisher, supra note 2, at 138.

16. Endangered Species Act Amendments of 1982, 97th Cong., 2d Sess., House of Repr., Rep. No. 97–835, Sept. 17, 1982.

taking" will not seriously affect the endangered species.[17] The permit can be revoked for noncompliance.[18] In return, environmentalists are assured that sufficient mitigation measures will be followed and that conservation plans necessary for an "incidental taking" permit will be fully funded by the developers.

Thus by cooperating with permit procedures and with each other, developers and environmentalists both may find it possible to co-exist. Developers are given long-range assurances that project regulations won't be changed and environmentalists may rest easier knowing a satisfactory conservation plan for the endangered species is funded and operational. With any luck, the end result could be the best of both worlds—intelligent, planned development and environmental protection tied together through mutual agreement.

Land Use Effects Since the 1978 and 1982 Amendments

Though weakened by the 1978 and 1982 amendments, the Endangered Species Act still contains a potential knockout land use punch. Even with the amendments the exemption process is lengthy and adverse environmental effects must be substantially mitigated.[19] The most recent land use success of the amended Act should give one a sense of *déjà vu*; once again a tiny, commercially valueless fish has halted a multi-million dollar project. The only difference is that this time it is a private developer being swallowed whole by a virtual guppy.

Barely four fifths of an inch long, the Devil's Hole pupfish has probably lived closer to extinction the past 10,000 years than any other endangered species. Exclusive to the Devil's Hole, a small, remote desert pool 75 miles west of Las Vegas, the Devil's Hole pupfish lives in the only water source for a Las Vegas based real estate development.[20] A water table drop of even one foot would doom the pupfish, and more than 12,000 acres of land surrounding Devil's Hole has been platted for a 23,000 lot subdivision.[21] Each of those 23,000 residential units would draw water from the same spring that feeds the Devil's Hole.

Because of the Endangered Species Act, a deal was made to save the Devil's Hole pupfish by transferring the land from the developer to the Department of the Interior.[22] The selling price was approximately $5.5 million. Without the Endangered Species Act, the developer could have sold the land, lot by lot, for as much as $420 million.[23] Because any proposed development in an area inhabited by an endangered species will be carefully scrutinized by federal officials and environmen-

---

17. 16 U.S.C.A. § 1539(a)(2)(A), (B).

18. Id. § 1539(a)(2)(B) and (C).

19. W. Harrington & A. Fisher, supra n. 2, at 138.

20. Adler, The Edge of Extension, Newsweek, Jan. 30, 1984, at 7.

21. Id.

22. Id.

23. Id. Lest these figures seem too appalling, it should be noted that the Devil's Hole pupfish could have incalcuable scientific value. Because of its Galapagos-like isolation, the pupfish may help settle an evolutionary debate between the old line Darwinians and the "punctuated equilibrium" theorists following Harvard paleontologist Stephen Jay Gould. W. Harrington & A. Fisher, supra note 2, at 120.

tal groups following the Endangered Species Act, the wise developer will check before he buys to avoid the kind of loss caused by the Devil's Hole pupfish.

 WESTLAW REFERENCES

"endangered species act" /s land /s use regulat!

section /s seven /s endangered /s species /s "critical habitat"

"endangered species act" /s hunt! fish! /s eagle snail

The 1978 Amendments

437 +3 153 /s 1978 /s amend!

The 1982 Amendments

section /s 9 /s endangered /s species /s taking

"endangered species act" /p 10(a) /p incidental /s taking

Land Use Effects Since the 1978 and 1982 Amendments

"devil's hole pupfish"

Chapter 14

AESTHETIC REGULATION AND HISTORIC PRESERVATION

Analysis

I. AESTHETIC REGULATION

§ 14.1 Introduction

What is beauty? Our individual preferences are conditioned by educational, social and environmental factors, and because of that, it would be impossible for any one person to be the final arbiter of taste. David Hume, a Scottish philosopher, has said that beauty in things exists in the mind that contemplates them.

Aesthetics is a subjective quality which eludes quantification. What is pleasing to the eye depends upon to whom the eye belongs. Thus, as a basis for regulation of land uses, statutes and ordinances grounded *solely* on furthering of aesthetic purposes have been, until recently, difficult to justify.[1] This chapter explores regulation of aes-

§ 14.1

1. Bufford, Beyond the Eye of the Beholder: A New Majority of Jurisdictions Authorize Aesthetic Regulation, 48 UMKC L.Rev. 125 (1980). See also Reisel, Aesthetics as a Basis for Regulation, 1 Pace L.Rev. 651 (1981); Note, Reasonableness of Aes- thetic Zoning in Florida, 10 Fla.St.U.L.Rev. 441 (1982); Note, State v. Jones: Aesthetic Regulation—From Junkyards to Residences, 61 N.C.L.Rev. 942 (1983); Comment, Zoning: Stronger than Dirt, 18 Wake For.L.Rev. 1167 (1982).

thetic values in three specific areas; sign control, architectural regulation and historic preservation. In each of these areas, aesthetic considerations loom large and particular attention must be given to the ways in which aesthetics relate to the public health, safety and welfare.

In land use control lore, an aesthetic control attempts to preserve or improve the beauty of an area. All zoning is to a certain extent based on the desire for beauty. Some of this country's first planning efforts arose from what was called the "city beautiful" movement. In one of the earliest zoning decisions, the Supreme Court of the United States in Village of Euclid v. Ambler Realty Co.,[2] validated zoning as a reasonable exercise of the police power, taking the view that law must respond to the changing demands and needs of urban areas. After Euclid and until 1954, however, aesthetics alone was not considered a valid purpose for land use measures. Courts required that such measures be coupled with more traditional grounds to be sustained.[3]

In 1954, Justice Douglas noted in Berman v. Parker[4] that public safety, health, morality, peace and quiet, law and order—which are some of the more conspicuous examples of the traditional application of the police power—merely illustrate the scope of the power and do not limit it. He further observed that the concept of public welfare includes values which are spiritual as well as physical, aesthetic as well as monetary. It is within the power of the legislature to determine that the community should be beautiful as well as healthy.[5] Subsequently, in People v. Stover,[6] the New York Court of Appeals determined that aesthetic purposes would support a restriction on the use of land. More recent cases extend legal support for the validity and necessity of aesthetic considerations in natural resource allocation and land use planning.[7]

Consideration of aesthetics in the promulgation of federal regulations was essentially guaranteed in 1969, with passage of the National

2. 272 U.S. 365, 47 S.Ct. 114, 71 L.Ed. 303 (1926).

3. See, e.g., Board of Supervisors v. Rowe, 216 Va. 128, 216 S.E.2d 199 (1975) (protecting property values); Cochran v. Preston, 108 Md. 220, 70 A. 113 (1908) (height restrictions in Washington Monument vicinity upheld on safety and aesthetic grounds).

4. 348 U.S. 26, 75 S.Ct. 98, 99 L.Ed. 27 (1954).

5. Id. at 29, 75 S.Ct. at 100.

6. 12 N.Y.2d 462, 240 N.Y.S.2d 734, 191 N.E.2d 272 (1963) appeal dismissed 375 U.S. 42, 84 S.Ct. 147, 11 L.Ed.2d 107 (1963) (regulation requiring removal of clothesline from front yard).

7. E.g., Citizens to Preserve Overton Park v. Volpe, 401 U.S. 402, 91 S.Ct. 814, 28 L.Ed.2d 136 (1971), on remand 335 F.Supp. 873 (D.Tenn.1972), opinion supplemented 357 F.Supp. 846 (D.Tenn.1973), order reversed 494 F.2d 1212 (6th Cir.1974), cert. denied 421 U.S. 991, 95 S.Ct. 1997, 44 L.Ed.2d 481 (1975) (recognizing that planners and bureaucrats must consider aesthetics); Scenic Hudson Preservation Conference v. FPC, 354 F.2d 608 (2d Cir.1965), cert. denied 384 U.S. 941, 86 S.Ct. 1462, 16 L.Ed.2d 540 (1966), appeal after remand 453 F.2d 463 (2d Cir.1971), cert. denied 407 U.S. 926, 92 S.Ct. 2453, 32 L.Ed.2d 813 (1972) (requiring consideration of power plant's visual impact on environment).

Environmental Policy Act.[8]   NEPA made consideration of aesthetic objectives a fundamental part of national policy by requiring an assessment of a project's impact on the built environment.   Congress intended that creation and maintenance of a productive harmony between man and the environment be a national goal, to the end that the nation may be assured safe, healthy, productive, and aesthetically and culturally pleasing surroundings.[9]   Enforcement of NEPA by courts has led to enactment of similar statutes in several states.[10]

In spite of the jurisprudential support given aesthetic control as a valid regulatory goal in recent years, problems still exist.   Courts are repeatedly forced to determine whether a particular aesthetic regulation is a proper use of the police power.   This often raises due process questions.   Measures based on visual compatibility principles, analogous to zoning rationale, are fairly easy to sustain, but if the compatibility requirements are vague, overbroad or ambiguous, serious due process and first amendment problems may be indicated.[11]   Sign control ordinances are particularly susceptible to first amendment attacks.[12]

Another charge frequently leveled at an aesthetics-based regulation is that the affected property has been taken.   These claims generally do not pose serious threats, however, for in most cases courts sustain the action as a valid exercise of a state's police power.[13]   Problems do on occasion arise where the adequacy of due process, in either the creation or application of the aesthetic control, is called into question.   A regulation as applied may in a few instances be deemed a taking, particularly if a landmarks ordinance prevents demolition of an historic building.[14]

On the whole, the courts' shift in favor of aesthetic-based regulation recognizes that pleasing surroundings are protectable as part of the public welfare.   Commentators have suggested that zoning ordinances enacted primarily for aesthetic objectives should be recognized as a legitimate means of implementing community values.   This would enable courts to discontinue upholding ordinances prohibiting uses that

---

8. National Environmental Policy Act of 1969, 42 U.S.C.A. §§ 4321–4370.

9. Id. § 4331.

10. E.g., West's Ann.Cal.Pub.Res.Code § 21000(b);   Minn.Stat.Ann. § 116B.02; N.Y.—McKinney's Envir.Conserv.Law § 8–0101–0117.   This sort of cause and effect situation is mirrored to some extent by the experience with the National Historic Preservation Act, and subsequently enacted similar state laws.

11. Costonis, Law and Aesthetics: A Critique and A Reformulation of the Dilemmas, 80 Mich.L.Rev. 355, 360–361 (1981). See supra §§ 10.2, 10.3.

12. See, e.g., Metromedia, Inc. v. San Diego, 453 U.S. 490, 101 S.Ct. 2882, 69 L.Ed.2d 800 (1981), on remand 32 Cal.3d 180, 185 Cal.Rptr. 260, 649 P.2d 902 (1982).

13. See Penn Cent. Transp., Inc. v. New York, 438 U.S. 104, 98 S.Ct. 2646, 57 L.Ed. 2d 631 (1978), rehearing denied 439 U.S. 883, 99 S.Ct. 226, 58 L.Ed.2d 198 (1978) (landmark regulation valid if part of an overall historic preservation scheme).

14. Lutheran Church in Am. v. New York, 35 N.Y.2d 121, 359 N.Y.S.2d 7, 316 N.E.2d 305 (1974). See also § 14.9, infra.

are aesthetically offensive, such as billboards, under the fiction that they constitute public health and safety hazards.[15]

WESTLAW REFERENCES

"aesthetic regulation"

aesthetic! /p land /s use /p beaut!

zon! /p preserv! improv! /p beaut!

cochran /s preston /p height

berman /s parker /s scope

people /s stover /s restrict!

overton /s volpe /p beaut! aesthetic!

n.e.p.a. /p assess! /s impact! /s environment! /p aesthetic!

aesthetic! /s regulat! /p "due process"

"first amendment" /p sign /p control /p ordinanc!

aesthetic! /p regulat! /p taking

§ 14.2   The Trend Toward Sign Control

Billboard and sign regulation is not a new phenomenon. People have long protested the unsightliness of billboards, and legislatures have attempted to appease them from time to time. Courts, however, in the early part of the twentieth century, were not receptive to these moves. In City of Passaic v. Paterson Bill Posting, Advertising & Sign Painting Co.,[1] the court invalidated an ordinance which imposed set-back and height restrictions, reasoning that aesthetic considerations were matters of luxury, and necessity alone justified exercise of the police power. Some later opinions were not quite so rigidly set, and courts allowed regulation of signs for traffic safety and health purposes or to preserve the scenery obliterated by the erection of signs.[2]

More recently, courts have recognized aesthetic concerns as being a valid justification for use of the police power.[3] An early opinion sustaining aesthetic values as sufficient grounds for a community to ban all off-premise signs was Cromwell v. Ferrier.[4] The New York Court of Appeals reasoned that exercise of the police power should extend to those aesthetic considerations which bear substantially on the

15. Dukeminier, Zoning for Aesthetic Objectives: A Reappraisal, 20 Law & Contemp.Probs. 281 (1955).

§ 14.2

1. 72 N.J.L. 285, 62 A. 267 (Err. & App. 1905). See also Commonwealth v. Boston Advertising Co., 188 Mass. 348, 74 N.E. 601 (1905); People v. Green, 85 App.Div. 400, 83 N.Y.S. 460 (1903); Bryan v. Chester, 212 Pa. 259, 61 A. 894 (1905).

2. St. Louis Gunning Advertising Co. v. St. Louis, 235 Mo. 99, 137 S.W. 929 (1911). Cf. General Outdoor Advertising Co. v. Indianapolis, Dep't of Pub. Parks, 202 Ind. 85, 172 N.E. 309 (1930).

3. This has been the case since Berman v. Parker, 348 U.S. 26, 75 S.Ct. 98, 99 L.Ed. 27 (1954). Undoubtedly Dukeminier, Zoning for Aesthetic Objectives: A Reappraisal, 20 L. & Contemp.Probs. 281 (1955), has been influential as well.

4. 19 N.Y.2d 263, 279 N.Y.S.2d 22, 225 N.E.2d 749 (1967), reargument denied 19 N.Y.2d 862, 280 N.Y.S.2d 1025, 227 N.E.2d 408 (1967). See also Oregon City v. Hartke, 240 Or. 35, 400 P.2d 255 (1965) (junkyard).

economic, social, and cultural patterns of a community or district. "Advertising signs and billboards . . . often are egregious examples of ugliness . . . just as much subject to reasonable controls . . . as enterprises which emit offensive noises, odors or debris." But elsewhere, an ordinance which attempted to require property owners to provide for "beauty, attractiveness, aesthetics and symmetry in commercial signs . . . " was invalidated.[5] The court distinguished between ordinances with a primary goal of furthering aesthetics, and those with other immediate goals, only secondarily considering aesthetics. The latter were a valid use of the police power, while the former were not.[6] The majority of states now hold a regulation based solely upon aesthetic considerations is legitimate.[7]

There are many ways to impose restrictions on signs, ranging from total exclusion from a given area, to limitation of location, size, height, and setback from the street. Distinctions are made between on- and off-premise signs, between those located in urban or residential areas, and between commercial and noncommercial signs. The first amendment protection afforded speech often comes into play when a statute or ordinance is not carefully drafted and infringes on the protected right.[8] If similarly situated signs are categorized or treated differently by the ordinance, an equal protection problem may exist.

 WESTLAW REFERENCES

passaic /s advertising /p "police power"

commonwealth +s boston +s advertising /p aesthetic! /p
   regulat! zon!

sy(aesthetic! /s valid! /s "police power")

cromwell +5 ferrier /p premise /p prohibit! ban banned
   banning

di("police power" /p substantial! /p bear*** /p community
   district)

"police power" /p substantial! /p bear*** /p community district
   /p aesthetic!

ordinance /p primar! immediate secondar! /p goal /p aesthetic!

ordinance /s only sole** /s base* /s aesthetic! beaut!

lasalle +s national +s bank +s evanston /p zon! /p
   valid!

sy("equal protection" /s sign billboard /s regulat!)

---

5. Mayor & City Council v. Mano Swartz, Inc., 268 Md. 79, 299 A.2d 828 (1973).

6. See also Donnelly Advertising Corp. v. Mayor & City Council, 279 Md. 660, 370 A.2d 1127 (1977) (ordinance upheld—aesthetics a secondary goal). Cf. Berberian v. Housing Auth., 112 R.I. 771, 315 A.2d 747 (1974).

7. Bufford, Beyond the Eye of the Beholder: A New Majority of Jurisdictions

Authorize Aesthetic Regulation, 48 UMKC L.Rev. 125 (1980). Sixteen states allow this sort of law, and another 16 authorize laws at least partially based on aesthetics. Only nine hold that such regulation is beyond the scope of the police power. Ten states have no reported decisions.

8. See infra § 14.4.

§ 14.3   Sign Regulation

Outdoor advertising and signs are not always controlled by zoning alone. Some municipalities attempt to regulate signs separately through a comprehensive ordinance. Statutes authorizing state sign control and enabling municipal regulation predate zoning, though courts have not always found them valid.[1] Private nuisance actions have also been used as a means of ridding certain locale of unsightly billboards.[2] The power to regulate and restrict outdoor advertising may even be found in state constitutional provisions, as was the case in General Outdoor Advertising Co. v. Department of Public Works.[3] The court found that this power could be delegated to municipalities, and its use could be justified to reduce traffic obstructions, to promote traffic safety and to avoid nuisances.

Similar regulations prohibiting signs near major highways and public places are traditionally considered valid.[4] Such regulations were upheld in New York State Thruway Authority v. Ashley Motor Court.[5] The court found that the regulations furthered the purposes of providing maximum visibility, preventing unreasonable distraction to drivers and interference with traffic regulation, preserving the natural scenic beauty, and promoting maximum safety and welfare of thruway users.[6] The court also suggested that the government had the power to apply regulations to existing signs, for it was the presence of the highway in the first place which gave the signs their value, inferring that no compensation was necessary.[7]

Attempts to regulate sign usage have traditionally led to taking challenges. One early theory upon which taking claims were based was that the sign erected on landowner's property became a fixture of the property, and therefore was realty, if that was the landowner's intent.[8] Such signs were treated differently if placed by the owner on property of another pursuant to an advertising lease. The current view is that fixtures attached to real estate under a lease are to be treated as real estate for valuation purposes, and when severed, the value attributed to the sign is treated as personalty and credited to the tenant.[9]

§ 14.3

1. St. Louis Gunning Advertising Co. v. St. Louis, 235 Mo. 99, 137 S.W. 929 (1911); City of Passaic v. Paterson Bill Posting, Advertising & Sign Painting Co., 72 N.J.L. 285, 62 A. 267 (1905); People v. Green, 85 App.Div. 400, 83 N.Y.S. 460 (1903). The use of zoning, of course, came later in 1926, with the holding in Village of Euclid v. Ambler, 272 U.S. 365, 47 S.Ct. 114, 71 L.Ed. 303 (1926).

2. See infra § 18.3, for discussion of private nuisance.

3. 289 Mass. 149, 193 N.E. 799 (1935).

4. E.g., Vt.Stat.Ann. tit. 10, § 321 et seq.

5. 10 N.Y.2d 151, 218 N.Y.S.2d 640, 176 N.E.2d 566 (1961), reargument denied 10 N.Y.2d 885, 223 N.Y.S.2d 1027, 179 N.E.2d 717 (1961).

6. Cf. West's Ann.Cal.Bus. & Prof.Code §§ 5200–5325.

7. Compare this rationale with a similar case, Kelbro, Inc. v. Myrick, 113 Vt. 64, 30 A.2d 527 (1943), which sidesteps the taking claim.

8. Teaff v. Hewitt, 1 Ohio St. 511 (1853).

9. 2 P. Nichols, Eminent Domain § 5.81(2) (rev. 3d ed. 1970). See City of Buffalo v. Michael, 16 N.Y.2d 88, 262 N.Y.S.2d 441, 209 N.E.2d 776 (1965); Rochester Poster Advertising Co. v. State, 27

Some states found that the existence of a right of removal is a proper basis for denial of compensation to the lessee for the value of his sign.[10] A few states have determined that advertising signs are personalty rather than realty, thus the state can require the lessee to remove the sign at his own expense.[11]

Under the Highway Beautification Act of 1965,[12] which prohibits signs within 660 feet of the right of way along interstate and primary highway systems, unless an area is zoned for commercial or industrial uses, compensation must be paid for the removal of signs predating the law. The act provided the stimulus for many states to control signs along highways or risk loss of federal funds. Funding for compensation has lagged, and at its current level it is doubtful that targeted billboards will be removed in the near future. Because the act only took aim at signs within 660 feet of federally aided highways, the proscription stimulated a proliferation of large billboards in rural areas set just beyond that line.

Justifications given for regulating signs through the police power have shifted from one emphasis to another. As with similar non-zoning regulations, zoning ordinances controlling signs along highways have been upheld to protect travelers. Other rationales [13] were stated to avoid the allegation that the regulation was being upheld solely on aesthetic grounds. Realistically, however, grounds for sustaining the regulation were based on either aesthetics [14] or the preservation of property, particularly in areas where signs would mar the historic or naturally scenic character of the area and interfere with the tourist industry.[15]

Some courts view preservation of property concerns as separate from aesthetic purposes. Aesthetic regulations have long been sustained when coupled with another legitimate police power purpose,[16]

Misc.2d 99, 213 N.Y.S.2d 812 (1961), affirmed mem. 11 N.Y.2d 1036, 230 N.Y.S.2d 30, 183 N.E.2d 911 (1967); Uniform Relocation Assistance & Real Property Acquisition Policies Act of 1970, 42 U.S.C.A. § 4655(1).

10. E.g., Mayor of Baltimore v. Gamse, 132 Md. 290, 104 A. 429 (1918).

11. E.g., Ghaster Properties, Inc. v. Preston, 176 Ohio St. 425, 200 N.E.2d 328 (1964).

12. 23 U.S.C.A. § 131.

13. Murphy, Inc. v. Town of Westport, 131 Conn. 292, 40 A.2d 177 (1944) (endangering public health by emphasis on advertisements for liquor, tobacco); St. Louis Gunning Advertising Co. v. St. Louis, 235 Mo. 99, 137 S.W. 929 (1911) (immoral acts might be performed behind signs, trash might accumulate).

14. See Dukeminier, Zoning for Aesthetic Objectives: A Reappraisal, 20 Law & Contemp.Probs. 218 (1955).

15. International Co. v. Miami Beach, 90 So.2d 906 (Fla.1956); Sunad, Inc. v. Sarasota, 122 So.2d 611 (Fla.1960) (proper to consider aesthetics but ordinance invalidated); City of New Orleans v. Pergament, 198 La. 852, 5 So.2d 129 (1941); State v. Diamond Motors, Inc., 50 Hawaii 33, 429 P.2d 825 (1967).

16. Little Pep Delmonico Restaurant, Inc. v. Charlotte, 252 N.C. 324, 113 S.E.2d 422 (1960), overruled State v. Jones, 305 N.C. 520, 290 S.E.2d 675 (1982) (aesthetics alone is sufficient); United Advertising Corp. v. Borough of Metuchen, 42 N.J. 1, 198 A.2d 447 (1964).

but aesthetics standing alone is now recognized as a valid exercise of the police power in many jurisdictions.[17]

Total exclusion of all types of signs from a municipality has not been allowed, for it may be unreasonable and violative of first amendment considerations. Exclusion of off-premise signs or billboards from residential areas has been held a reasonable application in light of compatibility and preservation of property value theories.[18] Courts have generally given their imprimatur to the regulatory purposes served by exclusion. In United Advertising Corp. v. Borough of Metuchen,[19] the New Jersey Supreme Court upheld a zoning ordinance absolutely prohibiting off-premise advertising throughout the municipality, including business and manufacturing districts, reasoning that the aesthetic impact of billboards was an economic factor relevant to property values. Another ordinance excluding off-premise signs throughout a township was upheld in Suffolk Outdoor Adv. Co. v. Hulse,[20] where the sign owners were given a three year amortization period within which to remove the signs.

Many of the sign cases involve the propriety of a classification which prohibits some signs and permits others. The off-site, on-site classification is often upheld because advertising is a distinct business that can be regulated, so such a classification does not violate uniformity of treatment and raise equal protection problems. The equal protection argument stresses that the aesthetic impact of a sign does not vary with its location, and that prohibiting or regulating billboards on that basis is invalid if on-premise signs are treated more favorably. Billboards have been treated separately and distinguished from other signs on the ground that the former are more likely to be unattractive, to restrict normal development, and be deliberately conspicuous.[21]

There is little case law concerning dimensional controls as a means of regulating signs. Laws controlling the size of signs have been upheld for such divergent reasons as public safety [22] and pure aesthetics.[23]

17. See Bufford, Beyond the Eye of the Beholder: A New Majority of Jurisdictions Authorize Aesthetic Regulation, 48 UMKC L.Rev. 125 (1980).

18. E.g., John Donnelly & Sons, Inc. v. Outdoor Advertising Bd., 369 Mass. 206, 339 N.E.2d 709 (1975); Naegele Outdoor Advertising Co. v. Village of Minnetonka, 281 Minn. 492, 162 N.W.2d 206 (1968). But see People v. Goodman, 31 N.Y.2d 262, 338 N.Y.S.2d 97, 290 N.E.2d 139 (1972), reargument denied 32 N.Y.2d 705, 343 N.Y.S.2d 1026, 296 N.E.2d 459 (1973) (off-premise signs totally excluded from resort island).

19. 42 N.J. 1, 198 A.2d 447 (1964).

20. 43 N.Y.2d 483, 402 N.Y.S.2d 368, 373 N.E.2d 263 (1977), reargument denied

43 N.Y.2d 951, 403 N.Y.S.2d 1029, 374 N.E.2d 1251 (1978), appeal dismissed 439 U.S. 808, 99 S.Ct. 66, 58 L.Ed.2d 101 (1978).

21. National Advertising Co. v. County of Monterey, 211 Cal.App.2d 375, 27 Cal. Rptr. 136 (1962).

22. Board of Adjustment v. Osage Oil & Transp. Co., 258 Ark. 91, 522 S.W.2d 836 (1975), appeal dismissed, cert. denied 423 U.S. 941, 96 S.Ct. 350, 46 L.Ed.2d 273 (1975) (to keep signs from falling on passersby).

23. People v. Goodman, 31 N.Y.2d 262, 338 N.Y.2d 97, 290 N.E.2d 139 (1972), reargument denied 32 N.Y.2d 705, 343 N.Y.S.2d 1026, 296 N.E.2d 459 (1973) (compatibility with natural beauty of Fire Island, N.Y.).

Height restrictions have been sustained on similar grounds.[24] Many ordinances which prohibit new signs also seek to require removal of existing ones as soon as possible. Already existing signs which do not comply with the ordinance are treated as nonconforming signs, and have been given the same protection as other nonconforming uses. Courts allow amortization schedules which provide for removal after a reasonable period.[25]

Compensation requirements under the Highway Beautification Act are generally strictly applied, and federal funding will be withheld if signs are removed and owners are not compensated.[26] In some jurisdictions, however, signs have been removed immediately and without compensation. In Markham Advertising Co. v. State,[27] the petitioners challenged a Washington state statute which prohibited billboards under certain circumstances, and declared it unlawful to maintain them after a certain date. The petitioner's signs had been lawfully erected prior to the enactment of the statute but became unlawful before the effective date of the Federal Highway Act which required compensation for forced removal; thus, the signs were removed and no compensation was paid. The court found that Congress had not intended to preempt state regulation of highway advertising but rather had intended to encourage state control by offering financial incentives. Therefore, language in the federal statute mandating payment of compensation was found inapplicable. Appeal to the United States Supreme Court was dismissed for want of a federal question.[28]

WESTLAW REFERENCES

private! /5 nuisance /p billboard sign

general +s outdoor +s advertising +s department +s
    public +s works /p constitution! /p power authori!

sy(regulat! ordinance /p prohibit! ban banned banning /p sign
    billboard /p highway /p power authori!)

sy(regulat! ordinance /s sign billboard /s use usage /s taking)

148k147 /p billboard sign

(ghaster +s preston /p compensat!) (sign billboard /p
    personalty /p remov! /p condemn!)

24. Sun Oil Co. v. Madison Heights, 41 Mich.App. 47, 199 N.W.2d 525 (1972) (ordinance limiting high rise signs to 20 feet valid).

25. For a good discussion of the amortization concept in connection with nonconforming uses, see, e.g., Harbison v. Buffalo, 4 N.Y.2d 553, 152 N.E.2d 42, 176 N.Y.S.2d 598 (1958).

26. 42 Op.Atty.Gen. 26 (1966). See also State v. Adams, 506 F.Supp. 60 (D.S.D.), affirmed 635 F.2d 698 (10th Cir.1980), cert. denied 451 U.S. 984, 101 S.Ct. 2316, 68 L.Ed.2d 841 (1981). But see Ackerley Comm. Inc. v. Seattle, 92 Wn.2d 905, 602 P.2d 1177 (1979) (statute applies only to signs within scope of its definition), cert.

denied 449 U.S. 804, 101 S.Ct. 49, 66 L.Ed. 2d 7 (1981).

27. 73 Wn.2d 405, 439 P.2d 248 (1968), appeal dismissed 393 U.S. 316, 89 S.Ct. 553, 21 L.Ed.2d 512 (1969), rehearing denied 393 U.S. 1112, 89 S.Ct. 854, 21 L.Ed.2d 813 (1969). See also Ryan Outdoor Advertising, Inc. v. United States, 559 F.2d 554 (9th Cir.1977); La Pointe Outdoor Advertising v. Florida Dep't of Transp., 398 So.2d 1370 (Fla.1981) (statute is unambiguous, no compensation for nonconforming illegally-erected billboards).

28. 73 Wn.2d 405, 439 P.2d 248 (1968), appeal dismissed 393 U.S. 316, 89 S.Ct. 553, 21 L.Ed.2d 512 (1969).

"highway beautification act" /s compensat!

"highway beautification act" /p fund***

sunad +5 sarasota /p aesthetic!

prohibit! ban banning banned /p billboard /p residen!

advertising +5 borough +5 metuchen /p property /s valu!

sign billboard /s classif! /p permit! prohibit! /p "equal
   protection"

nonconforming /s sign billboard /s amortiz! /p number size
   height

markham +5 advertising +5 state /p compensat!

preempt! /p state /p regulat! /p highway /p advertis!
   billboard

§ 14.4 Sign Control and First Amendment Conflicts

Sign controls often raise first amendment issues because messages on signs are to a greater or lesser extent protected speech. Generally, signs which convey noncommercial messages are accorded full protection under the amendment while commercial speech is given only limited protection.

Noncommercial speech may not be regulated strictly on the basis of its content, but reasonable time, place and manner restrictions may be imposed. Whether time, place and manner restrictions are reasonable is weighed against the alternative means for communication still available to the speaker. In State v. Miller,[1] the court found that an ordinance prohibiting political signs in residential areas was not justified on aesthetic bases alone. Alternative and effective means for conveying the message were not available to the plaintiffs in this case; thus, the ordinance was stricken.

Protection was granted to commercial speech contained in signs by the U.S. Supreme Court, in Linmark Assoc. Inc. v. Township of Willingboro.[2] Because the township determined that the high rate of home sales was due to panic selling by white residents, it enacted an ordinance banning "for sale" signs. The purpose was to forestall "white flight," because the governing body felt the absence of signs would diminish the fear that the change in racial composition of the community would reduce property values. Even though the "for sale" signs were considered commercial speech, the court invalidated the ordinance, holding that the ban restricted the content of the expression and was not solely a time, place and manner restriction. Though alternative means of communication were available, they were neither as effective nor as economically feasible as the prohibited signs. Finally, the Township failed to establish that the actual effect of the ordinance supported its purpose.

§ 14.4

1. 83 N.J. 402, 416 A.2d 821 (1980); Farrell v. Township of Teaneck, 126 N.J. Super. 460, 315 A.2d 474 (1974).

2. 431 U.S. 85, 97 S.Ct. 1614, 52 L.Ed.2d 155 (1977).

Commercial billboard regulation, although it raises free speech issues, has generally been upheld because of a state's interest in protecting the health, safety and general welfare of the community. Usually, time, place and manner restrictions are found to be reasonable.[3] But an ordinance enacted by the City of San Diego did not fare so well. Off-site billboards were completely banned throughout the city. On-site signs were allowed if they fell within the statutory definition, and certain exceptions were included to allow government signs, historical plaques, and time and temperature signs, for example. In other words, the ordinance generally permitted on-site commercial signs and prohibited those with no commercial content.

The U.S. Supreme Court, in Metromedia, Inc. v. San Diego,[4] found the ordinance to be unconstitutional on its face. Continuing to observe the distinction drawn between commercial and noncommercial speech and indicating that the former could be regulated while the latter could not, the court invalidated the ordinance, since it forbade noncommercial signs. Insofar as it regulated only commercial speech, the ordinance was found reasonable. As applied to noncommercial speech however, the ordinance was invalid. Using the four part test enunciated in Central Hudson Gas and Electric Corp. v. Public Service Commission,[5] the Court questioned whether the ordinance directly advanced the governmental interests in traffic safety and visual appearance of the city. Following the general rule, the Court did not disagree with the "accumulated, common sense judgments of local lawmakers and of the many reviewing courts" that billboards were a hazard to traffic safety.[6] Further, the Court noted that aesthetic judgments such as those made by the City were subjective and would be carefully scrutinized only if they were a public rationalization of an impermissible purpose.[7]

But the Court found the ordinance afforded greater protection to commercial speech than to noncommercial speech, and that the City did not adequately explain this disparate treatment. Insofar as San Diego chose to tolerate billboards, it could not limit their content to commercial messages only, choosing to value that form of communication over noncommercial communication.[8] Further the City could not limit

---

3. See John Donnelly & Sons, Inc. v. Outdoor Advertising Bd., 369 Mass. 206, 339 N.E.2d 709 (1975); Suffolk Outdoor Advertising Co. v. Hulse, 43 N.Y.2d 483, 402 N.Y.S.2d 368, 373 N.E.2d 263 (1977), affirmed per curiam 439 U.S. 808, 99 S.Ct. 66, 58 L.Ed.2d 101 (1978).

4. 453 U.S. 490, 101 S.Ct. 2882, 69 L.Ed. 2d 800 (1981), on remand 32 Cal.3d 180, 185 Cal.Rptr. 260, 649 P.2d 902 (1982).

5. 447 U.S. 557, 100 S.Ct. 2343, 65 L.Ed. 2d 341 (1980). The test is: (1) first amendment protects commercial speech only if it concerns lawful activity and is not misleading, (2) a restriction on commercial speech is valid only if it seeks to implement a substantial governmental interest, (3) directly advances that interest, and (4) reaches no further than necessary to accomplish the given objective.

6. Metromedia, Inc. v. San Diego, 453 U.S. 490, 509, 101 S.Ct. 2882, 2893, 69 L.Ed.2d 800 (1981), on remand 32 Cal.3d 180, 185 Cal.Rptr. 260, 649 P.2d 902 (1982).

7. Id. at 510, 101 S.Ct. at 2893.

8. See also John Donnelly & Sons v. Campbell, 639 F.2d 6 (1st Cir.1980), judgment affirmed 453 U.S. 916, 101 S.Ct. 3151, 69 L.Ed.2d 999 (1981).

noncommercial speech to selected topics; e.g., those exceptions allowed in the ordinance. The court reasoned that because some noncommercial messages could be conveyed on billboards throughout commercial and industrial zones, other messages had to be allowed as well. To do otherwise would be to regulate content impermissibly. The Court rejected the City's suggestion that the ordinance was a reasonable time, place and manner restriction, because noncommercial speech alternatives were insufficient, inappropriate and prohibitively expensive.

Because the plurality determined a total prohibition of outdoor advertising was not before the court, it chose not to address the question. Justice Brennan disagreed, however, and wrote separately to emphasize that the practical effect of the statute was to eliminate billboards as an effective medium of communication for any speaker desiring to express political or other noncommercial information.[9] He found that neither traffic safety nor aesthetic objectives, the avowed purposes of the ordinance, were sufficient to save it. If a community could show it had a sufficiently substantial governmental interest which was directly furthered and that a more narrowly drawn restriction would not promote that goal, Justice Brennan would be willing to concede that a municipality might justify a total billboard ban.[10]

An ordinance regulating sign usage on public property successfully withstood a recent constitutional challenge. At stake in Members of Los Angeles City Council v. Taxpayers for Vincent [11] was an ordinance prohibiting the erection of any type of sign on public property. Vincent, a candidate for local office, had placed campaign signs on the crossbars of power poles. The City promptly removed them. Vincent filed suit claiming the ordinance unconstitutionally abridged his political speech, protected by the First Amendment.

The United States Supreme Court analogized appellant's posted signs to billboards, reaffirmed its conclusion in Metromedia that a city has a sufficiently substantial interest in justifying content-neutral prohibition of billboards for aesthetic reasons,[12] and held that the ordinance was not invalid. Public property not by tradition or designation a forum for public communication may be reserved by the state for its intended purposes, communicative or otherwise, as long as the regulation of speech is reasonable and not an attempt to suppress expression merely because public officials oppose the speaker's view.[13] The ordinance curtailed no more speech than necessary to accomplish its purpose because it attacked the medium (posted signs on government property) rather than the message.

9. 453 U.S. at 525, 101 S.Ct. at 2901.

10. Id. at 528, 101 S.Ct. at 2903.

11. 466 U.S. 789, 104 S.Ct. 2118, 80 L.Ed.2d 772 (1984), on remand 738 F.2d 353 (9th Cir.1984).

12. 104 S.Ct. at 2130.

13. Id. at 2134. For further discussion of the Constitutional issues, see supra § 10.1.

WESTLAW REFERENCES

state +5 miller /p ordinance /s prohibit! ban banning banned /s political!

linmark +5 willingboro /p protect! /s commerc! /s speech sign

commerc! /p sign /p regulat! ordinace /p state /s interest

regulat! ordinance /p unconstitution! /p face facial** /p sign billboard

§ 14.5 Architectural Control

Many communities have adopted ordinances which provide for architectural design review. Like sign regulation, the standards or criteria to be applied may be included in the zoning scheme or may be enacted separately. Typically, a board is established to review designs in accordance with enumerated criteria including compatibility with surrounding area, effect of allowing the design on neighboring property values and certain common stylistic features. Some boards also attempt to prevent monotony by requiring that the designs not be too similar.

The leading case upholding architectural design review is State ex rel. Saveland Park Holding Corp. v. Wieland.[1] The ordinance under scrutiny provided that a building permit would not issue if the building were so at variance with existing structures that it would cause substantial depreciation in property values. Although the express purpose of the ordinance was to protect property values, the court characterized it as being based on aesthetics, and upheld it on both grounds.

A more recent case sustaining an architectural review board decision is Reid v. Architectural Bd. of Review.[2] The board had disapproved a permit for a single-story, ten-foot high house built of glass and concrete in a rough U-shape, which rambled through a grove of trees on a lot surrounded by a ten-foot fence. While the house otherwise complied with zoning requirements, it was to be built in an area of stately, older, two-and-a-half story houses. The architectural review board concluded that it should not be built, for it did not comply with the ordinance which required that the buildings maintain the high character of community development and protect real estate from impairment or destruction of value. The court held that maintenance of a high character of community appearance was within the scope of the general welfare, and while aesthetics alone would not be sufficient to sustain the ordinance, it was not enacted solely for that purpose. Not surprisingly, these cases also involved the issue of whether the standards were adequate to guide administrative decisions. The pur-

---

§ 14.5

1. 269 Wis. 262, 69 N.W.2d 217 (1955), cert. denied 350 U.S. 841, 76 S.Ct. 81, 100 L.Ed. 750. Cf. Hankins v. Rockleigh, 55 N.J.Super. 132, 150 A.2d 63 (1959) (ordinance invalid as applied).

2. 119 Ohio App. 67, 192 N.E.2d 74 (1963).

ported standards in both ordinances were vague, but the court did not find them so vague as to be an improper delegation of authority.[3]

A third case in this milieu is State ex rel. Stoyanoff v. Berkeley.[4] The court upheld a denial of a building permit by an architectural review board on grounds that the proposed building would not fit the architectural character of the neighborhood, and would reduce the property values of neighboring homes. The proposed residence was to be a pyramid-like structure with a flat top, and triangular windows or doors at the corners. This was found to have an adverse aesthetic impact in a community of conventional residences of rather substantial value.

An interesting complement to these three cases is LaSalle National Bank v. Evanston.[5] The city refused to change a zoning designation and allow building of high-rise apartments near Lake Michigan, partly on the grounds that the building would disrupt the city's attempt to effect a gradual tapering of building heights toward the open lakefront and park area, which was used for recreational purposes. The court found that aesthetic qualities were properly cognizable, and when coupled with reasonable restrictions on population density, the refusal to rezone was valid.

Although it is possible that the legitimacy of aesthetic regulation may vary with the kind of aesthetic control at issue, the courts have not made distinctions on these grounds. Statutes and ordinances perceived to be based exclusively or primarily upon aesthetic considerations have been either sustained or struck, according to the perception of validity of such regulation in a given jurisdiction. Although decisions upholding ordinances based solely on aesthetics continue to grow in number, it is likely that at least some courts will persist in requiring that additional grounds, such as protection of property values or density control, be present.

In addition to the general considerations affecting the validity of architectural controls, two constitutional issues frequently appear. Ordinances establishing procedures for architectural design review must set forth standards which are not unduly vague. Such measures must also be narrowly drawn and must further a sufficiently substantial governmental purpose to avoid running afoul of first amendment considerations.

The vagueness-due process challenge was raised in both Saveland Park and Reid, but each court held that the standards involved were adequate to support the factual determinations made in those cases.[6]

3. See also City of Scottsdale v. Arizona Sign Ass'n, Inc., 115 Ariz. 233, 564 P.2d 922 (1977) (cited design review in Saveland Park, Reid, and Stoyanoff as sufficient to support an ordinance providing for review of all signs designed and erected in city). Cf. Morristown Road Ass'n v. Mayor & Common Council, 163 N.J.Super. 58, 394 A.2d 157 (1978) (standards too vague, ordinance stricken).

4. 458 S.W.2d 305 (Mo.1970).

5. 57 Ill.2d 415, 312 N.E.2d 625 (1974).

6. See Reid v. Architectural Bd. of Review, 119 Ohio App. 67, 192 N.E.2d 74 (1963); State ex rel. Saveland Park Hold-

When standards incorporated into an ordinance are sufficiently certain that they can be understood by the regulated group, implemented by the administering agency, and applied by the reviewing court, the chances that the ordinance will survive judicial scrutiny are greatly increased.[7] Standards may be found in the consistency or patterns of community preference.[8] For example, communities may favor billboard controls[9] or preservation of historic-architectural "ensembles" such as the Vieux Carre.[10] Thus, the presence of expressly articulated standards, is exceedingly important. When combined with separation of powers considerations and the judiciary's inability to determine community aesthetic values, such standards will often warrant granting a legislative presumption of validity to an architectural control.[11]

Aesthetic regulation based on the offensiveness of the expression or architectural design can amount to censorship, and thus freedom of expression concerns are raised. Permit denials, such as those in Reid, Stoyanoff and Saveland Park, are in a sense content-based restrictions on expression rather than simply time, place and manner regulations. A connection between the offensive expression and a threat to a substantial governmental interest may be sufficient to rebut a first amendment challenge. The question becomes one of how to define a community's burden of proving that failure to regulate "design as expression" would threaten a substantial governmental interest. In Penn Central,[12] the court found that the interest in preserving landmarks was sufficiently substantial to withstand a taking claim. Whether the rationale would stand in the face of a first amendment challenge is yet an unresolved issue.[13]

WESTLAW REFERENCES

architectur! /p control ordinance /p "police power"
414k106

architectur! /p board /p review! /p design /p regulat! /p
zon!

rezon! /p refus*** /p reasonable /p density

ing Corp. v. Wieland, 269 Wis. 262, 69 N.W.2d 217 (1955), cert. denied 350 U.S. 841, 76 S.Ct. 81, 100 L.Ed. 750 (1955). Compare Historic Green Springs, Inc. v. Bergland, 497 F.Supp. 839 (E.D.Va.1980).

7. See, e.g., Morristown Road Assoc. v. Mayor & Common Council, 163 N.J.Super. 58, 394 A.2d 157 (1978).

8. See generally Costonis, Law and Aesthetics: A Critique and Reformulation of the Dilemmas, 80 Mich.L.Rev. 355 (1982).

9. United Advertising Corp. v. Borough of Metuchen, 42 N.J. 1, 198 A.2d 447 (1964); People v. Goodman, 31 N.Y.2d 262, 338 N.Y.S.2d 97, 290 N.E.2d 139 (1972), reargument denied 32 N.Y.2d 705, 343 N.Y.S.2d 1026, 296 N.E.2d 459 (1973).

10. Maher v. New Orleans, 516 F.2d 1051 (5th Cir.1975), cert. denied 426 U.S. 905, 96 S.Ct. 2225, 48 L.Ed.2d 830 (1976).

11. See Metromedia, Inc. v. San Diego, 453 U.S. 490, 101 S.Ct. 2882, 69 L.Ed.2d 800 (1981) (Rehnquist, J., dissenting), on remand 32 Cal.3d 180, 185 Cal.Rptr. 260, 649 P.2d 902 (1982).

12. Penn Cent. Transp., Inc. v. New York, 438 U.S. 104, 98 S.Ct. 2646, 57 L.Ed. 2d 631 (1978), rehearing denied 439 U.S. 883, 99 S.Ct. 226, 58 L.Ed.2d 198 (1978).

13. See Note, Aesthetic Regulation and the First Amendment, 3 Va.J.Nat. Resources L. 237 (1984) (examining First Amendment challenges to architectural and aesthetic review board decisions and exploring whether a building may be considered constitutionally protected speech).

II. HISTORIC PRESERVATION

§ 14.6 Early Historic Preservation

Historic preservation [1] began in the mid 1800's with a private attempt to rescue Mt. Vernon from an uncertain fate. At the time the only means for protecting a landmark of historical significance was private purchase by preservationists. The focus was generally local, and aimed at preventing destruction of a single building.[2]

Congress injected itself into the preservation field some time later when it began purchasing Civil War battlefield sites. This action resulted in United States v. Gettysburg Electric Railway Co.,[3] which involved condemnation of private property for the creation of a national battleground memorial. The Court rejected the narrow view that the condemnation was not for a valid public purpose, and held that preservation of an important monument to the country's past was a proper purpose. Thus, the tool of eminent domain was established as a valid method for protecting our historical heritage.

A more complicated and less well settled question was that of whether government regulatory powers could be similarly employed to limit uses or structures not inherently noxious, particularly without payment of compensation to the owner. Although regulation is now a well-recognized preservation technique, early decisions were not as broad minded about the application of the police power for such

§ 14.6

1. In the preface to the well-respected work, A Handbook on Historic Preservation Law, the editor, Christopher Duerksen, addresses what is meant by preservation law:

> Just what is "preservation law"? It is a collage, cutting across and drawing from several other established areas of law: land use and zoning, real property, taxation, local government, constitutional, and administrative. In many ways preservation law, particularly at the local level, is closest to land use and zoning; the rules are very similar. For example, the standards that dictate governmental behavior in enacting and administering zoning ordinances are virtually identical to those applicable to local landmark and historic district laws, and the constitutional doctrines governing regulation of private property are similar.
>
> But preservation law has outgrown its local law origins and now has its own

distinctive provisions—pertinent state and federal administrative procedures, an indigenous regulatory scheme, and special tax laws to name only a few. As a result, the days when preservationists had only to know how to run the local historical museum are gone. Today they must know local zoning and land-use law, how the federal income tax code works, what the state enabling law provides, and what the U.S. Supreme Court thinks about preservation ordinances and private property. Id. at xxii.

For an excellent overview of the development of historic preservation, see generally Rose, Preservation and Community: New Directions in the Law of Historic Preservation, 33 Stan.L.Rev. 473 (1981).

2. See C. Hosmer, Presence of the Past (New York: G.P. Putnam's & Sons, 1965).

3. 160 U.S. 668, 16 S.Ct. 427, 40 L.Ed. 576 (1896). See also Roe v. Kansas ex rel. Smith, 278 U.S. 191, 49 S.Ct. 160, 73 L.Ed. 259 (1929).

purposes. One of the first steps toward a more expansive use of regulatory power came in Welch v. Swasey,[4] where the United States Supreme Court upheld a Boston ordinance limiting building heights under the state police power, notably for fire prevention. Regulation as a preservation device thus began gaining acceptance.

Another prickly question remained. How far could regulation go before it became a taking which required compensation? In a later decision, the Court, speaking through Justice Holmes articulated the general rule that ". . . while property may be regulated to a certain extent, if the regulation goes too far, it will be recognized as a taking."[5] Four years later, the Court, in Village of Euclid v. Ambler Realty,[6] validated a zoning regulation which reduced the plaintiff's property value by almost 90%. The Court found that the burden was imposed in a nondiscriminatory manner, and the benefits accrued to all property owners as well; thus the regulation was reasonable. In Nectow v. Cambridge,[7] however, a zoning ordinance was struck down as unconstitutional. Clearly, land-use controls would not be automatically exempt from invalidation, but the legal groundwork was set for furthering historic preservation through use of the police power. Preservation grew slowly and cautiously.

About the same time, the use of the historic district as a preservation tool was gaining considerable support not just for economic but for architectural reasons. In 1931, Charleston, South Carolina, enacted the first law that was effective to protect an historic area, the city's pre-civil war district. The Vieux Carre, in New Orleans, was established pursuant to a Louisiana Constitutional amendment in 1936,[8] and in 1939, San Antonio passed a preservation law. By 1956, still only a handful of cities had enacted such laws. They were very controversial, but despite owner opposition, nearly all challenges to historic district ordinances were rejected.[9]

Federal legislation has also played an important role in the advancement of preservation. In 1906, Congress passed the Antiquities Act,[10] allowing the President to designate national monuments, primarily from federally owned sites. Ten years later, the National Park Service was created, and it soon became the primary focus for federal preservation efforts. During the depression Congress enacted the His-

---

4. 214 U.S. 91, 29 S.Ct. 567, 53 L.Ed. 923 (1909).

5. Pennsylvania Coal Co. v. Mahon, 260 U.S. 393, 415, 43 S.Ct. 158, 160, 67 L.Ed. 322 (1922).

6. 272 U.S. 365, 47 S.Ct. 114, 71 L.Ed. 303 (1926).

7. 277 U.S. 183, 48 S.Ct. 447, 72 L.Ed. 842 (1928).

8. See Louisiana—L.S.A.–Constitution Art. 14, § 22A (creating the Vieux Carre

Commission to preserve such buildings in the district as it deems to have archaeological and historical significance).

9. City of New Orleans v. Impastato, 198 La. 206, 3 So.2d 559 (1941) (upholding Vieux Carre Ordinance); Opinion of the Justices, 333 Mass. 773, 128 N.E.2d 557 (1955) (upholding creation of historic district commissions in Boston and Nantucket).

10. 16 U.S.C.A. § 431 et seq.

toric Sites Act,[11] which for the first time conceived of historic preservation as national policy. In addition, the Act extended the Department of Interior's authority beyond federally owned properties to identify and survey historic sites throughout the country. This program later became the framework for the National Register of Historic Places. Not much later came the National Trust for Historic Preservation Act,[12] which facilitated private participation in preservation by creating a non-profit congressionally chartered corporation. Finally, in 1966, Congress passed the National Historic Preservation Act (NHPA),[13] which has become the basis for most of the administrative and protective devices, as well as the financial incentives, through which national preservation policy is now implemented.

 WESTLAW REFERENCES
"historic preservation" /p defin!

§ 14.7　Preservation at the Federal Level

The National Historic Preservation Act (NHPA)[1] provides the authority for a number of activities which implement the federal historic preservation program:[2] i) the National Register of Historic places, identifying and listing historic and cultural resources;[3] ii) the criteria for listing on the national register, establishing standards for evaluating historic significance;[4] iii) the matching grants-in-aid program, encouraging preservation activities at the state and local levels;[5] iv) the Advisory Council on Historic Preservation, providing information on historic properties to the executive and other federal agencies;[6] and v) the "section 106" review process, for protection of federal resources.

Under the act, "historic resources of federal interest" are broadly defined, so that not only nationally significant properties, but those important at local and state levels as well, are eligible for designation.[7]

---

11. Id. § 461 et seq.

12. Id. § 468.

13. Id. § 470 et seq. See § 14.7 infra.

§ 14.7

1. 80 Stat. 915, Pub.L. No. 89–655, codified at 16 U.S.C.A. § 470 et seq.

2. See generally, A Handbook on Historic Preservation (C. Duerkson ed. 1983), p. 214.

3. 16 U.S.C.A. § 470a. An important aspect of the National Register is the National Historic Landmarks Program. Operated under the auspices of the National Park Service, the program provides for designation and protection of national landmarks. Once designated, a national landmark receives even greater protection from the impact of federal projects than

even the § 106 review process provides. See 16 U.S.C.A. § 470a(a)(1)(B). See also Duerksen, supra note 2 at 228.

4. Id. § 470a(a)(2); see infra note 7.

5. 16 U.S.C.A. § 470a(d), b, h.

6. Id. § 470i, j.

7. 36 C.F.R. § 60.4. The National Register criteria for evaluation are:

The quality of significance in American history, architecture, archeology, engineering, and culture is present in districts, sites, buildings, structures, and objects that possess integrity of location, design, setting, materials, workmanship, feeling, and association and

(a) that are associated with events that have made a significant contribu-

Listing on the National Register qualifies a property for participation in most of the federal incentive and protective programs.[8] Most properties find their way onto the Register through local initiative, followed by a process of state review and nomination in accordance with federal criteria.[9]

The National Historic Preservation Fund [10] provides matching grants to the states to carry out the purposes of the NHPA. The monies are used to conduct statewide surveys, prepare nominations to the National Register, and develop state preservation plans. In addition, the funds are used to support the necessary administrative structure of state programs, and financially assist the restoration of Register properties within the state.[11] This portion of the act has been a great impetus in establishing historic preservation at the state level, and its requirements for participation in the grants program have led to greater administrative uniformity among state activities.

The Advisory Council on Historic Preservation (ACHP) is a cabinet level body which advises the president and Congress on preservation matters. It also comments on federal projects which may impact on historic properties, and aids in coordinating activities of federal agencies affecting preservation. Its principal role, however, is the review and comment responsibility under section 106 of the Act.[12]

Section 106 [13] brings together all elements of the federal preservation program to provide the basic federal legal protection for historic properties. Federal agencies must seek the council's comments for any action they wish to pursue which may affect a property either on or eligible for inclusion on the National Register of Historic Places. Like NEPA,[14] the provision mandates that an evaluation and analysis process be followed prior to approval of federal projects affecting historic properties. However, the ACHP's recommendations are not binding, and a proposed action may proceed once the review process is completed, regardless of a disfavorable recommendation. This does not mean section 106 review is entirely without teeth; even a determination of

---

tion to the broad patterns of our history; or

(b) that are associated with the lives of persons significant in our past; or

(c) that embody the distinctive characteristics of a type, period, or method of construction, or that represent the work of a master, or that possess high artistic values, or that represent a significant and distinguishable entity whose components may lack individual distinction; or

(d) that have yielded, or may be likely to yield, information important in prehistory or history. Id.

8. 16 U.S.C.A. § 470f.

9. Properties may become eligible for inclusion on the register when nominated by: 1) a State Historic Preservation Officer, qualified local government, or individual, 2) the head of a federal agency, 3) the Secretary of the Interior, by designating the property as a National Landmark, or 4) by Congress. See Duerksen, supra note 2 at 197.

10. 16 U.S.C.A. § 470h. See also Id. § 470a(d).

11. Due to recent cutbacks in funding, most federal money is now being spent on surveying and documentation of historic sites and structures, and little money is available for the less critical programs.

12. 16 U.S.C.A. § 470j.

13. Id. § 470f.

14. 42 U.S.C.A. §§ 4231–4261.

whether it is necessary to comply can take several years to complete. It is important to note that the Section 106 review process is applicable only to federal agencies and agencies proceeding with federally funded projects. Thus, state or local regulation is necessary to impose any sort of review process on projects affecting historic properties that are proposed by state or local governments, or by private individuals.

In addition to the NHPA there are, scattered throughout the federal statutes, a number of other tools and incentives available to preservationists.[15] NEPA requires consideration of impact on cultural environment as part of the environmental impact statement process.[16] Several statutes provide federal aid for preservation through loans, grants and use of surplus government buildings.[17] The Public Buildings Cooperative Use Act[18] directs the General Services Administration to give preference to use of historic buildings for federal offices. There has also been a shift in the policy of the Internal Revenue Code from penalizing to encouraging property owners to invest in preservation.[19] The legal role of the federal government, in spite of the act, is largely confined to regulating its own activities with respect to historic properties. Despite its limitations, the act has had a marked catalytic effect on programs at state and local levels. All states and territories have enacted historic preservation laws, and at least 832 historic districts or landmark commissions had been created as of 1981.[20]

WESTLAW REFERENCES

"national historic preservation act"　/p　aid　/p　state local!

di("advisory council on historic preservation"　/p　agency)

n.h.p.a.　/p　"section 106"　/p　review!

ci(36　+4　60.4)

"national register"　/s　state　/s　nominat!

"national historic preservation act" n.h.p.a.　/p　develop!　/p　state
　　/p　preserv!　/p　plan planned planning

(miltenberger　+s　chesapeake) (save　+s　courthouse　+s　lynn)
　　(edwards　+s　first　+s　national　+s　bank) (aluli　+s
　　brown)　/p　restor!

16　+5　470f　/p　protect! incentive

"advisory council on historic preservation"　/s　review!　/s
　　comment!

"advisory council on historic preservation" a.c.h.p.　/p　binding bound

15. See e.g., The National Coastal Zone Management Act, 16 U.S.C.A. §§ 1451–1464. For a recent and insightful analysis of the CZMA as applied to Preservation objectives, see generally Schmitz, The Coastal Zone Management Act's Role in Historic Preservation, Vol. 4 No. 6 Preserv'n L.Rptr. (Dec.1985). See also §§ 13.17–.19, supra.

16. See supra §§ 13.2, 13.3.

17. E.g., 42 U.S.C.A. §§ 5304(h), 5318 (Block Grants and Urban Development Action Grants).

18. 40 U.S.C.A. § 611(c).

19. Tax Reform Act of 1976, 26 U.S.C.A. §§ 167, 168 (permitting accelerated depreciation); Economic Recovery Tax Act of 1981, 26 U.S.C.A. §§ 44, 48(g) (allowing investment tax credits).

20. Directory of American Preservation Commissions III (S. Dennis ed. 1981); Beckwith, Appendix of State & Territorial Historic Preservation Statutes and Session Laws, 11 N.C.Cent.L.J. 308 (1980).

"advisory council on historic preservation" a.c.h.p. /p "section 106"
  /p federal! /p agency fund***

n.e.p.a. /p consider! /p cultur! /p "environmental impact
  statement" e.i.s.

block "urban development action" + 1 grant /p preserv! /p
  historic!

"public buildings cooperative use act"

§ 14.8   State Historic Preservation Law

The 1980 amendments to the National Historic Preservation Act
(NHPA) greatly increased the states' role under the federal preservation scheme.   The diminished federal involvement, while reducing
funding, has given states the opportunity to assume greater responsibility for preservation and to better respond to the individual needs of the
state.   Various types of laws have been utilized: grants of power to
local governments to preserve historic resources through zoning, establishment of historic districts and commissions, creation of state agencies
with preservation powers, state registers of historic places, environmental policy acts which consider the adverse effects of government actions
on historic resources, and even inclusion of preservation policy in a few
state constitutions.[1]

States can delegate regulatory authority in several ways.   Most
provide localities with power to enact historic district zoning, and some
allow for landmark designation.[2]   General zoning power can generally
be used to protect historic areas, and to require special standards and
review procedures for actions proposed within them.   Regulations
which designate landmarks or establish historic districts have generally
been upheld by courts as a valid use of local authority to promote the
general welfare.[3]

Most states authorize local preservation bodies to acquire historic
properties.[4]   These may be acquired not only in fee simple but in less-
than-fee interests, such as facade or conservation easements.[5]   Acquisi-

§ 14.8

1. E.g., La.—LSA–Const. art. 14, § 22A.

2. Beckwith, Preservation Law 1976–
1980: Faction, Property Rights, and Ideolo-
gy, 11 N.C.Cent.L.J. 276 (1980). See e.g.,
West's Ann.Cal.Gov't Code §§ 50280–
50290; Colo.Rev.Stat. 24–80–1201 to 24–
80–1202; D.C.Code Encycl. §§ 5.801 to
5.805; West's Fla.Stat.Ann. §§ 380.012–
380.25; Hawaii Rev.Stat. §§ 46–4.5, 246–
34; N.Y.—McKinney's Gen.Munic.Law
§ 96–a.

3. See, e.g., Figarsky v. Historic Dist.
Comm'n, 171 Conn. 198, 368 A.2d 163
(1976) (denial of demolition permit by historic commission upheld where local preservation ordinance. incorporated by reference state enabling statute); A–S–P Assoc.

v. Raleigh, 298 N.C. 207, 258 S.E.2d 444
(1979) (approving legislative grant of authority to locality for creation of historic
district); City of Santa Fe v. Gamble-
Skogmo, Inc., 73 N.M. 410, 389 P.2d 13
(1964) (city had sufficient authority to impose criminal sanctions for violations of
preservation ordinance).

4. Beckwith, Developments in the Law
of Historic Preservation and a Reflection
on Liberty, 12 Wake Forest L.Rev. 93
(1976).

5. United States v. Albrecht, 496 F.2d
906 (8th Cir.1974). See generally Coughlin, Preservation Easements: Statutory
and Tax Planning Issues, 1 Preservation
L.Rep. 2011 (1982). A preservation easement may be created by purchase or dona-

tion power also includes that of eminent domain which results in condemnation for a public purpose and payment of just compensation. Localities also have the responsibility of raising funds to foster preservation and maintain the properties under their dominion.[6]

Acquisition of full ownership of property is expensive and often has the effect of removing property from the local tax base. These drawbacks have limited its use as a preservation tool. On the other hand, enabling local governments or other bodies to accept preservation easements, or enter into and enforce partial acquisition contracts and covenants, results in less cost but offers many of the same protective benefits.[7]

Another technique enjoying some recent success is the use of a revolving funds program to purchase, or to acquire options on historic properties. Once purchased, a structure is sold to a new owner who covenants to maintain the building's historic character. The money realized from this sale is then reused to purchase and protect other historic structures.

Some states have enacted tax laws to aid and promote historic preservation. Among the available methods are granting localities specific power to reduce tax burdens on historic properties[8] and giving tax credits for restoration of buildings in historic districts.[9] The state may in some cases provide financing to the locality to the extent revenues are reduced. Under such a scheme, if a structure is subsequently destroyed or put to incompatible use, the owner repays taxes saved.[10] One of the greatest barriers to use of this device by state and local government is the fear of lost revenue.[11]

State Historic Preservation Officers (SHPO) have taken on a more substantial role in the federal tax incentives programs since the Tax Reform Act of 1976 and the Economic Recovery Tax Act of 1981.[12] To

tion. Put simply, it is an agreement between a landowner and a locality or charitable organization giving the latter the right to monitor and protect the architectural and historic integrity of the property. The concept represents a statutory departure from the common law's hostility toward easements in gross. See § 14.10 infra and text accompanying notes 11, 12.

6. See, e.g., West's Fla.Stat.Ann. § 704.06; Mich.Comp.Laws Ann. § 5.3395; N.Y.—McKinney's Gen.Mun.Law § 119–aa to 119–dd.

7. The advantages are primarily financial. Because the cost of a typical facade easement is around 10% of the structure's value, the amount of money normally required to purchase just one historic structure can now be used to protect 10 structures (assuming similar value) through acquisition of only a preservation easement. An added benefit is that the cost of maintenance and repairs is borne by the owner, further lessening the locality's financial commitment. Finally, federal tax incentives in the form of charitable deductions for donation of easements make this preservation technique especially popular with property owners. See generally, Lord, The Advantages of Facade Easements, Legal Techniques in Historic Preservation, National Trust for Historic Preservation in the U.S., 35 (1971).

8. N.C.Gen.Stat. § 105–277(f); Or.Rev. Stat. 358.475–358.565.

9. Md.Code Art. 81, § 281a.

10. Wilson & Winkler, Response of State Legislation to Historic Preservation, 36 Law & Contemp.Probs. 329 (1971).

11. Powers, Tax Incentives for Historic Preservation, 12 Urb.Law. 103 (1980).

12. 26 U.S.C.A. § 46(a)(2)(F).

qualify for the credit, a taxpayer must incur qualified expenses for rehabilitation of a certified historic structure. This eligibility determination relies heavily on the SHPO's review of a lengthy application and recommendation to the regional office of the Secretary of the Interior. Any property or district on the National Register is automatically certified historic, and property within a registered district may also be certified if the enabling ordinance and the ordinance creating the district qualify under National Register Criteria. Once the structure is certified, the proposed rehabilitation work itself must also be reviewed and certified. In making the review, the SHPO follows the Department of Interior's "Standards for Rehabilitation and Guidelines for Rehabilitating Historic Buildings," to determine whether the work is consistent with the historic character of the building.[13] Finally, to qualify for the tax benefits, the project must be a "substantial rehabilitation."[14]

There are also laws or programs in several states within state environmental policy acts (SEPA), which require extensive review of planned activities. These acts essentially mirror the policy and provisions of NEPA.[15] In nearly every SEPA, historic properties are included within the definition of the environment, and a permit to demolish a registered property would probably come under review. This is an important supplement to preservation at the state level because activities which would be generally outside the scope of other laws may be covered by a SEPA.[16]

 WESTLAW REFERENCES

1980 /s amend! /s "national historic preservation act"

local! /s preserv! /s historic /s zon! "state register"

sy(state /s delegat! /s regulat! /s authori! /s district)

"general zoning power"

regulat! /p landmark "historic district" /p valid! invalid! /p welfare

state /p authority authoriz! /p local! /p preserv! /p acquir! condemn! purchase purchased purchasing compensat! "eminent domain" /p historic!

"preservation easement" "partial acquisition contract"

"revolving fund" /p purchas! acqui! /p property

"state historic preservation officer"

state /s tax taxation taxing /s law statut!   /s credit exempt! reduc! /p preserv! /s historic

371k241(1) /p exempt! credit! reduc! /p historic!

s.e.p.a. /p review! /p plan planned planning

---

13. See 36 C.F.R. § 67.5.

14. 26 U.S.C.A. § 48(g)(1)(C).

15. Yost, NEPA's Progeny: State Environmental Policy Acts, 3 Envt'l L.Rep. 50,090 (1974).

16. NEPA and NHPA, again, only regulate federal use of its own property or major federal actions with significant effect on the environment. A SEPA would catch state activities which otherwise would fall through the cracks in federal law.

§ 14.9　Historic Preservation at the Local Level

The most important preservation work occurs at the local level, and it is here that the major issues are encountered and resolved. It was from a local regulation which allowed designation of landmarks in New York City that Penn Central Transp. Co. v. New York [1] arose. There, the Supreme Court of the United States affirmed community power to adopt ordinances which control what owners of historic buildings can do with their properties.

It is no accident that local regulation plays such an important role in our preservation scheme. As noted above,[2] the NHPA provides protection from only the potentially intrusive projects of federal government agencies. Thus, even if a locality is listed on the National Register of Historic Places, additional protection is needed to prevent alteration or demolition of historic properties by private individuals or state and local governments. This protection usually comes in the form of a local preservation ordinance.

Generally, local regulatory schemes are fairly simple and are usually considered to be just another type of zoning control. A preservation program is typically initiated by a locality through appropriate enabling legislation, which establishes a preservation overlay zone, sets forth criteria for inclusion in the district, and creates some sort of a preservation review board. Under the scheme, owners of designated historic properties must seek board approval prior to proceeding with any proposed alterations to the property. The amount of authority vested in a review board varies and may extend to cover demolition and new construction or may be limited to regulating exterior alterations.

As might be expected legal challenges, including the taking challenge, are frequently raised and litigated at this stage.[3] Owners of designated property, dissatisfied with the review board's denial of a certificate of appropriateness,[4] often question the sufficiency of due process in both the creation [5] and application of the preservation ordinance. Many localities have successfully anticipated the problem and have thwarted such attacks through careful ordinance drafting. Seeking to avoid vagueness challenges, localities often incorporate NHPA review standards, for which a considerable body of interpretive

---

§ 14.9

1. 438 U.S. 104, 98 S.Ct. 2646, 57 L.Ed. 631 (1978), rehearing denied 439 U.S. 883, 99 S.Ct. 226, 58 L.Ed.2d 198 (1978).

2. See supra, § 14.7.

3. See, e.g., Penn Central, supra note 1.

4. A certificate of appropriateness is a fundamental aspect of any preservation ordinance. It is essentially a requirement that proposed changes to an historic structure within a designated district be reviewed by a preservation commission to ensure that the changes are in harmony with the character, significant features, and atmosphere of the structure or area. See generally, Recommended Model Provisions for a Preservation Ordinance, National Trust for Historic Preservation (1983), reprinted as Appendix A in a Handbook on Historic Preservation Law, infra note 6.

5. DeMendoza v. Town of Palm Beach, No. 80–2437, Fla. 15th Jud.Cir.Ct. (filed May 16, 1980) (challenging sufficiency of a survey).

case law already exists.[6] Safety valves, allowing for exception to the regulatory scheme where economic hardship would occur, are another means of dealing with a potential taking challenge.[7]

A good preservation or landmarks control program commonly contains three elements: 1) a survey, to establish the basis for designation and regulation; 2) a means of providing technical and economic assistance, to aid historic property owners, and 3) some sort of synchronization with the jurisdiction's comprehensive plan, zoning ordinances or other regulatory programs.[8]

The 1980 amendments to the NHPA emphasize surveys and inventories. Under the amended act, states must maintain surveys to be eligible for National Register nomination and federal funding programs.[9] Surveys are also useful in providing direction to a preservation program. Using a well-documented survey as a guide, a community can carefully and rationally select those areas or structures it deems most worth protecting.[10] An added benefit is that such documentation provides a record of the designation decision, useful in the event of a court challenge.[11]

While most historic preservation plans tend to focus on what a property owner may do with his designated property, another successful approach used in addition to a regulatory scheme is to provide landmark owners technical and economic assistance. The idea is to defuse economic concerns weighing against preservation and make participation easier on historic property owners. In Penn Central,[12] New York City used a TDR [13] system to mitigate the financial effects of building permit denial. Other measures include financial assistance through reduction of property taxes, direct grant or revolving fund programs, and donation of facade easements qualifying for federal tax deductions, as well as educational programs, providing technical assistance through publications and workshops.[14]

Coordination of a preservation program is important legally, since a growing number of states require local governments to have compre-

6. A Handbook on Historic Preservation Law, p. 83 (C. Duerksen, ed. 1983).

7. Id. at 87.

8. Id. at 37.

9. Pub.L. No. 96–515, §§ 201(a), 202 (1980), codified at 16 U.S.C.A. § 470a, b, e (requiring the states to maintain a statewide inventory and permitting the Secretary of the Interior to make 70% grants for state and local surveys).

10. South of Second Assoc. v. Georgetown, 196 Colo. 89, 580 P.2d 807 (1978), appeal after remand 199 Colo. 394, 609 P.2d 125 (1980). The ordinance here designated the whole town an historic district.

The Colorado Supreme Court struck the law because the local commission treated areas within the district differently, indicating district boundaries should have been more precise.

11. Bohannan v. San Diego, 30 Cal.App. 3d 416, 106 Cal.Rptr. 333 (1973); Manhattan Club v. New York City Landmarks Preservation Comm'n, 51 Misc. 556, 273 N.Y.S.2d 848 (1966). See also Duerksen, supra note 6.

12. See supra, note 1.

13. See supra, § 11.6.

14. See Duerksen, supra note 6 at 42, 43.

hensive plans which include a preservation element.[15] This is especially important when a preservation ordinance comes under attack in court. If a local government can demonstrate that preservation is part of its overall plan to promote general community welfare, the local preservation ordinance stands a much better chance of surviving judicial scrutiny.

Commentators have suggested that, in order to avoid invalidating early zoning ordinances, courts often held that the existence of comprehensive plans could be implied from the combined effect of zoning ordinances, regulations and maps.[16] Although none really existed, the finding of a comprehensive landmarks program was important to the success of New York's Landmarks Program in Penn Central.[17] By looking at the local landmarks law and the properties designated under it, the Supreme Court was able to satisfy the requirement, albeit by legal fiction, that zoning be "in accordance with a comprehensive plan." [18]

In addition to the legal benefits it provides, a coordinated preservation program has some practical advantages as well. A well-ordered preservation plan will make acquisition of federal funding easier for local governments.[19] Synchronization of building, fire, and housing codes with preservation policies can do much for the success of a local program, as building officials usually consider safety of the building first, and only secondarily look to its special aesthetic or historic qualities.[20]

Because most preservation ordinances are implemented through overlay zoning, it is especially important that the plan be consistent with the applicable zoning. Problems arise when a preservation ordinance forbids alteration or demolition of a certain landmark but the zoning classification provides an incentive to tear it down by permitting a more lucrative use. Downzoning may work to ease this sort of development pressure.[21] To be truly effective, historic preservation must go beyond mere design and move broadly into the zoning realm by

15. See, e.g., West's Fla.Stat.Ann. § 163.3177(6)(d), (f) which includes preservation as a mandatory element of a local comprehensive plan.

16. Haar, In Accordance With a Comprehensive Plan, 68 Harv.L.Rev. 1154 (1955).

17. See Duerksen, supra note 6 at 35.

18. 438 U.S. at 132, 133, 98 S.Ct. at 2663. See also § 2.13.

19. E.g., NEPA requires an environmental impact statement which includes consideration of the project's effect on aesthetics and the built environment. Citizens to Preserve Overton Park v. Volpe, 401 U.S. 402, 91 S.Ct. 814, 28 L.Ed.2d 136 (1971), on remand 335 F.Supp. 873 (D.Tenn.1972), on remand 357 F.Supp. 846 (D.Tenn.1973); W.A.T.C.H. v. Harris, 603 F.2d 310 (2d Cir.1979), cert. denied 444 U.S. 995, 100 S.Ct. 530, 62 L.Ed.2d 426 (1979).

20. Some recent progress was made in this vein when the National Trust for Historic Preservation, the American Institute of Architects and the Building Officials and Code Administrators got together and amended the Basic Building Code to provide specifically for restoration of landmarks. See B.O.C.A., Basic Building Code § 576.1 (1981).

21. Amdur v. Chicago, 638 F.2d 37 (7th Cir.1980), cert. denied 452 U.S. 905, 101 S.Ct. 3031, 69 L.Ed.2d 406 (1981).

considering, in addition, such matters as density of development and permitted uses.[22] This integration will help satisfy concerns expressed by courts, notably the Supreme Court in Penn Central, about comprehensiveness, and further strengthen the legal status of preservation in general.

 WESTLAW REFERENCES

city local! community /s control! ordinance regulat! /s historic!
    /s preserv! /s power! empower!

historic! /s "preservation ordinance"

historic! /s preservation /s ordinance program! plan planning
    planned /p enabl! /s legislat! law statut!

historic! /p property land /p board /p approv! /s alter!

historic! /s preserv! /p board /p "due process"

1980 /s amend! /p n.h.p.a.

south +s second +s georgetown

historic! landmark /p preserv! /p techn! economic! /p assist!

t.d.r. "transfer development right" & landmark historic!

comprehensiv! /s historic! landmark /s program! regulat! scheme

(florida +s statut! /s 163.3177) ("local government
    comprehensive planning act")

"overlay zoning"

amdur +s chicago

§ 14.10 Police Power Issues

When a locality adopts a preservation ordinance, typically three issues arise: whether the new ordinance treats property owners fairly, how it affects the interrelationships between city departments and other programs, and its cost to the city. A well thought out and carefully drafted ordinance can go a long way toward solving the second concern. Cities are increasingly providing for wider use of historic districts in their plans for the future.[1] It is possible, through revitalization of downtown areas, to increase the property tax base and to acquire federal funding through block grants[2] or Urban Development Action Grant[3] projects. Often, landmarks can be a tremendous asset in renewal of a city if building owners and local governments are willing to collaborate and adapt the building to new uses.[4]

---

22. C. Weaver & R. Babcock, City Zoning: The Once and Future Frontier, 120, 121 (1979).

§ 14.10

1. One way to do this may be patterned somewhat after the Federal Public Buildings Cooperative Use Act, 42 U.S.C.A. § 611(c). Cities can designate properties and use the space for offices. Designated properties owned by government can be sold to private entities for similar utiliza-tion with the proviso that the historic integrity of the building be maintained.

2. 42 U.S.C.A. § 5304h.

3. Id. § 5318.

4. For example, in Boston, Faneuil Hall; in Baltimore, Inner Harbor; and in Washington, D.C., Old Post Office. See Trustees of Sailors' Snug Harbor v. Platt, 29 A.D.2d 376, 288 N.Y.S.2d 314 (1968) (retained group of Greek revival buildings and adapted to new use).

Urban renewal projects must be carefully scrutinized relative to their effect on historic areas, however. In Waterbury, Connecticut, a local group brought suit against HUD alleging that review of a renewal project's impact on historic properties was too cursory.[5] The Second Circuit agreed, interpreting the NHPA to require a more meaningful review of federally assisted projects affecting historic properties. As long as HUD retained the authority to make funding approvals pursuant to grant and loan contracts, HUD was responsible for determining whether the urban renewal project would harm property *eligible* for listing or listed on the National Register.[6]

The cry of the unwilling property owner when his parcel is designated as a landmark is usually that of "taking." Prior to the Supreme Court decision in Penn Central, courts found their way around the issue using several rationales. The Fifth Circuit upheld the New Orleans Vieux Carre ordinance which called for preserving the "tout ensemble" of the historic French Quarter.[7] It reasoned that the ordinance sought a legal constitutional end using permissible means, since the operation of the Vieux Carre commission satisfied due process standards by providing reasonable legislative and practical guidance to, and control over, administrative decisionmaking. In Rebman v. Springfield,[8] a zoning ordinance which placed the plaintiff's property in an historic district around Abraham Lincoln's home did not result in a taking but was a valid exercise of police power for zoning purposes. Thus, denial of the building permit for proposed construction not in keeping with the character of the historical area surrounding Lincoln's home was appropriate under the ordinance. In a New York case, designation of a building as landmark was held not confiscatory when the owner was guaranteed a reasonable return on his investment with an option to demolish if no scheme to provide reasonable return could be devised.[9]

Whether regulation is a taking of the owner's property or a permissible exercise of the police power thus not compensable is a question not completely answered by Penn Central. Pressure from real estate lobbyists concerned about the extent to which courts allowed regulation to reduce property values led to the 1980 amendments to the NHPA. The act now allows a property owner to object to having his building automatically placed on the National Register.[10]

---

5. W.A.T.C.H. v. Harris, 603 F.2d 310 (2d Cir.1979), cert. denied 444 U.S. 995, 100 S.Ct. 530, 62 L.Ed.2d 426 (1980). See also Wisconsin Heritages, Inc. v. Harris, 460 F.Supp. 1120 (E.D.Wis.1978).

6. 603 F.2d at 321 (injunction permanent until HUD complied with both NHPA & NEPA).

7. Maher v. New Orleans, 516 F.2d 1051 (5th Cir.1975), cert. denied 426 U.S. 905, 96 S.Ct. 2225, 48 L.Ed.2d 830 (1976).

8. 111 Ill.App.2d 430, 250 N.E.2d 282 (1969).

9. Manhattan Club v. New York City Landmarks Preservation Comm'n, 51 Misc. 2d 556, 273 N.Y.S.2d 848 (1966).

10. See 16 U.S.C.A. § 470a(a)(6), accord 36 C.F.R. § 60. Note that while this measure may appear to make National Register listing more difficult, it is in reality a pro-preservation compromise. As originally introduced, the bill containing the 1980 NHPA Amendments required the affirmative support of a majority of residents of the proposed district. As enacted, the amendment instead requires that a majority of owners oppose the proposed listing.

Among complications of this nature are uncertainties concerning the taking issue and first amendment values, as well as uncertainties about the validity of facade easements and restrictive covenants vis-a-vis policies against long term restraints on property. Courts may be developing a greater willingness to validate the running and enforcement of recorded less-than-fee interests held in gross. For example, in United States v. Albrecht [11] the court sustained the right to enforce a restriction in gross pursuant to programs under the Migratory Bird Conservation Act. That interest was acquired by the federal government pursuant to a recorded agreement for environmental protection, despite a hostile state law. The agreement was held to have created a property right that could be transferred and enforced.

Authority for a governmental agency to conserve or preserve historic buildings or sites by various means, including accepting less-than-fee property rights, is generally conferred by enabling statutes. This authority may be granted to state agencies or charitable entities organized to preserve historic buildings and sites. Another type of law deals specifically with the creation, transfer and enforcement of interests in gross. Its purpose is to authorize the running of these interests against successors to the original parties, in spite of the lack of common law requirements for assignability and enforcement. Holders of conservation or preservation easements are often authorized to enter the land and take necessary action.[12]

Local ordinances frequently authorize preservation commissions to require affirmative duties of landowners through anti-neglect or minimum maintenance measures to prevent demolition by neglect.[13] In a typical scenario, the local historic district commission is empowered to identify buildings needing repair and notify owners. If work is not commenced within a certain time, a hearing is held. After the hearing, repairs may be undertaken at city expense and a lien placed on the property. May a preservation ordinance do this without effectuating an unconstitutional taking? [14] Restrictions on private property rights have been long in existence. Some of these, based on general societal considerations such as easements by necessity, regulation of water rights, and zoning, recognize a state's right to limit or control the use of private property.[15]

As a practical matter therefore the amendment does not substantially interfere with National Register listing.

11. 364 F.Supp. 1349 (D.N.D.1973), affirmed 496 F.2d 906 (8th Cir.1974).

12. See, e.g., Conn.Gen.Stat.Ann. §§ 47–42a to 47–42c, 7–131b to 7–131c; West's Fla.Stat.Ann. § 704.06; Md.Code, Real.Prop., §§ 12E to E–1; Mass.Gen.Laws. Ann. c. 184, §§ 31–33. See generally Coughlin, Preservation Easements: Statutory and Tax Planning Issues, 1 Preservation L.Rep. 2011 (1982).

13. Note, Affirmative Maintenance Provisions in Historic Preservation: A Taking of Property?, 34 S.C.L.Rev. 713 (1983).

14. More complete discussions of the taking issue are found at § 10.7 and at §§ 24.2–.6 of the Practitioner's Edition.

15. See, e.g., Charleston, S.C., Code §§ 54–23 to 54–35 (1977); Coral Gables, Fla., Code § 9.4 (1981); New Orleans, La., Code (Vieux Carre) art. III, §§ 65–35 to 65–40 (1978).

Inclusion of the taking clause in the Bill of Rights represented a compromise between absolute individual property rights and the government's right to take property,[16] but determination of what constitutes a taking is "a question of degree . . . and therefore cannot be disposed of by general propositions."[17] Several approaches have been used by the courts to make this determination, including physical invasion,[18] noxious use,[19] balancing of interests[20] and diminution in value tests. The latter adapts well to cases which do not involve physical invasion or noxious use problems. In Penn Central, however the Court determined that diminution of value alone was not enough and that one must focus on the uses that the regulation allowed as well.[21]

While the existence of an historic district, as a comprehensive scheme which includes both landmark sites and historic districts, will generally withstand judicial scrutiny,[22] taking problems are potentially greater with respect to designation of an isolated landmark.[23] Ordinances usually require a certificate of appropriateness before any exterior changes to the landmark can be made, and may also make affirmative maintenance demands.[24] To avoid a claim of taking, the ordinance may provide for exceptions to certain restrictions on the property if the landowner cannot get a reasonable return on his investment, or for other economic assistance.[25] If the cost of maintenance is prohibitive to the landowner, the likelihood that it will be deemed a taking increases. For example, if the owner were unable to restore from an economic standpoint, he must establish that it is

16. See, e.g., Powell, Relationship Between Property Rights and Civil Rights, 15 Hastings L.J. 135 (1963); Note, Property, Philosophy & Regulation: The Case Against a Natural Law Theory of Property Rights, 17 Willamette L.Rev. 527 (1981).

17. Pennsylvania Coal Co. v. Mahon, 260 U.S. 393, 416, 43 S.Ct. 158, 160, 67 L.Ed. 322 (1922).

18. E.g., Northern Transportation Co. v. Chicago, 99 U.S. (9 Otto) 635, 25 L.Ed. 336 (1878).

19. E.g., Hadacheck v. Sebastian, 239 U.S. 394, 36 S.Ct. 143, 60 L.Ed. 348 (1915); Mugler v. Kansas, 123 U.S. 623, 8 S.Ct. 273, 31 L.Ed. 205 (1887).

20. E.g., Pennsylvania Coal v. Mahon, 260 U.S. 393, 43 S.Ct. 158, 67 L.Ed. 322 (1922).

21. Penn Cent. Transp. Co. v. New York, 438 U.S. 104, 136, 98 S.Ct. 2646, 2665, 57 L.Ed.2d 631 (1978), rehearing denied 439 U.S. 883, 99 S.Ct. 226, 58 L.Ed.2d 198 (1978).

22. See id. at 130, 98 S.Ct. at 2662.

23. Compare, e.g., Maher v. New Orleans, 516 F.2d 1051 (5th Cir.1975), rehearing denied 521 F.2d 815 (5th Cir.1975), cert. denied 426 U.S. 905, 96 S.Ct. 2225, 48 L.Ed. 2d 830 (1976) with Penn Central, 438 U.S. 104, 136, 98 S.Ct. 2646, 2665, 57 L.Ed.2d 631 (1978), rehearing denied 439 U.S. 883, 99 S.Ct. 226, 58 L.Ed.2d 198 (1978). See generally, Pinkerton, Aesthetics and the Single Building Landmark, 15 Tulsa L.J. 610 (1980).

24. See, e.g., Gainesville, Fla., Code of Ordinances, ch. 31 (1983); Note, supra note 13.

25. Manhattan Club v. New York City Landmarks Preservation Comm'n, 51 Misc. 2d 556, 273 N.Y.S.2d 848 (1966). Transferrable development rights may be an alternate means to compensate an owner. See Penn Cent., 438 U.S. at 137, for a discussion of TDR's. See also Costonis, Development Rights Transfer: An Exploratory Essay, 83 Yale L.J. 75 (1973); supra, § 11.6.

impractical to sell or lease the property, or that there is no market for it at a reasonable price.[26]

Application of a landmarks law to noncommercial landowners can be problematic. If maintenance of the landmark either physically or financially prevents or seriously interferes with carrying out a charitable purpose, the regulation may be considered invalid. While the test enunciated by the New York court in Trustees of Sailors Snug Harbor v. Platt [27] has proven workable for charitable organizations it may not meet the rigid proscriptions of the First Amendment when applied to religious organizations. Courts have tended to sidestep this issue, although it is often raised. This may be due to the complexity of the question and difficulty of drawing a bright line, but the crux of a case generally involves the taking issue, and resolution of the first amendment problem may be unnecessary.

In Lutheran Church in America v. New York [28] the church protested the designation as a landmark of the former Morgan Mansion, which it had been using for offices. The church, which had planned to demolish the mansion and construct a building more suitable for its administrative offices, argued that the designation interfered with its ability to pursue charitable goals and was therefore a taking. Rather than considering whether the church could put the building to any use, the court determined that since the designation effectively prevented the church from continuing to use the building as it had been used, the application of the landmark ordinance was void.[29] This decision has been strongly criticized,[30] and its rationale directly conflicts with language in Penn Central and earlier zoning cases.[31]

In contrast, when the First Presbyterian Church of York [32] protested the designation of a Victorian house which it wanted to demolish to make room for church parking, the court did not find a taking. It held

26. Lafayette Park Baptist Church v. Board of Adjustment, 599 S.W.2d 61 (Mo. App.1980).

27. 29 A.D.2d 376, 288 N.Y.S.2d 314 (1968).

28. 35 N.Y.2d 121, 359 N.Y.S.2d 7, 316 N.E.2d 305 (1974).

29. Id. at 129, 359 N.Y.S.2d at 15, 316 N.E.2d at 310. Other cases which have invalidated landmark designations as applied to churches include: St. James Methodist Church v. Kingston, (No. 76–1239, Ulster county Sup.Ct., N.Y., May 6, 1977) (notice requirement of ordinance not met). But in Lafayette Park Baptist Church v. Scott, 553 S.W.2d 856 (Mo.App.1977), the court stated that demolition must be permitted only if economics of restoration are such that no other use would be feasible. But here, the church had constructive notice of property's location in historic district, and the designation remained.

30. See Note, Use of Zoning Restrictions to Restrain Property Owners from Altering or Destroying Historic Landmarks, 1975 Duke L.J. 999, 1013; Note, Environmental Control—Land Use—Historical Preservation, 1975 Wis.L.Rev. 260, 276.

31. 438 U.S. 104, 125, 98 S.Ct. 2646, 2659, 57 L.Ed.2d 631 (1978), rehearing denied 439 U.S. 883, 99 S.Ct. 226, 58 L.Ed.2d 198 (1978). See also Goldblatt v. City of Hempstead, 369 U.S. 590 (1962); Hadachek v. Sebastian, 239 U.S. 394, 36 S.Ct. 143, 60 L.Ed. 348 (1915).

32. First Presbyterian Church v. City Council, 25 Pa.Cmwlth. 154, 360 A.2d 257 (1976). See also Society for Ethical Culture v. Spatt, 51 N.Y.2d 449, 434 N.Y.S.2d 932, 415 N.E.2d 922 (1980), reargument dismissed 52 N.Y.2d 1073, 438 N.Y.S.2d 1029, 420 N.E.2d 413 (1981).

the ordinance valid under a reasonable use test, where, as in this case, the property was located within an historic district.

Ultimately, the most troublesome aspect of applying landmark laws to religious buildings is the imposition of financial burdens. Maintenance requirements can be fiscally oppressive, especially if the structure has outlived its usefulness to the congregation and cannot be sold. Another problem arises when funds earmarked for charitable purposes are required to be diverted to cover maintenance and repair costs. Tax relief or exemptions granted by federal, state or local schemes are meaningless to churches and synagogues because they already enjoy tax-exempt status.[33] On the other hand, it can be argued that the tax exemption given to religious/charitable institutions gives them a responsibility to help maintain the commonly-held values of our society. They are presumably non-profit institutions, devoted to goals above and beyond the mercenary and should be in a less favorable position to claim that they need to make a profit on their property.

The different problems focus on aspects of what is ultimately the same question, which is, how much can the government under guise of the police power regulate the use of private property before the regulation becomes a taking? Historic preservation has been established in the law as a valid public purpose. The rough boundaries have been drawn, and it is in refinement of those limits that the future challenges lie.

 WESTLAW REFERENCES

trustee +s sailor +s snug +s harbor +s platt

landmark historic! /s use usage /s adapt!

199k25.10(5) /p ''major federal action''

property /p landmark /p taking /p historic!

414k110 /p confiscat!

268k601.1 /p landmark historic!

taking /s ''noxious use''

certificate /s appropriateness /s landmark historic!

''model cities program'' /p ''urban renewal''

di(''department of housing and urban development'' h.u.d. /p
　　　control! /p federal! /s fund***)

---

33. See Comm. of Religious Leaders of the City of N.Y., Final Report of the Interfaith Commission to Study Landmarking of Religious Property 7–22 (1982); Note, First Amendment Challenges to Landmarks Designation Statutes, 11 Fordham Urb.L.J. 115 (1983).

Chapter 15

FARMLAND PRESERVATION *

Analysis

§ 15.1 Agricultural Land and Urban Planning and Land Development Control Law

Urban planners and attorneys for many years gave very little attention to farmland or agricultural uses. Although many if not most zoning ordinances included an agricultural land use category, farmland was generally viewed from the urban perspective as a temporary use or holding category. As the urban area expanded, farmland was to "give way" to residential, commercial or industrial uses. For planners, agricultural lands were those left blank or white on the land use map

---

* This chapter is based upon Chapter 4 "Protection and Preservation of Agricultural Lands" of Juergensmeyer & Wadley, *Agricultural Law* (1982, Supp.1985, Little, Brown & Co.). Permission has been granted by Professor Wadley and Little, Brown & Co.

unless they were already surrounded by development in which case the holding category concept was applied.[1]

Today, both planners and attorneys increasingly recognize the importance and even necessity for including agricultural lands as a permanent land use category in plans and land development control codes. In fact, there is growing recognition of the need to extend special preservation and protection concepts to prime agricultural land for many of the same reasons that historic[2] and environmentally sensitive areas[3] are accorded special treatment and protection.

By according special treatment to prime agricultural lands, societal needs to preserve food and fibre production are fulfilled and urban needs for open space and buffer zones are also met. The accomplishment of these goals is usually sought through use of the same planning and land use control tools encountered in other subject areas such as zoning, subdivision control, districting, clustering, and transferable development rights. Special modifications of the usual approaches and concepts are frequently required and are analyzed in the sections which follow.

WESTLAW REFERENCES

land +3 use /s regulation /s farm! agricultur!

di,sy(agricultur! farmland /5 preserv! protect! conserv!
    environment**)

united +s states +s gettysburg +s railway /p preserv!

"united states" congress! /s condemn! /s historic! memorial /s
    preserv!

welch +s swasey

pennsylvania +s coal +s mahon /s taking /s regulat!

euclid +s ambler /p regulat! /p reasonable!

nectow +s cambridge /p zon! /p constitution! unconstitution!

"vieux carre" /p histor! /p district /p preserv!

"new orleans" +s levy /p historic!

"antiquities act" /p monument

"national park service" /s preserv! protect /s woods forest

"historic sites act"

department +s interior /p authori! /p historic +s sites +s
    act

di("national register of historic places")

historic! /p preserv! /p congress! legislat! /p "non profit" /p
    corporat!

"national trust for historic preservation" /p corporat!

---

§ 15.1

1. Roberts, Getting Ready for the Ag Revolution, 49 Planning 4 (June 1983).

2. See supra Chapter 14.

3. See supra Chapter 13.

§ 15.2 The Need to Protect Farmland

The characteristics of prime agricultural land and of prime development land are almost identical—i.e. level, relatively free from vegetation, good drainage, accessible to transportation, and in large parcels. Consequently, severe tension exists on the urban fringe due to the competition between developers and farmers for use of the same land. Current economic conditions place a tremendously higher economic value on land used for development than on land used for agricultural production thus predetermining the victory of development interests over agricultural interests if only economic factors determine the outcome of the conflict. On the theory that large scale conversion of agricultural lands to urban uses threatens the future of the national or local agricultural sector, land use control authorities impose restrictions or provide incentives to prevent or deter conversion of agricultural lands to nonagricultural uses. The need for and justification of such farmland protection programs is grounded on the current high rate of conversion.[1]

From a national agricultural land base of almost 2.25 billion acres, it is estimated that 35,000 acres are lost every week to development.[2] Soil Conservation Service research indicates that roughly 5 million acres of rural land are lost yearly through urban development, through isolation as a result of urban development, and through destruction for the benefit of new water supply projects.[3] If these current trends continue, prime farmland equivalent in area to the entire state of Indiana may be withdrawn from agricultural production between 1980 and 2000.[4]

Rural lands are being urbanized at rates 5 to 10 times faster than the population growth rate. The loss of farmland is more severe in some areas of the country than others. Between 1950 and 1972, 17 states lost 20% of their taxable farmland, 9 states more than 30%, 4 states more than 40%, and the states of New Hampshire and Rhode

§ 15.2

1. Farmland preservation is quite controversial and the statistics differ considerably depending on which "side" is using them. The statistics used in the balance of this section are those generally used by proponents of farmland protection. The exaggeration of these statistics has been alleged by the Urban Land Institute which "believes that pressures for farmland preservation are based on inaccurate and incomplete information and on assertions and distortions rather than on rational analysis." Urban Land Institute, Has the "Farmland Crisis" Been Overstated?: Recommendations for Balancing Urban and Agricultural Land Needs, 1983 Zoning and Planning Law Handbook 235, 266 (Strom, ed. 1983) [hereinafter cited as Urban Land Institute]. See also Fischel, The Urbaniza-

tion of Agricultural Land: A Review of the National Agricultural Lands Study, 58 Land Economics 236 (1982) (NALS overstated farmland conversion rate by a factor of 2 or even higher); E. Roberts, The Law and the Preservation of Agricultural Land (1982).

2. H.R.Rep. No. 1400, 95th Cong., 2d Sess. 7 (1978).

3. Id. at 8. This figure varies greatly depending on the source. See, e.g., Merriam, Making TDR Work, 56 N.C.L.Rev. 77 (1978) (1.4 million acres); Roe, Innovative Techniques to Preserve Rural Land Resources, 5 Envtl.Aff. 419 (1976) (1 million acres); National Agricultural Lands Study, Final Report (1981) (3 million acres) [hereinafter cited as Final Report].

4. Final Report, supra note 3.

Island lost more than 50%. The overall result of continued suburban migration has been the loss of 119 million acres of farmland between 1954 and 1974. This is equal to an area three times the size of New England.[5]

Farmland protection programs, if they are to be successful, must respond to the factors which determine the conversion of farmland to nonagricultural uses. Many forces and factors are involved.

A primary factor contributing to the loss of prime agricultural land is the current spiral in land values. In a recent five year period the average per-acre price for all farmland increased approximately 65 percent.[6] The farmer on the urban fringe is placed in an especially uncomfortable position. Although possessing a different understanding of the land, of the relationship of people to the land, and of the problems and costs of land ownership, the farmer may not hold such an affection for the soil that he will hold out in the face of massive profits. The temptation to sell is undoubtedly connected to the proximity of the farmland to the urban fringe. Since suburban land values average 1,800 percent more when utilized for building purposes than for cultivation or grazing, the farmer is likely to take his profits and leave farming altogether.[7]

Another factor that must be considered in evaluating preservation alternatives is the changing nature of farmland ownership. Urbanites, investors, syndicates, retirees, and corporations have entered the agricultural land market in increasing numbers. In 1976 alone, 35 percent of farmland purchasers were made by local nonfarmers, non-county residents, and others.[8] Investors, both foreign and domestic, appear to view land acquisition as a hedge against inflation based on the proven expectation that land prices will outperform the general price index and the market for common stock. Urbanites and retirees, on the other hand, purchase suburban and rural land to escape the pace of urban life. Developers purchase rural land because it provides large, contiguous, relatively inexpensive parcels of land for commercial, industrial, recreational, and housing developments. Finally, farmers and agricultural corporations purchase additional acreage to take advantage of economies of scale. On the other side of rural land demand is the slowly disappearing family farm. The family farmer is confronted with factors such as an inability to compete against the large agricultural corporations coupled with pressure to sell at a profit.[9]

As the foregoing discussion suggests, whether or not a farmer will sell his land to buyers for nonagricultural use is determined by the

---

5. Bonner & Sidor, Issues in Land Use, 1975 Land Resources Today 4 (January 1975).

6. R. Gloudemans, Use Value Farmland Assessments: Theory, Practice and Impact 4 (1974).

7. Healy & Shurt, New Forces in the Market for Rural Land, 46 Appraisal J. 190 (1978).

8. Id.

9. See § 4.3, Farm Unit Size: Preservation of the Family Farm, J. Juergensmeyer & J. Wadley, Agricultural Law (1982).

interrelationship of complex socio-economic factors. These include: (1) demographic factors, such as the farmer's age and state of health and whether or not he has children who want to be farmers; (2) economic factors, including not only the fair market value of the land but also the profit that can be made from the land if it is farmed (these two factors are determined by such considerations as income tax, estate tax, transportation costs, energy costs, and the like); (3) transitional factors, such as the landowner's interest in pursuing a nonfarm occupation or moving to another climate; and (4) so called secondary factors, such as nuisance complaints by nonfarm neighbors about farm odors and pesticides, decrease in the availability of farm labor, supplies, and services, and increase in government regulation of farming activities.[10]

The quest for farmland preservation must be balanced against the needs and demands of the nonfarm public and against the direct and indirect social costs that any viable program will involve. A multitude of land use planning concepts are currently in vogue as potential "solutions" to the problem. They include zoning, cluster zoning, compensable regulation plans, negative easements and purchase of development rights, land banking, large lot zoning, open space zoning, planned unit developments, purchase and leaseback programs, agricultural service districts, transferable development rights, differential taxation, eminent domain, public rights of first refusal, and public and private land trusts.[11] The sections of this chapter which follow analyze and evaluate these various techniques, but it always should be remembered that they frequently are not responsive to the socio-economic considerations that create the problem.

It should also be remembered that farmland preservation viewed from a societal land use planning perspective involves complex competing needs and values. Land preserved for farmland is not available for urban expansion and consequently may have serious consequences in regard to the cost and availability of housing, commercial centers and industrial sites.[12]

  WESTLAW REFERENCES

"farmland assessment act"

protect preserve preservation /s agricultur! farmland /s urban
      city

---

10. See Keene, Agricultural Land Preservation: Legal and Constitutional Issues, 15 Gonz.L.Rev. 621 (1980); Juergensmeyer, The Future of Government Regulation of Agriculture, 3 No.Ill.L.Rev. 253 (1984).

11. An increasingly popular concept, which has important land use regulation consequences but is primarily a fortification of the "coming to the nuisance" de-

fense, is the so-called "right to farm" laws. At least 34 states now have such laws. See infra § 18.6.

12. If current urban development rates continue, it is estimated that 24 million acres of land will be required for urban development between 1980 and 2000. Urban Land Institute, supra note 1, at 258.

§ 15.3   Farmland Defined

An obvious prerequisite to the structuring of farmland protection programs is the identification of the land and uses deemed to merit protection. If the protective legislation or enactment defines agricultural real estate generally in terms of rural or open space lands, the protective blanket may be so broad as to include lands that have no real value for cultivation and grazing. If, alternatively, agricultural land is defined narrowly, buffer lands that effectively separate farmland from the urban fringe may not be protected. The importance of seeking a definition of agricultural lands does not lie in developing a hard and fast meaning for the term or in developing any hierarchy of definitional preference. The true value of such an inquiry is found in the realization that the definition of agricultural land is only one variable of many that must be assessed in any given land preservation and use plan.

The definition of "agricultural land" used in the National Agricultural Lands Study follows:

> "Agricultural lands" are lands currently used to produce agricultural commodities, including forest products, or lands that have the potential for such production. These lands have a favorable combination of soil quality, growing season, moisture supply, size and accessibility. This definition includes about 590 million acres of land that has no potential for cultivated crop use but is now in agricultural uses including range, pasture, or forestland. There were 1.361 billion acres of agricultural land in 1977.[1]

Another typical definition of "farmland" is "a piece of land consisting of a fixed number of acres which is used primarily to raise or produce agricultural products, and the customary buildings which accompany such activities."[2] The U.S. Department of Commerce in its 1969 census indicated that "farmland as defined in that census included all land contained within the physical boundaries of a farm including cropland, woodland, and pasture."[3]

Since many farmland preservation efforts concentrate on the protection of "prime farmland," that concept also merits definition. The U.S. Department of Agriculture's Soil Conservation Service defines "prime farmland" as:

> land that has the best combination of physical and chemical characteristics for producing food, feed, forage, fiber, and oilseed crops, and is also available for these uses (the land could be cropland, pastureland, rangeland, forest land, or other land, but not urban built-up land or water). It has the soil quality, growing season, and moisture supply needed to economically produce sus-

§ 15.3

1. National Agricultural Lands Study, Final Report xx (1981).

2. Rohan, Agricultural Zoning, 3 Zoning & Land Use Controls 17 (1978).

3. Comment, Preservation of Florida's Agricultural Resources Through Land Use Planning, 27 U.Fla.L.Rev. 130 (1974).

tained high yields of crops. . . . In general, prime farmlands have an adequate and dependable water supply from precipitation or irrigation, a favorable temperature and growing season . . . and few or no rocks. . . . Prime farmlands are not excessively erodible or saturated with water for a longer period of time, and they either do not flood frequently or are protected from flooding.[4]

The Soil Conservation Service of the U.S. Department of Agriculture is now involved in a nationwide program to map and identify prime farmland, but completion of the effort is not expected until 1986. Pending the completion of that project the Soil Conservation Service classifies rural land into eight categories on the basis of soil capabilities and limitations.[5]

A popular land use oriented definitional approach is to define "farmland" as "a parcel of land used for agricultural activities" and to then define "agriculture" as:

> The production, keeping or maintenance for sale, lease or personal use of plants and animals useful to man, including but not limited to: forages and sod crops; grains and seed crops, dairy animals and dairy products; poultry and poultry products; livestock, including beef cattle, sheep, swine, horses, ponies, mules, or goats, or any mutations or hybrids thereof, including the breeding and grazing of any or all of such animals; bees and apiary products; fur animals; trees and forest products; fruits of all kinds, including grapes, nuts and berries; vegetables; nursery, floral, ornamental and greenhouse products; or lands devoted to a soil conservation or forestry management program.[6]

WESTLAW REFERENCES
di farm!

define* definition mean*** /s agriculture

---

§ 15.4 Land Use Planning and Farmland Protection

The increased usage and importance of comprehensive land use planning at all levels of government are discussed elsewhere in this Hornbook. True comprehensive land use planning is recent in origin. Even more recent is the inclusion in the scope of planning activities of farmland preservation and protection considerations. Although controversial, this phenomenon is occurring at all governmental levels—federal, state, regional and local.

4. Report to the Congress by the Comptroller General of the United States, CED–79–109, Preserving America's Farmland—A Goal the Federal Government Should Support 2 (Sept. 20, 1979).

5. See Soil Conservation Serv., U.S. Dep't of Agriculture, Statistical Bull. No. 578, Potential Cropland Study (Oct. 1977).

6. H. Moskowitz & C. Lindbloom, The Illustrated Book of Development Definitions 23–24 (1981).

A. Federal

The concern of any agency of the federal government with the agricultural lands preservation and protection problem not only is of recent origin but also represents a dramatic change of position. As recently as 1974, a U.S. Department of Agriculture [USDA] study concluded that "Although thousands of acres of farmland are converted annually to other uses . . . we are in no danger of running out of farmland." [1]

The shift in USDA policy occurred the next year. By 1976, the Secretary of Agriculture announced a new USDA policy aimed at discouraging federal government activities that would convert prime agricultural land to other uses and at encouraging state and local authorities to advocate the protection of such land.[2] In 1978, USDA issued a revised and considerably stronger policy directed toward committing USDA agencies to intercede with all other federal government agencies when conversion of prime farmland is threatened.[3]

The second most significant federal government policy revision in regard to farmland presentation, was the action taken in 1976 by the Council on Environmental Quality [CEQ] directing all federal agencies to consider the loss of prime farmland when preparing the environmental impact statements (EIS) required by the National Environmental Policy Act of 1969.[4] Compliance was purely voluntary under the 1976 action but in 1980 CEQ made the requirement mandatory.[5]

In spite of the changes in federal agency policies, federal government programs were still considered the cause of the loss of thousands of acres of prime agricultural land annually. Continuing concern over such government activities led to the establishment in June 1979 of the National Agricultural Lands Study (NALS) to assess and propose remedies for the problem.[6] The recommendations contained in the final report of the NALS are broad and extensive and directed toward five objectives: (1) information sharing by state and local governments concerning successful agricultural lands preservation programs; (2) articulation of a national policy on agricultural lands preservation and its implementation; (3) federal support of state and local government programs; (4) financial assistance for protection programs; and (5) clarification of land information base statistics and data.

§ 15.4

1. U.S. Dep't of Agriculture, Econ.Res. Sem., Our Land and Water Resources: Current and Prospective Supplies and Uses, Misc.Publ. No. 1,290 (Wash.D.C.U.S. G.P.O.1974). See F. Schnidman, Agricultural Land Preservation: The Evolving Federal Role, ALI–ABA, Land Use Regulation and Litigation 100 (1984).

2. Report to the Congress by the Comptroller General, Preserving America's Farmland—A Goal the Federal Government Should Support, (CED–79–109) 7 (1979) [hereinafter cited as Report to the Congress by the Comptroller General].

3. Id.

4. Id. at 35.

5. CEQ, Memoranda for Heads of Agencies of August 11, 1980.

6. Report to the Congress by the Comptroller General, supra note 2, at 49–52.

To help accomplish these five goals, the study makes five categories of recommendations. The first category concerns the characteristics of successful agricultural lands preservation programs and how they can serve as guidelines for development of new programs. The suggestions are: (a) that agricultural lands preservation programs should be combined with a comprehensive growth management system; (b) that state governments should assume an active role in the programs; (c) that protection programs should be adopted before development patterns foreclose some or many options; (d) that accurate information should be used in developing the programs; (e) that able political leadership should be sought as a key element of success; (f) that agricultural land protection programs should support the economic viability of agriculture in the area; and (g) that considerable attention should be given to assuring that protection programs are legally defensible.

The second category of recommendations relates to "national policy and federal agency initiatives." Most of these recommendations are vague and general. The three remaining categories of recommendations are technical assistance and education, financial assistance, and information and research needs.

At least partially in response to the NALS recommendations, Congress enacted the Farmland Protection Policy Act as part of the Food and Agriculture Act of 1981.[7] This Act requires USDA to develop criteria for identifying the effects of federal programs on farmland conversion and requires all divisions and units of the federal government to use the criteria to identify and take into account the adverse effects of federal actions on preservation of farmland and how to avoid such adverse effects. The Act contains a specific prohibition of any legal challenges to federal programs or activities based on the Act.[8] Conflicting pressures in Congress to repeal and to strengthen the act are occurring.[9]

The Secretary of Agriculture has recently promulgated a rule for implementation of the FPPA.[10] This rule establishes criteria for identifying the effects of federal programs on conversion of agricultural lands to nonagricultural uses. Five "land evaluation criteria" are established pursuant to which parcels will be evaluated and assigned a score from 0 to 100 representing the value of the land as farmland in comparison to other land in the area. This "scoring" is to be performed by the SCS. The federal agency whose action might lead to conversion of the

---

7. Pub.L. No. 97–98 (Dec. 22, 1981), 7 U.S.C.A. § 4201.

8. Section 1548 provides: "This *substitute* shall not be deemed to provide a basis for any action, either legal or equitable, by any State, local unit of government, or any person or class of persons challenging a Federal project, program, or other activity that may affect farmland."

9. See S. 2004, the Farmland Protection Policy Act Amendments of 1983. 99th Cong., 1st Sess. § 2 (1983).

10. 49 Fed.Reg. 27,724 (1984) (to be codified at 7 C.F.R. § 658). The rule became effective on August 6, 1984.

agricultural land must assess the suitability of the tract in question for protection by using twelve "site assessment criteria." [11]

B. State and Regional

Most states do not have state comprehensive plans but Oregon and Florida are notable exceptions. Farmland and agricultural land use policies are given considerable attention in the plans of both states.

In fact, preservation of agricultural land is said to have been the primary motivation behind the adoption of the Oregon comprehensive planning statute.[12] The goals and guidelines for Oregon's agricultural lands are now formulated as follows: [13]

Goal: To preserve and maintain agricultural lands.

Agricultural lands shall be preserved and maintained for farm use, consistent with existing and future needs for agricultural products, forest and open space. These lands shall be inventoried and preserved by adopting exclusive farm use zones pursuant to ORS Chapter 215. Such minimum lot sizes as are utilized for any farm use zones shall be appropriate for the continuation of the existing commercial agricultural enterprise within the area. Conversion of rural agricultural land to urbanized land shall be based upon consideration of the following factors:

(1) environmental, energy, social and economic consequences;

(2) demonstrated need consistent with LCDC goals;

(3) unavailability of an alternative suitable location for the requested use;

(4) compatibility of the proposed use with related agricultural land; and

(5) the retention of Class I, II, III and IV soils in farm use.

A governing body proposing to convert rural agricultural land to urbanizable land shall follow the procedures and requirements set forth in the Land Use Planning goal. . . .

11. 49 Fed.Reg. at 27,726 (1984) (to be codified at 7 C.F.R. § 658.5).

12. T. Pelham, State Land Use Planning and Regulation 158 (1979). See also Juergensmeyer, Introduction: State and Local Land Use Planning and Control in the Agricultural Context, 25 S.D.L.Rev. 463 (1980).

13. Oregon Land Conservation and Development Commission, Statewide Planning Goals and Guidelines 6 (1975). The implementation of Oregon's agricultural lands preservation goal is discussed in Rochette, Prevention of Urban Sprawl: The Oregon Method, 3 Zoning & Planning L.Rep. 25 (1980). Key Oregon cases on point are Hood View Neighborhood Ass'n v. Clackamas County, 43 Or.App. 869, 604 P.2d 447 (1979); Meyer v. Lord & LCDC, 37 Or.App. 59, 586 P.2d 367 (1978); 1,000 Friends of Oregon v. Benton County, 32 Or. App. 413, 575 P.2d 651 (1978), petition denied 284 Or. 41, 584 P.2d 1371 (1978); Flury v. Land Use Board of Appeals, 50 Or. App. 263, 623 P.2d 671 (1981). See generally Coughlin, Oregon's Program of State Standards and Local Planning Regulations, in Coughlin & J. Keene eds., The Protection of Farmland: A Reference Guidebook for State and Local Government, 239 (1981).

A. Planning

1. Urban growth should be separated from agricultural lands by buffer or transitional areas of open space.

2. Plans providing for the preservation and maintenance of farm land for farm use should consider as a major determinant the carrying capacity of the air, land and water resources of the planning area. The land conservation and development actions provided for by such plans should not exceed the carrying capacity of such resources.

B. Implementation.

1. Nonfarm uses permitted within farm use zones under ORS 215.213(2) and (3) should be minimized to allow for maximum agricultural productivity.

2. Extension of services, such as sewer and water supplies into rural areas, should be appropriate for the needs of agriculture, farm use and nonfarm uses established under ORS 215.213.

3. Services that need to pass through agricultural lands should not be connected with any use that is not allowed under ORS 215.203 and 215.213, should not be assessed as part of the farm unit and should be limited in capacity to serve specific service areas and identified needs.

4. Forest and open space uses should be permitted on agricultural land that is being preserved for future agricultural growth. The interchange of such lands should not be subject to tax penalties.

Florida's first state comprehensive plan had little legal significance within the state of Florida because it was adopted only as a *guideline* for state activities.[14] It was important, nationally, however, in that it illustrated an alternate approach to planning for agricultural issues. It took a broader approach than the Oregon plan and treated farmland protection as just one of many concerns faced by the state's agricultural sector. It placed equal emphasis upon Florida agriculture's water, land, government regulation, energy, marketing, and farm labor problems.[15] The provision relating to "land" was as follows:

LAND

Objective E: Preservation of Agricultural Land. To prevent further harm to Florida's renewable resources lands through

---

14. West's Fla.Stat.Ann. § 23.0114(1). See J. Juergensmeyer & J. Wadley, Florida Land Use Restrictions § 4.02 (1979). A new state comprehensive plan was adopted by the Florida legislature in 1985. West's Fla.Stat.Ann. § 187.201.

15. Division of State Planning, Fla. Dep't of Admin., The Florida State Comprehensive Plan.

unregulated development, the state should embark upon a program to identify and preserve agricultural lands with special emphasis upon those agricultural lands most seriously threatened by urban development or other forces.

Policies. 5. Designate agricultural resources as essential, renewable resources of our environment that should be dealt with in environmental and socio-economic impact statements.

6. Define agricultural land as land having soil, climate, water, and topography so interrelated that, if prudently managed to protect the natural qualities of the land, it is favorable for the production of adapted crops.

7. Maintain Florida's 10-year statewide soil survey mission with increased priority given to rapidly urbanizing counties having agricultural, environmental, and other renewable resources lands so that proper consideration of the soil will be a factor in agricultural planning and developments.

8. Consider the protection of the natural qualities of the land and water and the capabilities and needs of the soils so as to discourage and discontinue soil wastage and soil erosion in all planning and developmental activities affecting Florida's lands.

Objective F: Tax Laws and Policies. The preservation of agricultural land should be encouraged through provisions in, and enforcement of, existing tax laws and policies at all levels of government.

Policies. 9. Establish policies that require new developments to pay for all services and facilities essential for their development in keeping with this objective and the objectives, needs, and resources of the local area.

10. Provide that agricultural land may be taxed at its value as farm land as long as it remains in agriculture, and raise the federal estate tax exemption to a more realistic present-day level.

Objective G: Property Rights Protection. Governments should recognize that property may be regulated to a certain extent, but ensure that compensation is provided to the property owner if the courts determine that the regulation is unreasonable and amounts to a taking.

Oregon and Florida also offer examples of regional planning. Florida's adoption of portions of Article 7 of the American Law Institute's Model Land Development Code [16] results in the institution of two

16. West's Fla.Stat.Ann. ch. 380 (The Environmental Land and Water Management Act of 1972). See J. Juergensmeyer & J. Wadley, Florida Land Use Restrictions, at ch. 23 (1979); Finnel, American Law Institute Model Land Development Code: A Critique, (pt. 11) 29 Land Use L. & Zoning Dig. 4 (1977).

distinct but interrelated regional land use planning and control concepts: (1) Areas of critical state concern and (2) Developments of Regional Impact. The idea behind "areas of critical state concern" is that certain areas of the state because of the nature of the land area, for example, prime agricultural land or environmentally sensitive land, are of such importance to the entire state that matters concerning their use or protection should be decided with state or regional government participation and not just by local governments. The development of regional impact concept is that certain types of development wherever they are located impact so significantly on the entire state or major portions thereof, that such developments should be undertaken only after state and regional considerations have been invoked.

C. Local

Another recent development in the land use control area is the requirement via state legislation that all units of local government formulate and adopt comprehensive plans that meet state specified standards. The important enforcement mechanism in such statutes is the so-called consistency requirement,[17] whereby the state statute requires all subsequent land use regulations by local governments to be consistent with the state comprehensive plan.

A specifically required element of such a plan normally includes planning for agricultural lands and related activities. Thus, the Florida act provides for a "future land use plan element designating proposed future general distribution, location, and extent of"[18] agricultural uses as well as the requirement that each local government comprehensive plan contain an "open space element."[19]

WESTLAW REFERENCES
7 +5 4201
"farmland protection policy act"
ci(49 +5 27716)

§ 15.5 Zoning of Farmland

In spite of recent changes and innovations in the land use control area, zoning remains the most frequently used and potentially the most effective land use control device to protect and preserve agricultural lands. Nonetheless, serious limitations exist on the effectiveness of zoning, in its traditional format, as a solution to the preservation problem.

The key characteristic of use categories under traditional or Euclidean zoning is that all use zones are "cumulative," meaning that all higher, i.e., more preferred, uses are permitted in "lower" categories.[1]

17. See supra § 2.13.   § 15.5
18. West's Fla.Stat. § 163.3177(6).   1. See supra § 4.3.
19. Id. § 163.3177(6)(e).

Since the urban planners who traditionally drafted zoning ordinances were development oriented, "agricultural use" was ranked at or near the bottom, meaning that uses ranked "higher" were frequently permitted in agricultural zones no matter how inconsistent or competing they were with agricultural activities. Even those traditional zoning ordinances that allow only agricultural and specified other uses in agricultural zones proceed to permit so many inappropriate uses that the result is the same.[2]

Modern zoning ordinances are increasingly noncumulative in nature: all or specified use zones are to be devoted exclusively to the designated use, and even so-called "higher" uses are excluded. Given the failures of cumulative zoning to protect agricultural lands as discussed above, it is not surprising to find that in many zoning ordinances of recent vintage land zoned for agricultural purposes can be devoted only to agricultural and closely related uses.[3]

Exclusive agricultural zoning, unlike agricultural zoning under cumulative ordinances, not only restricts the landowner of agricultural land but confers protection to the farmer by excluding incompatible uses. Such zoning, in theory at least, is a definitive tool for preserving agricultural lands and preventing their conversion to nonagricultural uses. Even if land speculators purchase farm land and take it out of agricultural production, strict enforcement of the zoning code should prevent any development on or changes of the land that would affect its ultimate suitability for agricultural production.

The problems encountered in using exclusive agricultural use zoning as a farmland preservation tool result not from zoning principles but from zoning practice. The farmer himself may find the stringency of the zoning protection economically unacceptable, and he or his vendees may resort to the normal avenues for zoning flexibility—variances, special exceptions, and rezonings—to obtain permission for profitable but ultimately incompatible uses, thus undermining if not defeating the protective goals of such zoning approaches.[4]

Since exclusive agricultural use zones are relatively new, little judicial attention has been given to them but most courts which have considered the issue have upheld them.[5]

2. See J. Juergensmeyer & J. Wadley, Florida Zoning—Specific Uses § 29 (1980).

3. See supra § 4.4.

4. See supra § 6.5.

5. See Joyce v. Portland, 24 Or.App. 689, 546 P.2d 1100 (1976); Gisler v. Madera County, 38 Cal.App.3d 303, 112 Cal.Rptr. 919 (1974); Still v. Board of County Commissioners, 42 Or.App. 115, 600 P.2d 433 (1979); Wilson & Noss v. County of McHenry, 92 Ill.App.3d 997, 48 Ill.Dec. 395, 416 N.E.2d 426 (1981); County of Ada v. Henry, 105 Idaho 263, 668 P.2d 994 (1983); Dufour v. Montgomery County Council

(Circuit Court for Montgomery County, Md., No. 56964, 1983). See also Zoning for Agricultural Preservation, 36 Land Use Law & Zoning Digest 3 (April 1984). See generally Wright, Some Land Use Issues for the Future, 3 Agric.L.J. 587 (1982); Batie & Looney, Preserving Agricultural Lands: Issues and Answers, 1 Agric.L.J. 600 (1980); W. Toner, Saving Farms and Farmlands: A Community Guide (ASPO Planning Advisory Service Report No. 333) (1978); J. Keene, Agricultural Land Protection: Legal and Constitutional Issues, in R. Coughlin & J. Keene, eds., The Protection of Farmland: A Reference Guidebook

A recent case in which the local governments non-exclusive agricultural zoning plan was not upheld provides some judicial guidelines for local governments. In Hopewell Township Board of Supervisors v. Golla,[6] the Supreme Court of Pennsylvania was confronted with a zoning code provision which permitted the owner of a tract of land in an agricultural zone to use the undivided tract as a farm with only one single-family dwelling or to establish as many as five contiguous residential lots of no more than 1½ acres and a single family dwelling on each lot. Plaintiffs did not challenge the agricultural zoning classification but only the reasonableness of the restrictions placed on their own land. The court held that this approach to farmland preservation placed an unreasonably severe limitation on permissible land uses and that it had an arbitrary and discriminatory impact on different landowners since under the ordinance the owner of a small tract of land could devote a larger percentage of his tract to residential development than the owner of a large tract.

The court suggested a cure for the ordinance's defects by stating: "Were the ordinance to permit the dedication of the 1½ acre lot to a single family residence per each X number of acres in the tract, this scheme would have a more equitable effect and would avoid impacting landowners on an arbitrary basis."[7]

 WESTLAW REFERENCES
414k279

farm /s land +3 use /s zon***

farm–land agricultur! /s zon*** /s exclusive

§ 15.6 Agricultural Districts

Agricultural districting is designed to bring about through voluntary compliance and local initiative the same quality of protection for farmland as that afforded by exclusive agricultural zoning. It was pioneered in California,[1] New York,[2] and Virginia.[3] Agricultural land-

for State and Local Government 254 (1981). For a discussion of the problems inherent in distinguishing agriculture uses from other uses in a zoning code, see Hamilton, Freedom to Farm! Understanding the Agricultural Exemption to County Zoning in Iowa, 31 Drake L.Rev. 565 (1982).

6. 499 Pa. 246, 452 A.2d 1337 (1982). The case is analyzed at Berger, Agricultural Zoning Held Invalid, 7 APA Planning & L.Div. Newsletter 10 (May 1983).

7. 499 Pa. 246, 452 A.2d 1337, 1344 (1982). Justice McDermott dissenting criticized the majority's setting its own standards rather than accepting the local government's. "There is only so much prime agricultural land in Hopewell Township. Perhaps when the majority's paternal interest recognizes that fact the Court can

represide and reallot the land even closer to its heart's desire." Id. at 1345.

§ 15.6

1. The agricultural districting statutes of New York and Virginia currently are considered the prototypes of agricultural districting. Their precursor and inspiration is said to be California's Land Conservation Act, West's Cal.Govt.Code § 51200–51295, which is known popularly as the Williamson Act. Myers, The Legal Aspects of Agricultural Districting, 55 Ind. L.J. 1, 2 (1979), reprinted in 2 Agric.L.J. 627 (1981). See also Gustafson & Wallace, Differential Assessment as Land Use Policy: The California Case, 41 Am.Inst. Plan 379 (1975); Comment, Condem-

2.–3. See notes 2–3 on page 493.

owners whose land meets specified acreage minimums can voluntarily form special districts.[4] Such status, depending on the exact provisions of the relevant statute, creates a binding agreement between the landowner and local authorities for a specified number of years during which the landowner receives special tax treatment and freedom from eminent domain. The authority of public agencies to install growth—stimulating public services in the area is limited, special assessments against the land are forbidden, and local governments are prohibited from enacting certain regulations of farming practices on the land unless public health and safety factors are involved.[5] If non-agricultural uses are made of the land during the "contract" period, heavy tax penalties are incurred.[6]

The major advantage and appeal of the agricultural districting approach to farmland preservation lies in its emphasis on voluntary compliance and local initiative. Other strengths, compared to previously and subsequently discussed approaches, include the retention of land ownership by the farmer, the stringent restrictions its voluntary nature allows on land use without raising taking issue problems, and its emphasis on local control, which thereby at least theoretically makes it responsive to local needs and problems.[7] Given these advantages, the popularity of this approach to farmland preservation is not surprising. By 1978 approximately one-half of the farmland in the state of New York was in agricultural districting.[8]

In spite of this popularity, the approach is not without its problems and disadvantages. The obvious disadvantage is the feature that already has been pointed out as a basis for the concept's appeal—i.e., it is entirely voluntary. Studies indicate that the effectiveness of the approach is limited by the fact that only those lands relatively free from

nation of Agricultural Property in California, 11 U.C.D.L.Rev. 555 (1978). For an overview of the current agricultural districting legislation, see Duncan, Toward a Theory of Broad-Based Planning for the Preservation of Agricultural Land, 24 Nat. Resources J. 51, 96–113 (1984). For comparisons of existing programs, see generally J. Esseks & J. McDonald, Incentives: Agricultural Districting, in R. Coughlin & J. Keene, eds., The Protection of Farmland: A Reference Guidebook for State and Local Government 76 (1981).

2. N.Y.—McKinney's Agric. & Mkts. Law §§ 300–307.

3. Va.Code §§ 15.1–1506 to 15.1–1513.

4. Any owner of agricultural land who meets the statutory acreage requirements (in New York the greater of 500 acres or 10% of the land to be included in the district and in Virginia at least 500 acres and no more than 3,500 acres to be included in agricultural districts) may apply to

the local governing body that then seeks the opinion of a planning body, holds public hearings, and then adopts, modifies, or rejects the proposal. The details of the New York and Virginia procedure are discussed in Myers, supra note 1.

5. Clayton & Abbitt, Land for Florida Agriculture, 1977 Fla.Food & Resource Econ. (Jan.-Feb.); Lapping, Bevins, & Herbers, Differential Assessment and Other Techniques to Preserve Missouri Farmland, 42 Mo.L.Rev. 369 (1977).

6. In New York, for example, conversion to nonagricultural uses during the contract period results in a penalty equal to twice the taxes levied against property in the year following conversion. N.Y.—McKinney's Agric. & Mkts.Law § 306.

7. See Geier, Agricultural Districts and Zoning: A State-Local Approach to a National Problem, 1980 Ecology L.Q. 655.

8. Myers, supra note 1.

urban fringe development pressures, that is to say, those lands that need protection the least, are placed in districts. Secondly, the special tax treatment, which constitutes the major advantage to the landowner, hampers the revenue raising authority of local governments and provides dubious incentives to retain agricultural district status. Finally, the limitations placed on governmental power in regard to regulation of the land in question and the location of public facilities, may hamper local government comprehensive planning and result in less desirable growth patterns in the long run.

 WESTLAW REFERENCES

"williamson act"

"agricultural districts" /s development

§ 15.7 Clustering, Open Space, Planned Unit Developments, and Minimum Lot Size

One of the most serious dilemmas encountered by owners of agricultural land occurs when adjacent land is developed for residential, commercial or other nonfarm uses. Once such development occurs, the farmer usually finds himself subjected to intense economic pressures to convert his farm to nonagricultural use because of the increase in value which results from neighboring development. The farmer also frequently discovers that his land no longer is well-suited to agricultural uses, since the normal odors, noises, and pollutants accompanying many agricultural activities are now nuisances in the eyes of his new neighbors.[1]

Cluster zoning, planned unit developments, and open space zoning are land use control techniques designed to alleviate such consequences of development by providing a land buffer on or between the developed land and the neighboring farmland.

Cluster zoning involves development of a tract of land in order to meet density maximums for the tract as a unit but places improvements on the tract so as to allow the preservation of open space or buffer areas on all or certain borders.[2] As a result, new development need not abut agricultural land, and the development/farming conflict is lessened.[3]

Local governmental use of the cluster concept to provide a buffer between areas of development and of agriculture is relatively simple in the sense that little or no change in basic zoning codes is necessary to allow such an approach. Most courts have recognized the permissibility of such an approach, even pursuant to Euclidian ordinances, since no variation of overall density or of permissible uses occurs. The develop-

§ 15.7   3. See supra § 4.13.

1. See infra ch. 18.

2. See Stroud, The Farm and the City, 9 Fla.Envtl. & Urb.Issues 4 (1981).

er who is required or encouraged to cluster his planned improvements
is not usually in a position to assert constitutionally based objections
since he is not denied the right to develop the overall density established by the local land use regulation. In fact, developers frequently
seek permission to cluster since there often are economies of design and
construction to such a development arrangement.[4]

The planned unit development (PUD) is grounded upon the cluster
concept but constitutes both a refinement of that concept and a departure from traditional Euclidian zoning approaches. The PUD combines
uses within a development so that various housing types—for example,
high-rise apartments, townhouses, single family dwellings, and condominiums—co-exist with open spaces, recreational areas, convenience
type commercial uses, and business/professional uses.[5]

The use of a PUD for the development of land adjacent to agricultural lands offers various protective aspects. As with clustering, buffer
areas that are not built upon can be placed between new improvements
and neighboring farmland. Furthermore, unlike clusters, the provision
for various commercial recreational, or business/professional facilities
within the PUD means that adjacent farmland is not needed as a
location for supportive services that inevitably accompany development. By providing for such nonresidential uses, the PUD offers
greater protection for adjacent agricultural land than does simple
cluster zoning. Although PUDs frequently receive even greater developer enthusiasm than clusters, local land use control authorities are
often less enthusiastic about the PUD since its combination of uses is in
conflict with one of the sacred cows of traditional zoning—separation of
uses. Additionally, approval for use of PUDs frequently requires the
existence of floating zones [6] within the zoning jurisdiction.

Open space zoning is a more drastic way of providing the type of
open space or land buffer between new development and neighboring
agricultural land that results almost automatically from clusters and
PUDs. The technique is much simpler, however, since land bordering
agricultural areas is designated in the relevant comprehensive plan as
being unavailable for development and is zoned for only recreational or
other nondevelopment uses. The problem presented by open space
zoning is that the economic value of land so zoned is nearly destroyed,
thereby entitling the landowner to contest the zoning designation as an
unconstitutional taking of property without compensation.[7]

Another related zoning technique frequently advocated as an agricultural lands preservation device is "large lot" zoning. By establishing high minimum lot area requirements such as 1 acre, 5, 10, 15, 18,
or, in one case,[8] 160 acres, residential development of rural land is

---

4. See supra chapter 7.

5. See supra § 7.15.

6. See supra § 4.10.

7. See supra § 10.7.

8. Wilson & Voss v. County of Mc-
Henry, 92 Ill.App.3d 997, 48 Ill.Dec. 395,
416 N.E.2d 426 (1981).

discouraged by increasing the cost of, and thereby decreasing the demand for, such property. Furthermore, if the land is developed, the low density of such developments has a minimal deterrent effect upon the continued suitability of adjacent or nearby land for agricultural use. The major disadvantage of using large lot zoning to protect agricultural land is the same encountered with open space zoning: the economic value may be so greatly decreased as to raise the taking issue. Furthermore, the exclusionary effects of large lot requirements provide still another basis for contesting their validity.[9]

WESTLAW REFERENCES

"planned unit development" /s farm! agricultur!

"minimum lot" /s zon*** /s agricultur!

§ 15.8   Transferable Development Rights

The application of the transferable development rights (TDR) approach to agricultural land preservation is of recent origin.[1] In fact, "development rights" as a separate element of land ownership was not appreciated in this country until lately, even though it has been the key to land use control in Great Britain for some time.[2]

---

9. See supra § 10.4. The leading "large lot" zoning cases are Ybarra v. Town of Los Altos Hills, 503 F.2d 250 (9th Cir.1974); Steel Hill Dev. v. Town of Sanbornton, 469 F.2d 956 (1st Cir.1972); Hay v. Township of Grow, 296 Minn. 1, 206 N.W.2d 19 (1973); Berenson v. Town of New Castle, 38 N.Y.2d 102, 378 N.Y.S.2d 672, 341 N.E.2d 236 (1975); De Caro v. Washington Township, 21 Pa.Cmwlth. 252, 344 A.2d 725 (1975); County of Ada v. Henry, 105 Idaho 263, 668 P.2d 994 (1983); Still v. Board of County Commissioners, 42 Or.App. 115, 600 P.2d 433 (1979).

§ 15.8

1. See D. Merriam & A. Merriam, Bibliography of the Transfer of Development Rights, Council of Planning Librarians Exchange Bibliography No. 1338 (1977); Carmichael, Transferable Development Rights as a Basis for Land Use Control, 2 Fla.St. U.L.Rev. 35 (1974); Costonis, The Chicago Plan: Incentive Zoning and the Preservation of Urban Landmarks, 85 Harv.L.Rev. 574 (1972); Costonis, Development Right Transfer: An Exploratory Essay, 83 Yale L.J. 75 (1973); Merriam, Making TDR Work, 56 N.C.L.Rev. 77 (1978); Schnidman, Transferable Development Rights: An Idea in Search of Implementation, 11 Land & Water L.Rev. 339 (1976); Moore, Transferable Development Rights, An Idea Whose Time Has Come, Fairfax County, Va., Feb. 16, 1974; Tustian, TDR's in Practice: A Case Study of Agriculture Preservation in

Montgomery County, Maryland, 1984 Zoning and Planning Law Handbook 223. For a discussion of the TDR approach and an explanation of the PDR (Purchase of Development Rights) Scheme, see Duncan, Toward a Theory of Broad Based Planning for the Preservation of Agricultural Land, 24 Nat. Resources J. 61, 113–135 (1984).

2. Great Britain sees development rights as created and allocated by society and "ownership" as only the right to continue using the land as it currently is being used. The owner is seen as having no inherent right to develop. The Town and Country Planning Act of 1947 effectively nationalized all development rights. The act repealed all zoning laws, established a permit system for development, expanded eminent domain powers based on existing-use value as the measure of compensation, and, most important, vested all development rights in the government. See Merriam, supra note 1. The act nearly ceased development altogether, and nationalization was repealed in 1953. The 1947 Act was criticized because of its economic distortions, its elimination of incentives to develop, its complexity, its costly administrative processes, the excessive discretion it gave to local authorities, and the over-politicizing of the entire system. In 1975, Great Britain passed the Community Land Act, which was to "enable local authorities and certain other authorities to acquire, manage and deal with land suitable for

The TDR approach designates certain land areas within a given jurisdiction as subject to severe regulations and designates other land areas within the jurisdiction as appropriate for development. Owners of the severely restricted land are allowed to sell their rights to develop, which they cannot exercise because of the land use restrictions, to the owners of land permitted to be developed. The purchasing landowners may be required to purchase the rights of the restricted landowners before they may develop, or the purchase of development rights may authorize them to develop at greater density than otherwise would be permitted.[3]

Although considerable support exists for using the TDR concept as an agricultural lands preservation device, the National Agricultural Lands Study treats the idea rather negatively:

> Transfer of development rights (TDR) programs have been instituted by 10 municipalities and two counties, but developers have shown little inclination to participate in them. It is possible that the newer programs, which have been adopted by large suburban counties, may include development locations where the market will support higher densities and where the county government will provide sufficient facilities and public services so that the developers will find it profitable to purchase and transfer rights. But so far, the right combination of factors has not been present.[4]

In evaluating the usefulness of TDRs, it first should be noted that the statistics used by the NALS are now out of date and actual experience with TDRs is considerably broader and more positive.[5]

development and to make other provisions for land in connection with public ownership." V. Moore, Community Land: The New Act 1 (1976). The Act in effect renationalizes development rights by giving the government the power to acquire at current use price all land needed for development. See also Carroll, Rural Land Use Control in Great Britain, 19 Nat.Resources J. 145 (1979).

3. See supra § 11.6.

4. National Agricultural Lands Study, Final Report 61 (1981).

5. A well-studied TDR regime directed toward farmland preservation is that of Montgomery County, Maryland. Tustian, TDR's in Practice: A Case Study of Agriculture Preservation in Montgomery County, Maryland, 1984 Zoning and Planning Law Handbook 223. Examples of TDRs include Collier County, Florida, which in 1974 adopted a TDR plan for its cypress swamp and designated 84 percent of the county's land as a special treatment (SP) zone requiring special permission prior to development. New Jersey has had the most activity with its TDR plan. The 1976

legislature approved $5 million for an agricultural preserve demonstration project. An estimated 10,000 acres will be preserved which, calculated at $500 a preservation acre, is relatively cheap.

St. George, Vermont, and Buckingham Township, Pennsylvania, are examples of TDR's potential as a land use technique. In St. George, the town bought 50 acres for a downtown center. In order to build, a developer must transfer to the town an equal number of development rights from an unimproved parcel away from the town center. The town, in exchange for the right to develop, gets a permanent restriction on the land donated by the developer and maintains control over the town's central area. To date, 18 rights have been transferred. Merriam, supra note 1, at 112–13. The Buckingham Township plan, designed with agricultural preservation in mind, gave each landowner in the agricultural district one development certificate per acre owned. Each owner could sell his rights to landowners in three higher density residential districts. "Conveyance of development rights requires the seller to re-

Furthermore, whatever complexities and difficulties are encountered in regard to implementation of TDR programs, their key potential advantage over virtually all other approaches to agricultural lands preservation is that restricted landowners receive compensation for their losses without the need for expenditure of public funds.[6] The compensation comes from payments made in an open market context by landowners economically benefitted by land use restrictions. In short, TDRs allow payment of compensation without cost to the taxpayer. Judicial approval of this concept has been encouraged by the U.S. Supreme Court's comments in the Penn Central case on New York City's transferable density plan.[7]

Finally, as far as the acceptability of the TDR concept is concerned, the basic principle is a familiar one to farmers. As Professor Torres has observed: [8]

> While in urban areas transferable development rights may be looked upon as a novel land planning device, in farm country the notion that the productive capacity of one area may be severed and transferred to another area is at least as old as the Agricultural Adjustment Act.[9] Depending on the crop being farmed, acreage allotments have traditionally been transferable between farms. . . .

> One crop that farmers, especially those farmers in developing areas, hope to harvest is the appreciated nonfarm development value of their holdings. . . . TDRs function much like the transfer of acreage allotments between . . . holders of development potential. . . . Like crops, development potential becomes merely another cash valued commodity.

 WESTLAW REFERENCES
transferable /s development /s right

§ 15.9   Conservation Easements

Conservation easements merit special attention as an agricultural lands preservation technique, even though their use is sometimes part of a transferable development rights plan or of the land banking or public and private trusts approach.[1]

strictively covenant his land and rezone the land into an agricultural preservation district permitting only one residence in every twenty-five acres." Id. at 114.

6. Bozung, Transferable Development Rights: Compensation for Owners of Restricted Property, 1984 Zoning and Planning Law Handbook 207.

7. Penn Cent. Transp. Co. v. New York, 438 U.S. 104, 98 S.Ct. 2646, 57 L.Ed.2d 631 (1978), rehearing denied 439 U.S. 883, 99 S.Ct. 226, 58 L.Ed.2d 198 (1978). The Penn

Central case is discussed supra §§ 10.7, 11.6, 14.9.

8. Torres, Helping Farmers and Saving Farmland, 37 Okla.L.Rev. 31, 40 (1984).

9. 7 U.S.C.A. § 1281 et seq.

§ 15.9

1. For an analysis of conservation easements and a bibliography, see National Trust for Historic Preservation, Information Sheet No. 25, Establishing an Easement Program to Protect Historic, Scenic

A conservation easement is created when a landowner restricts his rights to develop his own land in ways that would be incompatible with its use as farmland. The landowner burdens his land in the form of a negative restriction, thereby creating a negative easement in favor of other parcels of land or for the benefit of public or private agricultural lands preservation organizations. Unless the negative restriction is in some way limited, it will bind all future owners of the land.

Although such arrangements are generally referred to as conservation or preservation "easements," the same goals can be accomplished from a property law viewpoint through real covenants or equitable servitudes.[2]

Perhaps the greatest advantage to the use of conservation easements is that the farmer remains owner of all interests in the land in question except the right to use the property in a manner inconsistent with the restriction.

One of the best, and thus far most successful, agricultural preservation restriction programs is that recently instituted in Massachusetts.[3] It was established by the Massachusetts legislature in late 1977. By early 1984, $40 million had been appropriated for the purchase of deed restrictions offered by farmers to the state on a voluntary basis. Over 8,000 acres had already been restricted by that date and purchase of restrictions for nearly 9,000 more acres was pending. The program is especially significant since "Massachusetts has lost nearly three-fourths of its land in farms and one-half of its productive cropland,"[4] in the last forty years. The state officials work closely with a private entity, the Massachusetts Farm and Conservation Lands Trust. The entire program serves as a model to other states.[5]

The institution of comparable programs is proceeding at an impressive pace. At least 34 states have adopted such measures.[6]

 WESTLAW REFERENCES
conservation +5 easement /s agricultur! farm!

---

and National Resources (Washington, D.C. 1980). See also Dawson, Compassionate Taxation of Undeveloped Private Land (pt. 11), 3 Zoning & Planning L.Rep. 57 (Sept. 1980); Netherton, Environmental Conservation and Historic Preservation Through Recorded Land Use Agreements, 14 Real Prop.Probate & Trust J. 540 (1979). Barnes, An Alternative to Alternative Farm Valuation: The Conveyance of Conservation Easements to an Agricultural Land Trust, 3 Agric.L.J. 308 (1981); Horne, How an Agricultural Conservation Easement is Negotiated, 2 Farmland 2 (March 1982).

2. See infra §§ 19.3–.5.

3. Mass. Dep't of Food & Agriculture, Saving Farmland in Massachusetts: The Agricultural Preservation Restriction Program (1983). See Connors, The Agricultural Preservation Restriction Program in Massachusetts, ALI–ABA, Land Use Regulation and Litigation 313 (1983).

4. Id.

5. Id.

6. State-By-State Roundup of 1983 Preservation Actions, 4 Am. Farmland 3 (Mar. 1984).

§ 15.10 Land Banking and Farmland Trusts

The agricultural lands preservation technique of land banking involves purchase of farmland by governmental or public organizations for the purpose of insuring that the land remains in agricultural production. The use of land banking to control urban land development patterns has long been practiced in Europe,[1] but one of the most ambitious uses of the concept in the agricultural context has occurred in Canada, particularly in the province of Saskatchewan.[2]

In recent years, several American states have expressed interest in the Canadian land bank idea and considered the possible applicability of the concept to this country. To date, however, there has been no widespread acceptance of the idea. Where it has been adopted, it has been used principally as a device by which farmland may be made available to specific groups of individuals rather than as a farmland preservation technique. It is also significant to note that interest in the idea has been more intense at the state or local level and is only very recently finding significant support at the federal level.[3]

The American Law Institute (ALI) Model Land Development Code defines land banking as a "system in which a governmental entity acquires a substantial fraction of the land in a region that is available for future development for the purpose of controlling the future growth of the region. . . . "[4] The ALI definition requires that: (1) the land being acquired does not become committed to a specific future use at the time of acquisition and (2) the land being acquired is sufficiently large in amount to have a substantial effect on urban growth patterns.

Two aspects of the ALI definition are inapplicable when land banking is used to preserve farmland. First there is a commitment to a specific future use at the time of acquisition—namely, continuation of agricultural uses.

Secondly, the ALI definition presumes government involvement. In many instances in which farmland is "banked" for preservation purposes a government entity is involved. However, land banking for farmland preservation purposes is done on a private as well as a public basis. In fact, the major land banking efforts of agricultural lands preservation advocates are directed to private trusts.[5]

§ 15.10

1. A. Strong, Land Banking: European Reality, American Prospect (1979). See also Lapping & Forster, Farmland and Agricultural Policy in Sweden: An Integrated Approach, 7 Int'l Regional Sci.Rev. 3 (1982).

2. Young, The Saskatchewan Land Bank, 40 Saskatchewan L.Rev. 1 (1975). See also, Fitch & Mock, Land Banking, in The Good Earth of America 134 (Harris, ed. 1974); Note, Public Land Banking: A New Praxis for Urban Growth, 23 Case

W.Res.L.Rev. 897 (1972). The statutory authority for the Saskatchewan land bank was repealed in 1983.

3. See J. Juergensmeyer & J. Wadley, Agricultural Law § 4.14 (1982).

4. ALI Model Land Development Code Commentary on Art. 6. at 254 (1975).

5. See Fenner, Land Trusts: An Alternative Method of Preserving Open Space, 33 Vand.L.Rev. 1039 (1980); Lapping, Bevins & Herbers, Differential Assessment and Other Techniques to Preserve Missou-

The private land trust is a charitable organization that acquires and holds interests in agricultural land for preservation purposes. To qualify as charitable, the trust must exist for a charitable purpose and operate for the benefit of an indefinite group of persons. Additionally, the trust must satisfy various state laws relating to charitable organizations and numerous federal and state tax laws and regulations in order to qualify for receipt of tax deductible or tax exempt "charitable" donations.

Land trusts need not be organized as "trusts" in the technical legal meaning of the term. In fact, "land trusts" can and do exist as (1) unincorporated associations, (2) charitable trusts, or (3) charitable corporations. The last two of these—charitable trusts and charitable corporations—are clearly the preferable form of organization. The charitable corporation format has been chosen by the most significant agricultural lands trust—the recently formed American Farmland Trust (AFT).[6]

 WESTLAW REFERENCES
"model land development code"
"soil bank" (7 +5 1801)

---

§ 15.11   Preferential Assessment and Differential Taxation

The major source of revenue for most local governments is the ad valorem tax levied on real property. In most states, agricultural land is given special treatment regarding ad valorem taxes or "property taxes," as they are often called. The justification given for "special treatment" or the "differential taxation" approach usually combines two arguments.

The first argument is the farmland preservation theory. Agricultural land tax breaks save farmers money and make agricultural activities more profitable, consequently giving farmers an economic incentive to continue farming. The second justification given for treating farmers differently for property tax purposes is that agricultural activities do not make the demands on governmental services that urban land uses make. Farmers therefore are entitled to tax breaks because they otherwise would be paying more than their fair share of the costs of governmental services. Under this approach, any farmland preservation effects are merely incidental.

Whatever the justification given, the differential taxation or preferential assessment approach is commonly used. In fact, at least 48

ri's Farmland, 42 Mo.L.Rev. 369 (1977); Large, This Land Is Whose Land? Changing Concepts of Land as Property, 1973 Wis.L.Rev. 1039; McClaughry, A Model State Land Trust Act, 12 Harv.J.Legis. 563 (1975); Renter, Preserving Farm Land Through Zoning and a Community Land Trust, 1971 Land Use Control Ann. 169; Roe, Innovative Techniques to Preserve Rural Land Resources, 5 Envtl.Aff. 419 (1976).

6. The American Farmland Trust was incorporated in 1980 pursuant to the District of Columbia Nonprofit Corporation Act. See American Farmland Trust, Statement of Purpose (1980).

states[1] have statutory and/or constitutional provisions falling under generally accepted definitions of differential taxation or preferential assessment. Not surprisingly, differential taxation is also one of the issues most frequently written about in all of agricultural law.[2] It is also one of the most controversial. The most recent evaluations suggest that differential taxation for ad valorem tax purposes has had little, if any, effect on keeping land in agricultural production. Differential taxation for estate, gift, and inheritance tax purposes is considered much more important and considerably more effective in accomplishing preservation goals. Perhaps the most balanced evaluation of differential taxation programs is that of the National Agricultural Lands Study—Final Report:

> Although many states have used property tax relief as a tool in protecting agricultural land, only a small fraction of farm estates or farms which enjoy the tax benefits of differential assessment meet all the conditions necessary to make this incentive effective. The benefits of reduced taxation, however, are conferred broadly, with no proof required of each recipient that the public policy of

§ 15.11

1. For a recent listing of the citations for the various state statutes and constitutional provisions, see Dunford, A Survey of Property Tax Relief Programs for the Retention of Agricultural and Open Space Lands, 15 Gonz.L.Rev. 675, 696–97 (1980).

The editors of the newly published casebook on agricultural law contend that all states except Kansas "have laws that seek to reduce the burden of real property taxes on farmers." K. Meyer, D. Pedersen, N. Thornson & J. Davidson, Agricultural Law: Cases and Materials 853 (1985).

2. See R. Gloudemans, Use-Value Farmland Assessments: Theory, Practice and Impact (Int'l Ass'n of Assessing Officers, 1974); J. Wershow, Florida Agricultural Law, at chs. 2 & 3 (1981); Adamson, Preferential Land Assessment in Virginia, 10 U. Richmond L.Rev. 111 (1975); Cooke & Power, Preferential Assessment of Agricultural Land, 47 Fla.B.J. 636 (1973); Currier, Exploring the Role of Taxation in the Land Use Planning Process, 51 Ind.L.J. 27 (1975); Currier, An Analysis of Differential Taxation as a Method of Maintaining Agricultural and Open Space Land Uses, 30 U.Fla.L.Rev. 832 (1978); Dean, The California Land Conservation Act of 1965 and the Fight to Save California's Prime Agricultural Lands, 30 Hastings L.J. 1859 (1979); Ellingson, Differential Assessment and Local Government Controls to Preserve Agricultural Lands, 20 S.D.L.Rev. 548 (1975); Hady & Sibold, State Programs for the Differential Assessment of Farm and Open

Space Land, 256 Agric.Econ.Rep. 6 (U.S. D.A.1974); Henke, Preferential Property Tax Treatment for Farmland, 53 Or.L.Rev. 117 (1974); Juergensmeyer, State and Local Land Use Planning and Control in the Agricultural Context, 25 S.D.L.Rev. 463 (1980); Keene, Agricultural Land Preservation: Legal and Constitutional Issues, 15 Gonz.L.Rev. 621 (1980); Keene, A Review of Governmental Policies and Techniques for Keeping Farmers Farming, 19 Nat. Resources J. 119 (1989); Lapping, Bevins & Herbers, Differential Assessment and Other Techniques to Preserve Missouri's Farmlands, 42 Mo.L.Rev. 369 (1977); Myers, The Legal Aspects of Agricultural Districting, 55 Ind.L.J. 1 (1979); Nelson, Differential Assessment of Agricultural Land in Kansas: A Discussion and Proposal, 25 U.Kan.L.Rev. 215 (1977); Wershow, A British Answer to Ad Valorem Assessment Problems in Florida, 53 Fla.B.J. 490 (1979); Wershow, Ad Valorem Assessment in Florida—The Demand for a Viable Solution, 25 U.Fla.L.Rev. 49 (1972); Wershow, Regional Valuation Boards—A British Answer to Ad Valorem Assessment Problems in Florida, 21 U.Fla.L.Rev. 324 (1969); Wershow, Recent Developments in Ad Valorem Taxation, 20 U.Fla.L.Rev. 1 (1967); Wershow, Ad Valorem Assessment in Florida—Whither Now?, 18 U.Fla.L.Rev. 9 (1965); Wershow, Agricultural Zoning in Florida—Its Implications and Problems, 13 U.Fla.L. Rev. 521 (1964); Wershow & Juergensmeyer, Agriculture and Changing Legal Concepts in an Urbanized Society, 27 U.Fla.L.Rev. 78 (1974).

protecting farmland is being promoted. For this reason, tax policy is often viewed as a shotgun approach. Furthermore, unless differential assessment programs are combined with agricultural zoning and/or with agreements that restrict the land to agricultural use and/or purchase of development rights, there is no assurance that the beneficiaries of tax reduction or abatement will keep their land in agricultural use. Owners may simply enjoy reduced taxes until the time comes when they want to sell. In the case of death taxes, significant tax benefits are made available to large farm estates, even those that are not in serious jeopardy of being converted because of high death taxes.

In isolation, then, differential assessment is largely ineffective in reducing the rate of conversion of agricultural land. It does not discourage the incursion of non-farm uses into stable agricultural areas; it simply enables owners of land under development pressure to postpone the sale of their land until they are ready to retire. The incentives are not keyed into actual need, except in the case of the tax credit programs of Wisconsin and Michigan.

Nevertheless, differential taxation is a valuable component of a comprehensive agricultural land protection program. As a matter of equity, if a program prevents agricultural land from being developed, the owner should pay taxes only on its agricultural use value. Further, benefits such as these may serve as incentives to encourage farmers to participate in integrated agricultural land protection programs.[3]

 WESTLAW REFERENCES

"farmland assessment act"

ci(23 +5 638)

farm agricultur! /s "property tax" /s different prefer! better

---

§ 15.12   Constitutional Limitations on Farmland Protection Programs

The power of state and local governments to use land use planning and control techniques to protect and preserve agricultural lands is based on the police power. It is therefore subject to the same constitutional limitations and requirements that apply to all exercises of the police power.

The issues of constitutional limitation are explored elsewhere in this hornbook. The reader should consider carefully the following interrelated concepts in judging the constitutional validity of farmland preservation programs: (1) the taking issue, (2) the arbitrary, capri-

---

3. National Agricultural Lands Study: Final Report 55 (1981). See also Duncan, Toward a Theory of Broad-Based Planning for the Preservation of Agricultural Land, 24 Nat. Resources J. 61, 78–96 (1984); Dun- ford, A Survey of Property Tax Relief Programs for the Retention of Agricultural and Open Space Lands, 15 Gonzaga L.R. 675 (1980).

cious, and unreasonable standard, (3) the requirement of conformity to comprehensive plans, (4) the unlawful delegation of legislative authority issue, and (5) the exclusionary zoning prohibition.[1]

 WESTLAW REFERENCES

topic(148) /p regulation /s farm! agricultur!

constitution! unconstitutional +1 land +3 use /s regulat! /s agricultur!

---

§ 15.12

1. See supra ch. 10. For a recent discussion of the constitutional problems inherent in protecting farmland, See Hand, Right-to-Farm Laws: Breaking New Ground in the Preservation of Farmland, 45 U.Pitt.L.Rev. 289, 328–347 (1984).

Chapter 16

NEW COMMUNITIES

Analysis

I. INTRODUCTION

I. INTRODUCTION

§ 16.1 Introduction

The development of "new communities" is an increasingly common growth phenomenon in the United States—particularly in the sunbelt jurisdictions. New communities are distinguishable from other development approaches by several—or perhaps all of the following features. (1) They are developed under a single or unified management in accordance with a comprehensive and inclusive plan, calling for staged development; (2) they follow principles of urban design including balanced land uses and specified population density; (3) they offer scale-economic and fiscal viability; (4) they have geographic and social identity; (5) they provide a full housing mix, a primary employment and commercial base, a full range of public facilities, community services and cultural amenities; and (6) they provide for local government and citizen participation throughout the development period.[1]

New community development requires the application of many of the tools of planning and control described in earlier chapters. This chapter will discuss new communities generally and how the various land use planning and control law principles are adapted for use in such developments.

 WESTLAW REFERENCES

planned retirement new /3 community & "planned-unit
    development"

topic(414) & sy,di("planned-unit development" "new community")

§ 16.2 Defining New Communities

There is no precise meaning of the term "new community." In terms of newspaper advertisements for real estate developments, a new community may only be a large subdivision or a planned unit development. At the other extreme, it is an entirely new city or new town built on never before developed land, with a full range of land uses, its own economic base and its own government. In between the extremes are satellite cities, namely cities that are outlying but are yet part of a metropolitan area and are dependent on the economic base of the area.

A definition commonly used by United States government agencies is as follows:

> '[New] communities' are large-scale developments constructed under single or unified management, following a fairly precise, inclusive plan and including different types of housing, commercial and cultural facilities, and amenities sufficient to serve the residents of the community. They may provide land for industry or are accessible to industry, offer other types of employment opportunities, and may eventually achieve a considerable measure of self-sufficiency.[1]

Generally, the new community or new town concept contemplates development on undeveloped land, though there is a concept known in planning circles as "new towns in town."[2] The new town in town concept is one dealing with social, economic and physical redevelopment of urban core areas. The concept has generally been implemented in the so-called Model Cities Program.[3]

§ 16.1

1. This list is adopted from DeLucia, New Communities and Small Town America, 4 The Urban Lawyer 734, 735–736 (1972).

§ 16.2

1. U.S. Advisory Comm'n on Intergovernment Relations, Urban and Rural America 64 (1968). For other definitions, see Dames & Grecco, A Survey of New Town Planning Considerations, 11 Current

Mun. Probs. 265, 266 (1970); McDade, New Communities in America, 1965 Urb.Land 6, 7 (Jan.); Gibson & Simms, New Community Development, 11 Washburn L.J. 227 (1972).

2. Perloff, New Towns in Town, 32 J.Am.Inst. of Planners 155 (1966).

3. See Title I, Demonstration Cities and Metropolitan Development Act of 1966, now in 42 U.S.C.A. § 3301 et seq.

§ 16.3 History, United States [1]

The history of the United States is in large part a history of the settlement of the country through the establishment of new urban centers. While many of them just grew in a rather haphazard manner the English Crown granted charters for cities from an early day, and some of the cities were rather thoroughly planned.[2] From the beginning of the states, state legislatures gave charters to new cities, and early statutes in many states had provisions for incorporation of new cities.

Federal Promotion of New Towns

The orderly development of new cities as part of a national policy was first evident in the town site laws. These laws provided for the withdrawal of public lands and the establishment of town sites.[3] Reclamation lands were also available for town sites.[4] National Forest lands in certain states can also be used for town sites.[5] Although these laws authorize occupant platting or the delivery of title to a trustee for the establishment of a town, they are generally unworkable in modern times.[6]

Many company towns were also formed during the period 1830–1900. Such towns as Lowell, Massachusetts, Gary, Indiana, Kohler, Wisconsin, Pullman, Illinois and Kingsport, Tennessee were established as company towns.[7]

During World War I, the U.S. Housing Corporation built some twenty-five developments, which were subsequently sold.[8] Such communities as Yorkship Village, New Jersey, Noreg Village, Pennsylvania, and Cradock and Hilton, Virginia were built under the program.

§ 16.3

1. See generally U.S. Advisory Comm'n on Intergovernmental Relations, Urban and Rural America 67–76 (1968).

2. Glaab & Brown, Cities in the New Nation, in A History of Urban America 25 (1967). See § 2.2.

3. The town site laws were first passed in 1863, 1867 and 1874. See 43 U.S.C.A. §§ 711–31. Repealed effective Oct. 21, 1976 by Pub.L. No. 94–579, tit. VII, § 703(a), 90 Stat. 2789.

4. See 43 U.S.C.A. § 561. Pub.L. No. 94–579, tit. VII, § 704(a), 90 Stat. 2792 deleted provisions of § 561 authorizing withdrawal from public entry any lands needed for town-site purposes.

5. 7 U.S.C.A. § 1012(a); 16 U.S.C.A. § 478a.

6. Only 600 acres were disposed of as town sites in the period 1958–1967. U.S. Public Land Law Review Comm'n, One Third of the Nation's Land 226 (1970) [hereinafter cited as One Third of the Nation's Land].

7. J. Allen, The Company Town in the American West (1966).

8. 1 Report of the U.S. Housing Corp. (1920).

During the New Deal, the Resettlement Administration began a new program to establish model new communities. Three such communities were established: Greenbelt, Maryland; Greenhills, Ohio; and Greendale, Wisconsin—all established close to existing metropolitan areas.[9]

No lofty new town population distribution policy caused the establishment of the atomic communities, Richland, Washington, Oak Ridge, Tennessee and Los Alamos, New Mexico. They were created by the Atomic Energy Commission in 1947 to provide a community for the employees of the Commission. They were government "company" towns, and, as was the case with so many privately owned "company" towns, suffered from all the difficulties of benevolent and complex paternalism. Paralleling the fate of the Greenbelt towns, the atomic communities were eventually sold.[10]

The power of the federal purse to create new communities is considerable. For example, when the $200 million linear accelerator of the Atomic Energy Commission was located in the Chicago metropolitan area in the middle 1960's, there was little thought given to the notion that such a facility could be located almost anywhere and, as a unique scientific instrument, its location could generate a rather sizeable town.[11] Generally, large scale, new town stimulating federal investments have not been made with consideration to the possibility that they could serve a population distribution function.

Private Development of New Communities—The Business Context

Of course, new communities have been started over the years by real estate developers. In order to evaluate the private development of new communities it is important to understand the new community developer and the business context within which he operates.[12] One of the best ways to understand the new community developer is to think of the development industry as including a wide range of business entities with varying degrees of specialization. At one end of the scale is the subcontractor who installs wiring, plumbing and other mechanical systems into individual buildings. Next on the scale is the home builder who both builds houses and sells them, and the small residential developer who subdivides land and installs streets and sewers in the subdivision. Further up on the scale is the mixed residential and

9. See P. Conkin, Tomorrow a New World: The New Deal Community Program (1959); A. Mayer, Greenbelt Towns Revisited (1968), partially reprinted in 24 J. Hous. Nos. 1–3 (1967); C. Stein, Toward New Towns for America (3d ed. 1966); Mullarkey, The Evolution of a New Community: Problems of Government, 6 Harv. J.Legis. 462, 466–68 (1969). The communities were sold by the federal government pursuant to 1949 legislation. Act of May 19, 1949, 63 Stat. 68.

10. Atomic Energy Community Act of 1955, and 1962 amendments to the Act, 42 U.S.C.A. § 2301 et seq. See Mullarkey, supra note 9, at 463–66.

11. For example, Page, Arizona was created as the result of the Grand Canyon Dam project. Boulder City, Nevada and Norris, Tenn. were similarly created.

12. For a thorough discussion of large-scale development see Large-Scale Development: Benefits, Constraints, and State and Local Policy (Urban Land Institute 1977).

commercial developer who must deal with a broader range of uses and facilities; and, then, finally, the large scale mixed-use developer whose projects, as they increase in size, at some point became "new communities."

The main factors that distinguish the participants in the development process as one goes up the scale are (1) the increasing range of services and facilities that must be provided and, consequently, the increasingly broad range of expertise that the developer must possess; and (2) the increasing amounts of up-front capital that are needed to participate in the process.

The corollary of the up-front capitalization requirement is the sensitivity of large scale development to interest rates. Large scale development requires much more up-front investment with long-delayed return than small scale development. The New Communities Program was conceived in the 60's when interest rates of three to five percent were the historical norm. As interest rates skyrocketed in the 70's, the whole process became very impractical except in situations where market conditions promised very quick and extensive sales.

The likelihood of sales were also affected by changing demographics of the period. The planners in the 60's were anticipating that the baby boom generation would behave like its predecessors—marry early, raise children and create demand for new housing. Their failure to do so destroyed all of the forecasts on which the new towns were premised. The consequent drop in the birth rate has further reduced the likelihood that there would be the large explosion of people seeking new housing in the future that would support the marketing of a new community (but our predictions of demographics may be no more reliable than those in the 60's). There are, however, two major exceptions where successful markets have been found:

1. Retirement communities [13] reflecting the substantial increase in the elderly population; and

2. Resort oriented communities, such as Hilton Head or Vail, which reflect the dramatically increased amount of leisure time available.

Given the need for extensive amounts of capital and a wide range of expertise, the new community business is available only to large corporations with a steady source of capital to be invested for long range purposes. At various times oil companies and insurance companies have been in that position, but the current instability of capital markets discourages such long range investment.

 WESTLAW REFERENCES
42 +5 2301 & atomic

---

13. Many of the developments started in the 1950's were specialized retirement communities. See M. Barker, California Retirement Communities (1966).

§ 16.4 National Policy

There is no national policy on population distribution. There have been many recommendations for a national policy that would include a new community policy.[1] Bills attempting to increase federal involvement in new community developments have been periodically introduced in Congress.[2] During the late 1960's and early 1970's Congress did develop a number of housing and community development programs that could be viewed as a national policy on new communities. The purpose of this section is to trace the historical evolution, development and subsequent repeal of these programs.

These programs included the Surplus Land for Community Development Program announced by President Johnson in August of 1967.[3] It was primarily directed to the establishment of new towns in town [4] through the use of surplus federal lands. Much of the land was formerly used for military bases.[5]

Title IV of the Demonstration Cities and Metropolitan Development Act of 1966 [6] was entitled Land Development and New Communities, and it provided mortgage insurance for privately financed land development which included mortgage insurance for new communities. At the time of its passage it was the only federal program specifically established for new communities. Utilities, roads and other facilities could be financed by the insured mortgages. The Act was not utilized in any substantial way [7] and two years later it was largely displaced by the federal program for new communities established under the New Communities Act of 1968.[8]

New Communities Act

The obligations of the new community developer that were guaranteed under the New Communities Act were the costs of land acquisition and the costs of labor, materials and interest up to 80 percent of the value of land upon completion of land development or 75 percent of the

§ 16.4

1. National Comm. on Urb. Growth, The New City (1969); U.S. Advisory Comm'n on Intergovernmental Relations, Urban and Rural America (1968); [hereinafter cited as Urban and Rural America]; U.S. Nat'l Goals Research Staff, Toward Balanced Growth: Quantity with Quality (July 4, 1970); Freeman, Towards a National Policy on Balanced Communities, 53 Minn.L.Rev. 1163 (1969).

2. See, e.g., National Land Use Policy Act of 1970 S. 3354, 91st Cong., 2d Sess. and Urban Growth and New Community Development Act of 1970, P.L. 91–609, 84 Stat. 1770.

3. Based on authority in 42 U.S.C.A. § 1458, omitted pursuant to 42 U.S.C.A. § 5316 which terminated the authority to make grants or leases under this subchapter.

4. See supra § 16.2.

5. U.S. Dep't of Hous. & Urb. Dev., Development Standards for Surplus Land for Community Development (1969); U.S. Dep't of Hous. & Urb. Dev., Surplus Land for Community Development (SLCD), Summary Program Description. HUD News, HUD–No. 68–2208 (Sept. 13, 1968).

6. 12 U.S.C.A. § 1715 et seq.

7. See Urban and Rural America, supra note 2, at app. IV–A, for history of Act.

8. 42 U.S.C.A. §§ 3901–14 (repealed 1983). See generally Keegan & Rutzick, Private Developers and the New Communities Act of 1968, 57 Geo.L.J. 1119 (1969).

value of the land before development plus 90 percent of the cost of development. The national policy with respect to these new communities could be read from the conditions, standards and criteria contained in the statute and the regulations. These indicated a national policy to encourage new communities that had a full range of activities of a normal city, but that were better balanced and harmonious, and would have a favorable impact on the area in terms of conserving land, of minimizing transportation, of extending a range of housing choice and of promoting economic development and new job opportunities. The community must have been designed for a full range of people of various income and ethnic backgrounds. The new community must have been of significant size and accessible to major transportation facilities. It was to be located in an urban, urbanizing or rural area.[9] It must be carefully integrated with old development, if any.

The new community need not be completely self-sufficient, but should aim in that direction, and it could not be a single purpose community with only housing or with predominantly commercial or industrial development. A general plan and program for development was required. A full range of governmental and public services were to be available from state and local government, community organizations or other appropriate entities. The area within which the community exists was to have been covered by a comprehensive areawide plan or by ongoing planning, and the new community plan was required to be consistent with the area plan. Citizen participation opportunities were also required. New communities established with the help of the federal guarantee include Jonathan, Minnesota, St. Charles Communities, Maryland, and Park Forest South, Illinois.[10]

Urban Growth and New Community Development Act of 1970

The Urban Growth and New Community Development Act of 1970,[11] signed into law in 1971 as part of the Housing and Urban Development Act of 1970, added some policy making capacity for national planning. The new community development provisions of the Act were the most important. While the new Act incorporated most of the New Communities Act of 1968,[12] it also significantly increased federal incentives to stimulate new community development.

State land development agencies, defined to include local public bodies and agencies, could enjoy the benefits of the Act as well as the private developers covered by the 1968 Act. The formula for comput-

---

9. See generally Ricks, New Town Development and the Theory of Location, 46 Land Econ. 5 (1970).

10. For a list of federally assisted new communities, see R. Burby & S. Weiss, New Communities U.S.A., Table 18–1, at 401 (1976). For privately developed new communities prior to the federal program, see E. Eichler & M. Kaplan, The Community Builders (1967).

11. 42 U.S.C.A. § 4511, repealed by Pub.L. 98–181, tit. IV, § 474(e), Nov. 30, 1983, 97 Stat. 1239.

12. Pub.Law No. 91–609, § 727(a), 84 Stat. 1770, incorporated the New Communities Act 1968 described supra text accompanying notes 8–10.

ing the amount of debt that could be guaranteed was somewhat changed:

> State land development agency . . . 100 per centum of the sum . . . of the value of the real property before development and . . . the actual cost of land development, or . . . in the case of a private new community developer . . . 80 per centum . . . of the value of the real property before development and 90 percentum . . . of the actual cost of land development.[13]

Also, the 1970 Act made several significant additional kinds of financial assistance available. These included loans to cover interest charges on new community development debt for up to the first fifteen years. The interest rate was below market, namely at one eighth of one percent over the interest the United States paid on its own medium to long term obligations. The assistance was designed to solve the developer's problem of securing adequate "patient money"—funds necessary to acquire land and begin development though income from sales and rentals was many years off. The 1968 Act provided for supplemental grants (grants over and above those typically available for a particular type of facility) for three Federal aid programs to provide basic facilities in new communities (open space, sewer and water). The 1970 Act provided for supplemental grants of 20 percent for many more programs including urban mass transit facilities, highway construction, airports, hospital and medical facilities, libraries, colleges, neighborhood centers, land and water recreation, urban beautification and sewer treatment works. The maximum grant for any facility (ordinary plus supplement) was 80 percent.

In addition to these capital grants, revenue grants would be made to public bodies responsible for providing certain essential public services to the residents of the new community during the initial development period, before local tax revenues were sufficient from the area to pay for the services. Educational, health and safety services were covered. Further, grants of up to three-fourths of the cost of planning new community development programs were made available.

Technical assistance was provided to new community developers and, on specific authorization of the President, a new federal agency, the Community Development Corporation, was authorized to carry out new community demonstration projects on federal lands. Primarily, however, the Community Development Corporation was designed to be a specialized agency within the U.S. Department of Housing and Urban Development, that will be responsible for administering the entire program.

The federal government's new community policy has been described as a "disaster." [14] In January 1975 the Department of Housing

---

13. Pub.L. No. 91–609, § 713(c).

14. For a critical evaluation of the federal government's new community policy

and suggestions, see R. Burly & S. Weiss, *supra* note 10, at 58–65; Evans & Rodwin, The New Towns Program and Why It

and Urban Development closed the door to further applications under the Urban Growth and New Community Development Act of 1970. Although approximately 100 applications were submitted for new community development assistance, only 13 private applications were approved for loan guarantees and other grants and assistance totaling approximately $372 million. In 1983 the statutory framework for the national policy on new communities was repealed.[15]

 WESTLAW REFERENCES
42 +5 3901 & "new community"
42 +5 4501 & "urban growth"

§ 16.5   New Communities, Other Countries

New communities have been built and are proposed to be built throughout the world.[1] The policies of many foreign countries concerning the establishment of new communities are considerably more developed than those of the United States. Great Britain,[2] Israel,[3] Canada[4] and Scandinavia[5] are among the leaders and their experiences with new community development provide a wealth of information for the student of comparative new community policy.

The diversity and variety of functions which foreign new communities serve has been of particular interest to scholars of new community development.[6] These functions have been summarized in the following six categories: (1) To serve as capital cities, (2) to fulfill strategic or military needs, (3) to exploit natural resources or to develop the potential of the land, (4) to relieve congestion in existing large urban centers and/or to organize more rationally existing and future metropolitan growth, (5) to cope with population growth, movements of

Failed, 1979 The Pub. Interest 90–105 (Nat'l Affairs, Inc.).

15. Pub. Law No. 98–181, tit. IV, § 474(e), Nov. 30, 1983, 97 Stat. 1239.

§ 16.5

1. See, e.g., descriptions of new communities and new towns around the world in A. Gallion & S. Eisner, The Urban Planner 332 (2d ed. 1963); F. Osborn & A. Whittick, The New Towns (rev. ed. 1969); United Nations, Planning of Metropolitan Areas and New Towns (1967).

2. See, e.g., McFarland, The Administration of the English New Towns Program, 1965 Wash. U.L.Q. 17.

3. See, e.g., E. Spiegel, New Towns in Israel: Urban and Regional Planning and Development (A. Rookwood trans. 1967); N. Lichfield, Israel's New Towns: A Development Strategy, Vol. I (Jerusalem: State of Israel Ministry of Housing, August

1971); A. Berler, New Towns in Israel (Jerusalem: Israel Universities Press, 1970).

4. See, e.g., McFarland, The Administration of the Alberta New Towns Program, 5 Duq.L.Rev. 377 (1967); I. Robinson, New Industrial Towns on Canada's Resource Frontier (Chicago: University of Chicago, 1962).

5. See, e.g., I. Robinson, Small, Independent, Self-Contained and Balanced New Towns: Myth or Reality?, in H. Perloff & N. Sandberg, New Towns: Why—and for Whom? (1973).

6. See, e.g., I. Robinson, supra note 5; A. Shachar, The Role of New Towns in National and Regional Development: A Comparative Study; N. Lichfield, Economic Opportunity in New Towns; and, N. Sandberg. Can the United States Learn From the Experience of Other Countries? A Commentary, in H. Perloff & N. Sandberg, supra note 5.

population, or special features of a population, and (6) to be part of a national planning and development policy.[7]

Many of the new communities studied in foreign countries which are leaders in new community development fit several but not all of these categories. Many of the Israeli towns—those built to provide for the settlement of Jewish populations in areas facing security problems, particularly along Lebanon, Jordon, and Syrian borders—fall into category 2.[8] Many of the Canadian new communities were created in order to exploit natural resources.[9] The original London new towns plus the Scandinavian new communities fall into category 4.[10] Several of the British and Israeli new towns were developed to cope with some special population problem; e.g., either to deal with a declining population or economic activity, or to attract population to an undeveloped region.[11]

II. GOVERNANCE, PLANNING AND CONTROL

§ 16.6 New Communities Formation and Governance

State Legislation

While new community development can occur in many states without new enabling legislation, most state legislation [1] was not drafted with problems peculiar to large-scale, planned development in mind. States may find it desirable to enact new legislation.[2] For example, the state may wish to establish criteria for site selection and require that the new community fit within comprehensive plans for the area. The state might prefer to encourage renewal of badly developed existing towns rather than permit the creation of entirely new cities. Perhaps the state may wish to set growth limits or at least require the developer to adopt such limits for a particular area. Once the area for a new community is defined, marginal development along the borders of the area might be adverse to the new community unless some extraterritorial control is given.[3] The state might wish to establish guidelines for access to transportation and criteria for soil conditions, sewage and water capabilities. It might wish to preserve prime agricultural land and encourage development of new towns on other lands.[4]

In addition to these issues there may be difficult problems over the share of governance exercised by the developer, the county and the new city, if any, as well as the transition of government from one group to

7. I. Robinson, supra note 5 at 4.

8. Id. at 5.

9. Id.

10. Id.

11. Id.

§ 16.6

1. See generally Scott, Urban Growth Challenges New Towns, 48 Pub.Mgmt. 253 (1966).

2. Mandelker, Some Policy Consideration in the Drafting of New Towns Legislation, 1965 Wash. U.L.Q. 71.

3. See supra §§ 3.11, 5.9, 7.4.

4. See supra ch. 15.

another. The state may decide to give eminent domain powers to the developer, which will raise a host of questions, including those associated with the Miller rule [5] as to the effect of early acquisition and development on the just compensation to be paid for later acquisition. Perhaps some inverse condemnation [6] provisions should be included so as to compel developers to include lands which might not add to their profit but should sensibly be included and which present owners wish included. In addition, planning controls present difficult problems that might be resolved by state legislation. [7]

Incorporation

In many states, the developer cannot himself incorporate as a municipal corporation because of typical requirements for a minimum amount or density of population. [8] There may also be maximum or minimum areas required [9] and a minimum tax base. [10] The area might be required to have an urban character before it can be incorporated. [11] Incorporations across county lines are not permitted in many states. [12] Once incorporated, there may be similar barriers to annexation. [13]

Accordingly, it may be necessary, or at least desirable, for a state to have special legislation concerning new communities. One such proposal would have the following features:

A NEW COMMUNITY LOCAL GOVERNMENT ACT

Table of Contents

5. See supra § 20.10.

6. See supra § 20.7.

7. See infra § 16.7.

8. D. Hagman, Standards for Incorporation and Municipal Boundary Change Recommendations Based on a Study of Statutory and Case Law in the United States, pt. II Boundary Change by Administrative Commission, The Minnesota Experience 3–8 to 3–25 (1968).

9. Id. at 3–53 to 3–58.

10. Id. at 3–61 to 3–75.

11. Id. at 3–84 to 3–88.

12. Id. at 3–110 to 3–113.

13. Id. at 4–1 to 4–86.

Section 8: Appointment of the First Mayor and Creation of
             the City Council

Section 9: Adjustment of Representation on the City Coun-
             cil

Section 10: Area City Halls

Section 11: Powers and Duties of the Deputy Mayor

Section 12: Creation of a New Community School District
             and School Board

Section 13: Election Procedures [14]

Special Districts

Rather than permit incorporation of new towns as cities, some states have provided for the creation of multi-function special districts.[15] Florida is a contemporary example of a state utilizing special districts as an element of its new communities policy.

The Florida Uniform Community Development District Act of 1980 [16] was created to provide a uniform method for the management and public financing of land development infrastructures. Prior to its enactment, independent improvement districts had been created by both general law and special acts to provide special services and capital improvements for community and land development.[17] These districts were given broad and differing powers. The provisions for the creation of a special district also differed and included creation by petition and by local ordinance. As a result, the Florida New Communities Act of 1975 was created to provide the sole authorization for establishing community development districts.[18] However, this act failed to accomplish its purpose because it exempted districts created under other general laws and because the procedure for the creation of a district was too costly and restrictive. The Uniform Community Development District Act of 1980, was enacted to correct the shortcomings of the New Communities Act.[19]

The purpose of the act is two-fold. First it provides an alternative, streamlined method for financing the construction, maintenance, and

14. A New Community Local Government Act, 6 Harv.J.Legis. 484 (1969). See also article accompanying statute, Mullarkey, The Evolution of a New Community: Problems of Government. Id. at 462.

15. For a discussion of the use, and abuse, of such districts in California, see Willoughby, The Quiet Alliance, 38 S.Cal. L.Rev. 72 (1965); Comment, The Use of Special Assessment Districts and Independent Special Districts as Aids in Financing Private Land Development, 53 Calif.L.Rev. 364 (1965). For a discussion of the Pennsylvania experience with special districts in general, see Special Purpose Taxation Districts: Coming or Going?, 11 U.Rich.L. Rev. 87 (1976).

16. West's Fla.Stat.Ann. ch. 190.

17. For a history of independent improvement districts in Florida, see Hudson, Special Taxing Districts in Florida, 10 Fla. St.U.L.Rev. 49 (1982).

18. West's Fla.Stat.Ann. ch. 163, pt. V.

19. For a history of special district reform in Florida culminating with the Uniform Community Development District Act of 1980, see Kynoch & Van Assenderp, Growth Management Through the Uniform Community Development District Act, 9 Fla.Envtl. & Urb. Issues 22 (1982); Van Assenderp, Uniform Community Development District Act of 1980 and Local Government Home Rule, 56 Fla.B.J. 342 (1982).

operation of major infrastructures necessary for new community development. Prior to the act, a developer had to obtain financing from private lending institutions. Financing the necessary infrastructures was costly to the developer and development projects were often delayed because of the developer's inability to obtain adequate private financing.[20] The act authorizes the board of supervisors of a newly created community development district to issue bonds and bond anticipation notes and to engage in short term borrowing.[21] It also authorizes the board to issue revenue bonds which are secured by, and payable from, the revenue generated by the district's infrastructures and to issue general obligation bonds which pledge the full faith and credit of the district.[22] The board is also authorized to assess an ad valorem tax on all property in the district to pay the principal of, and the interest on, any general obligation bond of the district.[23] The board may levy a special assessment tax for construction of assessable improvements against any property benefited thereby.[24] Second, the act authorizes a district's board of supervisors to manage and maintain the infrastructures and community services once the development project has been approved by the appropriate local, regional, or state land regulatory agency.

An important feature of the Florida act is that it distinguishes development approval from the process of determining alternative ways to manage and finance delivery of basic services to development.[25] The creation of a community development district does not authorize approval of development, and neither vests any development right nor works any estoppel against planning, permitting or other local, regional or state government regulatory determinations about growth and development.[26] A developer is required to obtain a development order from the appropriate state or local land use regulatory agency prior to beginning construction on the development.[27]

An additional feature of the act is the relationship between the district and local government comprehensive planning. No petition for the creation of a district can be filed in any local government jurisdiction until the local government has promulgated all of the mandatory elements of its comprehensive plan.[28] The creation of the district must also be consistent with state and local government comprehensive

20. For a discussion of two differing perspectives on the effectiveness of Community Development districts in growth management, see Wilkes, Community Development Districts: The Delusion that Tax-Exempt Financing for Developers Improves Growth Management, 10 Fla. Envtl. & Urb. Issues 8 (1983); Van Assenderp, Community Development Districts: An Alternative Way for the Private and Public Sectors to Enhance Growth Management, 11 Fla.Envtl. & Urb. Issues 14 (1983).

21. West's Fla.Stat.Ann. § 190.011(9).

22. Id. § 190.016(8).

23. Id. § 190.021.

24. Id. § 190.022.

25. See Van Assenderp, supra note 19, at 341.

26. See West's Fla.Stat.Ann. § 190.002.

27. Id. § 190.004(3).

28. Id. § 190.005(1)(a)(7).

plans.[29] In essence, the district is not a development but is a special "tool" or "mechanism" which if established becomes a "limited, specialized, non-policy making form of local government mandated to implement municipal or county growth policy, planning and development conditions . . . which apply to private development."[30]

Since the act is the sole authority for creation of a community development district, there can be no variations in the management of a district after it has been approved. The board of supervisors need not exercise all of the powers granted to it, but it may not exceed the legislative grant of power.

A community development district of 1,000 acres or more is created pursuant to a rule, adopted by the Governor and Cabinet sitting as the Florida Land and Water Adjudicatory Commission, granting a petition by the developer for the establishment of a district.[31] A public hearing is held in conformance with the requirements of the Florida Administrative Procedures Act.[32] A record of the hearing is then delivered to the commission which shall review the petition and make the decision to grant or deny the petition.[33]

A community development district of less than 1,000 acres is created pursuant to a local ordinance. The county commission having jurisdiction over the majority of the land in the area in which the district is located, grants or denies a petition by a developer for establishment of the district. The county commission may make the determination to grant the petition using the same substantive and procedural requirements imposed on the Land and Water Adjudicatory Commission or may forward the petition to the Commission for processing.[34] Any existing taxing district which provides the same services as the independent community development district may petition to be reestablished as a community development district.[35]

The act provides the powers and duties of the board of supervisors and the procedures under which the district would operate including: (1) Election of the board of supervisors; (2) General duties of the board; (3) A budget system; (4) Disclosure of public financing provisions; (5) A water management and control plan; (6) Issuance of bonds, bond anticipation notes, and short term borrowing; (7) Taxation; and, (8) Special assessments.[36]

In addition to these powers, the board of supervisors is granted a broad range of general and special powers. Such general powers include, in part, the right to sue and be sued in the district name, the

29. Id. § 190.005(1)(c)(2).

30. See Van Assenderp, supra note 19, at 341.

31. West's Fla.Stat.Ann. § 190.005.

32. Id. For rules and regulations concerning public hearings and the procedures to create a community development district, see Fla.Admin.Code ch. 42–1.

33. West's Fla.Stat.Ann. § 190.005(1)(b) & (c).

34. Id. § 190.005(2).

35. Id. § 190.005(3).

36. Id. §§ 190.006–190.022.

right to enter into contracts, apply for coverage of district employees under the state retirement system, borrow money, adopt bylaws, and to acquire land either through purchase or lease.[37] The district also has the power of eminent domain over any land within the state except municipal, county, state or federal lands. The district may also take easements over any land, whether within or without the district, for the purposes set forth in the chapter.[38]

After a community development project has been approved, the district may carry out numerous special powers necessary for the management of the district. Included are the powers to construct and maintain facilities for water management, water supply, waste disposal, road construction, street lighting, parks, fire prevention, security service, and mosquito control.[39]

The district through its board of supervisors may also petition to expand or contract the boundaries of a district and to merge the district with other community development or special purpose districts.[40] A specific service provided by a community development district may be transferred by local ordinance to the general purpose local government within which the district lies. Such ordinance must provide for assumption of the debts of the community development district related to the service and must demonstrate the ability of the local government to provide services as efficiently and economically as the district.[41] Finally, if, within 5 years after the effective date of the adoption of the rule or ordinance creating the district, a landowner has not received development permit from the appropriate land regulatory agency then the district shall automatically be dissolved.[42]

Development Corporation

Rather than merely enacting legislation to facilitate new community development by the private sector,[43] New York has directly involved the state in this activity by creating a state urban development corporation.[44] The corporation is a state governmental agency.[45] Its membership consists of nine directors: the Superintendent of Banks, the Superintendent of Insurance, and seven others appointed by the Gover-

37. Id. § 190.011.

38. Id.

39. Id. § 190.012.

40. Id. § 190.046(1) & (3).

41. Id. § 190.046(4).

42. Id. § 190.046(7).

43. Indeed, the policy of direct state involvement in the urban development area is based upon legislative finding that private enterprise in unequal to the task in the State of New York:

[T]he unaided efforts of private enterprise have not met and cannot meet the needs of providing such facilities due to

problems encountered in assembling suitable building sites, lack of adequate public services, the unavailability of private capital for development in such urban areas, and the inability of private enterprise alone to plan, finance, and coordinate industrial and commercial development with residential development for persons and families of low income, and with public services and mass transportation facilities.

N.Y.—McKinney's Unconsol. Laws § 6252.

44. New York State Urban Development Corporation Act, id. §§ 6251–85.

45. Id. § 6254.

nor.[46] It has all the powers of any private corporation, including the power to create subsidiaries, the power to enter into agreements with any person (natural or corporate) for the management of a project, the power to provide advisory or technical assistance to any person, and the catch-all power "to do any and all things necessary or convenient to carry out its purposes and exercise the powers given and granted in this act." [47] As a state agency, it also has the power of eminent domain [48] and is immune from local taxation except for assessments levied to pay for local improvements.[49] To raise revenues the corporation has the power to issue bonds [50] and other notes of indebtedness [51] up to a limit of one billion two hundred ninety-five million dollars.[52]

There are, however, certain limitations upon the power of the State Urban Development Corporation to aid new community development. The New York State Constitution permits the state to act only in the areas of: (1) "low rent housing" for "persons of low income," (2) rehabilitation of multiple dwellings "for occupancy by persons of low income," and (3) clearance and redevelopment of "substandard and insanitary areas." [53] These constitutional restrictions are heeded in § 6260 of the New York State Urban Development Corporation Act which requires that in the case of a residential project there be shown "a need for safe and sanitary housing accommodations for persons or families of low income, which the operation of private enterprise cannot provide;" and, in the case of an industrial project, that the proposed project area is "substandard" or "insanitary." None of these limitations is stated in the statutory definition of "new community," [54] but all would presumably be applied to limit new community development to the same extent as other "urban renewal" projects.

County and Local Government

In most cases, however, government for new communities has been provided by a county and by a patchwork of special districts, so that government is nearly as fragmented as it is in developed areas. In some states, however, county government is specially designed for rural areas and may not afford the power necessary to accomplish urban

---

46. Id.

47. Id. § 6255(26).

48. Id. § 6263.

49. Id. § 6272.

50. Floyd v. New York State Urb. Dev. Corp., 33 N.Y.2d 1, 347 N.Y.S.2d 161, 300 N.E.2d 704 (1973).

51. N.Y.—McKinney's Unconsol. Laws § 6267.

52. Id. § 6268.

53. N.Y.—McKinney's Const. Art. XVIII, §§ 1 & 2.

54. The statute defines "new community" as

A plan or undertaking for the development of housing together with such civic, industrial, and commercial facilities and other ancillary facilities as the corporation may determine necessary, including the implementation thereof through one or more projects of the corporation and through such participation by private enterprise as may be necessary or desirable to carry out the development of such new community.

N.Y.—McKinney's Unconsol. Laws § 6253(16).

development, particularly where the development must be planned, staged and controlled if the promise of a better life style is to result.

Other arrangements to protect the public interest on an interim basis pending full development might include advisory commissions or the conference of additional jurisdiction over private new town development to the commissions established in several states to approve annexations and incorporations.

Private Government

The new town developer is in a dilemma concerning governance of the new town. On the one hand, he is inexperienced with governance and it represents an out-of-pocket expense that he would readily share with others. On the other hand, he fears loss of control over development plans and financial arrangements if he does not provide and control a private government.[55]

Therefore, while most new town developers take advantage of state, county and other local government there is always a private government. The private government often takes the form of government by contract, that is, government through a homeowners association which is an incorporated, non-profit organization that operates under recorded land agreements for the maintenance of private and common property and the provision of certain municipal-type services.[56] The homeowners association idea is not new to new towns since it is used in major subdivisions and in planned unit developments.[57]

However, two of the better known new towns, Reston and Columbia, rely on the homeowners association concept far more than the typical subdivision and, in fact, have adopted a two-tier association.[58] The town-wide association in Reston, for example, (1) operates and maintains common property; (2) enforces covenants, restrictions, reservations, servitudes, profits, licenses, conditions, agreements, easements, and liens provided in deeds; (3) assesses, collects and disburses charges created under deeds and (4) functions to undertake matters proper or convenient for the promotion of the peace, health, comfort, safety, or general welfare of the owners and inhabitants. These corporate purposes as conferred on the Reston Homes Owners Association are in effect private government equivalents of (1) proprietary activities of government, (2) land use controls, (3) taxation, and (4) the police power. The neighborhood association maintains common areas at the neighborhood level, may assess dues and may carry out architectural review functions in conjunction with the town-wide association.

55. Kraemer, Developing Governmental Institutions in New Communities, 1 Urb. Law. 268 (1969).

56. See Comment, Democracy in the New Towns: The Limits of Private Government, 36 U.Chi.L.Rev. 379 (1969).

57. See infra ch. 7.

58. In local government, a two-tier government is one that has a regional tier providing regional services and governance and a local tier providing local services and governance.

Since the new towns have these private governments, which may perform very much like typical municipal government, interesting questions are raised as to whether they will be treated as municipal corporations in law. For example, the members of the Home Owners Association in Reston are generally the developer, who retained one-third of the votes until 1985, and property owners. In Columbia, each property owner or tenant is a member of a neighborhood association, which chooses a delegate to the Columbia Council, which in turn in effect chooses the directors of the Columbia Association, the townwide government.

These property ownership based membership and voting rights schemes may well violate one-man-one-vote rules if the private government is equated with public government.[59] It is now well established, for example, that the franchise cannot be limited to property owners in local school and bond elections.[60] The courts have also held that a town law requiring a holder of elective office to be an owner of real property violates the equal protection clause,[61] that company towns cannot unduly restrict fundamental liberties,[62] and, of course, that private discrimination in the sale and rental of housing is unconstitutional.[63]

WESTLAW REFERENCES

florida /s "community development district"

(planned retirement new +2 community) "new town" (planned-unit "planned residential" /3 development) "home-owner association"

§ 16.7   Planning and Control in General

Local and Developer Plans

There are perhaps three ways of exercising planning controls over new towns. One alternative, which might be used when a public agency undertakes the development, is to use the model developed for urban renewal. In that scheme planning and control is made a responsibility of the local government.[1] Alternatively, a public authori-

---

59. See Comment, supra note 56, for discussion of this question.

60. Phoenix v. Kolodziejski, 399 U.S. 204, 90 S.Ct. 1990, 26 L.Ed.2d 523 (1970); Cipriano v. Houma, 395 U.S. 701, 89 S.Ct. 1897, 23 L.Ed.2d 647 (1969); Kramer v. Union Free School Dist., 395 U.S. 621, 89 S.Ct. 1886, 23 L.Ed.2d 583 (1969). See generally Hagman & Disco, One-Man-One-Vote as a Constitutional Imperative for Needed Reform of Incorporation and Boundary Change Laws, 2 Urb. Law. 459 (1970).

61. Landes v. Town of North Hempstead, 20 N.Y.2d 417, 284 N.Y.S.2d 441, 231 N.E.2d 120 (1967).

62. Marsh v. Alabama, 326 U.S. 501, 66 S.Ct. 276, 90 L.Ed. 265 (1946) (company town could not prohibit distribution of literature by a Jehovah's Witness). See also Amalgamated Food Employees Union v. Logan Valley Plaza, Inc., 391 U.S. 308, 88 S.Ct. 1601, 20 L.Ed.2d 603 (1968) (state could not prohibit peaceful nonemployee picketing of a privately-owned shopping center).

63. Jones v. Alfred H. Mayer Co., 392 U.S. 409, 88 S.Ct. 2186, 20 L.Ed.2d 1189 (1968). See infra § 10.4.

§ 16.7

1. See supra Ch. 17.

ty may be given the development power itself to preempt local control. The new town development corporation or agency would then be responsible for planning the new town. A state planning agency might be given review powers, although consultation with local governments might be required. Such a scheme would be similar to that established in England where the Ministry of Housing and Local Government operates much as might a typical state review agency, and, since the Ministry also participates in the financial arrangements, the Ministry exercises functions of review similar to those by the U.S. Department of Housing and Urban Development under the New Communities Act of 1968.[2]

A third alternative assumes that most new town development will be carried out by private enterprise, without significant modification of governmental organization, particularly state-local relations. Thus, as with ordinary subdivisions, local land use planning and control requirements will be adapted to the new town development.

Given the complex nature of new town development, it may not be possible or desirable to preregulate development in a precise way. As with any good planning, the plan for redevelopment of a new town might well state standards and policies rather than detailed regulations and should facilitate feedback and change when necessary or desirable. A proposed ordinance authored by Christensen[3] for adoption by a local government suggests a two-step approval process. Other model statutes vary only in particulars from the scheme described by Christensen, which is the latest in a series of proposals.[4] The ordinance establishes some general criteria and allows the developer to offer a generalized plan. The generalized plan would be subject to a public hearing and approval by the local legislative body. After approval, the legislative body would not again consider the plan but the planning commission would consider a more detailed final development plan. Legislative approval would be required only if deviation from the preliminary plan was significant. The final plan would not have to be approved at one time, for the development could be approved in stages. The final plan would have some regulatory features. For example, upon approval, it would "fix the uses of the various buildings and structures designated on the plan in the same manner as if zoned"[5] and would result in

2. See generally Mandelker, Some Policy Considerations in the Drafting of New Towns Legislation, 1965 Wash.U.L.Q. 71, 80–87.

3. See Proposed Ordinance for Land Use During New Town Development, 6 Harv.J.Legis. 536 (1969) and accompanying article: Christensen, Land Use Control for the New Community, 6 Harv.J.Legis. 496 (1969).

4. Very similar models are contained in Urban Land Institute, Model State Ena-

bling Act with Commentary for Planned Unit Residential Development (tech.bull. No. 52, 1965), reprinted in Babcock, Krasnowiecki & McBride, The Model State Statute, 114 U.Pa.L.Rev. 140 (1965). The Model Statute is in large part the basis for U.S. Advisory Comm'n on Intergovernmental Relations, 1970 Cumulative ACIR State Legislative Program, Planned Unit Development 31–91–00 (1969).

5. Christensen, supra note 3, at 516.

an implied dedication of streets and other areas to be used by the public . . . [and] an implied easement of passage over the streets shown on the plan or an equitable servitude to require that items indicated on the plan be maintained.[6]

On policy grounds there might be some objection to the proposal as not preserving enough control in the local government. In urban renewal, for example, which is undertaken by a public, not a private agency, the plan is rather rigid once approved. Urban renewal is typically as or more complex than new town development, so that complexity is not a sound reason justifying flexibility. The fact that a private rather than a public agency is involved in new towns should suggest more rather than less public control. On the other hand, the public subsidy in new town development is ordinarily considerably less, therefore justifying less public control, and some greater flexibility might be justified on the ground that we do not as yet have enough experience with new town development to know the desired quantum of public control.

The two-step approval requirement is not different from that in urban renewal or under typical subdivision ordinances, and final approval of subdivision plats by the planning commission rather than a legislative body is not unique. Indeed, the planning commission rather than the legislative body has total authority to approve subdivisions in many states.

If the developer and the local government are both sensitive to one another's needs and obligations, the new town should evolve in a desirable fashion. In some localities, however, local politicians might be opposed to or feel threatened by massive, new self-contained development. In those situations the developer might well prefer that a fixed rather inflexible plan be adopted so that he can argue a reliance interest that will preclude arbitrary changes. If the local politicians are favorably inclined to the new town, the developer would ordinarily prefer a rather general plan—one that can be changed.[7] Generally speaking, the public desires and the developer is attempting to develop an environment that will have market acceptance. The public's main interest should be that no major externalities of the new development are transferred to the surrounding area and that the developer keep his major promises to initial settlers. The initial settlers have a reliance interest on the developer's promises. These should not be lightly disregarded just because profits become thinner than the developer originally hoped as the project develops, costs escalate and the developer therefore wishes to build more intensively or eliminate improvements and services earlier promised.

6. Id. at 534.

7. Kaplan, The Roles of the Planner and Developer in the New Community, 1965 Wash.U.L.Q. 88.

Plan Changes

Once the planning is finalized, development begins and the plan may be adequate for a few years. However, new towns take many years to complete. Perhaps prior to final completion and surely sometime after completion, life styles will change, and the plan will become outmoded. Models have been offered to handle the problem.

The ULI and ACIR [8] models provide that all provisions of the plan relating to (1) use of land and the use, bulk and location of buildings and structures and (2) the quantity and location of common open space (with exceptions) and (3) the intensity of use or the density of residential units may be modified by the local government. However, the modification does not affect rights of residents to enforce the provisions. Moreover, the modification can occur only after a finding by the local government (or whatever public agency is exercising control) after a hearing, that the development or its environs are not adversely affected and that the modification is not granted solely to confer a special benefit. The models provide that residents may modify the provisions of the plan by a method provided in the plan. But the models do not specify a method.

Mandelker's model similarly provides for approval of plan changes by a local government or agency. Generally, administrative approval is allowed for minor changes and legislative approval required for major changes. However, the Mandelker model also does not indicate how changes are to be authorized by residents.[9]

It may be relatively difficult to change any features of the plan that have been implemented by covenants and restrictions. For example, one model legal document [10] indicates that restrictions and covenants run to the lot owners and their homeowners association and can be changed only by consent of 90 percent of the lot owners for the first 20 years and by consent of 75 percent of the lot owners thereafter. The Urban Land Institute recommends that covenants run twenty-five years, with no provisions for change during that time, but that they can be changed by majority vote thereafter.[11]

 WESTLAW REFERENCES

(planned retirement new +2 community) "new town"

(planned-unit "planned residential" /3 development)

    /s local +5 government

---

8. See supra note 4.

9. D. Mandelker, Controlling Planned Residential Developments (Am.Soc'y of Plan. Officials 1966).

10. U.S. Dep't of Hous. & Urb. Dev., Fed. Hous. Admin. & Veterans Admin.,

Suggested Legal Documents for Planned-Unit Developments 18, FHA Form 1400, VA Form 26–8200, (1965).

11. Urb. Land Inst., The Community Builders Handbook 404 (1960).

Chapter 17

URBAN RENEWAL AND
DOWNTOWN REVITALIZATION

Analysis

§ 17.1 Introduction

The urban renewal program has been one of the most complicated programs for physical control and redevelopment of cities that one could imagine.[1] In addition to the use of many methods of planning and land use control, urban renewal has been further complicated because much of it was federally funded, state enabled and locally administered. The federal program was partially administered from Washington and partially from regional offices, and in most localities the local government created but was not itself the renewal agency. Federal, state and local aspects of renewal, prior to the Housing and Community Development Act of 1974,[2] are described in §§ 17.1–17.6, and provide an historical perspective. After the 1974 Act, the adminis-

§ 17.1

1. The Model Cities Program, which is yet more complicated, deals much more significantly with social and economic matters and is not discussed in this book. It was authorized in 42 U.S.C.A. § 3301. See 1 National Institute for Education in Law and Poverty, Handbook on Housing Law, ch. 111, pt. 111 (1969); Hetzel & Pinsky, The Model Cities Program, 22 Vand.L.Rev. 727 (1969). In 1974, it was discontinued as

a separate program and became part of the Community Development Block Grants. See §§ 17.7, 17.8.

2. For historic treatment of urban renewal, see Johnstone, The Federal Urban Renewal Program, 25 U.Chi.L.Rev. 301 (1958); Comment, Urban Renewal—Essentials of the Federal Program, 48 Ky.L.J. 262 (1960); Comment, The Concept and Objectives of Urban Renewal, 37 S.Cal.L. Rev. 55 (1964).

tration of urban renewal was decentralized. Much of what currently goes on at the local level looks like old style urban renewal, but the primary role of the Department of Housing and Urban Development (HUD) now is to control the strings of the common purse. Another shift in emphasis of the programs has been away from large scale new construction to maintenance and revitalization of older, existing housing stock. The current practices incorporating decentralization and rehabilitation are covered in § 17.7 and § 17.8.

§ 17.2 History—Through Housing Act of 1949

State Laws

The use of public funds to acquire lands and resell them to other private parties, which was the key feature of the beginning of urban renewal, started long before the federal program was developed. New York initiated a program of acquisition of slum dwellings in 1941, by using the power of eminent domain to acquire the property and then turning the land over to limited-dividend redevelopment corporations.[1] The financial inducements generally took the form of partial tax exemption, issuance of tax-exempt bonds and legislation designed to allow redevelopment agencies to take advantage of federal aid for public housing. These inducements were not sufficient to bring about substantial redevelopment despite the presence of enabling laws in about half of the states by 1947.

Housing Policy

In 1949, Congress adopted the Housing Act of 1949 [2] which included a declaration of national housing policy. It noted the housing shortage and the need for the elimination of substandard housing through the clearance of slums and blighted areas, and the realization as soon as feasible of the goal of a decent home and a suitable living environment for every American family. The policy included primary reliance on private enterprise, encouragement of local public bodies to undertake programs, and government assistance to eliminate substandard and inadequate housing through the clearance of slums and blighted areas.[3] Title I of the Act was titled Slum Clearance and Community Development and Redevelopment.

Local Responsibilities

Title I provided that in giving financial assistance, the Administrator [4] was to consider whether local public bodies had a program of

§ 17.2

1. Law of April 29, 1941, ch. 892, [1941] N.Y. Laws 2039 (now N.Y.—McKinney's Priv.Hous.Fin. Law § 200 et seq.). See also Bettman, Draft of an Act for Urban Development and Redevelopment (Am. Soc'y of Planning Officials, Mar. 15, 1943); Comment, Urban Redevelopment, 54 Yale L.J. 116 (1944).

2. 63 Stat. 413 as amended, 42 U.S.C.A. § 1441 et seq.

3. 42 U.S.C.A. § 1441. Citations to U.S.C.A. in this section are to the Code as of 1949.

4. The Housing and Home Finance Administrator, 42 U.S.C.A. § 1460(j).

building, planning and land use controls that would lower housing costs and prevent the recurrence of substandard housing. The Administrator was also to encourage state and regional local public agencies to work together to solve community development and redevelopment problems.[5]

Federal Laws

Forty-year loans were provided to cover the expenditures of local public agencies for the assembly, clearance, preparation and sale and lease of land for redevelopment.[6] Where land was open or predominantly open, ten-year loans were available to localities to provide public buildings or facilities necessary to serve or support the new uses of land.[7] Fund advances to localities were available to enable them to make surveys and plans for preparation of projects, with the advances payable out of funds later received.[8] The obligations issued by localities to fund projects and the income of localities from projects were exempted from federal taxes.[9]

Federal Grants

The federal government also provided capital grants to localities, except for open land projects. With respect to other projects, the grant was up to two thirds of the net project costs.[10] The locality was required to finance one third of the net project costs.[11]

Conditions on Federal Grants and Loans

Conditions were imposed on entities seeking federal aid. A redevelopment plan for the project area approved by the local government was required. The local government also had to find that the financial aid was necessary and was consistent with needs of the locality as a whole to permit redevelopment by private enterprise. The redevelopment plan also had to be found to conform to the general plan of the locality.[12] The purchasers and lessees of land had to devote the land to the uses specified in the redevelopment plan and had to begin to build within a reasonable time.[13] A feasible method for temporary relocation of displaced families was required. The relocation facilities could either be in the project area or in other not generally less desirable areas. They had to be decent and safe, at rents and prices displaced persons could pay and so located to provide reasonable accessibility to the places of employment of relocatees.[14] A public hearing was required before land could be acquired.[15]

5. Id. § 1451.

6. Id. § 1452(a).

7. Id. § 1452(b).

8. Id. § 1452(d).

9. Id. § 1452(g).

10. Id. § 1453(a).

11. Id. § 1454.

12. Id. § 1455(a).

13. Id. § 1455(b).

14. Id. § 1455(c).

15. Id. § 1455(d).

Federal Administrator's Power—Public Housing

The federal administrator could reimburse state or local taxing authorities for any losses of real property taxes caused by the acquisition of property.[16] He could also require covenants and conditions on the project, including provisions that would assure that excessive prices were not paid for the land, to preclude persons holding land for speculation.[17] Public housing authorities redeveloping the land were to pay fair market value for the land they acquired.[18]

Definitions

Definitions were included in the Act.[19] Some of the important definitions included the following: A redevelopment plan was to indicate its relationship to such local objectives as appropriate land uses, improved traffic, public transportation, public utilities, recreational and community facilities and other public improvements and to indicate the proposed land uses and building requirements.[20] A project could include acquisition of slum or deteriorating areas which were predominantly residential. If areas were to be devoted predominantly to residential uses, a project could also include (1) nonresidential deteriorated or deteriorating areas, or (2) land which was open but not being developed because of obsolete platting, diversity of ownership, deterioration of structures or site improvements, and (3) open land deemed necessary for sound community growth.[21] In addition to acquisition, a project could include demolition and removal of buildings and improvements,[22] construction of streets, utilities and other improvements essential to preparation of sites,[23] and the sale and lease of land for development or redevelopment at its fair value for the uses provided in the redevelopment plan.[24]

The one-third financial participation required of the locality could take the form of cash, donations at cash value of land, the cost of demolition or removal work, the cost of improvements in the project area, and the cost of parks, playgrounds and public buildings necessary to serve the project area. If the parks, playgrounds and public buildings also served other areas, the cost could be prorated to qualify as the local contribution.[25]

The gross project cost was defined to include all expenditures of the local public agency plus the amount of local grants-in-aid furnished in forms other than cash.[26] The net project cost was the gross project cost

---

16. Id. § 1456(c)(3).

17. Id. § 1456(c)(7).

18. Id. § 1457.

19. Id. § 1460.

20. Id. § 1460(b).

21. Id. § 1460(c)(1).

22. Id. § 1460(c)(2).

23. Id. § 1460(c)(3).

24. Id. § 1460(c)(4).

25. Id. § 1460(d). The Report of the President's Task Force on Urban Renewal, Urban Renewal: One Tool Among Many 7 (May 1970) recommended that non cash contributions be eliminated since they "have been difficult to assess and . . . have aggravated complexity and delay in the initiation and settlement of projects." Instead, it was recommended that the federal share be increased.

26. 42 U.S.C.A. § 1460(e).

reduced by the total sales prices of all land sold and the capital values of land leased or retained by the local public agency for its own use.[27] A local public agency included any state, county, municipality or other governmental entity or public body authorized to undertake a project.[28]

 WESTLAW REFERENCES

State Laws

148k18.5 /p private!

public! /s fund*** /p acquis! acquir! /s land property

148k167(1) /p federal!

slum blight! /s redevelop! /s corporat! /p limit! /s dividend

268k967(1) /p housing

371k241.1(2) /p redevelop! renew! housing urban

Housing Policy

"housing act of 1949" /s slum blight! /s renew!

42 +5 1441 /s environment!

"housing act of 1949" /s "title I" /s redevelop! rebuild! renew!

"housing act of 1949" /s private

Local Responsibilities

"housing act of 1949" /p "title I" /p local! /p program plan planning planned

Federal Laws

"housing act of 1949" /s fund*** lend! loan! /s redevelop! renew!

"housing act of 1949" /p fund*** lend! loan! /p exempt! /p federal /p tax taxed taxation taxable

Federal Grants

"capital grant" /s housing

Conditions on Federal Grants & Loans

"housing act of 1949" /p redevelop! /p approv! /p local!

"housing act of 1949" /p fund*** /p private! /p redevelop!

relocat! /s redevelop! /s fund***

"uniform relocation assistance and real property acquisition policies act of 1970" 42 +5 4621 /p eligib!

"housing act of 1949" /p hearing /p acquir! acquis!

Federal Administrator's Power—Public Housing

"federal administrator" /p 1949

"federal administrator" /p housing

Definitions

"redevelopment plan" /p relat! /p "housing act of 1949"

42 +5 1460(c)

"housing act of 1949" /p "one third"

---

27. Id. § 1460(f).　　　　　　　　**28.** Id. § 1460(h).

§ 17.3 Evolution of the Federal Program 1950–1964

The federal urban renewal provisions were amended many times, the major change occurring in 1954. The programs became known as urban renewal rather than redevelopment as a result of the 1954 amendments to the Act which added rehabilitation and conservation features.[1] The program was no longer limited to clearance. This program was contained in 42 U.S.C.A. §§ 1450–1469(c)[2] which was entitled Slum Clearance and Urban Renewal.

In 1959, states were induced to increase their efforts by a requirement directing federal administrators to encourage states to establish agencies that could work on a statewide basis to help smaller communities which did not have the technical competency to undertake the program.[3] Through a series of amendments beginning in 1954, requirements that localities have building, planning and land use controls were strengthened. This requirement was called the Workable Program. Loans and grants were available only if a community had a Workable Program for community improvement.[4] The provisions were intended to insure that the need for future clearance would be reduced.

Loans and Advances

The loan provisions[5] were also frequently amended. To accord with the new clearance and conservation thrust, loans were made available to aid in preventing the spread of slums, blight or deterioration and to provide for rehabilitation and conservation. To accelerate projects, temporary loans were authorized which could be obtained prior to approval of an urban renewal plan and thus permit advance acquisition of lands and payment for the cost of demolition and removal of structures.

To provide start up costs and stimulate localities to act, provisions for advances were included. Advances could be made for studies of the feasibility of projects, plans for programs of voluntary repair and rehabilitation and plans for enforcement of land use controls (largely zoning and housing codes) and other preliminary work. Advances were also made available to finance the preparation of a General Neighborhood Renewal Plan.[6]

§ 17.3

1. Literature and studies had recommended this expansion of the program and referred to it as urban renewal. See M. Colean, Renewing Our Cities (1953); President's Advisory Comm. on Gov't Hous. Policies & Programs, A Report to the President of the United States 115 (1953). Colean was also chairman of the Report of the President's Task Force on Urban Renewal, Urban Renewal: One Tool Among Many 6 (May 1970) which recommended further emphasis on improvement of municipal services and on maintenance and rehabilitation of existing structures.

2. References in this section are to U.S. C.A. (1969), as amended through the end of the first session, 91st Cong.

3. See Steele, A State Renewal Program, 43 State Government 111 (1970).

4. 42 U.S.C.A. § 1451(c). See infra § 17.5.

5. 42 U.S.C.A. § 1452.

6. Id. § 1452(d). See infra § 17.5.

Grants

In 1954 and by subsequent amendments, grants were also made available for demonstration projects for the prevention and elimination of slums and urban blight. These grants were made available to nonprofit organizations as well as to public bodies. The grants could be for 90 percent rather than two thirds of program costs and were intended to induce localities to act to develop improved methods for elimination and prevention of slums and blight that would best guide renewal programs in other communities.[7]

Grants were also made available for open land if it was redeveloped for public or low or moderate income housing, so as to encourage that kind of housing. The maximum grants available were increased from two thirds to three fourths in municipalities of less than 50,000 persons as a further inducement to encourage urban renewal in smaller cities.[8] Grants were also made available, beginning in 1959, for the preparation of community renewal programs. These grants were limited to two thirds of the cost.[9]

Conditions for Federal Grants and Loans

The conditions for obtaining federal aid were also changed. Beginning in 1954, the redevelopment plan was called the urban renewal plan in order to embrace the new features of rehabilitation and conservation in addition to redevelopment.[10] Relocation provisions were made applicable to rehabilitation and conservation as well as to redevelopment, and for individuals and businesses as well as families. Many communities had not been adequately providing for relocation so a relocation assistance program was required for each project to determine needs for relocation, provide information and assistance to relocatees and to assure coordination with other governmental actions, particularly low-rent housing projects.[11] After the 1969 amendments, local relocation plans were reviewed by the Secretary every two years,[12] and prior to demolition or removal of residential structures replacement housing had to be made available unless there were a high vacancy rate in the area.[13]

Partially to encourage redevelopment for low and moderate income housing, the local agency was required to publicize the names of redevelopers acquiring land, the redeveloper's estimate of the cost of residential redevelopment and rehabilitation and the redeveloper's estimate of rentals and sales prices of proposed housing.[14] Further pressure in that direction began in 1966, when more housing was required to be built for low and moderate income families. At least half the housing in each community's urban renewal projects had to be for low

7. 42 U.S.C.A. § 1452(a).

8. Id. § 1453(a).

9. Id. § 1453(d). See infra § 17.5.

10. 42 U.S.C.A. § 1455(a).

11. Id. § 1455(c).

12. Id. § 1355(c)(3). See infra § 17.6.

13. 42 U.S.C.A. § 1455(h).

14. Id. § 1455(e).

and moderate income families or individuals and 20 percent of the units for low income families or individuals.[15]

Secretary's Power

Minor changes were made in the powers of the federal administrator of the program, who, after 1967, was the Secretary of Housing and Urban Development.[16] Because many redevelopers were building luxury hotels rather than low and moderate income housing, a specific determination of a need for hotels was required before they could be included in the urban renewal plan.[17] When local agencies did not carry out development as planned, the Secretary was directed to require evidence that projects had been and would be carried out as contracted before additional loans or grants could be made.[18]

Public Housing

To further encourage the development of low income housing, the 1959 amendments allowed the tax exemption required of localities before they could obtain federal aid for public housing to be considered a part of the local contribution.[19]

Definitions

Definitions were changed to mirror the expanded scope of renewal. An urban renewal project could include acquisition of air rights over highways and railroads which had a blighting influence if the rights would be developed for low or moderate income housing or if unsuitable for such use, for industrial or educational facilities.[20] In addition to previous activities, amendments authorized plans for programs of code enforcement or voluntary repair and rehabilitation, acquisition of property in an urban renewal area necessary to eliminate unhealthful conditions, lessen density, eliminate obsolete uses or prevent spread of blight and to promote historic and architectural preservation and provide land for public facilities.[21] A project could also include the construction of foundations and platforms necessary to utilize air rights; acquisitions for repair, rehabilitation and resale or relocation and restoration of structures of architectural or historic significance.[22] To encourage rehabilitation rather than demolition, the Secretary was required to find that the objectives of an urban renewal plan could not be accomplished by rehabilitation prior to making capital grants for demolition or removal.[23] Since too much nonresidential development was occurring, the focus on residential development was strengthened by measures requiring that an urban renewal area be predominantly residential in character and be redeveloped for predominantly residen-

15. Id. § 1455(f).

16. Id. § 1460(j). The urban renewal laws were amended to conform that legislation to the 1965 legislation creating the U.S. Department of Housing and Urban Development.

17. Id. § 1456(g).

18. Id. § 1456(h).

19. Id. § 1457(b). See infra § 17.6.

20. 42 U.S.C.A. § 1400(c)(1)(iv).

21. Id. § 1460(c)(5) & (6).

22. Id. § 1460(c)(7)–(10).

23. Id. § 1460(c).

tial uses, unless nonresidential use was necessary for proper development of the community. In any case, not more than 35 percent of capital grants could be made to projects not primarily residential.[24]

The local grant in aid requirements were amended to provide that part of the benefits from publicly owned facilities used by the public for cultural, exhibitional, or civic purposes or as a city hall, public safety building or public university, hospital or medical school, if built in or near a project area, could be counted as part of the local contribution.[25] If public facilities were paid for by special assessments, the assessments were to be deducted from the cost of the facility in determining the "in lieu of cash" local contribution.[26]

The definition of gross project cost was amended to include local expenditures for the new activities encompassed in the expansion of the program from redevelopment to urban renewal. The definition also excluded certain types of expenses as part of the gross project cost.[27] Amendments also provided that where publicly owned property was not taxed, the exemption could be considered part of the gross project cost and part of the local contribution.[28]

Additional Programs

In 1956, special provisions were made to apply when there was a flood, fire, hurricane, earthquake or storm such that the President determined the locality to be a disaster area.[29] In such an area typical requirements for urban renewal assistance were relaxed. The community did not have to have a workable program before beginning, the renewal plan did not need to conform to a general plan, relocation requirements were not as demanding, the area did not need to be a slum, blighted, deteriorated or deteriorating area.

In 1959 and subsequently, provisions were added so that if an educational institution or a hospital were built in or within one mile of the project area, the urban renewal project did not have to be predominantly residential before and after redevelopment and the expenditures made by institutions for acquisition of land, demolition of buildings and relocation could be counted as part of the required local contribution. An educational institution was restricted to public and nonprofit private schools of higher education and a hospital meant any public or private nonprofit hospital.[30]

In 1961, to provide urban renewal assistance to areas that are economically depressed as described in the Area Redevelopment Act, urban renewal was made available without the requirement that the land be predominantly residential before or after renewal.[31]

24. Id. § 1460(c).

25. Id. § 1460(d).

26. See infra § 17.6.

27. 42 U.S.C.A. § 1460(e).

28. Id. See infra § 17.6.

29. 42 U.S.C.A. § 1462. See id. 1855 et seq. for disaster area legislation.

30. Id. § 1463.

31. Id. § 1464.

WESTLAW REFERENCES

"urban renewal" /p amend! /p 1954 /p act

"slum clearance and urban renewal"

"workable program" /p loan! lend! fund*** grant!

Loans & Advances

42 +5 1452

"general neighborhood renewal plan"

Grants

housing /p "demonstration project"

42 +5 1453

Conditions For Federal Grants & Loans

"urban renewal plan" /s rehabilitat! conserv! redevelop! /s
     relocat!

"relocation assistance program" /p 1969

"united states housing act of 1937" /s federal! /s fund***

local! /s agency /p publi****** /p name /p redevelop!

1966 /p housing /s low moderate /s income /s family

Secretary's Power

sy("secretary of housing and urban development /p determination)

"secretary of housing and urban development" /p "urban renewal
     plan"

"secretary of housing and urban development" /p fund*** grant!
     loan! lend! /p local! /s agency

Public Housing

42 +5 1457

Definitions

"urban renewal project" /p air /s right

authori! /p plan pianned planning program /p "code
     enforcement" /p urban housing renew!

secretary /p "urban renewal plan" /p "capital grant" /p
     rehabilitat! demoli! remov!

42 +5 1460(c) /p residen!

"local contribution" /p urban renew! housing redevelop!

Additional Programs

disaster /p renew! /p urban!

393k82(5)

"area redevelopment act"

---

§ 17.4   Major New Federal Programs 1964–1973

Beginning with amendments in 1964, urban renewal legislation
was amended in an important way by the provision of federal grants
used to pay relocatees to mitigate the expenses of relocating.[1] In 1964
and by subsequent amendments, loans were made available for rehabilitation. Loans were made through local agencies to both owners and
tenants.[2]

§ 17.4   2. Id.

1. See infra § 17.6.

Amendments added in 1965 provided for rehabilitation grants, demolition grants and code enforcement grants.[3] Rehabilitation grants were made to property owners to assist in making repairs necessary to render property decent, safe and sanitary. Demolition grants were made to local governments to pay for the costs of demolition. Concentrated code enforcement grants were made to help localities with their code enforcement programs.

Two important provisions were added in 1968, the interim assistance for blighted areas program[4] and the neighborhood development program. The neighborhood development program (NDP)[5] was established to provide cities more flexibility in urban renewal. Prior to the neighborhood development program, a community determined boundaries of an area needing urban renewal and prepared a detailed plan for renewal which was the basis for federal grants and loans. In many cities, dealing with one small area at a time was not practical because of large residential areas with relatively evenly distributed deterioration and blight.

The neighborhood development programs consisted of urban renewal project undertakings in one or more renewal areas planned and carried out on the basis of annual increments. Generally, the requirements governing these activities were the same as those which governed assistance for regular urban renewal projects (with a workable program being required when any annual increment was authorized). One of the principal differences was that the loan or grant contract for an annual increment of a neighborhood development program covered activities in several contiguous or noncontiguous urban renewal areas, and the funding was based on the amount of loan and grant funds needed to carry out the activities planned during that 12-month period in each of the urban renewal areas contained in the program. Local grants-in-aid were to be calculated as though they were under the regular urban renewal program. Thus, the NDP was primarily a new way of making federal financial aid available.

 WESTLAW REFERENCES

"federal grant" /p relocat! /p urban /s renew!

1964 /p loan! lend! money /p rehabilitat! /p tenant

rehabilitation demolition "code enforcement" /1 grant!

1968 /p "neighborhood development program"

"neighborhood development program" n.d.p. /p "annual increment"

"annual increment" /p "twelve month" "action year"

---

3. Id.

4. Id.

5. 42 U.S.C.A. §§ 1469–1469c. The Report of The President's Task Force on Urban Renewal, Urban Renewal: One Tool Among Many 6 (May 1970) recommends maximum use of the NDP as a way of producing more flexible renewal. It also recommended an increase of efforts seeking to improve municipal services and maintenance and rehabilitation of existing structures.

§ 17.5   Urban Planning and Urban Renewal

Federal urban renewal legislation had no requirement that urban renewal conform to any metropolitan or regional planning. Despite this omission, under the National Environmental Policy Act,[1] an environmental impact statement was required with regard to any major federal action significantly affecting the quality of the human environment.[2] This cut across nearly all federal construction financing, and was designed to assure, to the fullest extent possible, that the expenditure of federal funds would not despoil the environment.[3] NEPA's policy is very broad, and necessarily includes concern for the quality of urban life,[4] and engenders coordination between federal, state and local governments. Agency action must conform to the policies and objectives of the express legislative intent.[5] Remember, however, that NEPA requirements only apply to federal actions.[6]

Local Planning

After the Housing Act of 1949, to obtain federal aid the local government had to make a finding that "the urban renewal plan conforms to a general plan for the development of the locality as a whole."[7] Fortunately, the requirement was not that there actually be a general plan in existence. In the early days, few cities had a general plan and it was not until 1954 that the federal government provided any substantial aid for general planning.[8] The requirement of conformity, however, was intended to stimulate local general planning,[9] and to meet the requirement in good faith, the local renewal agencies often prepared a minimal general plan.[10]

As with the urban renewal plan, a general neighborhood renewal plan [11] must conform "in the determination of the governing body of the locality, to the general plan of the locality as a whole. . . ."[12]

Workable Program for Community Improvement

In the Housing Act of 1949, in allocating slum clearance funds, the Administrator was to "give consideration to the extent to which appropriate local public bodies" modernized their codes.[13] The requirement

§ 17.5

1. 42 U.S.C.A. § 4321 et seq.

2. Id. § 4332.

3. Ely v. Velde, 497 F.2d 252 (4th Cir. 1974).

4. Nucleus of Chicago Homeowners Ass'n v. Lynn, 524 F.2d 255 (7th Cir.1975), cert. denied 424 U.S. 967, 96 S.Ct. 1462, 47 L.Ed.2d 734 (1976).

5. Aertsen v. Landrieu, 637 F.2d 12 (1st Cir.1980); W.A.T.C.H. v. Harris, 603 F.2d 310 (2d Cir.1979), cert. denied 444 U.S. 995, 100 S.Ct. 530, 62 L.Ed.2d 426 (1979).

6. For discussion of NEPA at greater length, see ch. 13 and § 14.7.

7. 42 U.S.C.A. § 1455(a)(iii). In the original Act the urban renewal plan was called the redevelopment plan.

8. See 40 U.S.C.A. § 461.

9. Mandelker, The Comprehensive Planning Requirement in Urban Renewal, 116 U.Pa.L.Rev. 25, 27 (1967).

10. 42 U.S.C.A. § 1455(a)(iii) indicated a plan must be in effect and stated the minimum requirements of the plan.

11. Id. § 1452(d).

12. Id.

13. Id. § 1451(a). Rhyne, The Workable Program—Challenge for Community

was later made mandatory, so that contracts for most types of federal aid for urban renewal and for some other federal programs required a workable program for community improvement.[14]

The workable program was to be an official plan of action for effectively dealing with the problems of blight within the community. Its ultimate goal was to establish well planned and organized residential areas utilizing both public and private resources, and to encourage needed urban rehabilitation.

To be eligible under the plan, a community had to have developed a housing code equivalent to one of the national model codes, a similarly enacted building code, and have made provision for periodic review of these codes. Localities were required to show progress in preparing, adopting or updating general plans.

Community renewal program grants [15] were an attempt to encourage localities to engage in or continue community-wide planning. The program was to include identification of blighted and deteriorated areas and determination of resources needed to renew them. HUD required certain conditions be met before a grant would be made.

The general neighborhood renewal plan [16] was established to allow for planning in areas too large for a single project but considerably smaller than an entire community. The plan provided an outline of renewal activities and indicated where feasible, types of land uses, population densities, rehabilitation requirements and portions of the area set aside for clearance. Costs were allocable to subsequent urban renewal projects,[17] and the statute required that the local agency promptly begin a project and that the project conform with the overall plan of the locality.[18] Funds could be advanced to local governments for project feasibility surveys, but were conditioned on the showing that certain requirements were met.[19]

 WESTLAW REFERENCES

ely +s velde /s federal! /s fund***

n.e.p.a. /p "urban life"

n.e.p.a. /p coordinat! /s federal! /s state /s local!

n.e.p.a. /p apply! applic! /p "federal action" /p defin!

Improvement, 25 Law & Contemp. Probs. 685 (1960).

14. 42 U.S.C.A. § 1451(c). See also U.S. Dep't of Hous. & Urb. Dev., Urban Renewal Handbook, RHA 7204.1, ch. 1 (1968). The Report of The President's Task Force on Urban Renewal, Urban Renewal: One Tool Among Many 6–7 (May 1970) recommended abandonment of the workable program because many communities had deliberately failed to adopt a program so as to exclude federally funded low income

housing. The Task Force recommended that all federal aid be denied to communities which exclude low and moderate income housing.

15. 42 U.S.C.A. § 1453(d).

16. Curry, The Community Renewal Program, 21 Fed.B.J. 358 (1961).

17. Id.

18. Id.

19. Id.

Local Planning

"housing act of 1949"　/p　"urban renewal plan"　　/p　fund***

"general neighborhood renewal plan"

Workable Program for Community Improvement

"workable program for community improvement"

"community renewal program"

§ 17.6　Urban Renewal and Traditional Land Development Control Measures

Urban renewal utilizes most of the development controls discussed in other portions of this book. A brief review of the more important interrelationships follows.

The general plan to which the various urban renewal programs had to conform was required to include a zoning ordinance and map establishing regulations and zone districts governing the use of land, and location, height, use and land coverage of buildings.

Since most urban renewal projects involved a mixture of uses, particularly where there was clearance and redevelopment, a planned unit development zone,[1] which might be called an urban renewal zone, could sometimes be utilized. To increase flexibility, the urban renewal zone might well employ FAR[2] and other flexibility zones such as potential classification, tentative, qualified and overlay zones.[3] Prior to acquisition, or even prior to adoption of an urban renewal plan, a temporary freeze might be put on development in potential urban renewal project areas so as to hold the area in status quo pending completion of renewal plans.[4]

Zoning outside a project area had to be sufficient to protect the area.[5] The zoning itself was done by the local government with which the local urban renewal agency worked.

Subdivision Control

Ordinarily, the land acquired was not disposed of to and developed by a single owner. Therefore, a subdivision of the land was required and the local public agency was required to prepare a preliminary subdivision plat. Public utility easements, both those existing and to be created, which would encumber the project were to be shown on the plat. Each disposal parcel must be identified by number, the area in square feet and the use permitted by the urban renewal plan. Other

---

§ 17.6

1. See infra § 7.15.

2. See supra § 4.7.

3. See supra § 4.14.

4. Such a freeze was upheld in Hunter v. Adams, 180 Cal.App.2d 511, 4 Cal.Rptr. 776 (1960). See Note, Constitutional Law: Restriction of New Construction in Urban Renewal Area Without Compensating the Landowner, 50 Calif.L.Rev. 549 (1962). See also supra § 5.13.

5. U.S. Dep't of Hous. & Urb. Dev., Urban Renewal Handbook, RHA 7207.1, ch. 3 (1968).

requirements imposed under state law for subdivision, if the division of land fell within the statutory definition, were to be observed.

Building and Housing Codes

The use of building and housing codes was an important aspect of urban renewal. Conformity with a nationally promulgated code was required under the Workable Program, and grants were made to localities to assist in carrying out code enforcement projects.[6] Interim assistance grants were available to municipalities to help alleviate harmful conditions in areas stated for clearance or rehabilitation, but which needed immediate action.[7]

HUD utilized local public and private agencies where feasible to make loans to owners or tenants of property to finance rehabilitation. To qualify for loans the property had to be located in an urban renewal area or in a code enforcement area where the rehabilitation was necessary to conform the property to the code requirements or to carry out the objectives of the urban renewal plan. Loans were also available if property was uninsurable because of physical hazards. These loans were made to the owner or tenant of the property to finance such rehabilitation as HUD determined necessary to make the property meet reasonable underwriting standards.[8] The applicant had to be a low income person, and unable to secure a loan elsewhere on comparable terms.[9]

HUD could authorize rehabilitation grants to families and individuals through a local public agency (LPA).[10] Grants were made to owner-occupiers of real property in an urban renewal area to cover the cost of repairs and improvements necessary to make the real property decent, safe and sanitary as required by codes or by other requirements of the urban renewal plan. The grant could also cover the necessary cost of repairs and improvements if the property were in an area (other than an urban renewal or code enforcement area) which the local governing body certified as containing a substantial number of structures which needed repair and improvement. Grants could also be made to owner-occupiers of property which had been determined to be uninsurable because of physical hazards.[11]

HUD could make grants to public bodies and nonprofit organizations "to assist them in developing, testing, and reporting methods and techniques, and carrying out demonstration and other activities for the prevention and elimination of slums and urban blight."[12]

---

6. 42 U.S.C.A. § 1468.

7. Id. § 1468a.

8. Id. § 1452b(a)(1)(C)(ii).

9. Id. § 1452b(a)(2).

10. Id. § 1466.

11. This grant could only rehabilitate the property to make it meet reasonable underwriting standards imposed by such plan. Id. § 1466(b).

12. Id. § 1452a(a).

Nuisance

The relation between code enforcement and acquisition of property with compensation and nuisance law raises an interesting issue concerning the line between the police power and eminent domain.[13] Part of the issue has been previously described,[14] in which the police power is used to require demolition of a building even though the building is in an area scheduled for redevelopment. If the property was acquired by the local agency, compensation would be paid for the building. However, if a building were so bad that it could be "taken" under the police power, why should society pay a slumlord for his nuisance when his building is taken? There are perhaps two answers: first, the state can be more generous than the constitution requires, and second, nothing in fact may be paid for a slum building. While the offer for the acquisition might state a certain sum for the building and a certain sum for the land, which may make the owner believe he is receiving something for the building, it is only the total amount to be paid that concerns the condemnor. In fact, if there were no building on the property, the lot owner might be paid more than an owner of property with a slum building on it. The matter may be complicated somewhat by the method of valuation used. Ultimately, paying for a slum building which is so bad that it warrants demolition must be justified on political, social or efficiency grounds, not because the constitution requires it.

HUD was authorized to make grants to local general purpose governments of two-thirds of the cost of demolition of structures which had been found to be structurally unsound, infested or potentially infested with rats, or unfit for human habitation, and which the locality had the authority to demolish. This program encourages use of the police power rather than eminent domain to rid an area of slum buildings.

Restrictive Covenants

Most urban renewal projects, particularly those dealing with redevelopment, involved complicated arrangements, agreements and controls over the reuse of land. HUD was also authorized to require covenants, conditions, or provisions (including those necessary or desirable to prevent the payment of excessive prices for the acquisition of land) as necessary to assure that the purposes of the statute would be achieved.[15]

The urban renewal plan was partially implemented and maintained through the use of agreements, restrictions and covenants, covering such matters as control of maximum densities, land coverage, setbacks, off-street parking and loading, building height or bulk permit-

---

13. See supra § 3.1, infra § 20.2. See also Dagin & Code, Property, et al. v. Nuisance, et al., 26 Law & Contemp. Probs. 70 (1961).

14. See supra § 8.7.

15. 42 U.S.C.A. § 1467.

ted or required, and restoration and maintenance of properties acquired or moved for historic or architectural preservation. Controls on rentals, sale prices, income limits, construction methods or materials, or financing methods were not imposed unless required by state or local law. However, redevelopment time limitations are imposed on developers as are measures to ensure that at least some housing will be available for sale or rental as low and moderate income housing. The time permitted to complete the obligations of a disposal agreement can be neither so long that it permits the redeveloper to hold the land for speculation nor so short as to be impractical. A declaration of restrictions may be employed to specify land use controls.

The restrictions were partially imposed to assure the constitutionality of urban renewal, for if the property were turned over for unrestricted use, urban renewal might not serve any public purpose and hence be invalid.[16]

Eminent Domain

Eminent domain procedures were undertaken pursuant to state law. State law provided for ordinary condemnation, in which title is transferred at the completion of court proceedings, and may provide for so-called quick-taking or right of immediate possession, in which title is theoretically transferred upon commencement of condemnation proceeding.[17]

While urban redevelopment could be accomplished through acquisition of land by eminent domain, an attempt to negotiate a purchase is the first step. With respect to several federal programs, including urban renewal, federal assistance is not available unless the local agency makes every reasonable attempt to negotiate a purchase.

State statutes defined and the federal law provided funding only for acquisition of certain kinds of property. Most state statutes define "property" to allow full opportunity to exploit federal funding. Financing acquisition under the federal statute was allowed for slums, deteriorated or deteriorating areas, obsoletely platted open land, open land needed for sound community growth if developed for residential use, air rights over transportation facilities, unhealthy, unsafe or unsanitary property, property necessary to promote historic and architectural preservation, land for public facilities, and property to be acquired for repair or rehabilitation and resale. In most instances, the area had to be one where public action was necessary to eliminate a slum, deteriorated or blighted area, or to prevent the development or spread of deterioration and blight. The generic term for these conditions is that the property is blighted.[18]

16. Foeller v. Housing Authority of Portland, 198 Or. 205, 256 P.2d 752 (1953); Davis v. Lubbock, 160 Tex. 38, 326 S.W.2d 699 (1959). See infra § 20.4.

17. Federal quicktaking provisions are in 40 U.S.C.A. § 258a. Almost all states have similar provisions.

18. That is, the property itself is blighted or leads to blight. Open land needed

Blight is an inexact term, though federal guidelines attempt to define it precisely. To be blighted, at least 20 percent of the buildings in an area must contain one or more building deficiencies and the area must contain at least two environmental deficiencies. Building deficiencies include defects that warrant clearance,[19] defects not correctable by ordinary maintenance, extensive minor defects collectively having a deteriorating effect on the surrounding area, inadequate construction or alterations, inadequate or unsafe plumbing, heating or electrical facilities and other similar deficiencies. Environmental deficiencies include overcrowding or improper location of structures, excessive dwelling unit density, conversions to incompatible uses, obsolete building types, adverse influences from noise, smoke or fumes, unsafe, congested or poorly designated streets, inadequate public utilities or community facilities.

Property which could be taken by condemnation was substantially similar to the property which may be acquired by purchase [20] under the statute. The constitutional provision limits the taking of private property for private use, and what constitutes a public use in the urban renewal context has evolved over the years.[21]

The taking of property for urban renewal would generally not have been possible under an actual use test [22] because most land is subsequently resold to different private parties. Condemnation may also be justified because property is in a condition sufficiently detrimental to public welfare (i.e. a slum) that its taking fulfills a public purpose, but the feature of resale to a private developer originally raised questions whether the public purpose remained. Courts found slums to be detrimental to the health and welfare of the community, that they could be eradicated only by taking the property for clearance,[23] and that such a taking was a public purpose. Urban renewal laws provided for the clearance not only of slum property, but of "blighted" property as well, meaning a slum in its incipient stage.

Courts were less willing to sanction condemnation when there were no existing symptoms of blight because less drastic means of slum prevention through the police power might be effective, such as through housing code enforcement. Courts had held, however, that the taking had to be reasonably necessary to the purpose of preventing conditions injurious to the public health and welfare. The conditions had to be more than aesthetically displeasing.[24]

for sound community growth is not blighted.

19. See supra §§ 8.6–.7, infra § 18.6 on condemnation under police power.

20. When property was acquired by negotiated sale, it was difficult for anyone other than the parties involved in the sale to challenge it in court due to standing requirements and the general rules against enjoining expenditures of federal funds.

21. See infra § 20.4 for other contexts.

22. See infra § 20.5.

23. Housing & Redev. Auth. of St. Paul v. Greenman, 255 Minn. 396, 96 N.W.2d 673 (1959); New York City Hous. Auth. v. Miller, 270 N.Y. 333, 1 N.E.2d 153 (1936).

24. See supra §§ 14.1–.5 for discussion of similar limitation on use of police power,

Even if the original condition of the land justified acquisition by eminent domain, it might have been possible to point to intended reuse to establish that eminent domain was actually being exercised for a private purpose or to confer a private benefit. Objections that urban renewal statutes authorized the taking of property for private use because property was to be redeveloped by and for private interests met with little success.[25]

Few subjects generated as much controversy and legal literature in urban renewal as relocation requirements. The federal statute required that there be a feasible method for the temporary relocation of individuals and families being displaced from an urban renewal area as a condition to receiving federal grants and loans.[26]

The 1969 amendment requiring a one to one ratio of housing demolished to housing provided, and another which required HUD to review the effectiveness of relocation programs in each locality every two years were intended to result in *de facto* adequate relocation housing.[27] The administrative requirements for relocation have evolved over the years in an attempt to make certain the requirement is met. The reasons for the less than successful implementation of the requirement stem primarily from the fact that urban renewal has many constituencies that press for project completion. The adequate relocation of the elderly, low income persons and the deprived can add much delay to a process already burdened by many time delays.

The statute also provided for payments to individuals, families, business concerns, and nonprofit organizations displaced because of acquisition, code enforcement, or voluntary rehabilitation activities in connection with urban renewal.[28]

Taxes were utilized to aid urban renewal. Under federal law, the interest on obligations issued by local public agencies for urban renewal projects was exempt from federal taxes as was all income derived from a project by the local agency.[29] These provisions allowed local agencies to borrow money at lower rates than they otherwise could and gave them more revenues with which to pay off the obligations. If project property were made available for a low rent public housing project, the

---

and subsequent evolution of aesthetic regulation.

25. Berman v. Parker, 348 U.S. 26, 75 S.Ct. 98, 99 L.Ed. 27 (1954); Housing & Redev. Auth. of St. Paul v. Greenman, 255 Minn. 396, 96 N.W.2d 673 (1959); Wilson v. Long Branch, 27 N.J. 360, 142 A.2d 837 (1958), cert. denied, 358 U.S. 873, 79 S.Ct. 113, 3 L.Ed.2d 104 (1958); Foeller v. Housing Auth., 198 Or. 205, 256 P.2d 752 (1953); Davis v. Lubbock, 160 Tex. 38, 326 S.W.2d 699 (1959); Miller v. Tacoma, 61 Wn.2d 374, 378 P.2d 464 (1963). Foeller is unusual in its requirement that a public

agency actually hold the property for a time. South Carolina was the only state where acquisition and resale to private parties is still held unconstitutional. Edens v. Columbia, 228 S.C. 563, 91 S.E.2d 280 (1956). Accord Karesh v. City Council of Charleston, 271 S.C. 339, 247 S.E.2d 342 (1978).

26. 42 U.S.C.A. § 1455(c)(1).

27. Id. § 1455(c)(3).

28. Id. § 1465(a).

29. Id. § 1452(g).

real property tax exemption was that required for federal aid for low income housing.[30]

 WESTLAW REFERENCES

"general plan" /p "urban renewal"

"planned unit development zone" p.u.d. /p "eminent domain"

"potential classification" tentative qualified overlay /1 zon!

hunter +s adams /p freez! froz!

Subdivision Control

local! /s preliminary /s subdivi! /s plat****

Building and Housing Codes

build! housing /s code /s "urban renewal"

"workable program" /s requir! condition!

h.u.d. /s financ! fund! /s rehabilitat!

h.u.d. /s financ! fund! loan! lend! /p "urban renewal" "code enforcement" /2 area

l.p.a. "local public agency"

rehabilitat! /p l.p.a. "local public agency"

Nuisance

nuisance /p "police power" /p "eminent domain"

Restrictive Covenants

h.u.d. /s covenant!

"urban renewal plan" /p restriction agreement

h.u.d. /p state local! /s statut! law /p control! /p rent rental

declaration /2 restriction /p land property

(foeller +s portland) (davis +s lubbock) /p urban /s renew!

Eminent Domain

di condemnation

di eminent domain

state /s law statut! /p condemn! /s "quick taking" "right of immediate possession"

urban /s renew! redevelop! /s negotiat! /s purchas!

define* defining definition /3 blight!

"police power" /p "housing code enforcement"

"urban renewal" /p "eminent domain" /p private /s use benefit purpose

"urban renewal" /p relocat! /p "feasible method"

42 +5 1452(g)

§ 17.7 Urban Renewal Since 1974

The Urban Renewal Programs stalled in the early 1970's due to an attempt by then President Nixon to consolidate federal funding for housing and similar areas into what was termed special revenue-sharing.[1] The initial proposal failed, but was followed by a similar

---

30. Id. § 1410(h).

§ 17.7

1. Urban Community Development Revenue Sharing Act of 1971, H.R. 8853,

proposal in the next session of Congress.[2] During the ensuing legislative debates, the administration placed a moratorium on new commitment grants until Congress folded them into the special revenue sharing program, but this attempt to strong-arm Congress failed.[3] A resolution was passed which essentially continued the categorical programs as they existed.[4]

With passage of the Housing and Community Development Act of 1974,[5] Congress expressed its dissatisfaction with the various complex, overlapping federal assistance programs. The Act attempted to consolidate them into a consistent system of federal aid to provide annual assistance, which would enable communities to rely on funding in their planning. It was also intended to encourage community development activities consistent with comprehensive local planning, and to foster coordination of community development activities between federal agencies and local entities.[6]

Title I of the Act essentially terminated federally funded urban renewal projects and folded them into a special revenue-sharing program of Community Development Block Grants (CDBG). Though the old urban renewal statutes no longer control the program they remain in the U.S. Code for definitional purposes. The current approach to renewal under the block grants retains many of the substantive functions of the old program. However, most of the responsibility for oversight rests with states and municipalities. The specific categorical programs replaced were:

1) Public facilities loan program, which had been authorized by Title II of the Housing Amendments of 1955,

2) Open Space Program, authorized by Title VII of the Housing Act of 1961,

3) Planning Advance Program, authorized by § 702 of the Housing Act of 1954,

4) Water/Sewer,

5) Neighborhood Facilities, and

6) Advanced Land Acquisition Programs, all authorized under Title VII of the Housing and Urban Development Act of 1965,

7) Urban Renewal,

8) Code Enforcement, and

9) Neighborhood Development Programs, all three authorized by Title I of the Housing Act of 1949, and

92d Cong., 1st Sess. (1971); S.1618, 92d Cong., 1st Sess. (1971).

2. Better Communities Act, H.R. 7277, 93d Cong., 1st Sess. (1973); S.1742, 93d Cong., 1st Sess. (1973).

3. Advisory Council of Intergovernmental Relations, Community Development:

The Workings of a Federal-Local Block Grant (Mar. 1977).

4. H.J.R. 719, Pub.L. No. 93–117 (1973).

5. Pub.L. No. 94128, 91 Stat. § 1111, 42 U.S.C.A. §§ 5301–08.

6. 42 U.S.C.A. § 5301(d)(1)–(4).

10) Model Cities Program, authorized by Title I of the Demonstration Cities and Metropolitan Development Act of 1966.[7]

Federal oversight of the use of block grant funds is slight, and cities are free to set their own priorities from a list of eligible activities which includes virtually all physical development.[8] The legislation also provided for needs of citizens in smaller communities by guaranteeing that thirty percent[9] of the amount appropriated for block grants would be set aside for use by non-metropolitan and rural communities which do not automatically qualify for entitlements.

Entitlement areas are those metropolitan cities and urban counties which, as defined by the statute, meet both legal and population size criteria.[10] The distributional formula is based on three factors: population, poverty population, and the extent of housing overcrowding.[11] Until 1981, Community Development Block Grant funding was automatic unless the Secretary of HUD determined an application to be inappropriate (a rare occurrence). Recent amendments have changed the presumption so that a local government now may receive funds only if it certifies it is following an approved current housing assistance plan.[12] Funds are distributed proportionally depending upon the city's population relative to other entitlement cities.

To qualify for Block Grant funds, a local government applying as an entitlement area must submit a final statement of community development objectives and projected use of funds, provide certain certifications,[13] and advise the public of the amount of funding available and range of eligible activities. One of the most important aspects of CDBG is the variety of flexible and creative uses to which the funds may be put to support revitalization and redevelopment. In addition to direct loans and grants, projects may be financed through conditional grants or forgivable loans, partial loans, guaranteed loans, and tax exempt credit agreements, for example.[14] The statement of objectives and method of fund distribution must be published and the applicant must also insure that the distribution system and activities within the area are consistent with its final statement, funds are timely distributed and address one of three objectives encompassed by the act, an annual report is prepared and that related laws are complied with.[15]

7. These programs appear at scattered locations in title 42 U.S.C.A. The Housing and Community Development Act of 1974 begins at 42 U.S.C.A. § 5301. Additional information about relevant programs can be found in U.S. Office of Management and Budget, Catalogue of Federal Domestic Assistance Programs.

8. 42 U.S.C.A. § 5305(a)(1)–(18). Compare with activities listed supra § 17.2.

9. 42 U.S.C.A. § 5306(d). The percentage allocated to the discretionary fund was increased from 20 to 30% in 1981.

10. Id. § 5302(a)(3)–(6). A nonentitlement area is one which is not a metropolitan city or part of an urban county. Id. § 5302(a)(7).

11. See DeLeon & LeGates, Community Development Block Grants: Redistribution Effects and Equity Issues, 9 Urb.Law. 364, 368 n. 5 (1977).

12. 42 U.S.C.A. § 5304(c).

13. Id. § 5304(a).

14. U.S. Dep't of HUD, Guide to Housing Rehabilitation Programs.

15. 46 Fed.Reg. 57,256 (1980).

The statement of community objectives required by the act incorporates some of the planning strategies used in categorical grant programs before the 1974 Act. For example, under 1981 regulations, applicants must have a three year plan for use of block grant funds, and activities should be capable of being implemented in a concentrated and coordinated manner.[16] An environmental assessment of a multiyear project must be performed [17] which should encompass the entire multi-year scope of activities.

An entitlement application shall include a summary of a Community Development and Housing Plan which profiles the community in a narrative form and enunciates a comprehensive strategy for neighborhood revitalization, housing, and economic development.[18]

The 1981 Omnibus Budget Reconciliation Act,[19] in which Congress consolidated 57 categorical grants into nine block grants, further extended the opportunity for state and local governments to participate in funding and allocation decisions. The Small Cities Community Development Block Grant Program, initiated by the 1977 Amendments to the Housing and Community Development Act of 1974, was modified. More money was set aside for the grants, and states now administer the block grants to cities within their own borders. Since each state opting into the program determines its own criteria for selecting cities to participate, officials will have the flexibility to choose those activities with higher priorities in that state. HUD's role is limited solely to that of review and audit of applicants.[20]

The Housing and Community Development Act of 1974 [21] phased out most of the then existing housing subsidy programs and created the new, highly flexible Section 8 Housing Assistance Payments Program. Localities were to develop a Housing Assistance Plan as part of their application for block grant assistance, and HUD used these plans to allocate housing subsidies. The Section 8 program applied not only to construction and rehabilitation, but monies could be set aside for rent subsidies to tenants in existing housing which complied with local housing standards. The program was expanded to allow local agencies to allocate subsidies at higher rent levels. This enabled owners of rental housing to complete a moderate level of rehabilitation.

Application for housing block grants is similar to that for community development block grants. Basic to both is the concept of eliminating undue federal influence in local decisionmaking, and reducing the difficulties, delays, and costs inherent in federal processing.[22]

16. 24 C.F.R. § 570.301(a), (6).

17. Id. Pt. 58.

18. Id. § 570.304(a), (b). Many of the components for block grant fund applications reflect portions of earlier urban renewal tools. See supra §§ 17.5, 17.6.

19. Pub.L. No. 97–35, 95 Stat. 358, 385–412, 42 U.S.C.A. §§ 1437–1439, 5301–5320.

20. See generally, Williamson, Community Development Block Grants, 14 Urb. Law. 283 (1983).

21. Pub.L. No. 93–383, 88 Stat. 633, title 2, § 201(a) (1976).

22. Nolon, Reexamining Federal Housing Programs in a Time of Fiscal Austerity: The Trend Toward Block Grants and

With the repeal of the workable program provisions of the Housing Act of 1949, the building and housing code enforcement provisions were also discontinued. The Housing and Community Development Act of 1974 sought to erase the view of code enforcement as punitive and tie it to the goal of providing decent housing and a suitable living environment for all Americans. The Act authorized rehabilitation loans and grants to private property owners and provided for coordination of code enforcement activities with other housing and community development programs so that revitalization could be addressed in a comprehensive fashion.[23] The Rehabilitation Guidelines (1980) are not mandatory but are for use to guide a locality in upgrading and preserving the nations housing and maintaining reasonable standards for health and safety. For example, units leased under the Existing Housing Program [24] must meet twelve performance requirements.[25] These cover such things as sanitary facilities, food preparation areas, space and security, thermal environment and electricity and water supply.[26]

Urban Development Action Grants (UDAG) were brought into existence by the Housing and Urban Development Act of 1977,[27] to complement the block grant program. These grants were intended to help eliminate physical and economic deterioration in severely distressed cities and urban counties through use of federal resources to leverage private capital investment. Eligibility for the program is strictly limited to metropolitan cities and urban counties.[28]

Federal regulations set forth the criteria for selection of projects for actual funding. Of primary concern is the relative degree of physical and economic stress among applicant locales, measured by differences in extent of poverty, growth lag and adjusted age of housing.[29] Other factors considered before a grant is made are the nature and extent of private participation in the project, the number of permanent employment opportunities created, and the increase in an area's tax base.

Action grants can be obtained for all activities that are included under the block grant program, and any additional community development and conservation activities which the secretary considers consistent with the legislative purpose.[30] The requirements for an urban development action grant are fairly strict. Applications should include a detailed description of public and private components of the project, estimated costs, a performance schedule, and assurances that the applicant has complied with the citizen participation requirements. The Act

Housing Allowances, 14 Urb.Law. 249 (1982).

23. 42 U.S.C.A. §§ 5305(a)(3), 5301(c).

24. Id. § 1473(g). This is also known as the Section 8, Housing Assistance Payments Program.

25. See discussion of performance standards supra § 8.1.

26. 24 C.F.R. § 882 et seq.

27. Pub.L. No. 95–128, 91 Stat. 111 (1977), 42 U.S.C.A. §§ 5318–5320.

28. 24 C.F.R. § 570.3(w).

29. 42 U.S.C.A. § 5318(d)(1).

30. Id. § 5318(b).

also requires the applicant to identify any historic buildings which are on or eligible for inclusion on the National Register of Historic Places, and determine what effect if any the proposed project would have on the buildings, and to assure the secretary that the applicant will comply with the requirements relating to historic buildings.[31]

Approval by HUD is preliminary, as the applicant must tender legally binding commitments from the private sector prior to using grant funds. Until those commitments are submitted and accepted by HUD the applicant cannot draw on its letter of credit.

On the whole, the program has been fairly successful. For example it is estimated that in its first year of operation it leveraged an average of eight dollars of private sector monies to every federal dollar for investment in distressed communities.[32]

One project, in Baltimore, Maryland, involved $10 million in UDAG funding for a second mortgage loan to build a new hotel in the Inner Harbor area, and pedestrian walkways to connect the hotel to a new convention center and shoreline attraction. There was $68,500,000 of private funds committed to the project, and over $6 million in local funds. The city is an equity participant in the hotel and shares the profits; the number of new permanent jobs created exceeds 1600. Most were to be filled by persons of low or moderate income.[33]

 WESTLAW REFERENCES
"special revenue sharing"

"housing and community development act of 1974" /p consolidat!
/s federal!

"housing and community development act of 1974" /s "title I"

c.d.b.g. /p renew!

c.d.b.g. "block grant" /p rural

"community development block grant" c.d.b.g. /p entitlement /s
city county area

"community development block grant" c.d.b.g. /p certif!

"block grant" c.d.b.g. /p statement /s objective

"block grant" c.d.b.g. /p three /3 year /s plan planned
planning planner

"1981 omnibus budget reconciliation act"

"small cities community development block grant program"

"section 8" /p rent /s subsid! /p housing /p local!

"existing housing program"

u.d.a.g. "urban development action grant" /p regulat!

e.d.a.g. "economic development administration grant"

---

31. Id. §§ 5318(c)(4), 5320.

32. C. Duerksen, Handbook of Historic Preservation Law, 310 (1983).

33. Ellison, Urban Development Action Grant Program: Using Federal Funds to Leverage Private Investment in Distressed

Communities, 11 Urb.Law. 424 (1979). See also Greene, UDAG: Federal Carrots for Private Economic Revitalization of Depressed Urban Areas, 3 Urb.L. & Policy 235 (1980).

§ 17.8 Current Trends in Urban Renewal

De-federalization of many government programs has returned increasing choices and challenges to the states. This trend can be seen in the urban renewal programs, particularly since the Housing and Community Development Act of 1974. Amendments to the Act have expanded the block grant format for urban renewal projects and collapsed more categorical programs into block grants.[1]

Federal involvement has generally been pared to a minimum and HUD's primary role in the urban renewal area is to review applications and audit the progress of applicants. State and local governments determine their own priorities and spending needs. Federal policy also seeks to involve private sector investment in urban renewal projects by making it financially advantageous for businesses to do so. The UDAG program is a prime example of this trend.

Incentives have been built into the federal taxation scheme to encourage rehabilitation of existing housing stock. The Tax Reform Act of 1976[2] provided for an increase in the amount of eligible rehabilitation expenditures that could be depreciated,[3] and revised the definition of low income rental units to be consistent with the Section 8 leased housing program.[4] In 1981, the Economic Recovery Tax Act expanded the incentives for rehabilitation of Certified Historic Structures by providing for investment tax credits.[5] Measures which specify allowable depreciation and call for recapture of excess depreciation were modified with regard to residential property rented to low-income families.[6]

Attempts to revitalize deteriorating areas by attracting commercial ventures have also been considered. There are two ways this can be done: by use of tax increment financing and designation of enterprise zones.

Tax increment financing is an innovative tool that local governments can use to raise their local share of funds for block grants or UDAG.[7] The *ad valorem* taxes levied on a redevelopment area are divided into two parts: that levied on the base value (assessed value at

---

§ 17.8

1. The UDAG program was established by the Housing and Community Development Act 1977, Pub.L. No. 95–128, 91 Stat. 111 (1977), and further changes occurred with passage of the Omnibus Budget Reconciliation Act of 1981, Pub.L. No. 97–35, 95 Stat. 358 (1981). See 42 U.S.C.A. §§ 5318–20.

2. Pub.L. No. 94–455, 90 Stat. 1525 (1976).

3. 26 U.S.C.A. § 167(k)(2)(A).

4. Id. § 167(k)(3)(B).

5. Id. § 48(g)(3)(A), (B). See also supra § 14.8.

6. Accelerated Cost Recovery System, 26 U.S.C.A. § 168. See also id. §§ 168(b) (4), 1245, 1250. And see Depreciation and Investment Tax Credit, 36 Tax L. 973 (Summer, 1983).

7. See, e.g., Reece & Confe, Urban Redevelopment: Utilization of Tax Increment Financing, 19 Washburn L.J. 536 (1980), Comment, Tax Increment Financing for Development and Redevelopment, 61 Or.L. Rev. 123 (1982) and Note, Tax Increment Financing, New Source of Funds for Community Redevelopment in Illinois, 30 DePaul L.Rev. 459 (1981).

the time the project began) is allocated to cities, counties, schools and other taxing districts, as usual; the tax levied on the increment (excess of assessed value over base value) goes to the redevelopment authority. The monies may be used to finance public costs of redevelopment or to repay bonds previously issued to raise revenue for redevelopment. The theory was that without such projects property values would not increase and taxes levied on the increment and allocated to redevelopment would not affect local taxing units. After the redevelopment is completed, the taxing units benefit from the increase in property taxes. Enabling legislation has been enacted in almost half the states largely as a result of the shift from federal urban renewal programs to block grants.[8] Enterprise zones are locally nominated, federally designated, economically deteriorated urban areas into which commercial activity is attracted and jobs created.[9] Several proposals have been presented to Congress but none has been adopted.[10] Generally the plans contain reductions of tax rates or fees, attempts to increase the level and efficiency of local services,[11] provisions to streamline government regulation, and incentives to obtain commitments from the private sector to provide jobs and job training for low income residents. Income tax incentives for businesses are split between employers and employees.

Twenty states have designated and operative enterprise zones functioning within their borders or statutes now on their books enabling such activity.[12] Virginia's plan [13] provides for tax incentives to encourage business participation in designated areas, and allows some regulatory flexibility at the local level by use of special zoning districts, ordinance exemption and permit process reform.

Questions regarding the effectiveness of enterprise zones concern whether such proposals will really attract business and serve to revitalize an area. Another problem surrounds the ability of government to defend its standards for an area and show that they relate to criteria for accomplishing revitalization and redevelopment goals. It is possible that such plans might result in unfair treatment of some firms to the detriment of others. Lack of federal aid to enterprise zone areas may also be a problem. The British experience with the programs indicates that tax breaks and regulatory simplification alone may not be enough.[14]

8. Comment, Tax Increment Financing, supra note 7, at 126.

9. See generally, Unger, Enterprise Zones: Some Perspectives on Anglo-American Developments, 5 Urb.L. & Policy 129 (1982).

10. McKee, Treasury Details Enterprise Zone Proposal, 15 Tax Notes 456 (May, 1983) (reporting on testimony before the Senate Finance Committee, April 22, 1983).

11. This is done by experimenting with contracts with private groups to provide the services, and trying to avoid monopoly

problems. See Community Communications Co., Inc. v. Boulder, 455 U.S. 40, 102 S.Ct. 835, 70 L.Ed.2d 810 (1982).

12. They are Arkansas, Indiana, Illinois, Kentucky, Minnesota, Mississippi, Missouri, Nevada, Oklahoma, Rhode Island, Texas, and Virginia, Connecticut, Delaware, Florida, Kansas, Louisiana, Maryland, Ohio, and Pennsylvania.

13. Va. Code §§ 59.1–270 to 59.1–284.

14. Callies & Tamashiro, Enterprise Zones: The Redevelopment Sweepstakes Begins, 15 Urb.Law. 231 (1983). See also,

The enterprise zone proposals raise yet another spectre for deteriorated areas. Some fear that a commercial gentrification might result, as rising property values begin to drive out poorer residents and marginal businesses.

Gentrification is a side effect of urban revitalization. As new residents move into an area and property values rise, lower income family units move out. The phenomenon is called displacement,[15] and is a problem because it is often very difficult for this group to find new housing. Relocation payments provided to those displaced by government intervention do not extend to cover persons displaced by gentrification. Studies have shown that lower income groups of displaced persons usually find less satisfactory housing at higher rents.[16]

Urban renewal, as a cohesive federal program to revitalize slums and blighted areas has been largely dismantled. Once-centralized control has been shifted to the states and localities, which determine their own needs and devise plans to meet them. Though the ultimate financial source for most funding is the federal government, as appropriations are cut, there will be increasing reliance on local resources and private sector investment.

 WESTLAW REFERENCES

"housing and urban development" h.u.d. /p review! +s applica!
    /p "urban renewal"

"housing and urban development" h.u.d. /p audit! /p applica!

"tax increment financing"

"enterprise zone"

"urban renewal" /p displac! /p relocat! /p expose cost
    expenditure

gentrification

Frank, Enterprise Zone Proposals: Incentives to Revive Our Decaying Inner Cities, 110 J.Legis. 425 (1983), and Unger, Enterprise Zones, Some Perspectives on Anglo-American Developments, 5 Urb.L. & Policy 129 (1982).

15. Salsich, Displacement and Urban Reinvestment: A Mount Laurel perspective, 53 U.Cin.L.Rev. 333 (1984).

16. LeGates & Hartman, Gentrification-Caused Displacement, 14 Urb.Law. 31 (1982); White, Gentrification, Tipping and National Housing Policy, 11 N.Y.U.L.Rev. & Soc. Change 255 (1983).

Chapter 18

NUISANCES

Analysis

---

§ 18.1 Introduction

Nuisance is a form of private land use control, although it is public in nature because it stems from a common law attempt by the courts to impose conduct on land users and does not arise out of contract. Zoning might be said to have emerged from private nuisance law as a more sensitive scheme for finding a place for every land use with every land use in its place. The nuisance law scheme, by way of contrast, classifies uses only grossly.

The spread of comprehensive zoning has decreased the use of nuisance law to prevent discordant land uses.[1] But zoning has raised expectations, and if the local legislative body fails to deal with incompatible development through zoning, persons still turn to the courts for protection through the application of nuisance law.[2]

Each party to a land use conflict (including nuisance actions) is seeking some measure of control over the local environment. The subject matter of land-use regulation is the distribution of this local environmental control.[3] There are several types of common law nui-

---

§ 18.1

1. Use of nuisance law reached a zenith in the 1920's and 1930's as landowners invoked it to relieve actual or threatened noxious uses in their neighborhoods. Ellickson, Alternatives to Zoning, 40 U.Chi.L. Rev. 681, 721 & n. 15 (1973).

2. Beuscher & Morrison, Judicial Zoning Through Recent Nuisance Cases, 1955 Ariz.L.Rev. 440. See also F. Schnidman, S.

Abrams & J. Delaney, Handling the Land Use Case § 7.1.6 (1984); Coquillette, Mosses From an Old Manse: Another Look at Some Historic Property Cases About the Environment, 64 Cornell L.Rev. 761 (1979); Rabin, Nuisance Law: Rethinking Fundamental Assumptions, 63 Va.L.Rev. 1299 (1977).

3. Freeman, Give and Take: Distributing Local Environmental Control Through

sances, public and private nuisance, nuisance per se, and nuisance in fact.

A public nuisance is an unreasonable interference with a right common to the general public which impairs the health, safety, morals and comfort of the community. It may be conduct which is proscribed by statute, and may not necessarily harm particular property rights in any way. Public nuisance is usually continuing in nature or has produced either a long term or permanent effect, and the actor would have reason to know of that effect on the common right.[4]

Private nuisance involves nontrespassory invasion of another's interest in the private use and enjoyment of land. One may be subject to liability for private nuisance only if one's conduct is the legal cause of the invasion of another's right. The invasion must be intentional and unreasonable, or unintentional and otherwise actionable under rules of negligence, reckless conduct or abnormally dangerous situations.[5]

Although theoretically quite distinct, the distinction between public and private nuisances may be of little practical significance. A public nuisance often is also a private nuisance,[6] individuals are frequently granted rights to sue under regulatory ordinances,[7] and many plaintiffs may be joined in one action.

A nuisance per se is defined as an activity, occupation, or structure which is a nuisance at all times and under any circumstances regardless of location. It is so as a matter of law. A nuisance in fact is an activity, operation or structure which constitutes a nuisance only because of its location, surroundings or manner of operation.

Most nuisances are nuisances in fact because most harm producing activity is lawful somewhere and even socially productive. It becomes unlawful only when its utility does not outweigh the harm to other interests.[8] This principle was recognized as early as the seventeenth century in England.

William Aldred's Case[9] was a private nuisance action brought to enjoin the operation of a pig sty next door to the plaintiff's dwelling.

Land Use Regulation, 60 Minn.L.Rev. 883 (1976). See also Juergensmeyer, Control of Air Pollution Through the Assertion of Private Rights, 1967 Duke L.J. 1126; Juergensmeyer, Common Law Remedies and Protection of the Environment, 1971 Un.Brit.Col.L.Rev. 215.

4. Restatement (Second) of Torts § 821B (1976).

5. Id. § 822. See, e.g., Lunda v. Matthews, 46 Or.App. 701, 613 P.2d 63 (1980); Conlon v. Farmington, 29 Conn.Supp. 230, 280 A.2d 896 (1971).

6. Venuto v. Owens-Corning Fiberglas Corp., 22 Cal.App.3d 116, 99 Cal.Rptr. 350 (1971).

7. See, e.g., West's Ann.Cal.Civ.Proc. Code § 731a (allows suit for damages but precludes injunction for allowed industrial or commercial uses); West's Fla.Stat.Ann. § 60.05(1) (same).

8. Balancing the utilities doctrine stems from dictum, not the holding, in St. Helens Smelting Co. v. Tipping, 11 Eng. Rep. 1483 (H.L.1865), but compare with analysis of "sic utere tuo" doctrine in Rocha v. Socony-Vacuum Corp., 54 R.I. 411, 173 A. 627 (1934).

9. William Aldred's Case, 9 Coke 57b, 77 Eng.Rep. 816 (K.B. 1611).

The court found the sty to be a nuisance, and that smell and light were protectible interests. This was an early, successful attempt to internalize social costs of certain uses of property. Courts were vested with the discretion to determine the extent of natural rights of property ownership that could be protected by court-fashioned remedies.

Since that time there have been changes and advances in technology which have caused some shifting of the rights which inure in property ownership.[10] Whatever the relative values of the competing uses, it seems that the initial assignment of legal rights does not determine which use ultimately prevails. The efficient value-maximizing accommodation of the conflict will be adopted, whichever party is granted the legal right to exclude interference by the other.

There are some cases in which the costs of transferring the property right are so high that voluntary transfer is not feasible. Placing liability on the party who causes the damage may not be the most efficient solution of the conflict. The common law of nuisance was an attempt to obtain optimal resource use by assigning property rights to the more valuable use between conflicting land uses.[11]

 WESTLAW REFERENCES

"public nuisance" /10 define* definition

di nuisance

"private nuisance" /s defin!

(lunda +s matthews) (conlon +s farmington) /p nuisance

"nuisance per se" /s defin!

"nuisance in fact" /s harm utility

"nuisance in fact" /p outweigh!

venuto +s owens-corning +s fiberglas

(morris +s ciborowski) (prah +s maretti) /p property

§ 18.2 Public Nuisances

Public nuisances may encompass such diverse activities as polluting water supply,[1] running a disorderly saloon,[2] maintaining a structure which endangers persons passing on a highway,[3] or running a business which generates noxious odors near the center of a city's business district.[4]

---

10. See, e.g., Illinois v. Butterfield, 396 F.Supp. 632 (N.D.Ill.1975) (airport noise); Morris v. Ciborowski, 113 N.H. 563, 311 A.2d 296 (1973) (same). See also Prah v. Maretti, 108 Wis.2d 223, 321 N.W.2d 182 (1982) (access to sun for solar heating as protectible property interest).

11. R. Posner, Economic Analysis of the Law 16 (1972). See Coase, The Problem of Social Cost, 3 J.L. & Econ. 1 (1960).

§ 18.2

1. Nelson v. Swedish Evangelical Lutheran Cemetery Ass'n, 111 Minn. 149, 126 N.W. 723 (1910).

2. Taylor v. State ex rel. Adams, 275 Ala. 430, 155 So.2d 595 (1963).

3. Boyle v. Neisner Bros., 230 Mo.App. 90, 87 S.W.2d 227 (1935).

4. Fort Smith v. Western Hide & Fur Co., 153 Ark. 99, 239 S.W. 724 (1922).

The state has inherent power to declare what constitutes a public nuisance.[5] In addition, many states have enacted legislation permitting municipalities to define what uses constitute a public nuisance.[6] A city may by ordinance declare a thing to be a nuisance which was not a nuisance at common law.[7]

Public nuisances may always be abated by the state, acting in the public interest,[8] and to the extent that charter powers, or legislative authorizations, or home rule powers permit, by a county or municipality which suffers special injuries to its local interests.[9] Injunctive relief in favor of the state has been freely allowed in cases of public nuisances.[10] In the absence of statutory provision therefore, compensation need not be made for the destruction or damage of property incurred in the abatement of a public nuisance.[11]

When a private individual suffers special injuries, different in kind rather than degree from those of the general public, he can generally recover damages notwithstanding the public character of the nuisance if proof of substantial injury is made.[12]

 WESTLAW REFERENCES

(nelson +s swedish +s evangelical) (taylor +s state +s adams) (boyle +s neisner) (fort +s smith +s western +s fur)

to(279) /p state /p authori! power! empower! /p declar! /p "public nuisance"

municipality /s declar! /s "public nuisance"

municipality /s ordinance /s "public nuisance"

(lane +s mount +s vernon) (commonwealth +s baker) (people +s lim) /p "common law" & nuisance

state /s abat! /s "public interest" /s "public nuisance"

compensat! /s "public nuisance" /s abat!

sy("public nuisance" /s enjoin! /s state)

"public nuisance" /s private /s damage /s special

---

5. Goldblatt v. Town of Hempstead, 369 U.S. 590, 82 S.Ct. 987, 8 L.Ed.2d 130 (1962); Lawton v. Steele, 152 U.S. 133, 14 S.Ct. 499, 38 L.Ed. 385 (1894).

6. Vernon's Ann.Tex.Civ.Stat. art. 1175(19); W.Va. Code 8–12–5(23).

7. Lane v. Mt. Vernon, 38 N.Y.2d 344, 379 N.Y.S.2d 798, 342 N.E.2d 571 (1976); Commonwealth v. Baker, 160 Pa.Super. 640, 53 A.2d 829 (1947). Cf. People v. Lim et al., 18 Cal.2d 872, 118 P.2d 472 (1941).

8. Copart Indus., Inc. v. Consolidated Edison Co., Inc., 41 N.Y.2d 564, 394 N.Y.S.2d 169, 362 N.E.2d 968 (1977), reargument denied 42 N.Y.2d 1102, 399 N.Y.S.2d 1028, 369 N.E.2d 1198 (1977).

9. State ex rel. Schneider v. Stewart, 575 S.W.2d 904 (Mo.App.1978); Village of Riverwoods v. Untermeyer, 52 Ill.App.3d 816, 12 Ill.Dec. 371, 369 N.E.2d 1385 (1977); State ex rel. Hoffman v. Swift Co., 127 Kan. 817, 275 P. 176 (1929).

10. Town of Greenwich v. Stepping Stone Enter., Ltd., 122 R.I. 132, 416 A.2d 659 (1979); Black v. Circuit Court of 8th Judicial Circuit, 78 S.D. 302, 101 N.W.2d 520 (1960).

11. 6 E. McQuillin, Municipal Corporations § 24.74 (3d ed.rev.1980). See also Miller v. Schoene, 276 U.S. 272, 48 S.Ct. 246, 72 L.Ed. 568 (1928).

12. Town of Surfside v. County Line Land Co., 340 So.2d 1287 (Fla.3d D.C.A.1977), cert. denied 352 So.2d 175 (1977); Woods v. Johnson, 241 Cal.App.2d 278, 50 Cal.Rptr. 515 (1966). Cf. Gilmore v. Monroeville, 384 So.2d 1080 (Ala.1980).

§ 18.3   Private Nuisances

Private nuisances generally encompass interferences with land, but may encompass interference with the occupants' comfort and health,[1] and, in some cases, with the occupants' peace of mind.[2] For example, some courts will enjoin the erection of gas stations or funeral homes in residential areas.[3] Other courts have held that funeral homes are not necessarily nuisances in a residential area and must be shown to cause material rather than mental discomfort.[4] The first view is analogous to nuisance per se; the second analysis resembles nuisance in fact. The variation is probably based on differing opinions whether peace of mind is a protectible interest, the interference with which will constitute a nuisance.[5]

Generally, activities which offend aesthetic sensibilities, such as interferences with sight or view, are not considered nuisances.[6] This is changing, however, in favor of aesthetic regulation for certain specific purposes, such as maintenance of property values,[7] elimination of visual pollution,[8] or preservation of historic areas and structures.[9]

Most nuisance cases turn on factual considerations, such as the use being made of the plaintiff's property, the use being made of the defendant's property, the character of the neighborhood, and the frequency and extent of the injury.[10] Other things considered include the social value of the respective uses, the suitability of the uses to the character of the locality, and the ability of the plaintiff or the defendant to prevent or avoid the harm.[11] A residential use in a residential area is generally protected against subsequent encroachment by busi-

§ 18.3

1. Reynolds Metals v. Yturbide, 258 F.2d 321 (9th Cir.1958), cert. denied 358 U.S. 840, 79 S.Ct. 66, 3 L.Ed.2d 76 (1959). See also McCastle v. Rollins Envtl. Servs., 514 F.Supp. 936 (M.D.La.1981).

2. E.g., Adams v. Snouffer, 88 Ohio App. 79, 82, 87 N.E.2d 484, 486 (1949); Jordan v. Luippold, 189 Okl. 189, 191, 114 P.2d 917, 918 (1941).

3. Phillips v. Adams, 228 Ark. 592, 309 S.W.2d 205 (1958) (construction of gas station enjoined in residential neighborhood); Powell v. Taylor, 222 Ark. 896, 263 S.W.2d 906 (1954) (operation of funeral home enjoined in residential area). See generally Annot., 8 A.L.R.4th 324 (1979).

4. State ex rel. Cunningham v. Feezell, 218 Tenn. 17, 400 S.W.2d 716 (1966); McCaw v. Harrison, 259 S.W.2d 457 (Ky.1953).

5. See supra § 4.22 (funeral homes).

6. Fontainebleau Hotel Corp. v. Forty-five Twenty-five, Inc., 114 So.2d 357 (Fla.3d D.C.A.1959), cert. denied 117 So.2d 842 (1960); Livingston v. Davis, 243 Iowa 21, 50 N.W.2d 592 (1951). Cf. Prah v. Maretti,

108 Wis.2d 223, 321 N.W.2d 182 (1982); Parkersburg Builders Material Co. v. Barrack, 118 W.Va. 608, 191 S.E. 368 (1937). The rule is different in some foreign common law jurisdictions which follow the English doctrine of "ancient lights."

7. See generally Puritan Holding Co. v. Holloschitz, 82 Misc.2d 905, 372 N.Y.S.2d 500 (1975); Note, Aesthetic Nuisances: An Emerging Cause of Action, 45 N.Y.U.L. Rev. 1075 (1976); supra ch. 14, "Aesthetic Regulation and Historic Preservation."

8. Mahoney v. Walker, 157 W.Va. 882, 205 S.E.2d 692 (1974).

9. See, e.g., Penn Central Transportation, Inc. v. New York, 438 U.S. 104, 98 S.Ct. 2646, 57 L.Ed.2d 631 (1978), rehearing denied 439 U.S. 883, 99 S.Ct. 226, 58 L.Ed. 2d 198 (1978).

10. See Beuscher & Morrison, Judicial Zoning Through Recent Nuisance Cases, 1955 Ariz.L.Rev. 440, for discussion of the impact of zoning considerations on judicial decisionmaking in nuisance cases.

11. Restatement (Second) of Torts §§ 826–31 (1976).

ness or industrial interests.[12] Conversely, where an area is not predominately residential, courts tend to permit whatever use is appropriate to the area, emphasizing the business necessity or social desirability of the defendant's activity.[13]

Courts may also consider potential future development as well as present usage to determine whether a particular use is so incompatible as to constitute a nuisance.[14] The degree of use rather than type of use may warrant finding of a nuisance.[15]

Generally, an intentional or unintentional invasion of another's interest in the use and enjoyment of his property is a basis for liability, regardless of the degree of care or skill exercised to avoid injury. It is not necessary to show that the conduct is negligent, reckless or ultrahazardous.[16] An otherwise lawful use may constitute a nuisance if it is part of a general scheme to annoy a neighbor, or if the main purpose of the use is to prevent him from the enjoyment of his own property.[17]

WESTLAW REFERENCES

"private nuisance" /s health /s comfort

"private nuisance" /p "peace of mind"

(adams +s snouffer) (jordan luippold)

"funeral home" "gas station" /p "private nuisance"

(cunningham +s feezell) (mccaw +s harrison)

sy(nuisance /s view /s interfer!)

"ancient lights"

sy(nuisance /s property land /s valu! /s reduc!)

nuisance /p visual! /p pollut!

nuisance /p social community /p valu! /p use /p property land

nuisance /p able ability /p prevent! avoid! /p harm!

(schlotfelt +s vincent +5 farmers +5 supply) (bortz +5 troth) (essick +5 shillam) & nuisance

oak +s haven +s western +s wayne

unintentional! /s inva**** /s use /s enjoyment /s property

---

12. Schlotfelt v. Vinton Farmers Supply Co., 252 Iowa 1102, 109 N.W.2d 695 (1961); Bortz v. Troth, 359 Pa. 326, 59 A.2d 93 (1948). See Freeman, Give and Take: Distributing Local Environmental Control Through Land Use Regulation, 60 Minn.L. Rev. 883, 894–962 (1976). But cf. Essick v. Shillam, 347 Pa. 373, 32 A.2d 416 (1943).

13. Daniel v. Kosh, 173 Va. 352, 4 S.E.2d 381 (1939). Legislation has become necessary to protect certain uses, such as farming, from threat of nuisance actions. E.g., West's Fla.Stat.Ann. § 823.14.

14. E.g., Oak Haven Trailer Court, Inc. v. Western Wayne County Conservation Ass'n, 3 Mich.App. 83, 141 N.W.2d 645,

affirmed 380 Mich. 526, 158 N.W.2d 463 (1967).

15. Macievich v. Anderson, 4 D.L.R. 507 (Man.Ct.App.1952). See also Parker v. American Woolen Co., 195 Mass. 591, 81 N.E. 468 (1907); Mitchell v. Hines, 305 Mich. 296, 9 N.W.2d 547 (1943).

16. Ryan v. Emmetsburg, 232 Iowa 600, 4 N.W.2d 435 (1942); Morgan v. High Penn. Oil Co., 238 N.C. 185, 77 S.E.2d 682 (1953); Russell Transp. Ltd. v. Ontario Malleable Iron Co., 4 D.L.R. 719 (Ont.High Ct.1952).

17. Hutcherson v. Alexander, 264 Cal. App.2d 126, 70 Cal.Rptr. 366 (1968).

§ 18.4 Remedies

Compensatory damages, measured by the character and extent of the injury to the plaintiff's property interest are always recoverable. Where an interference is permanent, claims for both past and prospective injuries may be joined in a single cause of action,[1] otherwise, successive actions must be had for actual, not prospective, losses.[2]

Where no adequate legal remedy exists, an injunction instead of or in addition to damages can be obtained. An injunction is possible where the injury is irreparable, even if the consequential damages are small.[3] Similarly, an injunction is possible where damages would not adequately compensate for the threatened loss or because otherwise there would be a multiplicity of actions at law.[4]

Most courts will balance the relative hardships, and if the hardship to the defendant is considerable, compared to harm to the plaintiff, the court will deny injunctive relief and award money damages.[5] Boomer v. Atlantic Cement Co.[6] was an unusual example of this type remedy. The defendant's cement operation caused dust and ground tremors which disturbed neighboring houses. Plaintiffs asked the court for injunctive relief. Yet, after balancing the benefits of the defendant's presence in the community, its investment and the number of people it employed against the amount of damage suffered by the plaintiffs, the court denied the injunction. It awarded permanent damages instead and barred future actions. However, some courts will issue an injunction as a matter of course where they have found a nuisance exists.[7] This is a much less frequent occurrence, however.

An injunction may be made temporary and conditional where the defendant can reduce or abate the interference by reasonable changes in the conduct of his activities.[8]

Damages and conditional injunctions appear to be the most efficient remedies for nuisance. Award of damages against a nuisance serves to internalize the costs and permits the defendant to make his own cost-benefit analysis of preventive measures. Conditional injunc-

§ 18.4

1. Northern Ind. Pub. Serv. Co. v. Vesey, 210 Ind. 338, 200 N.E. 620 (1936).

2. Ryan v. Emmetsburg, 232 Iowa 600, 4 N.W.2d 435 (1942).

3. Hart v. Wagner, 184 Md. 40, 40 A.2d 47 (1944). Cf. Waschak v. Moffat, 379 Pa. 441, 109 A.2d 310 (1954).

4. Hennessy v. Carmony, 50 N.J.Eq. 616, 25 A. 374 (1892).

5. Varjabedian v. Madera, 64 Cal.App. 3d 199, 134 Cal.Rptr. 305, affirmed in part and reversed in part on other grounds 20 Cal.3d 285, 142 Cal.Rptr. 429, 572 P.2d 43 (1977); McKinnon v. Benedict, 38 Misc.2d 607, 157 N.W.2d 665 (1968).

6. 26 N.Y.2d 219, 309 N.Y.S.2d 312, 257 N.E.2d 870 (1970), on remand 72 Misc.2d 834, 340 N.Y.S.2d 97 (1970), judgment affirmed 42 A.D.2d 496, 349 N.Y.S.2d 199 (1973).

7. Hulbert v. California Portland Cement Co., 161 Cal. 239, 118 P. 928 (1911) (where defendant's conduct mandates punitive treatment). See Smith v. Staso Milling Co., 18 F.2d 736 (2d Cir.1927). See generally Riter v. Keokuk Electro-Metals Co., 248 Iowa 710, 82 N.W.2d 151 (1957).

8. McCleery v. Highland Boy Gold Mining Co., 140 F. 951 (C.C.Utah 1904); Yaffe v. Ft. Smith, 178 Ark. 406, 10 S.W.2d 886 (1928) (temporary injunction, dissolvable upon payment of damages).

tions may facilitate the termination of a nuisance whose harm a plaintiff values greater than recoverable damages only. This situation is most common where the plaintiff is hypersensitive to injury or he has come to the nuisance.[9]

Normally, a potential use will not be enjoined unless it is a nuisance per se [10] or it can be shown that, in the absence of an injunction, harm is substantially certain to result. Injunctive relief in favor of private individuals is usually available in cases of public nuisances (if special damages are shown) despite the fact that equity will not normally enjoin a crime. At common law, a public nuisance was always a crime and punishable as such. Most states have enacted criminal statutes declaring that maintenance of a public nuisance is a misdemeanor.[11]

Although nuisance actions are not as prevalent now as they once were, they are often applied in novel ways. When government has been slow to act, plaintiffs attempt to enjoin uses which have a negative impact on the environment. Often the offending use is compatible with the zoning or comprehensive plan of the locality, but can be shown to have harmful effects on the health of those living nearby.[12]

Disposal of hazardous substances is an example of such a use. The magnitude of the hazardous waste disposal problem in the U.S. is practically incomprehensible. It is estimated that only 10% of the roughly 35 million metric tons of hazardous waste generated annually is being disposed of in a manner considered environmentally safe.[13] The federal government as well as each state has passed legislation concerning waste disposal, but in spite of these laws, statutory remedies do not adequately or satisfactorily address all the problems.[14]

Private nuisance liability requires proof of significant harm.[15] This is problematic for plaintiffs because proof of a connection between plaintiffs' injuries and defendants' prior acts is often difficult to obtain. Effects of hazardous waste disposal may not become obvious for many years.[16] A plaintiff's burden of proof can be exacerbated by the dearth of scientific knowledge of effects caused by modern chemicals and resulting by-products.[17]

9. Spur Indus., Inc. v. Del E. Webb Dev. Co., 108 Ariz. 178, 494 P.2d 700 (1972).

10. McQuail v. Shell Oil Co., 40 Del.Ch. 410, 183 A.2d 581 (1962).

11. See supra §§ 4.36, 8.7.

12. E.g., McCastle v. Rolling Envtl. Servs., 514 F.Supp. 936 (M.D.La.1981).

13. 43 Fed.Reg. 58,946, 58,947 (1978) (EPA estimates of disposal sites requiring government intervention proposed regulations for implementing Resource Conservation and Recovery Act of 1976).

14. See generally Tarlock, Anywhere But Here: An Introduction to State Con-

trol of Hazardous Waste Facility Location, 2 U.C.L.A.J.Envtl.L. & Poly. 1 (1982).

15. Stockdale v. Agrico Chem. Co., 340 F.Supp. 244 (N.D.Iowa 1972).

16. E.g., United States v. Price, 523 F.Supp. 1055 (D.N.J.1981), affirmed 688 F.2d 204 (3d Cir.1982). See generally House Subcomm. on Oversight & Investigations of Comm. on Interstate & Foreign Commerce, Hazardous Waste Disposal, 96th Cong., 1st Sess. (Comm.Print 1979).

17. E.g., Miller v. National Cabinet Co., 8 N.Y.2d 277, 204 N.Y.S.2d 129, 168 N.E.2d 811 (1960), remittitur amended 8 N.Y.2d

Against this problem, public nuisance[18] or combined public and private nuisance[19] actions have been more successful than private nuisance actions alone, in effecting abatement or recovering damages by private parties. In some cases, defendants' activity may be found to pose imminent danger to public health and safety, enjoined, and ordered cleaned up at the defendants' expense.[20]

Handling of toxic wastes meets almost all the criteria for considering such activity abnormally dangerous,[21] and courts are beginning to apply common law strict liability to the hazardous waste industry.[22]

 WESTLAW REFERENCES

"compensatory damage" /s nuisance /s permanent

damage /s nuisance /s successive! /s actual!

injunction /s irreparable /s injury /s nuisance /s damage

to(279) /p multiplicity

to(279) /p balanc! /p damage

deni! /2 injunction /s nuisance /s damage

"conditional injunction"

"c*me to the nuisance"

potential proposed /s use /p "nuisance per se" /p enjoin!

misdemeanor /s maintain! maintenance /s "public nuisance"

dispos! /s hazardous /s waste /s nuisance

(united +s states +s waste +s industries) (delaney +s philhern +s realty) (driscoll +s new +s transit)

r.c.r.a. /p nuisance

c.e.r.c.l.a. /s hazardous /s waste /s dispos!

"solid waste disposal act"

di("private nuisance" /s caus!)

279k49

"private nuisance" /s substantial! significant /s harm!

279kl

yeager +s sullivan +s o'neill

toxic /p dangerous /p strict! /s liab!

1025, 206 N.Y.S.2d 795, 170 N.E.2d 214 (1960).

18. City of Philadelphia v. Stepan Chem. Co., 544 F.Supp. 1135 (E.D.Pa.1982); McCastle v. Rollins Envtl. Servs., 514 F.Supp. 936 (M.D.La.1981), class action transferred to state court and injunction affirmed 415 So.2d 515 (La.App.1982).

19. Chappell v. S.C.A. Servs., 540 F.Supp. 1087 (C.D.Ill.1982). This was a class action for damages, following Village of Wilsonville v. S.C.A. Servs., 77 Ill.App.3d 618, 33 Ill.Dec. 163, 396 N.E.2d 552 (1979),

affirmed 86 Ill.2d 1, 55 Ill.Dec. 499, 426 N.E.2d 824 (1981), which enjoined SCA's activity and required a cleanup of the site.

20. Wood v. Picillo, ___ R.I. ___, 443 A.2d 1244 (1982).

21. Restatement (Second) of Torts § 520 (1976).

22. Ashland Oil, Inc. v. Miller Oil Purchasing Co., 678 F.2d 1293 (5th Cir. 1982); City of Bridgeton v. B.P. Oil, Inc., 146 N.J.Super. 169, 369 A.2d 49 (1976).

§ 18.5   Federal Common Law of Nuisance and Statutory Preemption

After Erie R.R. Co. v. Tompkins,[1] which held that unless a matter was governed by the constitution or acts of Congress, the law of the particular state was to be applied, federal courts were generally precluded from developing a body of common law, though it was still appropriate for determining some issues.[2] The federal common law of nuisance had come into play when state nuisance law was deemed inappropriate for solving disputes between states, or when an issue concerned federal statutes, policies or international law. Though the key cases have strong environmental overtones, they do involve a conflict over the proper use of land under certain circumstances. Protectible property interests of both a public and private nature were being interfered with, and courts were grappling with finding a method for assigning the external costs to the appropriate party.

The Supreme Court had stated that ecological rights of a state should be held to be a matter having basis and standard in federal common law.[3] Lower federal courts at first required a showing of interstate effect[4] such as air or water pollution.[5] This was subsequently modified,[6] and one circuit effectively equalled the court's authority under federal nuisance law to that of the commerce power exercised by congress.[7]

Illinois v. Milwaukee[8] (Milwaukee I), which preceded the 1972 and 1977 amendments to the Federal Water Pollution Control Act,[9] had held that an interstate public nuisance was a federal question, and in absence of a statutory remedy was governed by the federal common law

---

§ 18.5

1. 304 U.S. 64, 58 S.Ct. 817, 82 L.Ed. 1188 (1938), conformed 98 F.2d 49 (2d Cir. 1938), cert. denied 305 U.S. 637, 59 S.Ct. 108, 83 L.Ed. 410 (1938), rehearing denied 305 U.S. 673, 59 S.Ct. 229, 83 L.Ed. 436 (1938).

2. E.g., Textile Workers Union v. Lincoln Mills, 353 U.S. 448, 77 S.Ct. 912, 1 L.Ed.2d 972 (1957) (labor law); Clearfield Trust Co. v. United States, 318 U.S. 363, 744, 63 S.Ct. 573, 87 L.Ed. 838 (1943) (commercial paper); Hinderlider v. La Plata River & Cherry Creek Ditch Co., 304 U.S. 92, 58 S.Ct. 803, 82 L.Ed. 1202 (1938), rehearing denied 305 U.S. 668, 59 S.Ct. 55, 83 L.Ed. 433 (1938) (apportionment of interstate waters).

3. Illinois v. Milwaukee, 406 U.S. 91, 99, 92 S.Ct. 1385, 1391, 31 L.Ed.2d 712 (1972), quoting Texas v. Pankey, 441 F.2d 236, 246 (10th Cir.1971).

4. Parsell v. Shell Oil Co., 421 F.Supp. 1275 (D.Conn.1976), affirmed 573 F.2d 1289 (2d Cir.1977).

5. Reserve Mining Co. v. EPA, 514 F.2d 492 (8th Cir.1975), on remand 417 F.Supp. 789 (D.Minn.1976), affirmed and remanded 543 F.2d 1210 (8th Cir.1976), 431 F.Supp. 1248 (D.Minn.1977).

6. United States v. Solvents Recovery Serv., 496 F.Supp. 1127 (D.Conn.1980).

7. Illinois v. Outboard Marine Corp., 619 F.2d 623 (7th Cir.1980), judgment vacated 453 U.S. 917, 101 S.Ct. 3152, 69 L.Ed. 2d 1000 (1981), on remand 680 F.2d 473 (7th Cir.1982). See generally Fort, The Necessary Demise of Federal Common Law of Nuisance, 12 Loy.U.Chi.L.J. 131, 140 (1981).

8. 406 U.S. 91, 92 S.Ct. 1385, 31 L.Ed.2d 712 (1972).

9. 33 U.S.C.A. §§ 1250–1376; Clean Water Act, 91 Stat. 1566.

of nuisance.[10] The court warned, however, that new federal laws might in time preempt the federal common law. The 1972 and 1977 amendments substantially altered the existing statute, particularly in the permitting procedures and requirements.

Again, in 1979, Illinois sued Milwaukee, alleging that it had created a public nuisance by discharging excessive effluent into Lake Michigan.[11] The court granted an injunction and Milwaukee appealed to the Supreme Court. In Milwaukee II the Court reversed the lower courts and overruled its earlier decision, holding that the comprehensive regulatory scheme established by the FWPCA, as amended, precluded use of the federal common law of nuisance for water pollution.[12] The message sent by Milwaukee II to lower federal courts was that where congress has legislated a comprehensive regulatory scheme for a particular subject area, federal common law remedies were unavailable for environmental torts.[13] There is every indication that this reasoning applies to federal common law nuisance actions for abatement of air pollution because of pervasive regulation under the Clean Air Act.[14] Thus, it appears that statutory remedies supplant those originally available at federal common law, and an injured party must turn to state law.[15]

WESTLAW REFERENCES

di(nuisance /s preempt! /s federal)

sy(federal /3 "common law" /3 nuisance)

(textile +s workers +s union +s lincoln +s mills) (clearfield
    +s trust +s united) (hinderliter +s "la plata" +s river
    +s ditch) /p erie +s tompkins

"interstate effect" /p federal! /p "common law"

f.w.p.c.a. /p preclud! /p federal! /p "common law" /p
    nuisance

---

10. 406 U.S. 91, 107, 92 S.Ct. 1385, 1395, 31 L.Ed.2d 712 (1972).

11. Illinois v. Milwaukee, 599 F.2d 151, 155 (7th Cir.1979).

12. City of Milwaukee v. Illinois, 451 U.S. 304, 101 S.Ct. 1784, 68 L.Ed.2d 114 (1981), on remand 731 F.2d 403 (7th Cir. 1984), cert. denied ___ U.S. ___, 105 S.Ct. 980, 83 L.Ed.2d 981 (1985). See also Middlesex Co. Sewerage Auth. v. National Sea Clammers Ass'n, 453 U.S. 1, 101 S.Ct. 2615, 69 L.Ed.2d 435 (1980); United States v. Price, 523 F.Supp. 1055 (D.N.J.1981), affirmed 698 F.2d 204 (3d Cir.1982) (preemption by RCRA and CERCLA—superfund).

13. United States v. Kin.-Buc., Inc., 532 F.Supp. 699 (D.N.J.1982).

14. 42 U.S.C.A. § 7601, et seq.

15. Scott v. Hammond, Indiana, 519 F.Supp. 292 (N.D.Ill.1981), order reversed 731 F.2d 403 (7th Cir.1984), cert. denied ___ U.S. ___, 105 S.Ct. 980, 83 L.Ed.2d 981 (1985). See also Illinois v. Outboard Marine Corp., 680 F.2d 473 (7th Cir.1982). The Seventh Circuit reversed its holding that the state had a cause of action under federal common law of nuisance against an pollution source within the state, but was not precluded from pursuing a state nuisance action if pollution involved intrastate waters.

§ 18.6　Police Power Regulation and Nuisance Law [1]

The common law of nuisance is subject to legislative change. As stated by Holmes, J., "within constitutional limits not exactly determined, the legislature may change the common law as to nuisances, and may move the line either way, so as to make things nuisances which were not so, or to make things lawful which were nuisances." [2] The constitutional limits are twofold. First, the legislature may not authorize or legalize a private nuisance,[3] and second, most courts hold that the police power does not extend to declaring activities nuisances which are not nuisances in fact.[4] For example, it would be unconstitutional for a legislative body to declare the existence of houses in an area to be nuisance, when they were perfectly good houses, but the legislative body wanted them removed so the property could be acquired at less cost for a park. However, if an ordinance is reasonable, a use may be abated, once it has been found to be a statutorily declared nuisance, though without the statutory declaration a court might not find a nuisance in fact.[5]

The same result may be reached by courts which nominally require that the activity constitute a nuisance in fact, but defer to the legislative judgment that the required harm exists.[6] It is a common practice of local legislatures to declare that the violation of local land use regulations, such as zoning ordinances, and building and safety codes, constitutes a public nuisance. Thus, nuisances in fact may be elevated to nuisances per se by an exercise of the police power. For example, a Michigan enabling statute for municipal zoning provides that ". . . uses violating any provision of local ordinances or regulations . . . are nuisances per se." [7]

The existence of zoning ordinances has affected the common law of nuisances. When a zoning ordinance authorizes a certain use, that use cannot, by definition, constitute a nuisance per se. And, it is generally held that the use cannot constitute a public nuisance.[8]

§ 18.6

1. See supra §§ 4.36, 8.7, 18.4 n. 10.

2. Commonwealth v. Parks, 155 Mass. 531, 532, 30 N.E. 174 (1892).

3. Richards v. Washington Terminal Co., 233 U.S. 546, 553, 34 S.Ct. 654, 657, 58 L.Ed. 1088 (1914). The Court stated that while the legislature may legalize what otherwise would be a public nuisance, it may not confer immunity from action for a private nuisance of such a character as to amount in effect to a taking of private property for public use.

4. City of Scottsbluff v. Winters Creek Canal Co., 155 Neb. 723, 53 N.W.2d 543 (1952).

5. Township of Farmington v. Scott, 374 Mich. 536, 132 N.W.2d 607 (1965)

(court held a zoning ordinance precluding a swimming pool supply business in a residential zone to be reasonable and upheld an injunction based on an ordinance declaring nonconforming uses to be nuisances per se).

6. See City of Bakersfield v. Miller, 64 Cal.2d 93, 48 Cal.Rptr. 889, 410 P.2d 393, cert. denied 384 U.S. 988, 86 S.Ct. 1890, 16 L.Ed.2d 1005 (1966).

7. "The court shall order such nuisance abated and the owners . . . shall be adjudged guilty of maintaining a nuisance per se . . . ." Mich.Comp.Laws Ann. § 125.587.

8. Robinson Brick Co. v. Luthi, 115 Colo. 106, 169 P.2d 171 (1946). But see Eaton v. Klimm, 217 Cal. 362, 18 P.2d 678

However, the question of whether a given use does constitute a private nuisance in fact may be affected by the weight given by a court to the existence of a zoning ordinance permitting the use. The character of the area is an important factor in determining whether a nuisance in fact exists; and the existence of a zoning ordinance permitting or precluding uses is significant in determining the character of the area. Most courts regard proof of the existence of a zoning ordinance to be admissible as evidence of the character of the district and bearing on the question of whether a nuisance exists.[9] However, some courts consider the existence of a zoning ordinance to have no effect.[10] And some courts consider the legislative determination that the area is proper for the use to be determinative so long as the defendant is conducting his business in a reasonable manner.[11] This effect is achieved in California by statute,[12] precluding injunctive relief by private persons where the use is conducted in an appropriate zone and unnecessary or injurious methods of operation are not employed. However, the statute does not preclude the recovery of damages. Zoning also affects nuisance law where the protested use violates a zoning ordinance and a private individual sues claiming that the violation of the ordinance is a nuisance per se or a common law nuisance.[13] But other cases require actual proof that the violation of the ordinance was a common law nuisance as a prerequisite to injunctive relief by a private person.[14]

Another issue is the extent to which local governments may pass separate nuisance prevention ordinances without fully complying with special zoning procedures.[15] In those states that grant broad police powers to local governments, such ordinances could probably be adopted without using any special procedures. However, state zoning statutes may use broad enough language in describing the types of land use controls authorized by the statute that any ordinance exercising any such type of control may arguably be required to comply with zoning procedures even though the ordinance does not purport on its face to be comprehensive zoning.[16] The procedural requirements may be avoided in some instances where separate zoning enabling authority for the nuisance ordinance exists. In the absence of statutory guidance, some

(1933) (later codified in West's Ann.Cal.Civ. Proc.Code § 731a).

9. Rockenback v. Apostle, 330 Mich. 338, 47 N.W.2d 636 (1951).

10. Weltshe v. Graf, 323 Mass. 498, 82 N.E.2d 795 (1948).

11. Bove v. Donner-Hanna Coke Corp., 236 App.Div. 37, 258 N.Y.S. 229 (1932).

12. West's Ann.Cal.Civ.Proc.Code § 731a.

13. In Hopkins v. MacCulloch, 35 Cal. App.2d 442, 95 P.2d 950 (1939), defendant's use, illegal under a zoning ordinance, was enjoined and declared a nuisance mainly because it violated the ordinance.

14. Morris v. Borough of Haledon, 20 N.J.Super. 433, 90 A.2d 113 (Ch.Div.1952), judgment reversed 24 N.J.Super. 171, 93 A.2d 781 (1952).

15. See supra § 3.11.

16. See City of Escondido v. Desert Outdoor Advertising, Inc., 8 Cal.3d 785, 106 Cal.Rptr. 172, 505 P.2d 1012 (1973), cert. denied 414 U.S. 828, 94 S.Ct. 53, 38 L.Ed.2d 62 (1973).

courts look to the nature and purpose of the specialized measure.[17] If it deals with zoning concepts or its effect is to regulate the use of land, then compliance with zoning procedural safeguards may be necessary.

Farming

Certain farming activities may constitute a nuisance. A plaintiff who brings a private nuisance action against a farmer must show that the farming activity unreasonably interferes with the use and enjoyment of his land.[18] Courts consider factors such as the character of the neighborhood, proximity of the farm to plaintiff's home, intensity of the odors and consequential diminution of plaintiffs' property value [19] when a farm is the object of a nuisance action, the plaintiff has usually been a latecomer to the vicinity. Raising by farmers of the defense that the plaintiffs "came to the nuisance" [20] has not been a complete bar to such actions. It is, rather, only one of several factors balanced by courts.[21]

According to a recent study,[22] about 10% of the cropland lost each year is lost to urban development. In spite of agricultural use of the land which conforms to applicable health and safety standards or is otherwise reasonable and consistent with character of the area, plaintiffs who come to the nuisance often prevail.[23] And even though in Spur Industries, Inc. v. Del E. Webb Development Co.,[24] the court required Del Webb to indemnify Spur the cost of moving its feedlot, the land was ultimately converted to nonagricultural use.

Recently, a large majority of states have abrogated the right to bring a common law nuisance action against farmers under certain circumstances by "right to farm" statutes.[25] This reflects a concern for loss of agricultural land, recognition of the value of farmers to society, and perhaps a fortification of the "coming to the nuisance" defense.[26]

Most of the statutes provide that agricultural operations which have been in existence longer than one year cannot become either public or private nuisances by virtue of changed conditions in the surrounding area, if they were not nuisances when the agricultural

17. See Piper v. Meredith, 110 N.H. 291, 266 A.2d 103 (1970).

18. Jones v. Rumford, 64 Wn.2d 559, 392 P.2d 808 (1964).

19. E.g., Baldwin v. McClendon, 292 Ala. 43, 288 So.2d 761 (1974).

20. Restatement (Second) of Torts § 840D (1976).

21. Spencer Creek Pollution Control Ass'n v. Organic Fertilizer Co., 264 Or. 557, 505 P.2d 919 (1973).

22. Krause & Hair, Trends in Land Use and Competition for Land to Produce Food and Fiber, U.S. Dep't of Agriculture, Perspective on Prime Lands 16 (1975).

23. E.g., Pendoley v. Ferreira, 345 Mass. 309, 187 N.E.2d 142 (1963).

24. 108 Ariz. 178, 494 P.2d 700 (1972).

25. In the period 1977–1982, 34 states enacted such laws. E.g., West's Ann.Cal. Civ.Code § 3482.5; West's Fla.Stat.Ann. § 823.14; Neb.Rev.Stat. § 2–401–02–4404. See also § 15.2 supra.

26. Many of the statutes include preservation of agricultural land as a major legislative purpose. The threat of urbanization and susceptibility of agricultural operations to nuisance suits is explicitly stated as grounds for enactment of the Florida law.

operations began.[27] Some of the statutes list exceptions to the rule to avoid judicial erosion.[28] Others protect specific activities such as livestock feedlots,[29] or operations used for specific purposes, such as production of milk, eggs, or livestock.[30]

WESTLAW REFERENCES

"private nuisance" /s authoriz! legaliz!

"police power" /s "nuisance in fact"

"nuisance per se" /p ordinance /p nonconforming

"public nuisance" /s violat! /s zon! /s regulat!

"private nuisance" /p zon! /p ordinance regulat! /p permit! authoriz! /p use

Farming

"private nuisance" /s farm! /s use usage

"right to farm"

---

27. Note, Right to Farm Statutes—The Newest Tool in Agricultural Land Preservation, 10 Fla.St.U.L.Rev. 415 (1982). See also Note, Right to Farm in Oregon, 18 Willamette L.J. 153 (1981); Thomas, Defining and Protecting the Right to Farm, 5 Zoning & Planning Law Report 57 (Sept. 1982) & 65 (Oct. 1982).

28. West's Ann.Fla.Stat. § 823.14.

29. Iowa Code Ann. § 172D.2.

30. Md.Code, Cts. & Jud.Proc. § 5–308(a).

Chapter 19

"PRIVATE" LAND USE CONTROLS

Analysis

I. PRIVATE USE OF "PRIVATE" CONTROLS

II. PUBLIC USE OF "PRIVATE" CONTROLS

I. PRIVATE USE OF "PRIVATE" CONTROLS

§ 19.1 Introduction

In addition to nuisance law,[1] private landowners use a variety of devices, either singly or in combination, to effectuate land use planning by private agreement: defeasible estates, easements, and contracts respecting use of the land. Through these devices, restrictions may be imposed on the use of a single parcel of land owned or conveyed. More commonly, in a land planning context, restrictions are imposed for the purpose of controlling the use and occupancy of multiple parcels of land; for example, in connection with the development of land for

§ 19.1

1. See Chapter 15 supra.

residential subdivision purposes or in connection with the ownership, use and maintenance of areas made available to residents for common use in planned unit developments and condominiums.[2]

 WESTLAW REFERENCES

private /s covenant! agree! /s land property /s restrict! /s
use usage

di estate

§ 19.2 Defeasible Estates

All freehold and nonfreehold estates can be made defeasible in three ways: (1) determinable (2) upon condition subsequent or (3) subject to an executory interest (limitation). Each type will be illustrated in a land use control context.

Determinable Estates

If O, owner of Blackacre, conveys that parcel to A "provided that the land be used solely for residential purposes and if it shall ever cease to be so used the title to Blackacre shall revert to the grantor, O, or her heirs," O has created and A owns a fee simple determinable. Since A's interest is less than a fee simple absolute, O retains a future interest which is called a possibility of reverter.

If A, or his successors in interest, uses the land for other than residential purposes (a Burger Paradise Restaurant, for example) his (or their) title to the land in question will automatically terminate (i.e. the fee simple determinable estate terminates) and title automatically returns to O or her heirs. Although the example of a determinable estate just used is a fee, the same land use restriction could be created by private parties for a life estate or a term of years. For example, if O conveys to "A for life, provided that the land be used solely for residential purposes and if the land shall be used for any other purpose, A's title shall terminate and automatically revert to O or her heirs," A has a determinable life estate and use of the land for commercial purposes, for example, will cause an automatic reverter of title to O or her heirs. Similarly, if Landlord leases unimproved land to Tenant for ten years "provided that the land be used solely for agricultural purposes," then if tenant builds a shopping center, title will automatically revert to L.

Estates Upon Condition Subsequent

If O, owner of Greenacre conveys that parcel to A "upon the condition that the land be used solely for residential purposes and if the land ever ceases to be so used O, the grantor, or her heirs may re-enter and terminate the estate hereby conveyed," O has created and A owns a fee simple upon condition subsequent. (A's interest is less than a fee

2. For a discussion of plat restrictions see Ch. 7 supra.

simple absolute so O has therefore retained a future interest which at common law is called a "right of re-entry" but has been needlessly renamed "a power of termination" by the Restatement of Property.[1]

If A, or his successors in interest, changes the use from residential to any other use, commercial for example, O or if she is deceased, the person or persons who inherited her right of re-entry may take possession of the property (re-enter) and thereby terminate the interest (estate) of A or his successors.

Other estates may be made defeasible by being subjected to a condition subsequent. For example O might convey to A for life upon the condition that the land be used only for residential purposes or Landlord might lease to Tenant for 10 years upon the condition that the leasehold estate be used solely for residential uses.

The Distinction Between a Fee Simple Determinable and a Fee Upon Condition Subsequent

Automatic versus nonautomatic termination distinguishes the fee simple determinable from the fee upon condition subsequent. Consider the following examples. O owns two adjoining parcels, Blackacre and Greenacre. She conveys a fee simple determinable estate in Blackacre to A and a fee simple upon condition subsequent in Greenacre to A. The "restriction" (technically the defeasible event) in both is the provision that the land must be used only for residential purposes. A builds a Cheeseburger Paradise on both parcels. The title to Blackacre automatically reverts to O, since A's estate was a fee simple determinable and O retained a possibility of reverter. O doesn't have to do anything to regain title. It is hers automatically.

A change in use of Greenacre does not cause title to automatically return to O. A retains ownership *unless and until* O retakes possession and thereby ends A's estate. O's right of reentry is subject to being lost if it is not exercised before the applicable Statute of Limitations runs.

Fee Subject to an Executory Interest

The future interest retained by the grantor when she conveys a fee simple determinable (the future interest is called a possibility of reverter) and the future interest retained by the grantor when she conveys a fee simple upon condition subsequent (the future interest is called a right of re-entry) can only be created in the grantor or her estate. At common law these two future interests could not even be transferred other than by inheritance. Only after the Statute of Uses did the courts allow an estate to be made defeasible so that when the estate terminated title went to a third party rather than back to the grantor or her estate.

Consider the following defeasible estate. O conveys Whiteacre to A and his heirs provided that the land be used solely for residential

§ 19.2
1. Restatement of Property § 45.

purposes and if the land shall ever cease to be so used then title shall pass to B and his heirs. After the Statute of Uses, A was recognized as having a fee simple subject to an executory limitation (interest) and B was held to have a future interest called an executory interest. If the land was ever used for commercial purposes (Cheeseburger Paradise) A's interest was cut off and B had a fee simple absolute. B's interest (the executory interest) could be created to become possessory automatically (as in the example just given) or only upon B's affirmative act of taking possession of the property. Other estates, life estates and terms of years, for example, could be made defeasible through their subjection to an executory limitation.

The Usefulness of Defeasible Estates as Land Use Control Devices

Defeasible estates are very effective devices for restricting the use of land. The problem is that they are too effective in the sense that they are too permanent and inflexible.[2] The consequence of violating the land use restriction thereby imposed is loss (i.e. forfeiture) of all interest in the land—a rather drastic result in the eyes of even the most zealous public land use control advocate. Of course their enforcement can generally be waived through failure of the owner of the possibility of reverter, right of re-entry or executory interest to assert her rights but the potential windfall of regaining the property will create a strong predisposition to the contrary.

Furthermore, the assertion by the future interest owner of her rights will not necessarily guarantee the continuation of the private restriction. In fact, just the contrary may be the case. If the property subjected to a residential use only restriction in the examples above is more valuable if used for commercial purposes, the future interest holder may well make that change in use upon gaining title to the property since the restriction applied only to the owner of the defeasible estate and not to the owner of the future interest. In short, defeasible estates offer a large degree of control, but their usefulness is limited when the object of planning is to impose area-wide controls over the use of land. The right of reentry or possibility of reverter is personal to the grantor, his heirs or assigns and in some jurisdictions,[3] the interest may not be assigned. Thus, the restriction may be of no benefit to subsequent purchasers of any land sought to be protected.

Additionally, defeasible estates are inflexible planning tools. A title once made defeasible unlimited as to time is forever subject to the condition unless property is released or terminated, or, in a few states, circumstances have substantially changed. Forfeiture of estate is the only remedy for breach of condition, and the grantor may at any time terminate the estate by appropriate action if the condition is breached.[4]

---

2. See generally, Goldstein, Rights of Entry and Possibilities of Reverter as Devices to Restrict the Use of Land, 54 Harv. L.Rev. 248 (1940).

3. See, e.g., Ill.—S.H.A. ch. 30, § 37b.

4. Quatman v. McCray, 128 Cal. 285, 60 P. 855 (1900).

WESTLAW REFERENCES

"defeasible estate"

Determinable Estates

"determinable estate"

defin*** definition /p "fee simple determinable" /p "possibility of reverter"

to(154) /p "life estate" "term of years"

Estate Upon Condition Subsequent

"estate upon condition subsequent" /s "right of re-entry"

The Distinction Between a Fee Simple Determinable and a Fee Upon Condition Subsequent

fee +3 determinable "condition subsequent"

"right of re-entry" /s "statute of limitations"

Fees Subject to an Executory Interest

"statute of uses" /p defeas!

"conditional limitation" /p "executory interest" /p "fee simple"

The Usefulness of Defeasible Estates as Land Use Control Devices

defeasible /s estate /p land property /p use usage /s contro! restrict! plan planning planned

"possibility of reverter" /s interest /s assign!

defeasible /s estate /p terminat! forfeit! /p breach! /p condition

---

§ 19.3   Easements

Affirmative and negative easements constitute important private land use control tools. An affirmative easement is a nonpossessory right to make some use of land belonging to another person or entity. A negative easement is the restriction placed by the owner of land on his own use of his own land for the purpose of benefitting another person or entity. The best example of an affirmative easement is the "right of way" easement pursuant to which A, owner of parcel A, grants to B the right to drive across parcel A. An example of a negative easement is A's restriction of A's right to use parcel A for other than a one-story residence so as to benefit B.

Affirmative easements are regularly found in multi-parcel developments granting rights to individual lot owners in common property such as parks and parking lots and reserving to the developer rights across lots for wires, pipes and so forth. Ordinarily, easements must be created with the formalities applicable to any conveyance of an interest in land.[1] However, where a developer sells lots with reference to a map, on which open areas, parks or beaches are designated and representations are made that the squares or parks or beaches are for the

§ 19.3

1. See Cottrell v. Nurnberger, 131 W.Va. 391, 47 S.E.2d 454 (1948); Restatement of Property § 467 (1944).

benefit of lot owners, the purchasers are generally held to acquire affirmative easements in such open areas, parks or beaches by implication and representation.[2]

An easement may be either appurtenant to the land, that is, created to benefit land owned by the holder of the easement, or in gross for the personal benefit of the holder. The burden of an easement appurtenant or an easement in gross passes with the land to all takers.[3] The benefit of an easement appurtenant passes freely with the dominant estate, even without separate mention in the deed. The benefit of an easement in gross is not attached to any parcel of land, and there is a serious question whether it may be assigned, although the trend is toward free assignability if the original parties wish it.[4] There is a constructional preference for easements appurtenant.[5]

Negative easements—since they are restrictions—constitute a theoretically effective land use regulation device. The limitation on the use of negative easements in land use planning stems from historical convention. Affirmative easements are considered to be those which involve the privilege of going onto the land of another, the servient estate. Negative easements are considered to be those which merely preclude the owner of land subject to the easement from doing that which, if no easement existed, he would be entitled to do. The negative easements which have been traditionally recognized as interests in property have historically (in England) been limited to easements for light, air, view and lateral support. American courts have been somewhat but not totally more liberal in regard to the use of negative easements to impose restrictions on the use or improvement of property such as residential restrictions and setback requirements, and undertakings involving active duties such as construction of sidewalks are recognized by some courts, but subject to question by others.

 WESTLAW REFERENCES

"affirmative easement"

"negative easement"   /p   creat!   /p   convey!   /p   interest

to(141)   /p   negative

(wilkinson   +s   nassau) (putnam   +s   dickinson)   /p   easement

easement   /s   appurtenant   /p   benefit   /s   holder

elliott   +s   mccombs   /p   appurtenant

easement   /s   appurtenant   /s   benefit!

easement   /s   gross   /s   burden!

2. Wilkinson v. Nassau Shores, Inc., 1 Misc.2d 917, 86 N.Y.S.2d 603 (1949), judgment affirmed 278 App.Div. 970, 105 N.Y.S.2d 984 (1951), reargument and appeal denied 279 App.Div. 591, 107 N.Y.S.2d 559 (1951), judgment affirmed 304 N.Y. 614, 107 N.E.2d 93 (1952); Putnam v. Dickinson, 142 N.W.2d 111 (N.D.1966).

3. See C. Clark, Covenants and Interests Running with Land 65 et seq. (1947).

4. Stockdale v. Yerden, 220 Mich. 444, 190 N.W. 225 (1922); See Simes, The Assignability of Easements in Gross in American Law, 22 Mich.L.Rev. 521 (1924); See also § 19.9 infra.

5. Elliott v. McCombs, 17 Cal.2d 23, 109 P.2d 329 (1941).

to(141) /p easement /s gross /s assignab!

"negative easement" /p land property /p use usage /p control!
    regulat!

"negative easement" /p setback sidewalk

"negative easement" /s improvement

§ 19.4 Real Covenants

For centuries landowners have used contracts to control the use of land. If Mr. A owns parcels A and B, adjoining properties, and Mr. A sells parcel B to Mrs. B, it is very common for Mr. A and Mrs. B to contractually agree that their respective pieces of land will be used for residential purposes only. There is no problem with using this simple contract approach to land use control since if either party starts to build a Cheeseburger Paradise the aggrieved party can collect damages and/or obtain equitable relief through specific performance of the contract.

The problem arises if Mr. A has sold his land to Mr. C and Mrs. B has sold her land to Mrs. D. If Mrs. D starts to build the Cheeseburger Paradise, the judge will have great difficulty using contract principles to allow Mr. C to enforce a contract to which he was not a party against Mrs. D who was also not a party to the contract. Certainly before the expansion of contract law to include promissory estoppel and third party beneficiary concepts, contract law offered little hope of relief. Many years ago, when Mrs. Bs found themselves unable to obtain relief on contract law principles, their attorneys tried property law principles. "Your Honor, consider the contract between Mr. A and Mrs. B as more than a mere contract. Consider it a modification of the land ownership interests of the contracting parties, modifications that affect the land ownership interests that can pass to their successors in interest." In other words the argument was that the A–B contract modified the ownership interests so that successors in interest to the land in question took title subject to the modifications. At first, judges refused to accept this property law view of the A–B contract probably out of a fear that to do so would be a step back to the feudal tenure system in which land ownership rights and personal obligations were intertwined. Eventually, however, probably several hundred years ago, the courts "gave in" and held that noncontracting parties could enforce and be bound by such contracts (or covenants as they were called at the time). The judicial label for contracts that would be enforceable by and against subsequent landowners on property law theories was the now quaint "covenants that run with the land" or "real covenants."

Judges did not treat all contracts respecting land as "real covenants." Only those covenants which met and satisfied certain judicially imposed criteria were allowed to "run with the land." Today covenants will run with the land and bind successors to the estates of the covenanting parties only if the following requirements are met: (1)

the parties intend that the benefit and burden run with the land; (2) the covenant touches and concerns the land; and (3) privity of estate exists.

In order to establish that the parties intend that their successors in interest be bound, it is not necessary that the words "heirs and assigns" be used. The parties' intent or lack of it can be inferred from the language of the agreement[1] or from the circumstances surrounding its execution[2] in most jurisdictions. In fact, judges generally presume intent—if all other requirements for a valid real covenant are met—in all circumstances except one. No such presumption is made if the covenant related to something not yet in existence (not in esse) such as a party wall *to be built* and maintained.

In order to "touch and concern" the land, courts require that the covenant must operate to benefit the covenantee in his physical use of the land.[3] However, most jurisdictions apply the test developed in Neponsit Property Owners' Ass'n v. Emigrant Indus. Sav. Bank,[4] applying a test of whether the covenant in purpose and effect "substantially alters the legal rights which otherwise flow from ownership of land." Under such formulation, promises to do affirmative acts, such as promises to pay money for the upkeep of a common park or to construct a dam, the burden of which were historically considered personal to the covenantor except in circumscribed situations[5] may "touch and concern" and therefore run with the land.

The privity of estate requirement is the primary obstacle to the enforcement of covenants at law. Privity of estate is used in two senses: (1) vertical privity means succession to the estate of one of the contracting parties, and (2) horizontal privity, which requires either a succession of estate between the contracting parties or, more restrictively, mutual and simultaneous interests of the contracting parties in the land with respect to which the promise is made.[6]

All courts require vertical privity; that is, courts will permit enforcement of a contract only between the contracting parties or by or against one who succeeds to the estate of a contracting party. Thus, the grantee of the promisee may enforce against the grantee of the promisor: both the benefit and the burden of the covenant run because there is a succession of interest between the promisor and his grantee and also between the promisee and his grantee.

Some recent cases repudiate the need for horizontal privity of estate between the contracting parties, in addition to vertical privity.[7]

§ 19.4

1. Union Trust Co. v. Rosenburg, 171 Md. 409, 189 A. 421 (1937).

2. Clark v. Guy Drews Post of the Am. Legion, 247 Wis. 48, 18 N.W.2d 322 (1945).

3. See, e.g., Restatement of Property § 537 (1944).

4. 278 N.Y. 248, 15 N.E.2d 793 (1938).

5. See, e.g., Furness v. Sinquett, 60 N.J. Super. 410, 159 A.2d 455 (Ch.1960); Miller v. Clary, 210 N.Y. 127, 103 N.E. 1114 (1913).

6. See C. Clark, Covenants and Interests Running With Land 111 (1947).

7. 165 Broadway Bldg. v. City Investing Co., 120 F.2d 813 (2d Cir.1941), cert. denied

Others dispense with it when the question is whether the benefit of the covenant will run.[8] In this latter situation, the grantee of the promisee could enforce against the original promisor, although not against a grantee of the promisor unless privity of estate existed between the contracting parties.

In those jurisdictions which do require horizontal privity, some consider the requirement satisfied when there is a succession of interest between the contracting parties.[9] For example, a promise made by a grantor in a deed with respect to the land granted could be enforced by and against successors to the estates of the contracting parties. A few jurisdictions require horizontal privity in its most restrictive sense, a mutual and simultaneous interest in the land by both the promisor and promisee.[10] When horizontal privity in this sense is required, a relationship between the contracting parties such as that between landlord and tenant or dominant tenement and easement holders is necessary at the time the contract is made before it is enforceable by successors to the estates of the contracting parties.

 WESTLAW REFERENCES

"real covenant"   /p   contract!   /p   use usage

"real covenant"   /s   "run with the land"   /s   successor

108k84 breach!

108k84   /p   "heirs and assigns"

"real covenant"   /p   "touch and concern"   /p   benefit!

neponsit   /p   covenant   /s   touch   +2   concern

"privity of estate"   /s   define definition

"vertical privity"   /p   real land   /p   requir!

§ 19.5   Equitable Servitudes

Covenants which cannot be enforced at law because some technical requirement such as privity is lacking, may be enforced in equity as equitable servitudes on the theory that if a subsequent grantee takes with knowledge or notice of a valid agreement concerning the use of land, he cannot equitably refuse to perform.[1] Courts have increasingly disregarded the question of whether the covenant runs with the land and have merely considered whether the parties intended that the restriction should be imposed upon one tract of land for the benefit of another and whether the successor took with notice of the restriction.

314 U.S. 682, 62 S.Ct. 186, 86 L.Ed. 546 (1941); See also Reichman, Toward a Unified Concept of Servitudes, 55 So.Calif.L. Rev. 1179 (1982) (advocating the abolition of the privity rule).

8. Horn v. Miller, 136 Pa. 640, 20 A. 706 (1890).

9. See Lingle Water Users' Ass'n v. Occidental Bldg. & Loan Ass'n, 43 Wyo. 41, 297 P. 385 (1931).

10. Morse v. Aldrich, 36 Mass. (19 Pick.) 449 (1837).

§ 19.5

1. Trustees of Columbia College v. Lynch, 70 N.Y. 440 (1877); Tulk v. Moxbay, 41 Eng.Rep. 1143, 2 Phillips 774 (Ch. 1848).

Equitable servitudes may be created by express covenants contained in the deed of conveyance,[2] or by separate instruments containing mutual covenants executed by the respective owners of the tracts involved.[3] When the deeds or instruments are recorded, subsequent purchasers are charged with constructive notice of the restriction.[4]

Equitable servitudes may also be created by implication from the circumstances, as in the case of a building plan or scheme. A common plan or scheme may be shown by the developer inserting substantially uniform restrictions in all deeds by his preliminary statements of intention or public announcement of intention to create a general scheme, or by recording a plat showing a general scheme. The fact that a small percentage of deeds contains the covenant is not determinative; the court may look to the reliance of buyers and to the actual development of the tract to find that a general building plan had been agreed upon.[5] A subsequent purchaser may be put on inquiry notice, for example, by the fact that all the other lots in a development were developed for residential use only [6] and may be bound even though his deed does not contain the restriction.[7]

California takes the position that a common plan or building scheme can only be evidenced by the express words of the grantor and grantee. Thus, a covenant in a deed must describe the land intended to be benefited and state that the restriction is for the benefit of the described land.[8] While a developer may record a Declaration of Restrictions, the declaration must describe the whole area to be benefited and affirmatively declare that it is the intent of the subdivider to restrict the various lots for the benefit of the lots described. And the restrictions must be incorporated by reference in the deed.[9] The grantor's retention of a right to modify may negate the existence of a common plan.[10]

Where a general plan or building scheme exists, the restrictions may be enforced by lot owners among themselves. A purchaser may sue a later taker and vice versa.[11] And on the division of the land, one may sue another even though each claims through the same original grantor.[12] Where a general plan does not exist, surrounding lot owners

2. Hercules Powder Co. v. Continental Can Co., 196 Va. 935, 86 S.E.2d 128 (1955).

3. Trustees of Columbia College v. Lynch, 70 N.Y. 440 (1877).

4. Boyden v. Roberts, 131 Wis. 659, 111 N.W. 701 (1907).

5. Taylor v. Melton, 130 Colo. 280, 274 P.2d 977 (1954).

6. Sanborn v. McLean, 233 Mich. 227, 206 N.W. 496 (1925).

7. Id.; but see Riley v. Bear Creek Planning Committee, 17 Cal.3d 500, 131 Cal. Rptr. 381, 551 P.2d 1213 (1976) (buyer of subdivision lot who takes deed prior to recordation of general plan of mutual restrictions applicable to the entire subdivision is not bound by restrictions, despite actual knowledge of restrictions.

8. Werner v. Graham, 181 Cal. 174, 183 P. 945 (1919).

9. Martin v. Holm, 197 Cal. 733, 242 P. 718 (1925).

10. Humphrey v. Beall, 215 N.C. 15, 200 S.E. 918 (1939).

11. Boyd v. Park Realty Corp., 137 Md. 36, 111 A. 129 (1920); Snow v. Van Dam, 291 Mass. 477, 197 N.E. 224 (1935).

12. Sanborn v. McLean, supra; cf. Korn v. Campbell, 192 N.Y. 490, 85 N.E. 687 (1908).

may enforce a covenant if their land is expressly referred to in the covenant.[13]

Most jurisdictions enforce equitable servitudes on the theory that an agreement to restrict land creates an interest in the nature of a legal negative easement.[14] Courts which adopt an easement theory may deny enforcement to the grantor after he has disposed of all the lots in a development on the theory that he has no land to be benefited.[15] However, some courts hold that the grantor need not have property in the area in order to enforce the restriction.[16] And courts have upheld the right of homeowners' associations to enforce restrictive covenants even though the association owns no property on the theory that, in truth and fact, the homeowners' association is acting on behalf of property owners in enforcing the restriction.[17]

Courts which adopt an easement theory of equitable servitudes sometimes require that the Statute of Frauds be satisfied and that an equitable servitude be created by an instrument in writing.[18] Most courts do not concern themselves with the Statute of Frauds question at least where a common building scheme exists.[19]

 WESTLAW REFERENCES

"equitable servitude" /s creat! /s requir!

"equitable servitude" /s grantee /s notice

"equitable servitude" /p "constructive notice"

sy(uniform! /s restrict! /s deed /s scheme)

108k79(3) /p record!

108k70 /p equitable /s servitude

"easement theory"

(genung +s harvey) (kent +s koch) /p enforc!

homeowner community /s association /s enforc! /s restrict!
    /s covenant

---

13. Vogeler v. Alwyn Improvement Corp., 247 N.Y. 131, 159 N.E. 886 (1928); cf. Davis v. Huey, 620 S.W.2d 561 (Tex. 1981) (mutuality of obligation necessary if surrounding lot owners are to enforce restrictive covenant).

14. See C. Clark, Covenants and Interests Running With Land 148 et seq. (1947).

15. Genung v. Harvey, 79 N.J.Eq. 57, 80 A. 955 (1911). See also Kent v. Koch, 166 Cal.App.2d 579, 333 P.2d 411 (1958) holding that subdivider who had retained lot adjacent to a subdivision which lot had been used for parking while subdivision was being developed, was not entitled to enforce restriction against fences within subdivision.

16. VanSant v. Rose, 260 Ill. 401, 103 N.E. 194 (1913).

17. McNamee v. Bishop Trust Co., 62 Hawaii 397, 616 P.2d 205 (1980); Merrionette Manor Homes Improvement Ass'n v. Heda, 11 Ill.App.2d 186, 136 N.E.2d 556 (1956); Neponsit Property Owners' Ass'n v. Emigrant Indus. Sav. Bank, supra § 19.4.

18. Sprague v. Kimball, 213 Mass. 380, 100 N.E. 622 (1913).

19. See Thornton v. Schobe, 79 Colo. 25, 243 P. 617 (1925); Sanborn v. McLean, supra; Johnson v. Mount Baker Park Presbyterian Church, 113 Wash. 458, 194 P. 536 (1920).

§ 19.6   Modification and Termination

A restriction may be modified or terminated by the acts of the parties themselves: through merger by the same person acquiring the dominant and servient estates; through agreement of the parties creating the restriction that it should have a specified duration or scope; or through execution of a release by the dominant owner. However, a release by the grantor has been held ineffective where a covenant benefits other land than that retained by the grantor and other lot owners insist on enforcing the restriction.[1] Similarly, the original contract of tenants who owned shares in a corporation formed for the purpose of taking title to, controlling, and operating premises as a cooperative could not be modified without the unanimous consent of all the parties.[2]

A restriction may not be enforceable because of equitable considerations. For example, relief may be denied where there is undue delay,[3] where the relative hardship on the defendant is too great,[4] or where there is no benefit to the plaintiff.[5]

In addition, a restriction may not be enforced when, by reason of changed circumstances, enforcement would be inequitable and oppressive and would harass owners without benefiting adjoining property owners. Numerous cases hold that restrictions requiring that lots be used for single family residences may be lifted when the character of the neighborhood has changed so as to render enforcement inequitable. The cases weigh such factors as the extent of the surrounding commercial uses, increased traffic and noise, hazards to children, and the low value of residential use as opposed to commercial use.[6]

Most courts hold that a point in neighborhood transition may be reached at which the disproportionate hardship imposed on the burdened estate makes specific enforcement of the restrictions no longer practicable. They will then only allow damages for a breach of covenant.[7] While change in neighborhood conditions may justify the nonenforcement of restrictive covenants, that change will not operate to extinguish a right of reentry for condition broken [8] or a recorded legal easement.[9]

§ 19.6

1. See Rick v. West, 34 Misc.2d 1002, 228 N.Y.S.2d 195 (1962).

2. Tompkins v. Hale, 172 Misc. 1071, 15 N.Y.S.2d 854 (1939), affirmed 284 N.Y. 675, 30 N.E.2d 721 (1940).

3. Gage v. Schavoir, 100 Conn. 652, 124 A. 535 (1924).

4. Gilpin v. Jacob Ellis Realties, Inc., 47 N.J.Super. 26, 135 A.2d 204 (App.Div.1957).

5. Welitoff v. Kohl, 105 N.J.Eq. 181, 147 A. 390 (1929).

6. Wolff v. Fallon, 44 Cal.2d 695, 284 P.2d 802 (1955); Trustees of Columbia College v. Thacher, 87 N.Y. 311 (1882). See § 19.10 infra on zoning regulations as evidence of a change in conditions. But cf. Cordogan v. Union National Bank of Elgin, 64 Ill.App.3d 248, 21 Ill.Dec. 18, 380 N.E.2d 1194 (1978) (movant, who created restrictions himself, was unable to remove restrictions without unjustly injuring neighboring properties).

7. See Case Note, 62 Harv.L.Rev. 1394 (1949).

8. Murray v. Trustees of Lane Seminary, 1 Ohio Op.2d 236, 140 N.E.2d 577, (P. Hamilton County 1956). In some states, however, a change of conditions will extinguish a right of reentry.

9. Waldrop v. Town of Brevard, 233 N.C. 26, 62 S.E.2d 512 (1950).

Private restrictions may be terminated by legislative action. Many states have limited by statute the period for which possibilities of reverter, powers of termination and covenants or servitudes may be enforced.[10] Other states provide by statute that conditions which are nominal and of no substantial benefit to the party in whose favor they run are void and unenforceable.[11] Similarly, statutes of limitation may be applied to defeat an attempt to enforce a breach of condition or covenant.[12]

Interests may also be extinguished by condemnation or by tax sale. Normally, a tax deed extinguishes all prior titles, rights, interests, equities, liens and encumbrances in the land conveyed. However, because an easement is an interest in land it is not extinguished when the servient estate is sold for taxes.[13] Further, a tax deed will not extinguish an equitable servitude, even though of equitable origin, on the theory that it is comparable to a negative easement for the benefit of other land.[14]

WESTLAW REFERENCES

sy(merg! /s dominant /s servient /s estate)

easement servitude /s scope duration /s limit! /s agree!

easement servitude /p execut! /p releas! /p dominant /p estate

easement servitude /p releas! /p grantor /p enforc!

tompkins +s hale

easement /p enforc! /p hardship "undue delay" /p equit!

easement /p enforc! /p circumstance /s chang***

sy(restrict! easement /s enforc! /s character /s neighborhood /s chang***)

specific! /2 enforc! /p neighborhood /p restrict! easement

specific! /2 enforc! /p damage /s breach! /s covenant /s easement restrict!

"right of re-entry for condition broken" /p enforc!

waldrop +s brevard

legislat! law statut! /s limit! /s "possibility of reverter" "power of termination" servitude /s enforc!

"statute of limitation" /p enforc! /p breach! /p easement servitude

di(property land /s interest /s extinguish! /s condemn! (tax /2 sale deed))

easement /s extinguish! /s servient /s tax /2 sale deed

---

10. See Mass.Gen.Laws Ann. c. 184, § 23, limiting all to 30 years duration if otherwise unlimited as to time; R.I.Gen. Laws § 34–4–19, limiting rights of reentry and possibilities of reverter to 20 years and covenants and servitudes to 30 years, if otherwise unlimited as to time.

11. See Mich.Comp.Laws Ann. § 554.- 46.

12. See Wolf v. Hallenbeck, 109 Colo. 70, 123 P.2d 412 (1942); Nearing v. Bridgeport, 137 Conn. 205, 75 A.2d 505 (1950).

13. Engel v. Catucci, 197 F.2d 597 (D.C. Cir.1952).

14. Northwestern Improvement Co. v. Lowry, 104 Mont. 289, 66 P.2d 792 (1937).

§ 19.7 Constitutional and Policy Constraints

Since Shelley v. Kraemer [1] courts cannot be used to enforce private restrictions based on race, color or creed. Shelley decided that the equal protection clause of the 14th amendment precluded the use of the judicial arm of the state from enforcing racially restrictive covenants. Theoretically, such agreements were valid but could not be enforced.[2]

Racially restrictive practices were circumscribed even further in Jones v. Alfred H. Mayer Co.[3] There, Jones wished to buy a home in a subdivision of a suburban St. Louis County community. The Alfred H. Mayer Co. would not sell because Jones was black. Jones sued under the Civil Rights Act of 1886, which provided, in part, that:

> All citizens of the United States shall have the same right as is enjoyed by white citizens . . . to . . . purchase, lease . . . real . . . property.[4]

In Jones v. Alfred H. Mayer Co. the court held that the statute was constitutional under the 13th amendment, discovered that the statute meant what it said and held the Act bars all racial discrimination, private as well as public, in the sale or rental of property.[5] The ruling is broad enough to cover acts of individual owners as well as those in the development business such as the Mayer Co. The significance of the case was that no state action was involved, even in the enforcement of a private agreement. Purely private acts of discrimination on the basis of race are now barred in the selling or leasing of housing.

Today, despite Jones v. Mayer, racial discrimination is still exercised by some homeowners' associations. In a homeowners' association, every owner of a lot in the subdivision is a member, and the association is given the right of first refusal to purchase any lot offered for sale— the right is often exercised only when the prospective purchaser is not the right color.

Even if the activities of a homeowners' association do not violate the Constitution, their practices may be constrained by the policy against restraint on alienation. The policy against restraint on alienation has operated to deny enforcement to provisions in condominium and homeowner association bylaws restricting the ability of members to convey their interest in property.[6] However, the court in Gale v. York Center Community Cooperative, Inc.[7] found a covenant proper which allowed the cooperative to redeem a membership within a 12 month

§ 19.7

1. 334 U.S. 1, 68 S.Ct. 836, 92 L.Ed. 1161 (1948).

2. The court also held that damages cannot be recovered for a breach of a racial covenant. Barrows v. Jackson, 346 U.S. 249, 73 S.Ct. 1031, 97 L.Ed. 1586 (1953), rehearing denied 346 U.S. 841, 74 S.Ct. 19, 98 L.Ed. 361 (1953).

3. 392 U.S. 409, 88 S.Ct. 2186, 20 L.Ed. 2d 1189 (1968).

4. 42 U.S.C.A. § 1982.

5. Id.

6. See Northwest Real Estate Co. v. Serio, 156 Md. 229, 144 A. 245 (1929); Mountain Springs Ass'n of New Jersey Inc. v. Wilson, 81 N.J.Super. 564, 196 A.2d 270 (Ch.1963).

7. 21 Ill.2d 86, 171 N.E.2d 30 (1960).

period at a price fixed by independent appraisal or negotiation if it found a proposed transfer unacceptable. The court stated that there were social and economic considerations which favor partial restraints on alienation by cooperatives.[8]

 WESTLAW REFERENCES

court /p enforc! /p private! /p restrict! /p race color creed

damage /s recover! /s breach! /s race racial! /s covenant

"civil rights act" /p "state action" /p private! /p agree*****
　　/p restrict! covenant land property sale sell*** rent***

"civil rights act" /p "thirteenth amendment" /p race racial! /p
　　discriminat! /p sale sell*** rent***

"restraint on alienation" /p serio (mountain +s springs +s
　　wilson)

association /p bylaw /p "restraint on alienation"

partial! /p "restraint on alienation" /p cooperative

II.　PUBLIC USE OF "PRIVATE" CONTROLS

§ 19.8　Condemnation and Restrictions

A public body may acquire land by condemnation which is subject to restrictions. It is the general rule that the existence of a restrictive covenant affecting the value of the condemned land should be considered in determining the market value of the property condemned. For example, Staninger v. Jacksonville Expressway Authority[1] held that property restricted to a single family residential use, the highest and best use[2] of which was for business and multi-unit apartment purposes, should be valued in eminent domain at or near its value as restricted.[3] However, Town of Tonawanda v. State[4] held that property was to be valued without consideration of a restriction. The land was owned by a city and acquired from the county for $500 per acre. The deed from the county restricted the property to municipal purposes. The state condemned part of the site at a time when property in the area was selling at $7,000 per acre. Since the county could release the restriction and since replacement property would cost the city the market price for land being sold in the area, the court held the property should be valued as if not restricted.

The extent to which the owners of dominant tenements having the benefit of restrictions over condemned property should be compensated

---

8. See also Penthouse Properties, Inc. v. 1158 Fifth Avenue, Inc., 256 App.Div. 685, 11 N.Y.S.2d 417 (1936).

§ 19.8

1. 182 So.2d 483 (Fla.App.1966). See Annot. 22 A.L.R.3d 961 (1968).

2. See § 4.3 supra.

3. See also Central Land Co. v. Providence, 15 R.I. 246, 2 A. 553 (1886); State v.

Reece, 374 S.W.2d 686 (Tex.Civ.App.1964); Note, 31 U.Pittsburg L.Rev. 128 (1969).

4. 50 Misc.2d 3, 269 N.Y.S.2d 181 (Ct.Cl. 1966), judgment affirmed 28 A.D.2d 644, 280 N.Y.S.2d 780 (1967). See also Burma Hills Development Co. v. Marr, 285 Ala. 141, 229 So.2d 776 (1969).

for a change in use is a related question. The majority rule is that compensation is due on the theory that an equitable servitude is a property right, analogous to an easement, loss of which must be paid for by the condemning authority.[5] Other courts hold that equitable servitudes are merely contractual rights cognizable in equity and do not constitute sufficient property interests to be paid for when taken.[6] These courts reason that it would violate public policy to allow individuals by agreement to greatly inconvenience or burden the governmental exercise of the power of eminent domain. Courts are influenced by the fact that the harm to the owner of the dominant tenement is small compared to the added public expense under eminent domain if the public must compensate for the restriction. However, since individuals can achieve the same effect by creating easements, it seems reasonable to treat restrictive covenants the same as easements. Furthermore, if the public pays less for property burdened by a restriction it seems just to require payment to the owners of land benefited by the restriction. Perhaps a taking might be found only when the intended public use is "obnoxious" to the character of the dominant tenement.[7]

WESTLAW REFERENCES

di(restrict! /s use usage /s condemn! /s land /s "market value")

148k134 /p covenant

148k222(4) /p "market value" /p remainder

sy("market value" /p "eminent domain" /p "highest and best use")

"dominant tenement" /p compensa! /p "eminent domain" condemn!

"equitable servitude" /p "property right" /p compensa! /p "eminent domain"

§ 19.9 Covenants and Publicly Owned Lands

The public body may itself create covenants benefiting land that it owns. Public agencies frequently acquire interests in land and then permit its use under appropriate conditions. California, for example, permits cities, counties and various state departments to acquire scenic and conservation easements, and by covenants or other contractual arrangements to permit the owner of the property to use the property

---

5. United States v. Certain Land in City of Augusta, 220 F.Supp. 696 (D.Me. 1963); Southern California Edison Co. v. Bourgene, 107 Cal.Rptr. 76, 507 P.2d 964 (1973); Town of Stamford v. Vuono, 108 Conn. 359, 143 A. 245 (1928); Peters v. Buckner, 288 Mo. 618, 232 S.W. 1024 (1921); see Annot. 4 A.L.R.3d 1137 (1965).

6. Arkansas State Highway Commission v. McNeill, 238 Ark. 244, 381 S.W.2d

425 (1964); Ryan v. Town of Manalapan, 414 So.2d 193 (Fla.1982); State ex rel. Wells v. Dunbar, 142 W.Va. 332, 95 S.E.2d 457 (1956). See generally Case Note, Restrictive Covenants: Do They Apply to Public Bodies, 10 Fla.St.U.L.Rev. 667 (1983) (outlines majority and minority viewpoint).

7. 3 U.C.L.A.L.Rev. 258 (1956).

in a way which will not interfere with the purpose of the easement.[1] Similarly, redevelopment agencies may impose restrictions on property returned to private uses.[2] Enforcement problems may arise in an urban renewal context after the public agency disposes of all its land subject to the restriction. In those jurisdictions which hold that the benefit of a covenant cannot be held in gross, a covenant cannot be enforced by the agency unless it retains some land that the covenant benefits.[3]

The public body may execute covenants benefiting other land. Such covenants may be enforced against the public by successors in interest to the estate of the promisee.[4]

 WESTLAW REFERENCES

government! /s purchas! acquir! acquisition! /s easement

redevelop! /p agency /p restrict! /p property /p private! /p
    use usage

enforc! /p "urban renewal" /p public! /p agency

covenant! /p "privity of estate" /p public agency /p enforc!

§ 19.10   Zoning and Private Restrictions

The public has an interest in land use planning effected by private agreement. In a general way, restrictive covenants play a role in public land use planning in that planners may be able to achieve objectives beyond the scope of their regulatory powers by persuading developers to include restrictive covenants in the deeds to property contained in a subdivision. The FHA, for example, encourages the use of restrictive or "protective" covenants to maintain neighborhood character and values, even where residential zoning is present.[1]

Restrictions as a Substitute for Zoning

The Texas legislature has enacted a unique method of land use control which relies on private agreement. The statute provides that

§ 19.9

1. West's Ann.Cal.Pub.Res.Code §§ 5096.1–5096.28; see generally Netherton, Environmental Conservation and Historic Preservation Through Recorded Land Use Agreements, 14 Real Prop., Prob. and Trust Journal 340 (1979) (providing comprehensive analysis of conservation/preservation agreement laws). For a discussion of the use of restrictive covenants for historic preservation purposes, see supra § 14.8.

2. See, e.g., 42 U.S.C.A. 1455(b) permitting controls and restrictions to be used to ensure that purchasers or lessees and their assignees shall be obligated to devote the property to the uses specified in the urban renewal plan for the project area.

3. See One Twenty-Five Varsity Road Ltd. v. Township of York, 23 D.L.R.2d 465 (Ont.Ct.App.1960) where a covenant was held not to be binding on subsequent purchasers where the Township did not exact the covenant for the benefit of any of its land. See also § 19.3 supra.

4. City of Reno v. Matley, 79 Nev. 49, 378 P.2d 256 (1963).

§ 19.10

1. See F.H.A. Underwriting Handbook for Home Mortgages §§ 70440.1, 70440.4. For an analysis of privately held conservation easements, see Korngold, Privately Held Conservation Servitudes: A Policy Analysis in the Context of in Gross Real Covenants and Easements, 63 Tex.L.Rev. 433 (1984).

an incorporated city, town, or village which does not have a zoning
ordinance may sue in a court of competent jurisdiction to enjoin or
abate a violation of a restriction contained or incorporated by reference
in a duly recorded plan, plat or replat or other instrument affecting a
subdivision.[2] The statute further provides that any person who desires
a commercial building permit[3] shall file a certified copy of any instrument which contains a restriction on the use of the property with his
application, together with a certified copy of any amendment, judgment
or other document affecting the use of the property.[4] When the
applicant has complied with the statute and any local ordinance, the
city agency issues a permit for construction or repair which conforms to
all restrictions relating to the use of the property described in the
application.[5] Section 7 of the statute also provides that an administrative refusal to issue a commercial permit on the grounds of a violation
of restrictions contained in a deed or other instrument shall be review-
able by a court of appropriate jurisdiction. Section 7 also provides that
in the event of changed conditions of a subdivision, or any other legally
sufficient reason for modifying a restriction, a person refused a commercial building permit can petition a court of appropriate jurisdiction
to alter the restrictions to better conform to present conditions.

The legislation has given the City of Houston, which does not have
zoning, an alternative method for exerting limited police power control
over land use. Questions have been raised as to the constitutionality of
the Act as a whole, the most serious being that it represents an
unlawful delegation of legislative authority to the nongovernmental
parties who created the restriction.[6] The Supreme Court of Texas has
raised questions of the constitutionality of Section 7, but since the
constitutional questions listed by the court were not raised by the
parties, the court did not decide them.[7] Objections are also raised that
the device represents control without planning and that enforcement of
private restrictive covenants without planning or standards can be no
better than haphazard.[8]

2. Vernon's Ann.Tex.Civ.Stat. art.
974a–1 §§ 1, 2(a).

3. Defined as any building other than a
single family residence. Vernon's Ann.
Tex.Civ.Stat. art. 974a–2 § 2(4).

4. Vernon's Ann.Tex.Civ.Stat. art.
974a–2 § 3(a).

5. Vernon's Ann.Tex.Civ.Stat. art.
974a–2 § 3(b). Art. 974a–2 is limited to
cities over 900,000, so it applies only to
Houston.

6. See Comments, Houston's Invention
of Necessity—An Unconstitutional Substitute for Zoning? 21 Baylor L.Rev. 307
(1969); Municipal Enforcement of Private
Restrictive Covenants: An Innovation in

Land-Use Control, 44 Texas L.Rev. 741
(1966). See also § 5.3 supra.

7. City of Houston v. Emmanuel United
Pentecostal Church, Inc., 433 S.W.2d 680
(Tex.1968).

8. Comment, Municipal Enforcement of
Private Restrictive Covenants: An Innovation in Land-Use Control, 44 Texas L.Rev.
741 (1966). The author also provides the
historical background for Houston's refusal
to adopt a zoning ordinance and the resulting necessity for such legislation. But cf.
Ellickson, Alternatives to Zoning, 40
U.Chi.L.Rev. 681 (1973) (proposing greater
reliance on private nuisance actions for
damages).

Restrictions Complementing Zoning

While contract or conditional zoning can be accomplished by other means,[9] restrictive covenants may be used to complement zoning ordinances and give individualized treatment to a given area for which a zoning change is sought. For example, a municipal authority may reclassify land to a less restricted use if the applicant for rezoning agrees to special limitations on the use of the rezoned property which are not imposed on other land included in the same classification. Such "contract zoning" has been attacked as an unauthorized exercise of delegated legislative powers.[10] However, an increasing number of cases have approved the device as a legitimate manner of exercising the zoning power and achieving needed flexibility.[11] Although the device contemplates that the private agreement restricting use be legally binding, there are serious questions, and little case law, as to what form the agreement should take to ensure enforcement against subsequent owners of the reclassified land.[12]

Conflict Between Private Restrictions and Zoning

Private land use planning by agreement may conflict with public planning through zoning. For example, a prior covenant may restrict property to a residential use while a subsequent zoning ordinance allows a business use. The overwhelming number of cases involve suits to enjoin uses constituting a violation of a restrictive covenant, which uses a subsequent zoning ordinance purports to make a proper use.[13] Many courts hold that the restrictive covenant cannot be abrogated by the ordinance.[14]

A number of courts, while following this general rule, have admitted evidence of the zoning ordinance in order to show there has been a change in neighborhood conditions which would render enforcement of the covenant inequitable.[15]

9. See § 5.5 supra.

10. Hartnett v. Austin, 93 So.2d 86 (Fla. 1956); Baylis v. Baltimore, 219 Md. 164, 148 A.2d 429 (1959); V.F. Zahodiakin Eng'r Corp. v. Zoning Bd. of Adjustment, 8 N.J. 386, 86 A.2d 127 (1952).

11. Sylvania Elec. Prod., Inc. v. Newton, 344 Mass. 428, 183 N.E.2d 118 (1962); Bucholz v. Omaha, 174 Neb. 862, 120 N.W.2d 270 (1963); Church v. Town of Islip, 8 N.Y.2d 254, 203 N.Y.S.2d 866, 168 N.E.2d 680 (1960).

12. See Comment, The Use and Abuse of Contract Zoning, 12 U.C.L.A.L.Rev. 897, 907 (1965).

13. Berger, Conflicts Between Zoning Ordinances and Restrictive Covenants: A

Problem in Land Use Policy, 43 Neb.L.Rev. 449 (1964). See also Comment, Resolving a Conflict—Ohana Zoning & Private Covenants, 6 U.Hawaii L.Rev. 177 (1984).

14. Murphey v. Gray, 84 Ariz. 299, 327 P.2d 751 (1958); Whiting v. Seavey, 159 Me. 61, 188 A.2d 276 (1963); Strauss v. Ginzberg, 218 Minn. 57, 15 N.W.2d 130 (1944).

15. Key v. McCabe, 54 Cal.2d 736, 8 Cal.Rptr. 425, 356 P.2d 169 (1960); Wolff v. Fallon, 44 Cal.2d 695, 284 P.2d 802 (1955); Martin v. Weinberg, 205 Md. 519, 109 A.2d 576 (1954); Brideau v. Grissom, 369 Mich. 661, 120 N.W.2d 829 (1963); Hysinger v. Mullinax, 204 Tenn. 181, 319 S.W.2d 79 (1958).

Several courts [16] have stated that the more restrictive of the two controls governs.[17]   This approach is particularly appealing when the zoning ordinance in question is a cumulative ordinance. If for example, the restrictive covenant requires residential use of the property and the zoning classification is commercial, there is technically no conflict between the private and the public restriction since residential use—as a "higher" use—is permitted in "lower" use zones. Only if the zoning ordinance is noncumulative (i.e. only commercial uses are permitted in commercial zones) is there a conflict between the private and public restriction.

The Restatement and some commentators take the view that in the case of an absolute conflict, where, for example, a lot is restricted to residential use and zoned for exclusive commercial use [18] the police power prevails.[19]   However, it may be necessary to compensate the private owner for his loss of the benefit of the overridden restrictive covenant.[20]   A zoning amendment may be utilized to extinguish a restrictive covenant originally imposed by the city, on the theory that the original covenant was for the benefit of the city and the city could release it.[21]

There are other differences between restrictive covenants and zoning. For example, while zoning that excludes churches from residential areas is sometimes held invalid,[22] restrictive covenants having the same effect are usually enforceable.[23]

 WESTLAW REFERENCES

"farmers home" /p restric! protect! /p covenant

Restrictions as a Substitute for Zonings
974a–1

houston /p "police power" /p limit!   /p land property

Restrictions Complementing Zoning
"contract zoning" /s illegal!
"contract zoning" /s power
(sylvania +s newton) (bucholz +s omaha) /s zon! power

Conflict Between Private Restrictions and Zoning
"restrictive covenant" /p abrogat! /p ordinance regulat!

16. Bluett v. County of Cook, 19 Ill.App. 2d 172, 153 N.E.2d 305 (1958); City of Richlawn v. McMakin, 313 Ky. 265, 230 S.W.2d 902 (1950), cert. dismissed 340 U.S. 945, 71 S.Ct. 531, 95 L.Ed. 682 (1951); Szilvasy v. Saviers, 70 Ohio App. 34, 44 N.E.2d 732 (1942).

17. City of Richlawn v. McMakin, supra, so held even though it was faced with a more restrictive zoning ordinance.

18. See §§ 4.3, 4.5, supra.

19. Restatement of Property § 568 (1944); 8 E. McQuillin, Municipal Corporations § 25.09, at 36 (3rd rev. ed. 1965).

The Restatement position was adopted by the court in Grubel v. MacLaughlin, 286 F.Supp. 24 (D.Virgin Islands 1968).

20. Burger v. St. Paul, 241 Minn. 285, 64 N.W.2d 73 (1954). See § 19.8 supra.

21. Taylor v. Hackensack, 137 N.J.L. 139, 58 A.2d 788 (1948), judgment affirmed 1 N.J. 211, 62 A.2d 686 (1948).

22. See § 4.20 supra.

23. Abrams v. Shuger, 336 Mich. 59, 57 N.W.2d 445 (1953); Hall v. Church of the Open Bible, 4 Wis.2d 246, 89 N.W.2d 798 (1958).

108k72   /p   zon!   /p   "restrictive covenant"   /p   business residen!

108k49   /p   "restrictive covenant"   /p   abrogat! impair! supersed! destroy!

108k49   /p   "restrictive covenant"   /p   license zon!

414k234   /p   zon!   /p   restrict!

(key +s mccabe) (wolff +s grissom) (martin   +s weinberg) (brideau +s grissom) (hysinger   +s mullinax) /p enforc! /p covenant restrict!

cumulative /s zon! /s ordinance regulat!   /p high higher highest low lower lowest /p use usage

non-cumulative /s zon! /s ordinance regulat!

zon! /s modify! modifi! amend! /s "restrictive covenant" /p releas! extinguish!

108k73   /p   "restrictive covenant"

zone zoned zoning /s prohibit! exclud! exclus! /s church /p residen! /s invalid! void unconstitutional!

"restrictive covenant" /s prohibit! exclud! exclus!   /s church /s residen!

taylor +s hackensack /p zon!

Chapter 20

THE POWER OF EMINENT DOMAIN

Analysis

I. INTRODUCTION

Sec.

20.1   The Power of Eminent Domain.
20.2   Eminent Domain and the Police Power.

II. PROPERTY, PUBLIC USE AND CONDEMNATION ISSUES

20.3   Compensable Property Rights.
20.4   Public Use in General.
20.5   Judicial Review of Public Use.
20.6   Excess and Future Condemnation.
20.7   Inverse Condemnation.
20.8   Condemnation by Private Parties.

III. JUST COMPENSATION

20.9   Fair Market Value.
20.10   Governmental Actions and Fair Market Value.
20.11   Divided Fees.
20.12   Noncompensable Damages.
20.13   Severance Damages.
20.14   Benefits as Set Offs.

I. INTRODUCTION

§ 20.1 The Power of Eminent Domain

The federal government [1] and each state [2] and municipality [3] generally have the power of eminent domain over property within the territorial limits of their jurisdiction. This power to take property for public use is an attribute of sovereignty and inheres in the sovereign, though the power is activated by and may be conferred on non-sovereign entities by legislative declaration [4].

The United States Constitution fifth amendment provision, "nor shall private property be taken for public use, without just compensation," limits rather than grants the power of eminent domain. The fifth amendment was held applicable to the states in 1896,[5] but by that time the limitations of "public use" and "just compensation" had been imposed on all state governments by their constitutions or by judicial concepts of "natural justice." [6] Although these constitutional provisions do not explicitly prohibit the taking of private property for private use, they are read as doing so implicitly.[7]

 WESTLAW REFERENCES

di eminent domain

pritz +s messer

(federal! /2 govern!) "united states" /s limit! /s "eminent domain" /s jurisdiction

(cherokee +s nation +s souther +s kansas) /p taking "eminent domain" /p power /p federal! "united states" congress!

to(148) /p power /s sovereign! /s municipal!

"legislative declaration" /p "eminent domain" /p power /p delegat! confer

to(148) /p property /s "public use" /s sovereign! /s power /s delegat!

to(148) /p "fifth amendment" /s "just compensation" /s "private property"

to(148) /p fifth /s fourteenth /s amendment

"natural justice" /p "eminent domain" "fifth amendment"

"eminent domain" /p "fifth amendment" /p apply! /s state

§ 20.1

1. Cherokee Nation v. Southern Kansas Ry. Co., 135 U.S. 641, 10 S.Ct. 965, 34 L.Ed. 295 (1890).

2. Zurn v. Chicago, 389 Ill. 114, 59 N.E.2d 18 (1945).

3. Du Pre v. Marietta, 213 Ga. 403, 99 S.E.2d 156 (1957). A municipality may be granted power to take property outside of its boundaries. Harden v. Superior Court, 44 Cal.2d 630, 284 P.2d 9 (1955).

4. See, J. Juergensmeyer and J. Wadley, 1 Florida Land Use Restrictions—Police Power § 2.02 (1975).

5. Missouri Pac. Ry. v. Nebraska, 164 U.S. 403, 17 S.Ct. 130, 41 L.Ed. 489 (1896).

6. See Raleigh & Gaston R.R. Co. v. Davis, 19 N.C. 431 (1837).

7. See, Hawaii Housing Authority v. Midkiff, 467 U.S. 229, 104 S.Ct. 2321, 81 L.Ed.2d 186 (1984), on remand 740 F.2d 15 (9th Cir.1984).

sy(state /p constitution! /p prohibit! /p taking /p private /p
property /p public! /p use usage)

§ 20.2   Eminent Domain and the Police Power

Few subjects are as intriguing as the question of the line between
the police power and the power of eminent domain. The line to be
discovered and defined is the one between those cases which hold a
regulation valid and those which hold that a regulation constitutes a
taking and therefore is unconstitutional, since no compensation has
been offered.[1] Some cases are illustrative of the problem. In City of
San Antonio v. Pigeonhole Parking of Texas, Inc.[2] plaintiff had constructed a ten story parking garage on its corner lot with a driveway
onto an abutting street. Defendant city denied a permit to construct a
driveway onto the other abutting street and passed an ordinance
prohibiting the issuance of such permits. The court held the ordinance
was a legitimate exercise of the police power having the effect of a
zoning regulation. The court stated that although the right of access
must be compensated for when taken by eminent domain, no compensation for it is due when the police power has been reasonably invoked for
the protection of the health, safety, and general welfare of the public.

In Bino v. Hurley,[3] plaintiffs sought to invalidate a city ordinance
prohibiting bathing, boating, or swimming in a lake in which plaintiffs
had riparian rights and from which the city drew its water supply.
The court held for plaintiffs, stating that the riparian right to use the
lake for swimming, boating and bathing is a substantial and valuable
one, and that when government action deprives the individual of a
vested property right, it goes beyond police power regulation and
becomes an act of eminent domain. On the other hand, a Vermont
court has held that if bathing in a pond contaminates the city's water
supply, the riparian owner's use of his property right is not reasonable
and may be prohibited by the police power.[4]

In deciding this type of case, the courts often use a variety of tests.
If the court can conclude that there is no property right involved, then
the regulation will be upheld because, by definition, there has been no
taking of property. For example, in Just v. Marinette County,[5] the
landowner was denied the right to fill and develop lakeside wetlands.
The court considered the argument that the landowner had been denied
the "value based upon the changing character of the land at the
expense of harm to public rights"[6] and stated it was not a necessary

---

§ 20.2

1. See § 10.7 supra, for a complete dis-
cussion of the taking issue. See also,
Siemon, Of Regulatory Takings and Other
Myths, 1 Fla.St.U.L.Rev. 107 (1985).

2. 158 Tex. 318, 311 S.W.2d 218 (1958).

3. 273 Wis. 10, 706 N.W.2d 571 (1956).

4. State v. Morse, 84 Vt. 387, 80 A. 189
(1911).

5. 56 Wis.2d 7, 201 N.W.2d 761 (1972);
for use of Just in another jurisdiction, see,
Graham v. Estuary Properties, Inc., 399 So.
2d 1374 (1981), cert. denied 454 U.S. 1083,
102 S.Ct. 640, 70 L.Ed.2d 618 (1981).

6. Id. at 23, 201 N.W.2d at 771.

factor in the calculus. In short, the court opined that the landowner was denied an economic right rather than a protected property right. In so doing, the Wisconsin court obviously relied upon the U.S. Supreme Court's decision in United States v. Willow River Power Co.[7] in which the Court stated, "But not all economic interests are 'property rights'; only those economic advantages are 'rights' which have the law back of them, and only when they are so recognized may courts compel others to forbear from interfering with them or to compensate for their invasion." [8]

Since there is no property right to maintain a nuisance, if a noxious use is regulated, the courts tend to view the regulation as valid.[9] For example, in Miller v. Schonene,[10] cedar trees hosted a disease that did not injure them but was deadly to nearby apple trees. The court held that the cedar trees could be destroyed under the police power without compensation. Similarly, there is no property right in the public domain, so that a property owner cannot recover for high overflights over his land [11] or for property rights that are made valuable because of the presence of a navigable stream.[12]

Sometimes a court is willing to uphold a regulation on the basis of an emergency. For example, during wartime it was held proper to close a nonessential industry without compensation, so the manpower would then be available for more war related employment.[13]

Courts also often apply more general tests. For example, a regulation might be upheld if it produces great public gain with little private harm. That "balancing" test is close to the fairness test, which determines whether the public weal is furthered too much at the expense of particular individuals.[14] The two tests in turn are close to and not less vague that the test which does not so much look to the public benefit, but which upholds the regulation unless values are unreasonably impaired or there is no remaining use which will yield a reasonable return.[15]

Perhaps the most often used test, however, is one which states that a regulation is a taking if it is designed to benefit the public rather

7. 324 U.S. 499, 65 S.Ct. 761, 89 L.Ed. 1101 (1945).

8. Id. at 502. See, e.g., Comment, Environmental Regulation, Just Prevents Harm, 33 U.Fla.L.Rev. 615 (1981) for a discussion of the status of property rights and economic rights in Florida. But see Bryden, The Phantom Doctrine of Just, 1978 Am.Bar Fndn.Res.J. 397.

9. See § 14.7 infra.

10. 276 U.S. 272, 48 S.Ct. 246, 72 L.Ed. 568 (1928).

11. See § 10.7 supra.

12. United States v. Twin City Power Co., 350 U.S. 222, 76 S.Ct. 259, 100 L.Ed. 240 (1956), rehearing denied 350 U.S. 1009, 76 S.Ct. 648, 100 L.Ed. 871 (1956).

13. United States v. Central Eureka Mining Co., 357 U.S. 155, 78 S.Ct. 1097, 2 L.Ed.2d 1228 (1958), rehearing denied 358 U.S. 858, 79 S.Ct. 9, 3 L.Ed.2d 91 (1958).

14. See, Michelman, Property, Utility and Fairness: Comments on the Ethical Foundations of "Just Compensation" Law, 80 Harv.L.Rev. 1165 (1967).

15. Goldblatt v. Town of Hempstead, 369 U.S. 590, 82 S.Ct. 987, 8 L.Ed.2d 130 (1962).

than to prevent harm. Several legal scholars have tried their hand at stating this test more precisely, though none have been regarded as fully succeeding. A definition that will satisfy most everyone in close cases has eluded consensus.

An often quoted early statement of the test was formulated by Freund: "[I]t may be said that the state takes property by eminent domain because it is useful to the public, and under the police power because it is harmful. . . . " [16] Dunham reviewed many cases and concluded that

> where the legislation was upheld, the purpose and effect of the legislation was to allocate to a land use the costs which, but for the legislation, the activity would impose on other owners without compensation. In each instance where the legislation was struck down, the purpose and effect of the legislation was to compel one or more particular owners to furnish without compensation a benefit wanted by the public.[17]

In other words if the regulation prevents harmful externalities it is proper, but if it is to confer a good on the public, regulation is improper. In a hard case, the test is not helpful. For example, when a regulation imposes flight plane zoning,[18] is it to prevent buildings above the flight plane which would cause harm to passengers in airplanes or is it the acquisition by the public of the benefit of a highway in the sky? [19]

Sax gives the test a slightly different twist.

> [W]hen an individual . . . sustains a detriment to legally acquired . . . economic values as a consequence of government activity which enhances the economic value of some governmental enterprise, then the act is a taking . . . but when the challenged act is an improvement of the public condition through resolution of conflict within the private sector of the society, compensation is not constitutionally required.[20]

Applying his test, Sax concludes that flight plane zoning is compensable because by acquiring the highway in the sky the public is enhancing the value of its publicly owned airport. Others might note, however, that the zoning is merely resolution of conflict between the owners of private land and the passengers in and owners of privately owned airplanes.

Other scholars have suggested other tests. Haar offers the following for consideration:

16. E. Freund, The Police Power, Public Policy and Constitutional Rights § 511 (1904).

17. Dunham, A Legal and Economic Basis for City Planning, 58 Colum.L.Rev. 650, 669 (1958).

18. See § 4.19 supra.

19. Sneed v. County of Riverside, 218 Cal.App.2d 205, 32 Cal.Rptr. 318 (1963).

20. Sax, Takings and the Police Power, 74 Yale L.J. 36, 67 (1964).

§ 1. General Rule

Police power measures may be utilized to control the use of land in such a manner that the land shall not harm the use of other land and in addition shall contribute to the welfare of the community, unless

(a) The law discriminates between owners in such a manner that it denies equal rights under the law, or

(b) The regulation reduces control of the land to the extent that it deprives the owner of property without due process of law.

§ 2. Deprivation of Property—Taking

Police power measures do not deprive the owner of property without due process of law unless the effect of the measures is to cause harm to the individual greatly in excess of the public benefits.

§ 3. Public Benefits and the General Welfare

Determination of the social necessity of a particular police power measure is governed by the following factors:

(a) The degree to which the ordinance is designed to prevent uses which may conflict with each other,

(b) The social desirability of the ends to be achieved by the particular police power measure, and

(c) The necessity of utilizing the police power rather than other powers of government.

§ 4. Injury to Private Rights

Determination of the extent to which the application of a police power measure injures the proprietary rights of an owner depends upon the following factors:

(a) The extent to which economic use of the land is precluded by

(i) The statute,

(ii) The physical condition of the land, and

(iii) Surrounding uses, and

(b) The social desirability of the uses to which the land may economically be put.[21]

Waite would prefer to shift the focus away from the all or nothing police power-eminent domain continuum, focus on government activity in general, and decide the compensation question on the basis of effect:

'Taking' should only occur when the land or interests in land remaining to the owner immediately after the governmental action in question is not of practical utility. Lack of practical utility

---

21. C. Haar, Land-Use Planning 544–45 (1959).

. . . would be shown by inability to earn a reasonable return on the value of the entire tract, appraised immediately before, and without regard to, the action taken.[22]

Michelman believes the entire matter is too difficult for courts and that they are not competent to handle it. Therefore, he proposes that legislatures stop dropping the problem in the judicial lap and instead specify in greater detail the acts for which compensation should be paid.[23]

Bosselman suggests that a more active voice by the legislature would be welcome; a greater delineation by them of which acts constitute a taking. But, of equal importance to him is the expansion of the court's awareness of the policies behind land use regulations. Finally, however, he states that a better solution lies in the quality of drafting of regulations, which entails greater research and better compromises.[24]

 WESTLAW REFERENCES

"eminent domain" /3 "police power"

di police power

sy(ordinance /p legitimate /p "police power" /p compensa!)

deny! deni** /s permit /s taking /s "police power"

deny! deni** /s permit /s taking /p "police power" /p
    ordinance /p compensa!

to(148) /p deni! deny! /s permit /s reasonable

ordinance regulat! /p prohibit! /p bathing boating swimming /p
    riparian

substantial! /p valu! /p "police power" /p "property right" /p
    vest!

government! /p depriv! /p "vested property right" /p taking

compensa! taking "police power" "eminent domain" /p bathing
    boating swimming /p vest! /s property land /s right

148k84 /p compensa! taking "eminent domain" "police power" /s
    vest!

"property right" /p regulat! /p upheld! uphold! /p valid! /p
    taking

(just +s martinette) (graham +s estuary +s property) /s
    taking

regulat! /s taking /s property land /s compensa! /s factor

148k2 /p factor

148k270 /p government

22. Waite, Governmental Power and Private Property, 16 Catholic U.L.Rev. 283, 289 (1967).

23. Michelman, supra note 14 "The decisions suggest that the process is one of balancing the public good which the regulation is intended to secure against the deprivation of use value suffered by the owner of the restricted land." Anderson, A Comment on the Fine Line Between "Regulation" and "Taking," in the New Zoning: Legal, Administrative and Economic Concepts and Techniques 66, 81 (N. Marcus & M. Groves eds. 1969); McClain, Modern Concepts of Police Power and Eminent Domain, 1969 Institute on Eminent Domain 165; Comment, An Evaluation of the Rights and Remedies of a New York Landowner for Losses Due to Government Action—With a Proposal for Reform, 33 Albany L.Rev. 537 (1969).

24. Bosselman, Callies, and Banta, The Taking Issue, 318–319 (1973).

economic /2 interest right /p "property right" /p compensa!
to(279) /p regulat! ordinance /s valid!

"public domain" /s "property right" /s land stream water air

united +s states +s central +s eureka +s mining /p
    emergency

402k14 /p taking /s compensa!

goldblatt +s hempstead /p regulat! /p taking /p "just
    compensation"

regulat! /s taking /s benefit! /s public!

sneed +s county +s riverside /p air airport plane airplane

General Rule

"police power" /s zon! /s "equal protection" /s discriminat!

92k228.2

"police power" /p depriv! /p land /p "due process"

Deprivation of Property—Taking

"police power" /p "due process" /p land /p harm harmed
    harming hardship /p public! /p benefit!

Public Benefits and the General Welfare

social! public! /s necessary necessity /s "police power" /s
    factor criteri!

Injury to Private Rights

"police power" /p factor criteri! /p injur! harm harmed harming
    /p private! individual! /p land property /p right interest

haar /s "police power" land

michelman /p "eminent domain" "police power"

bosselman /p "eminent domain" "police power"

II. PROPERTY, PUBLIC USE AND CONDEMNATION ISSUES

§ 20.3   Compensable Property Rights

The "property" for which compensation must be paid includes future,[1] present, tangible, intangible, possessory and nonpossessory interests. There is no property right to continue a nuisance. Easements for example are property for which, when taken, compensation is due.[2] In United States v. Welch,[3] the condemnor took a strip of land by flooding it and in doing so cut off a farmer's right of way from his farm to the county road. The farmer was awarded damages for the resulting depreciation in the value of his farm. The court held that a private right of way is an easement for which compensation is due, whether it is taken by appropriation or destruction.[4]

§ 20.3

1. Stubbs v. United States, 21 F.Supp. 1007 (M.D.N.C.1938) (life tenancy, remainder).

2. See § 19.8 supra.

3. 217 U.S. 333, 30 S.Ct. 527, 54 L.Ed. 787 (1910).

4. See §§ 4.36, 8.3 supra.

Access as Property

The interests of an abutting owner in a public way are subject to reasonable interference by police power action without compensation. For example, the public interest in safety and convenience is considered to outweigh the abutting owner's interests when it necessitates reasonable, temporary obstruction of the way during repairs.[5] Another outweighing factor would be interference with passage along the way by diversion of traffic;[6] for example, insertion of a median strip can also be done without compensation.[7] However, compensation must be paid when the construction of a public improvement substantially interferes with the abutting owner's recognized rights.[8]

Compensable property rights include the right of the property owner to have direct access to a public street abutting his property,[9] and to view, light, and air[10] over that street.[11]

Courts differ as to what constitutes a substantial interference with the right of access. Some courts hold that the landowner has a right of access not only to the immediately abutting streets, but also from that street to advantageous intersections and to the general system of streets. Therefore, compensation may be due when the closing of an intersection makes the abutting street a cul de sac.[12] For example, in People v. Ricciardi[13] a property right was held to have been taken when a circuitous route was imposed. The defendant owned land abutting a highway that the state proposed to widen. The widened highway plan included a sunken park which would form an underpass beneath a railroad crossing the highway. According to the plan, all through-traffic would be on the sunken middle section. Defendant's customers consequently first had to travel some distance on the surface level roadway abutting defendant's property rather than have direct access to the new highway.

The majority held that defendant's easements of access to and visibility from the old through-traffic highway had been taken and

5. Farrell v. Rose, 253 N.Y. 73, 170 N.E. 498 (1930).

6. Riddle v. State Highway Comm'n, 184 Kan. 603, 339 P.2d 301 (1959).

7. People ex rel. Dep't of Pub. Works v. Ayon, 54 Cal.2d 217, 5 Cal.Rptr. 15, 352 P.2d 519 (1960), cert. denied 364 U.S. 827, 81 S.Ct. 65, 5 L.Ed.2d 55 (1960).

8. Bacich v. Board of Control, 23 Cal.2d 343, 144 P.2d 818 (1943); Rose v. State, 19 Cal.2d 713, 123 P.2d 505 (1942).

9. Brownlow v. O'Donoghue Bros., 276 F. 636 (D.C.Cir.1922); People v. Riciardi, 23 Cal.2d 390, 144 P.2d 799 (1943).

10. St. Peter's Italian Church Syracuse v. State, 261 App.Div. 96, 24 N.Y.S.2d 759 (1941); State ex rel. Dep't of Highways v. Allison, 372 P.2d 850 (Okl.1962).

11. Easements of light, air, and access exist only to abutting public streets and not to abutting lands, unless conferred by grant. Thus, in the absence of statute or grant, public acts on other land, which diminish the value of neighboring land by obstructing light and air, does not result in a compensable taking of a property interest in the neighboring land. Rand v. Boston, 164 Mass. 354, 41 N.E. 484 (1895).

12. Bacich v. Board of Control, 23 Cal. 2d 343, 144 P.2d 818 (1943) (right of access to the next intersecting street in both directions): Village of Winnetka v. Clifford, 201 Ill. 475, 66 N.E. 384 (1903).

13. 23 Cal.2d 390, 144 P.2d 799 (1943).

must be compensated. The dissent concluded that recognizing these easements of access and view implied property owners on an undivided highway would be due damages whenever a street becomes a divided limited access highway, or where the state erects structures that block the visibility of abutting owners.

The fears of the dissenters have not materialized, however, as evidenced by People ex rel. Department of Public Works v. Ayon.[14] In that case the court held that an abutting property owner was not entitled to compensation when a divider strip was placed in the middle of the street that would divert some southbound traffic from the street in front of his property. The court reasoned that the compensable right of an abutting property owner is to direct access to an adjacent street and the through traffic on it. Further, if that basic right is not adversely affected, even though access is impaired or traffic becomes circular a public agency may enact and enforce reasonable and proper traffic regulations without compensation although they impair the convenience or access and necessitate circuity of travel to reach a given destination.

WESTLAW REFERENCES

"compensable property right" /p interest

united +s states +s welch /p easement

Access As Property

interest /s abut! /s "public way"

reasonabl! /s interfer! /s "police power" /s compensa!

"police power" /s safe! welfare /p outweigh! /s private

farell +s rose /p abut!

92k81 /p balanc! /p private!

92k81 /p "police power" /s reasonable! /s interfer! /s private!

"police power" /s substantial! /s interfer! /s compensa!

compensa! /s property land /s right /s direct! /s access! /s street light air

people +s ricciardi /p "property right" /p taking

di("property right" /s easement /s access! /s compensa!)

148k106 /p compensa! /s abut! /s landowner /s taking

148k106 /p temporar!

148k106 /p obstruct! /s compensa!

268k669 /p compensa! /p "right of access"

148k85 /p compensa! /s taking /s access!

---

§ 20.4   Public Use in General

Exercise of the power of eminent domain is proper only for a public use and only where use of the power is necessary.[1] The public use

14. 54 Cal.2d 217, 5 Cal.Rptr. 151, 352 P.2d 519 (1960), cert. denied 364 U.S. 827, 81 S.Ct. 65, 5 L.Ed.2d 55 (1960).

§ 20.4

1. See § 20.5 infra on necessity.

limitation was first interpreted as requiring that the taking further a broadly conceived public good. However, as the scope of governmental activity expanded and as the unoccupied lands in both public and private domains dwindled, the exercise of the power of eminent domain became more frequent and more burdensome to the private sector. The courts began to impose stricter limitations, and by the middle of the nineteenth century, if there was no actual use by the public there was some likelihood a court would find no public use.[2] However, exceptions were created to accommodate uses established in the earlier period—for example, the mill acts authorized a private riparian owner to build a mill dam interfering with a neighbor's riparian rights on payment of compensation for such interference[3]—and to meet the country's changing needs. These exceptions began to swallow the rule by the end of the century. This century has seen the virtual demise of the physical use by the public test[4] and the rise of a benefit to the public or the public purpose test.

The expanded nature of the public use and necessity test is perhaps best told in the context of urban renewal.[5] The exercise of the power of eminent domain in the context of urban renewal was justified first to remove slums, then to prevent blight of developed property, then to remove blight from undeveloped property and finally merely to improve the appearance of neighborhoods. Even though urban renewal transfers privately owned property to other private owners, that does not defeat the public use test.[6] Furthermore, the test is met even though the public investment in the renewal is often more than the resale price of the property. Such a situation does not make the public action a gift of public property to private persons.

While the compelling need for eliminating slums and the appropriateness of using private enterprise for accomplishing that objective may have created a special situation in which the public use limitation is no longer much of an impediment in urban renewal, the limitation may be a more formidable obstacle in other situations. Judicial reaction to condemnation for private beneficiaries in other contexts has been mixed. An emphasis on the constitutionality of the program rather than an examination of who actually uses the property exhibits the federal judiciary's liberal propensity to defer to the legislative branch in this area.[7] State courts often examine the condemnation as such which undoubtedly leads to who may end up in possession.

Condemnation for parking facilities and for commercial and industrial development has been the subject of much controversy in state

2. Gravelly Ford Canal Co. v. Pope & Talbot Land Co., 36 Cal.App. 556, 178 P. 150 (1918).

3. Head v. Amoskeag Mfg. Co., 113 U.S. 9, 5 S.Ct. 441, 28 L.Ed. 889 (1885).

4. See Comment, The Public Use Limitation on Eminent Domain: An Advance Requiem, 58 Yale L.J. 599 (1949).

5. See ch. 17 infra for a more complete discussion of Urban renewal.

6. See, Berman v. Parker, 348 U.S. 26, 75 S.Ct. 98, 99 L.Ed. 27 (1954).

7. See, Gelin and Miller, The Federal Law of Eminent Domain, 16–17 (1982).

courts, while a project that was essentially property redistribution has been allowed by the U.S. Supreme Court.[8] Cities often seek to solve their parking problems by leasing parking garages constructed on a condemned site to private lessees. Courts find parking projects to be a public use since they relieve congestion and reduce traffic hazards.[9] However, the public character of the use is considered removed when the primary objective is private gain rather than public need.[10] That impermissible objective may be evidenced by retention of too little control over rates to be charged and rules of operation. Also, the existence of too much floor area not associated with parking operations,[11] or the fact that the contract for building the garage and the lease have specifications peculiar to the needs of a particular bidder has been troublesome.

Denihan Enterprises, Inc. v. O'Dwyer [12] is an example of the aforementioned. Here, a city and an insurance company contracted for the condemnation of property opposite an apartment house being built by the insurance company. The city also agreed to offer the lease at a public auction on terms specified in the contract. The insurance company was to bid for the lease at a specified amount and, if successful, construct a garage in accord with the contract and lease. Procedurally, the court overruled a demurrer because the project was so involved with a private purpose it rendered the condemnation invalid. Important factors for the court were that the contract provided for a garage only two stories in height above the surface; for half the roof to be a private landscaped park for apartment house tenants, and for the right of the lessee to rent thirty percent of the ground and basement space for commercial purposes. However, in Foltz v. Indianapolis,[13] a parking facility was considered a public utility. The court held that lack of regulations and the lack of control over the lessee's rates did not destroy the public use. The common law right of the individual to compel service from business classified as affected with a public interest without discrimination or extortion existed regardless of the lack of a statute to protect the public interest.

Where unblighted land is acquired for an industrial or commercial enterprise, many state courts have been more reluctant to find a public use. In Hogue v. Port of Seattle [14] for example, the Port Authority was concerned about the status of the area as a one-industry city and

8. See, Hawaii Housing Authority v. Midkiff, 467 U.S. 229, 104 S.Ct. 2321, 81 L.Ed.2d 186 (1984), on remand 740 F.2d 15 (9th Cir.1984).

9. City and County of San Francisco v. Ross, 44 Cal.2d 52, 279 P.2d 529 (1955); Larsen v. City and County of San Francisco, 152 Cal.App.2d 355, 313 P.2d 959 (1957); State ex rel. Hawks v. Topeka, 176 Kan. 240, 270 P.2d 270 (1954).

10. City and County of San Francisco v. Ross and Larsen v. City and County of San

Francisco, supra; Opinion of the Justices, 341 Mass. 738, 167 N.E.2d 745 (1960).

11. City and County of San Francisco v. Ross and Larsen v. City and County of San Francisco, supra.

12. 277 App.Div. 407, 100 N.Y.S.2d 512 (1950), affirmed 302 N.Y. 451, 99 N.E.2d 235 (1951).

13. 234 Ind. 656, 130 N.E.2d 650 (1955).

14. 54 Wn.2d 799, 341 P.2d 171 (1959).

attempted to achieve industrial balance by acquiring land, regardless of marginal characteristics, for redevelopment and sale or lease to private industry. The court found that the Authority was condemning fully developed land because it believed it could devote the land to a better economic use and that such a condemnation was not for a public use.[15]

However, in Courtesy Sandwich Shop, Inc. v. Port of New York Authority,[16] the New York court virtually accepted the higher and better use test rejected in Hogue. The court upheld the constitutionality of condemnation for a "World Trade Center" to centralize New York City's foreign trade facilities. The Court found facilitation of the flow of commerce and centralization of all activity incidental thereto to be a public purpose. Thus the condemnation power extended to property with activities functionally related to that purpose. Finally, this included even the use of portions of structures otherwise devoted to project purposes for the production of incidental revenue for the expenses of the project.

WESTLAW REFERENCES

di(exercis! /s "eminent domain" /s power /s proper /s
    public! /s use usage)

water /p "mill act"

test /s "public purpose" /p "eminent domain"

land /s "eminent domain" /p "public use and necessity"

"urban renewal" /p transfer! /p private! /p property land

constitution! unconstitution! /s program project /s "eminent
    domain" condemn! /s private! /s beneficiary benefit!

condemn! "eminent domain" /p "parking facility" /p private! /p
    lessee

denihan +s o'dwyer /p condemn! /p private!

constitution! /p condemn! "eminent domain" /p public! /p
    purpose use usage /p incident! /p revenue gain

§ 20.5 Judicial Review of Public Use

The constitutional limitations that the taking must be for a public use and necessity create justiciable issues. A legislative declaration of public use bears a strong presumption of validity. While most state courts make an independent determination of public use, they generally give great weight to the legislative determination. That is so even under some constitutions which provide for de novo judicial review of public use.[1]

Federal judges have proved particularly reluctant to invalidate a legislatively authorized taking. Under the "due process" test, the court

---

15. But see, Midkiff supra note 8.

16. 12 N.Y.2d 379, 240 N.Y.S.2d 1, 190 N.E.2d 402 (1963), appeal dismissed 375 U.S. 78, 84 S.Ct. 194, 11 L.Ed.2d 141 (1963), rehearing denied 375 U.S. 960, 84 S.Ct. 440, 11 L.Ed.2d 318 (1963).

§ 20.5

1. Hogue v. Port of Seattle, 54 Wn.2d 799, 341 P.2d 171 (1959) was decided under such a constitutional provision.

accepts the legislative declaration of a public use unless property is taken without due process of law. As one federal authority has concluded, "the issue of public use thus raises the question not of constitutionality of the condemnation, as such, but of the constitutionality of the program or project for which acquisition of the land is sought." [2] Puerto Rico v. Eastern Sugar Associates,[3] is a striking application of the due process test and of federal court deference. The court upheld condemnation under a land redistribution law. The court indicated that its sole concern was whether the taking deprived defendant of property without due process of law. The taking need not be one for use by the public or necessary for the public health if it is material to the prosperity of the community. The severity of Puerto Rico's problems no doubt influenced the court in its decision. Under the "federal" test, the federal government is allowed to take property required to carry out its constitutional purposes and authority, so long as due process is not denied.[4]

A later U.S. Supreme Court case is illustrative of and expands the Eastern Sugar Association holding. In Hawaii Housing Authority v. Midkiff,[5] the state of Hawaii attempted to redistribute lands. Historically the land in Hawaii had been owned by a few individuals. The state legislature provided for condemnation for the avowed public good of alleviating the evils of oligopolic land ownership. Justice O'Connor opined that "in our system of government legislatures are better able to assess what public purposes should be advanced by an exercise of the taking power," [6] and in fact "the 'public use' requirement is thus coterminous with the scope of a sovereign's police power." [7]

Questions of necessity—the need for making a given public improvement, for adopting a particular plan for it, and for taking particular property—are considered matters for the discretion of the legislature or its appointed administrative body.[8] In urban renewal, for example, the determination that a particular area is blighted and the definition of project boundaries are likely to be foreclosed from judicial examination.[9]

2. Marquis, Constitutional and Statutory Authority to Condemn, 43 Iowa L.Rev. 170, 173 (1958).

3. 156 F.2d 316 (1st Cir.1946), cert. denied 329 U.S. 772, 67 S.Ct. 190, 91 L.Ed. 664 (1946).

4. United States v. Carmack, 329 U.S. 230, 67 S.Ct. 252, 91 L.Ed. 209 (1946), rehearing denied 329 U.S. 834, 67 S.Ct. 627, 91 L.Ed. 706 (1947).

5. 467 U.S. 229, 104 S.Ct. 2321, 81 L.Ed. 2d 186 (1984), on remand 740 F.2d 15 (9th Cir.1984).

6. Id. 104 S.Ct. at 2331, 81 L.Ed.2d at 200.

7. Id. 104 S.Ct. at 2329, 81 L.Ed. at 197.

8. Note, "Necessity" in Eminent Domain Proceedings: Four Cases, 29 Mont.L. Rev. 69 (1967). A jury determination of necessity may be required by statute or constitution. E.g., Wis. Const. art. 11, § 2 once provided: "No municipal corporation shall take private property for public use, against the consent of the owner, without the necessity thereof being first established by the verdict of a jury. See § 17.7 infra.

9. Kaskel v. Impellitteri, 306 N.Y. 73, 115 N.E.2d 659 (1953), reargument denied, remittitur amended 306 N.Y. 609, 115 N.E.2d 832 (1953), cert. denied 347 U.S. 934, 74 S.Ct. 629, 98 L.Ed. 1085 (1954); Davis v. Lubbock, 160 Tex. 38, 326 S.W.2d 699 (1959). Davis, in fact, held that the trial de novo provision of the Texas Urban

A judicial issue arises as to questions of necessity only when fraud, bad faith, or abuse of discretion in the determination of necessity is charged.[10] Determinations of abuse of discretion, however, are difficult. For example, in Bristol Redevelopment & Housing Authority v. Denton [11] determining whether there was an abuse of discretion meant reweighing the facts. The court found it must determine whether the area to be acquired was in fact blighted in order to determine whether the condemnor had acted with legal authority. "Bad faith" is equally difficult to determine. Where the project is for a clearly public purpose and the motives of the condemnor are challenged, courts are reluctant to intervene.[12] In Deerfield Park District v. Progress Development Corp.,[13] for example, where the taking was challenged as an attempt to avoid racially integrated housing, the court refused to prevent the taking unless its sole and exclusive purpose was racially inspired.[14] Even where the land is in fact not used for the public purpose asserted as the justification for its taking or the use is shifted from a public to a private use, the condemnee can only invalidate the previous condemnation by showing collateral and extrinsic fraud,[15] a difficult task.

 WESTLAW REFERENCES

legislat! /s declar! /p public** /p use usage /p land
    property /p presum! /s valid!

"due process" /p legislat! /s declar! /p public** /s use
    usage /p land property /p taking condemn! "eminent
    domain"

federal! "united states" /p take taking /s property land /p
    authority authoriz! /p constitution! valid! /s purpose reason
       /p "due process" /p condemn! "eminent domain"

"public use" /s sovereign! /s "police power"

148k13

Renewal Law requiring an independent trial on the question of whether an area to be cleared was in fact a slum violated the separation of powers. The distinction between public use and public necessity is not always a clear one. Inclusion of good buildings for acquisition in an urban renewal project, for example, may be viewed as either.

10. State ex rel. Sharp v. 0.62033 Acres of Land, 49 Del. 174, 112 A.2d 857 (1955); Kaskel v. Impellitteri, 306 N.Y. 73, 115 N.E.2d 659 (1953), reargument denied, remittitur amended 306 N.Y. 609, 115 N.E.2d 832 (1953), cert. denied 347 U.S. 934, 74 S.Ct. 629, 98 L.Ed. 1085 (1954). Contra, People ex rel. Dept. of Pub. Works v. Chevalier, 52 Cal.2d 299, 340 P.2d 598 (1959). The legislative determination is conclusive under statutes affording conclusive effect to the condemning body's findings of necessity even if fraud, bad faith or abuse of discretion is alleged since to hold otherwise would thwart legislative purpose in mak-

ing such determinations conclusive and would open the door to endless litigation. Federal courts have long held that "[i]n the absence of bad faith . . . if the use is a public one, the necessity for the desired property as part thereof is not a question for judicial determination." Wilson v. United States, 350 F.2d 901, 907 (10th Cir. 1965).

11. 198 Va. 171, 93 S.E.2d 288 (1956).

12. See, e.g., Moskow v. Boston Redevelopment Authority, 349 Mass. 553, 210 N.E.2d 699 (1965), cert. denied 382 U.S. 983, 86 S.Ct. 558, 15 L.Ed.2d 472 (1966).

13. 26 Ill.2d 296, 186 N.E.2d 360 (1962), cert. denied 372 U.S. 968, 83 S.Ct. 1093, 10 L.Ed.2d 1042 (1963).

14. See § 10.4 supra.

15. Beistline v. San Diego, 256 F.2d 421 (9th Cir.1958), cert. denied 358 U.S. 865, 79 S.Ct. 96, 3 L.Ed.2d 98 (1958).

"urban renewal" /s determin! /s blight! slum /s adjudicat!
   judgment judged adjudged examin!

di("urban renewal" /s determin! /s blight! slum)

414k602 /p scope /p review!

414k702 /p decision! /p review!

414k602 /p boundar!

414k613 /p good bad /2 faith

268k628 /p necessity

268k299

268k63.1(5)

268k267 /p necessity

268k267 /p review!

148k68 /p "abuse of discretion" /s review!

148k68 /p court /s substitut!

148k300 /p arbitrar!

268k323(3) /p fraud!

"separation of powers" /p blight!

bristol +s denton

condemn! "eminent domain" /p "bad faith" /p motiv! /p
   "public purpose"

condemn! "eminent domain" /p collateral /p extrinsic /p fraud

§ 20.6   Excess and Future Condemnation

A condemnor may seek to acquire more land than is absolutely necessary for an improvement for the purpose of (1) not leaving odd-shaped remnants of land, (2) taking abutting land so that planning restrictions may be imposed to protect the public improvement from an inharmonious environment, or (3) taking surplus land to recoup the expense of the project by selling the land at a profit after the value is enhanced on completion of the project. These are varieties of excess condemnation. Unfavorable court decisions have led to constitutional amendments to expressly authorize excess condemnation.[1] These provisions, however, may expressly exclude or be construed by courts as not allowing excess condemnation for recoupment. In City of Cincinnati v. Vester,[2] for example, the court held that excess condemnation for recoupment purposes was not for a public use within the meaning of the state excess condemnation constitutional provision and that it violated the due process clause of the fourteenth amendment. The

---

§ 20.6

1. E.g., West's Ann.Cal. Const. Art. 1, § 14½: "The State, or any of its cities or counties, may acquire by . . . condemnation, lands for establishing, laying out, widening, enlarging, extending, and maintaining memorial grounds, streets, squares, parkways and reservations in and about and along and leading to any or all of the same, providing land so acquired shall be limited to parcels lying wholly or in part within a distance not to exceed one hundred fifty feet from the closest boundary of such public works or improvements . . ." See also Matheson, Excess Condemnation in California: Proposals for Statutory and Constitutional Change, 42 So.Cal.L.Rev. 421 (1969). Note, Excess Condemnation—To take or Not to Take—A Functional Analysis, 15 N.Y.L.F. 119 (1969).

2. 33 F.2d 242 (6th Cir.1929).

government, however, may be able to recoup its costs indirectly by taking land primarily to protect a public improvement [3] and then sell it to private interests with restrictions adequate to insure protection.

Land may be taken under the remnant theory to avoid leaving ususable patches of "blight" giving rise to excessive severance damages.[4] California, for example, authorizes the taking of remnants when a city or county condemns land for a street or highway and would have to pay for the part taken plus severance damages in "an amount equal to the fair and reasonable value of the whole parcel."[5] Similarly, condemnors needing only an easement have been allowed to acquire a fee when underlying land is likely to be seriously injured, resulting in large damage awards.

The acquisition of lands in advance of actual need in order to minimize costs is a variation of excess condemnation. Board of Education v. Baczewski[6] denied the taking for a school site needed thirty years in the future on the ground that the transaction was not necessary now or in the near future and was motivated by economy. A court may allow such a taking, within reasonable limitations, however, on the theory that public officials should be permitted to plan for the future.[7]

 WESTLAW REFERENCES
"excess condemnation"
sy("future condemnation")
excess! /p condemn! /p recoup!
remnant /p "eminent domain" /p land
148k138 /p "severance damages"
148k138 /p remain!
148k138 /p "consequential damages"
148k138 /p "partial taking"
board +s education +s baczewski

§ 20.7 Inverse Condemnation

Where property has been damaged by government action, owners may be able to recover through inverse or reverse condemnation. Inverse condemnation is

> a cause of action against a governmental defendant to recover the value of property which has been taken in fact by the governmen-

---

3. White v. Johnson, 148 S.C. 488, 146 S.E. 411 (1929) (affirming the protective theory).

4. People ex rel. Dep't of Pub. Works v. Superior Court, 68 Cal.2d 206, 65 Cal.Rptr. 342, 436 P.2d 342 (1968).

5. See West's Ann.Cal.Code Civ.Proc. § 1266. See § 20.13 infra.

6. 340 Mich. 265, 65 N.W.2d 810 (1954).

7. Carlor Co. v. Miami, 62 So.2d 897 (Fla.1953), cert. denied 346 U.S. 821, 74 S.Ct. 37, 98 L.Ed. 347 (1953); State Road Dep't v. Southland, Inc., 117 So.2d 512 (Fla. 1st D.C.A.1960). D. Shoup & R. Mack, Advance Land Acquisition by Local Governments: Benefit-Cost Analysis as Aid to Policy (1968). Note, Problems of Advance Land Acquisition, 52 Minn.L.Rev. 1175 (1968).

tal defendant, even though no formal exercise of the power of eminent domain has been attempted by the taking agency.[1]

Inverse condemnation has been most useful to property owners whose property has been damaged by the government. Since inverse condemnation is not based on a tort theory, the doctrine of governmental tort immunity can generally be avoided.

In order to be a taking, the condemnor must intend to take the property or at least to act in such a way that the natural consequence is to take the property.[2] When the governmental act is negligent, the issue is cast as one of governmental tort liability. In V.T.C. Lines, Inc. v. Harlan,[3] for example, the plaintiff sued for damages to its bus station and garage from emery dust used by the defendant city in sand blasting its swimming pool. The court found no taking, classifying the case as one of negligent acts of city servants while performing governmental functions, for which acts the government is immune.

Inverse condemnation may arise in a variety of circumstances. For example, the public may construct a drainage ditch so that it interferes with natural flowage, and land may be flooded and thus taken though no condemnation was intended. The public may build a road near the bottom of a hill which causes a landslide that undermines the foundation of homes at the top of the hill, thus leading to their damage.[4]

Inverse condemnation has been of particular utility in the airport noise cases. For example, it was used in Thornburg v. Port of Portland[5] to recover damages for impairment of use of property by disturbance from plane flights in the absence of physical trespass. It was also used in Sneed v. County of Riverside[6] to recover compensation from the imposition of flight plane zoning.

The Sneed case raises a most interesting question. Can a regulation be the basis for an inverse condemnation action? In Sneed the property owner alleged and the court held that by regulating through flight plane zoning, the government had taken the property and compensation should be paid. In effect, the property owner was able to convert the government's attempted regulation into an acquisition. If such a doctrine had widespread acceptance, legislatures would be loath to regulate. Typically they risk little by regulating in an unconstitutional manner because the regulation is merely held invalid. But if the

---

§ 20.7

1. Thornburg v. Port of Portland, 233 Or. 178, 180 n. 1, 376 P.2d 100, 101 n. 1 (1962). See also § 10.7 infra for a more complete discussion of the taking issue including inverse condemnation.

2. B Amusement Co. v. United States, 148 Ct.Cl. 337, 180 F.Supp. 386 (1960).

3. 313 S.W.2d 573 (Ky.App.1957).

4. Mandelker, Inverse Condemnation: The Constitutional Limits of Public Re-

sponsibility, 1966 Wis.L.Rev. 3; Comment, An Evaluation of the Rights and Remedies of a New York Landowner for Losses Due to Government Action—With a Proposal for Reform, 33 Albany L.Rev. 537, 549–56 (1969); Note, Inverse Condemnation, 3 Real Property, Probate & Trust J. 173 (1968).

5. 233 Or. 178, 376 P.2d 100 (1962).

6. 218 Cal.App.2d 205, 32 Cal.Rptr. 318 (1963).

risk is unwanted acquisition of property, for which government has to pay, government would be much more disposed to play it safe.[7]

Government may still be chilled in their approach to regulations which could be construed as a taking, in the wake of recent case law. In the U.S. Supreme Court decision of San Diego Gas and Electric v. San Diego,[8] there was language in the dissent which answered the question of whether there should be compensation for a regulatory taking with a yes.[9] Justice Rehnquist, who cast the deciding vote, wrote a concurring opinion which sided with the majority in dismissing the case on jurisdictional grounds, but which stated in all other aspects he agreed with the dissent.[10]

In an attempt to settle this amorphous area one authority has written that Brennan's interpretation [11] in San Diego Gas of Justice Holmes' landmark decision in Pennsylvania Coal Co. v. Mahon,[12] was incorrect.[13] Instead, according to the aforementioned author, Holmes recognized two very distinct powers and as such "When [a restrictive regulation] reaches a certain magnitude, in most if not all cases there must be an exercise of eminent domain . . . ."[14] Absent this exercise of the correct power no compensation would be due and the correct remedy would be to invalidate the overreaching regulation. In fact, Holmes and the Court in Pennsylvania Coal decided the case by concluding the statute was invalid, the writer emphasizes.[15]

The latest Supreme Court opportunity to clearly settle the taking issue was decided on technical grounds, as was San Diego Gas. The Court declared the substantive issue, in Williamson Co. Regional Planning v. Hamilton Bank [16] not "ripe" for determination. After dismissing the § 1983 action for lack of finality of available state remedies, Justice Blackman turned to the due process question. There he emphasized the distinction between the two governmental exercises and stated, should the government wish to accomplish the goals of such [overreaching] regulation, it must proceed through the exercise of its eminent domain power, and of course pay just compensation for any

---

7. Beuscher, Some Tentative Notes on the Integration of Police Power and Eminent Domain by the Courts: So-called Inverse or Reverse Condemnation, 1968 Urban Law Annual 1; Mandelker, supra note 56 at 47; Comment, supra note 4 at 544–56.

8. But see Dade County v. National Bulk Carriers, Inc., 450 So.2d 213 (Fla. 1984). Here the Florida Supreme Court reached the conclusion that a zoning regulation which constituted a taking without just compensation is invalid. Therefore, while the Court will strike the regulation no compensation is due.

9. 450 U.S. 621, 101 S.Ct. 1287, 67 L.Ed. 2d 551 (1981).

10. Id. at 636, 101 S.Ct. at 1296.

11. Id. at 633, 101 S.Ct. at 1294.

12. 260 U.S. 393, 43 S.Ct. 158, 67 L.Ed. 322 (1922).

13. Siemon, Of Regulatory Takings and Other Myths, 1 Fla.St.U.L.Rev. 105 (1985).

14. Id. at 117 (citing Pennsylvania Coal, 260 U.S. at 413, 43 S.Ct. at 159).

15. Id. at 110 (citing Pennsylvania Coal, 260 U.S. at 414, 43 S.Ct. at 159).

16. ___ U.S. ___, 105 S.Ct. 3108, 87 L.Ed. 126 (1985), on remand ___ F.2d ___ (6th Cir.1985).

property taken;[17] to provide otherwise would allow the government to "take" property through the exercise of either power.

 WESTLAW REFERENCES

di inverse condemnation

"inverse condemnation" /s defined

148k316 /p "inverse condemnation" /p taking

"inverse condemnation" /s tort /s immun!

"inverse condemnation" /p "drainage ditch"

di("inverse condemnation" /p airport plane airplane /s noise)

148k293 /p "inverse condemnation" /p trespass!

148k293 /p "inverse condemnation" /p zon! regulat!

148k266 /p "inverse condemnation" /p road

148k266 /p flood***

148k266 /p trespass!

regulat! /s taking /s "just compensation"

92k280 /p regulat! /p compensa!

148k2 /p compensa! /s zon! /s taking

§ 20.8 Condemnation by Private Parties

Under certain circumstances, private parties may be authorized by the legislature to bring condemnation actions. Public service corporations such as power companies and railroads have long held the power to condemn to meet their land needs. Such a corporation must be organized under the authority of the state to serve the public at reasonable rates and without discrimination, and provide a necessity or a convenience that can be provided only if the power of eminent domain is available.[1] More recently, the power has been given to such non-profit institutions as universities and hospitals. Some states, as a result of the post war housing shortage, have authorized private corporations to exercise the power of eminent domain for redevelopment.[2]

For historical reasons, because of abnormal local conditions, and in aid of trade or agriculture, certain essentially private uses have become recognized as proper objects for the exercise of the power of eminent domain. They include irrigation, drainage, reclamation of wetlands, mills and milldams, mines and mining, lumbering and logging, private roads, and clearing a doubtful title.[3] The power to condemn for such uses may be delegated to private parties: the legislature may declare a public use and the existence of public necessity for the condemnation of land for such use, and confer the right to select the property which is to

---

17. 105 S.Ct. at 3122, 87 L.Ed. at 150.

§ 20.8

1. Attorney General ex rel. Corporation Contr. v. Haverhill Gas Light Co., 215 Mass. 394, 101 N.E. 1061 (1913); Minnesota Canal & Power Co. v. Pratt, 101 Minn. 197, 112 N.W. 395 (1907).

2. Robinson & Robinson, A New Era in Public Housing, 1949 Wis.L.Rev. 695.

3. 2 P. Nicholas, The Law of Eminent Domain § 7.62 (rev. 3d ed. 1983).

be appropriated to that use.[4] The private condemnor, however, might have to make a stronger showing of his right of and justification for taking than if it were a public entity; his taking might be denied if another remedy less injurious to private property is available to it.[5]

 WESTLAW REFERENCES

di,sy(public /s service /s corporation /p land /p "eminent domain" condemn! taking /p power empower! authority authoriz!)

148k36 /p condemn!

148k47(1) /p authority authoriz! /s public! /s corporat!

148k47(1) /p electric! railroad /s power

148k13 /p public /s corporation

di(corporat! /s public! /s service /s "eminent domain" condemn! taking /s necessity convenien!)

corporat! /s public! /s service /p "eminent domain" /p nondiscriminat! discriminat!

private! /s corporat! /s "eminent domain" /s redevelop!

private! /3 use usage /s "eminent domain" /s irrigat! drain! mine mining lumber! log logging flume ditch

private! /3 use usage /p "eminent domain" /p title /s good clear "fee simple"

III. JUST COMPENSATION

§ 20.9 Fair Market Value

The fifth amendment of the United States Constitution, applied to the states by the fourteenth amendment, and most state constitutions require that "just compensation" be paid for property taken for public use. Either by constitution, statute or court-made rule,[1] the measure of just compensation for property generally is its fair market value. Usually fair market value is determined by a jury; however, there exists no Federal Constitutional right to a trial by jury in condemnation proceedings.[2]

Market value is defined as the price which the property would bring at the time of taking[3] if offered by a willing seller who is not obliged to sell to a willing buyer who is not obliged to buy.[4] Under constitutional provisions requiring compensation where property is

---

4. Linggi v. Garovotti, 45 Cal.2d 20, 286 P.2d 15 (1955); H.A. Bosworth & Son, Inc. v. Tamiola, 24 Conn.Supp. 328, 190 A.2d 506 (Super.Hartford County 1963).

5. Linggi v. Garovotti, 45 Cal.2d 20, 286 P.2d 15 (1955).

§ 20.9

1. See Juergensmeyer, Federal Rule of Civil Procedure 71A(h) Land Commissions: The First Fifteen Years, 43 Ind.L.J. 679 (1968).

2. United States v. Reynolds, 397 U.S. 14, 17, 90 S.Ct. 803, 805, 25 L.Ed.2d 12 (1970).

3. For the doctrines surrounding the time of assessment, see 3 P. Nichols, The Law of Eminent Domain § 8.5 (rev. 3rd ed. 1965 & recomp. 1978).

4. Housing Authority v. Kosydor, 17 Ill. 2d 602, 162 N.E.2d 357 (1959).

damaged, the difference between the fair market value of the property before and after damage is the measure of compensation.

In determining present market value, all factors which affect the price that a prudent purchaser would be willing to pay are to be taken into consideration. All uses to which people of prudence would devote the property are to be considered,[5] including the highest and best use, even though the property is not being used or taken for such use.[6] The uses to be considered may be limited by zoning or other regulation.[7]

There are three typical approaches used in determining fair market value: (1) sales or comparable sales, (2) cost or replacement cost less depreciation, and (3) capitalization of income.[8] A recent arm's length sale of property is the best evidence of market value if not explained away as abnormal.[9] The price paid by the owner is very weighty evidence if the purchase was recent and arm's length.[10] A contract by the owner to sell the property is important evidence, but a condemnee cannot artificially distribute value over different parts of the land in a contract, attributing a higher value to the part to be expropriated to increase compensation for that part.[11] An offer previously made by the condemnor is excluded from evidence [12] since it includes consideration for avoiding litigation, but a recent bona fide offer from a private party is admissible in some states.[13] However, evidence of offers is often rejected as unreliable, indirect, and inaccessible to cross-examination,[14] at least where evidence of actual sales exists.

Where sales data are not available for the property to be acquired, sales data on similar properties may be used. Data on properties too dissimilar may not even be admissible, but sales data on similar property, located in close proximity to the acquired property, and recently sold, are persuasive evidence of market value.

5. City of Redding v. Diestelhorst, 15 Cal.App.2d 184, 59 P.2d 177 (1936).

6. Olson v. United States, 292 U.S. 246, 54 S.Ct. 704, 78 L.Ed. 1236 (1934); Forest Preserve Dist. v. Lehmann Estate, 388 Ill. 416, 58 N.E.2d 538 (1944).

7. See § 5.13 supra, § 20.10 infra.

8. See § 12.6 supra.

9. Vanech v. State, 29 A.D.2d 607, 285 N.Y.S.2d 636 (1967); See also, Dasso, Changing Economic Conditions and the Condemnation Value of Real Property, 48 Or.L.Rev. 237 (1969).

10. Riley v. District of Columbia Redevelopment Land Agency, No. 12782 (D.C. Cir., May 17, 1956), judgment set aside and remanded, 246 F.2d 641 (D.C.Cir.1957) on the grounds that under the circumstances of a wide divergence between the price set in the recent credit sale of the condemned property to the condemnee and the lower valuations of the appraisers, and the un-

certain methods used by them in making their valuations, an explanation of "terms equivalent to cash" should have been given to the jury to enable them to reach a reasoned conclusion as to the relationship between the prior credit sale and the present fair market value of the property.

11. Municipality of Metropolitan Toronto v. Lowry, 30 D.L.R.2d 1 (Can.Sup.Ct. 1961).

12. Darien & W.R.R. Co. v. McKay, 132 Ga. 672, 64 S.E. 785 (1909).

13. Muller v. Southern Pac. Branch Ry. Co., 83 Cal. 240, 23 P. 265 (1890); City of Chicago v. Lehmann, 262 Ill. 468, 104 N.E. 829 (1914).

14. Brock v. Harlan County, 297 Ky. 113, 179 S.W.2d 202 (1944); State Highway Comm'n v. Triangle Dev. Co., 369 P.2d 864 (Wyo.1962), rehearing denied 371 P.2d 408 (1962).

Where sale or comparable sales data are not available, cost or replacement cost less depreciation may be the best evidence of market value. Cost may be used for nearly new buildings. Cost is particularly appropriate for valuing a building designed for a particular use such as a church or hospital. If the buildings are old, actual cost is not likely reliable, but replacement cost may be reliable. The cost of replacement with improvements of equal utility is generally the standard rather than the cost of reproducing an exact replica, which is called the reproduction cost. Once the replacement cost of the property is computed, it is then depreciated for wear and tear and functional obsolescence. Various methods of determining depreciation are used, including the regular accounting methods of straight line, declining charges, and sinking fund. But accounting methods of depreciation are seldom reliable guides to present value. Estimation by an expert on appraisal examination of the premises may be more accurate though expert observations are not easily subject to cross examination. In general, the cost approach lends itself only to valuation of land with improvements. However, in response to the shortcoming a "development cost approach" has been proposed in one jurisdiction.[15]

Capitalization of income is often the best evidence of the value of standard commercial buildings. For example, an apartment building is typically priced in private sales by considering the rental income of the property. Capitalized income is the present worth of future potential benefits of property or the net income which a fully informed person is warranted in assuming the property will produce during its remaining useful life. Yearly projected income is divided by a capitalization rate. The rate depends on the price of money and on an estimate of the security and duration of the income flow. Only profits attributable to the real estate itself can be considered since business profits are avoided as too speculative. An exception is made for rental income, which is considered of sufficient predictability. The net rental value of a building takes into account present rentals in the building, rentals from similar property, the terms of existing leases, and due discount for vacancies or rental losses. Expenses, including interest, taxes, and depreciation, are subtracted from the discounted rental income value to arrive at the net figure.

 WESTLAW REFERENCES

148k134 /p "fair market value" /s "highest and best use" /s
    land

148k303 /p date

148k136 /p "measure of damage" /s condemn! /s "market
    value" /s taking

to(148) /p "just compensation" /s jur** /s determin! /s
    "fair market value"

148k202(4) /p compensa! /p "fair market value"

15. County of Ramsey v. Miller, 316
N.W.2d 917 (Minn.1982).

148k222(5) /p compensa! /s "fair market value"

148k222(1) /p jury /s valu!

148k136 /p jury /p remain!

federal! /s constitution! /s right /p trial /p jury /p
    "eminent domain"

bauman +s ross /p jury

148k209 /p right

230k19(11)

170ak2068

148k263 /p jury /p damage

148k221 /p determin! /s valu! /s compensa!

148k219 /p valu! /s determin! /s jury

148k140 /p jury

to(148) /p "market value" /s pruden! /s purchas! buy!

148k130 /p factor

redding +s diestlhorst /p valu!

to(148) /p "market value" /p use usage /p zon! /p limit!

(people +s gas +s coke) ("los angeles" +s faus) (decatur
    +s becker) (davenport +s franklin) /p estimat! adaptab!

148k149(3)

148k202(7)

148k143 /p term! lease!

148k114

157k4749(20) /p condemn! "eminent domain"

148k202(1) /p propos! anticipat! contemplat!

forest +s preserve +s district +s lehmann /p use usage

"eminent domain" taking condemn! /p "special use" /s valu! /s
    benefit!

148k134 /p zoning +1 ordinance regulation

148k134 /p restrict! /p expropriat! appropriat!

148k134 /p "highest and best use" /s factor

148k131 /p factor /s consider! /s damage

148k138 /p "severance damage" /s portion

148k96 /p future

148k96 /p value

"fair market value" /s "capitalization of income" /s "eminent
    domain" condemn! taking

to(148) /p offer! /s condemnor /s exclud! /s evidence

157k533 /p "eminent domain" taking condemn!

(muller +s southern +s pacific +s railway) (city +s chicago
    +s lehmann) /p offer!

(brock +s harlan +s county) (highway +s triangle +s
    development) /p evidence

"similar property" /s "fair market value" /s condemn!

157k142(1)

148k131 /p "similar property"

157k142(3)

to(148) /p "market value" /p "replacement cost less
    depreciation"

"market value" /p cost /p church hospital /p taking condemn! "eminent domain"

148k133 /p "replacement cost" /p depreciat!

148k133 /p apprais! /p valu!

"eminent domain" condemn! taking /p "expert witness" /p apprais! /p "fair market value" /p cross /1 examin!

148k138 /p "prior to taking"

di("eminent domain" condemn! taking /s "reproduction cost" /s "fair market value")

"eminent domain" condemn! /p depreciat! /p "straight line"

di depreciation

148k133 /p "cost approach"

"development cost approach"

"eminent domain" condemn! /p "capitalization of income" /p commerc! /p property building land /p valu!

---

§ 20.10   Governmental Actions and Fair Market Value

A condemnee is not entitled to the enhanced value that the need of the government for his property has created.[1] Thus any speculative increase in value due to the probability of taking is excluded from the award.[2]

If a tract of land is taken, neighboring lands may increase in market value due to the proximity of the public improvement erected on the land taken. If the government later decides to take the neighboring lands, it must pay the enhanced market value.[3] However, if the public project included the likely taking of several tracts from the beginning but only some of the tracts are taken initially, the owners of the remaining tracts are not paid the enhanced value of the land ultimately taken, even where there is no certainty that the additional property will be taken.[4] For example, in United States v. Miller,[5] as a result of a dam project, it was necessary to acquire land to relocate a railroad. The land to be acquired was located in a "boomtown" caused by the construction of the dam. The condemnees were not allowed the benefit of the value added to their property by the previous condemnation of adjacent lands.[6]

Of course, it is difficult to separate fluctuations in value attributable to the improvement from those attributable to other causes. It is

§ 20.10

1. United States v. Cors, 337 U.S. 325, 69 S.Ct. 1086, 93 L.Ed. 1392 (1949).

2. Id. The dissent points out that in this case the excluded increment in price on the open market had resulted in fact from governmentally created shortage rather than speculation as to taking. Id. at 342, 69 S.Ct. at 1095.

3. United States v. Miller, 317 U.S. 369, 63 S.Ct. 276, 87 L.Ed. 336 (1943), rehearing denied 318 U.S. 798, 63 S.Ct. 557, 87 L.Ed. 1162 (1943).

4. Id.

5. Id.

6. Whether a taking is within the original scope of a project is an issue for the court rather than the jury. United States v. Reynolds, 397 U.S. 14, 90 S.Ct. 803, 25 L.Ed.2d 12 (1970).

also difficult to determine when the effect of the improvement began. The government created increment may be excluded by designating the authorization date of the project as the date of valuation.[7] However, this date of valuation may also exclude increment from other sources. In one case [8] a statute fixing the date of measurement of compensation as that immediately preceding the resolution establishing the necessity of acquiring the property was held to violate the requirement of just compensation. It was held to not just exclude all enhancement of the property's value after the date of resolution.

The rule excluding the effect of the governmental activity operates to the condemnee's advantage where proposed condemnation lowers the market value of the property to be condemned. For example, such depreciation often occurs after the declaration of blight in an urban renewal project area. While the declaration of blight is not considered a taking,[9] it may set events in motion that substantially impair values. Several years may ensue before property is acquired or all of it is acquired. Meanwhile, the project may be completely dropped.[10] Expecting their property to be taken, owners may let their buildings deteriorate. Tenants may move out. If they do, income falls, leading to low capitalized values if capitalization of income is used to measure value.[11] As the neighborhood deteriorates, vandalism might occur or perhaps purchasers cannot be found. Finally, when purchasers are found, the purchase price could be lower and if it becomes evidence of market value an inequity would occur.[12] Therefore, courts may require that the depreciation be disregarded.[13] Courts have not unanimously adopted the Miller approach. In A. Gettelman Brewing Co. v. Milwaukee [14] for example, the city intended to widen a street. One resolution provided for the widening of one side of the street, and a later resolution was to widen the other side. The court held that compensation could not include any amount for a decrease in the value of the property taken under the second resolution caused by the pendency and delay in the adoption and execution of the city's plan for making the first improvement.

Justice can usually be achieved by valuing the property as it was immediately before the first official step of the project,[15] usually the declaration of blight. However, news of the possibility of urban renew-

7. Mann, The Relevant Date for the Assessment of Compensation, 85 Law Q.Rev. 516 (1969).

8. State ex rel. Willey v. Griggs, 89 Ariz. 70, 358 P.2d 174 (1960).

9. Wilson v. Long Branch, 27 N.J. 360, 142 A.2d 837 (1958), cert. denied 358 U.S. 873, 79 S.Ct. 113, 3 L.Ed.2d 104 (1958).

10. Note, The Condemnor's Liability for Damages Arising Through Instituting, Litigating, or Abandoning Eminent Domain Proceedings, 1967 Utah L.Rev. 548.

11. See § 20.9 supra.

12. Comment, A Redefinition of Just Compensation for Takings in Urban Redevelopment, 6 Wake Forest Intra.L.Rev. 84 (1969).

13. Tharp v. Urban Renewal & Community Development Agency, 389 S.W.2d 453 (Ky.1965); City of Cleveland v. Carcione, 118 Ohio App. 525, 190 N.E.2d 52 (1963).

14. 245 Wis. 9, 13 N.W.2d 541 (1944).

15. E.g., City of Cleveland v. Carcione, 118 Ohio App. 525, 190 N.E.2d 52 (1963). See Annot. 5 A.L.R.3d 901 (1966).

al may touch off depreciation in the value of property before the actual declaration of blight.

Effect of Zoning on Value [16]

Where the evidence shows a "reasonable probability" of the removal or imposition of a zoning restriction in the near future, the effect of such probability on the minds of purchasers may be considered,[17] as may the effects on the value of other future events.[18] Government sometimes intervenes directly, through regulation, to lower property values. For example, in City of Plainfield v. Borough of Middlesex,[19] after property owners and a municipality could not reach an agreement as to lands which the owner wanted to sell and the city wished to purchase, the city rezoned the tract for parks, playgrounds and schools. One month later, the municipality declared the acquisition of the land necessary for public use. The court held that the municipality had unlawfully used its power to zone as a method of depreciating the value of the property and limiting the possible purchasers to the municipality.[20] Some statutes regulating or forbidding construction in areas to be condemned have been upheld, however.[21]

WESTLAW REFERENCES

(consumer +s power +s allegan) (united +s states +s "chandler dunbar") /p estimat!

di(condemnee /p entitl! /p enhanc! /p valu!)

di,sy(increas! /s property land /s value! /s "eminent domain" condemn! /s disregard!)

united +s states +s cors

16. See § 5.13 supra.

17. People ex rel. Department of Pub. Works v. Dunn, 46 Cal.2d 639, 297 P.2d 964 (1956). See also Department of Public Works & Bldgs. v. Association of Franciscan Fathers, 44 Ill.App.3d 49, 4 Ill.Dec. 323, 360 N.E.2d 70 (1976), judgment affirmed 69 Ill.2d 308, 13 Ill.Dec. 681, 371 N.E.2d 616 (1977). Michigan State Highway Comm. v. Abood, 83 Mich.App. 612, 269 N.W.2d 247 (1978). Compare H. & R. Corp. v. District of Columbia, 351 F.2d 740 (D.C.Cir.1965), holding that where there is a clash of credible testimony regarding the probability of a change in zoning, the matter should be submitted to the jury, and that a report to the zoning commission concerning the rezoning of land similarly situated to the land in question may be admitted as evidence as to property taken after publication of the report if the probative value of the report is found to outweigh the delay and confusion its admission would cause. The dissent protested that the report could not be considered relevant evidence to establish even a substantial possibility, much less a reasonable

probability, that rezoning would be based on it. Similarly, in Canada, the estimate a prudent man in the position of the condemnee would have made of the possibility of rezoning is to be considered in fixing compensation. Metropolitan Toronto & Region Conservation Authority v. Valley Improvement Co., 35 D.L.R.2d 315 (Can. Sup.Ct.1962).

18. Olson v. United States, 292 U.S. 246, 54 S.Ct. 704, 78 L.Ed. 1236 (1934). For the effects of subdivision, see Annot. 26 A.L.R.3d 780 (1969). For effects of restrictive covenants, see Annot. 22 A.L.R.3d 961 (1968).

19. 69 N.J.Super. 136, 173 A.2d 785 (L.Div.1961).

20. Accord, In re Urban Renewal Elmwood Park, 376 Mich. 311, 136 N.W.2d 896 (1965). But see Reservation Eleven Assn. v. District of Columbia, 420 F.2d 153 (D.C. Cir.1969).

21. Hunter v. Adams, 180 Cal.App.2d 511, 4 Cal.Rptr. 776 (1960); Headley v. Rochester, 272 N.Y. 197, 5 N.E.2d 198 (1936).

speculat! /p valu! enhanc! increas! /p probability likelihood /p
　　exclud! /p "eminent domain"

united +s states +s miller /p value /s "eminent domain" /
　　s enhanc!

adjacent enlarg! /s enhanc! /s project /s valu! /s "eminent
　　domain" condemn! taking

date /s assess! /s compensa! /s "eminent domain" condemn!

"eminent domain" condemn! /s statut! law regulat! /s date /s
　　compensa! /s measur!

propos! /s condemn! /s depreciat! /s "market value"

di(declar! /s blight! /s taking)

(tharp +s urban +s renewal) (cleveland +s carcione) /p
　　depreciat!

decreas! /s property land value! /s disregard! /s "eminent
　　domain" condemn!

Effect of Zoning on Value

"reasonable probability" /s zon! /s valu!

probable probability /p change /p zone* zoning /p ordinance
　　regulat! /p future /p purchas! buy!

olson +s united +s states /p future /p property land

urban +s renewal +s elmwood +s park /p valu!

268k621 /p redevelop!

mumma +s stansberry

henle +s city +s euclid

probab! /s rezon! /s enhanc! /s valu!

"eminent domain" condemn! /p remov! relocat! /p cost expense
　　/p delay! /p compensa!

"condemnation blight"

148k203(2) /p adjacent! adjoin!

to(148) /p "scope of the project"

148k124 /p contemplat!

148k124 /p anticipat!

(mines +s george +s creek +s coal) (kerr +s south +s
　　park) (shoemaker +s united +s states) /p anticipat!
　　propos! contemplat! enhanc!

valu! /s condemn! "eminent domain" /s proximate! /2 caus!

148k202(1) /p public /s project improv!

268k621 /p moratori!

92k278(1) /p prohibit! restrict! /p depriv! /p property land /p
　　build! construct! project

148k2(1) /p restrict! regulat! /p depreciat! decreas! reduc!

148k2(1) /p resolution

148k2(1) /p depriv! /p benefit

148k202(4) /p limit! /s zon!

148k202(4) /p "highest and best use" /s admissible

148k202(4) /p future /s zon!

148k222(4) /p limit /s use usage

148k222(4) /p benefit!

148k222(4) /p "highest and best use" /s consider!

148k124 /p date /s taking

148k222(1) /p determin!

148k131   /p   "replacement cost"

148k131   /p   "income method"

148k131   /p   "cost approach"

148k134   /p   approach method   /p   determin!   /p   "fair market value"

"eminent domain" taking condemn!   /s   "arm's length"   /s   "market value"

vanech   +s   state

"eminent domain" condemn!   /s   apprais!   /s   price

"cost of reproduction"   /s   "eminent domain" condemn!

148k131   /p   apprais!   /p   improv!

148k136   /p   "partial taking"   /s   portion

148k136   /p   "severance damage"   /s   portion

148k136   /p   single   /p   tract

148k136   /p   valu!   /p   element

§ 20.11   Divided Fees

When a fee is divided into several interests, such as a leasehold and a freehold, it is valued for purposes of eminent domain as an undivided fee, as if title were in one owner. The resulting money is then apportioned among the interest holders according to their respective rights.[1] The rule is applied, even though the aggregate value of the separate interests is greater than the value of the property as a whole, unless unusual circumstances justify a departure.[2]

The existence of a leasehold may affect the value of the property, not because of the multiple ownerships, but because of the nature of the lease. For example, if property is leased to a financially responsible tenant at a high rental, its value is enhanced. A lessor is compensated for the present value of rents reserved and for the present value of his reversionary interest; the lessee is compensated for the value of his leasehold for the balance of the term.[3] Since a reversion after a long-term lease, e.g. ninety-nine years, probably has no present value or only speculative value, the lessor is not entitled to compensation for the reversionary interest.[4]

In an ordinary lease situation, the lessor is awarded the difference between the valuation of the property as a whole and the lessee's

§ 20.11

1. City of Ashland v. Price, 318 S.W.2d 861 (Ky.1958). Contra, Boston Chamber of Commerce v. Boston, 217 U.S. 189, 30 S.Ct. 459, 54 L.Ed. 725 (1910) where several interests (fee; easement of light, way, and air; and mortgage) in one piece of property had depressed each other in value. Property burdened with an easement is generally valued in its existing condition and not as an unencumbered fee. Terminal Coal v. United States, 76 F.Supp. 136 (W.D.Pa.

1948); Baker v. Town of Arlington, 271 Mass. 415, 171 N.E. 462 (1930); See generally Horgan & Edgar, Leasehold Valuation problems in Eminent Domain, 4 U.San Francisco L.Rev. 1 (1969).

2. Sowers v. Schaeffer, 155 Ohio St. 454, 99 N.E.2d 313 (1951).

3. Department of Pub. Works & Bldgs. v. Metropolitan Life Ins. Co., 42 Ill.App.2d 378, 192 N.E.2d 607 (1963).

4. Id.

interest in the award;[5] the lessee's interest is the difference, if any, between the fair rental value of the property for the remainder of the term minus the rental established by the lease.[6] Since the apportionment between interest holders is not the concern of the condemnor and does not affect the amount it must pay, the manner of apportionment can be decided upon by the interest holders.[7]

A lessor may be compensated even though improvements to the leased property, which form the essence of the lease, have not been accomplished. For example, in Levin v. State,[8] the landowner had executed a lease, though buildings to be constructed for the lessee had not yet been started. The court found that the lease had been made in good faith with financially responsible tenants, that the landowner had obtained favorable rezoning, had spent substantial sums for plans and engineering work, had obligated himself to completion of agreed upon improvements, and had progressed substantially in clearing and grading the land. Under such circumstances, the court held it would be unjust to hold that the successful business venture of which condemnees had been deprived was worth nothing more than the present value of the barren land. The court considered the realities of commercial transactions and made an award based on the loss of potential income.

In most jurisdictions, condemnation of only a part of the property, where the remainder is still inhabitable,[9] or condemnation for use limited to a period of time shorter than the remaining term of the lease, does not terminate the lease, or even abate rent.[10] The rule may apply even where the temporary use by condemnation may contain options permitting extensions beyond the term of the lease. Where rent is not abated, the tenant must be compensated for the lost use of the property, and the landlord, naturally, need not be compensated for the present value of rents reserved.[11]

A mortgage on the property taken does not affect the valuation, except that the amount owed may be indicative of the value of the property.[12] The mortgagee is entitled to as much of the award as is necessary to satisfy the mortgage debt, and where only part of the

---

5. City of Ashland v. Price, 318 S.W.2d 861 (Ky.1958).

6. Id. In Krieger v. Baltimore, 234 Md. 382, 199 A.2d 363 (1964), where the property condemned was subject to a leasehold interest and a stipulated ground rent, the leasehold interest was valued by determining the present fee simple value of the land and improvements and by subtracting the stipulated amount of the ground rent.

7. Rankin v. Town of Harrisonburg, 104 Va. 524, 52 S.E. 555 (1905).

8. 17 A.D.2d 335, 234 N.Y.S.2d 481 (1962), affirmed 13 N.Y.2d 87, 242 N.Y.S.2d 193, 192 N.E.2d 155 (1963).

9. Department of Pub. Works & Bldgs. v. Metropolitan Life Ins. Co., 42 Ill.App.2d 378, 192 N.E.2d 607 (1963).

10. Leonard v. Autocar Sales & Ser. Co., 392 Ill. 182, 64 N.E.2d 477 (1945), cert. denied 327 U.S. 804, 66 S.Ct. 968, 90 L.Ed. 1029 (1946), rehearing denied 328 U.S. 879, 66 S.Ct. 1339, 90 L.Ed. 1647 (1946).

11. Department of Pub. Works & Bldgs. v. Metropolitan Life Ins. Co., 42 Ill.App.2d 378, 192 N.E.2d 607 (1963).

12. Vanech v. State, 29 A.D.2d 607, 285 N.Y.S.2d 636 (1967). Contra, Boston Chamber of Commerce v. Boston, 217 U.S. 189, 30 S.Ct. 459, 54 L.Ed. 725 (1910).

property is taken, the mortgagee is entitled to as much of the award as is necessary to compensate him for his interest in the part taken.[13]

 WESTLAW REFERENCES

fee /s divid! division /s interest /p valu! /p "eminent domain"

fee /s "eminent domain" /s apportion!

sowers +s schaeffer /p valu! /p separate! division divid!

"separate interest" /s valu! /s land property /s "eminent domain" condemn!

148k157 /p leasehold /s compensa!

148k157 /p improv!

148k157 /p reversion! revert!

148k154 /p interest

148k152(1) /p interest /p compensa!

148k155 /p compensa! /p valu!

to(148) /p leasehold /p affect! /p valu!

lessor /p compensa! /p condemn! "eminent domain" /p revert! reversion! /p interest

148k147 /p temporar!

148k82 /p lessor /p lessee

148k155 /p allocat!

to(148) /p "conflicting interest"

148k155 /p estate

148k155 /p prior

148k158

148k155 /p abat! /p rent

148k155 /p waiv!

"eminent domain" condemn! /s lease /s limit! /s terminat! abat!

manner method /s apportion! /s interest /s condemn "eminent domain"

"eminent domain" condemn! /s potential! /s income

148k155 /p temporar!

"partial condemnation" /p terminat! abat! /p lease! rent

partial temporary /s "eminent domain" condemn! /p abat! /p rent

233k191 /p lease!

148k154 /p entitl! /p debt

148k154 /p mortgage /p valu!

investor +s syndicate +s dade

---

§ 20.12 Noncompensable Damages

"Just compensation" does not generally require payment for destruction of a business, loss of profits, loss of good will, or relocation expenses occasioned by the loss of property through condemnation,

---

13. Investors Syndicate of Am. v. Dade County, 98 So.2d 889 (Fla.3d D.C.A.1957).

even though these losses and expenses would certainly affect any selling price set by an owner.[1] These elements are considered speculative and personal to the landowner rather than relating to the land, and thus not proper elements of compensation. The policy of noncompensation can work great hardships. For example, in Mitchell v. United States,[2] land was appropriated by the United States for military use. The land was especially adapted to the owner's business of growing a special grade of corn, and the owners were unable to establish themselves elsewhere. The court denied compensation for destruction of business, reasoning that neither settled rules of law nor statute provided for such compensation.

While a condemnee's business might be established elsewhere, he may well lose the advantage of good will accumulated over the years. Good will attributable to the owner himself, as distinguished from good will attaching to the location, is not compensable. Of course, a statute or state constitutional provision may provide compensation in these special situations,[3] though according to the U.S. Constitution it would not be required.

Relocation

Generally, the condemnee owner or lessee is also not compensated for his expenses in moving personal property,[4] although removal costs may be considered in determining market value, since it is an element bearing on the price a seller would set on his property.[5] Where the property is taken temporarily for a period less than the lessee's outstanding term, removal costs may be considered in the award, not as an independent item of damage, but as bearing on the rental value of the premises.[6] Such costs need not be considered when the whole of the lease is taken, since the lessee need not return and has no liability for the remainder of the lease.[7] In United States v. Westinghouse Electric & Manufacturing Co.[8] the United States condemned property leased by defendant for use by the Army for a specified term with a right to renew for additional yearly periods during the existing national emergency. The occupancy was originally for a period less than the remain-

§ 20.12

1. In Canada there is a right to compensation for loss of good will, In re McCauley & City of Toronto, 18 Ont. 416 (Ch.1889), and for "disturbance," Woods Mfg. Co. v. The King, [1951] 2 D.L.R. 465 (Can.Sup. Ct.), when property is expropriated. See also Klien, Eminent Domain: Judicial Response to the Human Disruption, 46 J.Urban L. 1 (1968).

2. 267 U.S. 341, 45 S.Ct. 293, 69 L.Ed. 644 (1925).

3. See, Ch. 73.071(3)(b) West's Fla.Stat. Ann.; Vt.Stat.Ann. tit. 19, § 221(2).

4. United States v. 5.42 Acres of Land, 182 F.2d 787 (3d Cir.1950); Housing Au-thority v. Kosydor, 17 Ill.2d 602, 162 N.E.2d 357 (1959).

5. Harvey Textile Co. v. Hill, 135 Conn. 686, 67 A.2d 851 (1949); State Highway Dep't v. Robinson, 103 Ga.App. 12, 118 S.E.2d 289 (1961).

6. United States v. General Motors Corp., 323 U.S. 373, 65 S.Ct. 357, 89 L.Ed. 311 (1945).

7. United States v. Petty Motor Co., 327 U.S. 372, 66 S.Ct. 596, 90 L.Ed. 729 (1946), rehearing denied 327 U.S. 818, 66 S.Ct. 814, 90 L.Ed. 1040 (1946).

8. 339 U.S. 261, 70 S.Ct. 644, 94 L.Ed. 816 (1950).

der of the lease term, but renewals eventually exhausted it. The court held that there had been a taking of the entire interest and that removal costs were therefore a noncompensable consequential loss. Since the total award for the occupancy in such a case cannot be determined on any rational basis until the duration of the occupancy is known, an award for removal costs is to be treated as a segregated item and payment delayed until it is known whether the government's occupancy has exhausted the leasehold.[9]

The condemnee receives no extra compensation, because the rental or purchase price of replacement quarters to which he relocates exceeds his condemnation award.[10]

 WESTLAW REFERENCES

148k200 /p loss

148k200 /p business

"just compensation" /s "good will"

148k122 /p take* own** /p gain! los*

148k134 /p "highest and best" /p seller buy!

148k107 /p "lost profits"

148k107 /p speculat! conjectur!

148k107 /p "partial taking"

148k107 /p adjoin! adjacent!

148k102 /p damage

148k102 /p special

148k102 /p own***

lustig (feigenbaum +s new +s britaine) /p "eminent domain" condemn! "just compensation"

(saint +s louis +s knapp +s stout) (arkansas +s state +s highway +s fox) (newark +s cook) and "eminent domain"

(housing +s authority +s savannah +s iron) (siner +s oil +s city) /p "eminent domain"

"economic unit doctrine"

united +s states +s general +s motors /p remov! /p "eminent domain" condemn!

condemn! "eminent domain" /p lease! term /p right /s renew! /p remov! relocat!

poillon +s gerry

148k95 /p consequential

(eljay +s realty +s argraves) (brothers +s ansonia) (seferi +s ives) (suffield +s thompsonville) /p "eminent domain" condemn!

special /2 use usage purpose /s enhanc! /s valu! /s "eminent domain" condemn! taking /s property land

"just compensation" /s destroy! destruct! ruin! /s business "going concern"

land property /p consider! /p future anticipat! /p profit /p "just compensation"

---

9. Louisiana Highway Comm'n v. Boudreaux, 19 La.App. 98, 139 So. 521 (1932).

10. See § 17.4 supra.

"non compensable" /s "just compensation" "eminent domain"
    condemn!

148k87 /p real

148k87 /p realty

148k87 /p business

148k107 /p "loss of business"

148k201 /p remov! mov! relocat!

yee +s kai +s teung

Relocation

92k228.1

condemnee /s compensa! /s mov! /s expense

condemnee /s compensa! /s remov! /s expense

"uniform relocation assistance and real property acquisition"

"eminent domain" condemn! /s compensa! /s remov! mov!
    relocat! /s personal** /s property

remov! /s cost expense /s personal** /p "eminent domain"
    condemn! /p "fair market value"

§ 20.13 Severance Damages [1]

If no part of a parcel of land has been acquired, the owner is not compensated for consequential injury suffered by the public as a whole and not peculiar to his property.[2] However, if only part of a parcel of land is acquired, the owner is entitled to recover for all damage to the remainder not acquired that is directly attributable to the taking or use of the land taken.[3] These damages to property not acquired that result from the use of the land taken [4] are called severance damages.

The measure of damages for a partial taking may be the market value of the land taken plus the difference before and after in value of the remainder,[5] or the difference between the value of the whole tract before the taking and the value of the remainder afterwards.[6] In determining severance damages, the court may, under the rationale of giving due consideration to all the factors which customarily enter into purchase and sale negotiations, allow the consideration of factors ordinarily excluded from evidence. For example, prospective earning power evidenced by past earnings have been considered in determining

§ 20.13

1. See also § 20.6 supra.

2. See § 20.2 supra.

3. City of Crookston v. Erickson, 244 Minn. 321, 69 N.W.2d 909 (1955).

4. Bauman v. Ross, 167 U.S. 548, 17 S.Ct. 966, 42 L.Ed. 270 (1897); Sisters of Charity v. The King, [1922] 2 A.C. 315 (P.C.) (N.S).

5. For a discussion of the methods of measuring damages in cases of partial taking, see 4 P. Nichols, The Law of Eminent Domain §§ 14.05 (rev. 3rd ed. 1981; Supp. 1985).

6. Under the latter method, the damages are part of the award for the taking. To add the "resulting" damages would double count damages. Commonwealth v. Sherrod, 367 S.W.2d 844 (Ky.1963).

severance damages though the damage may only be the result of a noncompensable traffic diversion.[7]

To qualify for severance damages, the property taken and that remaining must have constituted a single physical unit.[8] In People ex rel. Department of Pub. Works v. Dickinson,[9] for example, a part of a parcel of land leased by a wrecking business was taken. The parcel was owned by one of the partners in the business. Another parcel owned by another partner and also leased to the business, was separated by 500 feet but was connected by an easement. The second parcel was entirely acquired. The court denied severance damages to the remainder caused by the taking of the other parcel, stating that all elements of unity of property were not shown: unity of title, ordinary contiguity, and unity of use. The first two requirements were not met.

A condemnee is entitled to compensation for damages to the remaining land from the taker's use of land taken and not from the taker's use of other property, where it is possible to make such a differentiation.[10] The rule may be difficult to apply. For example, in People ex rel. Department of Public Works v. Elsmore,[11] the state acquired a portion of defendants' lands as a cleared strip for emergency and maintenance use at the side of a freeway roadbed. The defendant claimed severance damages from the presence of the freeway. Though no part of the land was taken for the freeway, the defendant contended there was a unity of use by the state that could not be separated by an imaginary line drawn between property used for a maintenance strip and the property used for the freeway. The court denied severance damages for the presence of the freeway, holding that the freeway was being built on land taken from others, and that there had been no proof of damage from the use of the land taken from them. To allow a condemnee to recover severance damages for the use of land other than that taken from him, the court holds, would impose a severe financial burden on the state and an embargo on the creation of new and desirable roads.

Similarly, in City of Crookston v. Erickson,[12] the city condemned tract A and portions of tracts B and C for a site for a sewage treatment plant. All of the structures were to be on tract A; a sewer line was to run under tract C. The tracts were owned by different parties. The trial court denied recovery for the reduction in market value of the uncondemned portions of tracts B and C caused by the proximity to the

7. Riddle v. State Highway Comm'n, 184 Kan. 603, 339 P.2d 301 (1959).

8. United States v. Miller, 317 U.S. 369, 63 S.Ct. 276, 87 L.Ed. 336 (1943), rehearing denied 318 U.S. 798, 63 S.Ct. 557, 87 L.Ed. 1162 (1943).

9. 230 Cal.App.2d 932, 41 Cal.Rptr. 427 (1964).

10. Campbell v. United States, 266 U.S. 368, 45 S.Ct. 115, 69 L.Ed. 328 (1924); Peo-

ple ex rel. Dep't of Pub. Works v. Elsmore, 229 Cal.App.2d 809, 40 Cal.Rptr. 613 (1964); Sisters of Charity v. The King, [1922] 2 A.C. 315 (P.C.) (N.S.).

11. 229 Cal.App.2d 809, 40 Cal.Rptr. 613 (1964).

12. 244 Minn. 321, 69 N.W.2d 909 (1955).

sewage treatment plant on tract A. On appeal, a new trial was granted as to tract B, to determine whether the part taken constituted an integral and inseparable part of the whole improvement. The judgment as to tract C was affirmed, on the grounds that as a matter of law, its use for a sewer line did not constitute an integral and inseparable part of the sewage plant.

 WESTLAW REFERENCES

200k85 /p contiguous! adjacent! adjoin!

148k136 /p destroy! destruct!

200k85 /p "eminent domain"

148k96 /p "severance damage"

di severance damage

"severance damage" /s define*

"economic unit" /p "severance damage"

148k96 /p physical!

148k96 /p portion /p "just compensation"

148k96 /p "partial taking"

148k136 /p severance

"measure of damage" /s "partial taking"

commonwealth +s sherrod /s damage

determin! /s "severance damage" /s consider! /s factor

lipari "pulp and paper" (wood +s severage) /p "eminent domain" condemn!

"severance damage" /p admissib! /p relevan! /p valu!

157k555.6 /p "severance damage"

anticipat! future prospective! /s profit! gain /s "severance damage"

prospective! future /s use usage /s "severance damage"

willing /s buy! /s sell! /s "severance damage"

148k203(2) /p severance

148k203(2) /p consequential

"intended use" /p condemn! "eminent domain" /p severance

(new +s jersey +s turnpike +s bowley) (mccandless +s united +s states) /p "eminent domain" condemn!

(rapides +s parish +s nassif) (austin +s carizzo) & severance partial

"quick taking" /s severance

148k137 /p severance /p unit

148k149(7) /p "partial taking"

148k149(1) /p "partial taking" severance

"eminent domain" condemn! /s "unity of property"

148k200 /p unit

148k200 /p entitl! /p severance

148200 /p partial!

148k200 /p parcel

148k96 /p unit /p severance

```
"severance damage"  /2  deny!
crookston  +s  erickson
```

§ 20.14 Benefits as Set Offs

In cases of partial taking, "benefits" may be conferred on the remaining land by the use of the land taken. The value of such benefits may constitutionally be subtracted from the compensation award so that they will accrue to the public rather than the condemnee. The aforementioned is the case in Federal Courts.[1] States differ as to whether benefits are to be set off at all, whether they are to be set off against compensation for the partial taking or only against severance damages; and whether all or only "special" benefits are to be set off.[2] Special benefits may be those which exceed the general benefit to the public, those which accrue when the public improvement is located on privately owned land upon which the government has condemned an easement, those which result from a physical improvement on the land, e.g., a highway which provides drainage for abutting land, or those to owners who benefit most. Special benefits are not generally offset when the benefit is one which a condemnee's neighbors, whose land is not taken, receive free of charge.[3]

In Territory of Hawaii v. Mendonca,[4] for example, defendant's land was taken for the construction of a limited access highway. Access to the new highway was a benefit, but was held to be a general rather than a special benefit and thus not offsettable against the value of the land taken. In ordinary highway condemnation cases, a special benefit arises from location on a way to which there is direct access. But in the case of a limited access highway, benefits to both abutting and nonabutting properties are the same, since access afforded to lots of tracts not abutting the highway is equal to that afforded defendant's land.

WESTLAW REFERENCES

```
148k146  /p  "special benefit"  /s  "set off"
148k200  /p  condemnor  /p  benefit
148k200  /p  enhanc!
148k200  /p  offset
148k146  /p  "just compensation"
148k146  /p  "public improvement"  /p  condemn!
148k146  /p  "partial taking"
148k146  /p  "set off" offset  /p  valu!
```

§ 20.14

1. See, United States v. Sponenbarger, 308 U.S. 256, 60 S.Ct. 225, 84 L.Ed. 230 (1939).

2. In re City of New York, 190 N.Y. 350, 83 N.E. 299 (1907). See generally Hagman, Special Benefits in Road Cases: Myths and Realities, 1964 Institute on Eminent Domain 135.

3. Territory v. Mendonca, 46 Hawaii 83, 126, 375 P.2d 6 (1962).

4. Id.

Appendix

WESTLAW REFERENCES

I. Introduction

This informational appendix is designed to aid the reader in the general use of the WESTLAW system and more specifically to demonstrate how WESTLAW can be used in conjunction with this text to help make research in the area of urban planning and land development control law swift and complete.

II. The WESTLAW System

WESTLAW is a computer-assisted legal research service of West Publishing Company. It is accessible through a number of different types of computer terminals. The materials available through WESTLAW are contained in databases stored at the central computer in St. Paul, Minnesota.

To use the WESTLAW service a "query" or search request, is typed into the terminal and sent to the central computer. There it is processed and all of the documents that satisfy the search request are identified. The text of each of these documents is then stored on magnetic disks and transmitted to the user via a telecommunication network. This data then appears on the user's terminal, where it may be reviewed and evaluated. The user must then decide if the displayed documents are pertinent or if further research is desired. If further research is necessary, the query may be recalled for editing, or an entirely new query may be sent. Documents displayed on the terminal may be printed or, on some terminals, the text may be stored on its own magnetic disks.

III. Improving Legal Research With WESTLAW

The WESTLAW system is designed for use in conjunction with the more traditional tools of legal research. In principle, WESTLAW works as an index to primary and secondary legal materials. Yet it differs from traditional digests and indices in that more terms can be researched, and more documents retrieved.

Through WESTLAW it is possible to index, or search for any significant term or combination of terms in an almost infinite variety of grammatical relationships by formulating a query composed of those terms. Unlike manual systems of secondary legal sources that reference only a few key terms in each document, WESTLAW is capable of indexing every key word. This enables documents to be located using terms not even listed in manual reference systems.

In addition to its expanded search term capabilities, WESTLAW, through its numerous databases, enables the user to research issues in any and every jurisdiction quickly and efficiently. The queries found in this text are primarily designed to access WESTLAW's federal and state case law databases. However, WESTLAW provides access to many specialized libraries as well. For example, WESTLAW contains separate topical databases for areas of federal and state law such as tax, securities, energy, and government contracts.

WESTLAW also includes the text of the United States Code and the Code of Federal Regulations, the Federal Register, West's INSTA–CITE™ Shepard's® Citations, *Black's Law Dictionary* and many other legal sources. Furthermore, because new cases are continuously being added to the WESTLAW databases as they are decided by the courts, the documents retrieved will include the most current law available on any given issue.

In addition, WESTLAW queries augment the customary role of footnotes to the treatise text by directing the user to a wider range of supporting authorities. Readers may use the preformulated queries supplied in this edition "as is" or formulate their own queries in order to retrieve cases relevant to the points of law discussed in the text.

IV. Query Formulation

a. **General Principles.** The art of query formulation is the heart of WESTLAW research. Although the researcher can gain technical skills by using the terminal, there is no strictly mechanical procedure for formulating queries. One must first comprehend the meaning of legal issue to be researched before beginning a search on WESTLAW. Then the user will need to supply imagination, insight, and legal comprehension with knowledge of the capabilities of WESTLAW to formulate a useful query. Effective query formulation requires an alternative way of thinking about the legal research process.

Using WESTLAW is a constant balancing between generating too many documents and missing important documents. In general, it is better to look through a reasonable number of irrelevant documents than it is to be too restrictive and miss important material. The researcher should take into consideration at the initial query formulation stage what he or she will do if too many, or not enough documents are retrieved. Thought should be given as to how the query might be narrowed or the search broadened, and what can be done if the initial search retrieves zero documents.

Some issues by their very nature will require more lengthy queries than others; however, it is best to strive for efficiency in structuring the query. Look for unique search terms that will eliminate the need for a lengthy query. Keep in mind that WESTLAW is literal. Consider all possible alternative terms. Especially consider inherent limitations of the computer. It doesn't think, create, or make analogies. The researcher must do that for the computer. The computer is designed to look for the terms in the documents in relationships specified by the query. The researcher should know what he or she is looking for, at least to the extent of knowing how the terms are likely to show up in relevant documents. Always keep in mind the parameters of the system as to date and database content.

The WESTLAW Reference Manual should be consulted for more information on query formulation and WESTLAW commands. The Reference Manual is updated periodically to reflect new enhancements of WESTLAW. It provides detailed and comprehensive instructions on all aspects of the WESTLAW system and offers numerous illustrative examples on the proper format for various types of queries. Material contained in the Reference Manual enables the user to benefit from all of the system's capabilities in an effective and efficient manner.

b. The WESTLAW Query Defined. The query is a message to WESTLAW. It instructs the computer to retrieve documents containing terms in the grammatical relationships specified by the query. The terms in a query are made up of words and/or numbers that pinpoint the legal issue to be researched.

An example of the kind of preformulated queries that appear in this publication is reproduced below. The queries corresponding to each section of the text appear at the end of the section.

The query appearing below is taken from Chapter 17, Section 17.3, subhead Additional Programs, and appears at the end of this section of the text.

    disaster /p renew! /p urban!

This query instructs WESTLAW to retrieve documents containing DISASTER in the same paragraph as a form of the root RENEW all within the same paragraph as a form of the root URBAN.

This query illustrates what a standard request to WESTLAW looks like—words or numbers describing an issue, tied together by connectors. These connectors tell WESTLAW in what relationships the terms must appear. WESTLAW will retrieve all documents from the database that contain the terms appearing in those relationships.

The material that follows explains the methods by which WESTLAW queries are formulated, and shows how users of *Urban Planning and Land Development Control Law* can employ the preformulated queries in this publication in their research of urban planning and land development control law. In addition, there are instructions that will enable readers to modify their queries to fit the particular needs of their research.

c. Selection of Terms. After determining the legal issue that is to be researched, the first step in query formulation is to select the key terms from the issue that will be used as search terms in the query.

Words, numbers, and various other symbols may be used as search terms.

The goal in choosing search terms is to select the most unique terms for the issue. In selecting such terms it is frequently helpful to imagine how the terms might appear in the language of the documents that will be searched by the query. Moreover, it is necessary to consider the grammatical and editorial structure of the document. This involves a consideration of how the writer of the document (i.e., judge or headnote and synopsis writer) has worded both the factual and legal components of the issue involved in the case.

Although traditional book research generally starts with a consideration of the general legal concepts under which particular problems are subsumed, WESTLAW research starts with a consideration of specific terms that are likely to appear in documents that have addressed those problems. This is so because documents are retrieved from WESTLAW on the basis of the terms they contain. The more precise the terms, the more relevant the search results will be. For example, in researching obscenity and the Twenty-First Amendment, inclusion of the unique terms "Twenty-First Amendment" or "equal protection" rather than say the common term "constitution" would retrieve more specific, and hopefully more pertinent documents.

Once the initial search terms have been selected for a query, it is important to consider synonyms, antonyms, and other alternatives for the search terms. A space left between each of these alternative terms will read as an "or" in WESTLAW. See section d: Query Formulation: Proximity Connectors.) The nature of the legal issue will determine which alternative terms are desirable.

d. The Format of Search Terms. Once the key search terms have been selected, it is necessary to consider the proper form in which the term should appear in the query. As WESTLAW is literal in its search for terms, and as a term may appear in a variety of ways, derivative forms of each search term must be considered. There are two devices available on WESTLAW for automatically generating alternative forms of search terms in a query. The first of these is the Unlimited Root Expander, the symbol (!). Placement of the ! symbol at the end of the root term generates other forms containing the same root. For example adding the ! symbol to "zon" in the following query:

zon! /s constitutional

instructs the computer to generate the words ZONE, ZONES, ZONED, and ZONING as search terms for the query. Yet time and space are saved by not having to include each of these alternatives in the query.

The second device used to automatically generate alternative forms of search terms is the Univeral Character, the symbol (*). This symbol permits the generation of all possible characters by placing one or more asterisks at the location in the term where the universal character is desired. For example, placing three asterisks on the root LEGISLAT in the following query:

legislat*** /s power

instructs the computer to generate all forms of the root term with up to three additional characters. Thus, the terms LEGISLATE, LEGISLA-TOR, LEGISLATION and LEGISLATIVE would be generated by this query. The symbol * may also be embedded inside of a term as in the following query:

int**state /s "due process"

This will generate the alternative terms INTERSTATE and INTRA-STATE without the need to enter both synonymous terms. As WESTLAW automatically generates plural forms for search terms (e.g., the endings -s -es and -ies) it is generally unnecessary to use the root expansion devices to obtain plural forms of search terms.

e. Proximity Connectors. Once the search terms and alternate search terms have been selected the next consideration is how these terms may be ordered so as to retrieve the most relevant documents. The connectors and their meanings appear below.

1. *Space (or).* A space between search terms is read as an "or" by WESTLAW. For example, leaving a space between the query terms PERMIT and EXCEPTION:

permit exception

instructs the computer to retrieve documents that contain either the word PERMIT or the word EXCEPTION or both.

2. *Ampersand (&).* The symbol & means "and." Placing it between two terms instructs the computer to retrieve documents that contain both of the terms without regard to word order. For example, inserting the & between the terms URBAN and RENEWAL:

urban & renewal

commands the computer to retrieve documents that contain both the term URBAN and the term RENEWAL anywhere in the text. The ampersand may also be placed between groups of alternative terms.

3. */p (same paragraph).* The /p symbol means "within the same paragraph." It requests that the terms to the left of the /p appear within the same paragraph as the terms to the right of the connector. For example, placing the /p between HISTORIC and PRESERVATION:

historic /p preservation

instructs the computer to retrieve documents in which both the terms HISTORIC and PRESERVATION appear in the same paragraph. The terms on each side of the /p connector may appear in the document in any order within the paragraph. As with the & connector the /p may be placed between groups of alternative terms.

4. */s (same sentence)*. The /s symbol requires that the search terms so connected occur within the same sentence. A /s placed between DEFEASIBLE and ESTATE

defeasible /s estate

will retrieve documents that contain the words DEFEASIBLE and ESTATE in the same sentence, without regard to which of these terms occur first in the sentence. As with the previous connectors, the /s may be placed between groups of alternative terms.

5. *+s (precedes within sentence)*. The +s symbol requires that the term to the left of the +s connector precede the terms to the right of the connector within the same sentence. The query

enumerated +s power

instructs the computer to retrieve all documents in which the word ENUMERATED precedes the word POWER where both words appear in the same sentence. This connector may also be used between groups of alternative terms. Thus, the query

enumerated implied +s power authority

commands the computer to retrieve all documents in which the terms ENUMERATED and/or IMPLIED precedes the terms POWER and/or AUTHORITY in the same sentence.

6. */n (numerical proximity—within n words)*. The /n symbol means "within n words," where n represents any whole number between 1 and 255, inclusive. It requests that the term to the left of the /n appear within the designated number of words as terms to the right of the connector. For example, in the following query:

tax /3 sale

the computer is instructed to retrieve all documents in which the term TAX appears within 3 words of the term SALE, without regard to word order. In addition, the + symbol may be used to require that the terms to the left of the numerical proximity connector precede the terms to the right of the connector. Thus, the query above could be altered to require that TAX precede SALE by no more than 3 words by replacing the /3 connector with the +3 connector.

tax +3 sale

Both the /n and the +n connectors may also be used between groups of alternative search terms. For example:

tax +3 sale deed

instructs the computer to retrieve all documents in which the word TAX occurs within the three words preceding the words SALE or DEED.

7. *" " (quotation marks)*. The " " (quotation marks) symbol is the most restrictive grammatical connector. When used to enclose search terms it requres that the computer retrieve only those documents in which enclosed terms appear exactly as they do within the quotation

marks. For example, placing the following words within quotation marks

"urban renewal plan"

commands the computer to retrieve all documents in which these terms occur in precisely the same order as they do within the quotation marks.

The quotation marks symbol is especially effective when searching for legal terms of art, legal concepts, or legal entities that occur together as multiple terms. Some examples are:

"due process" "equal protection" and "equitable servitude"

8. *% (exclusion/but not).* The % symbol may be translated as "but not." It instructs the computer to exclude documents that contain terms appearing after the percentage symbol. For example, to retrieve documents containing the terms EASEMENT within the same paragraph as APPURTENANT but not the term NEGATIVE, the following query would be used:

easement /p appurtenant % negative

Any document containing the word NEGATIVE would automatically be excluded in the document search.

The connectors described above may be used in a variety of combinations, enabling the user to fine-tune a query to meet his or her specific research needs.

V. Advanced Search Techniques

a. The Field Search. Within any given database a more specialized search may be conducted. Rather than searching the entire text of a case for a designated query term, the search may be limited to specific portions of the case by conducting a "field search." A search may be restricted to a particular field (or portion) of a document by incorporating the field name into the query, followed by the field search terms enclosed in parentheses.

The fields available for WESTLAW case law databases are described below.

1. *Title Field:* The title field may be used to retrieve a particular case on WESTLAW. The ampersand, rather than the v. is used between the names of the parties. Thus, to retrieve the case entitled *Village of Belle Terre v. Boraas* the following query would be used:

title("belle terre" & boraas

2. *Citation Field:* The citation field may be used for any document for which a citation exists in the WESTLAW databases. The proper database must first be selected. A numerical proximity connector is then used instead of the publication name to separate volume and page number. For example, to retrieve the case appearing at 94 S.Ct. 1536, the Supreme Court database must be selected. The following query may then be used:

citation(94 +3 1536)

3. *Court Field:* The court field permits searches for case law to be restricted to particular states, districts, or courts. The correct database in which to conduct the search must be chosen. For example, to restrict a search to cases from the United States District Court in New York the database "dct" must be chosen. The following query might then be used:

    court(ny) & urban /s blight

4. *Judge Field:* A search may be limited to the individual or majority opinion of a particular judge. To retrieve all cases in which Justice Powell has authored an opinion the following query would be used:

    judge(powell)

5. *Synopsis Field:* The synopsis field consists of the editorially prepared summary of the case found immediately after the title. By reading the synopsis it may be determined if the decision generally encompasses the legal issue being researched without reading the entire decision.

The synopsis field search can be especially useful in focusing broad queries which might retrieve too many cases if the entire case was searched. For example, the following query would limit retrieval to cases in which a contract for deed was a key element:

    synopsis(contract /2 deed)

6. *Topic Field:* The topic field contains the West topics and Key Numbers assigned to the headnotes in a case. A search in this field may be conducted by using either the West topic name or by using the West number designated for that topic. For example, the West digest topic of Zoning and Planning has been given the number 414. Thus, in order to retrieve cases classified under the digest topic Zoning and Planning either of these two queries could be used:

    topic("zoning and planning") /p ordinance regulat! /s wealth income

or

    topic(414) /p ordinance regulat! /s wealth income

7. *Digest Field:* The digest field contains digest paragraphs prepared by West editors. It includes headnotes, corresponding digest topics and Key Numbers, the title and citation of the case, courts, and year of decision. The digest field can be used to search for terms which are not among the West topic headings. For example, the following query may be used to research real estate finance law even though this is not one of the West topic headings.

    digest("real estate" /s financ***)

8. *Headnote Field:* A headnote search limits the search to the language of the headnote, exclusive of the digest topic and Key Number lines and case identification information. Thus, the headnote field is useful in conducting a search where exclusion of the topic name, the key number or the title of the case is necessary to cull only the most pertinent cases. For example, if the query includes statute or rule

numbers the digest field can be helpful to exclude unwanted citation and key numbers. The query found below is an illustration of this function. The search, run in federal case law databases will retrieve cases discussing insured mortgages under the National Housing Act.

    headnote(12 +10   1701) & insure* /5 mortgag**

9. *Opinion Field:* The opinion field contains the text of the case, court and docket numbers, and the names of the attorneys and judges participating. The opinion field search is useful in retrieving cases in which a particular attorney, judge or witness has been involved. The following format can be used to retrieve this information:

    opinion(irving /s younger)

NOTE

Terms may be searched for in clusters of fields by joining any number or field names by commas. This technique is illustrated below:

    synopsis,digest(toxic /p dangerous /p strict /6 liab!)

With this query documents containing the indicated search terms in either the synopsis of digest portions of the case will be retrieved.

b. Field Browsing. The WESTLAW fields listed above may be used in yet another way. This second method, known as field browsing, may be used with any query. Once a search has been completed, the documents retrieved may be scanned by entering the "f" command. A list of fields available for browsing is then displayed. Once a field has been selected, WESTLAW will display only the specified field(s).

The WESTLAW Reference Manual should be consulted for further instruction on using WESTLAW fields for searching or browsing.

c. Date Restrictions. WESTLAW may be instructed to retrieve documents appearing before, after or on a specified date, as well as within a range of dates. To use the date restricter the term DATE, followed in parentheses by the words BEFORE and/or AFTER, or the abbreviations BEF and/or AFT, or the symbols $\langle$ and $\rangle$ must be included in the query. Note that the month, day and year may be included to further restrict the search. Date restrictions should be placed at the beginning or end of the query and connected to the query by an ampersand. The following are examples of how the date restriction may be used within a query:

    date(after 1977) & "civil rights" /s immun! /s monell
    date(aft 1977) & "civil rights" /s immun! /s monell
    "civil rights" /s immun! /s monell & date ($\rangle$ 1977)
    "civil rights" /s immun! /s monell & date (aft may 10, 1977 and bef feb 28, 1981)

d. Key Number Searching. Searches may be performed using West Digest Topic and Key Numbers as search terms. When using this search technique, the query consists of the West Digest Topic Number followed by the letter k (or the symbol available on WALT keyboards) and then the Key Number classified as a subheading under the Digest Topic and Key Number. For example, to retrieve cases under the

Digest Topic classification of Zoning and Planning (Digest Topic number 414), and under its subsection or Key Number for Signs and billboards (Key Number 81), the following queries would be used.

414 k 81 or 414 ☜81

A complete list of Digest Topic and their numerical equivalents appears in the WESTLAW Reference Manual and is also available on-line in the WESTLAW database directory.

e. The FIND Command. The FIND command may be used at any point in a search to retrieve a particular case from WESTLAW. No matter what the database, a case may be displayed by typing FIND followed by the case citation. For example:

find 94 sct 1536

will retrieve the case of *Village of Belle Terre v. Boras* no matter what the database. To return to the original screen the GOBACK command is then entered.

f. The LOCATE Command. The LOCATE command may be used when viewing documents retrieved by a search query, to find documents within the search results which contain certain words or series of words. To locate a term LOCATE or LOC is typed followed by the ENTER key. On the screen which follows the LOCATE terms are then typed. The terms may or may not be words contained in the query. WESTLAW will then search the documents retrieved by the query to find the LOCATE terms. For example, to search the documents retrieved by the query:

268k967(1)

for those documents containing the term "housing" LOCATE, then ENTER followed by the term HOUSING would be typed into WESTLAW. Those documents containing the term HOUSING will then be displayed.

VI. Citation Research With WESTLAW

a. Shepard's ® Citations on WESTLAW. From any point in WESTLAW, case citations may be entered to retrieve Shepard's listings for those citations. To enter a citation to be Shepardized, the following format is used:

sh 84 sct 710

or

sh 84 s.ct. 710

or

sh 84sct710

When the citation is entered, Shepard's listings for the citation will be displayed. To Shepardize a citation it is not necessary to be in the same database as that of the citation. For example, a Supreme Court citation may be entered from the Pacific Reporter database.

   b. WESTLAW as a Citator. It is possible to retrieve new cases citing previous decisions by using WESTLAW itself as a citator. Using WESTLAW as a citator complements Shepard's Citations by retrieving very recent decisions not yet included in Shepard's. Because citation styles are not always uniform, special care must be taken to identify variant forms of citations.

Retrieving Cases that Cite Other Court Decisions. WESTLAW can be used as a citator of other court decisions if the title of the decision, its citation, or both, are known. When only the title of the case is known, use the following format:

   neuburger /5 portland

This query instructs the computer to retrieve all documents citing the case of *Neuburger v. Portland.* The /5 numerical connector requires that the term NEUBURGER occur within five words of the term PORTLAND.

   If the citation of the case is known, it may be added to the query to retrieve only those documents citing the correct case name and case citation. For example, to retrieve cases that have referred to the *Neuburger* decision by its citation, 603 P.2d 771, the following format may be used:

   603 +5 771

If both the citation & the case title are known, one or both of the case name terms may be used to retrieve all documents citing this case. The queries below illustrate this format.

   neuburger /5 portland /15 603 +5 771

or

   neuburger /15 603 +5 771

West's INSTA–CITE ™

INSTA–CITE, West Publishing Company's case history system, allows users to quickly verify the accuracy of case citations and the validity of decisions. It contains prior and subsequent case histories in sequential listings, parallel citations and precedential treatment.

   Some examples of the kind of direct case history provided by INSTA–CITE are: "affirmed," "certiorari denied," "decision reversed and remanded," and "judgment vacated." A complete list of INSTA–CITE case history and precedential treatment notations appears in the WESTLAW Reference Manual.

   The format for instaciting a case citation consists of the letters IC followed by the citation, with or without spaces and periods:

   ic 376 u.s. 254

or

   ic 376 us 254

or

   ic 376us254

VII. Special Features

a. Black's Law Dictionary. WESTLAW contains an on-line version of Black's Law Dictionary. The dictionary incorporates definitions of terms and phrases of English and American law.

The dictionary may be accessed at any point while using WESTLAW by typing DI followed by the term to be defined:

di betterment

To obtain definitions of a phrase, enter the command DI followed by the phrase without quotation marks:

di special assessment

If the precise spelling of a term to be defined is not known, or a list of dictionary terms is desired, a truncated form of the words may be entered with the root expansion symbol (!) attached to it:

di sub!

This example will produce a list of dictionary terms beginning with the root SUB. From the list of terms a number corresponding to the desired term can be entered to obtain the appropriate definition of SUBROGATION.

VIII. WESTLAW Hornbook Queries

a. Query Format. The queries that appear in this publication are intended to be illustrative. They are approximately as general as the material in the Hornbook text to which they correspond.

Although all of the queries in this publication reflect proper format for use with WESTLAW, there is seldom only one "correct" way to formulate a query for a particular problem. The queries reflect a wide range of alternative ways that queries may be structured for effective research. Such variance in query style reflects the great flexibility that the WESTLAW system affords its users in formulating search strategies.

For some research problems, it may be necessary to make a series of refinements to the queries such as the addition of search terms or the substitution of different grammatical connectors, to adequately fit the particular needs of the individual researcher's problem. The responsibility remains with the researcher to "fine-tune" the WESTLAW queries in accordance with his or her own research requirements. The primary usefulness of the preformulated queries in this hornbook is in providing users with a foundation upon which further query construction can be built.

Individual queries in this hornbook may retrieve from one to over a hundred cases, depending on the database to which they are addressed. If a query does not retrieve any cases in a given database, it is because there are no documents in that database which satisfy the proximity requirements of the query. In this situation, to search another database with the same query, enter the letter S followed by the initials DB, followed by the new database identifier. Thus, if a query was initially addressed to the District Courts (dct) database, but retrieved no documents, the user could then search the Courts of Appeals (cta) database with the same query by entering the following command:

    s db cta

The maximum number of cases retrieved by a query in any given database will vary, depending on a variety of factors, including the relative generality of the search terms and proximity connectors, the frequency of litigation or discussion of the issue in the courts and administrative bodies, and the number of documents comprising the database.

b. Textual Illustrations. Examples from the text of this edition have been selected to illustrate how the queries provided in this treatise may be expanded, restricted, or altered to meet the specific needs of the reader's research in the area of urban planning and land development control law. A portion of Chapter 17 section 17.6 subhead Nuisance of this text appears below. The footnotes have been omitted for purposes of brevity.

Nuisance

The relation between code enforcement and acquisition of property with compensation and nuisance law raises an interesting issue concerning the line between the police power and eminent domain. Part of the issue has been previously described, in which the police power is used to require demolition of a building even though the building is in an area scheduled for redevelopment. If the property was acquired by the local agency, compensation would be paid for the building. However, if a building were so bad that it could be "taken" under the police power, why should society pay a slumlord for his nuisance when his building is taken? There are perhaps two answers: first, the state can be more generous than the constitution requires, and second, nothing in fact may be paid for a slum building. While the offer for the acquisition might state a certain sum for the building and a certain sum for the land, which may make the owner believe he is receiving something for the building, it is only the total amount to be paid that concerns the condemnor. In fact, if there were no building on the property, the lot owner might be paid more than an owner of property with a slum building on it. The matter may be complicated somewhat by the method of valuation used. Ultimately, paying for a slum building which is so bad that it warrants demolition must be justified on political, social or efficiency grounds, not because the constitution requires it.

HUD was authorized to make grants to local general purpose governments of two-thirds of the cost of demolition of structures which had been found to be structurally unsound, infested or potentially infested with rats, or unfit for human habitation, and which the locality had the authority to demolish. This program encourages use of the police power rather than eminent domain to rid an area of slum buildings.

This excerpt discusses police power and eminent domain in connection with nuisance law. In order to retrieve documents discussing this point of law the following preformulated queries are given as a suggested search strategy on WESTLAW:

nuisance /p "police power" /p "eminent domain"

The query can be altered in a number of ways to tailor it to the needs of the individual researcher. For example, to restrict the search to discussions of building demolition the following query could be used:

nuisance /p demoli! /p building /p "eminent domain"

By adding the root DEMOLI! and the term BUILDING the query retrieves documents involving building demolition. Excerpts from one such document retrieved from the ALLSTATES database are shown below.

R   1   OF   1   P   1   OF   19   ALLSTATES   1
492 A.2d 1196
99 Pa.Cmwlth. 579

Joseph J. BALENT and George Barto, Appellants,

v.

CITY OF WILKES–BARRE, Appellee.

Commonwealth Court of Pennsylvania

Argued Dec. 10, 1984.

Decided May 31, 1985.

Owners of building which was seriously damaged by fire and was demolished by city filed petition for board of viewers to be appointed in order to assess damages. The Court of Common Pleas, Luzerne County, Patrick J. Toole, J., dismissed petition, and owners appealed. The Commonwealth Court, No. 2190 C.D. 1983, Colins, J., held that city's demolition of building did not constitute compensable taking because city did not appropriate property for public use.

Affirmed.

Kalish, Senior Judge, dissented and filed opinion.

R   1   OF   1   P   9   OF   19   ALLSTATES   1
492 A.2d 1196

Court of Common Pleas of Luzerne County dismissing their petition for the appointment of board of viewers. A building owned by the Appellants was damaged by fire and subsequently was demolished by the City of Wilkes-Barre (City).

Appellants contend that this demolition constituted a de facto taking and filed a petition for the appointment of viewers to assess damages. The City filed preliminary objections. Pursuant to the procedure in eminent domain cases, the trial court considered depositions, briefs and argument to determine whether in fact there was a taking compensable in damages.

The court sustained the preliminary objections and dismissed the petition, concluding that the action of the City in abating the **nuisance** by **demolishing** the **building** constituted a noncompensable exercise of the police power and was not one of compensable **eminent domain.**

The court did find that the building was structurally unstable and constituted a health and safety hazard and that, after notice from the inspector, Appellants boarded the building but did not make repairs; nor was there an appeal to the Board of Appeals pursuant to an appeal notice.

A local ordinance provides that whenever any building shall have been declared dangerous or unsafe by the building inspector's office, the building shall, unless made safe, be demolished. Wilkes-Barre, Pa., Code § 7–23, Ord. No. 32–76, § 1 (1976). While the Appellants have no quarrel with the ordinance permitting abatement of the nuisance, they contend that the City's action in demolition was an excessive, arbitrary and unreasonable use of the police power constituting a taking, compensable under the Fifth Amendment to the United States Constitution. U.S. CONST. amend. V.

Just how a query is altered will depend upon the research objectives of the individual.

IX. Ranking Documents Retrieved on WESTLAW: Age and Term Options

Documents retrieved by a query can be ordered in either of two ways. One way is to order documents by their dates, with the most recent documents displayed first. This is ranking by AGE. Using the AGE option is suggested when the user's highest priority is to retrieve the most recent decisions from a search.

Alternatively, documents can be ranked by the frequency of appearance of query terms. This is ranking by TERMS. When a search is performed with the TERMS option, the cases containing the greatest number of different search terms will be displayed first.

When a database is accessed by entering a database identifier, WESTLAW responds with a screen requesting that the query be entered. At this point the user may select which type of ranking, AGE or TERMS, is desired.

The queries offered in this hornbook were formulated and tested for relevancy with use of the TERMS option. Accordingly, in certain instances use of the AGE option with the preformulated queries may display less relevant, yet more recent cases, first.

X. Conclusion

This appendix has demonstrated methods that can be used to obtain the most effective research results in the area of constitutional law. The addition of WESTLAW references at the end of each section of the text opens the door to a powerful and easily accessed computerized law library.

The queries may be used as provided or they may be tailored to meet the needs of researcher's specific problems. The power and flexibility of WESTLAW affords users of this publication a unique opportunity to greatly enhance their access to and understanding of urban planning and land development control law.

*

Table of Cases

References are to Pages

Table of Statutes

WISCONSIN

STATUTES ANNOTATED

WYOMING

STATUTES 1977

CODE OF FEDERAL REGULATIONS

CODE OF FEDERAL REGULATIONS

FEDERAL REGISTER

EXECUTIVE ORDER

Index

References are to Sections

†

1237